THE STEEL INDUSTRY
1939–1959

THE
STEEL INDUSTRY
1939-1959

A STUDY IN COMPETITION
AND PLANNING

BY

DUNCAN BURN

CAMBRIDGE
AT THE UNIVERSITY PRESS
1961

PUBLISHED BY
THE SYNDICS OF THE CAMBRIDGE UNIVERSITY PRESS

Bentley House, 200 Euston Road, London, N.W.1
American Branch: 32 East 57th Street, New York 22, N.Y.
West African Office: P.O. Box 33, Ibadan, Nigeria

©

CAMBRIDGE UNIVERSITY PRESS

1961

Printed in Great Britain at the University Press, Cambridge
(Brooke Crutchley, University Printer)

CONTENTS

Book I
WAR AND PEACE AGAIN
(1939–1945)

Book II
FROM PLAN I TO NATIONALISATION
AND BEYOND

LIST OF TABLES

LIST OF FIGURES

LIST OF MAPS

PREFACE

This is a sequel to *The Economic History of Steelmaking, 1867–1939* published in 1940. I first planned on my publisher's suggestion in 1948 to bring the first book up to date by adding two or three chapters. But the extent of change in the industry in the countries covered grew so fast that this was soon impracticable. Hence the new book. It is complete in itself, but it starts conceptually as well as chronologically where the other leaves off, and I think the earlier history necessary for the full understanding of the recent phase. The years since the war have been exceptionally rich in institutional developments associated with the steel industry. In Britain and on the Continent new institutions specific to the steel industry have emerged, and they fall wholly within the scope of this book. In the United States the industry has been subject to the extending influence of Antitrust. No attempt is made here to describe the antitrust system in general; but its impact on the steel industry is surveyed. I should have liked to include an analysis of Russian planning: but the opportunity to observe it has not come my way. The writing of the book was finished in 1959, and only minor modifications have been made since then: it was not possible, for example, to make use of the annual reports of the Iron and Steel Board or the British Iron and Steel Federation for 1959.

When I wrote the first book I knew the industry only as an outside observer. During the war I was for the first four years on the staff of the Iron and Steel Control, part of the time as Deputy Director of Statistics. Membership of a United States–United Kingdom Metallurgical Mission in February–April 1943 involved me in joint operations with members of the American industry. In 1944 I was dealing with post-war prospects for steel at home and abroad in the Raw Materials Department of the Ministry of Supply. How far my judgements met with approval in R.M.D. should doubtless remain obscure. But I must after these experiences disclaim the complete academic detachment which I enjoyed before November 1939.

I am much indebted again to a great number of firms in many countries for the opportunity of visiting their works and for guidance by conversation and correspondence, and to members of the staff of the British Iron and Steel Federation who in addition to providing information have discussed with me the whole manuscript in its various stages, to my great benefit. I had much help at an early stage from members and staff of the Iron and Steel Corporation of Great Britain, and later from the staff of the Iron and Steel Board. I am grateful too to members and officials of the High Authority of the European Coal and Steel Community for comment and advice. My major debt is to Sir Robert Shone, now executive member of the Iron and Steel Board, with whom I have been discussing steel industry problems for twenty-five years. As our views have evolved I think our agreements have been more extensive than our disagreements, though the latter have often been more conspicuous. I have had the advantage of comments on various parts of the manuscript from several friends and former colleagues; those from Professor A. K. Cairncross, Mr Nathan Isaacs, Mr Felix Levy, Professor E. A. G. Robinson, Mr Donald Tyerman and Mr C. R. Wheeler have been particularly valuable. I had useful discussions at an early stage with Professor Dietrich Goldschmidt, now of Berlin, whose *Stahl und Staat, das Britische Experiment* (1955) deserves a wider audience; and at a later stage with Professor H. E. English, whose article 'British Steel: a Unique Record of Public Regulation' (*Canadian Journal of Economics and Political Science*) appeared too late for overt discussion in this book; but I knew the argument. Mr Andrew Robertson lightened the task of proof-reading. Without my wife's help, in many forms, the book would not have appeared: and my daughter Susan took on much of the burden of the index. Finally, I am again grateful for the helpfulness and discrimination of my publisher and printer—and for their patience.

D. L. B.

LONG MELFORD
May 1960

PRINCIPAL ABBREVIATIONS

A.I.S.I.	American Iron and Steel Institute.
B.I.S.C.	British Iron and Steel Corporation.
B.I.S.F.	British Iron and Steel Federation.
B.I.S.R.A.	British Iron and Steel Research Association.
E.C.S.C.	European Coal and Steel Community. [I have sometimes quoted from the provisional edition of the Annual Reports of the E.C.S.C., where each chapter is paged separately, and sometimes from the reports in their final printed form, where the pagination of each volume is continuous.
E.C.E.	Economic Commission for Europe.
E.E.C.	European Economic Community.
Econ.	*Economist.*
Econ. J.	*Economic Journal.*
E.H.S.	*The Economic History of Steelmaking 1867–1939*, by Duncan Burn.
F.T.C.	Federal Trade Commission (U.S.).
I.C.T.R.	*Iron and Coal Trades Review.*
I.S. Board	Iron and Steel Board.
I.S. Corp.	Iron and Steel Corporation of Great Britain (1951–53).
I.S.H.R.A.	Iron and Steel Holding and Realisation Agency.
I.S. Inst.	Iron and Steel Institute.
J.R. Stat. Soc.	*Journal of the Royal Statistical Society.*
P.A.C.	Committee of Public Accounts.
R.M.D.	Raw Materials Department of Ministry of Supply.

Stat. B.I.S.F.   *Annual Statistical Yearbook* of the B.I.S.F. (published in two parts, one giving United Kingdom figures, the other figures for other countries). (From 1955 the Annual Statistics for the U.K. were published by the I.S. Board and B.I.S.F. jointly: statistics of overseas industries in B.I.S.F. *Statistical Handbook*.)

Stat. Bull.   *Monthly Statistical Bulletin* of the British Iron and Steel Federation. (From 1955 the *Bulletin* was succeeded by *Monthly Statistics* issued jointly by the I.S. Board and B.I.S.F., but without the valuable introductory articles hitherto included.)

T.N.E.C.   Temporary National Economic Committee (U.S.).

BOOK I

WAR AND PEACE AGAIN

1939-1945

Chapter I

THE IMPACT OF THE SECOND WORLD WAR
1939–1945

In September 1939, war changed the problems of the steel-makers abruptly for the second time in a generation. From then until 1945 there was an interlude in the deliberate and con-certed application of the policies propounded or foreshadowed in the May Report, except where they could be made to serve the different purposes of war. Investment plans which give lowest costs in the long run, and prices which encourage the best distribution of resources in the long run do not win wars. The contribution of the industry to victory falls outside the scope of this book. But inevitably, as in 1914–18, the activities of the war years, and the experience of organisation for war, influenced developments in the years which followed. The central organisation in the industry gained in substance, ex-perience and prestige. New plant was called for, though not the plant that would have been put up in peace. There were changes in the relative costs and availability of raw materials, which in some degree persisted after the war and provoked changes in price policy which endured. Inevitably the financial strengths of firms and districts changed. These and analogous aspects of the war history form the main subject of this chapter. Mobilisation for war and the evolution of policy in the light of shifting and worsening conditions are traced briefly in the first section. It shows the growth of the central organisation in depth and breadth. It also explains why the reactions to the Second World War differed in important respects from the reactions to the first, and it puts in perspective some criticisms of the industry in these years which reflected pre-war controversy rather than wartime facts, and put an additional spice of malice and prejudice into post-war discussion. The second section of the chapter traces the changes in plant and technique; the third deals with costs, prices and profits. The preparations made by the industry and the Government for the return of peace, and the fortunes of the industry in other countries during the war are dealt with in later chapters.

1. EVOLUTION OF SUPPLY POLICY

The growth of the Steel Federation in its latest phase before the war had been looked upon by the Board of Trade as a useful basis for war organisation. For on this second occasion there were some, though quite inadequate, economic preparations for war.[1]

Until Munich these preparations conceived a 'war of limited liability', with relatively light demands on steel.[2] Therefore when the Government was pressed by Sir Andrew Duncan in the summer of 1938 to stock iron ore or pig iron[3] it decided not to do so. By 1939 it was realised that a war would require at least as much steel as existing capacity could provide, and that for the full use of the capacity large raw-material imports would have to be maintained. It was finally decided, but too late for action, to have strategic stocks of both ore and pig iron.[4] Apart from air-raid precautions virtually no physical preparations had been made in the industry when war broke out. But an administrative organisation had been prepared, and was ready to take over.

Based partly on the existing model it was a two-tier organisation. The Raw Materials Department of the Ministry of Supply took the place (and much of the staff) of I.D.A.C., and had the job of formulating policy, or of interpreting and transmitting

---

[1] W. K. Hancock and M. M. Gowing, *British War Economy*, ch. II.

[2] *Ibid.* p. 67.

[3] *E.H.S.* p. 501. Mr Frater Taylor is quoted saying publicly what the Federation said privately to the Government. At that time, but not later, blast furnaces were not fully occupied. Stocks of some 'strategic' materials needed for special steels had been started earlier—ferro-tungsten, ferro-vanadium and ferro-molybdenum, for example, by the Admiralty in 1937.

[4] *The Times*, 12 Aug. 1939, confirmed that the Ministry of Supply was discussing purchases with B.I.S.F., but discouraged the view that quantities had been settled.

policies determined by higher authority—and of supervising and assisting the execution of policy.[1] The Iron and Steel Control took the place (and most of the staff) of the Federation and was primarily conceived as an executive body to administer policies. In fact, it also often proposed, though it could not determine, the details of policy. The British Iron and Steel Corporation became the commercial instrument of the Control as it was of the Federation. Sir Andrew Duncan became first Steel Controller until he became President of the Board of Trade early in 1940, and later Minister of Supply, which he remained, except for a second spell at the Board of Trade when Lord Beaverbrook was at Supply, until the end of the war. The later Controllers,[2] and all the Deputy Controllers,[3] and the directors who looked after individual raw materials or steel products were drawn from firms in the industry; but the Control found the nucleus of its secretariat and of its price control and statistical sections in the Federation, and Steel House became its headquarters.[4] The Federation itself continued to operate but on a very restricted scale, and there were regular meetings between the senior officials of the Steel Control and the President's Committee of the Federation.[5] All these arrangements were very natural, but it was equally natural that they should invite suspicion. Perhaps because Sir Andrew was, for much of the

---

[1] E.g. the Cabinet, or the Production Executive, or, rarely, the Prime Minister himself. The Economic Section of the War Cabinet Secretariat played an important part at certain stages in the background, particularly in regard to shipping and import policy.

[2] Sir Charles Wright (see *E.H.S.* p. 356) and Sir John Duncanson, commercial manager of the Steel Company of Scotland before the war, and Mr C. R. Wheeler (G.K.B.).

[3] Mr R. Alsop (Consett), Mr A. G. E. Briggs (E.S.C.) (later Sir George Briggs), Sir A. M'Cosh (Bairds and Scottish), and Major J. Campbell.

[4] Thus the statement that the Control 'represents essentially the personnel of the Iron and Steel Federation in Government', often quoted from the *14th Report of the S. C. on National Expenditure* (1942–3), is substantially inaccurate, though in regard to the price problems with which the *Report* was chiefly concerned the formative impulses in the Control came from Mr R. M. Shone (later Sir Robert Shone), who was the head of the Economic and Statistical Section of the Federation, became its Economic Director in 1950, and is now a member of the Iron and Steel Board.

[5] The President's Committee was given full powers to act for the Federation during the war; it had some functions which nominally could have been important (below, p. 34, n. 1).

war, its Minister but also because it was ably staffed the Control sometimes seemed to civil servants in other departments rather exasperating and autonomous, too self-opinionated for an executive instrument, lacking proper respect for planners and programme makers; albeit under the stress of war, as will be seen, the steelmakers became very plan and programme minded.

Both the new bodies had wider functions and more power (derived from the Defence Regulations) than their predecessors. The R.M.D. was not, like I.D.A.C., in name merely advisory; the Control did not have to seek the consent of member firms. It covered more products and more stages of production than the Federation.[1] Initially it even had the duty of deciding who should have steel for 'civilian uses' and of issuing licences to them. Steel ordered for the services or for basic industries at this stage had an overriding priority. This arrangement soon proved unworkable. Under the 'Distribution Scheme' which displaced it in the summer of 1940 priorities were discarded. All steel likely to be available was allocated in specific tonnages quarter by quarter for specific uses or groups of uses by a central 'Materials Committee', which performed a similar function in the distribution of other scarce materials. Bulk allocations were made to various Government departments who sponsored the steel needs of groups of users and were responsible for issuing 'authorisations' to users within the limits imposed by the allocations. Thus the Control was relieved of all responsibility for deciding who should have steel. Its part in the scheme was to see that steel was only supplied against authorisations, to show for which departments the volume of authorisations appeared to outrun the initial allocations, and so to help in bringing about either more accurate estimates of needs or more rigorous control of authorisations.[2]

The primary function of the Control was to organise supplies of steel both from home and abroad, to provide as far as raw

---

[1] E.g. iron castings, drop forgings, wire products, tubes and springs were covered; and the Raw Material Section covered the import of ore, ore mining and quarrying, scrap collection and distribution, and ferro-alloy supply and distribution.

[2] The Control was left for some time with responsibility for the issue of licences for the direct export of steel, within a quantity laid down by the Materials Committee.

materials and shipping and capital resources permitted, and with the most economic use of the scarcest resources, the steel needed for the conduct of the war in the proper balance of sizes and qualities. This included advising how much raw material and steel should be imported and what new capital equipment should be installed, whether for ore quarrying or transport, or for producing more raw materials oversea to import, or for iron and steelmaking here.[1] Naturally almost all the executive work arising out of the decisions on the import and investment programmes fell on the Control. Here, too, there were major changes, if only in emphasis, between the task envisaged in 1939 and as it ultimately developed. The initial programme postulated large imports of ore, pig iron and scrap, and of semi-finished products from the Continent. The outbreak of war at once seriously reduced the rate of ore imports; there were delays as convoys were formed, and foreign ships withdrew from the ore trade before British ships could, or would, take their place. But conditions improved, and plans for 1940 were based on imports of 6 m. tons of iron ore, with heavy imports of the other bulky raw materials. Home ore quarries were rapidly increasing output, and there were at this date proposals for several new blast furnaces and for a new steelworks on the Midland ores.

The successive blows which ended the 'phoney' war and left almost the whole of Europe and her Atlantic coastline under German control forced an entire recasting of policy on steel. Swedish and North African ores, Belgian and French semi-products, and Scandinavian ferro-alloys and special steels were now denied to Great Britain; invaluable new bases were in German hands for sea and air attacks on her shipping. Optimistic raw-material import programmes could not be fulfilled; it was necessary to use shipping space for bringing in finished goods rather than crude raw materials, pig iron rather than ore, steel rather than pig iron. The stringency grew progressively till 1943. The entry of Japan cut off more raw materials (e.g. wolfram from Burma) and added new shipping difficulties

---

[1] The drafting of the case for a new expansion scheme for submission to the Treasury for financial approval was the duty, however, not of the Control but of R.M.D.

and service responsibilities for the Navy. Pig-iron imports from India were drastically reduced. The entry of Russia drew ships for supply convoys, and when in 1943 the submarine and air menace for shipping was mastered ships were needed in great numbers for the landings and campaigns in the Mediterranean and Normandy and the Far East.

Thus the Control was much more involved in planning imports of steel, and especially of American steel, than was expected. Only by this means was it able to meet growing home demands in spite of raw material scarcities. The output of steel ingots and castings was at its highest at the end of 1939 and in the first half of 1940;[1] in the later war years it fell significantly below this peak, despite increased home ore production, a prodigious growth in the transport of home ore to coastal furnaces, and an intensive drive for more scrap.[2] Nevertheless, home use of steel in 1942 was 30–40 per cent above the highest level before the war.[3] The almost complete cessation of exports helped much towards this. In autumn 1939 exports were still advocated 'to keep markets'; in 1940 some were judged necessary to earn foreign exchange, but after Lease Lend came into operation steel was only exported when the importer was enabled thereby to render in return an essential service.[4] Reduction of exports may be said to have 'contributed' 2 m. tons for additional home consumption. But imported steel, almost all American, con-

---

[1] In the autumn of 1939 output was at a rate of 13·86 m. tons a year; from March to June 1940 it averaged 14·04 m. tons. This has escaped the notice of the pamphleteers for nationalisation, W. Fienburgh and R. Eveley, *Steel is Power*, p. 104: 'Things improved later in the war. Output was high and healthy....The record of steel at war was the record of the steelworkers and technicians. The general administration of the industry was perhaps adequate but never inspired.' These authors, no doubt writing in a hurry, had a genius for getting things wrong.

[2] The output of steel ingots and castings and use of home scrap were as follows:

Steel (m. tons)	1937	1939	1940	1941	1942	1943	1944
Output of ingots	12·70	12·94	12·50	11·88	12·37	12·42	11·55
Output of castings	0·28	0·28	0·39	0·43	0·57	0·62	0·59
Home scrap used (excl. circulating scrap)	3·4	3·1	3·1	3·3	4·0	3·6	3·6

[3] Deliveries for home users totalled 11·3 m. tons of finished steel compared with approximately 8·25 m. tons in 1937.

[4] E.g. steel sold to oil producers helped to maintain oil supplies; tinplate to the Argentine provided cans for corned beef.

tributed 2·35 m. tons in 1941 and 2·60 m. tons in 1942.[1] Four-fifths of this was in semi-products, and all told it represented each year over one-fifth of the whole steel supply in those years.[2] In these circumstances there was no repetition in the Second World War of the building of new plant for heavy steelmaking which occurred (or more accurately was started, for much of it was finished later) during the First World War. The early plans for new blast furnaces were curtailed,[3] and the plan for a new steelworks on the Midland ores which before Dunkirk might have been thought to have been examined at too leisurely a pace, was dropped entirely. For this the Control was harshly criticised. The organisation, according to the *Manchester Guardian* early in 1941, had to balance its members interests against those of the nation at war. The memory of the paring away of excess plant after the last war, it was argued, remained an obsession, and expansion in the primary stages of production

---

[1] The figure fell to 2·07 m. tons in 1943. In the last four months of 1940 consumption was at the rate of 1·1 m. tons a year.

[2] The changing pattern of imports and exports is shown broadly in the following table, though there were important turning-points within particular years which the table obscures:

Imports of steel and raw materials for steel and exports of steel (thousand tons)

Imports:	1937	1939	1940	1941	1942	1943	1944
Iron ore	7,039	5,240	4,549	2,283	1,922	1,894	2,167
Manganese ore	284	325	247	314	421	445	316
Scrap	955	605	937	549	15	5	13
Pig iron	638	354	676	976	356	362	285
Ferro-alloys	78	73	94	100	67	35	56
Steel	1,214	1,315	2,222	3,051	2,756	2,278	1,395
	10,208	7,892	9,325	7,279	5,517	5,119	4,232
Exports:							
Steel	2,184	1,461	954	397	203	91	173

Stat. B.I.S.F. for 1939–44. Imports and exports of 'Other manufactures of iron and steel' have been excluded. Iron ore includes 'manganiferous ore'. Exports include direct exports only; they exclude exports by services for service use. The weight of steel is as imported or exported not in ingot equivalents. The addition of imports is relevant as an indication of shipping needed; this sort of sum was done for shipping programmes.

[3] Above, p. 7. The Ministry of Supply was, however, at the instance of the Control, urging in Aug. 1940 that the expansion of blast-furnace capacity, near home ores, including one scheme yet needing Treasury approval, should proceed as fast as possible.

was resisted in a war 'where weight of metal means everything'. Maintenance of sea traffic, it was even argued, prevented the industry rising to its full stature; it encouraged bulk purchasing, when we should only have needed ships for scientifically selected imports.[1]

In retrospect it is evident that if some of the steel imports had been replaced by an equal tonnage of iron ore in 1940–2 (as the Control might at one stage have preferred),[2] still more if imports as a whole had been less, there would unavoidably have been less steel in the country in the most critical years. It is problematical whether more new blast furnaces or a new steelworks would have increased supplies at all in 1942–3, though they would have reduced them sensibly during construction.[3] From 1943 onwards labour scarcities and the growing service demands on rail transport reduced the total use of steel.[4] As it was, munitions production was not seriously if at all hampered by lack of steel in bulk.[5] There were at times scarcities of qualities and shapes of steel required in exceptional quantities in war, such as armour, armour-piercing shot and shell, steels for aircraft and their engines, and for tanks, gun-forgings and ballbearings. The demands for alloy steel, forgings, armour-plate, drop-forgings, steel castings and seamless tubes were far beyond existing capacities. In these instances relatively little reliance

[1] *Manchester Guardian Trade Review*, 21 Jan. 1941, p. 37. The *Manchester Guardian* continued to be very critical.

[2] In the spring of 1940 the case for the full ore import programme, to make *more* steel at home, was still being put by the Control. Others were arguing the case for more steel imports on shipping grounds. The Control, it was being said, argued as though it had a right to ore and scrap imports, but as though it was less right to import steel (though much steel was, in fact, being ordered).

[3] A new blast-furnace plant would require some 30,000 tons of iron and steel, a new integrated steelworks more than twice as much. Probably any work of this kind would have curtailed other wartime expansion.

[4] New blast furnaces on the orefield, if they were to add to output, would have involved more transport of coke and pig iron or steel.

[5] In 1940 the programme of war-factory expansion was curtailed because steel would not be available in sufficient quantities for processing if the whole programme were completed. But the factories which *were* finished were only with difficulty supplied with labour in 1941. In 1943, as mentioned in the text, labour for munitions began to fall owing to the pressure of service man-power needs. Cp. Hancock and Gowing, *op. cit.* pp. 446 *sqq.* Also M. M. Postan, *British War Production*, p. 223 and passim.

was put upon imports and a great deal of new plant was installed. The fatal objection to an increase of ordinary capacity, namely, that there were no raw materials for it, did not apply; there were, on the other hand, serious objections to depending on distant suppliers, with the risk of loss at sea, for specialised products which were required quickly for timed programmes of armaments manufacture.[1] Importing was best suited to supply steel which could be bought in stock sizes. The British industry naturally saw with especial force the desirability of feeding British mills with imported 'semis', and the American industry saw best the scope for sending finished steel. Whether the line was drawn in the end perfectly it is hardly possible to say.

In the most tangible sense the organisation of steel supply in the war achieved its object. By and large supplies kept pace with the growth of war production in general, and did not limit it. How far the work was done in the quickest, most effective and economical way is a more subtle and searching question which falls outside the scope of this book. There were mistakes, delays and waste. For example, some steel was imported for stock which became 'dead stock', being in unwanted sizes or qualities. Some new plant was built which was never used for war.[2] In a measure the vagueness of Service programmes[3] at

---

[1] Deliveries of special products for such programmes (e.g. shell-steel armour or track links for tanks, drop forgings for aircraft, forgings for guns, high-tensile steel sections for Bailey bridges, or the constructional steel for Mulberry harbours) were planned, scheduled and progressed by the Control, whose directors could only have effective control over home production.

[2] See below, p. 18. It would be easy to multiply instances of mistaken policies. Thus, to take one more, there was a time, a short time, early in the war, when some users were advised to use cast iron instead of steel. But cast iron used more ferrous material. The right policy was to reduce the use of cast iron and turn blast furnaces making foundry pig to basic pig. This could have been done more promptly than it was, but the delay was not long.

[3] My first function in the war was to act as liaison between the Control and the Priority Departments of the Ministries and to draw up consolidated analyses of their steel requirements. They were astonishingly vague, not merely because the size of the programme was not known, but because the material needs of programmes of different sizes were unknown, in gross or in particular. Departments never did have comprehensive analyses of their requirements; but the statistics of the Distribution Scheme showed them how much was being used under their authorisation, and they were able to concentrate attention on the marginal changes in their needs quarter by quarter.

the outbreak of war and the rapid switches during the war made some errors of this kind unavoidable. Moreover, no staff is first-class throughout,[1] and few administrators are quite infallible. The public criticism of the Control was in the main ill-informed, belated where it referred to real weaknesses, and usually wrong,[2] though it may sometimes—as even bad

---

[1] This not only leads to misjudgements, it may rule out extensions of administrative activity. Thus, for example, a strong case was advanced for more concentration in some branches of the trade to use the best equipment more intensively. This would have needed administrative organisation to sort out and distribute a great complexity of orders.

[2] It is difficult for outside observers to pierce sufficiently to the heart of administrative activities to discover the real weaknesses; and partly because of this, no doubt, the critics relied too much on preconceptions, and failed to ask the right questions. An interesting instance is found in the Fabian pamphlet *The Raw Material Controls*, by G. D. N. Worswick, written early in 1942. He stated, as though it was more than a surmise, that 'The Control (the British Iron and Steel Federation) is fearful of the post-war position of an industry which has developed too much plant during the war'. He then argued 'it is no coincidence that the Control has from the beginning adopted the line that the industry could easily produce all the steel the nation could possibly require and some to spare'. Yet the Control, in addition to purchases on the Continent, had ordered nearly 500,000 tons of steel in America by the end of 1939. Expansion of iron-ore production, he says, 'should have been an essential part of our war effort'. He conceded that in 1942 'it is now taking place'. But he did not point out—perhaps he did not find out—that ore output in 1940 had already exceeded the 1939 level by over 20 per cent, and that by the autumn of 1940, as the official history puts it, 'The provision of hopper wagons had not kept pace with the enormous increase in the output of iron ore in the Midlands' (Hancock and Gowing, *op. cit.* p. 273). By early 1942 ore output was 40 per cent above 1939, ore transport in ton miles over 150 per cent above 1939. (The transport figure is a contemporary calculation for administrative purposes.) These typical instances could be multiplied. The pamphlet was still arguing that under the Controls of 1942 'the war effort cannot go "all out" in the way we are all agreed is essential to victory'. Having stated at one point that steel supply here was 'strictly limited by the number of blast furnaces', the author later argues 'we can no longer rely on a great neutral like the United States' (because now an ally?) 'to help us out with steel when we run short'. He nevertheless complains 'there is no evidence of any foresight, of any planning for the use of alternate sources or of substitute materials, in case the usual supply should dry up' (see below, p. 15). And yet when he observed accumulations of scrap, which were partly being stocked in anticipation of the ending of imports (there were also unsatisfactory qualities), he complained that these were not flowing into production. The author declares 'an essential requisite of planning ahead is that the planning body should know *exactly* (my italics) what are the available supplies of raw materials and what is the potential increase of these supplies'. How pleased Steel Control, Ministry of Supply and Cabinet would have been to have known even inexactly in advance the course of the first 12 months of war!

criticism may—have provided a stimulus to more energetic action.

The very fact that the wartime development policy was in its main features well designed for war purposes meant that it was not ideally suited for peacetime needs. But because the conditions in the Second World War were so different from those of 1914–18 the form of the compromise was different. There was, as has been seen already, much less new mass-production equipment. The defences of the older higher cost areas were again strengthened, but in rather less direct and obvious ways, which will appear in the remaining sections of this chapter. The growth of the central administration was of far greater importance than in the First World War.

2. THE WAR AND TECHNICAL EFFICIENCY

Over £60 m. was spent during the war on new plant for the iron and steel industry.[1] But little more than one-tenth of this was spent on the early stages of production in ordinary grade steelmaking, where on an average £10 m. had been spent every year in the last five years of peace and where very great additions were made in 1914–18. Some work started before the war was completed, and its cost is not included in this war expenditure; it included the last stages of the blast furnaces at Scunthorpe and Clydebridge, the strip mills at Ebbw Vale and Shotton, and the continuous rod mill which was a sort of compensation plant for Jarrow. In their fields these were important additions to capacity.[2] But otherwise there was very little during the war. Ore quarrying was both expanded and more fully mechanised;[3] and a lot of new hopper wagons were built to transport the additional ore. There were four new blast furnaces; the three of these which were integrated with

---

[1] As defined by the Control Orders. In 1958 prices this total would be somewhere between £150 m. and £180 m.

[2] See *E.H.S.* pp. 460, 464. It is not surprising that the sheet industry was the only branch of steelmaking to be 'concentrated' during the war, and that re-rolling came near to being concentrated, and tinplate was, in effect but not in name, concentrated.

[3] See opposite, n. 2.

steelworks—Margam, Round Oak and Consett—strengthened plants in older areas.[1] The only changes in plant for ordinary grade steelmaking were, with one major exception, incidental to providing for more supplies of some special products, particularly armour and bullet-proof plate. The exception was a new cogging mill set up by Messrs Steel, Peech and Tozer,[2] which was completed at a late stage in the war; it was to replace one which was subject to rather frequent breakdown and was moved to Workington where the load was less exacting. Apart from this there were no important new mills, even replacements; but there were a few new open-hearth furnaces,[3] several of them to make alloy steel for armour and bullet-proof plate; and for the same programme considerable new reheating capacity was built at plate mills, together with cooling banks, heat-treatment furnaces, and profiling machines.[4] Two firms[5] installed facilities to make lead-bearing steel, a 'free-cutting' steel which is easy to machine.

All this did not amount to very much. It possibly represented an addition of about 500,000 tons of open-hearth melting capacity,[6] and the elimination of some 'bottlenecks'. Some

[1] See *E.H.S.* p. 13: 271 (Round Oak); 464 (Consett); 361 (Port Talbot and Margam are adjacent). The fourth new blast furnace was at Wellingborough.

[2] At Templeborough, Sheffield. See *ibid.* pp. 367, 371–2.

[3] Most were additions to existing shops. There were four on the North-east Coast (including one each at Consett and South-Durham); one at Appleby Frodingham; two in South Wales (G.K.B. Cardiff and Briton Ferry); three in Sheffield (Hadfields and Steel, Peech and Tozer (2)); and seven in Scotland. Of these three were in a new Ministry of Supply plant at Linwood, destined to supply gun forgings and managed by Beardmore's. The remainder were at Colvilles and Lanarkshire Steel (*Stat. B.I.S.F.* 1938 and 1939–44). A few furnaces fell out of commission in other works; but in most of these there was probably no net fall in capacity.

[4] The principal developments were at Dorman Longs, Appleby Frodingham, South Durham, Colvilles.

[5] Steel, Peech and Tozers, and Lysaghts (Scunthorpe).

[6] Production from a larger number of furnaces fell, however, during the war below pre-war output because (1) there was rather less molten pig iron in the charge; in 1937 the average was 6·62 cwt. per ton of open-hearth basic ingots, between 1940 and 1944 it ranged between 5·99 cwt. (1944) and 6·51 cwt. (1942). (2) Cold pig iron charged averaged 3·04 cwt. in 1937; during the war it ranged from 3·55 to 4·10 cwt. (3) The pig iron was mostly more phosphoric, thus requiring more refining time. (4) More high-quality steels were made in the open hearth during the war; not only more alloy steel, but also more high-tensile, etc. For the overall figures, *Stat. B.I.S.F.* for 1937, Table 20, and 1939–44, Table 30.

mills could be fed with steel more continuously. Better balance of capacities would lessen costs.[1] The most generally important technical advances in the early stages of steelmaking came not from new plant, however, but from the need to use different and often lower grade raw materials—more low-grade ore, for example, and more basic pig iron—to use coal more efficiently because it was scarce, and to make, even in the bulk trade, more of the higher grade steels, such as high-tensile structural steel for Bailey bridges, silico-manganese steel for springs, steel for tube rounds and shell steel. This was apart altogether from the specialised alloy steels, where there were impressive developments both of properties and in economy of composition.[2]

In alloy steelmaking the rate of expansion was sufficient in the aggregate if the expansion had been appropriately concentrated to allow for a great increase in economic efficiency. Output was more than doubled, reaching a peak of 1·6 m. tons in 1943 compared with 0·8 m. ton in 1940 and a lower figure in 1939. The greater part of the increase was in steel made in electric furnaces, in which the highest qualities of steel are made. Here output was more than trebled, rising from 292,000 tons in 1939 to 992,000 tons in 1943. It has been seen earlier that Britain had lagged in this field; output in 1937 had been 215,000 tons.[3] Here certainly there was room for advance. But wartime considerations which affected the planning of this expansion limited its contribution to post-war competitive

---

[1] The profiling and heat-treatment plant often had little early post-war value, however, and was something of an encumbrance.

[2] The complaint that there was 'no planning...for the use of substitute materials' (above, p. 12, n. 2) was unfounded. The increase in alloy and tool-steel output reflected just such planning. The increase was made in face of serious scarcities of alloys. Some were scarce because old sources (e.g. Scandinavia for ferro-chrome, Burma for tungsten) were cut off, others, e.g. nickel, molybdenum, tungsten and vanadium, because requirements here and in the United States, for alloy steels and other uses (e.g. tungsten for tungsten carbide, molybdenum for high-speed steel, nickel for high nickel alloys) grew more rapidly than supply could expand. These scarcities were foreseen and provided against by stock-building, by devising new steels with less alloy content and by recovering more alloy from 'scrap'. The work was done ultimately in close collaboration with American metallurgists. It involved a close comparison of the alloys used by different makers in each specification of steel and in steels for comparable uses.

[3] See *E.H.S.* p. 483.

strength. To reduce the exceptional, and as it seemed dangerous, concentration of electric furnace steelmaking in Sheffield, where 90 per cent of the electric furnace ingot output was made before the war, almost all the new furnaces were put elsewhere. Most of the new plants or extensions were relatively small, with two or three medium-sized furnaces only, often installed in existing steelworks to reduce the amount of new construction or new ancillary plant needed.[1] Most did not have new rolling mills.[2] Some were sponsored by existing alloy-steel firms in Sheffield or Clydeside, some started by steel firms who had not hitherto made 'special' steels.[3] The largest and best-equipped new melting shop was built at Distington (near Workington), because, it was said, there was surplus electricity in the area. There were no local facilities for finishing alloy steel, and no local scrap. The plant was designed to send ingots to Scotland or Sheffield for rolling, and after the war the furnaces were dismantled. The same fate befell the largest new Scots plant at Mossend. Of the big new plants only the one put up at Openshaw near Manchester by the English Steel Corporation, the largest Sheffield firm, flourished commercially after the war. It had new mills and drop forges.[4] A Ministry of Supply plant at Linwood, near Paisley, was built to feed a gun forge which was dismantled at the close of the war, so that here again the plant was left with no satisfactory normal outlet. Thus when the new demand eased off it was the new rather than the old plants which went out of production.[5] The changing importance of the regions, and the relative revival of Sheffield, after the war, is shown in Table 1.[6]

[1] Instances are the Brymbo Steelworks, near Wrexham, managed by Firth Brown's of Sheffield, and Baldwins' Panteg plant.

[2] There were new cogging mills at Jessops, Colvilles and E.S.C. (Openshaw), and new bar mills at Colvilles (3), E.S.C. (Openshaw) and Baldwins.

[3] E.g. Baldwins, at Panteg.

[4] Some of the new melting shops however worked, in addition to Openshaw. The Corby plant, for example, made special tube steels; Brymbo made high silicon steel for electric sheets.

[5] There were a few new rolling mills for alloy steel, e.g. at Colvilles, Firth Browns and Jessops.

[6] About 34 per cent of all electric furnace steel was for castings in 1957. The proportion had increased after the war, and a rather smaller part of the electric steel for castings was made in Sheffield than of the ingots.

Some of the new electric furnaces installed were individually big by English standards, and in this respect they marked an advance economically when other factors were also favourable. New electric furnaces built at the same time in America were much larger still, and had greater operating economies.[1] Whether there was scope for these still larger units in British markets is no doubt open to discussion; some British experts thought there was.[2] In any event they offered a competitive advantage to the Americans, which they subsequently extended.[3]

Table 1. *Regional distribution of electric furnace ingot output*[a] *(percentages)*

	1939	1943	1946	1949	1951	1952	1957
Sheffield	90	41	60	51	52	54	56
Scotland	3	16	3	12	8	7	7
Lancs and part of Yorks	3	18	16	18	23	22	20
N.E. Coast		3					
N.W. Coast		13		2	3	3	4
Northants	1	5	13	10	8	8	8
Black Country		1	1	1	1	1	1
S. Wales	3	3	7	6	5	5	4
	100	100	100	100	100	100	100
Total (thousand tons)	212	726	345	544	575	630	794
Total, ingots and castings	292	992	479	740	819	930	1211

[a] Sheffield and Lancashire figures are part estimated, since in available data outputs of Openshaw are included in Sheffield.

[1] The largest British furnaces were 25–30 tons capacity, the United States 60, 80 and even 100 tons. Labour and refractory costs were lower for larger furnaces, and radiation losses probably less. Cheaper scrap handling may be possible.

[2] Some Sheffield members of a United States–United Kingdom Metallurgical Mission of which I was a member, which visited new United States plants in 1943, took this view.

[3] By using larger transformers the melting and refining time was greatly reduced, and with it therefore capital and overhead costs, so that some American operators claimed to have brought electric furnace costs close to open hearth by 1949. (*Iron Age*, 8 December 1949). By 1950 many British steelmakers, particularly in the steel-foundry trade, were replacing their transformers by larger ones in order to provide more electricity to get quicker outputs in their furnaces. United Steels at S. Fox's installed an 80-ton electric furnace for alloy steel in 1957 and began replacing open-hearth by large electric furnaces at Templeborough in 1960 for carbon steel. Tube Investments set up 60-ton furnaces in 1956 at Round Oak for tube steel.

The larger part of the war expenditure was on works capacity for making highly finished and often highly specialised products. The value of these after the war varied greatly, because they were not all equally adaptable to peacetime uses. The new plant for making drop forgings has almost all been used continuously since the war, both new hammers installed in existing works, and in new works which were 'strategically' dispersed. Many quick-acting American hammers were brought in and the efficiency of the industry was appreciably raised for relatively heavy work; and the new works set a high standard for welfare and working conditions.[1] Much of the expansion in the steel-foundry trade, on the other hand, proved of little or no value after the war, being designed for needs for which there were no peacetime substitutes.[2] Additions to existing foundries proved valuable later on; but the wholly new foundries turned out to be of little subsequent use. Two of the largest plants were actually not used during the war itself.[3] New gun-forging and armour plants similarly had little post-war value, though some of the equipment, machine tools for example, could be used in other works for other purposes,[4] and the buildings could be adapted to other industries.[5] Finishing trades such as these are, however, only on the fringe of the activities with which this book is mainly concerned.

Although the rate of re-equipment and development in ordinary steelmaking was slowed down by the war, and much of the other expansion done had little subsequent value, the

[1] For some early stages in the history of drop forging—the pressing of hot but not molten metal into moulds or 'dies'—cp. *E.H.S.* p. 63. Before the war both German and American hammers were being brought into this country. Hitherto the pressure was exerted on the hot metal by a heavy hammer dropped from a height. American and German hammers were not dropped, but power-driven; they worked faster and exerted more force.

[2] Typical instances are bomb castings, castings for tank caterpillar track links, and for aircraft engine cylinder sleeve linings.

[3] At Coltness and Burton. The explanation is possibly threefold—over insurance of supply, slow building, change in tank or bomb programmes.

[4] The electric furnaces for bomb foundries were too large for normal steel foundries and too small for ingot production; conveyors in foundries were of little use except for the original site and job.

[5] The largest bomb factory building (Stanton), for example, is used for making concrete pipes.

war gave the Control and the R.M.D. a large experience in investment control, with virtually absolute power, the sort of control which some people in the industry were seeking to obtain for the Federation in a much more limited form under other auspices before the war. The relevant criteria were entirely different, but methods of procedure were evolved. The Control at the outset had little technical advice at its disposal, its staff being initially drawn from the administrative and sales side of the industry. But it brought in a technical adviser for the steel-foundry programme in 1940;[1] the Tube Director brought in a technical adviser,[2] and in 1942 one was appointed who would cover all the Control's main activities.[3] A progressing organisation was also instituted to co-ordinate and hasten the work on expansion schemes at all stages, including the initial securing of consents and licences as well as the ultimate provision of materials and machines. These were to prove important instruments of central administration.

3. COSTS, PRICES AND PROFITS

All the elements of cost that enter into steelmaking rose during the war, but as during the First World War they did not keep in step. The prices of different ingredients rose at different rates, and the proportions in which they were available or were used also changed at different rates. The most dramatic and quickest changes were not unnaturally in the prices of imported raw materials, which shot up immediately on the outbreak of war. Not unnaturally, again, the devices invented by the Steel Federation to stabilise prices in 1937 when imported materials prices rose were invoked on a large scale to stabilise prices during the war, and were elaborated and built upon to become almost unrecognisable and to the average outsider incomprehensible. These measures, after a somewhat sluggish start, were

---

[1] Dr Paul Fassotte.   [2] Dr Jenkin of Tube Investments.

[3] The adviser was Dr Colclough, formerly a partner in Brassert's, an important firm of consultants associated in the thirties with Corby, Ebbw Vale, the Jarrow project, and the Herman Göring works at Salzgitter. After a distinguished academic record he for a time managed the open-hearth shop at Park Gate, and later became an expert on blast-furnace technology. Much of his advisory work at the Control was concerned not with expansion but with furnace operating.

made to succeed in their primary object, but they did so by concealing the real costs of steelmaking at individual plants, and by sacrificing any attempt at a rational distribution of profit. In effect, because 1936–7 was used as a profit ceiling on old investments they favoured old plants and old regions; and the strategic advantages of the West for wartime investment reinforced this effect. The stabilising measures involved also, though this was not perhaps perceived at the time, a reduction of average real profit. During the war this sort of thing was no disadvantage because of the extent of central control. It became important at the end of the war when future investments for peace were being planned, and the measurement of marginal costs, the costs of making specific contributions and additions to output regained significance.

Firms did not emerge from the Second World War as from the first with a lot of additional, often only partly completed, capacity, which imposed heavy financial burdens and commitments, bank loans which were converted into debentures and became a growing encumbrance during the twenties.[1] Instead, they had rather larger liquid resources after the Second War than when it began. In this respect the financial state of the industry was better after the Second World War. But so long as the wartime methods of price control, depressing profit margins and distorting costs continued even in part, forecasting by individual firms was exceptionally hazardous. And for various reasons, political and economic, the Federation and Government alike preferred to continue these arrangements for several years. Thus though firms could start reconstructing without the particular handicap imposed by the First World War (though not immediately recognised as a handicap) the industry was encumbered in another way. How this worked out is part of the story of the early years of peace, but it gives the details of price and profit control measures in the Second World War a significance they did not have in the First. The fact that they paved the way for stabilising relatively low prices for steel was of course disturbing for the economy as a whole as well as for the steel industry itself.

[1] See *E.H.S.* pp. 382 sqq.

Changes of cost usually preceded changes of price in steel during the war; and although after the earliest stages changes of cost themselves reflected price policies both in the steel industry and in other industries, it is convenient to survey first the changes of cost in some detail before examining the evolution of price policy and the course of profits.

(a) Costs

The different rates at which steelworkers' wages and the prices of the chief raw materials for steel rose during the war are shown in Table 2.

Table 2. *Changes in costs of material and labour, 1939–44*

January–June 1939 = 100; yearly averages except where specified.

	Price per ton in base period	1940	1941	1942	1943	1944
Imported materials:						
Iron ore (C.I.F.)[a]	25s.	170	318	317	334	335
Scrap (C.I.F.)[a]	73s. 6d.	187	234	194	67	139[b]
Steel: billets, blooms and slabs (C.I.F.)[a]	131s.	188	230	240	234	227
Home materials:						
Iron ore—Midland, F.O.T.[c]	3s. 5d.	125	130	138	145	150
Scrap, heavy, bought delivered to works[d]	56s.	127	129	129	129	129
special supplies[e]	None	225	225	225	225	225
Coal (average pit head)[f]	17s. 4d.	118	139	152	167	190
Coking coal (Durham, F.O.T.)[g]	16s. 3d.	137	155	172	186	219
Coke (Durham, F.O.T.)[g]	24s. 2d.	140	151	176	187	217
Rail transport[h]	—	110	115	115	115	115
Labour:[i]						
Average earnings per week	80s.	133	139	154	167	167
Average earnings per hour	20·8d.	120	130	135	145	151

[a] Trade and Navigation Accounts.

[b] The quantity of scrap imported when prices were low was small; possibly the price was low through price controls.

[c] The pre-war figure price is not for Jan.–June 1939, but for 1938, and is from the *Ann. Rep. of the Secretary for Mines*. The percentage increase is based on a large

sample of cost figures, and the rise in costs is treated as a rise in price. In wartime practice the rise of price would have been less than the rise of cost. The figures for 1940–2 are interpolated.

ᵈ The 1937 price was 65s. A levy added a further 14 per cent. Below, p. 24.

ᵉ These figures are based on information I obtained in the Control; they are percentages of the 1939 prices for heavy bought scrap.

ᶠ The initial price is for 1938; the series is based on data in the *Ministry of Fuel and Power Statistical Digest for 1948 and 1949*, p. 44.

ᵍ The figures are difficult. There were schedule prices, for several grades of coking coal and of coke; but sales on old contracts went on at old prices after schedule prices had changed. The price of coking coal rose, fairly steadily, from 1937 to 1939. The price of coke climbed steeply and fell even more steeply. The approximate figures are:

May 1937	32s. 6d.	July 1938	27s. 6d.
June 1937	35s. 0d.	Jan. 1939	24s. 2d.
Sept. 1937	37s. 6d.	Nov. 1939	29s. 2d.

The figures given can only be an approximation. Yorkshire figures moved fairly similarly but on a lower level. I have been helped by individual firms, the Federation and the National Coal Board, to all of whom I am grateful.

ʰ *Fourth Ann. Rep. Brit. Transport Comm.* 1951, p. 39. Railway rates rose twice in 1940, by 10 per cent in April, and by 5 per cent in December. They then remained stationary for the rest of the war. The figure 110 for 1940, given as an average, is merely approximate, slightly too high.

ⁱ Based on Ministry of Labour periodic surveys of earnings and hours of work. These were made for July in all the war years, and for January also from 1942 onwards. I have used the July figures for the table. I have taken steel melting and rolling only, and adult male workers only. I have assumed that the average earnings for Jan.–June 1939 were equal to those of Oct. 1938, which is the base year for the Ministry of Labour figures. The sliding scale addition rose above the Oct. 1938 level from February to May, and then fell below it. I have no data to compare average hours of work. This series differs from one which might be based on the Control's returns (summarised in *Stat. B.I.S.F.* 1939–44, p. 50); but these include a wide range of finishing trades with different wage-levels whose relative importance changed, and a growing proportion of women workers and clerical workers. The Ministry of Labour figures only give earnings per hour from July 1943; the earlier figures are interpolations, but I have based them on the increase of weekly earnings of blast-furnace workers, whose hours of work could not increase to the same extent as steelworkers owing to the necessary continuity of the operation in peace as in war.

Prices of imported materials thus rose much more than the other costs. They reflected the high shipping costs. The contrasted movements in prices of home-produced supplies—coal, home scrap, home ore and rail transport—reflect basically the different influence of wage increases in industries in which the importance of direct labour varies greatly, though they were also in part an expression of price policies.

The rise of foreign ore prices (C.I.F.) was naturally the most dramatic change, because for a product cheap in relation to its bulk and weight wartime freights and war-risk insurance quickly became the dominating elements of cost. These shipping costs alone rose to upwards of 50s. a ton, reaching from some sources 80s. a ton, compared with a normal freight range before the war of from 6s. 6d. to 15s. a ton. The price of ore in the country of origin, the F.O.B. price, rose only moderately, in general probably not more than 50 per cent. The rise in ore prices was more dramatic than important during the war because the quantity used fell so sharply. The rise in the C.I.F. prices of scrap and of steel—in this context especially of steel 'semis'—though less impressive in percentages than that of ore, was in the aggregate much more important at some stages of the war, namely, until the virtual end of scrap imports after 1941, in the first case, and until steel was imported under Lease Lend in the second. As will be seen below it remained even then a book-keeping burden for the steelmakers.

The much cheaper home ores which were a partial substitute for imported ores were of course low in iron and high in phosphorus, so that more fuel was needed to refine them both in blast furnaces and steel furnaces; the outputs of blast furnaces fell because more materials had to pass through for a ton of iron, so that adjacent steel furnaces had less liquid iron, and the steel-refining period was lengthened on this account as well as on account of the quality of the iron. Moreover, as has been seen, the ores had often to be taken long distances to coastal blast furnaces.

The cost of scrap from normal home sources rose least of all steelmakers' costs during the war except transport. There were increased costs of moving and preparing scrap which had to be covered, but scrap prices, as has been seen, are not determined primarily by cost of production; it was possible to keep them down during the war by the simple device of fixing maximum prices. This controlled price was not relied upon to bring in the extra home scrap which was wanted to replace imported raw materials, or to pay for collecting the new kinds of scrap which the war itself created—steel in blitzed buildings and in ships torpedoed or mined near the coast. For abnormal home scrap there were *ad hoc* means of collection, often fairly costly, but averaged over the whole this would have raised the average cost by less than one-fifth.[1] In fact the cost of these supplies, like the high cost of imported scrap, was paid for out of a central fund financed by levies on ingot output and on purchase of scrap.

Railway rates were moved up very moderately during the war. It was possible to increase the number of goods trains without a proportionate increase in all railway staff, to load goods trains as well as passenger trains more heavily, and to defer some repairs and maintenance. Output per man could thus be easily increased as traffic increased.[2]

The cost of getting coal by contrast rose more seriously than any other domestic item in steelmaking costs. Direct labour was by far the chief cost in coal-mining; wages were raised much more in coal-mining than in other industries,[3] and output per man fell seriously. The fall was greater in some coalfields than in others. It was greatest in some of the older areas, such as South Wales and Durham, whose costs before the war were already above the average, and least in the newer fields of the east Midlands. But the Government stepped in to insulate the users of coal from the effects of these disparities; the disparate cost changes were not reflected in prices. After the early stages of the war it was decided that all changes in coal prices should be uniform for coal from all mines and for coal of all qualities,[4] and for this purpose those mines whose costs rose more than the average, more therefore than the rise

---

[1] Scrap from salvaged ships cost on an average £7 per ton; old tram-rails cost over £8. The total amount of special scrap collected by the spring of 1943 was 1·3 m. tons.

[2] This was familiar at the time, but by far the most illuminating data are in the *Rep. Brit. Transport Comm. for 1951, loc. cit.*

[3] Average weekly earnings of adult male workers in manufacturing industry rose by 74 per cent between Oct. 1938 and Jan. 1945. Hours of work had risen by 5 per cent. Miners' earnings rose by 84 per cent a week between 1939 and 1944—and average shifts per week fell by 6 per cent.

[4] The policy was discussed in a White Paper issued in April 1945 (*Coal Charges Account* (Cmd. 6617), esp. pp. 8 sqq.).

in coal prices, were compensated out of a pool into which all mines contributed. The high-cost mines were subsidised by the mines with low costs.[1]

For steelmaking this policy was important in two ways. First, it meant that the rise in the price of coal in South Wales, Durham and Cumberland was much less than the movement of costs; in Yorkshire and Scotland costs and prices moved broadly together, in Nottingham prices rose more than costs. Thus some important old higher cost areas of steel production were favoured by a subsidy on coal which the newest low-cost areas did not have and to which they may have slightly contributed.[2] Secondly, in addition to evening-out the movement of prices in different regions the price policy may have had the effect of raising coking-coal prices more than the price of

[1] *Ibid.* passim. The net contributions or 'subsidies' for individual districts are given for 1943–4 on p. 13. There was also a net contribution to the Coal Charges Fund— in effect a subsidy—from the Treasury during the war. The figures for different districts are of course averages; some mines had larger and some smaller subsidies, or made larger or smaller net contributions to the Fund.

[2] The broad facts are shown in the following table (based on returns in the Ministry of Fuel and Power's *Statistical Digest* for 1944 and 1945):

	Cost per ton in 3rd qr. 1944		Percent-age in-crease of total cost since 1938	Percent-age de-crease in output per man-shift since 1938	Net payments to or receipts from coal charges levy	
	Total cost	Labour cost			Receipts	Payments
S. Wales and Monmouth	45s. 9d.	31s. 4d.	151	23	8s. 4d.	—
Durham	37s. 4d.	26s. 2d.	142	23	3s. 5d.	—
Scotland	32s. 6d.	23s. 7d.	114	13	—	1s. 7d.
Yorks	31s. 11d.	23s. 4d.	106	16	6d.	—
Notts	27s. 3d.	19s. 9d.	94	8*	—	2s. 9d.

*(increase)

The South Wales figure covers the anthracite as well as steam and coking coal. This raised the average cost and lowered the average output per man-shift, but the coking and steam-coal areas nevertheless received substantial payments from the levy. High-cost steel areas thus gained substantially from the subsidy. Places depending largely or wholly on Yorkshire coal—Scunthorpe, for example— received no such significant subsidy if any at all; Corby, which used some coal from South Wales and Durham, gained a little on account of this, but made a contribution to the Coal Charges Account for their Nottingham coal.

'average' coal. Coking-coal prices had already risen more than the average between 1937 and 1939, but the wartime trend was not a further projection of this, but rather an accidental continuation.[1]

The price of coke, for firms who bought from independent ovens, was often said to have risen even more than the price of coking coal, though the records show there was no great difference.[2] When the war opened the price of coke was still fixed by the sliding-scale agreement of 1937.[3] By the end of 1939, however, the Steel Federation thought that the original principle of the sliding scale was no longer fully appropriate; there might be increases in steel prices, due to high costs of imported ore, for example, which seemed no longer obviously to require or justify a rise in coke prices. A new sliding scale was negotiated, which lessened the variation of coke prices as steel prices moved, so that coke prices would rise less than on the old scale with any further rise of steel prices, and there was a provision that if steel prices were raised by a levy to pay for high-cost imports—as they had been in a measure ever since 1937—the operation of the sliding scale might be suspended in respect of such a rise. Shortly after this negotiation the Auditor General expressed the view that a sliding-scale system of this kind did not conform to established principles of Government costing for price-fixing; the price of the coke should vary with its own costs of production. This was accepted, though it was

---

[1] The trend was as follows. The figures in brackets give prices as percentages of 1937 prices.

	Realised average pithead selling price for all coal (U.K.)	Price of coking coal	
		Durham (at ovens)	Yorkshire (at ovens)
	s. d.	s. d.	s. d.
1937	15 11 (100)	14 9 (100)	13 7 (100)
1938	17 4 (109)	16 9 (113)	15 10 (117)
1944	33 3 (209)	33 11 (224)	30 10 (225)

Since costs of transport rose much less than the cost of mining it may be assumed that the pithead price of coking coal would have risen slightly more in relation to the average price than the delivered (at ovens) price. Rail freights in Durham were 3s. to 5s. a ton; e.g. Consett to Middlesbrough, 4s. 10d.; Brancepeth to Middlesbrough, 3s. 11d. In Yorkshire somewhat higher.

[2] Above, p. 21.   [3] E.H.S. pp. 475, 502.

not quite simply applicable, since coke is a joint product, together with gas, tar, benzol and other derivatives.[1] The average overall profit to be made was fixed at 4s. a ton; and the future prices of coke and by-products were adjusted to give this result in the aggregate. But the 'by-product' prices were raised less than the coke prices, presumably because of the circumstances governing the costs and prices of the 'by-products' when these were derived from other sources.[2] This would account for any tendency of coke prices to rise proportionately more than coal prices. They rose considerably more ultimately, though less fast, than they would have done under the new sliding scale of early 1940.[3]

Average earnings of workers in the steel industry, unlike those in coal-mining, moved close to the average in all industries. It was argued in a Treasury memorandum in 1929 that 'limitation of wages is probably more important than limitation of profits' in controlling inflation, 'since all other methods failing taxation (it might well have argued "including taxation") can be applied more easily to correct inflated profits than to correct inflated wage payments'.[4] This order of priorities was not, perhaps it could not be, observed during the war. But in the steel industry the basis on which wages were changed—the sliding scale whereby wages rose if the price of steel rose—was replaced very early in the war, in order, it would appear, to avoid a steep rise of wages on account of the high costs of importing foreign

[1] The amount of different by-products obtained varies with different coals; and some coke ovens carry their refinement much further than others. The value of the main products—gas, crude tar, sulphate of ammonia, benzol and breeze—was about 40 per cent of the value of the coke output in Durham in 1936–37, and close on 60 per cent in Yorkshire.

[2] The return from by-products rose by different proportions in different regions. Such figures as I have been able to examine suggest that the money yield per ton of coke from sales of crude tar, sulphate of ammonia, crude benzol, stripped gas and breeze in the year 1943 was about 33 per cent higher than in 1938 in Durham and Yorkshire, 50 per cent higher in Derby and Notts, and almost doubled in South Wales and Scotland. In the first three instances the rise was much less than for coke.

[3] When steel reached its peak price in Nov. 1940, the coke price according to the scale would have been about 37s. 6d. In fact it averaged about 40s. per ton in 1942, and rose by stages to 52s. 6d. in 1944. Steel prices would have had to be over £5 higher to have yielded this coke price by the sliding scale.

[4] Hancock and Gowing, op. cit. p. 48.

raw materials. In the earliest stages of the war the sliding scale would have operated unfavourably for the wage earners because it involved a time-lag. The price reduction of January 1939 had its main impact in the sliding scale in May 1939, when the sliding-scale addition fell sharply. Wage-rates, though possibly not earnings, would have remained below the 1938 level in the autumn of 1939 had the scale been adhered to. But steel prices were already being raised in response to the rising prices of imported material, and the cost of living was beginning to rise. This position was too paradoxical to be acceptable, or easily defended, and an 'anticipatory' addition of 10 per cent was agreed to in November. A further 10 per cent rise occurred in the spring, again reflecting the rising cost of imports, and this now looked menacing to those who were trying to prevent steel prices rising too fast. Unjustified by any change at home, such an increase, it was argued, must be inflationary. The Auditor General expressed a dislike for the traditional sliding scale which linked steelworkers' wages with the price of steel, as he had also done for the new sliding scale for coke. With a superb disregard for logic, a system which linked wages with the cost of living (with the implication that the standard of living could be wholly sustained in despite of the war) was substituted for the historic scale, and the historic scale, put into abeyance for the war, has not yet been restored.[1]

It was soon to become clear that wage-rates linked with the cost of living yielded, as could have been foreseen (and no doubt was foreseen by some of the negotiators), earnings which rose faster than the cost-of-living index.[2] In the middle of 1941 the Government issued the first White Paper on Personal Incomes, euphemistically entitled *Price Stabilisation and Industrial Policy*,[3] which pointed out that standards of life must inevitably be lower during the war. Even if wages moved with the cost of living the goods would not be there to buy. 'The vicious spiral', the White Paper argued, started with high prices inducing wage demands, and it urged 'both sides of industry' to prevent in all ways, including wage policy, any rise of costs. It still visualised

[1] *Min. of Labour Gaz.* Jan. 1941, p. 3.
[2] Hancock and Gowing, *op. cit.* p. 169.   [3] Cmd. 6294, July 1941.

higher earnings for higher efficiency and where wage-rates were very low. The T.U.C. retorted in a 'rejoinder' that 'any attempt to control movements for increases of wages is impracticable and undesirable', as it had been in 1914–18. They welcomed, self-righteously, the Government's statement that in negotiating through the usual machinery the unions had 'made no attempt to exploit the war situation in the interests of their members' (they had, in fact, doubtless in a fit of absentmindedness, already increased their share of the national income), and they supported the policy of controlling profits arising through the war.[1] This rejoinder showed that, as the *Economist* put it, the White Paper policy was 'honest but barren'. It became essential since wages were, if only moderately, out of hand, to 'render the size of the money income as unimportant as possible', by rationing and in other ways.[2] Price relations became progressively more irrational.

The Government's measures to check the rise in the cost of living, by subsidies and other means, became fairly effective from the middle of 1941. The cost-of-living index only rose 5 points from July 1941 to the end of the war. But the steelworkers' earnings were not held in check to the same extent. In the steel industry the structure of the sliding scale was subjected to two major adjustments, so that the additions for cost-of-living increases should become larger.[3] There were also minor adjustments having the same effect. There was no rise in the productivity of labour in the industry to justify this; on the contrary, during the war years productivity fell (except for highly specialised products made in much greater quantities than usual), due mainly to the use of different and often poorer raw materials, and a little to unfavourable operating conditions.

The marginal cost of steel evidently rose far more than the average during the war years. How far the average rose is a hazardous calculation. A fairly close guess of primary raw material costs can be made; the course of processing and maintenance and administrative costs must remain, in the absence of published records, obscure. The cost of iron ore for

[1] *The Times*, 23 July 1941. The 'rejoinder' was made by Sir Walter (now Lord) Citrine.　　　　[2] *Econ.* 28 July 1941.　　　　[3] *Min. of Labour Gaz.*

a ton of basic pig iron rose on an average by about 70 per cent by the end of 1944, and the cost of coke by about 130 per cent. Ore and coke together cost about 85 per cent more. (The price of pig iron was 75 per cent up by the beginning of 1945.) The main raw materials for basic open-hearth steel—ore and coke for the pig iron, plus scrap and fuel—rose by approximately 80 per cent. Since average hourly earnings rose by 55 per cent, and more labour was needed for a ton of steel, it would be reasonable to assume that labour costs, for identical products, rose by about 60 per cent. Maintenance and general overhead costs are unlikely to have risen by less than the cost of labour; they probably were higher, since plants were ageing and poorer raw materials reduced their output. Costs of new plant and building probably rose slightly more than wages, so depreciation in replacement terms also rose by 70 per cent or more.[1] The general implication of these figures seems that average costs at steelworks rose by about 70 per cent between the beginning of the war and the end of 1944.

(b) Prices and profits

The Steel Federation's price policy in 1937, whose object was to restrain the rise of steel prices in face of rising costs of imported raw materials, provided the inevitable model for the first stage of wartime price policy. The policy had, after all, been blessed by I.D.A.C., and the members of the staff of I.D.A.C., who had been most concerned with steel, were now handling steel for the Ministry of Supply (R.M.D.). The Federation's system, as Sir William Brown explained to the Committee of Public Accounts, was one 'to which the industry was accustomed, and it was working'. Its application to mitigate and average out the effect of rising imported ore prices was worked out before the war started, and the scheme was ready to put into immediate effect.[2]

Some products which were outside the Federation's orbit but within the Control's—most tubes, forgings and drop forgings, steel castings, some special alloy steels and re-rolled

[1] *Rep. B.I.S.F.* p. 32.
[2] *Rep. P.A.C.* 1941, p. 331. See also pp. xxv sqq. and 320 sqq.

products are typical—could not be brought within the Federation's method of price-fixing, because the range of sizes and shapes made was very diverse, the scale of demand changed quickly and therefore the condition of production, and there was no reasonable sense in which 'average costs' of 'representative efficient producers' in the past could be made the basis of current or future price. These 'fringe products' were subject to special forms of price control. But prices of the bulk products, where variations from 'average' cost on account of variations of size and shape are fairly standard and relatively small in relation to the average, were fixed in the first 15 months of the war by the old formula. Uniform delivered prices—uniform for home and imported steel alike—were retained. Prices were fixed to cover 'ascertained' costs and still leave a reasonable profit'.[1] But the burden of high marginal costs was in a large measure spread over the whole production by the use of a Central Fund created in November 1939 and financed by levies (which were accepted as manufacturing costs for the purpose of price-fixing), on the model of the Spread Over Fund of 1937, but with higher levies on both ingots and scrap.[2] The new fund was used at first mainly to enable imported ore and scrap to be sold at or close to pre-war prices, and imported pig iron and steel at British prices. It was also used to meet some high domestic costs, a few 'once-for-all' costs (such as obscuring the glare of steelworks at night), but most of them recurrent. Some high-cost home ore production was subsidised; so too were exceptional transport costs for ore and pig iron, and exceptional costs of collecting some types of scrap.

Under this system steel prices, although they did not follow marginal costs, nevertheless rose by 50 per cent within 15 months.[3] Thus while the policy was designed in keeping with

---

[1] Cp. the explanation of Sir William Palmer, *Rep. P.A.C.* 1941, pp. 320 sqq.

[2] The scrap levy, introduced at 2s. 6d. a ton early in 1939, became 9s. a ton early in the war. The more lucrative ingot levy, 5s. a ton before the war, rose to 49s. 6d. a ton.

[3] For details see 14th *Report Select Committee on National Expenditure* (session 1942–3), pp. 71–3, which gives the price increases for the main heavy products, distinguishing the parts of the increase due to levies for the Central Fund from those related to other cost increases.

the Government's initial intention that prices should rise only so far as increased payments unavoidably incurred by producers[1] required it, nevertheless, the rise which it involved was an important part of the experience which led to the second phase of price policy, the phase of more resolute stabilisation, expressed in the White Paper of 1941 already referred to. Rising steel prices were widely regarded as exceptionally inflationary (though the point was not closely analysed or clearly understood), since steel was a cost in practically all industries. The increase in November 1940 which brought prices of heavy steel roughly 50 per cent above those of 1939, which alarmed the critics, was only accepted and sponsored by the Ministry of Supply as a final increase, and on the understanding that if costs continued to rise other steps would be taken to ensure full production. Steel prices were thus the first to be 'pegged'. Almost six months later, after difficult negotiations, the 'other steps' were agreed upon.[2]

They proved to be a new and still more complex application of the Central Fund. Increases of cost and the 'appropriate' increase of price per ton continued to be assessed every quarter for all the main heavy products.[3] But the buyer was not charged this addition; nor was it in all instances paid to the seller. It was only paid to firms who were not already earning their pre-war ('standard') profits.[4] Firms who by selling at the stabilised prices earned their 'standard' got nothing more. Firms earning

[1] Higher wages and higher prices for coal had to be paid. Higher profits did not have to be paid, nor higher depreciation accumulated, though as a *cost* it was necessarily rising.

[2] The discussions were under way when the Committee of Public Accounts was examining the Ministry of Supply Accounts in 1941, and the position emerged in the answers of Sir William Palmer and Sir William Brown already referred to in these notes.

[3] I.e. the cost increases by the Ministry of Supply's investigating accountant (also the accountant of the B.I.S.F. and B.I.S.C., viz. Peat Marwick and Mitchell) and the tonnage payments by the Ministry's Advisory Accountant, Mr Macharg of M'clelland Ker's. H. Owen, *Steel—the Facts*, p. 65, says, 'The accountants', including all who were concerned, 'were appointed by the Federation'. This was an error. Mr Macharg was first asked in 1938 to report to I.D.A.C., who were prompted by the Comptroller and Auditor General to employ an advisory accountant (*Rep. P.A.C.* 1940, Q. 771).

[4] 'Standard' by criteria established by the scheme. Pre-war profits were adjusted in ways which are described below, p. 48.

below their standard were paid (out of a 'Prices Fund' financed from the Central Fund) a part or all of the assessed increase of cost. They received the whole only if after the addition they still did not earn their pre-war 'standard'. Otherwise they received only the amount necessary to bring them up to their pre-war profit standard.

There were some very high cost firms who still made losses on these heavy products after the whole of the price increase was paid; in these instances a further payment might be made from the Prices Fund to cover the losses. Or firms might ask, where their costs were very high, for an extra payment to bring their profits up to 25 per cent of the pre-war standard. The firms who chose to have their losses on the specific products made up were presumably making profits in other activities. In both classes of case the Ministry of Supply had the right to investigate the efficiency of the firms concerned, and in most substantial instances of the second—they were not very numerous—they 'took steps to strengthen the management'.[1]

This system operated till the end of the war. The prices paid by consumers for heavy steel products remained unchanged though costs still rose by possibly another 20 per cent, and makers, to varying extents, were compensated by 'tonnage payments' and in other ways from the Prices Fund.

The lighter more highly finished and specialised products were not subject to the system; their prices were often subject to revision in the light of the profits they yielded, and some large, indeed enormous, rebates were paid.[2] There were no tonnage payments for these products, though the Prices Fund was available for firms earning below 25 per cent of their pre-war profit.[3] In

---

[1] *S.C. on Nat. Exp.* p. 75. In three out of the four of these cases which had occurred up to autumn 1943 the Ministry took 'steps to strengthen the management'.

[2] Probably prices were not revised downwards quickly enough as the load increased. It seemed so to some people at the time. These were products for which new plant was built. It was leased, at wartime costs, to managing firms. The question was asked in mid-1940, how can the prices cover wartime rents and not give extremely high profits on old plant? The question implied a standstill in depreciation as well as a standstill in valuation of capital irrespective of inflation.

[3] *Ibid.* pp. 75–8. Payment to bring these firms up to the 25 per cent standard meant using a levy paid by ingot producers to help firms who did not make ingots.

most instances the hazards during the war were relatively slight and the load exceptionally favourable.

No increase was made in the levy for the Central Fund to provide for the new Prices Fund. But the Central Fund was already running in surplus when the new scheme was conceived; there was a balance of £3,670,763 in hand.[1] The levies had been calculated on the expectation that imports would be greater than in the end they were. This could be seen to be happening quite early, but it continued for some time after the final increase of November 1940. Whether it was at any stage a deliberate over-insurance is not clear,[2] but it enabled rising home costs to be financed until 1943 without running the Fund into deficit. Thereafter there was a deficit which was financed by the Ministry of Supply. In the latest stages of the war therefore stabilisation was subsidised. There was an element of artificiality in this since the Central Fund was still called upon after the introduction of Lease Lend to pay the difference between the amount which American supplies would have cost had they been paid for and the lower prices of English steel. By 1944, however, the stabilised prices of heavy steel were not covering the costs of steelmaking, including the costs of importing raw materials but excluding the notional 'cost' of putting American steel on the market. There was a real subsidy.[3]

[1] *S.C. on Nat. Exp.* pp. 71–3. This was out of a total of levies amounting at the time to about £16 m. In Nov. 1940 the Central Fund, hitherto a private Federation Fund, became a Ministry of Supply Fund. The levies continued to need the approval of the President's Committee, to whom proposed rates of levy were submitted before being formally submitted to R.M.D.

[2] It was tempting in estimating import needs to provide wide margins for possible losses at sea and other perils. But until the losses occurred no doubt the whole as estimated might be regarded as potential imports involving financial liabilities. There were times when programmes were expanding when the rate at which orders were placed in America fell considerably below the Corporation's general estimate of what would be placed, perhaps through uncertainty in dollar supplies. There were, later, revisions of import programmes downwards for which those who calculated the levies could not have made provision. In mid-1940 plans were to import steel from America at an annual rate of over 7 m. tons a year, but this took a too cheerful view of the shipping prospects. The Control in estimating probable output always recognised that import programmes would not be realised in full.

[3] If the cost estimates above (p. 30) are a reliable guide the subsidy by early 1945 would have been close on £2 a ton of heavy steel.

These complex and to the outsider puzzling arrangements attracted the critical attention year by year of the Public Accounts Committee of the House of Commons (aided and possibly abetted by the Comptroller and Auditor General, Sir Gilbert Upcott) and in 1943 of the Select Committee on Expenditure.[1] Their complexity itself was an object of complaint; some M.P.'s were never able to see daylight through them. The Committees were mainly concerned with three questions—was the price policy inflationary? Did it encourage efficiency? Did it give unreasonably high profits?

That a rise in steel prices was inflationary was well-nigh universally deemed axiomatic; but it was an infectious assumption rather than reasoned belief. Some of the wartime developments in the industry certainly epitomised inescapable or largely inescapable inflationary influences of the war. The use of a large proportion of low-grade home ore for example (which lessened the output of furnaces, increased fuel consumption, lengthened the refining processes and increased the amount of waste products) inevitably meant that more man-hours of work had to be paid for, directly and indirectly, in making a ton of steel, so that failing a reduction of average earnings either there were— to use the early post-war Treasury jingle—less goods for money to chase or more money chasing the goods. And unless it was counterbalanced by taxes the absorption of more of the industry's output for munitions would help to reduce the volume of goods which civilians could buy faster than their spending power was reduced. But it was not this sort of thing which engaged the attention of the critics of price policy.

The heart of their criticism was that since steel was used in so many industries, when the price of steel rose many other prices rose too; and 'since quite a number—of charges—are regulated on a turnover percentage the basic increase in steel prices may in its final effect on public expenditure be considerably magnified'.[2] It was of course easy to show that much of the

---

[1] *Proceedings of the Committee of Public Accounts*, published annually, and *14th Rep. S.C. on Nat. Exp.* (Session 1942–43). It is the practice of Chairmen of the P.A.C. to consult with the Auditor General before probing into the accounts of a department and cross-examining the senior civil servants concerned.

[2] *14th Rep. S.C. in Nat. Exp.* 1942–3, p. 73.

increase in steel prices merely transmitted the effects of rises of wages or falls of efficiency—in the steel industry itself or industries like the coal industry upon which it relied for raw materials and other supplies. These effects could only be avoided to the extent that other incomes derived from the sale of steel could be squeezed (which some of the critics no doubt wanted to happen). But it was argued that the snowball effect positively generated inflation, and that less inflation would have been generated if, for example, the Government had covered all the increased price of imports by a subsidy, and stabilised these prices. This was the most seductive suggestion,[1] though it was not without its difficulties. For example, had this been done in the early months of the war, when Government orders took less than two-thirds of steel output, steel prices would have remained more attractive for non-war purposes, and the net cost to the Treasury would have been greater because it would have provided the subsidy for the whole output, not merely the levy cost in the price of the two-thirds of the output used by the Department.[2]

A subsidy on imported materials would, however, certainly have lessened the steep rise of steel prices up to November 1940 —by perhaps one-half. Had steel prices been insulated from the added cost of imports but not from rising home costs they would have risen more slowly but probably more continuously than they did. They would then have been much less conspicuous as a symbol of supposed profits from war, and their psychological disturbance would have been less. But although the rise was dramatic and caught the public eye, no one seems to have asked whether its inflationary force in a mechanical sense could be more than trivial. How much did the turnover of the industry grow, and what was the snowballing coefficient? A rough estimate of the net turnover of the industry based on the Census of Production for 1937 gives rather less than £150 m. for 1937.[3] This would have risen to a rate of perhaps £165 m.

---

[1] Set out most fully in *Rep. S.C. on Nat. Exp.* p. 73.

[2] *Ibid. loc. cit.*; the Control put the consumption for Government purposes at 60 per cent only when it was decided not to have a subsidy.

[3] The gross output of the steel melting and rolling industry was £129·7 m. in 1937. This includes some ferro-alloys which must be excluded, and some duplica-

in the first half of 1939. By 1941 it was possibly £250 m. and the inflationary snowball would be a proportion of the difference between these, viz. £85 m.—almost certainly considerably less, though no figure can possibly be given.[1] The gross increase of turnover after 1941 must have been relatively small; after mid-1943 turnover presumably fell. Evidently an inflationary effect on this scale, even if it was correctly diagnosed, did not deserve all the attention it received from Parliamentary Committees, the press, some professional economists and some administrators (who may be most readily forgiven since they had least leisure for detached observation).

By the time this topic was most discussed—long after steel prices had ceased to rise—imports of finished steel from America were being provided under Lease Lend. The practice was continued, however, whereby the Central Fund was used to pay the Government the full nominal cost of this American steel, the steel being sold to users, including steel firms who used the American 'semis' at the British uniform price. On what theory this was done was obscure; perhaps it was merely a 'vestigial trace'. Even the Control treated it as inflationary, when it was bringing the Fund into deficit. It was wrong they argued to load steel prices with a levy to pay for the higher cost of American steel which would have been incurred if the American suppliers had had to be paid from this country. The logic would have been simpler had there not also been reverse Lease Lend, and if steel prices had not been stabilised. The

---

tion, e.g. bright bars as well as the black bars from which they are drawn. It includes also 'semis' for sheet, tinplate, wire rod, tubes. These must be eliminated, which can only be done roughly, and the gross value of tubes, sheets, tinplates and wire added to give turnover in 1937.

[1] The percentage added in each round of snowballing would be far less than 100 per cent—and much steel was sold to a final user; ship plates, for example; railway rails and a lot of other steel to railway companies (price increases would not in any event 'snowball' here); and much of the steel used in motor cars. Steel used in Royal Ordnance factories would not be subject to snowballing. Some degree of snowballing may have been called for—it possibly was—because it may have corresponded to increases of administrative cost and overheads in the user industry, which were conveniently if inaccurately reflected in the cost-plus or percentage process, but which would have been covered in some way in any case. This is not, however, germane to the argument here, which is concerned with scale.

practice was important in retrospect because it continued after the end of Lease Lend.

Those who emphasized individual price controls in countering inflation were in danger of mistaking symptoms for causes, particularly when the price was one, like the price of steel, whose influence on the cost of living (which in turn has an effect, partly functional, partly psychological, on wages) is slight and slow. At first sight those who regarded wage increases themselves as a cause of inflation might also be suspected of mistaking a symptom (a particular kind of price increase) for a cause. But this was a special case. Higher wages were among the major costs which were accepted as a justification for higher prices; and because they were accepted they were 'validated' or substantiated by increases in money supplies, first in bank advances and ultimately in increased Government expenditure, which were not countered by increased taxes. Because it was accepted that wages should rise to compensate for rises in the cost of living (which was raised by high import prices) and should rise additionally (as an incentive) to remunerate special effort, and because the purchasing power was made available for this through the monetary mechanism, although civil consumer supplies were falling relatively to the volume of civil employment, it was legitimately argued that rising wages were in an important degree inflationary, a source of too much money chasing too few goods. The full sequence of reactions was, however, obscured in the unintentionally superficial discussions of the inflation allegedly caused by higher steel prices, which were still carried on intensively even late in 1943, two years after the prices had been stabilised. The preoccupation with this topic probably reflected both distrust of the logic of the new budgetary attack on inflation introduced with a flourish in 1941, which was based on national income calculation,[1] and even greater doubts (which proved justified) whether the attack would or could be made with sufficient vigour. Yet the newer policy was at least in theory capable of being aimed

[1] Professor R. Stone, who with Professor James Meade was responsible for the calculation, has told the story in *Lessons of Britain's War Economy* (edited by D. N. Chester), pp. 83 sqq.

at the core of the inflationary problem, the unbalance due to rising money earnings, falling efficiency and falling supplies of consumer goods.[1] Partial and opportunist price-pegging was largely irrelevant.

Nevertheless, stabilised prices for steel had a reassuring look, incongruous as it was to fix them while other related prices continued to rise. As the period of stabilisation lengthened, however, the assumption that a rise would be inflationary became ingrained. Hence, it was concluded, increases of price must be delayed as long as possible and kept as small as possible by the use of all expedients short of state subsidies (and in some circumstances including these), without references to changes in the prices of other goods save in so far as these raised the average cost of making steel. Possibly in the later stages of the war this desire to keep steel prices down almost at all costs was encouraged by the knowledge that because America, to take a short cut, had had less inflation her steel prices were much lower in the domestic market than English prices at the current rate of exchange (although when loaded with the high transport cost of the war the steel was dearer when imported into this country). The attitude persisted after the war, and indeed, as will be seen, after American prices had risen, and in spite of dollar scarcity, and after the devaluation of sterling. It became part of the ideology which rather incongruously the Steel Federation, whose leading officials had always been attracted by stabilisation, was to share for many years with the Ministry of Supply.

But in wartime the universal readiness to allow steel price policy to be so greatly influenced by the desire, however illogically interpreted, to avoid inflation was tacitly a recognition that price relations and the relation of prices and costs had lost their peacetime significance. The makers and users of steel had rapidly lost their freedom to choose raw materials, orders, scale of output or investments. Prices could not be expected and were not wanted to bring efficiency in these fields. They might

---

[1] It was possible by this method to take account of the whole effect of imports not paid for—not merely to allow, as was proposed for steel, for the increased cost of imports, which was not really logical.

still have been used to stimulate efficiency in the use of the labour and materials which were put at the manufacturers' disposal. The most cogent criticism of the fixing of steel prices during the war was that in its second phase, after stabilisation, it could not have this salutary effect. In the first phase, when high marginal costs which hurt some makers more than others were met by a policy of levies and subsidies on the pre-war model but on a vastly extended scale, and before the Prices Fund, there was a stimulus to efficiency. Indeed, it could be argued that the system of the Central Fund was much less afflicted in war than in peace with the vices which have been discussed earlier.[1] The distortion of costs which in peace would rule out the right selection of materials and investments mattered little with the growth of central direction; but the fixed uniform delivered price[2] provided an incentive to induce the best use of materials and plant, since the profit it gave was larger if costs were kept down. Even the fact that the uniform price was still a delivered price was not open to the same objections in war as it was in peacetime. Orders were more and more placed by central authority; the steelmakers would not be tempted to incur high expenditure on delivery costs by the desire to get orders since they would not be short of orders, but there was no scope for prices during the war to bring about a more rational distribution of consumption.[3]

But the system lost its logic when profits no longer varied directly with efficiency. Stabilisation was achieved at the expense of such virtue as the old system had as a source of incentives. Under the Prices Fund arrangements many firms could allow their costs to rise within certain fairly wide limits

[1] *E.H.S.* pp. 502–3.

[2] There were some extras for deliveries to areas remote from any steelmaking district; but the uniform price applied to the areas where the greater part of the steel was consumed.

[3] Transport costs for some important products rose less than the percentage rise of railway rates, an indication that deliveries were in a measure rationalised. The danger even in wartime of delivered prices in time of scarcity was, and is, that makers will favour even among their normal customers those to whom it is cheapest to send steel. The Control was, of course, concerned from time to time with ensuring that particular customers were not unduly favoured at the expense of others. It would be claiming too much to say they were invariably successful.

without suffering any fall in profits, and they had therefore no financial motive for striving after lower costs. Firms who earned over their standard profit without any help from the Prices Fund had the stimulus when it was introduced, and for what it was worth, of the 20 per cent Excess Profits Tax post-war refund; firms who, having received the full 'price increase' from the Prices Fund, still earned less than their pre-war standard, earned lower profits if their costs rose and vice versa; they had an incentive. But firms who needed less than the whole notional 'price increase' from the Prices Fund to bring them up to their pre-war standard could have higher costs without being worse off until they fell into the previous category. Firms making losses and firms making below 25 per cent of their standard after full payment of the price increase had no financial incentive.[1]

What, then, it could be reasonably asked 'was the urge to do well'?[2] Yet the Select Committee on National Expenditure who did most to shed light on these problems in public discussion were themselves uncertain how important this lack of consistent financial incentive was. 'It is practically impossible to get conclusive evidence;...all well-managed firms, if only for the sake of maintaining their future competitive position, strive to maintain standards of efficiency.'[3] Prudential and patriotic motives combined to encourage efficiency. Moreover, administrative action was often taken to promote it under the duress of war scarcities, the scarcity of coal for example.[4] And although the price system did not provide consistent incentives it was consistent with maximum efficiency in the industry for war—it was not an obstacle to any kinds of cost reduction then in reach.

Lurking behind these discussions on inflation and efficiency the criticism that steel prices were too profitable was never far away. To the Socialist who found it 'hard to stomach' that even

[1] *S.C. on Nat. Exp.* p. 74.   [2] *Rep. P.A.C.* 1941, Q.3618.
[3] *S.C. on Nat. Exp. loc. cit.*
[4] The Iron and Steel Research Council, for example, organised a series of regional conferences on fuel economy in 1942, and reports were published. The frequent analyses of cost changes made it possible for the price-control authorities to seek explanations of high or rising items, and they did so.

in wartime steel was only to be had by 'bribing a capitalist to produce', any profit was too high;[1] but the arguments more usually deployed were that the steel industry earned profit above the standard accepted by the Comptroller and Auditor General as 'reasonable' in sales to Government departments, and that to continue the pre-war rate during the war was to pay too much because the pre-war profits were themselves too high.

As early as 1937 the P.A.C. had queried whether steel prices approved by I.D.A.C. were necessarily 'reasonable' for purchases by Government departments. I.D.A.C. had not been created to give this assurance—so the Treasury spokesman[2] put it—but for other purposes, which Sir Gilbert Upcott took to be securing the efficient organisation of the industry and having a general oversight of iron and steel prices as between the producer and the general consumer.[3] How a price might be reasonable to general consumers and unreasonable for a Government was not explained; but this discussion prompted I.D.A.C. to appoint its advisory accountant[4] to help it examine the audited costs which the Steel Federation submitted for price-fixing. In 1940 the P.A.C. returned to the subject when examining the contracts for Anderson Shelters. Here the cost of steel was six-sevenths of the whole cost. The Home Office placed the first contract with the British Iron and Steel Corporation, and relied upon I.D.A.C. to say that the prices were reasonable; I.D.A.C. relied in turn upon an examination of the results of cost investigation by the Federation's accountant, as it did not see the accounts of individual firms. Normally, as Sir Gilbert Upcott pointed out, when Government contracts were large and non-competitive the prices were agreed 'after an investigation by Government accountants of the accounts of particular firms'. Was the reference to I.D.A.C. adequate? Under the chairmanship of Mr (now Lord) Pethick Lawrence the P.A.C. thought not.[5]

The shelter programme was an unrepresentative lead into the problem of steel prices. It encouraged the illusion that even

[1] Owen, *op. cit.* p. 73.   [2] Mr (later Sir) Frederick Bridges.
[3] *Rep. P.A.C.* 1940, pp. 96–7.   [4] Above, p. 32.
[5] *Rep. P.A.C.* 1940, pp. vi–viii and 96–105.

individual *orders* for steel for Government contracts might be individually costed and priced—an idea which the Treasury representative still found it necessary to discuss, and to dismiss as impracticable, before the P.A.C. as late as 1943.[1] Members of the P.A.C. were, more practically, concerned lest the average profit which all steelmakers earned from uniform prices concealed very high profits for a few. But as the methods of control were developed by the Ministry of Supply, and partially understood by the P.A.C., this too was seen to be a false trail, though the exigence of the P.A.C. may have helped to make it so. Sir Gilbert Upcott, in the early discussion of wartime prices, drew attention to another more technical uncertainty. 'The determination of costs', he declared, 'involves matters of opinion on which different conclusions may properly be reached by different persons in the light of the standpoint from which they are acting and the purpose which they have in view.' Summaries of costs and profit margins in steelmaking drawn up by the Federation and I.D.A.C. accountants were thus figures on which he could not pass an opinion.[2] The accounting problems did raise delicate matters of judgement, and if any part of new capital expenditure, for example, could be treated as a production cost, evidently the profit margin could be made to look narrower as a result. But after Sir Gilbert had had access to the full information no more was heard of his rather querulous professional scepticism, though later critics have repeated his doubts without noting his subsequent satisfaction. He stated, indeed, that the Ministry of Supply's advisory accountant had taken 'book figures of capital which may sometimes be lower than the value which would be used where profits on Government contracts are fixed'. The steel companies in assessing the book value of their assets had written off more than the inland revenue rate.[3] This would make the profit percentage in steelmaking seem rather higher by comparison with

---

[1] *Ibid.* 1943, Q.4948 (Sir Frank Lee).   [2] *Rep. P.A.C.* 1941, Q.3550.
[3] *Min. P.A.C.* 1943, Q.4543. Owen, *op. cit.* p. 64, asked 'What is capital employed?': was it 'real', valued by a surveyor? 'all'—whether met in a particular process or not—or money capital including debentures. It was typical he should ask thus without finding out that the answer was available in a document he quoted, and that the answer was favourable to the industry he attacked.

those in other industries subject to Government cost investigations than they really were. The Select Committee on National Expenditure made a very different approach to the valuation of the steel industry's capital in 1943, which must be put beside Sir Gilbert's judgement. The book value of plants, the committee argued in its report, 'may be misleading...if such assets consist of plant which in fact ought to be regarded as obsolete'.[1] This revived doubts which were apposite before the war—but much less so as the war progressed—whether the prices fixed under cover of the tariff imputed a higher value to some of the industry's plant than could have been sustained in 'fair' international competition. In the new wartime circumstances plant which was in use was not obsolete. The use of pre-war profits as a standard in the war was little more than a convenient way of ruling out high profits from war and avoiding political changes of industrial structure not needed to win the war. It was not the outcome of esoteric discussions of 'right' levels of profit in war. But if the pre-war valuation of capital were to be revised during the war it was at least as reasonable to ask that all pre-war capital values should be revalued upwards to keep pace with inflation as that some should be revised downwards to simulate values under perfect peacetime competition. But this disturbing question was never asked in the P.A.C. or the Select Committee; half consciously it may have been seen to be politically inconvenient. As a price-fixing though not as an income-taxing authority the Treasury recognised very early in the war that depreciation allowances were inadequate in estimating profits if they were based on the original value of assets.[2]

These were blind spots in the discussion as the P.A.C. wrestled year by year to discover whether the return on capital in the steel industry exceeded the return which the Treasury (and so the Auditor General) thought 'reasonable' in individually costed contracts. The P.A.C. included several members who thought steel prices had been too high before the war—the reductions in January 1939 had, indeed, met with much resistance in the industry, and were less than I.D.A.C. first pro-

[1] *14th Rep. S.C. on Nat. Exp.* p. 68.
[2] Below, p. 46.

posed[1]—and these members certainly seemed to have hoped to find in this comparison of profit percentages a reason for bringing steel prices down. The dispute was enlivened by a misconception bred in the P.A.C. in the early years of the war that the Treasury had brought down the rate of profit deemed 'reasonable' in other industries.

Mr Pethick Lawrence asked the Ministry of Supply officials giving evidence before the P.A.C. in 1941 whether they 'still regard 10 per cent (on capital) as a normal and reasonable rate of profit? Would not $7\frac{1}{2}$ per cent be more appropriate'? He was told there were a number of instances where less than 10 per cent had been allowed, that 10 per cent had never been 'laid down as a rule', that any higher figure would be exceptional, that the 'general tendency now would be (as the Treasury witness put it) to harden up on the 10 per cent, and to bring it down in the direction of the figure which you named as being the more appropriate target now'.[2] The change of policy was

---

[1] The 1938 price negotiation was an interesting one, and has never, I think, been closely examined. It showed some development of price-fixing method. The Federation has stated that 'the last pre-war price alteration...was a reduction based not upon costs but upon the state of the market with a view to stimulating demand'. (The view was set out in *The Times*, City Notes, 16 Oct. 1939.) Discussions with others involved in the negotiation lead me to conclude that this is not quite a complete picture. I.D.A.C. believed a price reduction was needed even if only because the public were determined there should be no high profits from rearmament. They thought the public would conclude from balance sheets that prices were too high. I.D.A.C.'s criterion here was in a sense political; but they believed that moderately efficient firms could have done satisfactorily with lower prices at the end of 1938 with no increase of load. The Associations within the Federation, however, were concerned for their marginal members. I.D.A.C. did not want to countenance a price structure whereby prices would have to be especially high when trade fell off, i.e. when the load was unfavourable for costs. Thus there were still unsettled questions concerning what profits were reasonable. I.D.A.C. thought also, as the Federation did, that a reduction would stimulate demand, though they believed a larger change than the change finally agreed was needed for this effect. The conflict of view between I.D.A.C. and the Federation may have been in part a stage conflict, not only in the sense that negotiators usually start with a negotiating margin. For I.D.A.C. to suggest a larger reduction than it thought reasonable might help Federation leaders to persuade its member associations to go part of the way, and this could be concerted. There are no published documents on this last stage of pre-war price policy.

[2] *Min. P.A.C.* 1941, Q.3480 sqq. Discussions between Mr (later Lord) Pethick Lawrence, Sir William Brown (Ministry of Supply), and Mr J. H. Woods (later Sir John Woods) (Treasury).

46   THE IMPACT OF THE SECOND WORLD WAR

thus suggested to, not drawn from, the witnesses, but on this slender basis the P.A.C. Report registered as in process of achievement what would, indeed, have been a radical change, imposed by administrative action, for which no reason was advanced. The Auditor General in turn quoted the P.A.C. conclusion in his report.[1] Two years later the Treasury made it clear to the P.A.C. that no such change had ever taken place: 'if there has been the impression that $7\frac{1}{2}$ per cent was the standard, and that that applied to the great majority of cases, there has definitely been a misunderstanding...there is a standard starting point, but the efficiency and risk can both be judged and the profit margin adjusted accordingly'.[2]

What virtue lay in either of the percentages, why they should be a starting point or an average or normal, was not discussed. The zeal of those who, like Mr Douglas,[3] sought 'some kind of economic principle involved', and asked why the profit rate at its lowest, when there was no risk and little efficiency and payment for management was allowed for separately, was so much above the gilt-edged rate, was not rewarded; though the Treasury witness hinted (and the Auditor General underlined it) that all these comparisons of rates were of dubious relevance for the doctrinal issue because the 'profits' were not all profits (since depreciation was only allowed on the original costs of the assets before striking the profits, whereas replacement costs were constantly rising) and could not prudently be all paid out as dividends.[4] The comparisons of pre-war and war figures were all vitiated by the progress of inflation.

When the average rates of profit earned in steelmaking were ultimately reported to the P.A.C., from 1943 onwards, it became clear that in the heavy sections of the industry where prices had formerly been controlled by the Federation the average profit percentage was less in 1941–2 than in 1936–7,

[1] Since the Chairman of the P.A.C. and the Comptroller and Auditor General often consult closely in preparing the committee's examination of expenditure (as mentioned earlier), cross-references in the reports thus deserve to be carefully observed.
[2] Sir Bernard Gilbert (Treasury), *Min. P.A.C.* 1943, p. 482.
[3] Labour M.P. for North Battersea.
[4] *Min. P.A.C.* 1943, p. 410, Q.4943, 5876 sqq.

and about the same as the average for all Ministry of Supply 'costed contracts' (which in 1941 was 9·68 per cent),[1] but that in the parts of the industry within the Control but outside the Federation, making the 'fringe' products, profits were higher in 1941 than in 1936–7. In subsequent years percentage profits on both heavy and 'fringe' products fell much below their pre-war standard. The range of profits in the heavy sections was considerably wider than before the war, but the highest was not above the highest of 1936–7.[2] In the 'fringe' sections some very high profits were made, but substantial 'rebates' were made retrospectively. The main figures are shown in Table 3.

Table 3. *Rates of profit of steel firms,*[a] *1936–37* and
during the war (as percentages of capital employed)

	Heavy products (incl. sheets)	Fringe products[b]	Whole industry
1936–7	10·5	14·7	11·8
1941–2	9·8	15·7	11·8
1942–3	9·5	13·5	11·1
1943	9·2	13·3	—
1944	8·0	10·2	—

[a] The figures for 1936–7 and 1941–2 are in Min. P.A.C. 1943, Q. 4932; for 1942–3 in *ibid.* 1944, Q.4714; for 1943–4, and for 1944–5, *ibid.* 1945–6, p. xix.

[b] This includes alloy steel, re-rolled products, steel castings, forgings, wire and wire rope, tubes, bolts and nuts. The division was not carried out with complete rigour; integrated heavy steel firms who made some fringe products were at least in some cases included wholly under 'heavy'. Tinplates do not appear to have been covered in these figures; they were included in my estimate of turnover (above, p. 37).

This picture was not the one which the disputations in the early years of the war—in Parliamentary Committees and outside them—foreshadowed. And the questions of equity into which contemporaries plunged with such obscurantist zeal drew attention from more humdrum functional questions—how, for instance, were rates of profit likely to affect the ability of the steel firms individually, as well as collectively, to finance

[1] *Ibid.* 1943, Q. 4983
[2] *Min. P.A.C.* 1945–6, p. 58. Five firms made losses of from 0·3 to 13 per cent; six made profits of from 2·6 to 12·6 per cent. Before the war all made profits ranging from 6·8 to 12·7 per cent.

further development after the war? For such questions percentages were less relevant than quantities and aggregates, and
these were not published. Where additional capital was employed by firms the Prices Fund allowed 10 per cent on this in
the profits 'standard'. It has been seen that additions of
capital equipment costing about £60 m. were made during the
war for the war. But much of this, perhaps over half, was
provided by the Government. Only what was privately
financed counted for the 10 per cent. But firms also had to
employ more capital on account of increased costs of stocks and
work in progress, and to finance production in new plants built
and paid for by the Government but rented to firms who provided the management. As a rough guess—it is no more—it
may be hazarded that 'capital employed' rose from about
£180 m. to £240 m. during the war.[1] If this is approximately
right—it almost certainly represents the order of magnitude—
then aggregate profits rose between the beginning of the war
and the height of the industry's war activities from a rate of
about £21·5 m. a year to one of about £26·5 m. at the peak.
But the extra £5 m. was not earned every year. Part of it was
apparent but not real, since allowances for depreciation did not
rise *pari passu* with the replacement cost of plant, which had
risen by 80 per cent since 1938 by the end of 1944.[2] Nor was
the additional profit evenly divided—there were gains and losses.

[1] This is from Aug. 1939 to, say, the end of 1943. After this date investment
was beginning to wear a post-war look. The official valuation of capital before the
war took an average of 1936–7; but although these years were perhaps roughly
acceptable guides for profit *rates* they were not equally good for estimates of
capital, since there was a lot of expansion both in 1936–7 themselves (the value
in 1937 was possibly itself from £5 m. to £10 m. in excess of the average of 1936–7)
and between 1937 and Aug. 1939 (another £15 m. to £20 m.?). This included the
strip mills at Ebbw Vale and Shotton and large schemes at Colvilles and
Appleby Frodingham, which were in no sense war preparations. The figures
concerning the increase of capital employed given in the *Rep. P.A.C.* 1943, p. 415,
stated that there had been an increase of 50 per cent; but these figures used
1936–7 as the pre-war reference, and included the strip mills. The figures were
described by Mr Shone (Q. 4970) as 'in part,...a measure of the technical
development...over the past five or six years'.

[2] This was the subject of a complaint by the Steel Federation to the Chancellor
as early as 1941. For the Prices Fund calculation of standard profits an addition
of 20 per cent to the income-tax depreciation was allowed. This, however, was
a small concession—admitting a principle but not applying it rigorously.

It has been seen above that profit-earning was partially insulated from the vagaries of raw material costs, but with no pretence at equity; imported ore prices were all subsidised, but coal prices only to the extent that the coal industry equalised prices, which had a discriminating effect on steelmaking firms. Again, while some high raw-material costs were pooled exceptional operating costs were not. The impact of these elements in the control system was accidental, not governed by design; a stable aggregate profit for ordinary steels covered a redistribution between firms which reflected both accidents of war and accidents of control. The earning of additional profits due to increased capital investment on the other hand, and the management of State factories, depended on the relative fitness and adaptability of companies for special war work. They might be fitted by their location strategically, as Colvilles were, for example, for the manufacture of alloy steel. (Steel output in general, as well as alloy-steel output, rose in Scotland when it fell in all the major districts except Sheffield.)[1] Location was naturally not all that counted; Colvilles were also experienced in making alloy steels, though their output before the war was relatively small. The affiliations of particular steelmakers with particular finishing trades were often a determining factor in decisions on wartime expansion; thus though Stewarts and Lloyds were unfavourably placed as regards their profit standard, both because Corby only just came into use in 1936 and because the international tube trade was in a state of conflict in 1936–7, and were also discriminated against by the Coal Charges Act and other wartime cost practices, they also stood to gain because war created great new demands for tubes and associated products;[2] and Corby also had scrap as a basis

---

[1] Ingot output exceeded the 1937 level in Scotland in 1940 and 1943 by 6 per cent and 3 per cent respectively. It was lower in all war years on the North-east Coast, and in South Wales except in 1940. Above, p. 17, for electric furnace ingots. The Scots were quick to see the possibilities of this situation: 'Strategic factors transcend all else' it was claimed; 'the drift south has probably been permanently stopped' (*Scotsman*, 2 Dec. 1940).

[2] Tubes, for example, for rockets, sten guns, 'Pluto'; and for aircraft (though this was more in Tube Investments' line of country). Stewarts and Lloyds made shells through New Crown Forgings; here again their tube techniques were the starting-point.

BEH

for some electric steelmaking.[1] Every firm was in this way a special case; and its part in war production which yielded profits above the pre-war standard was not dependent on long-term advantages of site or plant.

Thus in general, as in all industries, profits became a diminishing proportion of the gross receipts of the steel industry, and did not grow in step with wages and salaries or with the cost of new equipment. And in particular since the selective forces of competition, which were already prevented before the war from providing for wholly natural selection, were now almost completely subdued, changes which would have occurred in the relative position of firms were delayed, perhaps avoided, perhaps in a sense reversed. As the war closed, the resources of firms were less than ever rationally adjusted to normal economic circumstances; they bore little relation to their managements' skill in adjusting production and investment to changes in relative values of raw materials and in markets. But it was also singularly hard to judge what 'normal' (or more circumspectly 'peacetime') circumstances would be when efforts were made in these years both to read the future of the industry and to shape it. They form the subject of the next chapter.

[1] Since the Bessemer converters could only use part of the 'circulating' scrap, this provided a raw material for electric furnaces uniform in quality. Since the war Corby has had an open hearth shop built, which uses the scrap.

Chapter II

PRELUDE TO PEACE
1943–1945

By the time the Select Committee on National Expenditure published its report on wartime price-fixing in November 1943 the time had gone by when such a report could affect the course of the war. So, indeed, the committee seems to have recognised. 'The need for evolving the best possible technique' for fixing prices 'will not necessarily cease when the war ends', they argued in their report.[1] A growing amount of attention was being focused by this time on the reconversion of the economy from war to peace. For just as more was done to prepare for the war before 1939 than before 1914, so more was also done to prepare for peace on the second occasion. The Ministry of Supply had already asked the Steel Federation five months before the report was published a long series of questions to elicit its views on post-war problems. Arrangements had been made for the trade unions directly concerned to be consulted too. The Ministry was preparing to make its own examination of the industry's future. And outside the official world, the Labour Party and Trades Union Congress also began (or should one say began again?) in 1943 to make plans for the industry in peace.

When the Select Committee reported, the ball was in the steelmakers' court, where it had been sent by the Ministry. This chapter starts therefore with the evolution of their proposals. This is followed in the second section by the departmental reactions; and this in turn in the third section by the story of the hardening of Socialist views.

[1] *Rep. S.C. on Nat. Exp.* 1942–43, p. 16.

1. THE STEELMAKERS PROPOSE

The Ministry's questions to the Steel Federation were concerned essentially with the early transitional period which
would immediately follow the war. How much steel would be
needed after the war, and in what shapes and qualities? What
were the prospects for employment? Should any key workers be
brought back quickly from the army after the war to maintain
activity? What raw materials, and what steel, should be
imported? What new plant would be wanted, especially from
America, and how much would it cost? What powers should
the Control retain after the war and for how long? Analogous
questions were posed by other Ministries to industries which
they sponsored, at the instance of the Board of Trade.[1]

The Federation at an early stage suggested sensibly that these
questions should be considered in relation to 'the direction in
which the industry would be travelling in the long run'. The
Ministry agreed, and thereafter the discussions within the
Federation—in its Post-War Reconstruction Committee, the
'Under Fifties', as they were called[2]—and in the Ministry
itself, with some assistance from the Cabinet Secretariat, were
focused as much on permanent reorganisation and adjustment
as on the transition from war to peace. This work fell rapidly
into two sections, which may be conveniently opposed as
constitutional and constructional, and they may be examined
in that order.

(a) A self-governing industry

The Ministry's questions plunged the Federation into a contentious discussion of its future constitution, concerned above
all with its powers over capital investment, and the range of
finishing industries and raw-material supplies which should be
brought under its wing. The problems left by the May Com-

---

[1] Hancock and Gowing, *op. cit.* pp. 535, 540, refers to the new departmental
activity in regard to post-war developments of their controls, though it gives no
details of what was done on steel.

[2] *I.C.T.R.* 8 Feb. 1944. The President's Committee of the Federation selected
a group of the younger but very senior executives for the committee, men for the
most part in their forties. The chairman, Sir Alexander Dunbar, was not so young.

mittee's Report and pushed aside by the outbreak of war were revived. A few hardy individualists still opposed even the sort of regulation of major capital expansions whose earliest operation was recorded in that Report.[1] Under this arrangement, it has been seen, any major proposal for expanding capacity was submitted for examination to an *ad hoc* committee of the Federation, whose members were so selected as to include some disinterested persons not directly affected as competitors; their report was submitted to I.D.A.C. so that it could be 'reviewed in the public interest', but it imposed a moral obligation only. Most firms seem to have agreed that this at least must continue. But the May Report said the Federation should do more, should be prepared to examine schemes proposed by 'outsiders' as well as by its own members, and to initiate schemes of its own when its members were apparently not proposing all the developments which were 'in the public interest'. It should not merely 'vet' plans but make them. So then the question had to be answered—whom could the Federation choose to do these tasks—so that the 'national interest' would be served and not stifled? And if this hurdle were overcome, and the decisions were right, would they become effective if they had moral force only?

No prominent steelmaker in the late thirties believed in free trade or free competition.[2] But some, notably Sir William Firth and Sir Allan Macdiarmid, who were most adventurous in introducing new methods or moving to new sites, feared that a strong Federation would crab any new enterprise which disturbed established concerns and areas. They believed in co-operation and association so long as it led to the right results. The 'right results' were that violent price fluctuations should be avoided, and severe price competition ruled out by agreement, but new plants (such as they themselves had or wanted to have) with high capital costs and low prime costs should be enabled to run with a full load when demand fell off, the loss of business being concentrated, also by agreement, in the old high-cost plants. The adventurous firms wanted quite naturally

[1] *E.H.S.* pp. 462 sqq., 503 sqq.
[2] Mr Arthur Chamberlain, of Tube Investments, was such a believer, but was not a steelmaker, only a steel user and manipulator.

the best of the competitive and the protective-cartel worlds. Their experiences and attitudes provide a vivid background for the constitutional discussions of 1943–4.

Sir William Firth openly stated in 1934 that he thought statutory powers—an Enabling Act—would be needed if these desirable results were to be achieved.[1] He had found the other leading Welsh steelmakers unco-operative in his major enterprise. Partly it was that they regarded him as a merchant, with good ideas perhaps but no administrative skill, no skill in picking people, and technically incompetent. But they were unprepared to work closely with each other, and some thought his radical ideas were bad.[2] In 1935 he tried, and failed, to persuade other steelmakers in Wales and Lincolnshire to combine with him in putting up the first wide strip mill.[3] Thereafter he thought the sheet trade used all their competitive sales skill and market contacts to hurt his prospects of entering the high-grade sheet trade (in which Richard Thomas had hitherto not operated, but for which the new mill would provide the best product). When a year later he had made the dramatic decision—without discussions with Sir Andrew Duncan or the Federation—to build such a mill, not in Lincolnshire, as he first suggested, but at Ebbw Vale,[4] he claimed that the Government should preserve the tinplate trade for South Wales, and 'make it unmistakably clear that an established and organised industry in an important industrial area could not be interfered

[1] *The Times*, 16 July 1936, when Sir William in his chairman's speech at the Annual Meeting quotes an earlier dictum.

[2] As I understand it Sir Charles Wright (Baldwins) was not prepared to work with Firth or to collaborate more closely with the Beale family (in G.K.N.) than was already involved in the working of G.K.B. Lysaghts (part of G.K.N.) remained deeply attached to the old-fashioned way of making motor-car sheets, of whose production by these methods as they controlled them they were, as I found myself, very proud. Sir Samuel Beale (chairman of G.K.N.) was a less impressive figure than his father (Sir John Beale) had been, and the Lysaght influence in the firm threw the weight of the firm against the idea of a strip mill in the mid-thirties when Sir Charles Wright was for his part converted and beginning to plan the Port Talbot venture. Cp. below, p. 80.

[3] *Ibid.* 29 July 1938. I believe the firms approached were Baldwins, G.K.N., Lysaght's and the United Steel Companies. The latter had flirted with the idea of a wide strip mill. Firths' proposed strip mill was to be built at Grimsby; the steel to be made at Scunthorpe.

[4] *E.H.S.* p. 460.

with by industrialists in outside areas'.[1] Ambitious outsiders, geographically, the argument now ran, should be crabbed by the state. Not so, however, ambitious insiders. For the prospectus he issued when capital was raised for Ebbw Vale early in 1937, announced that the new continuous mill would be run at full capacity, but that Firth was prepared to restrict production in the older tinplate plants of Richard Thomas on a *pro rata* basis with other firms, 'so as to maintain, in co-operation, ...orderly competition'.[2] Since 1925 the tinplate trade had been one of the parts of the steel trade which had run a pooling scheme, the Tinplate Conference, whereby firms were allocated specific proportions of the trade. If they sold more than their quota they paid into the pool, if they sold less they drew money out. Three firms partly owned by consumers (e.g. the Elba works, which was partly owned by an oil company[3] and partly by Baldwins) were outside this arrangement, and normally ran full—to the understandable annoyance of Sir William Firth— but otherwise all were in. The prospectus statement was therefore a challenge to an arrangement now over a decade old.

This programme was never put to the test. Sir William's plans suffered from misjudgements and ill luck. The building of the new Ebbw Vale works in a period of rising prices ran into unexpected delays and incurred unforeseen costs. Over £3 m. was needed more than he had stated in the prospectus of January 1937.[4] Discrepancies of this order were not yet (as they were after the war) deemed trivial. He was forced to seek large additional financial support from the City, and this was only granted on condition that he 'co-operated' with the Federation on terms which may have been dictated by some of his principal rivals. Sir Charles Wright of Baldwins and Mr S. R. Beale[5] of Guest Keen Nettlefolds (who controlled Lysaghts) became members of his board. A Control Committee was set up which was led by Mr Montagu Norman, Governor of the Bank of England, and a close friend of Sir Andrew Duncan (himself a director of the Bank).[6]

---

[1] *The Times, loc. cit.*   [2] *The Times*, 26 Jan. 1937.
[3] Asiatic Petroleum Co. (Shell).   [4] *The Times*, 5 July and 29 July 1938.
[5] Later Sir Samuel Beale.   [6] *The Times, loc. cit.*

In public Sir William Firth accepted control 'without misgivings', and welcomed competitors as directors; it could not be 'to our disadvantage', and must strengthen co-operation in the industry.[1] A year later, in summer 1939, these competitors resigned; with their association, Firth stated, Richard Thomas had 'obtained the agreement of the tinplate industry to satisfactory quota arrangements for the manufacture of tinplates at Ebbw Vale'.[2] He did not reveal how the terms compared with those in the challenging prospectus. Three more distinguished steelmakers, among them Macdiarmid, now joined the board (on which at different times between 1938 and 1940 the chairmen of companies making half the British output of steel ingots served), and Firth himself was relieved of part of his load of responsibility, remaining chairman but no longer managing director. He still 'welcomed the influence' of the Control Committee and the Federation on the destinies of Richard Thomas, which he expected to 'prevent the building of modern plant in excess of the country's normal demand'. The British industry could thus, he argued, open up a new line in policies, and avoid the mistakes of the Americans, who had pioneered the wide strip mills but had built far too many.[3] A year later he was no longer even chairman. What 'irreconcilable breach within the Board' caused his dismissal was not made known; but at the first annual meeting after his deposition by the Control Committee Firth complained that 'our steel was being diverted to others, and the majority of our sheet mills were idle through shortage of steel while competitors were operating almost fully'.[4] Evidently he no longer liked the way the available work was distributed. He made it seem doubtful whether he ever had liked it, despite his earlier emollient phrases; for he now roundly declared that 'two years ago in very dirty weather some pirates pushed us on the rocks and boarded us'. They were 'disguised as national interests'. Whether his facts were right, how far he had a legitimate complaint, how far what happened was under

---

[1] The Times, loc. cit.   [2] Ibid. 9 Sept. 1939.
[3] Ibid. loc. cit.
[4] Ibid. 31 July 1940. Mr E. H. Lever the new chairman said at the end of 1944 that the revised quota arising from the erection of Ebbw Vale had never been fixed (ibid. 30 Dec. 1944).

stress of war, was never satisfactorily explained in public. Lord
Dudley, acting as chairman, thought silence was best. 'We had
no desire to join (the board)...we still have no desire to be
here, but we are taking our place (Firth thought it was his
place)...in the highest national interest.'[1] This deity, as her
votaries so often find, could only remain inviolate when veiled.
Mr E. H. Lever (later Sir Ernest Lever),[2] Joint Secretary of
the Prudential Assurance Company, and an actuary, who had
been trustee for the Debenture holders, became Firth's successor, and Mr Latham, who left the board in 1938, returned
to be managing director. As chief collaborator with Whitehead
he had a record of great success in running a high-capacity
re-rolling mill.

Thus preparations for the post-war steel world could proceed
without the disturbing unpredictable, ungovernable Welsh
figure, who was wont to say incredulously—'they say I'm
difficult to work with'. But the second dissident progressive,
Allan Macdiarmid, remained. He was an accountant, but he
had risen to eminence in the industry through the usual
channels. The Corby scheme was well timed. Construction
started when building and engineering costs were low.[3] Progress was not marred by misjudgements nor, after the initial
opposition, dogged by ill luck.[4] When Firth made his ill-fated
decision to go to Ebbw Vale and to forego the possibility of
making cheap steel, Macdiarmid's daring and foresight were
being vindicated by commercial success. He was making good
steel for welded tubes cheaply. His dry comment in 1936 that
progress would be achieved by the troublesome fellows like

[1] *Ibid.* 31 July 1940. [2] He was knighted in 1954.
[3] In the report drawn up by the Federation at the invitation of the Government
in the later months of 1945 it was stated that the cost of an integrated plant in 1935
(including blast furnaces, steel melting and rolling mills) to make billets was
equivalent to £8. 12s. for each ton of output per year. The cost when Stewarts
and Lloyds built—as they started in 1934—was almost certainly less. By 1939
the cost was said to be £13. 10s. by 1945 £23. 10s. (*Iron and Steel Industry Reports*
by B.I.S.F. and Joint Council to the Minister of Supply, May 1946, Cmd. 6811,
p. 35).
[4] The opposition succeeded, by disparaging the prospects of Corby in the City, in
reducing the capital available for the first stage of building; this led to some compromises, which possibly accentuated early teething troubles, particularly in the
first stage of rolling. But there was nothing on a scale to offset the great gain.

Firth and Whitehead, who would not play with their fellows, rather than by the vote of the majority, reflected his own experience and was impressive because of his success. He thought it unlikely that any firm with a continuous mill would be allowed to run at full capacity in a slump by agreement with other makers, and feared that it would be forced to pay excessively for 'quotas' to increase its load. He found it hard to believe, at this time, that a committee of steel firms would vet each other's plans in a disinterested way, or that a body of disinterested people could vet them competently. He was inclined to agree with Firth that even if the Federation made the right decisions they would not become effective unless backed by an Enabling Act.[1] He was probably deeply impressed by the rebuffs suffered by Sir Andrew Duncan who, when he was, in his own words, 'playing himself in', failed in the Jarrow controversy to secure either of his alternative objects, to have a new works on the Tyne or on the Tees, based on co-operation between the North-east Coast firms, and failed over Ebbw Vale, whose revival he did not wish.[2]

Macdiarmid's association with the Federation remained uneasy at the outbreak of war; the tube-makers' associations were not affiliated to the Federation,[3] and much to the chagrin of I.D.A.C. Stewarts and Lloyds refused to pay levies into the Spreadover Fund in respect of the ingots which they made themselves into tubes.[4]

But Macdiarmid's approach to these problems had never been, as his handling of tube-trade affairs from 1929 onwards showed, a *laissez faire* one. He played a large part in negotiating

[1] I found this was Macdiarmid's chief preoccupation at my first meeting with him before the war.

[2] Sir Andrew Duncan explained his attitude on both these projects at some length to me at the time. The North-east Coast project he regarded as merely delayed.

[3] Cp. the list of affiliated associations in *Rep. I.D.A.C.* p. 116. It is of interest that Macdiarmid was not one of the representatives of the Steel Federation who appeared as witnesses before the May Committee. He appeared, as an individual, for his firm. Mr Benjamin Talbot of Cargo Fleet was the only other steelmaker in the same category. Firth appeared with the Federation, but also on his own.

[4] P. 31. These schemes had been designed to help firms—who were in the majority—using costly imported raw materials, at the expense of those using cheap home raw materials. See *E.H.S.* pp. 475, 502.

the first International Tube Cartel,[1] which lessened the tube imports into this country, secured a good export quota, and ensured access to foreign technical development and knowledge.[2] At home he made an arrangement with other makers of welded tubes whereby they undertook to buy most of their strip from Stewarts and Lloyds, who undertook to supply a high proportion of their needs at low prices commensurate with those of the continental imports on which most production was formerly based. Thus he ensured a larger outlet for Corby strip, took much of the immediate sting out of the case for letting foreign strip imports in free of duty,[3] but also strengthened his hand in settling quotas for welded tube production which enabled Corby to have a good load. There were quotas, fixed prices and some pooling of orders for welded tubes, and agreements with other large steelmakers and tubemakers not to enter the Corby range. The two leading tube firms were closely linked through an exchange of shares. In all a wide assortment of restrictive agreements—a 'co-operative scheme', as Macdiarmid put it, which 'provided for the creation of the most up-to-date tube works in the world'.

Macdiarmid approached the problem of association as a tubemaker, not as a steelmaker. But the steelmakers were anxious, naturally, that so large a firm as Stewarts and Lloyds, whose chairman was the outstanding personality in the industry, should co-operate with them fully. So, for that matter, was I.D.A.C. before the war, with whom Stewarts and Lloyds negotiated over the prices of tubes and over their trade associations, national and international, directly. No doubt it was part of the process of wooing by the Federation (with I.D.A.C.'s blessing) that led to the inclusion of Macdiarmid on the board of Richard Thomas in 1940. By the middle of the war Macdiarmid, while still regarding sectional associations as the proper basic units of collective organisations in industry, had moved

[1] E. Hexner, *The International Steel Cartel*, p. 158.
[2] Macdiarmid made this point in an article in the *Sunday Times*, 15 Aug. 1943, in which he described—not as fully as one would like, but very frankly—the organisation of the tube industry from 1929 onwards.
[3] Because the existing tube firms who would otherwise have suffered did not suffer. But the system did preclude newcomers from getting cheap strip.

sufficiently to become one of the sponsors of *A National Policy for Industry*, which represented a long step towards the idea of federation. This 'national policy', sketched in a pamphlet issued in autumn 1942 and signed by 120 industrialists from large companies, of whom sixteen were steelmakers, recommended as 'an essential condition of progress' that all manufacturing industry should be 'more fully and comprehensively organised' in a hierarchy of associations under a central council for industry, with an Industrial Tribunal appointed by the Government to protect the interests of small producers and consumers and of large firms in danger of pirates.[1] The Steel Federation could evidently find a place in such a hierarchy. When the discussion of the Federation's powers over investment was formally restarted in 1943 and the drafting of a new constitution was begun, Macdiarmid's role was now not only active but positive. The wooing, in the most obvious sense, had been successful. In March 1944 Macdiarmid succeeded Sir James Lithgow as President.[2] Who was the victor—and on what terms?

Perhaps no one had won. For by 1943 they were not fighting quite the same battles. War and other experiences had brought the contesting views closer together.

To begin with, it was not now a question whether to establish a stronger central control over investment than the Federation exerted in 1937–8. A much stronger control existed—but it was exercised by the Government, with the advice of the Iron and Steel Control; and although the outside world was taught to regard the Control as the Federation in sheep's clothing the steel firms knew this to be erroneous. The questions they naturally asked were—would the strong all-pervading central control continue, and who should exercise it? Already by the

---

[1] The statement was issued in Nov. 1942, and prominently discussed in the Press (e.g. *The Times*, 11 Nov.). With its claim that 'the idea of service' can be carried more fully into practice 'without changes in the social system' this was presumably a reaction in the cold war carried on on the political front, as will be seen later, by the advocates of nationalisation throughout the war.

[2] I once asked Sir Andrew Duncan how Presidents were chosen. He replied that he did not know—it just happened somehow, there was no rule—but the choice always seemed to be good.

end of 1943 it was becoming clear that the Government intended to continue to control capital investment, in all industry,
at least during the transitional years from war to peace, because,
in the current jargon, there would be so many claims on scarce
investment resources, and priorities must be given to ensure that
'first things came first'. Most steelmakers—the proceedings of
the Under Fifties and the President's Committee alike suggested
—felt instinctively that they must organise a voluntary scheme
of control themselves if only to avoid having priorities imposed
without the firm's views being, in their view, adequately
represented.

This would have predisposed most of the industry's leaders
towards stronger Federation control of investment in any event;
but most were convinced for quite different reasons that
priorities, and something more were not merely unavoidable
but desirable in the foreseeable future. All judged, naturally,
from their own plans and projects. All firms in varying degrees
had put off normal replacements in the war. All had put pre-
war development schemes into cold storage. Many visualised
good markets after the war, and thought they should expand
capacity. There was war damage to make good, civilian markets
here and abroad had been starved, and the Continental makers
would be out of action for a time at least. The firms thus had
more investment projects, collectively, to carry out simultaneously than ever before the war, and by 1944 they were
becoming anxious to get on with them. But they knew there
would be fewer facilities for carrying them out. Much of the
new plant of the thirties had come from America and Germany.
There would be a restriction on dollar purchases after the war,
and imports of German plant could not be counted on. Scarcity
of plant alone would thus impose a severe restraint on investment. In addition, building labour was relatively scarcer and
became less efficient during the war, and the Prime Minister
declared in 1943 that the first claim on it would be for houses.
There was threatened therefore a kind of jam, a degree of delay,
which had not occurred before the war; and while the steelmakers set out to alleviate it (making a strong case for importing
American plant, for example, seeing whether any useful German

plant would be available as reparations, and seeking the expansion of the manufacture of steelworks plant here, in which Macdiarmid was active),[1] they recognised a new potent argument for orderly restriction and co-ordination of investment.

It was, however, only an argument for temporary organisation for as long only as plant and building labour and materials *were* scarce. But no one participating in the Federation discussion ever seems to have visualised anything temporary. This reflected another wartime change. Far more of the leaders in the large firms were convinced by 1943 than had been so convinced in 1937 that if British steelmaking was to be competitive and efficient by world standards modernisation would need to be more radical and faster than before the war, with more specialisation and concentration, and larger and therefore fewer works. The risk which Macdiarmid had rated high before the war that radical change would be hampered or made unprofitable by the quotas, tariffs and price-fixing of the Federation and I.D.A.C. now therefore seemed less. Early in 1945 Mr John E. James[2] told the shareholders of the Lancashire Steel Corporation that the steelmakers were considering the possibility of 'centralising the manufacture of different iron and steel products in respectively suitable areas throughout the country, to cheapen cost by the use of mass-production methods and the elimination of unnecessary transport charges'.[3] Such changes, as the Under Fifties recognised in 1943, especially if they were to come quickly, must be based on co-operation between neighbouring firms or firms making similar products; they would not occur if individual firms went ahead with their own projects of modernisation in isolation. If all existing firms were patched—even thoroughly modernised within the scope permitted by their scale and their range of output—and the existing pattern of production was thus preserved, this would rule out the greater savings permitted by more radical change,

---

[1] Sir Allan Macdiarmid became a director of Davy and United Engineering Company. One reason given for this was that if a steel firm was linked with a plantmaker the latter could be relied upon to treat all information as confidential; hence the steelmaker could state his problems more completely.

[2] He became Sir John James in 1949.

[3] *Financial Times*, 20 Mar. 1945.

by concentration in fewer works and some changes of location. Hence the Under Fifties seemed to speak the language of some pre-war critics. Projects of radical change take longer to mature than proposals for patching; the Under Fifties thought that inadequate schemes would not be effectively stopped by the moral embargo which the Federation might impose (but had not imposed) before the war, and that the Federation would need to be able to veto schemes, and to supplement the proposals put forward by firms (as I.D.A.C. had suggested in 1937 it should be prepared to do) by its own proposals based on world-wide surveys of market prospects and technical change. Some also thought that radical schemes would need to be collectively sponsored as a means of obtaining capital, since depreciation allowances and controlled profits provided too little.

The determination to pave the way for radical change was primarily due to a much greater respect for, and fear of, American achievements. This was only in part due to the war. The completion of the Ebbw Vale and Shotton wide strip mills, for example, showed other sheet and tinplate makers, and the workers, irrevocably that they must change, and that the days of the small independent mills were numbered. Though they struggled to get good compensation, and there were prolonged negotiations over a tinplate redundancy scheme, the inevitability of concentration of production in a few large units was plain to all in 1941.[1] By and large more steelmakers were persuaded of the value of American practices during the course of the war, because more had close contacts with American works and could exchange detailed information. They were more fully aware of the advantages reaped before the war by the greater American firms from large-scale mechanised equipment in increasing the average output of the worker and increasing productivity. There was little disposition to challenge the crude comparisons published by Dr L. Rostas

[1] This became very clear in the discussions in, and about, the Essendon Committee which was set up in July 1941 (*Financial Times*, 25 July 1941) to work out which works should be closed, and on what terms, since output was greatly curtailed during the war. It was recognised to be unlikely that all works so closed would reopen after the war.

in 1943, which set out the relative productivities before the war in steelmaking in the U.S.A., Germany and the United Kingdom as 168:114:100 respectively.[1] The steelmakers were able to get more refined figures referring to the production of comparable products.[2]

But it was not necessary for steelmakers who in 1943 said modernisation should be faster and more radical to confess to, or even be conscious of, any error of judgement before the war, because there was a great expansion of capacity in America during the war. New plant (much of it integrated and all of course modern) to make over 20 m. tons of steel of ordinary grades was put up between 1941 and 1944, and firms were allowed to pay for it out of depreciation within five years.[3] Expansion which could not be justified in the United Kingdom was concentrated in the United States for the Allied cause, and as a result American firms would want to sell much more steel after the war than before, and about a quarter of it would be made with new plant. If all the plant, new and old, were used much more American steel would evidently be available for export. 'America will hold the key to the post-war world markets' the Federation declared!

The danger of this was perhaps exaggerated in 1943–4 by steelmakers and steel users, partly it may be because American steel prices did not rise as fast as British steel prices rose during the war. Prices were more easily stabilised in America, where a much smaller proportion of food and raw materials was imported than into Britain. Hence by 1943–4, with the dollar exchange rate pegged, home steel prices in Britain were 20 per cent higher than home prices in the United States.

The Federation claimed, perhaps wrongly, that before the war British prices (except for sheets) had been slightly the

[1] *Econ. J.* Apr. 1943, p. 46. These were the figures for steel melting and rolling; for blast furnaces they were 361:115:100. The figures were popularised in an article by Sir George Schuster in *The Times*, 24 June 1943. For earlier figures e.g. *E.H.S.* pp. 417, 434. Mr Rostas for the first time used the British, American and German Censuses of Production for a broad survey of comparative productivity.

[2] There was some correspondence with American firms and through the British Purchasing Mission in the United States on the man-hours required for specific products.

[3] Details of the expansions were given in *Iron Age*, 27 May 1943, and 3 June 1943.

lower.[1] Since American wages were double the British wages this was not, as was sometimes implied, a proof of the efficiency of the British industry; it showed, indeed, that the American industry had better raw materials, better markets, or better plant—had in one or more ways a comparative advantage, which gave it a much higher labour productivity. Productivity lower than American was of course common to the majority of British industries; steelmakers sometimes felt they were singled out in this respect unreasonably. It would have been an asset to steel users to have cheaper steel where, as seemed possible, the use of American methods allowed it.

When, as a result of the vagaries of wartime price changes, and not because of a change in productivities, British prices were above American prices, British steelmakers, who believed costs could be appreciably reduced by radical change in Britain, were perhaps more ready to coerce obstructive colleagues, and they were certainly more anxious to conciliate public opinion. There was a recrudescence of criticism from large consumers, especially from the motor-car industry, with Sir Miles Thomas, as so to speak, the lineal descendant of Lord Nuffield, amply supported by Mr G. W. Lucas,[2] who represented the sellers, not makers, of motor cars, and who later became better known as a Labour peer. England must export more than ever in future—the theme was becoming familiar in 1944—yet how would it be possible if steel were dear? The steelmakers recognised that they had more than ever to demonstrate their zeal for efficiency, which put a premium on the dramatic rather than the humdrum.

As reasons for more investment control seemed to multiply, some of the resistances to it and to other forms of collective action weakened. The habit of working together during the war almost certainly made more people ready to go on working together; and the war made problems of planning seem simpler

---

[1] For prices at works this was so in 1937, not in 1938. American prices rose in booms, fell in slumps. Their delivered prices naturally had higher transport costs. My impression from published *realised* 'at works' prices is that for heavy steel products average prices from 1926 to 1938 were not significantly different.

[2] He was President of the Motor Agents' Association, and was elevated to the peerage as Lord Lucas in 1946. (For Lord Nuffield's earlier part see *E.H.S.* p. 495.)

than they had seemed in peacetime and made the practice of planning familiar and so less frightening. And there was by 1943, or so it seemed, a prospect of getting new personalities into the Federation—not merely a new president, for that happened in the course of things, but new directors and even a new Chairman.[1] The forceful personality of Sir Andrew Duncan, while no doubt in the wings, was not on the stage in these wartime discussions.

So when the Federation drafted its new constitution[2] it incorporated a suggestion made first by the Under Fifties in autumn 1943, and included among its standing committees an Economic Efficiency Committee. Its composition was in form at least less heavily weighted by experts and Federation staff than was first proposed, and it was still only advisory and consultative. But it was charged with the duty of 'making general surveys in order to co-ordinate modernisation on a national basis'. It was both to examine schemes put before it and to propose schemes, and in principle at least it was to cover all branches.[3] By the time the Constitution was adopted, in March 1945, such a committee had already been advising the Control and R.M.D., since the later months of 1944, which schemes of capital investment they should sponsor under their existing powers. The Federation had asked firms to submit their projects under two heads, those necessary to maintain output after the war, and those necessary to meet urgent new demands. The sifting of these lay with the new committee, whose initial staff included the Control's technical adviser and the head of their Plant Progress department. By the end of 1944 they had recommended the licensing of schemes involving £20 m., and were

[1] E.g. Mr I. F. Elliott, who had been Managing Director of the B.I.S. Corporation before the war, left in 1942.

[2] The constitution was not published until many years later, but copies appear to have been issued to the press. It was commented upon in some detail, often with evident but unacknowledged quotations, in most of the London papers on 14 March 1945. Some papers, notably the *Manchester Guardian*, returned on several days to the topic. The weeklies also commented: e.g. the *Economist*, and *Tribune*, 17 Mar. 1945. For the latter the constitution was a 'blueprint for fascism'.

[3] The *Manchester Guardian*, 21 Mar. 1945, commented on this committee; the Government must either have its experts on the committee or set up a parallel body outside.

examining proposals to cost over £100 m.[1] It was a first step towards a five years' plan.

There was a dissident minority,[2] but none of the dissident firms were now, as they had been before the war, among the largest. The fears of former large dissidents—above all Stewarts and Lloyds, since Firth had been displaced—were met by other changes in the Federation constitution, which strengthened the position of sectional associations (henceforth to be known as Conferences) representing different branches of production and placed control more firmly in the hands of company chairmen or their immediate associates. Full membership of the Federation was henceforth to be confined to Conferences. The Federation was thus to be more purely federal, since these Conferences were to be protected from growing interference from the centre. Thus, for example, to take the instance dearest to Macdiarmid, purely tube affairs would not come before the Federation. This was in keeping with the principle of organisation set out in the *National Policy for Industry*. Whether the relation was very clearly conceived is not certain. An attempt was made to clarify it by saying that 'decentralisation of management must go together with centralisation of policy', but this was hardly a declaration of independence for the Conferences. The second change was possibly more clearly conceived in practical, if not in theoretic, terms. Membership of the Council of the Federation and (with one exception) of its Executive Committee was to be confined to persons responsible for top management in their companies. Council members would be chosen by Conferences, the numbers from each Conference being in proportion to the net output of its member firms; but no paid official of a Conference could be chosen. The Executive Committee would be appointed by the Council from its own members and each Conference would be represented, so that, as it was explained, this Committee would 'consist of leaders with power to act, chosen democratically by the various sections'. The industry, Macdiarmid argued, would

[1] The figure was put at £120 m. by *The Times*, 25 Feb. 1945; this may presumably be taken to be a Federation estimate.

[2] *I.C.T.R.* 17 Mar. 1945; 'the statement that the constitution was adopted by an overwhelming majority means that there are some dissident firms'. Among the bigger dissidents, it is believed, was Cargo Fleet.

thus not be allowed to fall a victim to bureaucratic control even by the permanent officials of its own central organisation. The Federation's chief executive officer was still to be chairman of the Executive Committee—but his chief function, as the constitution defined it, was to execute policies determined by the Committee, not to design policy. He might act as an impartial adviser for individual firms or for Conferences should they invite him, but the idea of 'independent chairman', as the function had been built up by Sir Andrew Duncan, was under a cloud. The Federation, as one of the trade journals put it, 'must be the servant of the industry, and not its master'; and the *Manchester Guardian* commented that 'big industrial organisations are often more bureaucratic than government departments. But the steel constitution shows that the danger has been appreciated.'[1]

The iron founders, drop forgers and the steel founders were apparently not satisfied with the new safeguards, though they may also have thought that to keep outside the Federation might save them from nationalisation. They perhaps saw in what was happening little more than a reallocation of power between individuals and firms. They still feared that the Federation would be run for big steelmakers, and so they decided, unlike the tubemakers, that their trade associations should remain independent and not become Conferences within the Federation.

Those who drafted the new Constitution hoped to allay such fears by giving to all firms in Conferences a right of appeal to arbitration, and they visualised that the Government would set up an independent tribunal as a final arbiter—'on the same lines as I.D.A.C.', Macdiarmid said, 'but with different terms of reference'.[2] It would 'help to ensure', he said, 'that the Government was being adequately served', and to it 'appeals could be made by any parties feeling themselves aggrieved,

---

[1] *Iron and Steel*, Apr. 1945; *Manchester Guardian*, 15 Mar. 1945. I have been helped by glosses made to me on clauses of the new constitution by the President during the drafting. The constitution defines the powers of the independent chairman loosely and inconspicuously, though not less conspicuously than the former constitution, whose text was published in the May Report.

[2] *The Times*, 18 May 1945.

whether they represented shareholders, labour or consumers'. They did not, however, want the Government to take an active part in the detail of planning. They wanted 'self-government within the framework of Government policy'.[1] The Government's views on strategy in the siting of works, on the capacity of the industry, and on social questions arising out of location, were entitled to respect. But any oversight, except in regard to price-fixing, should be 'at the highest possible level'[2] only. 'The industry's operations must be open to scrutiny',[3] but 'they must avoid the stifling of initiative by dictation or bureaucratic control'. Macdiarmid thought it might be useful for a very senior civil servant to attend meetings of the principal Federation committees, where he could immediately say whether proposed Federation policies were in accord with Government policy.

On import and price policy the Federation stood in these wartime discussions almost exactly where it had before the war. The home market for steel must be secured for the home industry—whether by tariffs, import quotas and licences, or international agreement. There must be no encroachment upon the plant load of British works by unnecessary imports. Import restrictions were the way to low prices by giving domestic plants full employment. Exports must be secured, and if necessary prices for export sales must be below the protected home price. Free international competition could only be contemplated if the home prices for steel were the same in all countries—if, that is, the conditions which prompted exchange and trade were absent. The ideal would be to restore and extend international agreements—'market-sharing agreements' made by industries, as they frankly put it, though they steered clear of the word 'cartel'—whereby 'manufacturing nations will only export to each other's domestic markets such products, and in such quantities, as may be necessary to meet a shortage of

---

[1] The phrase was quoted from a Federation statement by the *Manchester Guardian* 17 Mar. 1945. Macdiarmid (*loc. cit.*) improved on it; the new constitution was to ensure that the industry shall develop 'as a self-governing body within the framework of Government policy and free enterprise'.

[2] *I.C.T.R.* 16 Mar. 1954.

[3] Sir Allan Macdiarmid's chairman's speech, *The Times*, 18 May 1945.

supply'—and thus tariffs could be dispensed with.[1] Unfortunately, the need for a high degree of organisation for the orderly conduct of trade in a world where so many countries had been industrialised was not well understood by public opinion, and the American administration was fanning anti-trust prejudice. So the ideal was not immediately attainable; there must be tariffs, quotas, and subsidised exports. If in the long run the Government approved of the policy of proceeding by international agreement between industries, which would result presumably in quotas only, then the Federation would be prepared for the Government to take an active part in deciding with the Federation the policy to be adopted, though negotiation would rest with the Federation.[2]

The Federation thought, with some justification, that all this was the gospel according to I.D.A.C. Their approach to price policy in general bore the same pre-war hallmark. There was no overt disposition in the Federation to depart from the basic elements of former policy which had been agreed with I.D.A.C., namely, that there should be no price competition,[3] that prices

---

[1] In a speech at Sheffield Sir Alexander Dunbar stated that international arrangements of some kind were absolutely necessary, and went on to say that pre-war trade agreements between Governments were not nearly so beneficial to this country as international cartels such as the steel cartels arranged by industrialists (*Financial News*, 31 Jan. 1945). A comment in *Iron and Steel*, Mar. 1945, suggests that Dunbar was arguing that no Government (therefore no nationalised) industry had succeeded in international trade, hence the industry must remain private enterprise; 'but the Government must mainly take the responsibility for efficiency of the steel industry and influence the price levels of its raw materials'. This may merely have meant the Government must be satisfied the industry was efficient, but it was open to other interpretations.

[2] There was, it was argued, a change here, in that before the war agreements were shown to the Government after they had been concluded.

[3] It has been suggested to me that I.D.A.C. did not say there should be no price competition, but merely that maximum prices should be fixed. The relevant parts of the May Committee *Report* are §§ 81-5 and 96, which are too long to quote in full, but the following extracts seem to be conclusive. 'A uniform national price including delivery charges has definite advantages both to the producer and consumer. *It facilitates the working of an association arrangement for price control* (my italics), tends to greater price stability etc...' (§ 81). 'Prices fixed by associations in the past have been naturally minimum prices, and there has been no objection to members charging higher prices.... The setting up of the Federation's organisation and the limitation of competition has of course modified this and the public interest is to secure that the prices fixed are maximum prices.... We requested an assurance

should be fixed and should be based on the costs of efficient firms (which by custom meant that the costs of firms making a small part of output should be neglected in fixing prices and that the average costs of the others should be accepted as a guide), and that there should be supervision by an impartial body (such as I.D.A.C.) appointed by the Government. The idea that one firm might offer steel to a customer at a lower price than another firm, even though the first firm could make it and deliver it more cheaply, or at a higher price, perhaps for earlier delivery, was still anathema.

But it was seen that to say prices should be based on costs provided no rigid formula—it was 'a guide, not a rule', as Sir Winston Churchill was to say later in another context. The costs of future production on which prices must be based were not facts but forecasts; capital costs were of necessity arbitrary estimates; and prices still had to be fixed with an eye on the market. So price policy must, the steelmakers said, be flexible. They thought, after wartime experience, that the bias of price-fixing under state supervision was likely to result in prices being too low, allowing too little for the rising costs of depreciation and modernisation. Most of them, however, seem to have expected that market conditions would force them after the war to keep their prices low. The flexibility they sought in particular was the power to discriminate more between different

that where prices had been fixed with our approval they should be regarded as standard prices not to be exceeded' (§ 84). 'One effect of fixing standard prices... has been to preclude the producer from quoting firm prices...for deliveries over a relatively long period....If prices are to be related to costs of production the period for which they can be reasonably fixed is dependent on the conditions existing....This is an inherent disadvantage of the system of price regulation' (§ 85). The implication all the time is that associations will join in the price-fixing, that for them prices are minima, for the Government maxima, hence they are fixed and standard. It is clear that price competition was not favoured, still less sponsored; it was not part of the machinery visualised by I.D.A.C. as necessary to secure efficiency, and it was not expected. I.D.A.C. accepted the principle of deferred rebates, which was a means of forcing firms into the trade associations, and the associations would manifestly continue to regard fixed prices as minima. 'If one manufacturer remains outside an organisation and by selling at lower prices is enabled to operate at full capacity, it is within his power to make a larger profit than the conforming members whilst benefiting from their corporate actions. It appears to us essential...that the organisation should be entitled to frame rebate schemes which discourage an individual producer from refusing to join it' (§ 96).

customers. Before the war exports were sold at prices below
home prices; now it was proposed (as it had been, but possibly
not in public, in 1939) that special reductions should be made
to certain classes of consumer, among them manufacturers of
goods for export, and perhaps shipbuilders and motor-car
makers, who were large consumers and therefore were deemed
to qualify for special concessions even when their orders did not
attract quantity rebates.[1] This device seemed perhaps to offer
the chance of charging in general prices which gave margins
reasonably in keeping with capital costs while enabling the
steelmakers to meet the embarrassing and damaging complaints
of substantial customers whose competitors had cheaper steel,
and for whom the cost of steel was a large part of their total cost.

It would not, however, be left to individual firms to decide
what concessions should be made; this must be done by the
Federation or a member association. The Federation marked
out one class of consumer for relatively higher prices than in the
past. Independent re-rollers did not as a group pay the whole
cost of delivering 'semis'—billets, sheet bars, slabs and the like
—to their works.[2] This cost was spread over the whole output of
such 'semis', including those used where they were produced,
which incurred no transport cost. Thus steelmakers who re-
rolled their own 'semis' did not get the whole advantage of
integration. To raise the price of billets and other semis (or
'intermediate products', as they were now called) would therefore, it was argued, promote technical and economic efficiency.
This was true so long as there was no other source from which
re-rollers could normally buy cheaper 'semis'. The relatively
low level of billet prices still reflected the former competition
of imports of cheap Continental steel. Yet it was not now suggested by the Federation that the re-rollers should be free to

[1] In Jan. 1939, the Federation was considering making special concessions to
motor-car makers and shipbuilders. The May Committee *Report* of 1937 had
approved of such policies, on the time-honoured basis that 'each case should be
considered on its merits'; the principle was to help exports of goods in which the
cost of steel was a large part of total costs, and of course other countries did it. If
all countries were to avoid it it would be better (*Rep. I.D.A.C.* 1937, pp. 53-4).

[2] The profit margin allowed in the billet price was also less than that on other
heavy products. This was well known (cp. *The Times*, 26 Feb. 1945); but at this
time I believe there was no proposal to alter it.

import steel again if it paid them to do so. It is no wonder
therefore that over the fixing of prices the Federation judged it
desirable, even merely in respect of price policies of this type,
that there should be supervision in detail by an impartial
authority.

Away from the main work of shaping a new constitution for
the Federation, a second work of reorganisation, nominally
uncontentious, was also undertaken in 1943, the reorganisation
and expansion of the industry's collective research by the
establishment of a Research Association. It aroused some mis-
giving among those who had led the joint research committees
of the Federation and the Iron and Steel Institute, and the
Sheffield members of the Federation Committee which was
responsible for the reorganisation—who had been very influential in past research—clearly thought that the Association
would turn out to be primarily for the benefit of the heavy
trades and, if not a menace to the Sheffield firms who had built
up imposing research organisations of their own, of little value
to them. There was something in this; but it did not rule out
the possible value of the new proposal. The constitution of the
Association was drafted, however, under the influence of the
makers of heavy-steel products who dominated the Federation,
so that it was not encumbered by the past tradition in conducting joint research.[1] Set up in 1944, it was a token,
Sir James Lithgow said, of the Federation's recognition of its
obligation to maintain efficiency.[2]

(b) Practical planning

By the time the Federation had its new constitution drafted it
was also as it said 'well ahead with practical planning'. It had
set out, in the light of economic and technical conditions as it

[1] The Scots' influence was strong in these discussions (which almost seemed a
contest of Scotland versus Sheffield). The Scots were led by the chairman of the
Committee, Sir James Lithgow. Sir Andrew McCance was first President of the
Research Association. The personal situation was eased by the untimely death of
Dr W. H. Hatfield, Research Director of Firth Brown, who died during the Committee proceedings. Dr Swinden, Research Director of United Steel, a second
distinguished Sheffield member, died shortly after.

[2] The *Manchester Guardian*, 27 Mar. 1944, commenting on the announcement, said
that the initial annual payment, £250,000, was not much for the job in hand.

saw them, and in varying degrees of detail, its view of the pattern in which the industry when planned in a practical manner, that is, for the immediate post-war years, should be cast—how much steel it would make, the amounts of different raw materials it would need and their sources, the site and location of the works. The majority of the firms, individually or in groups, had put forward their specific plans of development, in greater or less detail, and many of these had passed through the rather large mesh (as it seemed to one observer) of the Federation's first screens. Thus when the Ministers and departments began, at the end of 1944, to come to grips with the post-war problems of steel whose consideration they had stimulated in the spring of 1943, they had before them not merely the project of a constitution, they had also a circumstantial indication of how the new powers sought by the Federation would be used if they were granted. They could also, if they chose, observe the momentum imparted by the mere operation of the industry within its existing pattern towards the maintenance of that pattern.

To formulate the general framework of a plan the Federation deemed it essential to determine the total post-war capacity of the industry. So practical planning started with a guess that consumption of steel at home would be 14·5 m. ingot tons within a year of the end of the war, and not much more five years later.[1] Some critics thought the guess too high, others too low; but on the assumption that the home market was to be preserved for the home steelmaker and that there would be some exports, it was held that home demand would certainly justify bringing steel-melting capacity up to 15 m. tons. Some people thought the target must be 20 m. tons. The Iron and Steel Trades Confederation advocated this because otherwise when the industry was modernised there would not be jobs for all the present workers.[2] Company chairmen who supported

---

[1] This was because there would be much abnormal replacement work immediately after the war; normal demand, it was supposed, would be for different purposes, and a different balance of products. I compounded the first 'estimates'.

[2] *The Times*, 25 June 1945, referring to a pamphlet issued by the Confederation calling on members to 'Vote Labour'. This claimed that 'present directors...will be well content to maintain a nominal capacity of 15 m. tons—with a yearly out-

this higher target,[1] however, agreed it would be difficult enough to reach 15 m. tons quickly. All were, of course, in the fashion, expansionists; they must 'develop the industry to the greatest possible extent'. Where should expansion occur, and what form should it take?

It was to begin with a question of raw-material supply. There would be less scrap to import than before the war, because the Americans would use their own, though there would for a time be battle scrap. The first guess was that 750,000 tons a year would be imported, which was soon seen to be rather high. On this assumption, to make 15 m. tons of ingots would, it was calculated, require 2·5 m. tons more blast furnace capacity than before the war, an increase of about 30 per cent. Instead of the ratio of scrap to pig iron used as raw material in steel furnaces being 60:40 as before the war, it was argued, it must be 40:60.[2] This in turn would require more ore, home or imported, and more coke. Where should the ore come from?

Steelmakers who had been obliged to use more home ore during the war in coastal plants designed for richer imported ores were anxious to return to their normal furnace 'burden' as soon as they could; it would give them more liquid pig iron for their steel furnaces and so lessen melting times and increase steel outputs. To import more ore was thus the simplest way of increasing steel supplies quickly; the Federation recommended reducing consumption of home ore to its pre-war level as soon as possible, and bringing in as much ore from oversea as in

put of between 10 and 12 m. We have urged that if the number of workpeople at present dependent on the industry…is to be assured of continuous employment and an increasing standard of life an output of between 18 and 20 m. tons will be necessary.' The Confederation stated that the B.I.S.F. aimed at importing 'semis', with profit to the steel firms but no employment for the men. It was on the side of the angels in one thing, viz. more development in Northamptonshire, but only on the assumption that production was maintained everywhere else. The *Manchester Guardian* commented on the Confederation's proposals sensibly (26 June 1945), that to build capacity for 20 m. tons would be 'an act of faith rather than of planning' and was quite out of the question for three or four years at least, and possibly five or six, because of the investment claims of other industries.

[1] It was said that Mr James of the Lancashire Steel Corporation was the chief of these.

[2] The ratio had only been 60:40 in the depth of the slump.

1937-9 or if possible more. What was good for existing plants in order to boost output was, however, of little relevance in deciding where to build new furnaces, and what ores they should use if the object was to keep production costs low. The Federation was well aware of this. The answer must be based on forecasts of post-war costs of imported and home ores, and of coal. All were very obscure. The Federation was guarded in its comments, but in the undertones, emphasis and omissions the deep-seated preference and interest of the old coastal areas left an unmistakable mark.[1]

The use of home ore, it was said fairly enough, is heavily penalised when fuel prices are high. Hardly anything was said, however, in public—except by Macdiarmid on behalf of his own company—of the distorting effect of the Coal Charges Account,[2] the specially heavy burden of the real costs of coal in South Wales and to a lesser extent on the North-east Coast. Scarcity of coke was likely, it was said, to be a critical factor discouraging the use of home ore because it needed more fuel than imported ore. The scope for the reduction of coke consumption in smelting iron ores which was demonstrated by the low coke consumption in the Corby furnaces was not conspicuously referred to. The industry, it was argued, must have the benefit of Government advice on the extent to which the use of home ore—which must be on the ore fields to be economic—should be maintained or increased as a security for defence purposes, as though the costs of using home ore might rule it out if there were no strategic case in its favour. Home ore reserves were perhaps smaller, it was said, than I.D.A.C. had supposed; careful investigation would be essential before reliable estimates could be made of the size of the steel industry which could be based on them. This was apparently not urgent. But the industry should be allowed as soon as possible to explore the foreign ore position so that it could, on technical grounds, define its wishes (or as was commonly said its 'needs') relative to sources of supply.

[1] Sir Alexander Dunbar made the conclusion clear enough. 'Much as he liked the policy of using home produced materials nevertheless he was convinced that after the war we must revert largely to the use of imported ores of high iron content' (*I.C.T.R.* 25 Feb. 1945).

[2] Above, p. 25. For Macdiarmid's comment, *The Times*, 18 May 1945.

As for costs, the Germans, it was assumed, would be out of the market for imported ore,[1] hence it would be a buyers' market. The F.O.B. prices might be expected to be little higher than before the war. Freights would probably fall sharply (since there would be a surplus of shipping when the war was over) and might settle about 50 per cent above the normal in non-boom years before the war.[2] This suggested an average C.I.F. price of 30s. a ton after the war, compared with an average of 22s. 6d. in 1937.[3] Home ore prices had risen by more than 50 per cent during the war. Moreover, it was possible to lower prices of imported ore by having better loading and unloading facilities (the existing ones were now acknowledged to be bad) and better, bigger ships, whereas the cost of home ore would steadily rise as deeper ore was used.

The implication seemed to be that the industry might still expand in all the old centres rather than in the new. This was more explicitly stated when the proper size of plant was discussed. The industry was planning, as Mr John E. James said, for mass production and specialisation; which might be expected to lead to fewer, larger, plants. How large should they be? Not mammoth, as in America (where there were several plants of 2–6 m. tons capacity) was the answer. Little economic or technical advantage was to be gained in an integrated steelworks[4] by adding capacity 'beyond (say) 500,000–800,000 tons per annum', a very wide tolerance.[5] Where operations were based on local scrap a cold-metal plant of 250,000 tons might

---

[1] Although the British attitude towards the scale of German steel output after the war was more liberal than the American, Russian and French views, and from the first sponsored the figure which for the Western sector amounted to 11 m. tons, it was visualised that this would be made largely from domestic ores and scrap, with a relatively small import of ore.

[2] This view of freights became the basis of the first arrangements for subsidising ore imports after the war. Below, p. 205.

[3] And 28s. 6d. in 1938, 25s. Jan.–June 1939.

[4] I.e. one with blast furnaces.

[5] In contemporary newspaper discussions, based necessarily on data derived from the industry, the size of an efficient plant was often put surprisingly low. Thus, for example, *The Times*, 26 Feb. 1945, speaks of 'the building of an integrated works, involving probably an optimum output of 500,000 tons a year for a single works'. Figures of this kind were published in the first steel plan early in 1946, but they had been prepared by the end of 1944.

in certain (not precisely defined) conditions be completely efficient in terms of production cost. No cold-metal shop could be fully efficient it was argued making more than 600,000 tons (there were, of course, those who argued that no cold-metal plant could be efficient for mass production steelmaking at all, but this point was only made obscurely, in technical discussions)[1] although hot-metal plants might be operated successfully up to 1 m. tons a year, at which point it was claimed the Americans were tending to duplicate shops.[2] These standards of size would allow modernisation without tears. The ability to use units of such modest scale made possible a considerable degree of dispersal of production and employment, it was claimed, without any real loss of technical efficiency.

Could it be that these ideal standards for maximum efficiency were influenced by the plans which the firms individually were preparing, that they underwrote decisions which had been made, and were not designed to shape them? No single British works made as much as 800,000 tons of ingots a year; no firm could say from experience that it had not gained from making more than 800,000 tons. The great majority of British plants were still small even by the Federation Standards. The distribution of output according to size of works making over 50,000 tons each in 1939 is given in Table 4. Thus only three made more than 500,000 tons in 1939, and each of these had two melting shops.[3] It was no doubt tempting to put the ideal within the limits of what seemed practical, and what seemed likely. The Federation's standards demanded no revolution; if total ingot output could be raised by one-fifth and a bunch of the smallest

---

[1] Cp. G. A. V. Russell's lecture in *Proc. Cleveland Institute*, 18 Dec. 1941.

[2] In discussions with Mr Quincy Bent of Bethlehem during the meetings of the United States–United Kingdom Metallurgical Mission in 1943, at which two prominent British steelmakers were also present, Mr Bent told me that he regarded 1·5 m. tons as the point at which it became desirable to duplicate, because the managerial problems became too unmanageable. At the Bethlehem Works there were three units of this size.

[3] The remaining 0·6 per cent of the output, 360,000 tons, was made by sixty-four works of varying sizes, the largest making approximately 30,000 tons. The firms either made castings or alloy and special steels; but makers of high-speed and tool steel only are not included. In a few instances works under common ownership were operated so that some ingots made in one were rolled or put through finishing stages in another.

plants eliminated—as was proposed—the rest could all, on these standards, be modernised and retained.

Table 4. *Distribution of output according to size of works, 1939*

Output of ingots or castings (thousand tons)	No. of Works	No. integrated with blast furnaces	Group output (thousand tons)	Proportion of total output (%)
50– 99	13	1	1,070	8·1
100–199	16	3	2,300	17·4
200–299	8	6	2,010	15·2
300–399	11	9	3,790	28·8
400–499	4	3	1,820	13·8
500–675	3	2	1,860	14·1
Total	55	24	12,850	97·4

By and large this was what the schemes put forward by the firms and recommended for licensing by the Federation by the end of 1944 and early in 1945—which formed the more concrete aspect of practical planning—proposed to do. Indeed, while the general discussions on size of works focused attention on steel-melting capacity, in the individual schemes greater cost reduction seems to have been looked for from changes in the programmes and equipment of finishing mills, which depended commonly upon more specialisation and standardisation of product and more regional concentration. The scale of finished product programmes almost invariably seemed to have deter-mined furnace capacity (though they hardly thought in these terms) rather than to have been designed to absorb the output of a melting shop of ideal size. Sometimes the character of the finishing mill did require a markedly higher ingot output; but this was consequential, not the prime motive of change. As a consequence these projects seemed to be visualised as creating demands for raw materials at specific places which must be met, and the question whether these materials could be ad-vantageously and cheaply assembled there appeared of secondary or tertiary importance.

This particular character of the schemes was often plain, not least in the most spectacular and most publicised project, which caught the public eye, the plan to build a wider wide strip mill in South Wales at Port Talbot. A mill capable of making strip 6 ft. wide—of a size made for the first time in the United States in 1935[1]—was deemed by all the experts to be obligatory in this country at the end of the war. A technical report confirming this was made for the Control in the winter of 1943. The same kind of mill was, as will be seen later, deemed no less obligatory for several other European countries. The only questions asked were: who should build and run it, and where should it be sited? But these were treated as questions which concerned only South Wales, and largely as a stage in the conflict over the tinplate redundancy scheme, a scheme for the payment of compensation to owners of old works for closing down when large efficient mills were built to take their place. The Principality's exclusive right to make tinplate and the continued concentration of a large part of the steel manufacture there were deemed axiomatic.

Port Talbot was brought into the picture at least partly because Baldwins' plate production there urgently needed to be modernised. They had, as Sir Charles Wright said, examined many schemes in detail in the hope of putting down 'modern plant to look after those sections of the trade which the company has been able to serve in the past'.[2] Examination started before the war; from 1935 Baldwins were considering the feasibility of putting down a very wide strip mill for which they contemplated linking up with Lysaghts, but the project made slow progress. By the war it had become clear that the old scale of operations of Baldwins and its closer associates would not alone permit the use of modern method. A continuous strip mill could, as the Americans were showing during the war, make some qualities of plate as well as sheet, but the scale of Guest Keen Baldwins and Baldwins combined businesses in plates and sheets was not enough to occupy such a mill,[3] and the compromise type of mill

---

[1] The Bethlehem Steel Co. installed an 80 in. mill in 1935. In 1936 two further very wide mills were installed in the United States, one of 80 in., the other 96 in. During the war these mills made over 1 m. tons a year each.

[2] *I.C.T.R.* 8 Dec. 1944.

[3] These two firms, who were very strongly represented in the Control (above, p. 5), made about 250,000 tons of tinplate and sheet and 125,000 tons of plate in South Wales before the war.

for smaller outputs which was being tried out in the States was said to be unsuccessful.[1] Baldwins were thus ready to amalgamate. Richard Thomas were far more important than Baldwins in the tinplate trade; they had, as the *Economist* said, the only good tinplate plant in the industry, and although price controls and other war circumstances were unfavourable for them, they had amassed large liquid reserves for further improvement, and they recognised that they must replace their vast holding of old-style tinplate plant by new-style plant.[2] But they had no coastal site such as Port Talbot; and they were no doubt conscious of the unsuitability of an inland site such as Ebbw Vale for making steel in Wales. This circumstance probably made them ready to approach, or to respond to, Baldwins,[3] though the position remains puzzling; since, assuming the new plant must be in South Wales, Port Talbot was not in itself an ideal site for a major modern works, though there was a little existing plant which could be utilised. It was argued forcefully, though probably incorrectly, that on technical grounds, and according to American experience, it was virtually essential to use high-grade imported ore for the new sheet process. Sites for so large a works are not common, but an alternative near Barry was strongly, though not publicly, advocated, where the largest ore ships then visualised (up to, say, 20,000 tons) could be docked. The main drawback at Port Talbot was that the bar of the harbour only allowed ships of 25 ft. draft to dock there, so that the larger ore ships of 10,000 tons and more, and over 30 ft. draft, which had the lowest freights, were excluded, the largest ships which could enter being of about 8000 tons. Whether it was an additional drawback that the Port Talbot site was a sandy beach is still disputed; it involved an immense amount of pile driving, but provided immense supplies of sand as a building material. The board of Richard Thomas

[1] Presumably the Steckel Mill, which has since been used in Luxembourg, Belgium, and Germany, sometimes being replaced as markets grew.

[2] *Econ.* 28 Aug. 1944.

[3] I do not know who made the first formal move proposing amalgamation. But it was Baldwins who initiated the Port Talbot plan. The *Economist* seemed to treat the affair as though Richard Thomas were the instigators (*Econ.* 17 Nov. 1944); that may have referred chiefly to the formalities.

concluded, nevertheless, that Port Talbot was the right site, and to amalgamate.[1]

Political influences may have played a part in this. In October 1944 Mr Dalton, then President of the Board of Trade, in a debate on South Wales affairs, said that he would only consider the tinplate redundancy scheme 'when it is established that the new plants will be sited in accordance with the national interest'.[2] He would be no party to the dislocation of the Welsh tinplate industry; the idea of a strip mill on the Humber, which he said had been mooted again, was anathema to him. 'We must remember what happened before the Ebbw Vale plant was set up.' The mantle of Lord Baldwin had descended on Mr Dalton. But given the acceptance of South Wales for which the firms concerned, despite Mr Dalton's pretensions, may have been wholly responsible, the President's concern may have been primarily that some of the new plant to be put up should be farther west than Port Talbot, since most of the older tinplate works were clustered round Swansea and Llanelly. Mr Dalton expressed satisfaction when it was announced in January 1945 that the hot strip mill and major steelworks would be at Port Talbot, but the site of the cold reduction mills was yet to be finally settled and 'one will, unless some insuperable technical or economic difficulty is encountered, be located in the Llanelly area'. Port Talbot and Llanelly he stated were 'excellent sites for the new plants, and fit well into the pattern which we (still the coalition) are now working out for the post-war industry in South Wales and Monmouthshire'.[3] Whether his views influenced the decision or not, his declaration effectively committed the Government to support the major new steel expansion scheme and the major decision on location of the early post-war years, before any rigorous assessment of the general raw-material cost position had been presented to the responsible

[1] Some special compensatory advantages were put forward for Port Talbot: that oil could easily be brought by pipe-line from Llandarcy to fuel the open-hearth furnaces, and that there was an untapped source of good coking coal near by, which could be cheaply mined. This has so far been a disappointment economically.

[2] *Hansard*, 17 Oct. 1944, col. 2322–3. Mr Dalton became Sir Hugh Dalton and in 1960 Lord Dalton.

[3] *The Times*, 29 Jan. 1945. (A statement in lieu of a speech.)

Ministry, the Ministry of Supply,[1] and before an opportunity had presented itself to consult any of the main ore-importing merchants, who were most experienced in regard to freights and unloading installations.

The formal announcement of the intention to build at Port Talbot was preceded, as it had to be, by the merger of Richard Thomas and Baldwins, which provoked another bitter dispute between the Richard Thomas board, who rushed their proposals through without giving sufficient information in the eyes of the responsible journals to permit of judgement, by methods which savoured of dictatorship, and some of its shareholders who, led by Sir William Firth, felt that Baldwins, whose plant was mainly old and who had only a small part in the tinplate trade, did too well out of the terms.[2] Investors seemed to agree; 'the market reactions in general', as *The Times* put it with urbane restraint, 'might be interpreted as a feeling that in the short run Baldwins stand to gain more than its partner in the fusion'.[3] Whether (and if so how) the market indicated that in the long run the balance might be redressed for Richard Thomas shareholders *The Times* did not vouchsafe. But it returned often to the argument that 'there are no doubt answers that are at present hidden from shareholders' to all the awkward questions raised by Sir William Firth[4] in what was manifestly his last throw. The *Economist* was less satisfied; 'there has been no adequate consideration of the terms of fusion...the complete rejection of demands for information are indefensible'.[5] But both, in common with the 'City' columns of all London papers, thought the fusion itself desirable because of its 'paramount object'[6] as described by Mr Lever, namely, that it would '*accelerate materially* [my italics] the steps necessary to rebuild export trade particularly in the tinplate industry. One of these steps is the extension of the continuous strip mill process.' The phrase read oddly seven years later when the wheels of the cold reduction plant at length began to turn. A fusion was

---

[1] As far as I know the Ministry of Supply had not expressed approval of the site.
[2] I have been informed of this by persons who might have been consulted.
[3] *The Times*, 11 Dec. 1944 (City Notes).
[4] *The Times*, 7, 11, 22, and 29 Dec. 1944.
[5] *Econ.* 6 Jan. 1945.   [6] *The Times*, 7 Dec. 1944.

necessary, it was held, before the funds for a new integrated steelworks with hot and cold strip mills, whose cost ran easily into eight figures, could be procured.[1] The first of the cost guesses was £15 m. The project was assessed in the financial columns wholly in City terms—not as an industrial problem—as though the precise site and nature of the plant might be irrelevant. Yet if Port Talbot was not indispensable Richard Thomas need hardly have accepted terms which appeared to favour Baldwins,[2] though the board may have been prepared to make a sacrifice to secure the services of some of the Guest Keen Baldwins technical management.[3] The formation of Richard Thomas and Baldwins was to be part of a wider merger that was contemplated, and Mr Dalton in announcing his approval of Port Talbot referred to Guest Keen Nettlefolds, the Briton Ferry Steel Company and the Llanelly Steel Company as prospective participants. Colonel Bevan of Briton Ferry had welcomed the merger as a 'magnificent move' on its first announcement, when Richard Thomas promised to behave as 'big brother' to the lesser members of the tinplate trade.

Nothing else in the 'practical planning' in the last 18 months of the war competed with this *cause célèbre* in individual importance or publicity. Cognate with it was a decision to introduce

---

[1] *The Times*, 7 Dec. 1944.

[2] Apart from the favourable terms, since the Baldwin holdings were to be managed by Baldwins (Holdings) the control of one third of R.T.B. was consolidated in the hands of the Baldwin directors on the new board. Mr Lever said that since their interest was wholly in ordinary shares they would suffer with all ordinary shareholders (cp. *The Times*, 30 Dec. 1944). His argument neglected the point that the new shareholding group, because coherently organised, would have a privileged position, and could exert more power than the original holders, so that though they would no doubt, as he said, try and act in the common interest of all, their judgement carried disproportionate weight. He did not attempt to meet this objection, and his attitude showed in this again a failure to perceive the 'democratic' claims of ordinary shareholders in joint stock company management. *The Times* (City col. 22 Dec. 1944) recognised that the obvious way to avoid this objection to the scheme was for the ordinary shares to be paid not to 'Baldwins Holdings Ltd.' but to each individual shareholder of Baldwins. But the comment was made that even if this were done Richard Thomas shareholders might think the sum paid was too much.

[3] It was my impression that G.K.B. had a stronger team than Richard Thomas, and that the handling of the steelmaking at Ebbw Vale had not commanded universal confidence.

the new electrolytic process of putting the tin on tinplates at Ebbw Vale, another American process, a further blow to the traditional small plants and to the ample labour force of the South Wales industry. It was to be located at Ebbw Vale because the thin sheets for tinning had to be provided in coils from a cold reduction mill. The process saved not only labour but tin, since it provided a much thinner coating, too thin at the outset for some purposes.[1] This difficulty was to be overcome by putting a thicker coat on one side, but this came later.

In the heavy-steel trade the most arresting plan arose out of Dorman Long's decision to install a Grey Mill (or universal beam mill), more than 40 years after this type of mill had been invented in America by an English immigrant and used first on the Continent in 1902, in America in 1908.[2] Like the strip mill it was to have a new melting shop and blast furnaces to feed it, and Dorman Longs also planned to install efficient equipment for unloading and preparing their imported ore. The new mill would make 'broad flange beams', so called rather oddly, since it is the web of these beams which can be made most conspicuously wider than in the conventional mills.[3] They were acknowledged now to be unmistakably of great importance for structural engineers,[4] though before the war their use was discouraged.[5] In Germany it had been found possible by skilful roll-cutting to make beams of this type up to a 24 in. web in conventional heavy-section mills.[6] In America more than half the beams made were rolled in universal mills. Thus this second project in practical planning was also concerned with making

[1] Electrolytic tinning was used commercially in a small way in 1937 in the United States. There were three production lines by 1942, and 25 under construction. *Iron Age*, 2 Dec. 1943.

[2] See *E.H.S.* p. 286. The universal beam mill had a considerable history in France and Germany—back to the eighteen-sixties—before Grey's development in 1897.

[3] In the United States mills the web could be made up to 36 in. wide. The flanges could be wider too, because they do not, as in conventional beams, taper. Conventional beams had a maximum web of 24 in.

[4] There were several advantages; for example, riveted fabrication was avoided for the larger beams, while it was possible to vary the thickness of web and flanges much more, which allowed more flexibility in design.

[5] I understand that imports were specially restricted.

[6] I am indebted to Mr G. A. V. Russell for information on this.

up for lost time. It was widely rumoured that it might promote the co-ordination of heavy-section rolling on the North-east Coast, and even the elimination of the Skinningrove Works, and the amalgamation of Cargo Fleet and Dorman Longs, which for long had been the daydream of those who fancied regional co-ordination. The larger firm wanted it to increase its load as a basis for 'rationalising', and the smaller possibly found it less attractive because even in 1939 Dorman Long had still much dead plant to cut out. The Sankey Report referred to the proposal;[1] Sir Andrew Duncan hoped it would grow out of the Jarrow negotiations and then decided it would have to wait upon a change of leadership at Cargo Fleet. Cargo Fleet's own plans for immediate post-war development were modest; they proposed, for example, to adapt a plate mill to roll wider plates and to replace a steam by an electric drive; but for such things they did not, initially at any rate, seek Federation support.

Dorman Long's rather distant neighbours in the North-east at Consett made it plain in their plans for urgent reconstruction that they had no thought of reviving the idea of moving to a seaboard site on the Tyne. This was implicit, in fact, in the decision to build the new blast furnace of 1941.[2] They sought permission successfully, as an urgent need for keeping steel output up in the years of reconstruction, to modernise completely their decrepit and high-cost plant starting with another blast furnace and the melting shop. At the outset it was not certain on what finished product they would concentrate. The ore was to be brought by telpher from a new unloading point on the Tyne to the hill site of Consett which still, like Ebbw Vale, got some of its coking coal from local mines. The plant 'tied up with string' always has the first claim for restoration when it can be said that immediate output is at stake. The tale of North-east projects was completed by a plan to install a new light-section mill (especially for window-frame sections) with a new standard of accuracy for this country at the Darlington Rolling Mills, a re-rolling subsidiary of Dorman Longs,[3]

---

[1] *E.H.S.* p. 437.   [2] Above, p. 14.
[3] Via Bolckow Vaughans; *E.H.S.*, pp. 374, 439.

Crittalls and Henry Hope. This, too, was a project which secured early consent.[1]

In Scotland Colvilles most urgent object was to replace the melting-shop at Dalzell, with enlarged capacity, where it was argued the old shop could no longer be safely maintained and repaired. The plant as a whole had high costs, not only because it had no blast furnaces but on account of its bad layout,[2] which had been worsened by the installation of a new rod mill, in itself a good mill, in 1938. This proposal was not approved as quickly as Colvilles would have liked, but it was approved. Colvilles proposed also to extend their blast furnaces and steel plant at Clydebridge. The Lancashire Steel Corporation's main preoccupation was the increase of wire-rod capacity, without excess and suitably co-ordinated. The most noteworthy proposals for development on the cheap home ore came from Lincolnshire, the principal one being put up by the United Steel Companies. They, as well as Dorman Longs, contemplated making universal beams as part of their post-war reconstruction at Scunthorpe.[3] They gave up their plan when they heard of Dormans, possibly because they realised that Dormans with their large constructural engineering interest would command a great part of the market, though Appleby-Frodingham would have lower costs. They did, however, plan to replace the oldest of their Lincolnshire blast furnaces and melting shops and the section mills, which although they had been the only consistently profitable part of the combine, had hitherto often been 'starved for expenditure'.[4] Obsolete plant,

---

[1] See for example *Financial News*, 3 Apr. 1945, when the work was already in hand.

[2] *E.H.S.* p. 368.

[3] P. W. S. Andrews and Eliz. Brunner, *Capital Development in Steel*, p. 295. The text gives the impression that what was in mind was a Grey Mill; but I was informed by Mr Gerald Steel that their plan was to use a conventional mill in the manner referred to above (p. 85).

[4] *Capital Development in Steel*, pp. 289 sqq. It was planned to expand the up-to-date blast-furnace plant and give up using one dating from 1865, to build a new melting shop near this blast-furnace plant to displace the former 'Frodingham' shop, to build a new cogging mill to take larger ingots, and to revamp the section mills (among other things replacing steam by electric drives) and provide new ancillary equipment. Even after these changes there were to be left two hand-charged blast furnaces.

wasteful in its use of fuel, had thrived on the cheap ores which were used with only moderate efficiency.[1] As usual modernisation promised expansion. United Steel's plans for other of their branches were comparatively modest, but they included expansion of steel capacity at Steel, Peech and Tozers to match the new cogging mill,[2] with possibly a new bar and rod mill;[3] and within a scheme which proposed to reduce the steelmaking capacity at Workington to 200,000 tons a year because its costs were inevitably high,[4] they included a plan to 'claim a much larger share' of the rail trade, on which Workington had always specialised. Stewarts and Lloyds concentrated their development proposals almost wholly on facilities for making more weldless tube, particularly for the oil industry. At Corby they had a pre-war project for ore preparation to carry out, and wanted to build an open-hearth plant to use their works scrap; but they had more ambitious plans for new steel and tube capacity at their remaining Scots works and at Bilston, where they proposed to patch up the old blast furnaces a little as well. The small hand-charged high-cost furnaces there had used the puddle cinder, the waste product of the wrought-iron trade, rich in iron, of which there had been great stocks in the old 'iron' country; but the reserves were drying up, and since these furnaces would be quite uneconomic to work on home ores it was planned to charge imported ore, which also gave with least trouble the right kind of pig iron. They proposed no immediate development of their welded tube production; during the war the plants other than Corby closed. Stewarts and Lloyds main concern over welded tubes was lest other firms developed electric welding facilities.[5] Stewarts and Lloyds proposed only a moderate increase in their steel capacity. It should be con-

[1] The Appleby plate mills were much more efficient, though not so profitable; rather far away from shipbuilding.

[2] Above, p. 14.

[3] There were plans also to introduce into the continuous billet mill an improvement made first at Salzgitter, whereby alternate rolls were horizontal and vertical; the billet was not twisted.

[4] It was recognised that high cost of coal and ore was a handicap.

[5] Sir Allan Macdiarmid was concerned in 1944 that one important firm which had agreed not to enter the welded tube trade—thinking in terms of the Fretz-Moon process—had decided to go in for making electric welded tubes.

sidered, they argued, solely as steel for tubes, and not as steel in general, but most of it was on this occasion in smaller works in old areas. In south Staffordshire the Earl of Dudley also proposed to replace the melting shop at Round Oak by one of larger capacity, 250,000 tons a year. It was just the minimum which the Federation were to find could be economic in special circumstances.

Such was the picture which, in greater detail, the Ministry of Supply in its various guesses had to consider at the end of 1944. It was not at the date a complete picture. The industry claimed rightly during the nationalisation debates that it had been making investment plans long before the Labour Government came into office, but it naturally had not made all its plans. It was a cumulative process. At this stage in the preliminaries of central planning two processes were going on side by side, the preparation of a schematic analysis of the markets, raw material supplies and costs and of the economies of 'scale' of production on the one hand, and the preparation and collation of particular projects on the other. The second probably had more influence on the first at this stage than the first on the second. And the preparation of particular projects reflected the outlook and aspirations of the individual firms. These sought zealously, quite naturally and rightly, what they could do with their own facilities as a starting-point, in their own trades, in their present locations. This approach was likely to promote greater technical efficiency, but not necessarily economic efficiency. It would tend to lead at most to the best technical solution of a series of limited local problems, the more efficient supply of the products normal to the various existing locations on a scale determined partly by the present distribution of markets, using raw materials to which the firms had access. It would not tend to result in radical adaptation to changes in the basic raw-material situation and in relative advantages of different sites. It was liable to result in a perpetuation of the existing pattern of production, with everything on a larger scale if total output were larger. There was a risk, to put it no higher, that little attention would be given to the possibility of establishing new low-cost plants whose costs were bound to remain for a long time, on account of natural advantages of site, below the average.

Ideally the processes of central analysis should have revealed any gaps and defects in the accumulation of particular projects. Some gaps were recognised—a lack of new plans for billet production, for example, which was no doubt a reflection of the low-profit margins allowed, was recognised fairly quickly. Were there more fundamental deficiencies? That was a question to which the Ministry of Supply might be expected to find the answer.

The Government also naturally wanted to know how the projects put forward would affect prices and employment. In answering the Federation turned back, perhaps inevitably, to generalities. There was, it argued, such a wide spread between the costs of high- and low-cost plants, in so far as the cost figures collected for price-fixing were a guide, that even if the prime costs of new plants were no better than those in the best existing plants it would be right to build new plant to replace the worst existing plant. Although the cost of fixed capital development had risen more during the war than the cost of labour,[1] nevertheless, total costs in a new plant would be less than prime costs in the old, though the favourable margin would not always be great.[2] The figures were not all equally conclusive, because the high-cost plants made a different assortment of sizes and

[1] *Iron and Steel industry* (May 1946), p. 32; the cost of a new billet plant was said to have risen from £13. 10s. per ton of capacity to £23. 10s. i.e. by 70 or 80 per cent. For the rise in the cost of labour see above, pp. 21–2, 27–9.

[2] *Ibid. loc. cit.* gave the following table:

Comparative costs at new plant and plant displaced

	Old plant prime cost		New plant		
Product	20% highest cost	Next 20%	Prime cost	Capital charges	Total cost
	£ s. d.	£ s. d.	£ s. d.	£ s. d.	£ s. d.
Pig iron	7 17 0	7 11 0	6 0 0	1 5 0	7 5 0
Billets	13 17 6	13 0 0	10 7 6	2 0 0	12 7 6
Plates	17 0 0	16 3 0	13 12 6	2 15 0	16 7 6
Sheets	23 10 0	22 4 0	17 5 0	3 15 0	21 0 0
Tinplates	36 5 0	33 15 0	25 0 0	5 5 0	30 5 0

shapes, and satisfied different markets from those supplied by the low-cost plants, though there was overlapping; they earned higher average prices.[1] Also the costs were distorted by war conditions. But it was stated that a new integrated plant, good in all parts, would have lower costs than any existing plant— perhaps £1 a ton lower, assuming the same raw materials were used. How much lower costs would have been, assuming the use of the cheapest raw materials at the most favourable sites, required a supplementary calculation.

The Federation thus held out no hopes of sensational price reductions as an outcome of new capital investment (they hoped for much more by a fall in the price of coal). In the end the case for change seemed to rest largely on the need to replace old plant that was wearing out, the scope for installing new plant which would make new products or new qualities, and the growing demand for steel (hence, the assumption followed, for more steelmaking capacity *here*). Employment prospects were assessed on the same basis. The use of more modern methods would reduce the amount of labour needed to make a ton of steel; but a larger proportion of pig iron would be used, which would require more labour. The guess was that 15 per cent more workers would be employed by the plans in hand— within say five years. No one in the Federation dreamed that savings of labour on the scale which American productivities would have offered were a practical 'target'.

2. THE DEPARTMENTS PONDER

It fell naturally to the Ministry of Supply to chart the course of the steel industry in the transition period. This involved both unwinding the war machine and starting a peace machine, albeit it might only be a temporary one. In the autumn of 1944 the Ministry was asked in addition to study the measures needed —in the as yet untarnished jargon of the new orthodoxy—to establish an efficient steel industry which would play its full

[1] I have been shown figures for light re-rolled products which showed that the few largest works had an average realised price which was 96 per cent of the average for the whole trade, whereas the small works had an average realised price of 108 per cent of the average for the whole trade.

part within the national economy in expanding the export trade, and contribute to the maintenance of full employment. It was to do these things in consultation with the Board of Trade (and where necessary, for example in assessing future demand, other departments) and it called in aid from the Cabinet Office for the second. Although these tasks were intimately related they were pursued somewhat independently, though there was overlapping on the periphery. The second was one of the 'separate studies of the post-war future of particular industries' to which the official history refers without having room for any detail.[1]

For the transition it was necessary to decide whether relaxations should be made in the system of allocating steel, what imports or exports of steel could be hoped or provided for in the early years of peace, how far prices should still be subsidised —and, as already remarked, what schemes of capital investment should be sponsored. It was here that the work necessarily impinged on long-term plans. In theory some decision had to be made at short notice before long-term plans were agreed in order to prevent a fall of output. But these could not fail in the larger cases to influence the pattern of development for long to come. The Consett proposals provided an outstanding instance. Here, as has been seen, an expansion of output was proposed at an old plant now fully dependent on imported ore but 12 miles inland. This posed most of the major concrete problems of planning. Was Consett a good site for further expansion? Or was this an instance when plant which had worn out should be replaced elsewhere? Before the war there had been talk of moving to Tyneside.[2] Strong arguments could be advanced, from a national standpoint, for concentrating the import of ore at a few points capable of unloading large ships (of 12,000 tons or more) quickly, since this would lower both unloading costs and freights. The development planned for Consett visualised some expansion of output[3] and provided for quick unloading of

---

[1] Hancock and Gowing, op. cit. p. 54.

[2] See E.H.S. p. 464. The consultant Brassert advised a shift to the coast in 1922.

[3] Output rose to about 520,000 tons of pig iron and over 500,000 tons of steel ingots by 1950. Steel output doubled again by 1960.

big ships. But plant which could unload a 12,000-ton ship in a day, and thus give big specialised ships a quick 'turn round', could not be fully employed supplying blast furnaces making together only about 350,000 or 500,000 tons of pig iron a year. Nor would the scale of working allow the use of blast furnaces of the size now normal for new American installations, where almost all the new furnaces made 1000 tons or more a day.[1] Moreover, the steelworks were to have the minimum capacity which in the Federation's estimate allowed for efficiency,[2] but was below one-half the minimum which many Americans recommended.[3] Thus the new Consett raised a forbidding assortment of planning problems.

There was, it may be surmised, what appeared to be a short cut through these and similar difficulties.[4] The Ministry, it could be argued, must assume that if a firm advanced a project it had assured itself of the commercial soundness of the scheme. All the Ministry had to do, the argument could run, was to confirm that, in a broader sense, the project was needed urgently, and so must be given a prior claim to scarce investment resources 'in the national interest'. The Ministry did not have to promise the project would be profitable; it did not undertake to provide protection or subsidies, or even to accept the plant automatically as efficient for purposes of price-fixing. Firms would indeed in these circumstances be expected to estimate profitability without knowing the future economic framework within which it would operate. On this supposition it was open to the Ministry to argue that the cost reduction offered by a scheme must be adequate, since the sponsoring firm was prepared to take the risk. It was not so clear that the firms themselves would acknowledge the risk in this form. How

[1] In America 46 blast furnaces built or enlarged had an average capacity of 1000 tons a day. Only four new furnaces had a capacity of below 300,000 tons a year, and 15 had capacities of from 425,000 to 465,000 tons a year (i.e. 1150–1300 tons a day). Full details in *Iron Age*, 3 Jan. 1944.

[2] Above, p. 27.

[3] From my limited experience I would say *most* Americans.

[4] For example, an early proposal was to build a wholly new melting shop at Dalzell (see above, p. 87) and a proposal to modernise the Darlington Rolling Mills (a re-rolling plant). Both these schemes and the Consett one were allowed. This may have been right; I am only concerned to show what was involved.

many firms, it may be wondered, would have revised their projects in 1944 had it been announced that there would be no tariffs, no central fund to spread the costs of costly raw materials, a free price for scrap?

Those charged with the task of finding the ways to make the industry permanently efficient did not ostensibly run into the difficulty of having openly to pass judgement on individual investment proposals. They accepted the view which the Federation advanced that the rapid completion of a substantial volume of modernisation and new construction was needed; that was clear from the 'priorities' based on their work.[1] The general argument seemed irrefutable; it was never challenged. There was a small tiresome minority who thought many specific proposals unsound, but it did not question the need, by implication urgent, for heavy investment. The steelmakers claimed that Britain was catching up other countries in efficiency before the war, but was checked by the war when only halfway to success; her steel prices were now well above the American, and her fuel costs in particular, which were still a larger part of total steel-making costs than they need be, had become of overwhelming importance because of the lamentable rise of coal prices during the war. All this called urgently for modernisation, but in addition the growth of Britain's engineering industries, the destruction and disorganisation in Europe, and the world's pent-up hunger for machinery made it desirable to add capacity for making more steel. So the general decision on a programme, the kind of decision which Sir Oliver Franks (who in 1944 was second secretary of the Ministry of Supply and in 1945 became Permanent Secretary) was later to dignify as the Government function in central planning as he conceived it,[2] seemed easy to make, and valid for any future form of régime in or for the industry, cartel or competitive, free trade or protective, private

[1] Below, p. 95.
[2] Sir Oliver Franks, *Central Planning and Control in War and Peace*, pp. 35 sqq. E.g. 'A Government committed to central planning...has to do more than define its attitude to future contingencies and elaborate its responses, legislative or administrative, to existing needs. It has to practise strategy and plan a campaign in as real a sense as any commander....Like him it must give hostages to fortune and say what it will make happen.'

or public ownership. There must be a big programme of development for steel, and it must give more scope for large-scale operations (which would raise efficiency), provide new finished products for export, and reduce fuel costs. Here were the simple priorities which the industry must interpret in a detailed plan, which the industry must then accept as imposing an obligation.[1]

Such priorities rose, so it seemed, above the conflict over organisation, having as it were an absolute validity. Yet how were they arrived at? They were, once they departed from the mere assertion that large investments were needed, inevitably based on the data given by the Federation or the firms about plans and projects already in hand, and about costs present and future, and the scope for cost reduction. And because they grew in this way, they were less non-committal than they looked. The general priorities in reality awarded individual priorities to the particular schemes on which they were founded. Moreover, the priorities committed the Government (and by implication those who advised them) as much by what they did not refer to as by what they included—most clearly in regard to location, the issue which had been raised so conspicuously by the conflict over Corby, Jarrow and Ebbw Vale before the war. They provided a general cover for virtually all the schemes which firms were drawing up, and avoided drawing attention to the controversial issues and the impossibility of getting concentrations and lowest costs without locational adjustments. Thus preferences to schemes which would advance large-scale production would embrace all schemes which involved expansion, without providing a means of making sharp distinctions

---

[1] See the Remit to the British Iron and Steel Federation in *Iron and Steel Industry* (May 1946), p. 7. The steel industry were asked by the Government for 'a plan to be carried out in five years' to 'secure the rapid completion of a substantial volume of modernisation and new construction', adequate to 'put the industry on an efficient operating basis'. 'In formulating the plan priority should be given to new plant at the finishing end of the industry which would increase exports; to schemes to reduce fuel costs and consumption; and to schemes to enable a greater proportion of output to be produced by large scale methods.' It was added that the Government were 'aware of important factors not directly related to the efficiency of the plants, such as the price of coal, which may place the British industry at a disadvantage'.

between those which were really large and those which were not; preferences for schemes which promoted fuel economy would give high marks to blast-furnace developments based on imported ores, and preference for plants to make new products covered the South Wales strip mill and Dorman Long's beam mill.

But the question—where should expansion occur—was left discreetly alone. Was Port Talbot the right spot for the strip mill? What were the relative merits of Lackenby and Scunthorpe for making broad-flange beams? The general question did not go by default; it was raised, and in effect, though not in so many words, the priorities implied a judgement that these things did not for the moment matter; they were not urgent. The Federation view, that is, was for practical purposes accepted, along with its forecast that imported ore might be expected to cost about 30s. a ton, and that on this basis the ratio of home and imported ore costs would be as from 2d. to 3d. a unit of iron in the first to 7d. a unit in the second.[1]

Even on this basis and with coal prices evened out by the Coal Charges Account the cost of the blast-furnace burden was astonishingly cheaper when home ore was used, and it was unlikely that the advantage would be wholly dissipated by higher capital and labour costs and higher costs of steelmaking arising from the low iron content of the home ore save possibly at a few exceptionally favoured sites, which did not include Port Talbot. A rough calculation in the middle of 1944[2] showed that the blast-furnace burden would cost from 70s. to 75s. a ton in Northants on the ore field and 100s. to 105s. a ton using imported ore at a coastal site, if home ore cost 4s. to 5s. a ton, imported ore 30s. a ton, with coking coal at the current rates. The ratio remained fairly constant, but Table 5 is based on coking-coal costs in the last half of 1944 and the early part of 1945. Coal prices, it has been seen, were steadily rising, which was unfavourable to the use of home ore so long as imported ore prices were, in this theoretic calculation, pegged.

[1] Above, p. 77.
[2] I published these figures in a paper to the Economic History Society (*Econ. Hist. Review*, 1947, p. 96).

Two calculations are given for the use of imported ore burdens, one assuming the use of 18 cwt., the other 16 cwt. of coke, because the low figure was a projection of what could be

Table 5. *Relative cost of blast-furnace burdens*

	Ore[a]	Coking[b] coal	Lime[c] stone	Rail transport On ore[d]	Rail transport On coal[e]	Total
	s.	s.	s.	s.	s.	s.
Northants (using 3·3 tons home ore and 1·0 ton coke)	14	51	—	—	15	80
Coast:						
(a) Using 1·8 ton imp. ore and 0·9 ton coke	54	48	4	—	5	111
(b) Using 1·8 ton imp. ore and 0·8 ton coke	54	43	4	—	4	105
Inland 'Coastal':						
(a) Using 1·8 ton imp. ore and 0·9 ton coke	54	48	4	6	3–5	115–117
(b) Using 1·8 ton imp. ore and 0·8 ton coke	54	43	4	6	2–4	109–111

[a] Cost of home ore at works located on ore field; of imported ore at docks or works located by dock. I assume 1·8 tons of 54 per cent ore; the cost of 54 per cent iron at 7d. a unit would in fact be just over 30s. a ton. The cost of 96 units at 7d. a unit would be 56s. Often iron ore is replaced in part by scrap, cinder, etc., but these are additional costs which cannot be schematised in this way.

[b] Assuming 1·5 tons of coking coal a ton of coke, and an average price in Northamptonshire based on two-thirds Yorkshire and one-third South Wales coal. The Yorkshire price averaged about 33s., the South Wales and North-east Coast about 36s. a ton.

[c] It had proved possible to use 'self-fluxing' mixtures of home ores, almost dispensing with limestone.

[d] These figures cover rail charges on ore to sites like Consett, Ebbw Vale, Clydebridge, and (prospectively) Shotton, and canal charges to Irlam. The figures are for most instances probably too low.

[e] I assume a railway rate of about 3s. 6d. per ton to a deep-water site, but give a range to allow for sites where roughly half the coking coal was mined at the works site—for example, at Consett or Ebbw Vale. This is a diminishing asset, and inland sites are not invariably near mines (e.g. Clydebridge, Irlam, Shotton). Hence as an average this figure is too low for inland sites.

7   BEH

done, not a record of contemporary achievement, whereas the coke consumption at Corby was already 20 cwt. and had been for periods lower. The Corby coke consumption reflected in part the fact that the 'fines' in the ore were sintered. To keep consumption down to 15 or 16 cwt., a ton of iron using imported ore would require either the use of selected ores of exceptionally favourable quality (possibly above 55 per cent, easy to reduce and in good mechanical condition), or the introduction of new ore preparation plant and some sintering. It would involve therefore additional operating costs. Naturally, as more imported ore was wanted, and as existing good sources became exhausted, it would be necessary to turn to less good ores. Smelting costs are inevitably higher in using home ore, not only because more fuel is needed but also because more materials (including more airblast) must be handled. In 1944 operating costs in an efficient works using home ore were about £1 a ton. Costs in an equivalent works using imported ore might thus have been about 14s. a ton, but the works would have produced less gas and slag as by-products per ton,[1] so that the net gain in operating cost would have been certainly less— possibly much less—than 5s. a ton. The difference in capital cost would possibly have been greater, perhaps nearly 8s. a ton.[2] One further extra cost in smelting is to be allowed for, the cost of sintering. Since the best foreign ore practice would normally require some sintering a net allowance of 5s. a ton is probably excessive.[3] The margin in raw-material costs of between 25s. and 35s. would thus have been reduced by from 15s. to 18s.

For basic Bessemer steel this was the end of the calculation. The high phosphorus of the pig iron made from Northampton-

[1] The value of these by-products was high; in one home ore works for instance it was 12s. a ton in 1944.

[2] The capital cost of a blast-furnace plant per ton of output was £3. 5s. in 1936; it might be reckoned at £10 a ton in 1944. If depreciation and interest were taken at 14 per cent and capital cost at 40 per cent more for home ore the difference was 8s. a ton.

[3] In one estimate for a reconstruction in 1946 the total cost of sintering (which was already practised at the works) was put at 6s. a ton of sinter. Recent practice in using imported ores at some works involves sintering all the ore, which reduces coke consumption below 15 cwt. per ton of iron.

shire ore suited it to this process, for which the scope was clearly widening. The process had, as has been seen, the singular advantage that all three major cost elements, fuel, labour and capital, were cheaper in it than in the open-hearth process. It became known in 1944 that the Germans were increasing the range of good steels made by the process by reducing its nitrogen content. For the open-hearth process pig iron from home ore was more expensive to use because of the phosphorus; so that on the cost assumptions in these calculations the costs at a Northamptonshire site might not have been much less than the costs on a well-located plant on deep water. Of existing deep-water sites only Cardiff and Teesside qualified.[1]

One of the cost assumptions was that the price of coal in the coastal areas would continue to be lowered by a subsidy based on coal in the east Midlands, and it was also implicit that South Wales or Durham coking coals would still be mixed with the cheaper Yorkshire and Nottinghamshire coking coals in Corby practice, though Lincolnshire practice showed that the proportion of the best coking coals so mixed could be greatly reduced if not eliminated. In terms of real costs therefore a calculation, which at current money costs equated North-amptonshire costs with those at the best deep-water sites, would conceal a net advantage for Northamptonshire. There was a probability that the net advantage of Lincolnshire might prove greater. Coke consumption in smelting had not come down there to the Corby level, but it was being reduced, and the access to coking coal was much better. Northamptonshire could offset a further rise in transport costs (which had risen very moderately in the war) by skill in blending the nearer coking coals, but relative remoteness from coking coal was a weakness, though not a major one, unless it was to be expected that the cost of rail transport would ultimately rise *more* than (at the moment it had risen *less* than) other major costs above its pre-war level.

In more general terms this was the kind of problem which

---

[1] The factors covered in these paragraphs do not cover all aspects of the comparative costs; but as will be seen later they include all that is needed for a balance on the point at issue.

those who tried to forecast future costs in different locations had
to face. The cost of coal had risen disproportionately during the
war, which reduced the cost advantage of the home ore sites.
Administrative measures to moderate the rise of coal prices had
accentuated this to the further disadvantage of these sites. In
looking forward the Federation took the view that the other side
of the account would also turn to the disadvantage of the home
ore sites, that just as coal prices had risen more than most other
elements of home costs since 1936–9, imported ore prices would
(when the war was over) rise less.

Was it likely that prices of imported ores would be among the
prices which rose relatively little, less, for instance (to give it a
precise sense), than average wage-rates in all manufacturing
industries, which rose by the end of 1944 to 146 per cent of the
1939 level? It was easier to find reasons against this view than in
its favour. Engineering and shipbuilding wages had risen more
than the average and were unlikely to relapse: by mid-1943
average hourly earnings of all workers in shipbuilding and
marine engineering were 72 per cent and 61 per cent higher,
respectively, than in 1938, and the rise continued.[1] Largely as
a result the cost of new ships was 80 per cent or more above the
pre-war cost by 1944. The earnings of merchant seamen had
also risen at an exceptional rate, which was a token of the war
risks they undertook. It was most unlikely that the whole of
their relative gain, and the improved accommodation for ships'
crews and better standards of food that went with the rise
in earnings, would be lost after the war. There was a slight
risk that acute competition might bring freights down when
war was over because of the great amount of wartime
shipping (largely in America), but it was more likely that this
would be too embarrassing for the Americans, who were
high-cost shippers, and now owned a great deal of shipping,
and were in a strong position not only while rates were controlled, but because they could withdraw 'surplus' ships out of
service, to avoid a slump in freights. All this suggested that
'normal' freights were likely to remain more above pre-war

[1] *Min. of Labour Gaz.* 1944, p. 34. Earnings rose sharply through 1944, from
131 to 146 per cent.

levels than the 50 per cent increase visualised by the Ministry of War Transport, which by the end of 1944 (though not when it was first forecast) was broadly equal to the increase of 'average wages' since 1938. Considerations more specifically related to the ore traffic reinforced this. The ore trades were helped before the war by the export of coal—ships brought ore in and took coal out. This was particularly an advantage for South Wales. It was obviously not going to be quickly if ever fully restored after the war; Britain would have less coal to export to the ore producers. From another angle, the nearer foreign ore fields, in northern Spain, were being exhausted,[1] so that a larger proportion of ore would have to come from relatively distant ore fields. Therefore, even if each specific ore freight was no more than 50 per cent higher the average freight on all ores would be up by more than 50 per cent. It was planned, for example, to get more ore from Sierra Leone. This influence was likely to become more important as the volume of imports increased.

The knowledge that Germany would be out of the market for a long time—the period was apt perhaps to be deemed almost permanent—made it arguable, as has been seen, that iron-ore prices in the exporting countries themselves, the F.O.B. prices, would be extremely low. Some F.O.B. prices had been kept low during the war; but of course the trade had been small and many of the trades, the Mediterranean ore trade for example, had been cut out. There were, however, reasons for doubting whether the absence of Germany would have quite the effect at first expected except for a very short spell. Some of the ore-mining or port facilities had been destroyed and had to be restored, supplies would not at once be on a pre-war scale. Britain with little coal was a less attractive buyer. Standards of living appeared to have risen relatively in the ore-mining areas, in Sweden, the Mediterranean and West Africa, which raised the costs in local currencies (apart from inflation) of mining, transport, reconstruction and development, and though Germany would be absent it was soon clear there would be other buyers, Dutch, Belgian, French, Italian and Polish in

[1] Below, p. 326.

Europe[1] for example, and the United States, whose great
Mesabi deposits were not enough to support for long the
increased scale of output. There was good reason, in fact, to
expect the 'terms of trade' to be less favourable for British
importers. Because of the devaluation of sterling since before
the war, wherever America was buying sterling prices were
likely to be relatively high by comparison with pre-war prices.
Increased American ore imports came in 1944 almost exclusively
from South America, but naturally American buyers would be
disposed to buy European and African ores in large quantities
if these sold at prices which did not reflect changes in the rate of
exchange. Even if the volume of American purchases was low
the influence of American price levels on the market was thus
likely to be appreciable. For familiar reasons dollars were
usually preferred to sterling. So long as conditions allowed
exporters to keep prices up subsidies which had in certain
instances kept pre-war prices down—the subsidy, for example,
to the railway from Ouenza to the coast[2]—were of course
unlikely to be restored. Political considerations were likely to
favour generous prices for certain ores at least initially—the
F.O.B. price for the first purchases of French North African
ores, for example, was fixed, for obvious political reasons, at the
high price (as it then seemed) of 30s. F.O.B. charged by the
Spaniards—so the trade got off to a bad start from the buyer's
standpoint. It proved possible in 1945-46, when demand for
ore was at its lightest, to bring this F.O.B. price down by hard
bargaining to a figure barely 50 per cent above the 1937 average;[3]
but this was resisted and lasted for a very short time only.

---

[1] By the early summer of 1944 the Belgians, for example, were negotiating here
to obtain Swedish ore. At this time French ore was not available; but it soon became
clear that dear and scarce coal was also a driving force. Belgium sent a mission to
Sweden in July 1945 to arrange for the purchase of ore. *Metal Bulletin*, 10 July
1945. By 1945 it was clear that possibilities of getting coal would determine in part
the markets for Swedish ore; e.g. Poland agreed to supply coal and coke and to
receive iron ore and machinery from Sweden (*Financial News*, 12 July 1945). The
same copy of the paper reported that foreign ships unloading here could not get
coal to take out.

[2] The French Government, part owners of the Ouenza mine, subsidised the rail
rates before the war; it was 15 francs a ton, about 2s. a ton, for 200 miles.

[3] The 1937 F.O.B. average was 14s. 6d. a ton for Ouenza ore.

There were thus a multitude of reasons, in respect of freights, the terms of trade, the weakness of sterling, which made it likely that the estimate of 30s. C.I.F. for imported ore prices was too low, and these reasons were set out at the time.

On this foundation it was urged at the end of 1944 that a higher estimate should be used in current planning of investment.[1] Since it then seemed likely that severe competition would make it imperative to enjoy the lowest cost possible, the implications of a higher price for imported ore seemed to be simple. They were: (1) that preference should be given to expansion on sites suited to the cheap use of home ores; (2) that when possible the basic Bessemer process should be used since it would make the most of the low cost of the home ores; (3) that in developments and 'modernisation' based on imported ore (there was bound to be a lot of this), preference should be given to schemes which allowed the cheapest assembly of the main raw materials; apart from the avoidance of railway freights on ore it was desirable to keep the sea freights on ore down by making the use of large ships possible; (4) that if it seemed risky to build a major works for wide strip which was to depend entirely on home ore then it was desirable to choose a site where home ore or imported ore could be used to almost equal advantage. A possible choice was on the south bank of the Humber, near Grimsby at Immingham, with good access to cheap Yorkshire coking coal (and water access to Durham coking coal), proximity to home ores, and deep water for imported ores, the site which Sir William Firth once flirted with.

It is perhaps not surprising in retrospect that the probability that imported ore would be relatively costly was for practical purposes disregarded, and not allowed to influence priorities. How far the priorities implied a belief that imported ores would be

---

[1] I have followed closely in the analysis of imported ore price prospects an analysis I first made in the summer of 1944. At this time, with 1943 wage-rates and coking-coal prices only available, my unduly cautious judgement was that 'while it would probably be unreasonable to forecast that ore prices would rise 50 per cent above the average of 1939 (that is, to 37s. 6d.), on the other hand anything below 30s. a ton for a 55 per cent ore seems unlikely'. Towards the end of 1944 in revising the document in the light of more recent data I argued, still with undue caution, that imported ore was 'unlikely to be less than' 7d. a unit (that is, 32s. for a 55 per cent ore) 'and likely to be higher'.

relatively cheap, on the other hand, is uncertain; it is possible to read them as a skilful evasion of judgement on this crucial issue of fact, though as mentioned earlier they could not in their practical effect be non-committal.[1] Sometimes the forecast of high prices for imported ore was challenged. It was even argued, for instance, that a price of 30s. was an extremely high figure, because although only one-third above the 1937 average, and less above the 1938 price, it was nearly double the 1933–6 average.[2] (Those who so argued forgot that prices had fallen sharply after 1929.) The forecast of freights being 50 per cent above pre-war levels was even described as 'alarming'.

Such comments showed how hard it was for busy people with no economic background to grasp the significance of creeping inflation, devaluation, the changing terms of trade, and the prospect of stable high demand.[3] But some of those concerned were certainly able to avoid these pitfalls. Decisions may have been made on grounds of practicability and timing. In the end political considerations enter into decisions of this order, but at what stage and in what form, whether by direct or indirect means, it is not possible from the outside to judge. The administrator advising a Minister may think it his function to put forward the best, on his estimate, that can secure agreement; it is wrong to suppose that matters omitted from a published document are necessarily matters not understood. Moreover, the reluctance of the civil servant (even the temporary civil servant) to challenge the judgement of the practical man, faulty though this often proves to be, is understandable. The argument that to use home ores would give much lower costs was no longer supported by a leading consultant, as it had been by

[1] When the industry produced its plan later there were nominal concessions to the claims of home ore development; but as will be seen since they had no 'priority' they could be disregarded (below, pp. 177 sqq).

[2] At the peak in 1937–8 the price of French North African ores had been over 37s. 6d. a ton.

[3] Sometimes people who were oblivious of these things for the United Kingdom were singularly alive to the economic weaknesses of other countries. The prospect that our inflation and balance of payments difficulties may have some similar effect, might even lead to our devaluing, was passed over in silence by people who pointed to inflation in French North Africa and said that they would have to deflate or devalue, so either way we would get imports cheaper.

Brassert before the war. The leading consultants, as well as the Ministry's principal advisers on raw materials during the war, were now behind the 'practical planning' of the firms. One of the firms mainly concerned in the Port Talbot plan held extensive iron-ore leases, where quarrying was very cheap, near Banbury;[1] surely it had every reason to use home ore if to do so was a good idea? Some leading Federation officials did not conceal their view that to revive pre-war criteria betokened prejudice, if not neurosis.

Administrators asked to advise on priorities in planning after planning had started were indeed faced with an invidious choice, though perhaps it did not appear so as clearly at the time as it does now. Should they list as priorities only the things which might be ideally best, even though no one as yet proposed to do them? Or should they confine themselves to sorting out, by broad precept, among the projects actually in a design stage those which should take precedence? The second was the only course which could be justified by the argument of the White Paper on Unemployment Policy that control was needed because investment resources were scarce. The first course was the one which most people would think planning to consist of, but to adopt it might be to check avoidably (even though healthily and for a short time only) the rate of investment in steel, which was capable of being represented as an odd thing for anyone to do who also believed that a large well-directed investment was urgently needed in the industry for the good of the country. It is thus at least not surprising that those who were faced with these issues should try to avoid holding too many things up or turning too many things down, and should incline towards the second course. Such, broadly, was the explanation given by Sir Andrew Duncan later of what occurred.[2] So much was under way that it had to be accepted. In retrospect this has an air of inevitability which was not present at the time.

Once the general decision was made it could be buttressed by arguments which looked strong. The steel firms were putting

[1] At Hook Norton.
[2] In discussion much later, and shortly before he died.

up a lot of plans which would reduce costs, even if they would not reduce costs as much as possible. There were some very big schemes among them, and there was some zeal for co-operation. That firms should propose so much, though it fell short of the best possible, was a sign of grace. The best must not be allowed to stand in the way of the good. Those who criticised the plans might, after all, be merely cranky; they were not numerous or influential. Planners must be sensible, content to compromise. And if, as seemed likely, the demand for steel was going to go on increasing, and the capacity for making steel here to be added to steadily for some years, then did it matter overmuch if works to use more imported ore came first, and works to use more home ore came later? It was never proposed that all steel should be or could be made from home ore, for the supplies were not inexhaustible, and they occurred only in the east Midlands and therefore were not well placed for steelmaking to serve all markets and absorb all scrap. On strict marginal doctrine no doubt the cheapest should come first; but it was not certain that the home ore plant would be a lot cheaper, and since no one was *planning* such a plant was it not better to accept what was easily available? It could not be a mistake to have a new wide strip mill; this in itself would probably reduce the cost of making sheets and tinplate by £2 a ton or more, and make better sheets and tinplates. To do this at a different site than Port Talbot might bring additional savings, but these, according to estimates from persons within the industry who must be regarded as experts, might be no more than 5s. a ton. It was even uncertain, on expert advice, whether the lowest cost sites of all for steelmaking were suitable for a strip mill, since the cheap home ores were hard to use for high-grade steel—the Americans had never succeeded in making strip from low-grade ore. (They had, of course, never needed to!)

This kind of approach fell in happily with one of the few strands of industrial policy on which there was bipartisan agreement—the encouragement of development areas. While the Ministry of Supply was studying the post-war problems of the steel industry Mr Dalton was busy committing himself to support the Port Talbot scheme, which he welcomed effusively in January 1945.[1] It was never argued openly that works should be sited in development areas even though their costs were as a result higher than they would be elsewhere; the preferred argument was the familiar one evolved before the war,[2] that if the value of social capital was taken into account costs would be lower than they appeared. But the plain fact was that costs of steelmaking would often be higher in Development Areas than they need be elsewhere. By an odd irony those who stressed the disadvantage of building new houses or a new community for a new steelworks on a new site with low costs (because of the loss of social capital at old sites) were not deterred from sponsoring 'new towns' for other objects.[3] As interpreted in regard to steel the policy sacrificed the future to the present. However, departments had a clear lead on this matter from Ministers, which they were hardly at liberty to oppose except on unshakable evidence. Thus everything conspired to create an intense and misleading conformism; the civil servants followed their Ministers' lead, firms in Development Areas and the steel industry collectively sought public approval as they fell into line—the line of least resistance—and Ministers then found reason on all sides to suppose that they were not merely being politic but were even right.

There was in all the discussions of this period a conspicuous lack of interest in the stimulating effect which might have been exerted in the British industry by one or two more works whose costs were on the lowest possible level, the Corby level, including one in the sheet trade.

The momentum gathered by the 'practical plans' born within the industry by the end of 1944 was possibly too great to be resisted; and if this was so priorities in these circumstances were little more than a formal necessity, bringing in their train the licences, permits and financial facilities which were needed for capital investment in the post-war world. But Governments and civil servants are reluctant to acknowledge when they bow to the inevitable; though their choice may be *faute de mieux* or submission to *force majeure* it has always to be 'in the national

---

[1] Above, p. 82.   [2] See *E.H.S.* p. 465 and passim.
[3] Indeed, Mr Dalton sponsored one near to his own constituency.

interest'. And hence presumably a works which was granted licences and permits was in fact though not in theory for price-fixing purposes efficient, with a legitimate expectation of profits.

Again the question was relevant: what did the firms who made these plans presume about the shape of economic conditions to come? Would all the plans have gone forward if it were known that firms were not infallibly to be protected from imports, that low-cost production would not have to subsidise high-cost, that there would be no 'pooling' to average costs of ore or scrap or (through the Coal Charges Account) coal, no embargo on the export of scrap to keep the home price below world levels, no subsidies on imported ores?

Had the test been applied it might have made little difference at the end of 1944. Firms planning to build new works or extensions based on imported ores, which they were led to believe might be moderately cheap, had good reason to suppose that once they had built their plants it would not be worth while for other firms in the United Kingdom to build competitive plants, even though these other firms could have much lower raw-material costs. The history of the industry had shown that such competitive building did not happen, at least in this country. New plants were progressively more costly to build, and the annual capital cost far exceeded any likely margin in raw-material costs.[1] In such circumstances, as has been shown earlier, the durability of plant added to the imperfections of the market, and various forms of integration became potent sources of inertia.[2] Competitive plant (which 'priorities' would rule out for the time being) would only be justified if the market grew rapidly. Trade Union leaders and managements of established firms often had strong motives for taking advantage of this inertia—their managerial interests naturally, and local social, political and property interests, for example; and real, though it might be shortsighted, solicitude for their staffs. They were often aware of this; a director of one of the large companies

---

[1] The capital cost of a new steelworks and strip mill was by the end of 1945 close on £40 a ton; the capital cost per ton of strip would thus have to be reckoned at about £5 a ton.

[2] *E.H.S.* ch. XI *passim*.

when asked to give a purely technical appraisal of a large scheme put forward by his firm paying no respect to social and personal factors said he could not possibly do so. They were less and less concerned as owners of the works and more and more as managers. Yet even from the standpoint of an owner, because of the way the price mechanism worked and the traditions of moderate dividends which were being established it was quite on the cards that higher costs would not involve a reduction in net earnings. Thus any new plant could expect to be fairly secure provided there was a market for its product; the choice of a relatively high cost site would have no dramatic unfavourable repercussions. In these circumstances the threat of more rigorous competitive conditions might have proved innocuous, and those who bestowed priorities might still have found themselves giving bouquets to the irresistible forces of inertia. The test, however, was not applied, and would have been hard to make effective.

Nothing illustrates this so forcibly as that while the priorities which emerged from the Ministry of Supply's survey of the steel industry did become known, nothing was published of the reaction in the survey to the Federation's plans for a 'self-governing industry'. The Federation's views were informally publicised[1]; reactions to them 'on the official level', which if they reflected the general policies expressed by the Government on monopoly and international trade policy were unlikely to have been favourable on all points, were not.

It did not escape comment that the pre-war régime of protection and international cartels whose restoration the Federation sought had been justified at the time by the Continental dumping under whose pressure it could be argued British steel-making had retrogressed. If dumping could be eliminated, preferably by international agreement of the kind it was hoped would evolve out of the negotiations which started at Hot Springs,[2] the special need for protection would have gone, and

---

[1] Almost all the more striking phrases coined in expounding these views found their way into newspapers or periodicals, as the quotations in the previous section of this chapter will illustrate.

[2] Hancock and Gowing, *op. cit.* pp. 545–6.

there would be no case for raising home prices to subsidise exports. In the immediate post-war years, with import licences and currency restrictions and good markets, the British industry might be able to make up for lost time, so that provided there was no dumping protection should not again be needed.

But the decision could, and indeed must, wait on events. As for international cartels, this was a matter, too, which could not be decided for one industry alone; it again was not urgent, and must be settled by the international trade talks with the United States and other allies. The Americans in the State Department and many others (as the Federation too noticed) did not like cartels.[1]

The proposal that there should be fixed prices, by implication minimum prices, not merely maxima, was also one which advisers dealing with the steel industry alone could if they chose happily put aside for later decision. The issue could not be determined for steel in isolation; there would be a Government policy on cartels and price-fixing. Fortunately, the question of minimum prices would not arise quickly. Scarcity of steel, and import licensing, would mean that the Government must fix maximum prices. The overriding need seemed to be to keep prices down. Everyone thought the same, or so it seemed.

Deep thought was given to the question how was it possible to fix prices so that only efficiency would be remunerated. It was, indeed, proposed that prices should be based on the costs of the most efficient firm. But so long as it seemed desirable to have the output of almost all existing capacity it was necessary that prices should be fixed which would keep the least efficient in production. It should, nevertheless, remain possible for firms with low costs to attract business by charging less than the maximum prices; indeed, if this did not happen surely it would be necessary to direct business to them, to load the best plants fully? If, however, there seemed a need to have minimum prices (if, that is, destructive competition occurred), then the only minimum which could be justified must be based on the costs of the most efficient plant alone, certainly not on the average of all plants which in the eyes of the Federation were efficient. But it was not an immediate issue.

[1] Hancock and Gowing, *loc. cit.*

The same was felt about the methods used to spread costs of exceptionally costly imported raw materials, and to even out the price of coal and, rather more surprisingly, about the manner of keeping the price of scrap low. These practices obviously ruled out price competition as a means of sorting out the firms who were economically efficient from those who were not, and ruled out the possibility of comparing the relative advantages of steel or other materials in any application by comparing prices, because there was no measure of marginal costs. But to eliminate all this paraphernalia at once would force prices up, especially while imported ore was still close to its maximum cost. It may be surmised that this was the reason why the elimination of these 'artificial arrangements', as they were often called, was also marked out as for the future, and therefore something on which no immediate decision was needed. Not even an announcement of intention.

There was one problem which could not quite so logically be put aside for the future. If the Government were to go on fixing priorities and deciding about price policies there must be some instrument through which it must work. The idea that this work should again be an activity of a tariff advisory committee (which was hardly appropriate if tariffs were to be reduced by international agreement) did not prove universally attractive; nor the idea of a body solely concerned with steel (because it might become too narrowly interested in steel). A proposal for an Industrial Commission which would carry out the functions undertaken by the Government in a range of industries had some support. But for the time being the jobs could still be done by the Ministry of Supply—and the Coalition was completely unable to agree upon this kind of question. This too could, after all, wait.

So the net visible outcome of departmental effort was contained in the day-to-day decisions on investment projects and in the letter sent from the Ministry of Supply to the Steel Federation. This letter, referred to earlier and sent by the Ministry during the Caretaker Government, though it could equally well have come during the Coalition (it was a chance of timing), asked the Federation to draw up a plan inspired by the

Government's priorities.[1] The organisation of the industry and its constitutional relation to the Government must await the result of the General Election. The Federation had had a partial success. Its 'practical planning' had by and large been accepted and given an official *cachet*. Objections to its constitutional proposals, if any had been entertained, had not been expressed openly and could be regarded with equanimity unless they had the support of one or other of the main political parties.

3. PHILOSPHERS DECIDE

Remote from the practical planning and constitution making of the Steel Federation, and almost as remote from the departmental inquiries, socialists, too, were deciding in the later years of the war what the steel industry's shape would be if the decision rested with them. The Iron and Steel Trades Confederation, like the Federation, was asked to submit its views on reconstruction to the Ministry of Supply. The Trades Union Congress gave its Economic Committee the task of drafting a programme for reconstruction, and this inevitably covered 'basic' industries including steel. So did the Labour Party's Central Committee on Reconstruction set up in 1943. And perhaps because the secretary of the latter, Professor Laski, was one of the two Labour Party representatives on the former in 1943 and 1944, the approach of the two bodies showed considerable similarity.

Professor Laski was prominent among those socialists for whom Labour's participation in Mr Churchill's Government in 1940 was to be a means of achieving both victory and socialism.[2] At an early date he set his face against a coalition after the war —'the time had come to renew the foundations of the state', and it must be by way of socialist planning 'by men who believe in the principles and purposes of planning'. The war was an

[1] Above, pp. 94-5.
[2] Kingsley Martin, *Harold Laski*, p. 142. Professor G. D. H. Cole seems to have taken a similar position. The *Daily Herald* announced on 21 Oct. 1941 that he was forming a political group to advocate things—among them it was understood the nationalisation of steel—which the Labour Party could not now officially advocate.

outcome of capitalism: 'We want to use the necessities of war to lay the foundations of peace...power is on our side.'[1]

Steelmaking was one of the few industries for which a socialist constitution—indeed, three socialist constitutions—had already been devised before the war. The basic approach was simple. Control by private ownership had not operated, and could not operate, in the national interest; but if the industry were publicly owned it would be run in the national interest. The only problem was to devise the right machinery. Exponents skated lightly over the difficulties of choosing the right people, except that some thought the key men ought to be socialists. For them at least there could be, so it seemed, no difficulty in identifying the national interest. It was easier to assume this at the beginning of the period than at the end; and the shifting emphasis in the interpretation of national interest by nationalisers during the thirties would have had some significance for minds less controlled by controversial commitments.[2]

The steel industry was not included under its own name among the first Labour Party lists of industries to be nationalised which was made soon after the First World War, though it was probably implicitly there as a part of the armaments industry. When most armaments were made and designed and developed by private firms these firms thrived on war and busily sought markets in countries who were at odds with each other. This catholic response to demand laid them open to two not mutually consistent criticisms, that they fomented wars and that they helped their country's enemies. Since armaments were made of steel, and some famous steelmakers—Vickers and Krupps for example—were also makers of armaments, steelmakers as a whole, with their satellites the makers of ferro-alloys and the scrap merchants, became subject to the same dual accusation. 'Steel has no fatherland'; steelmakers were conspirators against peace and merchants of death. This emotive fantasy has been progressively undermined as arms manufacture has come more under state control or ownership, not least because the change

---

[1] Martin, *op. cit.* p. 142.
[2] *Ibid.* p. 151, says with a kindly interpretation that Laski's had become 'a one track mind'.

has coincided with an increase in the material and intellectual resources devoted to arms. In the inter-war years those close to the steel industry, who knew what most steelworks really made—the trade unionists, for example—were never under its spell. Yet the emotional appeal of proposals to nationalise steel has continued to gain something from this irrelevant argument—it was revived during the war[1]—designed to demonstrate that the private owner-ship of this industry must militate against the national interest.

Distress in the inter-war years culminating in acute depression in the early thirties gave the main impetus to the movement, and brought the trade unions in. The Confederation sought protection against imports as early as 1925 from countries where labour was sweated. Five years later under the stress of the 'economic blizzard' which, as they said, had swept over all the Western countries, the Confederation submitted a scheme of national reorganisation to the Board of Trade in August 1930. They did so partly in lieu of the Sankey Report—'there was nothing to be got from an unpublished report'. They recom-mended the immediate appointment of a Central Board or Council 'charged with advising on practical schemes of eco-nomic organisation of the industry on the basis of providing for a production of not less than 12 m. tons of crude steel per annum'. The schemes would provide for amalgamations, organisation of raw-material supplies, control of imports and prices, and (a peculiarity not repeated in later schemes) for a labour reserve above the number required for an output of 10 m. tons a year. Any public credit should be cheap. Though the industry would be controlled it would not be nationally owned.[2] In May 1931 the confederation published a variant of this scheme, calling upon the Government to 'place' direction and development 'of the industry in the hands of a public (utility) corporation'.[3] This again left the question of ownership

[1] See, for example, Fenner Brockway and Frederick Mullally, *Death Pays a Divi-dend*, 1944. The argument linked on naturally to the one that the war was an outcome of capitalism, of which it was a facet. Cp., for example, Worswick, *Raw Material Controls*, p. 2.

[2] Sir Arthur Pugh, *Men of Steel by One of Them*, pp. 457-8.

[3] *What is Wrong with the British Steel Industry*, p. 21. On this page it is just a 'public corporation, on p. 22 a 'public utility corporation'.

hazy, but may be treated as the first sketch of a constitution for a nationalised steel industry. It was not merely proposing a Board to complement private enterprise.

In all countries the 'blizzard' induced demands for more intense economic nationalism; and the Confederation's proposals fell into the prevailing pattern though the unions also endorsed the principles of the World Economic Conference of 1927.[1] The Confederation wanted national control as a means of compelling rationalisation, but this was in form only a little more far-reaching than was suggested in the Sankey Report.[2] They modelled these largely on the German pattern, unaware of the critics in Germany who were tracing the still greater acuteness of the slump in the German industry at the same time to the very extent of rationalisation therein.[3] The prime source of trouble in the industry here was traced by the union to the 'enormous' wartime increase of capacity, which bore no true relation to post-war demand, so that the industry dropped into the 'inevitable slump'.[4] In this situation the steel industry 'suffered exploitation by other trades and sections of the community',[5] hence steel prices had fallen in relation to wholesale prices in general. What was needed was strong organisation, capable of exercising control at home and of making terms with steelmakers abroad. Prices should be fixed, and raised. Imports should be prohibited or restrained. 'Fair trade and security' should be established by international negotiation. Hours of work should be reduced so that all the labour in the industry could be absorbed.[6] And there must be planning to avoid the spectacle 'of additional mills being erected while the trade was operating 20 per cent below its productive capacity', and of 'a minority of producers threatening the whole stability of the trade by a refusal to co-operate with their fellow producers for the common interest'.[7]

So trade union socialists, whose 'wider vision' enabled them

[1] *What is Wrong with the British Steel Industry*, p. 17.
[2] *E.H.S.* pp. 436–40.   [3] *Ibid.* pp. 443–6.
[4] *What is Wrong with the British Steel Industry*, pp. 9–10.
[5] *Ibid.* pp. 10–11.   [6] *Ibid.* p. 13.
[7] *Ibid.* p. 14. (The passage refers specially to tinplates, but is of general application.)

to see that 'the needs of the twentieth century call for a conscious planning and regulation of the national economic life',[1] came singularly close to the policies associated popularly with cartels —restriction of competition, at home and abroad, restriction of output and of capacity, division of markets, a damper on expansion on new sites and protection for old sites, higher prices. The Labour Government of the day had, as the Confederation pointed out, already made a start in applying some of these principles to the coal industry. There 'the regulation of output and prices' were 'but devices to counter the effects of cut-throat competition, and to secure an economic price for the coal owner and fair wages and shorter hours for the mine workers'.[2]

Three years later the Economic Committee of the Trades Union Congress[3] sponsored a second plan for steel nationalisation, which was also first devised by the Confederation, and was endorsed by the Labour Party Conference in 1934. But although, as will be seen, the proposed organisation was different, the objects to be secured through the plan, the 'national interests' which private ownership could not secure, had changed little. Here again the 'tremendous increase in productive capacity, out of all proportion to post war demand'[4] was the source of 'surplus capacity'. 'Due to the absence of adequate co-ordination' it had been impossible to secure 'good enough terms' from the International Steel Cartel.[5] The contrast presented by the German model, with its central selling and dual prices, keeping prices up at home without endangering exports, was again emphasised. This later analysis admitted technical failings in the British industry with less reserve than the first; it spoke of 'the failure of many' works to adopt the

---

[1] *What is wrong with the British Steel Industry*, p. 4.

[2] *Ibid.* p. 17. The reference was to the Coal Mines Act of 1930; described briefly by W. H. B. Court, *Coal*, p. 19. Cp. also A. Beacham, 'The Coal Industry', pp. 116, 128, 136–7, in *The Structure of British Industry* (ed. Burn), vol. I.

[3] *Trades Union Congress Annual Report*, 1934, pp. 188–205. The Chairman of the Committee was Arthur Pugh, who was secretary of the British Iron and Steel Trades Confederation from 1917 to 1936; Ernest Bevin and Walter Citrine were members. Mr Dalton was one of the representatives of the Labour Party who attended; Herbert Morrison was a substitute member.

[4] *Ibid.* p. 195.   [5] *Ibid.* p. 197.

most modern practices.[1] And it necessarily took account of the changes implied in the proposed new constitution of the Steel Federation in 1934. In doing so it showed how much more of the same sort of thing it wanted itself. 'No attempt has been made as in Continental countries to regulate production and no comprehensive machinery exists for pooling orders or allocating quotas on a basis which favours efficiency or the elimination of redundant plant.'[2]

Two years later still, in 1936, a third plan of nationalisation was set out by a city journalist (afterwards a civil servant) who wrote under the pen name of 'Ingot', and had the ideological assistance and criticism of the New Fabian Research Bureau, and especially of Mr Arthur Pugh (later Sir Arthur Pugh), Mr Mitchison and Professor G. D. H. Cole. Not only was his a new plan, but even more markedly than in 1934 there had to be a new 'case', a new emphasis in setting out the objects of nationalisation and identifying the 'national interest'. For now the industry was becoming prosperous again under private enterprise. The industry was escaping from the effects of over-expansion,[3] but it was advancing, 'Ingot' argued, towards an inflationary boom; capacity was being expanded again 'when demand was at the top'. 'Ingot' was forced to ask whether the next depression could be avoided without socialism. It could no longer be argued with conviction that rationalisation was altogether impossible without socialism. Something—a compromise no doubt—was certainly happening. Advantageous terms had been made with the European cartel. 'Ingot' fully expected that central selling would be established before the industry was socialised. He conceded, with a shade too much enthusiasm, that 'since the tariff was imposed great advances

---

[1] *Trades Union Congress Annual Report*, 1934, p. 195. The earlier *Report* spoke of the 'considerable advance' in technical matters, and objected to the Prime Minister's sweeping assertions about bad plant. The unions' delegation in Europe (*E.H.S.* p. 422) had found that 'the modernity and equipment of certain units of plant here was equal to and in some cases superior to iron and steel plants which had been seen on the Continent'. The *Report*, however, duly concluded (p. 12) that conscious national planning was needed to keep plant suitably up to date.

[2] *Trades Union Congress, Annual Report*, 1934, p. 197.

[3] Ingot, *The Socialisation of Iron and Steel*, p. 112. Ingot attributed the over-expansion in Europe to the dislocating effect of the Versailles Treaty.

have been made on the technical side'.[1] Some £20 m. had been
invested since 1931. 'The expenditure of, say, another £25 m.
would put the industry in the first flight.'[2] The danger now was
the development of strong central organisation in private hands,
'self-government'. 'The idea of the producers' monopoly is the
very root of Fascist organisation.'[3]

The economic power of the industry was now too great to be
left in private hands. Instead of firms being likely to do too
little they might do too much. Stewarts and Lloyds had moved
to Corby, Guest Keens had deserted Dowlais, and Sir William
Firth had only just not taken tinplate making from South Wales
to Lincolnshire. Such moves were based on the narrow cost
estimates of the owners only. What 'may be economic and
necessary from the point of view of technical efficiency may be
wasteful from that of national interest'.[4] In socialist planning
alone 'everything can be taken into account'. 'Ingot' complained that the organised industry would raise prices ('the
essential nature of capitalism...is to make maximum profits'[5]),
and the imposition of the new tariff, which the trade unions had
sought as they sought higher prices, was a 'victory for the producing interests over the consuming interests'.[6] The steel
industry was indeed 'the very centre' of the British industrial
system. 'On its activity', 'Ingot' declared, putting the cart
neatly before the horse, 'depends the progress of the trade
cycle.' Hence steelmaking was 'a key point in the economic
structure for planning'. 'Ingot', unlike the trade union
socialists, took a global view; as the depression argument for

---

[1] *The Socialisation of Iron and Steel*, p. 51.

[2] *Ibid.* p. 153. Despite an impressive familiarity with the relevant Blue Books
and company reports Ingot was unfamiliar apparently at close quarters with the
processes and plant. Thus, for example, of the North-east Coast he said: 'first of
all, the technical position is good': an astonishing remark to any one who knew
the plants.

[3] *Ibid.* p. 121.

[4] *Ibid.* p. 125.

[5] *Ibid.* p. 125.

[6] *Ibid.* p. 124. Ingot continues: 'This balancing of interests is the fundamental
purpose of capitalist government, and differs entirely from a Socialist government's
purpose to abolish capitalism and work the economic system in the public interest.'
How this can differ from a balancing of group interests (even if non-capitalist groups)
he left wholly to the imagination.

nationalisation had become becalmed the 'basic industry' argument was launched.[1]

Attempts to control monopoly combines, 'Ingot' asserted, not without some reason, 'have never been particularly happy'. The only way for combines to be 'effected in the right direction, is for them to be ordered under a régime of public ownership' Almost as he published the Jarrow controversy flared up, and it seemed for many to clinch the argument. Steelmakers, if not the Steel Federation, effectively stood in the way of building a wholly new plant even on an old (though disused) site.[2] Possibly what they did was right, though hardly their manner of doing it. This incident which distressed not only the socialists but *The Times*, prompted (it has been seen) the final development in the functions of I.D.A.C.[3] But subsequent socialist propaganda wrote this off as entirely make-believe. Socialists took no initiative, indeed no part, in discussing the standards which I.D.A.C. might apply over prices or investments. Stripped of its politics the case for Jarrow was shaky. To have a wholly new works on a deep-water site where it would relieve unemployment sounded well. But was it desirable to build a new works on a small site without room for expansion? Jarrow could not have become the nucleus of a large works which would have marked a step towards the concentration of production which was needed for lowest costs. No calm retrospect, however, seems to have been taken. The Jarrow scheme was defeated, it was argued, by the interested opposition of other steelmakers, who threatened to undermine it by 'unfair' competition and so choked off the newcomer. There was some truth in this, but it did not prove that the newcomer should have been welcomed by planners, that it could have stood up in a competitive world. But it was allowed to become a symbol

[1] *The Socialisation of Iron and Steel*, p. 124.

[2] *E.H.S.* pp. 461–4. A full account of the Jarrow controversy must wait for the opening to public examination of all the records. I have read more of them than I had when I wrote my original account, and my present judgement is that it would have been a mistake to build at Jarrow, if for no other reason than that the site was too small for a modern plant. The methods used in discouraging the scheme leave an unpleasant impression; but so do the political methods used in advocating it.

[3] *Ibid.* p. 466.

of the national interest in eclipse, a depressed area not relieved as it should have been, a victim of the restrictive practices of monopolists. To argue as the socialists did first that in the depression the weakly organised unprotected industry suffered from over-expansion here and in Europe, and later that in the boom the strongly organised protected industry expanded too little, was not inherently contradictory and might have been true. But the emphasis on Jarrow showed that in fact the socialists' approach to steel problems was doctrinaire and emotional, ungoverned by realism—an exercise in political algebra, a manipulation of symbols which were not in conformity with their nominal concrete counterparts. Socialists had a guide to monopoly, a simple rule. It meant high profits, high prices, low output. They saw what they were looking for. They showed no interest in the precise adaptations of the steel industry under protection, in its methods of keeping down boom prices by averaging raw-material costs, with their profound implications for investment and price policy, for example, or in its publicity-conscious readiness to make concessions to public sentiment, its anxiety to justify its ways to men. The risks that investment might be not too little but misdirected, that the misdirection might be due partly to short-sighted consideration for vested interests of labour as well as of capital, and that prices might at times be not too high but too low, and in general vary too little or too late to have a useful influence on investment or consumption, passed them by; they were either not observed or not understood or not thought important.

When war came the simple rule was, as has been seen, still applied. The public interest was again in eclipse; restrictive monopoly acting through the Control, which was merely the Steel Federation in sheep's clothing, refused to build the new plants which the prosecution of the war demanded, for fear of having too much capacity after the war. But they raised prices and profits excessively. How much of this was fantasy has been seen. It was early evident to those at all closely in touch with the industry in the war, as they were naturally aware that scarcity of raw materials, not of plant, imposed the limit on output. To the outsider it was inevitably more obscure. But the outsider might not be concerned if he thought, like one academic Fabian, that while 'the argument that the Controls are a hindrance to the war effort is powerful, the argument that they would wreck any attempts at reconstruction is overwhelming'.[1] In effect socialist thinking on steel owed nothing in these years to anything that happened after 1936.

The Iron and Steel Trades Confederation were perhaps vaguely aware of this.[2] The most serious practical problem they had to face was the impact of the strip mill and hence tinplate redundancy. At one time they visualised that five strip mills like Ebbw Vale would meet all foreseeable demands for Welsh tinplate.[3] They assumed that private ownership would continue for some years, and so advocated a central authority with greater powers than those of the British Iron and Steel Federation, but subject to control by a Government authority. When they were asked for their views on long-term policy they reaffirmed, almost in an aside, their belief that public control of the trade is essential, and that the T.U.C. scheme of 1934 'constituted the declared policy of the Confederation on the question'.[4] They reproduced the old scheme, with no new glosses. The T.U.C. Economic Committee put the steel industry high in the list of those meet to be nationalised—it was a 'secondary priority' after fuel, power and transport and on a par with cotton—and they added laconically that 'for the nationalisation of this industry the T.U.C. has already published a detailed programme'. Again, it was the plan of 1934.[5]

This plan, as has been seen, was the second to be evolved by

---

[1] Worswick, *Raw Material Controls*, p. 13.

[2] They had taken a favourable view of the May Committee's *Report* and the policies of 1937; and Sir Arthur Pugh in his history, referring to this, said 'the industry succeeded in reshaping itself and so developed its resources and increased its productivity that when the Second World War broke out the industry was in a position to meet the immediate needs of the country, and when the war ended to make a contribution second to none towards its economic recovery' (Pugh, *op. cit.* p. 533).

[3] The plants were to be at or near Llanelly, Swansea, Neath—Port Talbot, Gorseinon and one farther east.

[4] Mr John Brown and Mr Lincoln Evans (later Sir Lincoln Evans) (*Daily Herald*, 29 June 1945), Secretary and Assistant Secretary of the Confederation, both wrote in support of nationalisation in 1944-45.

[5] *T.U.C. Ann. Rep.* for 1944, p. 399.

the Confederation. The details of both are mainly of antiquarian interest. The first, in 1931, proposed a public utility corporation, under which there should be regional Managerial Boards[1] who were to be allowed 'such local autonomy as will secure the fullest degree of initiative to produce the best results consistent with a sound national policy'. Only the powers of the centre were defined, and it is hard to see what the regions were left to do.[2] The second constitution[3] differed in a major respect, for instead of regional boards there were to be sectional boards as the second stratum of organisation. This seemed to follow the structure of the new Federation, but the purpose of the change was not explained. The powers of the centre seemed slightly, but very slightly, less.

The chief interest of this plan was its concern, not found in the first, with the 'status of labour by hand and brain' within the socialised industry. The 'general conduct of the industry' should 'find its genesis in the workshop', through the media of representative councils. These should be consulted in appointments to Boards. For this purpose the trade unions must put their house in order and be suitably unified to 'conform' to the organisation of the industry. 'A new conception of industrial management and administration must be inculcated. A healthy discipline of workshop self-government must be developed in which authority is related to merit rather than to social distinctions. It must be the discipline inseparable from successful team work, embodying the spirit of the sports field, each and all being expected to play the game in their respective fields of activity.' Nevertheless, 'terms of remuneration' and other such things would still have to be fixed, stripped naturally of the distinctions between manual and non-manual labour, and inspired by real copartnership. 'As schemes of socialisation

---

[1] Cp. the proposal of the Sankey *Report* (1931) for regional consolidation (*E.H.S.* p. 437).

[2] *What is Wrong with the British Steel Industry*, pp. 22–3. Broadly, the central authority was to arrange an adequate supply and distribution of raw materials, to distribute orders and market the finished products, to negotiate with other countries, to prohibit, restrict or regulate imports, to fix prices (bearing in mind the need to encourage major users) and to co-ordinate research.

[3] *T.U.C. Ann. Rep.* 1934, pp. 189 sqq.

develop, a proper relation between the various industries and services in fixing standards of remuneration must be established', with some aid from Parliament. And in case irreconcilable differences remained despite the mood and machinery of nationalisation, the 'right to strike and likewise the right of lockout must be preserved'.[1]

This emphasis was to prove a diversion; and 'Ingot', in the third blue-print in 1936, said scarcely a word on this kind of thing.[2] He returned to the original preference for an organisation based on geographical regions, not on sections of the industry defined by their products. His choice, like the Confederation's, was determined largely, he explained, by the need to avoid the 'inevitable bureaucracy of an over-centralised undertaking'. But like the Confederation he did not succeed in endowing the regions with any evident autonomy. There must be no interregional competition; the central board would decide which regions were suitable for development, and which products each region should make; it would control production, prices and markets (by central selling); it would arrange for the interregional business in raw materials and semi-products, organise raw-material supplies, attend to all transport questions, and have full control of finance. Otherwise the regions would be autonomous.

The same jealous regard for central control led 'Ingot' to a second important departure from the T.U.C. plan of 1934, for he rejected the public corporation as the proper form of central organisation. His major objection was 'the sketchy nature of the Government control' it would permit. 'Left to itself the Steel Board is bound to over-extend capacity in periods of good demand, or fail to reduce prices as demand falls.'[3] He wanted more Parliamentary control. So a Minister of Heavy Industry should be *ex officio* chairman of the Board. But the job should be permanently delegated to an Under Secretary for Steel,[4] who would devote all his time to being head of the Board. With political control thus assured—a socialist politician would know

---

[1] *T.U.C. Ann. Rep.* 1934, pp. 204–5.
[2] The workers' position was last but not least in his reasons for nationalising.
[3] Ingot, *op. cit.* p. 181.   [4] *Ibid.* p. 133.

the national interest, so the appointment of leaders under him would present no difficulties—it would be safe to use experts for the management and there was 'no essential reason for the statutory representation of trade unions'. But the leaders 'should as far as possible be active sympathisers'.[1]

Thus the 'intellectual' was at odds with the producers, the unions. It was a traditional opposition in the party. In another guise it was perpetuated during the war. For in the formulation of policy for after the war it was the 'philosophers' who were not absorbed in war administration, who, sometimes to their chagrin, were having no practical experience of government, who were able to plan, plead, infiltrate and whip up support most continuously in party discussions. When the question had to be decided—should nationalisation of steel be part of the Labour Party's programme for the first post-war election—the leader of the resistance was one of the Labour Ministers in the coalition who had had closest contacts with the steel industry. Perhaps he was aware how useless all the blue-prints of 1934 and 1936 would turn out to be; perhaps he merely appreciated that the more orthodox parts of the nationalisation programme would present sufficient unforeseen difficulties, and that it was better, at least in the interim, to continue the existing controls, of whose effectiveness and potentialities he was naturally aware. No Minister could be hoodwinked by the fantasy that a restrictive industry had overruled the intentions of Government, and by the end of 1943 all Ministers knew that steel supplies had been adequate, and that output was being reduced because there were too few workers to use all the steel that would otherwise be provided.[2] But for the philosophers the pre-

[1] Ingot insisted that any compensation offered to shareholders should be proffered 'solely as a matter of expediency, and on no account as a matter of principle —it must be assessed so as not to be a heavy burden' (op. cit. p. 130). Expediency would, however, be guided by some considerations of equity, pp. 136 sqq.

[2] Thus Mr Herbert Morrison (later Lord Morrison) skilfully avoided accusing the steel industry while setting out in general terms the case commonly levelled against it for its pre-war policies as 'an imaginary case'—of 'an industry producing essential goods', profitable with expanding markets until the big slump. Then unable to compete, and unwilling to make changes, its leaders got together, formed a ring, got a tariff, fixed a minimum price, bought up 'surplus plant' 'took care not to produce too many essential goods', and so on. 'It might happen that one or two

war blue-prints, though they shelved even the theoretic analysis of crucial issues, price policy and investment policy and the measure of efficiency, as well as the practical issue of 'choosing the chaps', gave the illusion that the problem of reorganisation 'in the national interest' if not exactly easy had been or could be mastered.

The pre-war mood on the right as well as the left had in a way encouraged this assumption. I.D.A.C. too, for example, was enjoined and prepared to judge whether prices or investment plans were right in the national interest, without the aid of any guiding principles. The blue-prints showed, or so it seemed, that there were several ways in which it could be done. If 'full employment' was not to be sabotaged by restrictive monopolists it must be done. So the philosophers insisted, and so steel went into the party's nationalisation list. With a logic hard to follow now, though many people were then ready to pass over its oddity, this was commonly supported by reference to the great advances made in America which had not been made here, and which by implication could only be made in this country under national ownership.[1] The question then asked by practical minds, uneasily committed, was 'How little need be nationalised?' It became a question of practical importance—though one to which those who asked could find no satisfactory answer—when Labour had a resounding victory in the election of 1945.

of the most modern and efficient plants among them were deliberately prevented from operating at full capacity.... They didn't have a plan, just a month to month piecemeal opportunist habit of action, unrelated to any conception of the future or of national needs. They didn't really have a policy—just an urge to get away from the hazards of free competition.... It had the elementary commonsense to offer its work people a share in its returns if they would accept a partnership in its restrictive policy.... This is not a fancy picture. It is by and large a perfectly fair account of a substantial fraction of British industry...between the wars. It reveals an industry comfortably dying on its feet.' But during the war a quick reverse of the policy of decay, 'a partnership between State and industry...revivified the failing powers of our producers'. So to the problems of policy—'public ownership where it is appropriate, stimulating public control elsewhere'. But 'let the hysterical and the hasty not seek to commit us before we know where our country's need may point us' (H. Morrison, *Prospects and Policies*, pp. 40–5. (A speech in April 1943)).

[1] E.g. *Tribune*, 2 May 1945; Mr Dalton, in an election speech, *Daily Mail*, 4 June 1945; Mr Ernest Bevin, in an interview in the *News Chronicle*, 11 June 1945.

BOOK II

FROM PLAN I TO NATIONALISATION AND BEYOND

Chapter III

FROM PEACE TO PLENTY:
A CHRONICLE
1945–1959

The wartime interlude from the concerted pursuit of the I.D.A.C.-Steel Federation policies for the orderly collective development of steelmaking under supervision came to an end, as the last chapter has shown, before the end of the war. The war organisation, the Control, had evolved ingenious elaborations of pre-war devices which could be applied in peacetime to continue to stabilise relatively low prices, and it had planned wartime capital development. From the end of 1943 preparations were made by the Federation for planned developments for peace, and a start was made on the work and indeed in some of the works.

In sharp contrast the interlude from competition which the war brought did not come quickly to an end. It could be foreseen that the post-war period would begin as a sellers' market, but it had been visualised that there would be a day of reckoning, not long to be deferred, when British steel would have to meet either American or Continental competition, and many had supposed that the low United States prices of the war years would then be a menace to exports from Britain both of steel and of goods made of steel, unless productivity and efficiency in the British industry were rapidly increased. Such was the picture continually painted, even by steelmakers, to stress the urgency of thorough rehabilitation of British steelmaking. But the day of reckoning had not come in the form visualised even by 1958.

The year 1958 saw the third and most serious setback since the war in consumption of steel in the 'West'. The first came in 1949, the second in 1953–54. On the first two occasions steel output in Britain and steel exports from Britain continued to

BEH

rise. The largest falls in output occurred in the United States, but there were falls in some Continental centres and falls in their exports too. On neither of these two occasions was there a simultaneous decline or severe check to growth in industrial activity in all the important industrial countries. Though there was some price-cutting competition, with some Continental producers and sellers making the running, there was no question in the first two recessions of the British steel industry, or the industries using British steel for 'indirect' exports of steel, being at a disadvantage through British steel prices. British steel prices, for a variety of reasons, were much the lower. The falls in consumption and exports were brief, and the sense of steel scarcity was quickly restored by the end of 1950 and of 1954. In 1958 the acuteness of the competitive situation was greater. Again the dominant feature was a fall in American consumption and output, a more severe fall than in 1949 or 1953-4, and again the price cutting in exports was led by the Continental producers, who were selling at low prices in the United States itself. By this time, however, home prices on the Continent had also come down in relation to British; the approach of competition in forms visualised in 1944, though not from America, seemed at least more likely than on any earlier occasion since the war.

It is convenient, before turning in subsequent chapters to study particular aspects of the steel industry's growth since the war and the policies adopted in regard to the industry, to map out in outline in the present chapter the main features of its development and those elements of general economic and political development which are a necessary complement.

The post-war years can be appropriately broken into the three periods[1] referred to above, each terminated by a fall of Western steel output and consumption, and a revival of competition in export trade, periods in which the 'leaps and bounds' have been more conspicuous than the 'rebounds'. Figs. 1 (p. 133) and 3 (p. 142) show respectively the course of production and of exports diagrammatically for main producers and exporters.[2] For the cyclical movements monthly figures must

---

[1] Referred to in the text as periods 1, 2 and 3.
[2] For outputs since 1870 in all countries see Table 105.

often be consulted. This division into three parts is manifestly convenient *konjunktur*-wise; it also happens to be convenient, no doubt largely by chance, in regard to changes of policy and organisation in the steel industry, and in regard to the flow and flux of Governments' policies and attitudes towards the industry in Britain and in the rest of Europe.

The three sections which follow each fall roughly into two parts, the first dealing with the course of production, export and consumption in the United Kingdom, United States and the Continent, the second with the political changes of policy in regard to steel and the changes of organisation, national or international, having a political or governmental or inter-governmental source.

1. RECONVERSION AND RECONSTRUCTION,
1945–1949

World steel output in 1947, though not output in each producing area, equalled the highest pre-war output (1937), but it was not till 1949 that world output was approximately equal to the highest wartime figure. The quick restoration after the war of a level of steel consumption high by previous standards for civilian uses was parallel to what happened in 1919–20, but was not followed by violent collapse as in 1921. Instead, there was further advance, until the slight recession in 1949, six months of uncertainty and no disaster.

Among Western countries steel consumption in this period was, almost inevitably, most resilient in the United States. At its peak in the war consumption in the United States was 55 per cent higher than at its highest in the thirties (1937), though only 35 per cent higher than in 1929. The highest wartime consumption was passed in 1948.[1] The fears that there would be no peacetime outlets for much of the steel capacity used in the war were belied by the event. Instead, new expansion of capacity

---

[1] For consumption figures—or, more precisely supply for home use, Table 7, p. 135. Before 1950 there are no published statistics for changes in merchants' or consumers' stocks.

Table 6. *World production of crude steel, 1937, 1943, 1945–58 (m. tons)*

	1937	1943	1945	1946	1947	1948	1949	1950
U.S.A.	50·57	79·32	71·16	59·47	75·80	79·14	69·62	86·46
E.C.S.C.	33·64	28·31	4·24	11·92	15·73	22·49	28·22	31·26
U.S.S.R.	17·42	9·84	12·11	13·09	14·27	18·60	23·23	26·87
U.K.	12·98	13·03	11·82	12·70	12·72	14·88	15·55	16·29
Eastern Europe[a]	8·48	6·02	1·79	3·55	4·88	6·33	7·30	8·60
Rest of Europe[b]	2·01	3·13	2·14	2·17	2·34	2·78	3·17	3·44
Latin America[c]	0·11	0·39	0·44	0·72	0·83	0·88	1·08	1·27
Commonwealth[d]	3·72	6·19	5·85	4·96	5·82	6·18	6·13	6·46
China	0·44	1·18	0·90	0·03	0·05	0·03	0·10	0·67
Japan	5·71	7·53	1·93	0·55	0·94	1·69	3·06	4·76
Total	133·51	157·74	112·90	109·54	133·80	153·36	157·86	186·43

	1951	1952	1953	1954	1955	1956	1957	1958
U.S.A.	93·93	83·19	99·65	78·85	104·50	102·87	100·64	76·12
E.C.S.C.	37·09	41·13	39·00	43·10	51·72	55·78	58·86	57·06
U.S.S.R.	30·90	33·96	37·50	40·78	44·56	47·93	50·24	54·02
U.K.	15·64	16·42	17·61	18·52	19·79	20·66	21·70	19·57
Eastern Europe[a]	10·01	11·25	12·71	13·39	14·70	15·83	16·78	17·78
Rest of Europe[b]	3·65	4·00	4·46	5·15	5·81	6·50	7·26	7·05
Latin America[c]	1·56	1·81	1·88	2·09	2·18	2·13	2·56	2·76
Commonwealth[d]	7·09	7·62	8·24	8·03	9·49	10·35	10·69	10·54
China	0·89	1·33	1·74	2·19	2·81	4·49	5·17	8·00
Japan	6·40	6·88	7·54	7·63	9·26	10·93	12·37	11·93
Total	207·62	208·05	203·65	220·13	265·45	278·93	287·43	266·06

[a] E. Europe: Czecho Slovakia, E. Germany, Hungary, Jugoslavia, Poland, Rumania.

[b] Rest of Europe: Austria, Denmark, Finland, Norway, Spain, Sweden, Switzerland.

[c] Latin America: Argentina, Brazil, Chile, Mexico.

[d] Commonwealth: Australia, Canada, India, S. Africa.

took place, and there were complaints in 1947 (as there were in the United Kingdom) that the steelmakers were too slow in this.[1]

[1] Cp., for example, evidence of Otis Brubaker, Director of Research, United Steelworkers of America, testimony to the *Special Senate Committee to Study Problems of American Small Business*, 11 Sept. 1947. This committee also had evidence from the Bureau of Labour Statistics on steel demand for full employment (e.g. paper submitted 20 June 1947). The trade union criticism of steel 'barons' was expressed by W. Reuther, *The Steel Monopoly and Your Job*, 25 July 1947. The steel firms said that if there had been no coal and steel strikes there would be no scarcity.

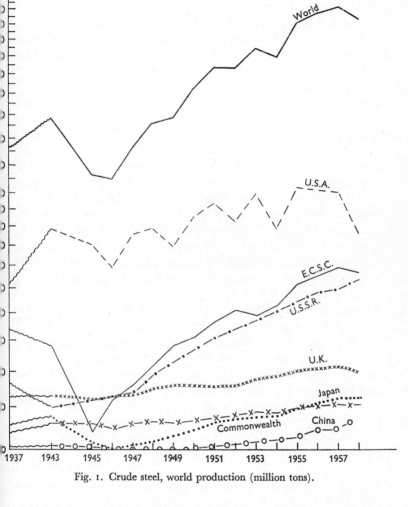

Fig. 1. Crude steel, world production (million tons).

American exports in these years were high by pre-war standards (cp. Fig. 3, and Table 9, p. 141), as had also been feared; but they were high because there were large unsatisfied demands, not because United States steelmakers were finding outlets for surplus capacity and selling at low prices. After wartime price controls were relaxed in 1946 rapid inflation (which was not surprising, or to most people unexpected in view of the accumulated savings and associated wartime deferred purchasing, plus liberal hire purchase terms and world scarcity of food and other commodities) carried American steel prices well above the British.[1] The volume of United States exports in period 1 was largest in the earlier years and when home demands were most exigent, and was smaller in 1949–50 when home demand fell off and output fell. In large measure the United States exports were financed, directly or indirectly, by American Economic Aid overseas, the continuance of immediate post-war aid being signalised by the announcement of Marshall Aid in 1947.

The first brief but shaking reversal of trend in the United States came at the end of 1948. Industrial production was 12 per cent lower in July 1949 than in July 1948 and unemployment up by 1,500,000.[2] 'Post-war inflation on a worldwide scale was over', it seemed, and 'countries needed once more to concern themselves with the problem of unemployment'.[3] Wholesale prices fell by 10 per cent. Farm prices fell by 20 per cent in the United States; worldwide post-war food scarcity was over. Gross private investment was one-quarter lower in 1949 than in 1948, mainly because heavy stocking was replaced by heavy unstocking.[4] United States imports of *all* commodities fell by 15 per cent in the first half of 1949; imports from Europe fell by one-third. The sharp fall in steel output was a reflex of this general recession; as was natural and for the familiar

---

[1] The *Iron Age* composite index rose by only 3 per cent over the 1941–4 level by the end of 1945, but 12 per cent by the end of 1946, 33 per cent by the end of 1947 (*Iron Age*, 2 Jan. 1958, p. 324). It is naturally not intended in this book to account for all the conjunctural swings in all the countries covered, but merely to record the aspects necessary to provide the context of steel developments. A useful brief survey of the waves of price increases in the United States since the war, 'Prices, Wages and Productivity in the United States 1946–1957', by Ewan Clague, United States Commissioner of Labour Statistics, was published in *Labour News from the United States* (26 Apr. 1958) by the United States Information Service.

[2] *National and International Measures for Unemployment*. Report by a group of experts, United Nations, 1949, p. 8.

[3] *Ibid. loc. cit.*

[4] For the statistics, see *Economic Report of the President*, Jan. 1958, p. 125. The fall in fixed capital investment in industry and trade was about 10 per cent.

reasons it was more acute in degree than the fall in industrial output all told. It looked as though the transit from peace to plenty was complete. By the time the setback was becoming familiar, and the subject of United Nations experts' reports, it was, as the experts knew, tailing off.

Table 7. *Steel consumption in the United Kingdom, 1937, 1943, 1946–50 (in m. ingot tons)*

Year	Ingots and castings made	Steel from (+) or to (−) steel-makers stocks	Re-usable steel	Imports	Exports	Net exports	Home deliveries
1937	12·98	−0·08		1·48	2·92	1·44	11·62
1943	13·03	+0·20	0·25	2·77	0·12	−2·65[b]	16·13
1946	12·70	+0·15	0·81[c]	0·48	2·30	1·82	11·64
1947	12·72	+0·30	0·85[c]	0·46	1·73	1·27	12·60
1948	14·88	−0·16	0·63[c]	0·50	1·98	1·49	13·87
1949	15·55	−0·25	0·52	1·09	2·36	1·27	14·55
1950	16·29	−0·11	0·48	0·56	3·15	2·59	14·29

[a] From the *B.I.S.F. Annual Statistics*. Only the figures for ingots and castings are precisely comparable before and after 1946. There is no figure for re-usable steel for 1937. No figures of consumers' and merchants' stocks are available.
[b] Net import.
[c] Presumably inflated by disposals from war stocks.

In Britain output and exports rose continuously in period 1, but at the end of the period there was a check in consumption. In annual figures it appears as a fall in 1950; but the level in the later months of 1949 was below that of the earlier months.[1] As consumption fell exports were higher. Consumption was never as high in period 1 in the United Kingdom as it had been at its highest in the war; it did not compare with the American record in this. But it rose rather faster than the first officially proffered published estimates had forecast. The figures are given in Table 7. Thus consumption already almost equalled the pre-war peak by 1946, and thereafter was higher.

Though consumption practically reached the pre-war peak

[1] The three highest months in the first half were above the three highest in the second.

in 1946 the output of crude steel (ingots and castings) did not exceed the 1937 figure till 1948, when it did so handsomely. That consumption rose above the pre-war peak sooner than production was due in part to the large supplies of second-hand material and war surpluses in the years 1946–8,[1] but there was also a fall in net exports below the 1937 figure, though average net exports in the years 1946–9 were higher than from 1934 to 1938. Imports and exports both fell below the average of the last five pre-war years in 1946–9, exports being restricted in the interest of the home market by licensing.

The big rise in crude-steel output in 1948–9 was faster than the rise in pig-iron output, and depended greatly upon increased imports of scrap from West Germany, which became immediately easier to obtain after currency reform; the dependence made the raw-material position of British production precarious, but this may not have been clearly perceived by all concerned.[2]

Steel consumption in Britain reflected industrial development. Total industrial output approximately reached the pre-war peak in 1947, and was about one-fifth higher in 1949. This rapid growth was possible only because many industries expanded considerably in the war, and as these were mainly metal-using industries this in turn explains why the steel consumption rose faster than industrial output in general. Even so steel supplies did not expand fast enough to satisfy the demand—at the prices charged for steel—and, just as in the United States, though more continuously, there were complaints of scarcity and the industry was often accused of being restrictive.

---

[1] Steel that becomes available after buildings, machines or other structures wear out or are no longer needed does not necessarily all become scrap. Old rails, for example, can be re-rolled and used as billets; cuttings from plates used for small products, e.g. spades. No figures on second-hand steel supplies before the war are available. Hence some addition must be made to pre-war consumption figures for comparison with post-war.

[2] It did not seem precarious if the Marshall Plan for German steelmaking in 1948 was regarded as durable. It visualised a steel ingot output of 10·7 m. tons in 1951, using 4 m. tons of circulating and bought scrap. Output in 1950 was 11·8 m. tons, in 1951 13·1 m. tons, with 5·6 m. tons of scrap for steel, and 1·5 m. tons of scrap for blast furnaces. *Stat. Bull.* Mar. 1948. The *German level of Industry and Scrap Supplies*, and the *Statistisches Jahrbuch für die Eisen u. Stahl Industrie*, 1952–3, p. 9.

The industrial expansion of this period depended partly on American aid, in various forms, which was a source of vital imports of raw materials, food and machinery on which the expansion of the economy partly rested. It was constantly emphasised that this dependence should stop and Britain become, in the jargon of the day, 'viable'; but viability was not achieved by 1949, though British exports had been increased to a degree which, when looked at in isolation from what was needed for the balance of payments and rebuilding a reserve, seemed satisfactory. It would be inappropriate here to explore how far Britain's position remained precarious as a result of too much inflation or too little increase of 'productivity', or to too much inflation in other parts of the sterling area to which United Kingdom loans and releases of sterling balances contributed. The setback in America, and the fall in American imports, showed Britain's position to be precarious; it created payments difficulties in many countries, which limited their buying of imports from all sources. But in hard-currency countries British exports lost ground against American on account of price as well as design. British exports fell off in the beginning of 1949, in advance of falls which occurred in several other countries (including the United States, where the fall was acute, but not Germany) later in the year. This was the setting in which devaluation of sterling became unavoidable in September 1949, and for Britain this may be taken as marking the end of period 1.

Sterling was devalued by 30 per cent in terms of dollars; and as a consequence Britain's exports to countries who did not also devalue to the same or a lesser degree were at the outset by that amount cheaper. But her imports were dearer. This was of importance to the steel industry. In period 1 pig-iron makers reverted to their pre-war degree of reliance on imported ores, the pressures described above for a return to the old order having succeeded. Furthermore, as has just been observed, in the later part of the period there was a great reliance on imports of scrap. The full significance of these situations was not immediately obvious, though it was not to be concealed for long.

Steel production on the Continent did not recover by 1949

to the 1937 level, and, indeed, did not do so till 1951. This was primarily due to the delayed start of rapid recovery in West Germany, a combined outcome of destruction, disorganisation and uncertainty. Reconstruction was deferred much longer in the Ruhr than after the First World War, it was not until just before currency reform in mid-1948 (and more notably after it) that a movement of great vitality manifested itself. The Ruhr's neighbours depended so much on Ruhr coke that what happened there was necessarily reflected in all the steel industries of the north-west of the Continent. Nor were they able to make up for deficiencies of Ruhr coke by supplies from Britain, because the United Kingdom coal industry also recovered only slowly from the dislocation and reduction of output induced by the war (not of course comparable to what happened in the Ruhr) and the growing pains, if that is the right term, of nationalisation. Britain curtailed her exports drastically. American coal came to the Continent, a portent whose significance was not grasped at once. Inadequate fuel supplies kept French, Belgian and Luxembourg steel output to 45–50 per cent of capacity in 1946 and 60–65 per cent in the autumn of 1947.[1]

French, Belgian and Luxembourg steelmakers used more imported ores (which were dearer ores), largely from Sweden, instead of relying almost exclusively on the Lorraine 'minette', and these imported ores being richer in iron used limited supplies of coke to greater advantage. More low-grade scrap was also used in blast furnaces, in France, Belgium, Luxembourg and Germany. The Lorraine coal and steel industries made great efforts which ultimately had some successes to increase the proportion of coal of poor coking quality which could be mixed with high-grade coking coal to make metallurgical coke. There was, moreover, much investment in the French industry, in particular under the first 'Monnet' five-year plan for the modernisation and expansion of all French industry; and this investment in France, and some in other Continental producing

---

[1] *Committee of European Economic Co-operation*, Report of Meetings, July–Sept. 1947 (Tech. Rep.), vol. II, p. 182. In 1945 5·9 m. tons of American coal was sent to Europe; in 1946 17 m. tons, and for the first half of 1947 16·5 m. tons. The figure was expected to be at its highest in 1948 (the estimate was 41 m. tons) falling progressively to 5 m. tons in 1951 (*ibid.* pp. 109, 125).

areas, in Benelux for instance and in Italy, was fed by American aid and provided with American machinery, most conspicuously with American strip mills. But by 1949 France, though she made more steel than in 1937, still made less than in 1928–9; Belgium just touched her 1937 output, Italy, Luxembourg and the Saar lagged some way behind their pre-war peak, and West Germany made only 62 per cent of her output in 1936.[1] The figures for the main Continental producers except Sweden are given in Table 8 (Fig. 2). They were the countries which were to form the European Coal and Steel Community.

Table 8. *Steel production in countries of 'Little Europe',*
1937, 1943, 1945–58 (m. tons)

	1937	1943	1945	1946	1947	1948	1949	1950
W. Germany	15·19	15·25	1·21	2·50	3·01	5·47	9·01	11·93
France	7·79	5·05	1·63	4·34	5·64	7·12	9·01	8·52
Belgium	3·80	1·64	0·74	2·26	2·84	3·86	3·79	3·72
Luxembourg	2·47	2·13	0·26	1·27	1·69	2·41	2·24	2·41
Holland	0·04	0·15		0·13	0·19	0·33	0·42	0·48
Italy	2·05	1·70	0·39	1·13	1·66	2·09	2·02	2·33
Saar	2·30	2·39	0·01	0·29	0·70	1·21	1·73	1·87
Total	33·64	28·31	4·24	11·92	15·73	22·49	28·22	31·26

	1951	1952	1953	1954	1955	1956	1957	1958
W. Germany	13·29	15·56	15·18	17·16	21·00	22·82	24·12	22·43
France	9·68	10·70	9·84	10·46	12·39	13·19	13·87	14·38
Belgium	4·97	4·99	4·43	4·89	5·76	6·28	6·17	5·92
Luxembourg	3·03	2·95	2·62	2·78	3·17	3·40	3·44	3·33
Holland	0·55	0·67	0·85	0·91	0·97	1·03	1·17	1·42
Italy	3·01	3·48	3·44	4·14	5·31	5·81	6·68	6·17
Saar	2·56	2·78	2·64	2·76	3·12	3·32	3·38	3·41
Total	37·09	41·13	39·00	43·10	51·72	55·85	58·83	57·06

On the Continent, as in the United Kingdom and the United States, consumers were commonly asking for more, and there were steel 'famines'. It was said by the precursor of O.E.E.C. in 1947 that even after receiving imports of United States steel Continental countries were 'falling short of their steel budgets' to the extent of 25 per cent. Such figures are always suspect;

[1] Based on output in West Germany in 1936.

scarcities are immense until they become superfluities. At the end of the period, as German output began to grow fast—it nearly doubled from 1948 to 1949—the market for the other steelmakers of the north-west Continent, especially their export

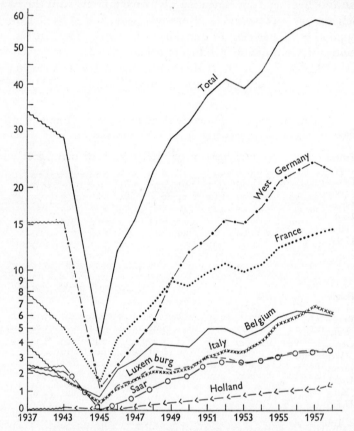

Fig. 2. Output of crude steel, E.C.S.C. (million tons).

market, declined seriously. For some months output in these countries fell off, and exports and export prices fell sharply. The annual statistics give only a slight indication of the flutter in 1949; but that is because for this purpose annual figures are insufficient. In Belgium and Luxembourg the monthly average of exports in 1949 was, as can be gathered from Table 9, about 360,000 tons; but in the first three months it was 415,000 tons, in the last three 280,000 tons. France had a similar experience. The early months of 1950 saw an improvement, but not up to the average for 1949, still less to the level of the first quarter. For Belgium–Luxembourg the first three months' exports averaged 335,000 tons. In West Germany exports as well as output of steel continued to rise (see Table 9 and Fig. 3, p. 142).

Table 9. *Exports of ingots, 'semis' and finished steel (by country of consignment) (thousand tons)*

	1946	1947	1948	1949	1950	1951	1952
Belgium–Luxembourg	1,448·9	2,085·8	3,215·9	3,544·6	3,256·3	4,721·3	4,672·0
France and Saar	156·9	279·5	768·8	1,847·8	3,180·9	3,609·7	2·584·9
Germany (West)	—	—	122·0	493·9	1,623·3	1,968·2	1,732·8
Japan	0·1	0·3	12·5	212·5	541·9	930·4	1,549·0
United Kingdom	1,722·0	1,280·0	1,452·0	1,738·0	2,356·7	1,915·7	1,875·3
U.S.A.	4,110·2	5,663·3	3,793·9	4,128·5	2,396·5	2,746·3	3,597·8
Total	7,438·1	9,308·9	9,365·1	11,965·3	13,355·6	15,891·6	16,011·8

	1953	1954	1955	1956	1957	1958
Belgium–Luxembourg	4,196·9	4,456·9	5,433·6	5,925·8	5,795·3	5,876·8
France and Saar	3,402·4	3,679·5	4,876·4	4,392·9	4,262·4	4,424·8
Germany (West)	1,772·8	2,401·1	2,580·4	3,586·6	4,869·7	4,594·3
Japan	785·8	1,094·4	1,751·0	1,178·6	895·9	1,540·4
United Kingdom	2,006·9	2,167·1	2,520·5	2,469·6	2,929·9	2,527·0
U.S.A.	2,674·0	2,471·0	3,642·2	3,912·6	4,808·4	2,622·7
Total	14,838·8	16,270·0	20,804·1	21,466·1	23,561·6	21,586·0

Period 1 was the heyday in Britain of the Attlee Government. The result of the election of 1945 brought the promise of nationalisation for steel. But the political dispute over the British industry's future was unexpectedly prolonged just as the sellers' market was; and as is the way in such affairs the ebb and flow of party opinions and party fortunes thrust into

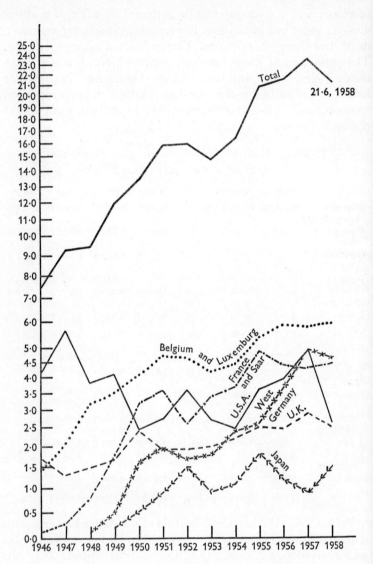

Fig. 3. Exports by country of consignment (million tons), 1946–58.

relative oblivion the economic questions which were at stake. The Labour Party was not ready to nationalise the industry when it came into office. The Federation was asked to complete its plan, which it did, co-ordinating the plans of firms and adding to them, and the result received the Government's hardly qualified blessing. When the wartime Steel Control was wound up in 1946 the Government set up, as a holding operation, a new supervisory body, the Iron and Steel Board. It soon became evident that the Government and the Labour Party were even less united in favour of nationalising steel after the election than they had been before it; and the inclusion of trade union members on the Iron and Steel Board lessened union support for the more radical measure. The nationalisers (led, according to popular rumour, by Mr Aneurin Bevan, the hero of Ebbw Vale, though Sir Stafford Cripps and Mr Ernest Bevin were strong supporters) won in the struggle. But by the time the Bill became an Act, in November 1949, the Government were losing ground in the country, and because they foresaw difficulties in finding people to man the nationalised Corporation they delayed bringing it into force until 1951, outside Period 1.

Thus this period may, politically, be dubbed the period of the first Board and first Plan. The next two chapters which deal with the events of this period take it from this point of view. What was the impact of the plan and the board on the industry's evolution? The period was characterised by the importance attached to quantitative planning, not only in regard to steel. At the outset such planning was very generally held to be imposed in many sectors by post-war scarcities and the problems of transition. There must be priorities. In steel, rationing based on the wartime system remained throughout the period. The 'price mechanism' was in disrepute, and this was reflected in the handling of profits and price policies. The full impact of prices was in many aspects overlooked. The emphasis in steel price policy was on keeping prices both low and stable; and, for most of period 1, Government subsidies were used in association with some of the pre-war and wartime devices to bring this about. By 1948, however, the subsidy bill was mounting. By the end of period 1 the Government had brought this policy, which could be regarded as one covering the transition from war to peace, to an end, and the role of levies and subsidies organised inside the industry had been made more important. By this time too the period of scarcity seemed passing. The plans of the firms to expand were bearing fruit—though what was done departed significantly from the 'Plan' of 1946. The end of rationing was being discussed.

In Europe period 1 witnessed the beginnings of economic co-operation, and the emergence of two institutions which concerned themselves among other things with steel—the Economic Commission for Europe (E.C.E.), and the Organisation for European Economic Co-operation (O.E.E.C.). The steel scarcity was one of the typical embarrassments facing European recovery in which they were expected to assist. The precursor of O.E.E.C. issued a technical report on steel in 1947.[1] In this, after surveying the scarcity, the authors proposed ways of making the best use of available raw materials (suggesting for example that Germany should be enabled to use imported ore to save coke). They surveyed the prospects even as far ahead as 1955, and made out the case for imports of American coal and steel to fill critical gaps. Meetings were instituted to draw up Europe's steel budget at regular intervals to lay bare deficiencies.

The E.C.E. undertook a similar task. It had the advantage of covering the Eastern bloc (though there was not complete co-operation), but the disadvantage of lacking executive functions,[2] although at the outset it took some part in administrative decisions.

Towards the end of 1948 the O.E.E.C. steel committee was given the task of approving steel investment schemes in Europe which were to benefit from American aid. The E.C.A. authorities decided they could not authorise $100 m. for a number of

---

[1] Referred to earlier, *Committee of European Economic Co-operation* (C.E.E.C.) *Report of Meetings, July–Sept. 1947*, vol. II (Technical Reports), pp. 179–220.

[2] Because, however, it had no executive power, its officials were not responsible to Ministers who had policies, so the E.C.E. officials were freer to express views. To some extent the same people went to the committees of all the bodies, the E.C.E. the C.E.E.C. and the Control Commission meetings in Germany during the occupation; these were in a large measure meetings of the same people under different hats.

schemes, most of them already under way, unless they were all approved as economic from the standpoint of an integrated Europe. They were all approved quickly.

The C.E.E.C. report of 1947 had suggested that after the current investment plans were finished steel capacity would still be deficient by 3–4 m. tons.[1] A slight note of doubt seemed to be sounded at the O.E.E.C. Council meeting in February 1949. Investments 'should be developed rationally and in concert', it was concluded ponderously, 'along lines which will best help to correct the balance of payments, but...will also avoid the creation of surplus capacities'. There were voices that suggested that when all the steel plants that all the companies were building were completed (and all the oil refineries and power stations), there might be too much steel, oil and power.[2] Late in the autumn the E.C.E. published the first of its now regular series of studies on steel trends, whose broadest conclusion was that on existing plans, and according to the best forecasts they could make of demand for steel, Europe's steel capacity would exceed markets by 8 m. tons in 1953.[3] There had always been experts looking over their shoulders even at the height of America's post-war 'boom' who foresaw its deflationary end. The authors of the report were concerned only, in the report, to find ways of avoiding the 1953 surplus. But many observers were beginning to think the surplus was much closer at hand. They were bothered by the falling outputs and exports of France and Belgium, the rapid growth of German output, and the German search for exports. Some German steel folk were talking of the need for cartels in early summer 1949. By the time the E.C.E. report was published recovery in the United States was well under way, though this was not universally perceived. As it became certain period 1 gave way to period 2.

---

[1] *Rep. C.E.E.C.* p. 197.
[2] Cp. for all this the second half of an extremely interesting and well-informed article in *Econ.* 2 Apr. 1949, pp. 619–20. (I found at the time that steelmakers' criticisms of plans were directed generally against those of countries who were small producers—Italy, Austria, Norway, Holland.)
[3] *European Steel Trends* (Nov. 1949), p. 67. There was an unpublished O.E.E.C. report to much the same effect; but O.E.E.C. documents, if published, had to be more diplomatic.

2. REARMAMENT CYCLE, 1950-1953

The character of period 2 was derived from the economic consequences of the Korean war. But already before this started
(which was in July 1950) industrial output in the United States
had been restored to its earlier high level. New expansion of
Government purchasing based on war needs, and organised in
a semi-war economy, was thus superimposed from July in the
United States 'on the top of substantial business recovery in the
private sector'.[1] The somewhat hectic results, inside and outside
the United States, are familiar. In the United States a new
wave of investment, encouraged again by accelerated depreciation, added 20 m. tons of new steelmaking capacity between
1950 and 1953. The expansive effect was more or less expended
everywhere before the end of 1952, though the tailing off did
not coincide everywhere; it presents a rather untidy picture.
The Korean stimulant brought boom conditions and expansion
to metal industries in Europe as well as the United States, and
provoked exigent demands for commodities, some to use, some
to stock, and much prospecting for and investment in new
sources of supply of many materials. The exigent demand was
reflected in inflated commodity prices. Recession when it came
thus hit commodity suppliers as well as the industrial countries,
which induced balance of payments difficulties and some check
on their importing.

Recession occurred in Europe in 1953. In 1952 the E.C.E.
Steel Committee wrote: 'During the rearmament period
immediately ahead effective demand for steel will probably be
limited to production possibilities: over the long term the
problems will be the development of steel demand for the
maximum consumption of steel that can be produced with the
capacity now being created'.[2] By 1953, earlier perhaps than
was foreseen in the report of 1952, the 'long-term' problem had
become the actual one. 'In 1953 the situation changed', the
next E.C.E. survey of trends reported, 'and on the whole supply

---

[1] Clague, *op. cit.* p. 4.
[2] *Steel Production and Consumption Trends in Europe and the World*, E.C.E. Apr. 1952,
p. 3.

exceeded demand.'[1] This report examined in particular why steel demand was so relatively sluggish on the Continent, why it kept up so much better in Britain,[2] though they were apprehensive since investment was looking somewhat sluggish in Britain so that the balance between it and the steel industry's growth might not be enough 'to promote a continued growth of demand for steel in years to come'.[3]

The contrast between what happened in the United Kingdom and the rest of Europe in this period was certainly striking, as the graphs and statistics show. The contrast between the United States and Europe was also striking. In the United States steel output, and consumption, fell sharply in 1952, but this was a result of strikes at the end of the year. There was a great recovery of output in 1953.[4] The falling off in activity in the United States occurred right at the close of period 2, and in annual statistics of steel production appears exclusively as an affair of 1954.

That steel output in 1954 in the United States was 10 m. tons less than in 1953 (when it had established a new record, 6 m. tons above the previous peak) gives the appearance of a severe setback; but this 'business downturn...could hardly have been called a recession, except in certain parts of the economy'.[5] Government purchases were reduced by nearly $ 8 billion; which caused sharp declines in war-expanded industries, including capital equipment industries, and including steel, whose business also fell by reduction of stocks, and a reduction of demand for exports in Europe. It was remarked at this time that the United States steel industry did not compete vigorously for more of the world export trade, which in 1954 expanded. The explanations given by the E.C.E. steel experts were that it is difficult to get into competitive markets quickly (especially into markets for relatively small orders), American costs were above European costs, and firms did not wish to cut export prices in a way which would lead to

[1] *The European Steel Market in 1953* (Jan. 1954), p. 1.
[2] *Ibid.* p. 44 and *passim.*   [3] *Ibid.* p. 58.
[4] Early in 1953 the high level reflected pent-up demands unsatisfied during the strikes.
[5] Clague, *op. cit.* p. 5.

cut prices at home, and were content to see a proportion of their plant idle, some being obsolete and some overdue for repairs.[1]

That demand fell off sooner on the Continent than in the United States may be explained by the fact that the stimulus of rearmament there was more indirect, taking the form partly of offshore purchases and purchases of components, materials and machine tools by the United States and United Kingdom, and of business resulting from the growth in demand for commodities and shipping with its worldwide repercussions. This indirectness made the Continental position more immediately vulnerable, though it is also probable that expansion was less diverted by and dependent upon rearmament than in the United States and United Kingdom. The check to the steel industries on the Continent was much more acute than in industrial production *in toto*, due to the fact that steel stocks had been accumulated as an insurance when demand was exigent. Stocking had been helped by imports from the United States and Japan. In Germany steel consumption became static for a time, but hardly declined.

There were falls in Europe's exports (and still more in orders for them) and a slight fall in aggregate steel exports; falls acute in some markets, but partly offset by increases in other markets. There was a large fall in the United Kingdom market, which was not mainly due to a fall in demand; large falls in South America, partly due to payments difficulties, partly to more local production; significant falls in Commonwealth countries, notably Canada, Australia and New Zealand; and in all parts of Africa. Falls too in Switzerland, Sweden and Finland. But exports to the United States, China, Russia, Eastern Europe, and oddly enough to the North-west European steel-producing countries, rose (see Table 10).

The declines in steel use, steel exports and engineering exports in European countries, reflected and were reflected in a lower rate of investment. To this Government policies to balance budgets, a reaction after the spending sprees which defence had seemed to make imperative, and a reaction too to the quickened

[1] E.C.E. Report on *The European Steel Market in 1954* (June 1955), p. 21.

Table 10. *World trade in semi-finished and finished steel, by destination, 1951–8*
(*in thousands of metric tons, actual tonnage*)

Destination		1951	1952	1953	1954	1955	1956	1957	1958
World trade in steel	Total	18,613	18,675	18,477	20,285	26,121	27,532	29,770	29,175
(Excluding intra-E.C.S.C. trade)		16,760	16,554	15,706	16,307	20,978	22,792	25,464	23,953
Importing regions and countries									
1. Western Europe	Total	5,995	7,658	7,197	8,561	12,034	12,199	11,762	10,539
(a) E.C.S.C. countries		2,263	2,777	3,481	4,647	6,198	5,843	6,556	6,344
(E.C.S.C. imports from third countries)		411	655	710	729	1,054	1,103	1,249	1,122
(b) United Kingdom		464	1,534	880	440	1,517	1,304	781	445
(c) Other western European countries		3,267	3,346	2,836	3,473	4,319	4,052	4,425	3,749
Denmark		440	348	366	437	485	451	475	438
Finland		329	395	172	396	418	394	424	352
Norway		386	389	419	428	569	499	529	422
Sweden		746	747	536	693	803	650	812	706
Spain		29	66	83	119	266	245	235	202
Switzerland		672	569	399	601	799	877	851	558
Turkey		115	205	312	136	219	150	138	168
Yugoslavia		66	111	128	139	129	96	193	196
2. Eastern Europe[a]	Total	696	1,000	1,165	1,115	1,470	1,901	2,551	2,916
3. U.S.S.R.		156	211	279	239	163	614	747	710
4. North America		3,601	2,604	2,772	1,716	1,877	3,248	2,890	2,808
(a) United States		2,043	1,486	1,488	618	768	1,174	908	1,413
(b) Canada		1,558	1,118	1,284	1,034	1,109	2,074	1,973	1,396
5. Latin America		2,856	2,001	2,138	3,127	3,321	3,039	4,109	3,597
(a) Argentina		964	403	385	1,106	1,422	832	985	1,468
(b) Brazil		305	269	196	538	227	159	313	255
(c) Chile		83	66	63	50	57	83	83	84
(d) Colombia		114	117	247	232	200	201	191	82
(e) Mexico		425	307	205	218	243	348	378	283
(f) Venezuela		380	375	376	395	494	642	1,219	615
6. Africa		1,452	1,593	1,339	1,351	1,572	1,548	1,735	1,772
(a) Union of South Africa		412	402	349	253	321	350	453	377
(b) Algeria		188	209	130	126	165	173	214	403
(c) Morocco		219	197	130	157	169	103	73	1
7. Middle East		804	625	703	862	1,173	1,038	1,129	1,333
8. Far East		1,892	1,866	2,263	2,228	3,133	3,930	4,796	4,519
(a) China (mainland)		589	506	794	554	715	659	1,578	1,580
(b) India		166	207	287	443	56	269	963	1,470
(c) Japan		25	26	93	45				105
9. Oceania		971	79	366	770	1,079	591	581	512
(a) Australia		785	518	173	494	700	352	214	152

[a] Excluding the U.S.S.R.

inflation of 1950–2, contributed. From the end of 1953 conditions began to look more favourable—the worst seemed over in the commodity markets, industrial credit was easier, but still in April 1954 experts were speaking of 'stagnation' in investment activity on the Continent; stagnation being the new jargon which embraced a condition in which there was still much new investment, but with a changing pattern, with absolute falls of volume in some, said to be key, sectors, plenty of openings taken in others, but building in particular held up by dearness of materials and of capital.[1]

The British experience in period 2 was wholly atypical. This happened because the United Kingdom was in the anomalous position of meeting this time of acute demand for steel with a falling output of steel. She could not at once replace the scrap from Germany, which was absorbed in Germany as the German industry rapidly expanded, by alternative raw material. Allocations of steel, given up in the late spring of 1950, were thus restored for another spell in 1951–2. Britain set about increasing imports of steel, but so did the United States and Germany, who was short of ship plates. Both Britain and Germany suspended duties on imports of steel; and Sir Winston Churchill made the provision of more steel by the United States an object of his first visit to the United States after he again became Prime Minister in 1951.

Home supplies of steel were perhaps lower in 1950 than in 1949, and only a little above the 1949 figure in 1951, when it had been possible to get some more imports and check exports. Official figures show consumption slightly up in each year, because consumers and merchants had built stocks up in 1949 and drawn on them in 1950 and 1951, after which, in 1952, they began adding to stock again, quite substantially. The 1952 figure is, however, for 53 weeks, and reduced to a 52-week basis it shows a slight fall of consumption. The annual figures are given in Table 11. Such figures cannot be precisely right, and there were important trends within the years. Thus in 1950 output was at its highest in the first half, before the Korean war,

---

[1] Cp. *Second General Report of the European Coal and Steel Community*, p. 131, published in April, but necessarily written rather earlier.

and consumption was no higher at the end than at the beginning;[1] in 1951 the rate of consumption, seasonally adjusted, rose in the middle of the year, but fell back at the end when steel output fell sharply, and for most people unexpectedly. Consumption was 4 per cent lower in the first half of 1952 than in the second half of 1950. At this point restriction of metal-using industries by steel scarcity was serious.[2] Since defence orders absorbed about 5 per cent of the output of the metal and engineering industries in 1950, but over 8 per cent in 1951 and

Table 11. *Steel consumption in the United Kingdom 1950–3*[a]

| Year | Crude steel output | Second-hand steel | Drafts from (+) or supplies to (−) stocks[b] | | | | Consumption |
			Steel industry	Merchants or consumers	Imports	Exports	
1949	15·55	0·52	−0·25	unknown	1·09	2·36	14·55
1950	16·29	0·48	+0·07	+0·27	0·56	3·15	14·52
1951	15·64	0·54	+0·67	+0·33	0·52	2·61	15·09
1952	16·42[c] (16·10)	0·44	−0·14	−0·64	1·77	2·56	15·29 (14·99)
1953	17·61	0·30	−0·31	−0·39	1·11	2·76	15·65

[a] From the Iron and Steel Board's *Special Report on Development in the Iron and Steel Industry*.

[b] Stock figures are more complete for these years than for the earlier years, owing to the inclusion from 1950 of figures for stocks held by merchants and consumers. The 1949 figures are not fully comparable.

[c] Figure for 53 weeks. The figures in brackets are corrected to 52 weeks.

[1] There are quarterly estimates of consumption in the article by Shone and Fisher in *J.R. Stat. Soc.* 1958, p. 300. The quarter figures, seasonally adjusted, for 1950–53 and given in annual rates of steel finished are (in m. tons):

	1950	1951	1952	1953
1st	10·820	10·884	10·452	11·320
2nd	10·264	11·288	10·836	11·132
3rd	10·635	11·012	11·240	11·512
4th	10·832	10·844	11·176	11·688

The possibilities of error are greater in this kind of figure the shorter the period.

[2] *Ibid. loc. cit.* The point was clear in contemporary statistics; cp. *The Times, Financial and Commercial Review*, 13 Oct. 1952, articles on 'Setback in steel production' and 'Restraints on industrial production'.

10 per cent by the beginning of 1952, the limited supplies of steel forced many steel-using industries to contract, including motor car and ship-building. Output was curtailed by steel scarcity.

Steel scarcity in Britain began to lift at the end of 1952, and British steel output rose sharply in 1953, but there were for a time conflicting trends. Industries which had been restrained by steel shortage could now expand, and many did. But, under the impact of the forces which led to recession in Europe, there was a fall in many kinds of engineering exports, and an aggregate fall of such exports. The net effect of all the trends was a rise in steel consumption (in the first quarter of 1953 it was 5 per cent *above* the rate in the same quarter 1950), and though world export markets for finished steel were contracting the United Kingdom steelmakers, whose exports had been contracted at the height of the boom (when steel imports were raised), now reversed the process. Cutting prices and returning into normal markets, they increased the volume of their exports though at a lower profitability. This made the British steel industry's position look more resilient than the Continental when the E.C.E. made its 1953 survey, where they rated the effects of constricted supplies in Britain in the boom too low. In 1953 the rationing which had been restored in 1951–2 was again removed. This may be regarded as a symbol of the end of period 2.

Politically period 2 was in Britain the period of nationalisation and denationalisation, and on the Continent the European Coal and Steel Community was created. The second Attlee Government named the day, the vesting day, 15 February 1951, on which the Iron and Steel Corporation of Great Britain was to acquire and manage a large part of the steel industry for the nation. By this time the Government was falling out of public favour, and the steelmakers succeeded in a policy of passive resistance to drastic change during the short period between vesting day and the fall of the Government.

The succeeding Conservative Government, returned in October 1951 immediately deprived the Corporation of power to impose changes, and by the Steel Bill which became an Act in June

1953 they dissolved the Corporation, and set up the Second Iron and Steel Board to supervise the industry, and a Holding and Realisation Agency to hold the assets of the Corporation and dispose of them back to private ownership as soon as it could be done on reasonable terms. The opponents in the controversy over ownership and control betrayed no great cleft of opinion as to what should happen, concretely, in steelmaking. There was no conflict over the pattern of growth, and there was complete continuity of policy from one Government to the other in respect of price stabilisation, in whose pursuit the levy system reached its apogee in 1951–3, though the new Government was legislating nominally to provoke efficiency through competition. The political struggle over ownership provides the framework for the discussion in Chapter VI of the industry's development in period 2—and as for period 1 the treatment of international aspects is only incidental, the main consecutive treatment of these being left till Book III.

The international development was of great prospective importance in period 2, and the establishment of the European Coal and Steel Community provided a new and potentially more exacting setting in which the British industry must compete. The economic impulse to the plan for the Community came from the worsening economic prospects of the end of period 1. There was also a political impulse, which gave it its emotional appeal; it was to bring France and Germany irrevocably together and make war between them impossible, to achieve this being of particular importance if Germany's return to independence and power was to be acceptable in France. The Schuman Plan, drawn up by the French foreign minister and inspired by the head of France's industrial planning commissariat, Jean Monnet, envisaged the setting up of a large area of free trade and free competition in the coal and steel industries of Europe. The area should have appropriately conceived rules for investment and prices, and controls to sustain full employment, and a supra-national authority with power to act, and take the necessary executive steps. Under its umbrella the lambs and lions of Europe would lie down together in peace.

By the time the Constitution had been drawn up by the six countries who chose to join (France, Germany, Italy, Belgium, Luxembourg and Holland), the economic clouds of 1949 had blown away. When the High Authority of the Community opened its office in the summer of 1952 everything seemed set fair. But in 1953 the clouds were gathering again. As in 1949 the E.C.E. saw gloom three years away; there would be too much capacity for making sheets by 1956 in the new-style American plants now springing up, so policy must be devoted to creating new demands for sheets, and to replacing export markets which were becoming self-sufficient.[1] But as in 1949 the trouble was nearer at hand, and the High Authority found itself first facing the difficult task of governing the steel industries of the Community when steel was hard to sell and output and prices falling. The outlook still seemed to its economic advisers sombre when it produced its second report early in 1954, though some favourable winds were seen to be blowing.

3. BOOM AND RECESSION, 1954–1958

Nevertheless, 1954 proved to be one of two successive years of fast expansion in Europe, including the United Kingdom, which in turn were followed by two more years during which the rate of expansion progressively declined. In this period the upturn in the United States came later than in Europe, and the downturn when it came was more acute. In retrospect 1953 itself is seen in Europe as a period in which rising consumption was a prelude to an intense investment boom which owed little or nothing in any country to new Government expenditure, and was more widely spread than the investment of period 2, though not of course uniform in intensity everywhere. It was particularly intense in Germany and (to a lesser but still impressive extent) in France, and more intense as well as earlier in Europe than in the United States.

Indeed, in the middle of 1954 people were asking how it was

---

[1] *The European Steel Industry and the Wide Strip Mill*, E.C.E. Geneva, 1953, *passim.*

that Europe was beginning to fare so well and not suffer repercussions from the recession (or as some preferred to call it, adjustment) in America which though not deep, lasted, or at least so it seemed at the time, almost till the end of 1954.[1] The answers to the query, why so little effect in Europe, were broadly: that United States military expenditure overseas rose in 1954 though direct economic aid was reduced by a lesser amount, and there was no serious fall in United States commodity imports in 1954 because purchases and stocks had been adjusted in 1953 with sufficient prescience. Thus the United States position did not create new payments difficulties, as it was feared might happen, to prevent a recovery in world export demand. The import restrictions in oversea export markets removed in 1953 were not restored.

The upturn was encouraged in all countries though in varying degrees by Government policies to increase demand; by tax cuts, for example, and favours for investments, reductions of interest rates (most influential possibly in Germany and France), easier credit policies (under which hire purchase expanded fast in many countries).

In Britain Tory freedom had come into its own by the beginning of period 3, and Mr Butler's attachment to expansion was allowed full rein. Food rationing and control of softwoods went, as well as steel rationing, in 1953; the latter removed the indirect control which directed a given proportion of motor-car output into export markets. Initial allowances which survived the capital investment restraints of 1949 and 1951 but were withdrawn in 1952 were back in the 1953 Budget, and replaced in respect of certain types of new fixed assets by the Investment Allowance in 1954.[2]

The encouragements to buying consumer durables were quickly effective; new motor cars registered in the United

---

[1] For a good short contemporary discussion of the move from the peak in the spring of 1953 to the low point in the autumn of 1954 cp. Tarshis in *London and Cambridge Economic Bulletin* (abbreviated as *L. and C. Bull.*), Mar. 1955.

[2] For a succinct account see *Report of Commissioners of Inland Revenue* for 1957, p. 7. The initial allowances were a form of accelerated depreciation; the investment allowance is in addition to normal depreciation (which still amounts over time to the full value of the assets).

Kingdom rose by 60, 30 and 30 per cent respectively over the previous year's figures in 1953, 1954 and 1955 (or in hard figures by 109,000, 91,000 and 115,000).[1] The pace of industrial investment necessarily responded more slowly. Gross investment in fixed capital in industry and distribution fell in volume from 1950 to 1951 and again from 1951 to 1952, cumulatively by 3 per cent. It rose 5, 11 and 15 per cent in 1953, 1954 and 1955.[2] House-building, which may be classed with consumer durables, rose faster sooner; by 20 per cent in 1952 over 1951, and 30 per cent in 1953 over 1952, and a little more in 1954, after which it was checked. The volume of exports of manufactures, which had fallen 8 per cent in 1952, did not recover at all in 1953, and did not reach the 1951 average in 1954. Imports, on the other hand, rose by 10 per cent from 1952 to 1953, and this was not solely because more raw materials must be imported to sustain more exports; food imports rose faster than imports of materials.

Revival in the United States followed much the same pattern as in Europe. The relaxations, moderate tax cuts, more liberal mortgages, freer credits, were mild, and there was no special encouragement of investment. Government buying had fallen sharply and stocks too, from the peak in spring 1953 to the 'low' in summer 1954, but consumer buying was up; wage-rates rose, and less personal income was saved. Businesses were liquid; investment in capital goods fell only slightly, and relatively slight encouragement was needed to stimulate more. Confidence that it was only readjustment after Korea (not drastic enough to be called reconversion) was sustained by high-powered propaganda. 'Although it may be impossible for an economy to lift itself by its bootstraps', it was sardonically remarked, 'many seem to believe it can do so by its own vocal chords.'[3]

---

[1] There were striking increases also in refrigerators, washing machines, radios, etc. Cp. *The European Steel Market in 1956*, E.C.E. p. 14.

[2] The figures in 1948 prices (£ m.) were:

1950	1143	1953	1165
1951	1122	1954	1297
1952	1106	1955	1484

[3] L. Tarshis, in *L. and C. Bull.* Mar. 1955, p. v.

By the end of 1954 the buying of motor cars had begun to rise
to a new unforeseen high level, and this, with buying to re-
plenish stocks, set off a new wave of investment, and carried
steel consumption rapidly to a new peak in 1955.

By this time the pattern of expansion, its repercussions on
balance of payments, and the inflation which it promoted and
on which in turn it thrived, were causing many European
governments to reverse their policies.[1] This happened notably
in the United Kingdom, where a first step was taken with a
mild increase of bank-rate to $3\frac{1}{2}$ per cent towards the close of
1954. A full array of monetary restraints was assembled progressively, the credit squeeze, higher bank-rate, more onerous
hire-purchase conditions, higher purchase taxes, reductions of
investment plans in the public sector and the suspension of
investment allowances, the whole being rounded off in February
1956,[2] though a heavier dose of the mixture was still to be
administered in September 1957.[3]

The effect of the measures in different industries was not
uniform. Demand for consumer durables was effectively
checked quickly by hire-purchase restraints, and purchases fell
rapidly in the latter part of 1956.[4] But though it was a way of
delaying such purchases, these revived a year later when people
had accumulated the necessary larger deposits. Industrial

[1] Cp. *Economic Survey of Europe for 1955*, E.C.E. pp. 3–4 and *passim*.
[2] By Mr Macmillan.
[3] By Mr Thorneycroft.
[4]

		Plant and machinery	Building except housing	Road vehicles
			(seasonally adjusted, (£ m.)	
1955	3rd qr.	784	558	205
	4th qr.	798	627	203
1956	1st qr.	777	604	226
	2nd qr.	754	627	232
	3rd qr.	777	622	176
	4th qr.	802	656	173
1957	1st qr.	823	670	173
	2nd qr.	828	652	208
	3rd qr.	837	646	223
	4th qr	873	684	233
1958	1st qr.			268

(from *L. and C. Bull.* June 1958, p. ii).

investment in plant and buildings went on rising continuously through 1956 and 1957, for most of the time vigorously though in the end less so; at the close private industrial investment was slightly falling, but this was more than offset by industrial investment in the public sector. Investment in commercial vehicles sagged and revived from mid-1956 to end 1957 like purchase of private cars.[1] Physical stocks and work in progress rose every year in the United Kingdom in period 3 to the end of 1957, then fell till 1959.

Period 3 was not marked anywhere by acute scarcities of raw materials like those which were a serious drag in period 2. In part this was a consequence of the earlier scarcity, with its dramatic price increases and somewhat feverish expansions. There was, however, scarcity of coal in 1955 in Europe, relieved by greater imports from the United States. Contrary to earlier expectations[2] these had not yet been, and did not look like being eliminated. Freights rose correspondingly. Estimates of minimum amounts of primary fuels necessary for Europe in 1975 showed, or so it seemed, that rapidly growing imports of oil and possibly coal would be needed. Shipbuilding plans were expanded; the Suez crisis added a further stimulus, and 1955–6 saw an intensification of shipbuilding everywhere.

The broad effect on steel consumption in the United Kingdom of these varying trends and policies, the sources from which the supplies of steel were built up, and the repercussions on imports and exports, are set out broadly in Table 12.

Rapid expansion of consumption from 1953 to 1955 (about 7 per cent a year for the first two years) was thus followed by a slowing down to an almost static position and then by a fall. The way changes evolved in period 3 can best be seen from the deliveries of steel to particular industries given in Table 13.

[1] Registrations of new motor cars were as follows (in thousands):

	1955	1956	1957	1958	1959
1st qr.	124	119	81	141	147
2nd qr.	138	124	125	156	184
3rd qr.	120	86	115	129	140
4th qr.	120	72	106	130	176

[2] Above, p. 138, n. 1.

Table 12. *United Kingdom steel consumption, 1953–8*
(in ingot equivalents, m. tons)

Year	Crude	Second-hand	Steel-works	Merchants or con-sumers	Imports	Exports	Consump-tion
1953	17·61	0·38	−0·31	−0·37	1·11	2·75	15·66
1954	18·52	0·35	+0·15	+0·16	0·47	2·90	16·75
1955	19·79	0·30	−0·39	−0·32	1·86	3·36	17·88
1956	20·66	0·31	−0·21	−0·77	1·77	3·29	18·47
1957	21·70	0·32	−0·01	−0·40	0·95	3·93	18·63
1958	19·20	0·28	+0·21	+0·75	0·58	3·41	17·61
1959	20·19	0·28	−0·03	+0·69	0·50	3·72	17·91

The column heading "Drafts on (+) or additions to (−) stock" spans the Second-hand, Steel-works, and Merchants or consumers columns.

Thus steel for motor cars[1] shot up by one-third in two years, then sagged, then went ahead again.[2] Steel for constructional engineering rose steadily till the first quarter of 1958, then dropped heavily. Steel for building and contracting rose fairly continuously with only a short setback from mid 1958. Miscellaneous engineering rose steadily to a sort of plateau from 1956 to mid 1958, then dropped a little for about a year. Steel for shipbuilding started at an unrepresentatively high figure, fell back for 18 months, revived steadily till the beginning of 1958, then lost ground steadily. Steel for railways dropped sharply in 1954–5, revived in 1956–7, fell dramatically thereafter.

[1] Steel for drop forgings and springs is closely associated with motor vehicles, cycles and aircraft, and the changes in this item may be largely added to the motor-car figures. It is familiar that the expansion of car output created much indirect demand for steel—which appears, for example, in the building and contracting, machine tools, iron and steel, electrical machinery and equipment figures, etc.; but how much cannot be identified.

[2] This movement appears to have been reflected in total demand impressively; the Shone and Fisher figures of quarterly consumption, seasonally adjusted, are (in thousand tons at annual rates):

	1954	1955	1956	1957
1st qr.	12,212	12,772	13,892	13,468
2nd qr.	12,240	13,140	13,768	13,328
3rd qr.	12,500	13,396	13,412	13,804
4th qr.	12,812	13,600	13,188	13,716

Table 13. *Deliveries of finished steel according to using industry (quarterly, in thousand tons)*[a]

	Constructional engineering	Building and contracting	Shipbuilding and marine engineering	Misc. non-electrical engineering	Electric machinery etc.	Motor vehicles, cycles, aircraft	Drop forgings, laminated springs	Railways		Coal mining	Machine tools	Total
								Rolling stock	Others			
1953 4th qr.	248	71	262	226	96	296	128	206	85	155	12	3021
1954 1st qr.	267	70	251	240	104	322	131	221	89	170	12	3211
2nd qr.	262	78	235	232	99	309	129	195	86	179	11	3090
3rd qr.	206	76	188	199	88	276	121	165	66	160	9	2746
4th qr.	255	84	193	238	105	342	146	185	74	170	12	3220
1955 1st qr.	261	96	201	245	110	379	155	185	76	175	13	3425
2nd qr.	257	98	199	246	113	373	154	184	65	175	13	3409
3rd qr.	237	87	176	220	97	311	133	161	51	151	11	3050
4th qr.	289	104	232	263	111	375	171	198	64	178	15	3681
1956 1st qr.	295	104	232	276	118	379	174	216	83	178	15	3877
2nd qr.	289	114	236	277	104	318	170	208	81	190	15	3702
3rd qr.	237	98	199	250	87	249	132	190	66	154	13	3055
4th qr.	309	109	261	282	103	253	149	228	102	185	16	3598
1957 1st qr.	318	111	252	290	117	266	150	213	107	193	16	3664
2nd qr.	304	109	255	275	108	321	149	206	108	192	13	3554
3rd qr.	246	111	212	251	97	328	135	177	87	171	13	3229
4th qr.	321	117	260	281	116	378	170	203	103	191	14	3764
1958 1st qr.	315	113	250	286	133	390	169	186	113	190	13	3705
2nd qr.	284	115	245	279	122	345	147	150	105	174	13	3387
3rd qr.	194	107	171	222	109	312	105	102	80	120	11	2731
4th qr.	203	101	183	247	126	327	131	111	88	131	12	3016
1959 1st qr.	205	99	183	249	122	383	143	98	79	145	10	3044
2nd qr.	227	134	165	267	127	433	154	82	79	142	13	3246
3rd qr.	198	136	137	242	115	385	142	59	52	118	11	2951
4th qr.	281	146	150	305	135	457	185	68	67	123	15	3604

These are not a complete guide to the use of steel in particular industries. Tinplate was in all the totals, but not subdivided in the industry columns until 1957. Sales to small users, sales through merchants, and finished steel imports (cp. Table 14 on page 162) were not subdivided according to using industries. A considerable part of the imports of sheet and plates could be credited to the motor-car and shipbuilding industries.

The deliveries for machine tools were at their peak in 1956, fell back from the spring of 1957 and did not revive again till the end of 1959. In coal-mining there was a steady rise until 1958, and then a fall as coal stocks rose. The particular intensity of the use of steel for building and contracting and motor vehicles at the peak of the boom stands out notably; these two groups together took one-quarter of all the steel in the first quarter of 1958, and accounted for over 36 per cent of the increased consumption in period 3.

The rapid growth of steel consumption in Britain in 1954–5 was possible partly because steel ingot output rose, the falling away of German scrap supplies having been made good mainly by increased blast-furnace capacity in Britain, though other sources were drawn upon for overseas scrap, and rather more pig iron was imported, a considerable part of it from Russia.[1] In 1954 it also depended a little on the use of stocks, and in 1955–6 quite substantially on a rise in imports of steel. The products mainly imported, and the main supplying countries are shown in Table 14. The figures are taken back to 1952 when there was also a large import, but much less concentrated on plates and sheets, and not so dominated by the needs of makers of motor cars and of ships.

Imports on the scale of 1955–6 were costly, but they were not, at their highest (i.e. in 1956), as costly as the imports of iron and steel in 1952.[2] There was, however, a big jump from 1954 to 1955—£40 m. in finished steel, £46 m. in raw materials for steel, including ingots and semi-products to be finished in the United Kingdom. It was tempting to underline, perhaps with some exaggeration, the rapid growth in buying private motor

[1] The total imports (thousand tons) from 1952, with the Russian contributions in brackets, were:

1952	624 (nil)		1955	671 (263)
1953	693 (nil)		1956	548 (303)
1954	338 (120)		1957	317 (225)

The other main sources were: Austria, France, the Netherlands.

[2] Imports of *finished* steel were slightly higher in 1955 (£54 m.) than in 1952 (£46 m.); but much more semi-product steel came in in 1952, and if imports of pig iron, iron ore, scrap and ferro-alloys are taken into the sum 1952 remains the year of highest expenditure.

cars in Britain after restraints were removed as a source of this increase of steel imports, not offset by a parallel growth in motor-car exports. The fall in car exports late in 1955 and in 1956, when other countries, particularly Germany, were increasing their export sales, may have been partly due to diversion of effort from exporting to the home trade, but it was only temporary. Car exports set a new record in 1957, and the value of direct and indirect exports of steel rose throughout the period 1953–7 considerably more than the combined cost of steel imports and imports of materials for steelmaking.

Table 14. *Imports of steel into the United Kingdom, 1952–8* (*in thousand tons of finished or semi-finished steel*)

	1952	1953	1954	1955	1956	1957	1958
Total	1526	914	364	1514	1403	753	461
Main products:							
Ingots and 'semis'	808	558	104	508	404	247	86
Wire rods	150	47	6	49	44	14	21
Bars under 3 in.	145	28	1	92	111	13	17
Heavy sections	44	18	14	56	81	59	28
Plates	72	86	32	60	191	104	54
Sheets	76	14	173	457	200	164	194
Tinplates	1	—	—	88	47	4	—
Main sources:							
U.S.A.	574	110	94	748	392	289	115
Belgium	310	197	44	211	352	139	88
Luxembourg	186	101	19	53	57	24	6
France and Saar	124	110	45	6	181	47	13[a]
W. Germany	105	34	40	83	196	104	63[b]
Netherlands	16	5	47	80	57	40	110
Italy	11	37	8	—	—	4	7
Sweden	25	30	20	23	40	24	25
Austria	3	75	34	21	14	10	4
Canada	27	27	—	90	16	14	4
Australia	2	133	21	—	1	10	4

[a] Excl. Saar.　　　　[b] Incl. Saar.

Revival in the United States in 1955 was impressive and carried the index of industrial output by the end of the year to a level 5 per cent higher than at any earlier date. The average for the year was 8 per cent over 1954. The 'cherished goals of our society'—'full employment, rising incomes, a stable dollar' —had all been achieved, so the President claimed. But people asked, was the economy really well adjusted?[1] One major impetus was exhausted before the end of the year; the prodigious level of car sales, over 8 millions in one year, had begun to fall. The new mainspring was the rate of business investment, in new plants and equipment and in stocks. The former rose steadily from an annual rate of $30·2 billion in the first quarter of 1955 to 42 billion in the first quarter of 1957; stocks which fell at an annual rate of $1·7 billion in the last quarter of 1954 rose at an annual rate of $6·6 billion in the last quarter of 1955; thereafter almost the same rate of growth was maintained throughout 1956. In 1957 the rate of fixed investment in plants and equipment became static at $42 billion, which meant a slight fall since prices were rising. The increase of stocks stopped, and in the last quarter they fell, at an annual rate of $3 billion. The second major impulse was thus also exhausted. There remained some growth in Government purchases, not enough to offset the other reversals of trend. A general decline set in in the closing months of 1957, which continued in 1958. Car sales which began to fall off at the end of 1955 fell heavily in 1956, did not recover in 1957 and fell again in 1958. Buying of some other consumer durables, and house building, dropped in 1956–7. Steel consumption had reached its highest point in period 3 in 1955. This level was not sustained by the business investment boom in 1956 (though industrial production as a whole rose 3 per cent), and there was a further fall of steel use in 1957, and a more severe drop in the first half of 1958. Steelmaking capacity followed a strikingly different course from steel output; it grew by 5 m. tons in 1956 and 7·3 m. tons in 1957, reaching almost 140 m. short tons (or 125 m. long tons) by the beginning of 1958, though it was still growing. Capital expenditure, which had been $1·75 billion in the industry in 1957, was expected to fall back to $1·00 billion in 1958.[2]

Government policies passed through several phases after the moderate encouragements of expansion of 1953–4. By the end of 1955 'the Federal Reserve system shifted from a policy of

---

[1] Cp. L. Tarshis in *L. and C. Bull.* Mar. 1955, 'The American economy—adjusted to what'?

[2] *Iron Age*, 13 Feb. 1958. Capacity rose to 132·5 m. long tons by Jan. 1960.

active ease to one of moderate restraint'; but the Government was mainly preoccupied with 'extending prosperity to the less flourishing parts of our economy', which meant the farmers. A year later, with wages rising faster than productivity, counter-inflationary policy had grown more imperative for 'our enter-prise economy'. By January 1958 the 'paramount task' had changed again; it was now 'to facilitate readjustments in the economy essential to the resumption of sustainable economic growth, but to do so without reviving inflationary pressure'.[1]

The slowing down did not reduce United States imports in the aggregate until 1958, but it marked the end of early prospects of increased sales for many primary producers, and it caught some of their expansion programmes, in copper-mining for example, in mid-stream. Imports of several commodities were sustained for several months better than their consumption, sometimes possibly through contractual obligations, sometimes because prices of imports were lower than or were reduced in advance of the prices of American home supplies of the same materials. Whatever the explanation, it had the effect of building stocks and further depressing prices. While in general, therefore, manufacturers were reducing stocks of raw materials —stocks of steel for instance—the reverse occurred with several primary commodities.[2] The paradox of commodity imports building stocks in a period of general de-stocking was associated with a growth of manufactured imports, notably from Japan and Europe, and including steel from the Continent. These imports continued to rise in 1957 though, like so much else, at a diminishing pace.

Growth of output in Western Europe was fastest in 1955, as in the United States, and fell off progressively in 1955–8, but the rates of growth, though falling, remained higher than in the United States, and output was still, though slowly, rising at the beginning of 1958. In most European countries, as in the United Kingdom, fixed investment grew in 1957, though at a diminish-ing pace. In West Germany it ceased to expand, and vigorous

---

[1] *Econ. Report of the President*, Jan. 1956, p. iv; Jan. 1957, p. v; Jan. 1958, p. iii.

[2] E.g. copper, lead, zinc, synthetic rubber (which would presumably react on the price of natural rubber, stocks of which did not rise).

growth of output there in 1957 depended upon still growing exports. Export markets were conspicuously beginning to weaken at the end of 1957, a reflection in part of declining expansion everywhere, including the United States, and the falls in demand for commodities and in commodity prices. Hence in 1958 the E.C.E. recorded that expansion was checked not only in countries where it had been deliberately damped down but even in countries which 'did not introduce or reinforce restrictive measures in 1957'—Belgium was the outstanding instance—the source of the check being 'more spontaneous demand factors—in particular weakening export demand'.[1] There was, conspicuously, a fall in export demands for steel; export became more competitive, there was price-cutting in many markets, first by Continental sellers of steel, and in January, February and May 1958 the United States Steel Corporation announced it was reducing its export prices.[2] It seemed that since contraction of demand was at least partly due to restrictions by countries in balance-of-payments risk, effective export demand could best be revived by credits from the few countries with ample reserves—by the United States and Germany—and this was proposed.

Decline in demand for steel exports in 1957 came primarily, as will be seen from Table 12, from falls in the imports of large steel-producing countries. On the Continent Germany imported less. The United Kingdom and the United States imported less. In each case expansion of productive capacity in the steel industry was coming to fruition faster than consumption was expanding. Consumption was indeed either contracting or was expanding less than at the time most of the steel expansions were started. France, where industrial expansion remained vigorous, imported more steel in 1957. Apart from the contractions of imports into these major steel-making countries there was no general contraction for the year as a whole, but there was a weakening in the closing months. There were also some declines in markets where domestic production was growing, while the rapidly expanding output and export of Japan was making important inroads in several

[1] *Econ. Bulletin for Europe*, May 1958, p. 2.   [2] Below, p. 514.

markets within, or half within, the Western orbit; for example, India, Pakistan, the Philippines, Australia, British Africa, the Middle East and South America (notably in Argentine). Russia, it has been seen, was sending pig iron to Britain, but not steel; the immense growth of her steel output, which was such a salient feature of period 3, was expressed relatively little in exports, and these mainly to the satellites. But some was sold in the West; some steel, for example, in Finland and Sweden from 1954 onwards.

In the first half of 1958 the 'weakening' of markets outside the major producing countries (whose imports are by their nature unstable) became more pronounced. British exports fell in value in the first five months of 1958 10 per cent below their level in the same months in 1957. Germany, France, Sweden and the United States also experienced falling exports at the beginning of 1958.

How far the recessions were due to restrictive policies, how far they could be reversed by taking off brakes (many *were* taken off by mid-1958) or by planning expansions, was now much discussed.[1] For how long would steel supplies be plentiful? How far they were due to lack of balance in expansion and investment projects, a lack of matching, exaggerated forecasts of potential demands, and whether this could be lessened in the next cycle, when it started, these were questions which were not asked as much as might have been expected or hoped, though it was observed that the fall in the American demand for motor cars might have an important moral, and one that could be of great significance for steel.[2]

The United States, last in, as it were, to the period 3 boom and first out of it, led in the recovery from the recession.

---

[1] A characteristic, and useful (albeit a little over-dramatic and not all in proportion) survey of the United States recession and its impact in Europe was published in the *E.C.E. Bulletin*, May 1958, pp. 41 sqq. While stating flatfootedly in an unsubtle phrase (I think in retrospect it will be regarded as doctrinaire) that the downturn was 'called forth through persistent central bank action' (p. 44) it accepts the view (p. 45) that 'resumption of production at the previous maximum levels would hardly have sufficed to call forth a renewed expansion of industrial investment to the levels of 1957'.

[2] I found no one who was prepared to regard this downturn of United States demand for cars as 'called forth through central bank action'.

'Recovery began in the late spring (1958) and proceeded at an increasingly rapid pace' until the third quarter of 1959 when there was 'growing evidence that the rate of increase in output' was slowing down, though no downturn was yet in sight'.[1] Industrial production passed its former peak level in the first quarter of 1959 and was 4 per cent above it in the last quarter. Personal consumption and higher government purchases provided the initial impulse; by the end of 1958 there was more house-building, and the process of reducing stocks had been reversed. Stock building was very vigorous by mid 1959. Capital investment in industry which had dropped acutely, was now recovering—but remained below the boom level. The number of cars sold remained far below the 8 million sold in 1955 and of those sold a much higher proportion came from Europe.

For the United States steel industry the first half of 1959 was dominated by the possibility that wage negotiations would lead to a strike in July. This led to more purchases for stock. Output of steel rose from 4·94 million tons of ingots in April 1958 to 10·33 million tons in March 1959. Quotas were now imposed by firms for most products: and some mills were stopping taking orders because they were booked to the end of June. Even so the industry did not operate above 95 per cent of its full capacity. There was in these months a striking rise in imports from Europe—first mainly to the West Coast, later to the Middle West by way of the St Lawrence Seaway—which helped to build some stocks but was also a response to exceptionally low Continental prices for some products—bar and wire were the ones about which the American technical press commented most. How much of the 'fast and furious' activity was for stock, how much for expanding business was uncertain. As July approached there was more emphasis on the extent if it was for the latter: but consumers' stocks rose, according to experienced commentators—there were no formal statistics—to about 22·5 m. tons of finished steel, and warehouse stocks to 3·25 m. tons; both much above the normal.[2] The stocks were

---

[1] M. W. Reder, 'The United States Economy at Mid Year', in *L. and C. Bull.*, p. ii. *The Times Review of Industry*, Sept. 1959.
[2] *Iron Age*, 20 Aug. 1959, p. 91.

said to be being dissipated during the first six weeks of the strike by over 1 m. tons a week (about 1·35 m. ingot tons). Together with an ingot output of about 350,000 tons a week from works not closed by the strike, and imports of about 100,000 tons a week, this implied a rate of consumption around 90 m. tons a year, or just over 70 per cent of the steel industry's full capacity. This kept the rest of industry working at a high level with surprisingly little interruption for six weeks, after which the deficiencies grew severe. There were premium prices, dealers sold above the makers' prices, and foreign steel prices rose above domestic. Nevertheless, high industrial activity was based on steel supplies well below the full capacity of the steel industry. After the strike, with the industrial output index at a new peak and car output better, steel *consumed*, not merely stocked, was put at 80 per cent of capacity.[1]

In Europe the recession—or some would say merely the slowing down and pause in advance—became most pronounced when the United States recovery from a certainly deeper recession had been in progress for several months. Steel outputs were still at low levels in the first quarter of 1959. They would have been lower still in 1958-9 but for the vigorous demands of the motor car industry and of shipbuilding. This apart, trade and industry's investment in fixed assets flagged in 1958. On balance, however, the activity of engineering and metal-using industries in general on the Continent fell little and fared better than that of industry in general. In the United Kingdom, as seen earlier, it was different. That less steel was in fact bought on the Continent (though not so much less as in the United Kingdom) was due to a considerable extent to reductions of stocks: the statistics on this are incomplete.[2] The Continent secured a larger part of world export trade in 1958 (while the United Kingdom and United States both lost ground). The American buying of imports provided one of the sources of recovery of demand for steel on the Continent in the early part of 1959: first particularly for France, whose prices were low

[1] *Iron Age*, 25 Feb. 1960.
[2] They are analysed in the E.C.E. Survey of *The European Steel Market in 1958*, ch. II.

owing to devaluation, and in Belgium and Luxembourg (who cut their prices most severely), and then for Germany. The reversal of the policy of stock reduction, the continuing advance in car outputs, rising demands for other consumer durables, a housing boom in Germany, revived activity in public investment—but only a slow recovery in private industrial investment led to a rapid recovery in Continental steel production by the end of Spring 1959. By the middle of 1959 it seemed 'fully booked' for the rest of the year. Recovery in the United Kingdom was more gentle.[1]

Period 3 spanned the first five years of the E.C.S.C. on the Continent and of the new Iron and Steel Board in the United Kingdom, where also most of the firms which had been nationalised were sold back to private ownership in this period. Period 3 saw no dramatic changes of régimes, but the practical significance of the changes of period 2 now began to unfold; their effects, for instance, on price policies, development, investment, cartels, and combines and international relations. At the end of this period the formation of the European Economic Community seemed certain to change further the environment in which the iron and steel industry would develop, and the efforts for a still wider area of freer trade in Europe, or for alternative groupings, were liable to bring about further changes. What they would be, still more what their impact would be, remained obscure in 1959.

[1] The following Table shows the comparative course of recovery in industrial production and steel output in a selection of countries. The indices of production (i.p.) are calculated from the seasonally corrected series published by the National Institute of Economic Research in their *Review*, the base chosen being the 3rd qtr. 1957; the United States figure had been at a peak (108 if 1953=100) for the first three quarters and fell in the 4th qr. Steel output (s.p.) is given in million tons a quarter.

Quarter	U.S.		U.K.		W. Germany		France		Italy		Japan	
	I.P.	S.P.	I.P.	S.P.	I.P.	S.P.	I.P.	S.P.	I.P.	S.P.	I.P.	S.P.
4 1957	96	22·3	99	5·5	102	6·3	103	3·7	100	1·7	98	2·8
1 1958	90	16·8	99	5·5	103	6·1	107	3·8	100	1·6	99	2·8
2	89	16·9	97	5·1	103	5·5	105	3·6	99	1·6	97	2·9
3	94	19·1	97	4·3	103	5·5	105	3·3	101	1·5	99	3·0
4	97	23·3	98	4·5	106	5·3	103	3·6	104	1·5	107	3·2
1 1959	100	27·2	99	4·6	107	5·3	104	3·6	106	1·5	113	3·5
2	106	30·2	102	4·7	109	6·3	108	3·8	106	1·6	120	3·9

By the side of institutional changes the results of research and development were again in period 3 perceptibly influencing prospects in steelmaking. The most conspicuous impulse to change in the early post-war years had been the wide strip mill, an American impulse; and the general effort to obtain the advantages of large-scale operating, by the use of bigger units and more elaborate engineering, was also a pervasive effect of American achievement. The research and development which began to have significance in the fifties was concerned with variations in iron and steel smelting or casting processes. For several years the E.C.E. published surveys of these technical advances. While some were to improve quality, and some promised cost reductions equally open to all producing centres, and some might favour small as against large plants, an important group of changes which promised an alternative to the blast furnace in the primary stages seemed certain to change the comparative advantages of different producing countries. They would make the possession of large coking coal reserves less important and the possession of cheap electricity and large supplies of natural gas more important.

All this at once reflected and was likely to encourage the progressively widening geographical range of steelmaking, which the production figures bring out. From 1951 to 1957 output in Japan grew from 4·8 m. tons to 12·5 m. tons. This was an exceptional rate of growth, much higher than in Russia, and was characteristically in a country with no domestic ores and with coal of only a medium quality. For Japan before the Second World War it had seemed better to expand steel-making in Manchuria.[1] The greater geographical spread of steelmaking, whose full details are in Table 105, is indicated broadly here (Table 15). In all these areas the rate of increase after 1950 was well above the world average (55 per cent), and in all except 'Other Europe' and the Commonwealth it was above the Russian rate (87 per cent). Expansion of output in E.C.S.C. (88 per cent) was also above the world average, but in 1950 E.C.S.C. had still not recovered her 1939 output. The rises in United Kingdom and United States outputs were

---

[1] Her output on the mainland, however, was over 6 m. tons in 1939.

appreciably below the world average; the United States, however, was peculiar in having much idle capacity.

Table 15. *Steel outputs outside main producing areas*
(thousand metric tons)

	1939	1950	1957
Central Europe[a]	8,676	9,682	19,500
Other Europe, excl. E.C.S.C. and U.K.	1,997	2,831	5,100
Commonwealth	4,044	6,563	11,400
Latin America	243	1,283	3,000
China	538	681	5,310
Others[b]	102	61	1,000

[a] Includes Austria, where steel output rose from 0·9 m. in 1950 to 2·5 m. in 1957.
[b] The chief producer here is Korea.

How far all this widespread expansion had ushered in an age of plenty in steel had yet, in 1959, to be proven. That it opened the way for a more competitive world (even though some of the new works only thrived on heavy protection) was plain. International comparisons were beginning to acquire an immediate practical significance by period 3 which they lacked in the earlier periods, and the final chapters look at the developments of period 3 from this angle.

Chapter IV

THE FIRST PLAN

1945–1950

The first landmark in the steel industry's history after the
Second World War was the development plan presented to the
Government in December 1945, and published by the Government six months later.[1] It marked the culmination of the work
started back in 1943. But, by the time it was being finished,
the dominant personalities had changed again, and the balance
of power had swung back closer to the pattern of 1935. Macdiarmid had died in the summer of 1945, a severe loss because
he was not only President of the Federation but, on the record,
the industry's most adventurous leader. Sir Ellis Hunter, who
took his place as President, was to remain so, contrary to precedent, for over seven years. He was soon to become famed for
the tenacity with which he clung to the policies he supported.
Sir Andrew Duncan returned as independent chairman in
September 1945 and, with Mr Robert Shone, who became the
Federation's Economic Director, was again, in the months
when the plan was taking its final shape, the architect of the
Federation's policy. This triumvirate was to lead the Federation
throughout its ultimately successful opposition to nationalisation.[2]

The Federation's plan grew, naturally, out of the 'practical
planning' of the later war years; and much of it had already
become familiar by partial statements of the Federation and the
firms. But when the known details were presented together as

[1] *Reports by the British Iron and Steel Federation and the Joint Iron Council to the
Ministry of Supply*, Cmd. 6811 (May 1946). The first of these is referred to in the
notes as *Rep. B.I.S.F.*

[2] Sir John Duncanson, Steel Controller from 1943 to 1945, became Commercial
and Technical Director of the B.I.S.F. in Aug. 1945. He made the first public
statement on the progress of the steel plan on behalf of the Federation (*The Times*,
23 July 1945). He left to become managing director of Lithgows in 1949, and
later a director of the Lancashire Steel Corporation.

a whole, and with new supplements, they presented a prospect that could not fail, at first sight, to dazzle. Expenditure of £168 m. in 7½ years was contemplated with the dual purpose of modernising and expanding (in both senses, i.e. making more steel and a wider range of finished products). Modernising was to play the larger role, and at the end two-fifths of the industry's equipment would, it was projected, be new. The general changes envisaged are given in Table 16. It had to be assumed, though such an assumption is not always justified,[1] that 'modernisation' would mean the use of the best type of plant for what was undertaken (i.e. having regard to the scale of operation and the materials to be used). It was not suggested that the changes would put Britain in the lead in large-scale steelmaking. The most spectacular schemes, referred to earlier, were to introduce or extend the use of American practices here —the wide strip mill in South Wales and the broad-flange beam mill on Teeside.[2] But obviously a programme on this

Table 16. *Development as percentage of existing capacity 1946*

	Replacement (%)	Additional capacity (%)
Blast furnaces (for steelmaking)	40	24
Steel furnaces	30	13
Billet mills	38	22
Plate mills	30	—
Joist, heavy section and rail mills	26	—
Sheet and tinplate mills	33	12
Wire rod mills	11	11
Light section, bar and strip mills	22	12

ᵃ Based on Table IV of the *Rep. B.I.S.F.* This table does not include plans for new coke ovens.

[1] I was surprised to find how much of the plant put in just before the war proved unsatisfactory, and was altered, either at once or shortly after the end of the war, including blast furnaces and rolling-mills. Some instances given in the report itself—not the ones I have in mind—are referred to in the text.

[2] Above, pp. 79–86. It was to be a *wider* strip mill, but not the first in the United Kingdom; the beam mill, however, as seen earlier, was to be the first. There was a superbly misleading remark in the report to the effect that when the new—third—strip mill was completed 'no other country will be similarly equipped except the United States' (*Rep. B.I.S.F.* p. 29). It did not go on to say that the United States had over 20 such mills before the war.

scale could do a lot to help the British industry to catch up, and even go ahead of some countries if development there was checked.

This would have been true, however, of a mere list of the schemes proposed by the individual companies. There was, after all, a most impressive (and in part disastrous) programme of new plant building after the First World War.[1] What was the contribution of 'planning' to the plan? What was to be done, or not done, as a result of the Economic Efficiency Committee and Government priorities? The answer was to be found in proposals to ensure 'the full loading of efficient plant', and in two projects for new plants.

'Full loading of efficient plant' was described as 'the fundamental basis on which modernisation plans have been drawn up'. The approach was first to ensure efficient planning in each district, and second to ensure the 'proper relationship of capacity between districts'. Three illustrations were given. On the North-east Coast instead of nine steelworks (owned by four firms) and most engaged on a mixed range of production, it was envisaged there would be five, each specialised on a particular product, one on heavy structural steel (a new one at Lackenby), one on rails and special billets (Cleveland), one on billets and light sections (Cargo Fleet), two (Redcar and Consett) on plates. This visualised the disappearance of the Skinningrove Works, the South Durham plate plant of the South Durham and Cargo Fleet group (which would be kept going on light and medium plates 'for the limit of its useful life'), and two of Dorman Long's works (Acklam and Britannia). The Cargo Fleet group would thus cease to produce heavy steel finished products. The dream of the North-east Coast consolidation was, so it appeared, at last to come true. 'A similar degree of concentration', the report stated, 'will be secured in other districts.' Nothing comparable was in fact indicated for them.[2]

---

[1] See *E.H.S.* pp. 356 sqq.

[2] In Scotland, as the report said, the concentration of production in *firms* had gone almost as far as it could. Some further rationalisation of Colville's production was suggested; the very small plant of Bairds and Scottish was to continue, with

The type of change visualised 'on a national scale' was illustrated from the rail trade. Instead of eleven firms making rails as in 1937 the business would be concentrated in four only, who would be able to have specialised plant for handling, straightening and so on. The four plants were to be Colvilles (125,000 tons), United Steel at Workington (190,000 tons), Dorman Longs (200,000) and Guest Keen Baldwins (135,000 tons); and the quotas (whose variation and geographical distribution reflected tradition rather than the distribution of demand or costs) visualised an increase of 40 per cent in the total trade. 'Similar rationalisation' was to be achieved 'in heavy sections, sheets and tinplate, as well as in billets, where 8 continuous mills will produce 3·7 million tons, or over 90 per cent of the output of ordinary billets'. Some proposed details of other rationalisations were scattered through the report. Thus for plates: the 'largest sizes of commercial plates' were to be produced only at the Dalzell works;[1] Park Gate and Guest Keen Baldwins would give up rolling plates, and their 'tonnages' would be 'transferred' to other companies[2] (in the first case to another district); the North-east Coast arrangements have been seen; a new four-high mill was to be built at a site yet to be chosen in Scotland for light plates.[3] This was not a complete picture, but illuminating. Three new wire rod mills were contemplated—at Lancashire Steel,[4] Richard Johnsons[5] and possibly Lysaghts (Scunthorpe); the first and last were to be associated with new continuous billet mills. This was all to replace imports; in itself it gave new business to all involved. That is the easiest form of planning. Lancashire Steel would, however, give up making rails and heavy sections, their output being too low for good costs;[6] Lysaght's business in sheet bars was a victim of the new continuous strip mill.

a hope that consultation would lead to exchange of orders to secure more efficient loading of the mills. The Blochairn and Hallside steel-melting plants and the Hallside mills were to be closed. In South Wales the problems were wholly different, due to the fact that the small works were doomed by the strip mill. Cp. above pp. 80 sqq., 121.

[1] *Rep. B.I.S.F.* p. 19.   [2] *Ibid.* pp. 16, 22.
[3] *Ibid.* p. 19. There was to be a four-high plate mill at Consett also, p. 26.
[4] Above, p. 87.   [5] At Manchester.
[6] *Rep. B.I.S.F.* p. 21.

A steelmaker might thus in these proceedings be asked to cease producing some products 'in the interests of concentration'; when this happened 'the possibility of the manufacture of other products for which his plant is suited, provided that such product can be made efficiently' would be examined.[1] In regard to products other than rails the schemes were not yet cut and dried—'full concentration which may ultimately be necessary will not in all cases be secured from the plans of the next five years'.[2]

The *Report* did not establish how far the North-east Coast firms were committed to the plan announced, nor on what terms. Was there to be amalgamation? ('The site for the new billet plant, as well as the speed of concentration, will depend', the report said, 'upon co-operation and technical arrangements still to be worked out between the firms.')[3] Nor did it show how the rail treaty had been negotiated; still less how, in fact, the claims of different firms were weighed when quotas of capacity were negotiated or how firms had been persuaded, or were going to be persuaded, to give up participating in some trades, and to 'transfer their tonnages'. It might not always be so convenient as at Irlam or Port Talbot, where the firms were anxious rapidly to expand their most profitable business, nor perhaps would all firms be equally content to commit themselves to an 'eggs in one basket' policy. The traditional development of steel firms in most countries has been to broaden their range of products as they have grown older. What persuasion was to be used to persuade firms to drop out of business altogether was still harder to imagine.

The object—concentration for larger scale production—was unexceptionable; but whether the machinery existed to bring it about quickly, if at all, or (which is equally important) to make the best decision, was not shown. It is now known, for example (as seen earlier, though the *Report* did not refer to it; it gave decisions, but not the range of choice from which decisions were taken), that United Steel gave up a project to make broad-flange beams because Dorman Longs proposed to

---

[1] *Rep. B.I.S.F.* p. 28. [2] *Ibid. loc. cit.*
[3] *Ibid.* p. 18.

build a new universal beam mill. United Steel's was much the less ambitious adventure. It is reasonable to ask in retrospect whether they were wise to give up their more modest plan— it looks as though they were not—or would indeed have been wiser themselves to have thought in terms of a universal mill.[1] In the planning context the simple question is whether the best site and most enterprising management were destined for the job, whether 'planning' tipped the scales in the right direction. (It is irrelevant whether the authors of the plan were asked to tip it.) The same question arises over the rail plan. Geographically it is hard to justify the northerly and westerly siting of all of the four selected plants. United Steel made strong claims for Workington where the rail trade was to solve their development area problem.[2] It would have appeared more rational to have had one east Midland site for rail making as an object—it was obviously not an urgent need—even though it meant that a production new to the east Midlands (and which no east Midland firm was seeking) should have started there. Or was 'rationalisation' in this planning not to include such radical departures?

This conclusion is at first sight hard to accept in view of the proposals for two new steelworks, the second contribution to the plan which appeared to arise from the planners rather than the firms.

One new steelworks was to be on the Northamptonshire ore field. 'Cost considerations', the *Report* said, 'on balance do show some advantages to steel based on home ores', but only for the 'commoner steels, particularly billets'.[3] Hence this new plant, which 'will be sponsored by the United Steel Companies and Stewarts and Lloyds', was to meet the increased demand of the Midland re-rollers for their 'extended production programme'; initially it would have finishing mills for two-fifths of its billets only, with a chance of more under later plans. This plant, it was made clear, was not to be one of the first parts of the plan to be started; and, indeed, it could not be, because

---

[1] The answer might be 'no', because Dorman Longs had so large a hold on the structural engineering business itself.

[2] Andrews and Brunner, *op. cit.* p. 277. [3] *Rep. B.I.S.F.* p. 12.

12   BEH

there were no plans.[1] The other new plant, put forward more tentatively, was to be in Scotland. Dalzell was a fixed star in the future firmament, despite all earlier criticism. It was to have a new open-hearth shop.[2] But the future of the rest of the Colville steel plants was left highly uncertain. The Hallside and Blochairn melting shops were to go; the three plants improved before the war, Glengarnock, Lanarkshire and Clydebridge,[3] would receive a 'limited expenditure', but one or more might be displaced by a 'new Clyde plant'. All the changes immediately proposed 'provide a basis for a long-term policy based on constructing improved dock facilities for handling imported ore, ore preparation plant, new blast furnaces, and new and increased open hearth capacity at a new plant on a riverside site'. It was to start with a continuous billet and sheet-bar mill (to make Scots re-rolling and sheet industries self-contained), to replace the existing re-rolling capacity of Colvilles, and to include the four-high plate mill for all Scots light plate referred to earlier. This plant was to be the 'nucleus around which the future developments of the Scottish steel industry will be planned, as soon as economically practicable, having regard to the efficient balance and life of the existing plants on other sites'.[4] Meantime the two fixed developments in Scotland were the melting shop at Dalzell and extensions to the Clydebridge blast furnaces.[5]

The *Report* contained a long discussion of the reasons governing the first of these decisions in a general section on location, which concentrated on one of the location issues only, namely, the relative merits of using home and imported ore, and so evaded the equally important issues of the siting of plants using imported ores, and of concentrated or rationalised

---

[1] *Rep. B.I.S.F.* pp. 22–3.   [2] *Ibid.* p. 19.

[3] Where some furnaces were in any event to be dismantled, though they evidently might be replaced (*ibid. loc. cit*).

[4] *Ibid.* p. 12.

[5] Cp. above, p. 87. The site chosen in 1936 was clearly open to criticism if the arguments for a coastal site were thus valid. The case for expansion after the war, however, rested on the advantages in making more intensive use of existing services and lowering overheads. The plant was from an engineering standpoint good, and was said to have been much less costly in construction than some contemporary plants.

production altogether. And on the ore issue, though the *Report* came to a quantitative conclusion, it offered no quantitative arguments. Since the generalities had been chewed over so much, quantities alone were of interest. The conclusion was that a number of 'considerations appear to confine the extension of steel output on a home ore basis to a maximum figure of the order of an additional one million tons'. What were the considerations?

Five were adduced: (1) difficulties of obtaining labour; (2) the coastal areas were close to coal mines and scrap supplies; (3) if too much steel is produced on one site distribution costs become too high; (4) 'technical factors (for example, the more exacting demands on the steel used in the continuous strip mill) make it necessary to envisage certain types of steel production being developed to an increasing extent on the richer imported ore'; (5) the reserves of home ores 'available at an economic cost' are limited. As was remarked in the most perceptive and penetrating contemporary comment on the plan by an economist,[1] only the first of these could be accepted without qualification and it would not justify the upper limit; it was relevant to the rate, not the amount, of change. The availability of coal and scrap in coastal areas as a factor favourable to costs there was naturally already accounted for in the conclusion that the home ore sites had a net manufacturing cost advantage. The *Report* did not suggest what this net advantage was; nor did it point out that the costs of getting coal had moved very unfavourably in South Wales and Durham, but that the price of coking coals there was in effect being subsidised from other coal regions, particularly the east Midlands, where coal was cheapest to mine. Nor did it point out that some of the coastal regions, and notably South Wales, were scrap-importing regions; the argument of accessibility was thus misleading. All these factors entered into the 'cost-at-works' comparison; the evidence available suggested that this had moved in favour of home ore during and since the war.[2] The third argument might conceivably lead to the conclusion that Stewarts and Lloyds had

[1] Brian Tew, in *Econ. J.* Sept. 1946.
[2] Above, pp. 99 sqq. Cp. Tew, *Econ. J.* Sept. 1946, p. 489. Also *Econ.* 20 July 1946.

increased their costs by concentrating production of welded tubes for the whole of the United Kingdom at Corby. The distribution of markets for other districts was not portrayed—how much Scots steel, for example, came into the Midlands—nor was there any measure of the Midland markets which were within easy reach of the east Midlands, though the size and rapid growth of these was clear enough before the war. Had the planners who were allocating quotas of trades regionally worked out how much of, for example, the rail market could be most cheaply reached from a southerly east Midland site?

The trump card for the imported ore argument was the assertion that the low-grade ores could not be used for the new wide strip mill and for some kinds of tube steel. Non-technical men would take a serious risk in dismissing this—even though the French intention to use their low-grade phosphoric home ore to supply steel for strip mills made the British claim seem dubious, and as was pointed out at the time the unsuitability was not absolute,[1] since Lincolnshire steel was to be taken to be rolled at Ebbw Vale.[2] But at most this argument could merely be that British steelmakers had not yet found a cheap way of using these ores for the kind of steel they thought the strip mill needed;[3] an absolute limit on the use of home ores could not rest on this. The evidence was that most products could be made from home ores.

There remained the argument of ore reserves—the one valid basis for some ultimate limit of capacity. This was of course a well-recognised limiting factor.[4] There remained room for elucidation—what were the reserves? The last published survey dated from 1939.[5] It included the corrections made in December 1937 by the Iron Ore Producers to the Geological Survey's estimate of reserves made in 1917. Their conclusion

---

[1] Tew, *Econ. J.* p. 490.

[2] It still was in 1954—and possibly later—being used for electrical sheets, steel of exceptional quality.

[3] It later appeared that great difficulties were met at Port Talbot in making the steel they wanted even out of their imported ores.

[4] See *E.H.S.* p. 505.

[5] *Report of the Committee on the Restoration of Land Affected by Iron Ore Working*, H.M.S.O. 1939, pp. 19–24 and 96–102.

was that there were in the east Midlands 82,834 acres of probable reserves, with a possible addition of 20,006; and of this it
was likely that about 80,000 acres would be quarried, the rest
mined. The average yield per acre, mined and quarried, was
25,600 tons in 1937[1] (the Geological Survey had estimated on
a higher average). So the prospective tonnage of ore was about
2·760 m. tons.[2] It was possible to argue that as a large part of
the reserves were in Northamptonshire and the average output
per acre was rather less there, the reserves should be put nearer
2·250 m. tons. This was not the last word by 1946; by that time
the reserves had already been found to be larger. At what rate
was it reasonable to use them?

The plan visualised the use of Midland ore for steel at the
rate of 11 m. tons a year as a maximum. A further 3–3·5 m. tons
would be used for foundry iron.[3] At this rate reserves, as estimated in 1939, would have lasted for 150–200 years. This was
beyond all recent precedents, as the shift in the sources, foreign
as well as domestic, from which this country has drawn iron ore
since the beginning of modern steelmaking shows. It was far
longer than the life of a steel plant. Why it became mandatory
in this one case was not explained. Nor, indeed, why the
diminishing returns in these orefields should receive such
emphasis (with no factual support) while diminishing returns
in oversea mines received no recognition at all.[4]

Such then was the background to the decisions that one new
steelworks should be built in Northamptonshire to make
primarily billets, a product which because its price was controlled (for the historical reasons set out earlier)[5] at a relatively

---

[1] 10,882,000 tons of east Midland ore was mined or quarried in 1937, and the
acreage was 425, of which 49 was mined.

[2] The Geological Survey has since revised its 1918 estimate, and its most recent
assessment puts these east Midland ore reserves at 3400 m. tons. Cp. below, pp. 634,
679.

[3] *Rep. by Joint Iron Council* (in *Iron and Steel Industry*, May 1946), p. 44. On a pre-
war basis 3·75–4·4 m. tons of home ore were required for post-war plans in iron
foundries; but some of this had been haematite, some from Cleveland; and after the
war more special irons were to be made from low phosphoric ore, and more in
Scotland (where home ore would *not* be used).

[4] The point was well made by Tew, *Econ. J.* Sept. 1946, p. 490.

[5] See *E.H.S.* pp. 471 sqq.

unprofitable level did not find its way into plans made by firms on their own initiative to the extent that the re-rolling demand might seem to justify. (It will be recalled that the Jarrow scheme was more unattractive because of the decision that this plant should not enter the more profitable finishing trades.) How far the two firms who were to sponsor it were committed, and whether they wanted to be committed, was not shown in the *Report*. They had both very large commitments in other directions which were likely to strain their resources, personal as well as financial.

Although the most dogmatic conclusion in the plan was the extremely limited scope for more steelmaking in the east Midlands, nevertheless the report made much of the fact that 'the main increase in capacity' visualised in the plan 'is in plants based directly on the home ores. The total increase in the Lincolnshire and Northamptonshire areas amounts to almost 60 per cent.' It was, however, only 30 per cent of the new steel-furnace capacity which was to be installed, because in other areas more old capacity was going to be abandoned, unless perchance demands were so high that it was retained. Even so, despite the emphasis of the report on the east Midlands expansion, the capacity of the major older areas was to remain proportionally as important at the fulfilment of the plan as in 1937. It was hardly an accident; indeed, the section dealing with the future of the Scots industry started quite frankly—'It is proposed that in the present developments Scotland shall make provision for the same proportion of the steel production of the country' as in 1937.[1]

The projected distribution of capital expenditure also emphasised the concentration on the larger of the older centres; 63 per cent of the expenditure was to be in South Wales, the North-east Coast and Scotland, 24 per cent in Lincolnshire and Northamptonshire.[2]

The contrast between the inter-regional rigidity of the plan

---

[1] *Rep. B.I.S.F.* p. 19.

[2] The figures were South Wales, £41 m.; North-east Coast, £35 m.; Scotland, £29 m.; North-west Coast, £1·3 m.; Sheffield, £5·5 m.; Lancashire, Flintshire, Staffordshire, etc., £17 m.; Lincolnshire, £19·2 m.; Northamptonshire, £20 m. Total, £168 m. (*Rep. B.I.S.F.* p. 13).

and the proposals for new works and for rationalising within regions was striking. The *Report* showed, directly or by implication, and presumably its authors were aware of this, that many of the sites at which important expansions were to take place could not enjoy minimum or near-minimum costs in the use of the raw materials on which they would be based. As was emphasised in the book to which this is a sequel, plants could not all use the cheapest raw materials. But that was not the issue.

Table 17. *Distribution of steel ingot making, 1937, 1946 and (as planned) 1953*[a]

	Output in 1937		Capacity in 1946	New building	Net addition to 1946	Future capacity	
	(thousand tons)	%	(thousand tons)	(thousand tons)	capacity	(thousand tons)	%
S. Wales	2,629	20·2	3,000	850	250	3,250	20·4
N.E. Coast	2,825	21·7	3,050	1,100	200	3,250	20·4
Scotland	1,895	14·6	2,000	1,100	300	2,300	14·5
N.W. Coast	385	3·0	360	—	−110	250	1·6
Sheffield	1,739	13·4	2,100	200	—	2,100	13·2
Lancs, Flint, etc.	1,072	8·3	1,000	675	150	1,150	7·2
Staffs, etc.	702	5·4	700	250	−50	650	4·1
Lincs	1,299	10·0	1,350	825	275	1,625	10·2
Northants	439	3·4	540	835	835	1,375	8·6
Total	12,984	100·0	14,100	5,835	1,850	15,950	100·0

[a] Based on Table 11 in *Rep. B.I.S.F.* p. 24. The output in 1937, and the percentages, are added. The different increases in capacity during the war will be observed. The North-east Coast had lost a little ground to South Wales during the war, and the new plans confirmed this. Sheffield was to make no further advance—naturally. The Lancashire figure for 1937 included the output of ingots for rolling at the Crewe works, which, however, was given up before the war; hence the fall of the Lancashire percentage registers a change in 1937–8.

The discussion of the project for a new Scots works implied the desirability of siting a works using imported ore on deep water.[1] The passage concerning the site of the new strip mill went further; it emphasised that for cheap production it 'should be on a seabord with the necessary facilities for handling suitably sized vessels' (but it stopped short of mentioning that Port Talbot was not large enough to accommodate vessels over 7000 tons).[2] The *Report* drew attention to some of the drawbacks

[1] *Ibid.* p. 19.   [2] *Ibid.* p. 14.

of the Shotton site, where John Summers were to increase the capacity of their strip mill, replace and expand their steel-melting capacity, and add blast furnaces. 'Shotton is not situated in so favourable a position for the assembly of the raw materials, coking coal and ore, as some of the other coastal plants,[1] and it is visualised that the plant will operate on a rather higher proportion of scrap than for the country as a whole.'[2] The drawbacks are manifest; ore had to come to Birkenhead and then by rail, coking coal from Lancashire where it was costly to mine, or from north Staffordshire, or from farther afield. Equally it was not a good site for the use of scrap; there was no local supply, hence in the scrap price schedules deliveries to Shotton were above the normal. If the wartime manner of keeping scrap prices down, by monopoly action, continued, the mixing of a lot of scrap with a little dear pig iron might give a nominally low raw-material cost for steel. From a national standpoint the scheme meant a commitment to use ore, coke and scrap in large quantities at a site where it was expensive to collect all three. The Shotton proposals were a natural consequence of the decision to build a strip mill there in 1936; a warning of the danger of choosing a high-cost site for the new process. Ironically the Shotton project was an almost isolated instance in the plan—apart from the Margam scheme, which would displace many small open-hearth shops making steel and tinplate bars—of a step to increase integration of processes.[3]

The *Report* drew attention to the lack of balance in some of the newest British plants; Ebbw Vale and Cardiff both made too little steel for their rolling mills, and at both, the *Report* said, capacity could not be sufficiently increased; hence ingots would

---

[1] It is one of the idiosyncrasies of the *Report* that works in Scotland, the North-east Coast and South Wales are all labelled as coastal area works, though, of course, Consett, Ebbw Vale, Dalzell and Clydebridge, to name no others, were no more 'coastal' than Scunthorpe.

[2] *Rep. B.I.S.F.* p. 21.

[3] Although the argument is a strong one that because of the initial error in locating the strip mill the steelworks and blast furnaces had to follow, it is striking that one of the most impressive United States strip mills (the Irvine works, near Pittsburgh) is a pure re-rolling plant receiving slabs from other United States Steel Corporation sources.

be brought from other west Wales works and for Ebbw Vale from Lincolnshire. It also emphasised forcibly one weakness, not the major one, in the proposals for making sheets and tin-plates in South Wales. The intention, foreshadowed in the early discussion, was to carry out the finishing processes, including cold reduction, at three plants each at some distance from the hot strip mill at Port Talbot; one near Llanelly, one near Swansea, and the third Lysaghts works at Newport. (Here a three-stand mill 'recently installed' was to be provided with more powerful drives and more ancillary equipment to retain the firm's trade in motor-car sheets.) 'There can be no doubt', the *Report* stated, 'on technical grounds and on the basis of economy that the lowest capital expenditure and operating costs would be obtained by the integration' of hot and cold rolling. But 'it is thought that it might be undesirable to concentrate so large a part of the sheet and tin plate trade in... Ebbw Vale and Port Talbot, with the resulting movement of population and loss of industry in many villages and towns'.[1] Was the *Report* inviting someone else to argue that what was most economic was also in this case desirable?

At this one point where the *Report* declared that the proposed compromise would lead to avoidably higher costs it could have argued that it was following Government policy. How far did the plan as a whole by compromises in the interest of existing sites and areas sacrifice lower future costs while lessening the immediate outlay and disturbance? The *Report* emphasised the extent to which, in order to get big units the plan was in fact proposing the displacing of mixed collections of plant, some of which had costs not appreciably higher than those of the pro-posed new plant. 'Unless this issue is faced, as it has been, the reconstruction is a patchwork job and does not achieve the best long term result. Further...on balance the (future) changes of cost are almost certain to involve a relative worsening of the position of the older plants.' It was admirable doctrine. But clearly the number of works at which the plan visualised expensive modernisation was such that it ruled out economies of large scale of the kind enjoyed not only in America but in north-

[1] *Rep. B.I.S.F.* pp. 15–16.

west Europe.[1] The comparison was not discussed in the *Report* though the point was picked up by some of the less popular critics, notably in the *Economic Journal*. A plan for so much 're-equipment *de luxe*' could not be regarded as mainly a plan of improvisation for quick results or because capital was scarce. It did not look forward to rapid concentration at fewer, better (in some instances new) sites. On an optimistic estimate the plan promised an ultimate average output of 600,000 tons a year sometime after 1953. The *Report* gave the illuminating cost data referred to earlier which[2] purported to show that total costs in new plants were less than prime costs in the plants producing the 20 per cent (for some products 40 per cent) of output with higher costs. The figures were not in logic conclusive; for this context what is most striking is that they gave no indication of the variation of costs in a new plant according to location, scale of production, scrap/pig-iron ratio, steelmaking process, or degree of integration. In showing, however, how greatly the cost of new plant had risen—much more than the cost of labour —it might have suggested, but in fact did not, that the case for radical change was for the time being less strong than before the war except where, in addition to cost reductions due to new plant, there could also be cost reductions from lower costs in buying and assembling raw materials.

The final section of the *Report* dealt with the phasing of the plan to insure that the urgent things came first, that there was the minimum interference with production, and that 'the major items are reasonably spaced according to plant making capacity'. Priorities were to go to some patching which would give quick results, and to some which would give some doomed works 7-10 years more life, and to plant needed for new products (especially wide-strip and wide-flanged beams, which were 'urgent national needs' and 'essential for the export

---

[1] *The Report* (p. 31) gave information concerning the size of new steelworks proposed which were slightly different from those suggested at the end of 1944, but not larger. 'The steel-melting plants proposed have an output of between 600,000 and 800,000 tons per annum. In a few cases a start will be made with 400,000 tons, and there is one cold metal plant of 250,000 tons which will be an efficient unit based primarily on scrap.'

[2] Above, p. 90, n. 2.

trade'). On the other hand, what could only be done slowly— and anything requiring new houses—must come late; in particular, the projects put into the plan by the planners, such as the new plant in Northamptonshire. Moreover, while the work to be done at once must be decided on at once (much was already under way), the timing of deferred or newly conceived jobs could be left till later. The amount started would be governed partly by the limited supply of steelworks machinery; the *Report* discussed the proper size of the industry which supplied this on the assumption that peak demands for machinery (as for steel) were satisfied by imports. Everything obviously had been thought of.

The most conspicuously weak part of the *Report* was the first, dealing with the future demand, but it was also the least relevant. Home demand, it was suggested, would be 13 m. ingot tons in 1953, compared with the 14 m. to 14·5 m. tons in 1950 (i.e. five years after the war) which was the 1944 figure.[1] The criticism that this had been too high was tacitly accepted. Exports were put at 3 m. ingot tons; the industry would aim not at a higher than pre-war figure, but at exports of higher average value. Assuming home demand would not normally be at its peak they took 15·5 m. tons as the average total demand, of which 500,000 tons could be got from imports.[2] Whether if demand fell the imports would be reduced before home production was reduced was not discussed; but there seemed to be no rational basis for the import figure other than as a sort of cushion. Home demand was projected on a graph, which showed an approach surprisingly simple-minded for this *Report*. A trend was projected from the curve of the five-year moving average from 1910 to before the war. The war demand was neglected, because this procedure could be used with approximate success to link consumption before 1914 with consumption in the 'black decade' and in the thirties (including the depression), it was blandly assumed that history would, as it were, repeat itself.[3] This was inviting the charge of restriction. But it exercised no governing effect on the plan; an upper limit set by demand had

[1] Above, p. 74.   [2] *Rep. B.I.S.F.* p. 10.
[3] *Ibid.* pp. 8–9.

little part to play so long as investment was to be limited because of scarcity of resources by priorities and licences; and as the *Report* itself said the programme 'does not mean that a 15 m. ton output could not be appreciably exceeded if necessary'. Part of the capacity billed for elimination as inefficient 'could be retained for a further period'; and for the later stages of the plan 'readjustment in the plan could be effected'. The plan, after all, was not final and irrevocable.

Time alone would show its mutability. Few of its readers were able to criticise any of it save its odd assessment of demand. Immediate interest centred naturally on the Government's attitude. Steel House had presented the first planning government with their first plan. What would they make of it? First they submitted it to an inter-departmental committee, whose membership and terms of reference, of course, were undisclosed. Rumour had it that the technical expert called in to help was one of the Federation planners. The economist consulted was not one of those who had been in on the earlier discussions about post-war steel. The advantage of the fresh mind was thus sought with discrimination. Mr Lyttleton said the 'expert committee' had found the plan 'complete and adequate', and he no doubt knew.[1] The long period between the delivery of the plan in December 1945 and its publication the following May reflected not the intensity of the committee's work but the Government's difficulty in deciding what to do about nationalisation. When they had decided, and their policy was debated, they too blessed the plan. Sir Andrew Duncan could claim legitimately that the plan, for whose preparation 'the best combined brains and technical advice in the country were available, had met with no serious criticism in the debate'.[2] 'It is a valuable report', said Mr Morrison. Neither he nor the Minister of Supply, Mr Wilmot, had 'any fundamental quarrel with it.... It is an able and valuable contribution to the discussion of the problem.'[3] By this time it was hardly a discussion any longer, for it was known that twenty-seven schemes in the plan (costing £16 m.) had been approved, and licences had

---

[1] *Hansard*, 27 May 1946, c. 857. Mr Lyttleton became Lord Chandos in 1954.
[2] *Ibid.* 28 May 1946, c. 1026.   [3] *Ibid.* 28 May 1946, c. 1108.

been issued in respect of them, and another 40 (to cost £48 m.) had been approved. The first twenty-seven included the beginnings of many of the major schemes, so that the real commitment was greater than these figures showed. It included most of the controversial proposals of the firms, but none of the controversial addition of the planners.[1] Many of the approvals had been given by the Coalition;[2] some had been given since, though Mr Wilmot explained that 'while awaiting the Federation's report I was forced to hold up the approval of schemes which were coming separately from various companies'. He had, however, 'now gone forward with approving all the major schemes which are ready to start'.[3] Priorities, apparently, to the schemes which were first thought of and prepared. The time, he said, had come for decision and action. Had he said that the opportunity for decision had passed it would have been more purely descriptive.

In this first steel debate of the new era, a foretaste of dreary wastes ahead, neither the plan nor any criteria that might be applied to it in whole or in part, were discussed. Neither Government nor Opposition had anything to add or subtract. There were pleas for development areas—Mr Dalton said again 'I insisted on South Wales' for the strip mill—but there was no attempt to assess gains and losses. The fact that two of the North-east Coast companies, Skinningrove and South Durham,

[1] Some details were given in answer to a question in the Commons: *Hansard*, 20 May 1946 (c. 17–19). The 40 included Dalzell. The 27 included (according to the answer) Colvilles' Clydebridge blast furnaces; Dorman Long's ore preparation and unloading plant; G.K.B.'s preliminary work on the Margam site; Lysaght's sheet-mill modernising; electrolytic tinning at Ebbw Vale; John Summer's melting shop; improvements to Whitehead's re-rolling plant; new boilers at Workington; the melting shop and section mills at Appleby Frodingham; tube-work developments at Newport, Clydesdale and Mossend; a new open-hearth melting shop and coke ovens at Corby. The list given was not exhaustive, for as seen above the Consett scheme was sanctioned in part earlier (this was implied in the *Report*, p. 17) and the Darlington light section re-rolling plant also (above, p. 86).

[2] Sir Andrew Duncan asked 'whether it is the case that the bulk of the sanctions had gone through the Building Executive before the General Election'; Mr Wilmot said half had been *sanctioned* before. The other half have started since. A curious evasion. *Hansard*, 27 May 1946, 852.

[3] *Ibid. loc. cit.* The impression emerged that Colvilles had had to wait longer than they liked to get approval for their Dalzell scheme.

whose works 'might have to go out' in the second round of planning, had protested[1] was discussed solely as a token of the need for Government compulsion. There were complaints of restriction—the plan only offered 'a paltry 500,000 tons' more for exports at a cost of £168 m.,[2] and 'We in Scotland believe that in the White Paper the expansion of the steel trade is not sufficient'.[3] Mr Clem Davies showed that he was aware the *Report* was not beyond more refined criticism—'it is nothing but a compromise, and merely patching'—but this sounded like an echo, and like an echo faded out.[4] No one probed into the way in which the plan was put together (though at least one firm whose proposal was accepted, but not ultimately carried out, thought the Federation's experts took remarkably little time in examining it),[5] or asked how the Government chose experts to give advice on these matters. To do so would have been indiscreet on either side of the House; the Government side would not wish to disturb faith in the Government's ability to plan, and the Opposition would not wish to cast doubt on the Federation's wisdom.

It remained to be seen how far the plan, so uncritically accepted, would influence future development, how far the parts injected by the central planning body itself would be carried out, how far the plan would be modified and for what reasons.

[1] *Hansard*, 27 May 1946, c. 844 sqq.

[2] *Ibid.* c. 874, Stanley Evans.

[3] *Ibid.* Alex. Anderson, from Motherwell, c. 899. He was horrified that 'We are faced at the end of the war with a position in which our industry cannot supply the world demand!'

[4] *Ibid.* c. 912. (In *Hansard* the word is, 'patchy', but I am assuming one should read 'patching'.)

[5] Officials of the firm commented vigorously on this to me.

Chapter V

THE FIRST STEEL BOARD
1946–1949

1. PURPOSE AND PERSONS

Little was said at all, in the first post-war debate on the Government's steel policy, about the Control Board which, as seen above, was to bridge the gap between the wartime Steel Control and nationalisation. It was 'to see that the industry is carried on', that it had adequate raw materials despite their scarcity, 'that the modernisation schemes proceed smoothly and rapidly'. It was to be responsible for the regulation of production and distribution, and for advice on prices. And, Mr Wilmot added fatally when he first announced his plan, the Board would 'also act as my advisor on questions arising in the preparation of the scheme of nationalisation'.[1] Advice only, he explained in the later debate, on detailed technical matters.[2] But he had provoked the first short phase of passive resistance. The Federation would not co-operate with the Minister on the Board until the Ministry agreed that the members were not expected individually or collectively to advise on nationalisation,[3] and so long as it took this stand no directors from member firms would join the Board. The Minister after trying to persuade the chairman of the nationalised Iron and Steel Corporation of South Africa to act as chairman,[4] gave way on the point and the Board was finally set up in September.[5]

Its constitution followed the contemporary pattern set, for example, in the 'Working Parties'. The chairman was 'independent'; Mr Wilmot chose Sir Archibald Forbes for the role, the financial director of Spillers, originally an accountant, who

[1] *Hansard*, c. 850–1, and 17 April 1946, 1693.   [2] *Ibid.* 27 May 1946.
[3] *The Times*, 2 Aug. and 19 Aug. 1946.
[4] *Ibid.* 2 Aug. and 19 Aug. 1946.
[5] *Ibid.* 6 Sept. 1946.

had been made deputy permanent secretary of the M.A.P. and later held other M.A.P. offices during the war, and was now looking for fresh fields to conquer. He had the almost indispensable qualification for those called to central administrative office in the steel industry—he was a Scot. His was the only full-time appointment. There were two representatives of the employers, Mr Latham,[1] who was to have been the next President of the Federation, and Mr Mather, who had expressed his resolve to save Skinningrove from extinction; and two representatives of the workers, Mr (now Sir) Lincoln Evans and Mr Callighan, Secretary of the Blast-furnacemen's union, whose main experience was in the north-west, and who had attracted attention late in 1945 by contrasting 'a policy of concentration of production' with 'wise planning' which would 'locate new plant developments in the existing centres of production on a fair basis'.[2] The claims of the old districts and small works would not go unrepresented on the Board. Sir Alan Barlow, formerly deputy secretary of the Treasury, was a second independent member; a third, Sir Amos Ayre, shipbuilder, was appointed later, as a consumer.

The Board's history was unspectacular. No doubt it deliberately kept out of the public eye, and the Government had no wish to dignify it as more than a temporary makeshift. When in the spring of 1949 the members of the Board (except the trade unionists) refused a further term of office, and the staff carried on without its directors, they received their largest bouquet from the Federation.[3] This eulogy was as unqualified as it was lacking in supporting detail when it surveyed the Board's functioning as supervisor of production, development and prices. It was also a classic in the lore of planning of the early post-war type so notably rationalised by Sir Oliver Franks in 1947, a type whose appeal had lost some of its magic by 1949.[4]

[1] Above p. 57.
[2] Quoted by a Special Correspondent in *The Times*, 9 Jan. 1946. He had also said 'it should be compulsory on firms to use a fixed proportion (20 per cent) of home ores in a blast furnace'.
[3] *Stat. Bull.* Oct. 1949.
[4] Above, p. 94.

In this chapter the Federation's analysis of policies and of the Board's part in the industry's life is taken as the starting-point in examining what happened in these formative years. Supervision of production, which meant in effect dealing with scarcities, the development of price policies, and the interplay between planning and development are treated *seriatim*.

2. ADJUSTMENT TO SCARCITY

In supervising production the Board, as the Federation put it, 'acted primarily as the channel through which, in one direction, the industry's requirements were represented to the planning authorities, and, in the other, the industry was kept informed of the national plan'. Planning departments could rest satisfied that the industries' applications for fuel, imports, the use of land, building licences, investment permits, or price changes, 'bore the sanction of an authoritative public body'. It was as though the Federation looked forward to scarcity and rationing for ever, the centraliser's dream. In reverse the Board told the steelmakers at an early stage what demands for steels were likely to develop 'when national programmes were being elaborated...not when orders came flooding in'.

Whether the course of events was profoundly altered by all this is doubtful. There were no overt signs that in handling the manifold scarcities—of steel in general, some kinds of steel in particular (billets, for example, and light re-rolled products, and sheets), imported ore, coke, silica bricks, and so on—it behaved very differently, or more or less effectively, than the earlier organisation. It inherited some of the Ministry officials who had been doing this work for years. In any case these were the dying problems. Its forecasts did not show any marked prescience, either for the near or more distant future. The step forward in production in 1948 was not foreseen, and no sufficiently urgent steps were taken to forestall the pig-iron scarcity of 1950–51 or to avert what was to prove the most serious scarcity in the early fifties, that of plates. Different opinions about this in 1947, which received little public discussion, shed the most interesting light on this aspect of the Board's work.

Within the Board's first year home consumption of steel almost reached the height visualised in the plan as to be reached in 1953,[1] though a substantial part was satisfied from second-hand material. It was recognised that more steel would have been used had it been there. By the end of 1947 steel was, according to the Economic Survey, the 'principal limiting factor'[2] in British industry, and a new estimate of future steel requirements was being made by the central planning body in the Treasury (not the body which made the steel plan). Indeed, the estimates given by the Iron and Steel Board for Marshall Plan forecasts had already lifted the estimated home consumption in 1948 to 14 m. tons, rising to 14·5 m. tons in 1951. The central planners' inclination was to put the 1950 figure much higher, at 16 m. ingot tons. This was based partly on investment plans of some major industries—collieries, shipbuilding, railways, petroleum (which were now submitted to an Investment Programmes Committee)—which included statements of steel requirements, and projections of consumption in user industries based on probable employment and 'average consumption per employee' in different pursuits. This was broadly the method used for the forecast made in 1944 (of which the inquirers of 1947 appear to have found no trace!);[3] but by 1947 the estimates of investment for reconstruction were suffering from the sort of elephantism which infected early wartime estimates, and the whole procedure, followed rigorously, allowed nothing for the possibilities of substitution or economy in use. In a large measure the treatment of the figures was merely a hunch.[4] The Federation pointed out appositely that

[1] This was not clear in the statistics published by the Federation at the time, because these did not show the use of second-hand steel till later.

[2] *Econ. Survey*, 1948, p. 27.

[3] They also projected a curve based on five-year averages (as the Federation did) to confirm their main estimate; but they did not flatten it off (why indeed should they?). Instead of a freehand extension they applied a precise formula. This presumably combined two oddly assorted rises, one due to recovery from the severity of the slump, the other in part to rearmament. The estimate was made on the assumption that rearmament made no difference in 1935–39; but the view was unjustified.

[4] As it had to be; but there are fashions in these things. Some of the detailed forecasts, which were passed to me for comment, seemed grotesquely high, and two at least proved in different ways to have been so. The Coal Board had very

since the war steel was in fact being used as a substitute for other scarce materials, such as timber.[1]

While the high figure was challenged the conclusion that in the immediate future more steel was wanted quickly was universally accepted. This conclusion seemed inescapable. The allocation scheme had broken down under the strain of post-war working and the Chancellor announced it would be revised;[2] the authorising departments had authorised more than their allocations, and steelmakers consequently could not be found to honour all the authorisations; orders could not be placed, deliveries were badly delayed. Such circumstances breed panic ordering, and panic stocking; the alarms of late 1947 doubtless exaggerated the real scarcity.

The prospects of getting any more steel quickly were, however, rated very differently by different experts early in 1948, and the decisions then taken, or not taken, were probably in a small way a watershed.

In the export and production drive inaugurated after Britain had been forced to end the convertibility of sterling in September 1947 the target for steel ingot production in 1948 was set at 14 m. tons.[3] From September to November 1947, however, ingot output already exceeded this rate (it was 14·1 m. tons, compared with 13·1 m. tons a year earlier), and the question was asked what would prevent a further advance through 1948, when large steel supplies were so anxiously sought.[4] The orthodox answer was that the high output of steel ingots late in 1947 (which was improved upon early in 1948) depended upon the use of stocks of pig iron and scrap; the output of the former could not be much raised because coke was scarce and poor in quality, while the chance of getting more home scrap was limited and German scrap seemed impossible to extract.

The unorthodox view, which hailed from within the industry,

ambitious forecasts for its investments; and the railways were to use 750,000 tons a year on wagons, and 1·3 m. tons finished steel in all. Had they not been limited by restraints on investment they could hardly have reached such figures. But to suggestions that these were high figures the reply tended to be: Perhaps, but if *these* demands don't mature others are sure to be bigger.

[1] *Stat. Bull.* Feb. 1948, p. 3.   [2] *The Times*, 15 Oct. 1947.
[3] *Ibid.* 13 Sept. 1947.   [4] *Ibid.* 26 Nov. 1947.

though how widely it was held was hard to judge,[1] was that there was a quicker way to increase output than was being followed; that in view of the greater scarcity of capital equipment for all purposes than had been expected the right course was to forgo for the time being some of the radical reconstruction of the industry according to the plan, and substitute a policy of increasing output from existing works by jobs of a 'comparatively minor nature', which would fall far short of building even a 'greenfields Department', let alone a greenfields works.[2] Naturally the principal greenfields works, in South Wales, must go forward because of the need for sheets and because it was well under way. But, the argument was, output at most existing works could be increased by 20 per cent, in some cases by much more, by balancing the various stages. 'Most cogging mills in the country could do 30-40 per cent more without alteration to the mill proper by paying attention to regular feeding of well-heated ingots.' Finishing mills, too, could be used more intensively; they might need more heating furnaces or cooling equipment. Steel-furnace capacities could be greatly increased in rebuilding, outputs could be raised by using better fuels, larger ladles, better charging equipment; blast-furnace outputs could often be increased if the profiles were improved on relining, if hearths were enlarged, more tuyères introduced, better gas offtakes installed, and if the furnaces were driven harder, all of which promised lower coke consumption per ton of iron.[3] There were also some idle furnace stacks, which could be activated if provided with a little additional ancillary equipment.[4]

[1] It was sponsored, though not publicly, by one of the leading technical experts of the industry; I was informed that the view was in its general aspects if not necessarily in all details supported by at least two substantial firms, including one of the six largest firms.

[2] I am quoting from a survey shown to me in Nov. 1947.

[3] There were a few striking instances in which outputs were increased and coke consumption reduced by these methods. One leading scientist connected with the industry whom I consulted on this expressed the view that coke consumption was higher than need be in a large part of the industry because the managers played for safety by using too much.

[4] I knew of four; but there were no doubt more. It seemed to me right they should be activated though I thought the extra equipment might be delayed.

The possibility that 'patching' in this sense might be the right policy had been pointed out by one commentator on the plan when it was published. His term for it was 'urgent improvisation'.[1] Now it was reinforced by the experience that all capital works (including new steel plant) were being delayed by scarcities of materials, components and the like, and were rising in cost, and becoming fruitful very slowly. It was reinforced too by what was learned after the war from the records of German steel companies of the development of Ruhr steel-making under the Hitler régime when these Western works were starved of capital for the benefit of other, strategically more remote, areas. The response in the Ruhr had been to balance the capacities of different parts of plants up to the level of the most productive section by relatively small developments and makeshifts, the result being higher outputs than from equivalent units of plant in this country, and reduced costs. The same policy was adopted there after the war.[2]

Success in more rapidly expanding steel output seemed to depend primarily on getting more pig iron. There was a disposition to say that coke provided an upper limit, but that need not have been so if the Government and Coal Board had been

[1] 'If the resources available...are sufficiently limited there is almost no case where "patching" would not be more advantageous...than building on a new site...but the *Report* does not appear to base any of its recommendations on the assumption that the aftermath of war makes it necessary to discount the future more heavily...the expenditure of £168 m. in 7½ years resulting in a net increase of only 2 m. tons a year...cannot seriously be treated as a plan for urgent improvisation' (B. Tew, in *Econ. J.* Sept. 1946, p. 491).

[2] Mr G. A. V. Russell (see *E.H.S.* p. 443) showed me extremely interesting data based on an early visit to Germany by some members of the steel industry after the war. I was able later to observe the development of balancing practices in German works after the war. Thus at Oberhausen in 1949 I found that two ingots (at different stages of reduction, naturally) were being rolled in one pair of cogging rolls at once; they informed me that the steam engine in use had plenty of reserve power, which they now were using; the engine was old and they were prepared to risk breaking it. It was still working in the autumn of 1953, but foundations for a new cogging mill were being laid nearby. This works also increased capacity at various stages by, for example, top pressure in blast furnaces, used only when high outputs were required; by preheating liquid iron by an oxygen lance before charging to converters, by blowing the converters with part oxygen (which diminished the length of blow by 20 per cent), and in other ways.

persuaded to remove the obstacles.[1] The steel industry was getting less than its allocation at the end of 1947.[2] First-rate coking coal was being used for purposes other than coking,[3] and more coke ovens providing domestic coke could have been used to make furnace coke. Some transfers occurred.[4] It was a simple problem of priorities.[5] After coke shortage ore shortage was pleaded; if there *were* more coke, you could hardly use more home ore, because there was a scarcity of wagons, and because it used such a lot of fuel.[6]

While it was staunchly held that nothing more could be done over pig iron to increase supplies the plan was departed from freely to increase steel melting capacity, as will be seen later, by uncovenanted expansions of melting shops. This had the effect, which it was sometimes said the resistance over short-term blast-furnace development was intended to avoid, of perpetuating the subdivision of production, and so in effect putting new obstacles in the way of concentration and radical modernisation, without providing a solid basis for a larger output.[7]

When the Economic Survey for 1948 appeared, in February, the November forecast of 14 m. tons was repeated. But by this time the Federation, though not yet the Board, was beginning to have second thoughts. In May the target was raised to 14·5 m. tons;[8] in the end output was 14·88 m. tons. This, however, was due almost entirely to greater success than was

[1] There were regular liaison meetings between the Federation, the Coal Board, and the Ministry of Fuel and Power.

[2] Coke quality was poor also. Under the stimulus of public discussion coke supplies for blast furnaces improved at the end of 1947.

[3] According to the *Plan for Coal* (Oct. 1950), p. 55, out of 110·2 m. tons of coal produced in 1948 within the types suitable for carbonisation (i.e. for gas or furnace coke) 49·7 m. tons were sold to the carbonisation industries.

[4] *Nat. Coal Board Ann. Rep. for 1948*, p. 77.

[5] But it was not usually so described by those who talked about it in public. Increase was often related to the possibility of building new coke ovens. It was desirable to build more coke ovens, and I had the impression that the National Coal Board hung fire a little on this. There was much talk of silica bricks as a limiting factor on coke-oven building—which I gathered later proved to be exaggerated. But for emergency supplies of coke all these matters were irrelevant.

[6] This elegant roundabout is based on an unpublished official document.

[7] Little seems to have been done by improvisation to meet rolling mill bottlenecks; for example, to increase billet output quickly by unconventional means.

[8] *Hansard*, 13 May 1948, c. 2278.

expected in getting more scrap from home sources, partly by a vigorous scrap drive which had surprising success in the steelworks themselves.[1] Imports of scrap (800,000 tons) fell a little short of the Survey's forecast, but in the last two months of 1948 they reached a rate of almost 1·35 m. tons a year. They had been released, in a sense, by Germany's currency reform; but before they flowed there were several months of United States–United Kingdom negotiations, supplemented by O.E.E.C. negotiations.[2]

So by the end of 1948 steel was more plentiful and raw material stocks (pig iron and scrap), which fell (at a declining rate) through 1947 and the first quarter of 1948, were rising,[3] to that there was no immediate pressure on steelmakers to be provident over the provision of pig iron or ore. This situation lasted through 1949; raw material stocks continued to rise. By the end of 1949 demand for steel was also less exigent. Hence although the Federation had been led by the end of 1948 to accept a steel ingot capacity of 18 m. tons as a target, and to start thinking of a second five-year plan to achieve this figure,[4]

---

[1] Pig-ron output in 1948 was 9,276,000 tons compared with the forecast of 9,200,000 tons; but consumption in steelmaking was 31,000 tons less than the forecast 7·1 m. tons. More went into iron foundries than the survey proposed. (Cp. *Stat. Yearbook B.I.S.F.* and *Econ. Survey*, 1948, pp. 27–8). The *Economist* attributed the greater output to 'technical advance, the team spirit, and determined efforts in the procurement of raw materials (*Econ.* 15 Jan. 1949). Home scrap provided 4,550,000 tons instead of a forecast 3,700,000. With the derived circulating scrap this will have provided rather over 1 m. tons of extra raw material for steel. An interesting earlier assessment was made in *Stat. Bull.* Apr. 1948, pp. 3–4.

[2] *Econ.* 9 Oct. 1948, gives an account of these discussions. O.E.E.C. set up finally an *ad hoc* committee to propose allocations of scrap from West Germany and other O.E.E.C. countries. The agreement between the United Kingdom and United States Governments proposing the setting up of such a committee in which the United States should be a full member, together with recommendations to be sent to the Military Governors in the Zones was published in an *Exchange of Notes on Ferrous Scrap Exports*, Cmd. 7938 (1948). Prior to currency reform the amount of commercial scrap coming forward was negligible; and to the evident annoyance of the Federation the United States–United Kingdom Control Commission was offering facilities for the import of 1½ m. tons of Swedish ore into Germany, a policy presumably for reducing coke consumption in pig iron. Cp. *Stat. Bull. loc. cit.*

[3] The turning point was the second quarter of 1948. Cp. *ibid.* July 1948, p. 2.

[4] *Ibid.* Sept. 1948. This figure, it explained, was the outcome of a new Government survey of demand; the situation, it explained, was now easier to assess.

it also expressed confidence that 'all foreseeable demands' could be met, though there were still scarcities of particular products such as sheets, tinplate and wire rod. Imports were easier to get, and were no doubt expected to fill up the gaps. The Government still assessed the demand higher than the steelmakers.[1] The current was, however, against them. The first E.C.E. steel report, it has been seen, foreshadowed capacity ahead of demand.[2] Demand in some countries was not sufficient by autumn 1949 to sustain output.[3] In February 1950 the Federation was agreeing with the E.C.E. that scarcity and dearness of steel since the war had had the effect in Europe (but not, one was left to infer, in this country) of encouraging many steel development plans 'which will inevitably result in inefficient and dispersed production'.[4] Two months later the steelworkers' trade union, whose secretary Lincoln Evans had been on the Steel Board, declared in its journal that the 'steel shortage, except for sheets and tinplates, is virtually over, and the Government should now discontinue, or at least modify, controls for which...there is no further need.[5] Home consumption of new steel when demand thus seemed to be satiated was very close indeed to the figure forecast in 1944; it was 14·0 m. tons in 1949, 13·7 m. tons in 1950.

The new trend in market development, which occurred after the Board had retired, was a more potent influence on invest-

[1] *Econ.* 15 Oct. 1949, pp. 861–2. The Federation stated at frequent intervals the case *against* expecting too large a permanent demand for steel. Thus in Feb. 1948 (*Stat. Bull.* p. 3), 'Home deliveries of finished steel will doubtless be insufficient to meet all potential requirements: for demand has been swollen by wartime arrears of maintenance and development work as well as by the shortages of other materials. (Steel is replacing timber for pit-props and railway sleepers and in the construction of railway wagons: while the shortage of glass containers has increased the demand for tinplate)'. In the *Stat. Bull.* for Mar. 1948, the B.I.S.F. argued that the extra steel estimated as needed for the new export targets of Nov. 1947 was 500,000 tons; this would be reduced by the revision of the export targets in the *Econ. Survey* for 1948. Output of steel was, however, to be over 1 m. tons higher in 1947, so how would steel be a limiting factor?
[2] Above, p. 145.   [3] Above, p. 145.
[4] This illuminating sentence from *Stat. Bull.* Jan. 1950, was quoted by *Econ.* 25 Feb. 1950.
[5] Quoted from *Man and Metal* by *Econ.* 22 Apr. 1950. Earlier requests that the control should go—rejected possibly on the advice of the Board—'may have been a little premature'.

ment than the suggestions earlier for getting the most out of existing capacity. The Federation seized the occasion to correct the misconception that attributed post-war scarcity to lack of capacity, when it was 'primarily due to raw material deficiencies'.[1] It did not point out the precarious character of Britain's scrap supply, of which 2 m. tons a year now came from Germany, and the expansion of pig-iron production and capacity seems to have been allowed to lag. The significance of this was not immediately evident.

3. FIXING PRICES

(a) State subsidies ended

The Federation in its eulogy of the first Board gave especial prominence to the Board's contribution to price-fixing. The Board was asked by the Government 'to examine afresh the principles according to which prices and costs had been related to each other, to decide whether they were still valid, and if so, in what ways their application needed revision',[2] and it stayed in office after its appointed two years to complete this review. When it had at length completed the task, in the spring of 1949, the Board agreed with the pre-war Federation-I.D.A.C. procedure in fixing maximum prices, which (as seen earlier) consisted of adding to the average costs of efficient firms 'standard margins' for depreciation and profit. This agreement must have been gratifying to the Federation; and the only new thing which the Board did in this connexion was to suggest new standard margins, which should be reviewed again in two years. One of the considerations which the Board took into account was the need for a 'reasonable return on capital'. What was deemed a 'reasonable return', and what level of working in relation to capacity was taken as normal in calculating the standard margin per ton which would provide this as well as adequate depreciation and obsolescence were not disclosed.[3] Some changes in the

[1] Quoted by *Econ.* 25 Feb. 1950, p. 455.
[2] *Stat. Bull.* Oct. 1949, p. 5.
[3] To assume a high level of normal utilisation—say 90 per cent of capacity—might yield relatively low margins: there were critics who suspected the margins were consistently (and still in 1960) too low on this account.

margins, not changed it was said since before the war, were no doubt desirable. The specific changes in the margins were not stated. There were, it was indicated, increases of some on highly finished products and reductions of others.[1] But altered margins had less effect on prices than a second change made at the same time, at the instance, according to the Federation, of the Government and the industry, and not on the Board's initiative. This change was the removal of state subsidies on imports of raw materials. The Board's part in this was to decide how much prices must be raised to carry this intention out.

The main result of the Board's price review was the biggest jump in steel prices since the war, as Table 18 shows. In one obvious sense this reflected a decision that prices should cover costs. But the Federation accepted that broadly before the war, in the sense that prices should cover *average* costs. What was the Board's attitude, in accepting the broad basis of Federation-I.D.A.C. policy, towards all the other elements emerging in pre-war policies, above all the spreading of exceptionally high raw-material costs, the depression of scrap prices, the maintenance of uniform delivered prices, and the elimination of price competition? Before turning to this it is necessary to trace the movements of costs, in forecast and fact, during the reconversion and reconstruction years, and the immediate adaptation of price policy when war ended, which provided the background against which judgements were made by the Board.

The changes in prices and the main cost items from 1944 to 1949 are shown in Table 18.

When the Board took office—it held its first meeting in October 1946—the chief wartime price-control innovation, the Prices Fund, had already been wound up and well-nigh forgotten. The Federation was anxious early in 1945 that prices should be fixed after the war as close as possible to 'permanent

---

[1] When Mr Strauss announced the withdrawal of subsidies and raising of prices in the House of Commons he stated that the new prices were 'designed to provide no more than a reasonable return on capital employed in each section of the industry, and on the best calculation possible' (Ministers usually think it necessary to call those available 'the best possible') 'will give no increase but probably some reduction in the total profits of the Iron and Steel Industry'.

Table 18. *Material and labour costs and prices, 1944–49*
(per ton, except first two columns)

	Level of rail freights	Earnings per hour	Coke		Iron ore[a]				Basic pig iron		Heavy melting scrap		Soft basic billets		Heavy plates		Sheets	
					Home		Imported											
		d.	*s.*	*d.*	*s.*	*d.*	*s.*	*d.*	*s.*	*d.*	*s.*	*d.*	*s.*	*d.*	*s.*	*d.*	*s.*	*d.*
Dec. 1944	100	31·3	54	0	4	10	84	0	115	6	72	3	250	0	308	0	455	0
Mar. 1945	100	32·1	54	0	4	10	72	0	130	6	72	3	250	0	308	0	455	0
Dec. 1945	100	32·1	—		4	10	72	0	150	6	72	6	257	6	314	6	—	
Aug. 1946	108	34·6	58	6	5	5	56	2	155	0	72	11	262	6	319	6	497	6
Oct. 1947	134	37·4	58	6	7	2	55	1	169	6	75	4	277	6	348	6	521	0
Jan. 1948	134	38·5	54	6	7	9	55	2	178	6	75	4	282	6	353	0	521	0
June 1948	134	39·7	67	10	7	9	57	2	182	6	75	4	287	6	353	0	521	0
Aug. 1948	134	40·8	70	4	7	9	57	2	185	0	75	4	287	6	—	6	521	0
Apr. 1949	134	41·4	70	4	8	2	57	10	197	6	75	4	341	6	414	6	601	0
Apr. 1949 as percentage of Dec. 1944	134	132	132		170		80		171		104		137		135		132	
As percentage of 1937	155	200	220		200		255		210		114		217		195		191	

[a] The ore figures are annual averages. The imported ore figures are C.I.F. values: the home ore figures are average annual values returned to the Ministry of Fuel and Power. The 1949 percentage figures relate to 1945 ore prices.

post-war costs', so that the price level then established could be stabilised. It would then, the theory went, not mislead long-range planners or provoke speculative buying, and it should contribute to the avoidance of booms and slumps.[1] This policy required that prices should be raised, though for various reasons the Federation wanted to restrict the increase to the minimum. There was the risk of future overseas competition, the myth that steel price increases are inflationary, and fear of the political repercussions from raising prices. By the end of the war (it has been seen) costs were well above prices. The 'Central Fund' (a Ministry fund) was running into deficit, and prices were then being kept down by subsidy.[2] Some of the excess of costs (but not all) would last. How much of it would become 'normal'? That was one of the problems to be faced. It was still thought of, of course, in terms of 'average costs'. But the Federation also expressed its hope that the 'price artificialities' introduced during the war to meet cost abnormalities, to allow the stabilising of prices irrespective of cost trends and ensure maximum output during the war, should be dispensed with. It would be wrong, they argued (because it was not consistent with rewarding efficiency and enterprise), to subsidise high-cost plants after the war, and needless to compensate firms for using abnormal raw materials because within a short time they should have access to normal supplies (above all of imported ore). Hence the Prices Fund, used to ensure that firms not earning their pre-war (standard) profit did not make losses and earned something nearer to (though not above) their standard, should be dispensed with. These two aims—to fix prices as low as possible in relation to 'permanent post-war costs', and to get rid of 'artificialities'—determined the pattern of the Federation's policy, because it was only possible to do the first by maintaining some state subsidy where abnormal high material costs continued, and the second by changing the form of subsidy. Hence the proposal was that certain exceptional costs,

---

[1] Above, p. 39. Mr Shone was well known to be an advocate of using interest rate changes and avoiding price changes as a means of controlling the trade cycle. (Cp. his contribution to *Some Modern Business Problems* (1935), pp. 218–19.)

[2] Above, p. 34.

in particular the high freights on imported ores and the high cost of imported scrap, should be defrayed by direct state subsidies. The extent of the first of these was to be based on the controversial forecast whose foundation has been examined earlier that freights on imported ore might be expected to fall to 50 per cent above pre-war.[1] The extent of the second would of course be determined by the gap between prices of home and imported scrap. It was further assumed that the practice of keeping scrap prices low should be perpetuated; but since as a result pig-iron prices must always be much higher than scrap prices an ingenious proposal was made that the levy-subsidy device evolved before the war to spread the burden of high-cost imported raw materials should be used in a new role, namely, to spread some of the advantage enjoyed by steelmakers who used a high proportion of cheap scrap. This would allow the greatest advantage to be taken of the cheapness of scrap in keeping steel prices low.

These proposals became the basis on which the Ministry of Supply, retaining its wartime functions, began to fix prices after the war; they provided the starting-point for the Board in its comprehensive review.

The state subsidies were conceived from the start as temporary. It was recognised in the industry early in 1945 that to keep imported ore prices down helped firms using imported ore to the disadvantage of those using home ore. Hence the steelmakers did not wish at that time, under the influence possibly of Macdiarmid, to deal with this problem by a levy-subsidy arrangement, since this would have been in their view obviously unfair to home ore firms who were handicapped by the high cost of fuel. The state subsidy seemed to offer advantages for all steelmakers by keeping prices lower than they would be if all costs were to be covered by price; presumably this, viewed against the background of the boom and slump after 1918, reconciled home ore users to the additional benefit secured from the subsidy (as was supposed temporarily) by their rivals.

There was no change in this temporary subsidy arrangement until June 1948. Imported ore prices, it has been seen in

[1] Above pp. 77, 101.

Table 18, remained far higher than had been optimistically forecast; and the Government had paid close on £1 a ton subsidy on all the ore brought in. It was decided therefore in June 1948 to give the subsidy only on the excess of freights above 100 per cent over the pre-war standard. Even then the burden remained heavy. On ore freights alone there was still a subsidy of 14s. per ton of ore, which the Federation said in its averaging way amounted to 10s. 6d. per ton of steel if spread over the whole steel supply.[1] By the time the decision to eliminate the subsidies was announced, however, other elements in the subsidy bill were rising; above all the new availability of German scrap at commercial prices, which revolutionised the steel supply in the United Kingdom by the end of 1948, involved a heavy and growing subsidy, and there were growing imports of steel at high prices. The bill rose as shown in Table 19. According to Mr Strauss, who had succeeded Mr Wilmot as Minister of Supply, the loss in the first five classes would have reached £25 m. in 1949–50, if no change were made, and half of this would be on account of scrap.

Table 19. *Exchequer losses in respect of steel supplies*
(thousand pounds)

	1946–47	1947–48	1948–49 (est.)
Imported ore freights	6·775	7·050	6·000
Imported scrap	206	367	5·410
Imported pig iron	6	66	766
Home ore	665	792	900
Imported semis	1·600	1·900	2·574
Imported finished steel	300	914	3·150
Total	9·552	11·099	18·800

This represented an average cost of almost £2 a ton of finished steel, which was now to be incorporated in steel prices. The manner in which this should be done was in a sense the most significant decision of the Board. For in their turn they had recourse to a characteristic Federation levy-subsidy averaging arrangement.

[1] *Stat. Bull.* June 1948, p. 4.

(b) 'Price artificialities' retained

The desire expressed by steelmakers in 1945 to get away from the 'price artificialities' of the war did not, it has been seen, extend to getting away from the equalising devices introduced before the war. On the contrary, they found in these a second means of keeping down prices despite the rising cost of pig iron. The disparity between scrap and pig-iron prices had been widened during the war; for though pig-iron prices rose proportionately less than steel prices, scrap prices had been kept down even more drastically.[1] By the end of the war, however, more was being 'lost' in making pig iron than in making steel, and the payments from the Prices Fund on account of pig iron were consequently high. The largest readjustment of relative prices needed before the Prices Fund could be dropped therefore was an increase of pig-iron prices, the first step of which occurred in March 1945,[2] the second following in a general revision of steel prices in December. Hence the first post-war price adjustments further widened the gap between pig-iron and scrap prices. The process was to continue for some years, as Table 18 shows. The price of scrap rose between 1944 and 1949 by 3s., the price of pig iron by 82s. a ton. (Even so, the margins allowed on pig iron were low, it is stated, compared with those for finished steel, and lower in practice than in intention because adjustments came *after* costs had risen.[3])

It was evident by the end of the war that this would discriminate against those steelworks which used a lot of pig iron and in favour of those who used a lot of scrap, as it had, on a smaller scale, in 1937–8.[4] So the Federation and the Control urged that when basic pig-iron prices were raised in 1945 the users should have the levy they paid per ton of ingot reduced by

[1] Above, pp. 21 sqq.
[2] *The Times*, 9 Mar. 1945. Pig-iron prices alone were raised on this occasion.
[3] It has to be emphasised that margins were not published; and when important firms state that margins were less good on one product than on another those who fixed the prices may (and sometimes do) say this was because the firm's practice was more efficient for the one than for the other. In the absence of full details some uncertainty is unavoidable.
[4] See *E.H.S.* pp. 475 sqq.

an equal amount per ton. Thus if the pig-iron prices which they used to make steel went up by 10s. per ton, as was first planned, the 'pig-iron remission' on the steel they made should be 10s. per ton of pig iron charged.[1] In fact since the first rise was 15s. the first remission was 15s., and when pig iron went up again in December by 20s. the pig-iron remission was increased to 35s. per ton. When this happened the pig-iron remission was the only payment for which an ingot levy was required. The levy of 9s. per ton was still raised on bought scrap, in effect raising its price. The ingot levy was fixed at 17s. 6d.[2] These levies and remissions were unchanged in 1948, though the price of pig iron had now mounted from 150s. 6d. to 182s. 6d. per ton. Thus the arrangement 'still leaves pig iron costly in relation to scrap', the Federation commented, 'but it goes some way to spreading over the whole industry the extreme burden of the rise in pig iron costs'.[3] Some way, but not all the way. Hence in effect firms making steel from a lot of scrap and a little pig iron were favoured at the expense of firms using a lot of pig iron and a little scrap, though the steady expansion of steelmaking depends on the greater use of pig iron. Such a situation necessarily relied on an allocation of home scrap—mainly informal, in that merchants sought first to supply their normal customers in presumably their normal proportions; not wholly informal, because there were special instructions where the Federation wanted changes, wanted, for example, stocks of scrap to be built up at Port Talbot or (on a smaller scale) at Round Oak in anticipation of the opening of the enlarged steel-melting shops there. Since prices were both fixed and low, competition could play no part.

How would the Board face this 'artificiality'? They left it alone, presumably uncriticised, and added a further instalment. The elimination of state subsidies threw a heavy additional cost on steelmaking, but the rise in costs would not have been equally divided between all steelmakers. It would have fallen most on

---

[1] The 'one for one' principle, if it had been consistently applied, would have preserved the lack of balance between pig-iron and scrap prices which had been created before the war. But the margin would have been less important owing to inflation.

[2] *Financial Times*, 24 Jan. 1946.   [3] *Stat. Bull.* June 1948, p. 3.

users of imported ore, imported scrap and imported 'semis', and least on users of home ore. The decision (made presumably on the advice of the Board) was that most of these extra costs should be averaged and spread over the whole industry by a new ingot levy of 26*s.* per ton (which would carry the excess costs of imported ore and scrap) and a levy of 13*s.* per ton of 'semis' which would be included in the price of 'semis'. According to the *Economist* it was the *industry* which proposed to finance the new costs 'by reverting to a system of levies', which is indeed very likely.[1] But whoever proposed it, the Board and Minister had to agree, and as has been seen it was not a case of 'reversion'; the new ingot levy was in addition to the existing one of 17*s.* 6*d.*[2] Nevertheless, the agreement of the industry had extra significance since it was adopting a policy which in 1945, when Macdiarmid was President of the Federation, it had rejected as unfair to users of home ore. Now at length the low costs of plants based on home ore would again be used to bring down the costs of firms based on imported ore and imported scrap—more comprehensively than they had been in 1938–9 when Macdiarmid had refused to play in respect of Corby steel ingots used in making tubes.[3]

Possibly, as the *Economist* and other papers[4] argued, it was impractical to do anything else, to attempt to 'allocate' the additional costs to those concerns who used the imported materials. Indeed, the whole of this episode showed the grim effects of attempting to keep prices of one commodity stable too long, at what was initially too low a level, in a period of steadily rising prices. Even as it was the rise in April 1949 invited the comment that steel prices having been kept extremely low when steel was desperately scarce (*vide* the *Economic Surveys* of 1947 and 1948, when therefore it would have been sensible to discourage the more frivolous demands and make the holding of stocks costly) was raised sharply when demand for steel seemed to show signs of flagging. 'An increase in the price of a key

---

[1] *Econ.* 2 Apr. 1949. Though this passage is slightly misleading the whole article is important and enlightening.

[2] The combined ingot levy was in fact 51*s.* a ton.

[3] Above, p. 58.

[4] *Econ. loc. cit.* see also *The Times* (City Notes), 31 Mar. 1949.

industrial material', the *Economist* commented, 'does not accord very happily with pressure to reduce the cost of exports and of construction work at home.' It was the beginning of the period of difficulty which was the prelude of devaluation. There may have been political considerations behind the change, but they were not simple to disentangle. It had no doubt been good publicity for the steelmakers to keep prices low, but not good that their prices should be called subsidised. For the Government it would have been hard to raise prices merely to check a fall in profit margins while also maintaining and raising subsidies, and perhaps it seemed convenient to get prices up under private enterprise; to save the nationalised concern they were creating the embarrassment of having to raise prices early in its career. All the parties may have been calculating thus. But all probably felt forced by economic circumstances; unless prices were to remain permanently divorced from costs a drastic step must be taken, and the longer it was delayed the worse it would be.

(c) *International price comparison*

As it was home and export prices for most forms of steel were still lower than in America and on the Continent. The Federa-

Table 20. *Home prices of steel in the United Kingdom and other countries*[a] *(all prices in sterling)*

		U.K.		U.S.		France		Belgium		Italy		Australia	
Products	Date	£	s.	£	s.	£	s.	£	s.	£	s.	£	s.
Angles	June 1948	16	18	17	0	24	10	18	5	—		11	14
	Apr. 1949	19	13	22	15	23	4	19	3	—		13	2
Plates	June 1948	18	13	19	7	29	2	19	8	37	5	—	
	Apr. 1949	21	14	23	1	27	0	20	11	42	4	13	10
Re-rolled	June 1948	19	13	20	11	25	2	17	18	29	16	11	6
bars	Apr. 1949	22	9	23	12	23	15	18	7	32	19	13	2
Sheets	June 1948	25	1	23	5	34	5	27	18	47	10	—	
	Apr. 1949	28	6	26	18	32	9	27	18	63	14	26	16
Tinplate	June 1948	1	17	1	13	3	2	3	0	—		—	
	Apr. 1949	2	0	1	18	3	3	3	0	—		—	

[a] *Stat. Bull.* Mar. 1949, where particulars are given of sizes, minimum quantities, process, etc., including extras for open hearth where prices are for Thomas steel. The oversea prices include an estimate for transport cost to consumers' railway station.

tion published tables to this effect every time a significant increase of prices occurred.[1] This was not what had been expected in 1944, though it was no longer surprising in 1949, because inflation in America and the severe handicaps in Europe (such as dear coal, delays to re-equipment in Germany) were by now familiar. Nevertheless, the figures, some of which are given in Table 19, could be used as a token of greater relative efficiency which was persuasive on a superficial view. Such comparisons, it must be repeated, involve immense hazards. The B.I.S.F. always added an average transport cost to foreign figures because British prices were 'uniform delivered' in the sense described above. Foreign prices vary for different consumers according to real costs of delivery, real costs for *some* makers. However, these prices were broadly a reliable guide. Belgian home prices, it will be seen, for Thomas steel were lower in most products than British prices for open-hearth steel after the rise of 1949. American prices were above the British except for sheets and tinplate. French prices were at least a little higher on all products. Italian prices were a great deal higher, Australian notably lower. No information was given, understandably, about variation in extras, nor about concessions when there were any.

The E.C.E. in its first report on steel gave a table which

Table 21. *Home market and export prices in United Kingdom, Belgium and United States January 1949 ($ per metric ton)*

Product	U.K.		Belgium			U.S.	
				Organ-ised	Free-market		
	Home	Export	Home	export	export	Home	Export
Heavy steel: Joists	71	91	67	98	127	72	90
Plates (10 mm.)	74	94	76	109	148	75	93
Light steel: Round and squares (under 76 mm.)	80	104	69	100	119	74	93
Wire rods	77	—	72	107	131	80	92
Sheets (1 mm.)	99	110	105	136	191	95	112

[1] E.g. *Stat. Bull.* June 1948, and Mar. 1949.

widened the comparative picture in some respects usefully. It gave prices in dollars per metric ton, which was to become more and more the common basis of comparisons. In all three countries export prices ran above home prices at this date, but in Belgium the disparity was much greater than in the United Kingdom or United States. As was soon to be seen, this particular date caught the Belgian export price at an extremely high point; by the time the report was published the position had crumbled.

(d) Price-fixing to promote competition

The Federation was not content, however, to rely merely on this aspect of steel prices in defence of the industry's price structure. From 1948 onwards it presented in a series of articles what amounted to an apologia for the structure. These included a reprint of a striking paper read by Mr Shone, their Economic Director, to the British Association. This series seemed called for no doubt by the political conflict over the ownership of the industry which is traced in the next chapter; but it is particularly relevant to the present context, more particularly as neither the Board nor the Ministry ever set out in any detail the reasons for the policies they adopted. The plain implication of the Federation's exposition was that the mind behind the price structure was a Federation mind, though the blessing of the Board and Government was needed. While the origin of the structure, and the development of a logical argument in its favour, may rightly be traced in the Federation, it would be wrong to regard either as having the unanimous support of the industry; there were always important critics among the leading firms, but they chose not to come out in public, though the rule was inconspicuously and most discreetly broken from a rather narrow viewpoint in 1952.[1]

The Federation claimed that the price-control arrangements provided competition in a form which was better than existed when there could be price competition, and that the 'artificial arrangements' did not mask real costs, but instead sometimes helped to reveal them.

[1] See an article by Fred Stones, *J. Ind. Econ.* Nov. 1952, p. 32.

The virtue of competition was to be measured by its effectiveness in bringing pressure to bear on firms to lower their costs and raise their efficiencies. Under the former conditions the inefficient firms were not quickly eliminated, though the efficient ones might be impoverished. Mr Shone emphasised the acute effects in steelmaking of the succession of booms and slumps as the explanation of the inoperativeness of competition in its old form. Firms which lowered prices were not thereby able to get much more business because demand was inelastic in the short run. In the long run the finances of the inefficients were restored by the boom prices.

The Federation argument was that the form of competition which is sponsored—within a régime of externally fixed prices based on the costs of efficient firms—would do what price competition had seemed not to do in this country, would bring, for example, more pressure to bear on inefficient firms to lower their costs, lead to the quicker elimination of firms which remained inefficient and the faster establishment of large-scale methods where they were appropriate. The starting-point of the argument was one repeated often in the war. If a firm had to make a clearly specified article to an externally fixed price it was in the firm's interest to keep its costs as low as possible. Profits could only be raised by greater efficiency. If, in addition, the price is fixed in relation to average costs, with a narrow profit margin only, then every successful effort to reduce costs by one firm squeezes the margin of profit of the others, and those who fail to improve will fare progressively worse and fall out of production because they make losses. The fixed price is an invitation to reduce costs; but when costs are reduced the advantage of doing so will at once be partially taken away. Indeed, as Mr Shone pointed out, in addition to this automatic effect of the reduction of average costs, once firms had responded as the price-fixing authority thought sufficiently to a situation of relative scarcity by increasing capacity the margin itself could be narrowed. It had in fact been done; 'where rapid expansion of output was needed the Steel Board fixed prices above [this] marginal cost level. In other cases where modernisa- of capacity seemed less desirable, because the saving in prime

costs at a new plant would be insufficient to offset the high
capital cost, they did not fix a price even as high as the marginal
cost at a new plant.'[1] Provided prices are not raised in booms,
or lowered in slumps, the pressure will be continuous; there
will be no opportunity for weak firms to restore their finances
out of boom high prices. There was no question under such a
system 'of giving profits to all producers however high their
costs'; there were also, on the other hand, no quotas, no
restrictions on any firm's output. Evidence was published which
was intended to illustrate the validity of this ingenious theory
from the actual working of competition in the industry. The
Federation published for three quarters (IV, 1947, II and IV,
1948) charts showing the margins earned (before charging
depreciation) on sales of heavy products by all the forty-two
firms who made and sold them. Six of the forty-two firms sold
in the first quarter (which in this respect is fairly representative)
between 60,000 and 80,000 tons each in a quarter, and together
provided 41 per cent of total sales, five selling from 30,000 to
60,000 provided 20 per cent, six selling from 20,000 to 30,000
provided 11 per cent, those (twenty-four) selling less than
20,000 tons thus provided 28 per cent. These charts showed that
some firms made large losses in all three quarters. A diagram
showed the margins rising from a loss of £2. 12s. 6d per ton (for
the least successful firm) to an equal profit for the most successful. Losses were made on some 140,000 tons in the first quarter
(out of 1,070,000 tons), on over 200,000 tons out of 1,080,000 in
the second, and on 300,000 out of 1,100,000 tons in the third.
Eight firms made losses in each quarter; seven others had losses
in two quarters only, and four in one quarter only. These are
not the only remarkable features of these figures. There were,
for example, some striking fluctuations of fortune from one
quarter to another; one firm appears to have increased its
margin from 12s. per ton to 38s. from one quarter to another
when the average margin fell; another (selling about 50,000 tons
a month) had a fall from 25s. to 2s. 6d.; one turned a loss (on a
small output) of £2. 12s. 6d. into a profit of 5s. Competition

[1] *Stat. Bull.* Aug. 1949, p. 9. This procedure was described with apparent
approval.

in this form evidently had very erratic results. A third notable feature was that the largest margins were made by firms with small sales. In the first quarter only seven firms earned margins of over 30s. per ton, of whom five sold about 5000 tons each in a quarter and the two others sold respectively about 20,000 and 10,000 tons. Five of these same firms had the best margins in the second quarter, and three in the third. Only fifteen firms in the first quarter, thirteen in the second, and ten in the third, making about 30, 35 and 28 per cent of the total sales, earned 20s. profit margin, which was about 5 per cent on turnover, and presumably less on capital employed.[1] Only one of the six firms with largest sales made over 20s. margin in all three quarters; two others did so in two out of the three quarters. The average return seems to have been rather less than 5 per cent in the first quarter, and progressively less in the later ones.[2]

These charts were arresting. Here it seemed was an industry where a surprisingly large number of firms competed against each other, and they were accepting without complaint price-fixing which left many of them with a loss at a time of exigent demand and gave no large producer a high margin of profit. But as the Federation itself indicated, this was too simple a view. The firms were not all competing against each other. Not all made all the types of heavy product which were subject to individual price-fixing and few made the whole range of sizes and qualities in any single type of product. Within each heavy trade there was an amount of specialisation—Colvilles for example, made the widest and thickest heavy plates; Cargo Fleet made the only wide flange beams; there were some patent piling sections, special high-tensile structural steels, and free-cutting steel billets. (Hence in the production of specific products there was often little, even no, competition at all.) Nor did the firms only make heavy products; with few if any exceptions they made some of the more highly finished products as well—sheets, tinplate, re-rolled bars, rods and sections, wire,

---

[1] This depends naturally on the basis of calculating capital employed. New plant cost certainly more per ton of annual capacity than the value per ton of the product.

[2] Cp. chart in *Stat. Bull.* Mar. 1949, p. 3.

hoops and strip, tubes, forgings or drop forgings, tyres, wheels and axles. Apart from this many were linked with engineering and other manufactures.

Hence 'it should not be concluded' as the Federation put it 'that firms are making a loss overall' because they are losing on some products.[1] Normally they were making profits on other products. In general the more finished products gave good profits. Mr Shone set the position out usefully rather later, in 1952: 'There has been a fairly persistent tendency for the margin on semi-finished steel particularly—and in heavy steel generally—to be lower than that earned on later finishing operations. This may have been due in part to political considerations, which tend to make it difficult to increase the prices of controlled products in periods of rising costs. More highly finished products have not generally been subject to the same rather special degree of public watchfulness, so that their margin has generally been good. . . . Public watchfulness can be exercised more precisely in the case of primary products.' It 'has been more concerned with the danger of prices being too high and is only slowly coming to realise that there may be an equal danger of their being too low'.[2]

This put a new complexion on the charts. Heavy product *sales* accounted for about 40 per cent of the steel ingot output; the larger part of the steel industry's output was sold in the higher profit categories with regard to which no data on margins were published. Sales of heavy products even 'at a loss' might in fact be making a useful contribution to overheads. Some of the billet production at low margins may have resulted from Federation pressure to provide billets when they were very scarce from plant that was more efficiently used for other products. Some of the production 'at a loss' was no doubt the result of 'coupled bargains', whereby as a member of a steelworks' staff was to put it in 1952[3] firms undertook to take 'unremunerative' orders linked with remunerative. The erratic distribution of profit margins under control drove firms to build up 'balanced programmes' of orders, balanced, that is, to

[1] *Stat. Bull.* June 1948, p. 3.
[2] *J. Ind. Econ.* Nov. 1952, p. 46.   [3] *Ibid.* p. 35.

offset low margins by high ones.[1] There was thus no reason to suppose that the 'losses' of many firms making heavy products betokened that their plants were 'on the way out'. And instead of the narrow margin of profit fixed under control being an incentive to firms to do their best to reduce costs it might, being discriminatingly small, discourage investment in these branches. If the margin were raised, however, the squeezing effect so much emphasized would be reduced. One peculiarity of the charts remains: why were there so many firms with small sales of heavy products making wide margins? Some may have been large firms whose sales of heavy products were a small sideline, but none of the large-scale producers of ordinary quality steels seem to fall into this category. The more probable explanation is that there were small firms making profitable specialities.

The Federation coupled with its profit-margin charts other evidence to show how its policy had worked in the long run. The relative failure and success of firms competing under externally fixed prices could be illustrated, the argument ran, by the fact that firms expanded at different rates between 1938 and 1948. Statistics and charts were published to substantiate this.[2] They showed for ingots, heavy and medium plates, heavy rails, tyres, wheels and axles, and hot-rolled hoop and strip, that between 1938 and 1948 expansion of output had varied greatly from firm to firm. Almost all firms, in all the groups, had expanded. Except in the case of heavy rails none had gone out of production. What did the figures prove? They showed for several individual firms sizeable expansions. But 1938, chosen no doubt because it was the last full pre-war year, was a poor year. Ingot output had been 25 per cent higher in 1937. Hence increased outputs since 1938 were not wholly, or on the average mainly, due to expansion.[3] And for most of the period since then there had been war, when the fortunes of firms were not determined by their competitive efforts. Since the war

---

[1] *Ibid.* p. 35.

[2] A table illustrating this for ingots was published in *Stat. Bull.* Oct. 1948, p. 4; charts covering ingots and other products named in the text were published in *ibid.* Aug. 1949, p. 8.

[3] Average ingot output in 1948 was 45 per cent over 1938, but only 16 per cent above 1937.

investment in new capacity had been subject to permits which could not be obtained automatically, so that post-war growth was not a pure reflection of competition. It was impossible from this kind of data to make the comparison which these diagrams were supposed to represent. If they are taken at their face value they suggest that competition under fixed prices with demand rising allowed almost all firms to expand, and did not lead to the elimination of any high-cost firms, save possibly in rail-making. Here, however, the Plan stated that some firms were withdrawing by arrangement, not as a result of competition (though no doubt because other business promised more profits), but in the interests of rationalisation.[1] The Plan foreshadowed, too, that some firms were giving up, for example, making plates, in the interests of radical rationalisation, not because they were being eliminated by competitive pressure.[2] It was reasonable, nevertheless, to argue that if prices had always been fixed to remunerate the least profitable plant these things might have been harder to bring about, though this was probably not true in all the instances.

Though the charts did not prove the Federation's case, this did not dispose of it. It resulted from the inadequacy of the material dealt with in the charts as proofs. To show that firms expanded at different individual rates from 1938 to 1948, and that their proportionate importance in different trades varied and that their rates of profit varied, was to show something which would have been true of the industry, and could have been illustrated by similar charts, under the earlier régime, which nevertheless, Mr Shone argued, and he could have given

---

[1] Above, p. 175.

[2] Above, *loc. cit.* Like the charts of margins the charts of outputs 1931–48 suggested that comparisons could be made between firms who were not in fact competing against each other. Small ingot producers, for example, increased their output collectively by 66 per cent, whereas ingot output as a whole rose by 45 per cent only. The Federation drew attention to this (*Stat. Bull.* Oct. 1948, p. 4) without however indicating how much this was due to the growths of alloy and special steelmaking; the output of electric furnace steel in 1948 was 240 per cent higher than in 1937. Even if the situation of ingot makers producing sheets, or tubes, or ship plates on a large scale is considered it is quite obvious that since their products were not only different but not complementary different rates of expansion did not necessarily reflect the sorting out effects of competition.

good reasons, had not been characterised by quick elimination of inefficients, or expansion likely to give the greatest overall efficiency.[1] Mr Shone would appear to argue that the total expansion had been faster from 1938 to 1948 because of the régime, but the charts could not establish this, nor could this be anything but optimistic speculation.[2] Their limitation as proof is paralleled by the narrowness of the premise of the whole argument, which was that the succession of booms and slumps have 'made the orthodox competitive determination of prices quite inappropriate'. This was true if orthodoxy meant competitive price-cutting unlimited; but as Mr Shone also recognised the 'market determination of prices' in these circumstances would itself not follow the pattern of orthodoxy. Moreover, the resistances to elimination which made severe price-cutting ineffective are not removed by a system of fixed prices. Old firms with large reserves and established reputations, firms making specialities, firms enjoying tied markets which enable them to 'weather the storm' of a depression though they are not the lowest cost producers, do not lose these strengths with the new type of price fixing. Did the resistances in fact prove less important? And how were the administrative difficulties of price-fixing overcome? How was the 'right' margin of profit fixed? Did the fact that the profit margin for controlled products was lower than for products with no control distort investment from a 'perfect competition' normal? Questions of this kind can only be answered by reference to specific development, by some attempt to compare what actually occurred with what might have occurred; though some light can be shed by comparisons of British experience with that of steel industries under other régimes, notably the American (so much the model in matters technical) and the German.[3]

These matters are returned to later. There remains, however, a further element to examine in the Federation exposition of price policy, the defence of the so-called 'artificial arrangements'.

---

[1] *Stat. Bull.* Aug. 1949, p. 7.
[2] *Ibid.* p. 6.
[3] No doubt the Russians too; but there is not yet the same type of evidence.

(e) Levy-subsidies: practice and theory

The Federation, and no doubt all others concerned, were conscious that the 'special arrangements' affected competition between firms, and between countries. It has been seen that the Federation leaders were very conscious that the arrangements over imported ore helped users of these materials at the expense of users of home ore, and it must have been clear to all that the scrap arrangements *could* help large users of scrap and *must* bring British costs down relatively to those of countries where scrap prices were settled in a competitive market.

The arrangements themselves were introduced, developed and varied to meet specific circumstances: first the boom prices of imported raw materials of 1937–8, then the wartime situation, then the transition from war. They were perhaps all at times regarded by some of their advocates as *ad hoc* and temporary; but as the provisional which endured they were progressively explained, justified and in some ways refined. It may be that the doctrine ultimately revealed was complete and explicit from the start; it looks more likely that it evolved. Its precise form acquired increasing interest as time passed both because some of the practices seemed to be progressively regarded as permanent and because analogous practices, and doctrine, began to be evolved in Europe in respect of scrap.

In 1948 the doctrine presented was still rather rough and ready. 'In all cases the arrangements are designed to deal with some currently abnormal cost factor, and [they] affect firms quite independently of whether they are efficient or inefficient, or whether they are making profits or losses.'[1] There was no pooling of profits, or subsidy for the less efficient at the expense of the more efficient. They were part of a price-fixing policy which 'has regard to the long-term cost position of the industry',[2]

[1] *Stat. Bull.* Jan. 1948, p. 3.
[2] *Ibid.* Oct. 1948, p. 3. Mr Shone was soon to put it much more precisely in his address to the British Association: 'I would personally prefer to see an independent authority, capable of judging fairly as between producer and consumer, fix prices on the basis of full information at a level corresponding to long

rather than the short-term position. This would allow steel-producing firms to make their plans on a proper assessment of real costs and potential steel users to gauge the future steel market situation accurately.

This was, indeed, seductive simplicity. But to say the arrangements 'affected firms quite *independently* of whether they are efficient' is not to say their effect is *neutral*, and leaves the relation of the efficient and inefficient firms unaltered. Did they in fact tend to have a regular bias, and was it possible to avoid this? What constitutes efficiency in this context? Is a firm regarded as efficient because it has placed itself well for getting some cheap raw materials, or is this to be ruled out, as the effect perhaps of past decisions, which might earn a rent, which if substantial might even allow some current inefficiency in operations? What exactly is a 'currently abnormal cost factor', and for how long may it be abnormal? How were long-term costs defined, how were they forecast, and were successful methods of forecasting found? To what scale of output would they be related, and to what scale of imports of steel, at what prices?

These points were not brought out clearly. In regard to ore it has been seen the starting-point in the subsidy was the supposition that freights would settle at 50 per cent above the pre-war level. For this unrealistic figure as it proved there was substituted in 1948 the figure of 100 per cent.[1] In discussion of the ore subsidy in 1948 the hope was expressed that as freights fell in relation to other prices the subsidy would be reduced and ultimately disappear (as it did for a short time in 1950). The implication was that 'abnormal' meant a change from a past ratio. It looked like nostalgic inflexibility. The possibility was still entertained of a return to a coal outwards/iron ore inwards pattern in shipping. Meantime with no term set to the period of abnormality firms using imported ore were continuously helped and those using home ore were not. When in 1949 the levy-subsidy arrangements took the place of the state subsidy

---

term marginal cost, i.e. the cost of efficient units taking into account the possibility of new units coming into the industry—and let the pattern of production settle around this level' (*ibid.* Aug. 1949, p. 7).

[1] Above, p. 206.

the home ore users were once more helping the imported ore users.[1] It never seems to have been proposed that imported ore users should be debited with the excess cost of their ores, to be recovered from them later when prices were lower. On the basis adopted only the home ore users could suffer. It was occasionally suggested that this could be justified not only by the hope that imported ore prices would one day be brought down but by the fact that home ore-quarrying and mining costs would one day be raised, as the cream was skimmed. That the same creaming was happening with imported ore was then overlooked.

However 'normal' and 'abnormal' were interpreted it was implicit that a central judgement would be decisive, either a decision that ore and freight markets were to be deemed normal, or that home and imported ore prices should be in a particular ratio. There was no promise of ultimate market freedom once the post-war abnormalities were over. Nevertheless, this was not ruled out; nor was it inevitable that the system must be so administered as to mask real costs, though it had been so administered up to 1949. It did not have to be so.

Whether this could be said of the arrangements on scrap was more doubtful. There were two problems. First, did the arrangements influence unsatisfactorily the proportions in which steelmakers in different places used scrap, and lessen the inducement to invest in the expansion of the manufacture of pig iron? Secondly, was their effect in reducing the general level of steel prices desirable? The Federation made no bones about admitting in 1948 that users of scrap were benefited compared with users of pig iron as the arrangements were then working. The purpose, it was stated, was to 'mitigate the effects' of the steep rise in pig-iron costs; the result 'leaves pig iron costly in relation to scrap, but it does go some way towards spreading over the industry the extreme burden of the rise in pig iron costs'.[2] Some way, but not all the way. Four years later Mr Shone set out a more advanced doctrine whereby it was suggested that levies and subsidies could be so adjusted as

[1] *Stat. Bull.* June 1948, p. 4.
[2] Quoted above, p. 208, from *Stat. Bull.* June 1948, p. 3.

to compensate fully the user of pig iron for the artificial cheapness of home scrap. For as Mr Shone rightly emphasised this was the basic artificiality.[1] This *could* lead to distortion. To avoid this 'a close examination of the relativity of scrap and pig-iron prices over a period of years and in various countries when free market conditions obtained in both shows that scrap is normally somewhat cheaper than pig iron, being, on the average, about 75–80 per cent of the pig-iron prices'. The levy on scrap and the remission on pig iron were 'designed to have the effect of bringing the cost of scrap to the steelmakers up to the relationship to pig iron indicated'.[2] At this stage, in 1952, the object was thus stated, from an authoritative source, to be the maintenance of the cost of scrap below the cost of pig iron at an almost fixed ratio based on past (for most countries long past) experience of the average of competitive pig-iron and scrap prices.

Was the ratio right historically? What was the range within which the pig iron-scrap ratio moved in competition? Had the average relation in a free market, if properly established, any relevance? And if it had, and it was properly discovered, what validity did that give the whole scheme, including the artificially low price of scrap and the use of the ingot levy to cover costs of imported scrap or special collections of home scrap?

How prices of scrap moved in the free market, when steel prices as well as scrap prices were subject to price competition, appears to have escaped rigorous examination. A brief survey of this and of the factors which influenced it, and of the flux in supply which was in part cause and in part effect, is given in Appendix 1. Historically the average scrap/pig iron price ratio was rather above the 75–80 per cent in the periods surveyed. What stands out was the great fluctuation, between a minimum of 62 and a maximum of 107 per cent in the period 1919–39 in the United States and United Kingdom. These corresponded with slump and boom. In a slump the supply of scrap from processing (including 'circulating' scrap obtained from rolling mills within the industry and scrap arising when steel is cut and machined or otherwise processed by consuming industries)

---

[1] *J. Ind. Econ.* Nov. 1952, pp. 49–50.   [2] *Ibid. loc. cit.*

is large in relation to a falling output of steel; to sell it its price might well fall below the prime cost of 'hot metal'. In a boom the supply of scrap might ultimately be slightly more elastic than that of domestically produced pig iron; the price would rise to attract and pay for exceptional—for example, imported —supplies, the maximum being set by the price of steel, not the cost of producing pig iron (though the cost of *importing* pig iron could exert a governing influence). It is hard to see that the average of prices determined in these ways (only the extremes have been mentioned and this over-simplifies) could have any particular significance or be appropriate for any sequence of years from 1946 to 1957 during which demand for steel was almost continuously exigent and not wholly satisfied. If anything the price of scrap might in such a period be expected to be higher in relation to pig iron than the 'average' ratio would determine. The object of the formula applied as set out was to ensure that firms using relatively high proportions of pig iron in steel melting were not at a disadvantage compared with those using relatively high proportions of scrap, and clearly it was intended or implied that the inducement to expand pig-iron production would be just adequate when such expansion was 'required'. There seems no theoretic reason why the average should ensure this.

In a sense this was ultimately acknowledged, because the percentage was changed, was in fact raised.[1] This was not based upon a new historical retrospect; it implied that a review was made of the impact of the cost relations in practice. There was therefore no suggestion any longer that a 'neutral' decision of what was 'right' was being based on past experience. Indeed, even if the right data could be found such a plan was impossible. The ratio was necessarily a decision involving implicitly if not explicitly a judgement of the extent to which it should seem desirable to firms in planning to increase their steel output to do so by increasing pig-iron output. Since the ratio was, initially at any rate, fixed by the Federation, this decision, though made at the centre, was presumably found acceptable by the firms; it represented to some extent their own estimate

[1] Below, p. 610.

of what was a desirable (or as they might have said right) relation of scrap and pig-iron costs. This was a long way from the situation in which inducements to expand more or less on a pig-iron basis were determined by market influences.

Since costs of making pig iron vary from firm to firm, and the price of scrap, though fixed, varied under the price-control arrangements from district to district by specific margins, being higher in regions which were not self-sufficient and lower in regions which produced more scrap than they used, the inducements to use more pig iron or more scrap were not made uniform to all users by the 'special arrangements'. But any change in the levy-remission arrangements changed the inducements for all users. It would do so without automatically increasing the inducements to suppliers of scrap, producers or merchants, to try and supply more or less. A central decision was needed to organise (and subsidise) special collections or increase imports.

If the pig iron/scrap price ratio favoured scrap—as it was acknowledged in 1948 it had done consistently so far since the war—this would increase the pressure of demand for 'exceptional' supplies, those which could only be obtained by special arrangements at higher prices (financed from the Central Fund), and would discourage expansion of iron smelting.

It is hard to see by what mechanism under this system any steelmaker could increase his supply of scrap *at the expense of* another steelmaker (since he could not offer a higher price) except as a result of administrative intervention, or by the acceptance on the part of scrap merchants of an implied allocation scheme. Firms might, for example, be able to rely on getting a higher proportion of what was available if they installed new steel-melting capacity but not otherwise. Administrative intervention occurred; for example, as mentioned above, scrap firms were asked to build up stocks of scrap at the new Margam works and the expanded Round Oak works in 1950.[1]

---

[1] Prices were used to help in this. The scrap price was supposed to be fixed to attract all normal supplies. Regional price differences were changed periodically in the light of changes in 'requirements' of users, to ensure that scrap merchants would be best remunerated when supplies flowed in *desired* quantities to each user. There were thus price inducements to distribute according to a desired pattern!

There was, however, no reason why the pig iron/scrap price ratio as fixed by the levies and remissions should always favour scrap; the reverse was possible, though it had not happened up to 1948, and the 75–80 per cent ratio of 1952 still favoured scrap. But the system which ran alongside it whereby imports of scrap at world prices were sold to steelmakers at home scrap prices, and the additional cost in buying the scrap was paid for first by state subsidy and later out of the Central Fund based on the ingot levy, would appear to involve a permanent bias in favour of firms using a high proportion of scrap to pig iron, in situations, that is, where expansion of output depended most on imports. This was of course the 1937 situation perpetuated. The ingot levy was collected as much from firms using little bought scrap as from those using much. There have, it is true, been times when the ingot levy was continued at a level in excess of what was needed to finance imports, which put the Central Fund in surplus. All firms were contributing to a reserve out of which subsidies could be paid on high-cost imports later on. The firms who would benefit most were themselves contributing, but not in isolation or in proportion to future gains; some firms who would gain much less, perhaps nothing, were contributing an amount equal in proportion to their ingot output. Here there was an element of steady bias, the same type of bias as was implicit in the arrangements over iron ore.

It remains to consider the implications for competition of the practice of keeping home scrap prices low by administrative action while other prices, and scrap prices elsewhere, rose. Basically this was the most controversial of the 'special arrangements' for scrap. It lies at the root of the others. So long as scrap prices in the United Kingdom were kept exceptionally low by a ban on the export of scrap coupled with price-fixing (or with co-ordinated purchase arrangements by the steelworks), steel prices could be kept low in relation to prices of other competitive raw materials or prices of steel in other countries where the same practices were not followed. To keep scrap prices down in a boom (and up in a slump) might be consistent with maintaining steel prices in accordance with long-period marginal costs—and it was then plausible to argue that steel was fully subject to the competition of alternative materials, as the Federation argued—and subject to fair competition in export markets. But this could not properly be argued (though the claim was indeed made) when the depression of scrap prices was permanent. Its effect varied from year to year, but has rarely in the post-war period been negligible; on a rough calculation the extra cost of scrap for British steel if the scrap prices had been the same in the United Kingdom and the United States would have been:

	s. per ton		s. per ton
1946	10	1953	50
1947	35	1954	20
1948	45	1955	45
1949	20	1956	70
1950	55	1957	45
1951	70	1958	20
1952	55	1959	25

Had scrap prices been free, users in the home market who bought steel would have had some compensation for higher steel prices in higher prices for the scrap they sold.[1] This would not have helped all of them equally, and it would not have covered the major part of the increase in steel price to any user.[2] Hence in a period of steady inflation the policy of keeping scrap prices pegged inevitably assisted steelmakers in competition with makers of other raw materials as well as in competition with steelmakers overseas. It was a policy of discriminating administrative intervention which was bound to keep the prices of steel below the long-term trend of prices.[3] The comparisons between steel prices and those of other

[1] This would not have been so for overseas buyers, the value of whose scrap was determined in another 'market'. This might have been advanced as an argument for dual pricing of steel—higher prices for export—but as far as I know was not.

[2] Because the bought scrap content of the steel is more in almost all cases than the scrap discard in processing. If we assume a 55/52 ratio of pig iron to scrap in the charge, and 25 per cent of the ingot output as circulating scrap, then 27 per cent will be bought scrap, i.e. roughly 34 per cent of the finished steel output (which will be 75 per cent of the ingot output). The recovery of scrap for sale by users as a result of discards in processing steel will be about 5–20 per cent.

[3] I.e. lower than it would have been had the only factors bringing changes in relative prices been changes in relative efficiencies or in costs of imports.

materials in the United Kingdom and steel prices in other countries could obviously not be accepted as appropriate guides to relative efficiencies as it was sometimes suggested they might be.

It may well be asked whether the distorting effect of the special arrangements matched in importance the complexity of investigation and analysis which their understanding requires. That their influence on prices and in bringing the raw-material costs of firms nearer together, to the benefit in particular of firms using a lot of scrap and using imported ore,[1] was significant has appeared in figures above, and will appear again in later chapters. What has to be established is the impact this had on the expansion of firms and the pattern of investment. Can it be said that expansion of capacity was concentrated less than would seem likely where raw-material costs would be expected to be lowest (making due allowance of course for the pull of the market), or less than would seem appropriate on pig iron? And if so can this be attributed at least partly to the special arrangements? Or was it an outcome of the inertia, inertia which is to some extent implicit in the nature of the industry and its plant but to which personal and political factors contributed? Were the 'special arrangements' behind the prices and distortion in investment policy to be traced to the same source—rather than regarded as cause and effect? These are questions to be returned to later.

(f) The price changes of 1949

Though there was no explicit evidence that the Iron and Steel Board accepted the apologia of the Federation on price policy it seemed safe to assume that no profound difference of principle divided them, and the detailed changes made whose broad features have been shown earlier in Table 18, imply this. Superficially the changes made by the Board in 1949 made a concession to a point of view which in its early days, when billets were very scarce, both it and the Federation had opposed. The price of billets was raised in 1949 more than that of other heavy products.

---

[1] And imported pig iron; but this is a smaller matter.

In 1947 it was often said within the industry as well as out-side it that the low margin of profit on billets discouraged the growth and aggravated the scarcity of output. One *riposte* to this, with which the Board appeared to concur, was that there was ample administrative machinery to deal with the scarcity and see that the best use was made of rolling mill resources and that new extensions were made as circumstances justified; higher prices could do nothing. Some works declared that they kept off making billets on mills which could produce other products because billets did not pay; and in one plant it was said that if the price were attractive, a continuous mill could be built quickly in the firm's workshops and fed from an existing cogging mill which was underemployed. That the profit margin on billets was especially narrow is not, and was not, in dispute.[1] But the price jump of 1949 was in fact especially high not to give a more attractive margin but to help pay for the high cost of imports, and it included the levy mentioned above. The complaint of low margins on billets remained. There were some other changes in differentials which betokened an attempt to adjust prices rather more closely to costs. Instead of a common base price for angles and joists two bases were established. There were changes 'bringing up to date the lists of extras and allowances for quantities, sizes, etc.' as the Federation put it. 'Bringing up to date' was a slightly euphemistic description for a small operation; but there were increased quantity rebates, and there were also increased deductions for auto-body sheets, a product in regard to which the industry had for long toyed with the idea of giving special privileges and to which it conceded a special reduction in 1948. Why concessions to particular users could not be given wholly in

[1] Cp., for example, R. M. Shone, on Steel Price Policy, in *J. Ind. Econ.* vol. 1 p. 46, already quoted above: 'Nevertheless it is true to say that there has been a fairly persistent tendency for the margin on semi-finished steel particularly—but also in heavy steel generally—to be lower than that earned on later finishing operations.' The delivered price of billets delivered to pure re-rollers was at this time the same as the price attibuted to billets used in integrated works making their billets and re-rolling them. Hence for such integrated works the price might normally be satisfactory, and such indeed was claimed by those responsible for fixing prices. The profit of firms like G.K.B. at Cardiff whose billets were used in an associated plant which was adjacent support this.

quantity rebates available to all users was not explained. Zone extras for areas remote from works were increased, but the general practice of having for most products uniform delivered prices for large zones centred on steelworks remained unchanged.[1]

(g) Price policy and profits

Before passing to the third field of the Board's activity, its part in central planning, it may be asked whether it is possible to trace the impact on profits of the price procedures of the Federation Board and Government. The profits percentages in the industry published for the war period by the P.A.C. ceased for the post-war years. But useful as these were because they provided a uniform series for showing that wartime profits were not high they were inadequate for the more subtle problems of the early years of peace. The most illuminating figures come indeed from outside period 1; they are the accounts of the Iron and Steel Corporation of Great Britain for the brief period when a large part of the industry was, for the first if not the last time, nationalised. They can be usefully supplemented by the statistics of company profits published by the Inland Revenue Commissioners.

How easy it was to strike the wrong balance from highly generalised profits figures for short periods was made clear when the Productivity Team which, under the auspices of the Anglo-American Council of Productivity, visited the United States in 1951 to compare efficiencies in the two industries and trace the source of the differences. They compared figures for one year, 1950, to show how profits restraint in the United Kingdom placed the British industry at a disadvantage compared with the American in matters of investment. Their attempt revealed the pitfalls into which any such comparison, between two industries in the same country, or the same industry in two countries, may lead. The higher profitability of American steel-

---

[1] Hence anomalies persisted, and remained in 1960. Plate prices were uniform with no zone extras in the North-east Coast and Northern Joint Areas and Scots Zone I; there was a 2s. 6d. extra in the large Midland Area (see Map 1). Thus prices were as low in Barrow as in Middlesbrough, but 2s. 6d. higher near Scunthorpe, where they were as high as in Birmingham, Liverpool, Preston or Barmouth. Yet Scunthorpe had the lowest cost steel.

making, they asserted, had the result that 'the American money
market has shown itself more ready to invest "risk" capital in
the steel industry than its British counterpart'. The American
industry, they showed in a diagram, had earned 25¾ per cent
on capital employed in 1950, the British 13½ per cent in the
year 1949–50. This contrast might 'be taken to indicate the
future expectations of the steel industries in the two countries'.[1]

A single year is rarely representative; 1950 was the peak year
in the first 12 years of peace for the American industry's profits
after the deduction of tax,[2] whereas 1949–50 was far from being
the peak year in Britain, being surpassed, for example, in 1951
and 1952 when the report was being written. An equally
fundamental defect of a different order was that the report said
nothing about the scale of 'capital employed', which sounds
a more concrete concept than it is. 'Book values' are highly
esoteric, influenced greatly by rates of depreciation, special
write-offs, changes in the value of money, etc., so that precise
comparison is ruled out. It might be surmised that the American
industry, far more elaborately equipped than the British, with
more mechanical aids and more complete integration with
raw material supply, and about thirty strip mills, might have
more capital employed per ton of capacity than the British
industry; but in fact the two employed nominally approximately the same (the British being only slightly lower) at the
time of this comparison, after devaluation had raised the
sterling equivalent of the American figure drastically. Prior to
devaluation the British industry had (in this sense) much more
'capital employed' per ton of capacity than the American, a
Gilbertian situation which put 'capital employed' (in the form
used in this comparison) in perspective.[3]

There was another aspect of American development which

---

[1] *Productivity Team Report, Iron and Steel*, published by Anglo-American Council
of Productivity, June 1952, pp. 119, 123.

[2] Figures from 1948 to 1954 are on p. 232. Figures 1955–58 were: 7·8, 7·25, 7·3,
6·5.

[3] In 1948 the value of capital employed per ton of ingot capacity was £16 in the
United States, and rose to £22 after devaluation in 1950. The British figure was
little under £20. No doubt the American figures were low partly because of the
quick 'write-off' during the war, but this does not disturb the validity of the
point made above.

hardly supported the team's thesis that high returns were needed to secure capital—as some of the team's members were possibly aware—for the American industry had invested heavily in the thirties, although it suffered more from the depression than the British industry and earned on an average only 2·16 per cent on 'capital employed' from 1930 to 1938.[1]

A comparison of profits after taxation as a percentage of turnover is the simplest way to compare profits in the two industries as a source of funds for investment. The percentages

Table 22. *Profits after tax as percentage of turnover in steelmaking*[a]

	U.S.	U.K.
1948	6·7	6·9
1949	7·2	6·6
1950	8·0	5·5
1951	5·8	6·6
1952	4·9	6·5
1953	5·6	4·9
1954	6·0	5·9

[a] The United States figures are based on the tables published annually in *Iron Age*. Figures for 'Primary iron and steel' in Federal Statistics covering presumably much more of the industry (but firms of different classes) were close to but consistently below the *Iron Age* figures. Conversely for the United Kingdom the Iron and Steel Corporation of Great Britain figures for 1951 and 1952, calculated from the annual accounts, were below the series in the table for the United Kingdom, which is based on the Inland Revenue Statistics in the *Annual Reports of the Commissioners of Inland Revenue*. These cover not only steel, but iron foundries, and a sample analysis in the *Report* for 1952 showed that the half of the sample with the higher ranges of profit were on average firms with less than the average turnover.

[1] The *Report* went out of its way to say that comparison of profits in 1949–50 'will not...account for the present physical state of the industries, since the year 1950 was unrepresentative of conditions during the life of much of the existing plant'. It did not say in what ways it was different—a sign of discretion. The financial history of the American industry in the inter-war years was surveyed in two T.N.E.C. volumes: Part 31, *Investment Profits and Rate of Return for Selected Industries*, Part III, pp. 17739 sqq. (the figure in the text is based on a table on p. 17760) and Monograph No. 12: *Profits, Production Activities and New Investment*, by Martin Taitel, esp. pp. 115–22.

were surprisingly similar in the United States and the United Kingdom; the figures in Table 22, though not perfectly comparable, are probably a reliable guide. If British figures were available for the larger steel firms only, and so more precisely comparable with the United States figures, the parallel would probably be closer. In 1951–52 the figures for the Iron and Steel Corporation of Great Britain were almost identical to the American for the same years.

Again, 1950 was an exceptionally good year for the American industry. But there was no striking normal advantage in these figures, especially with what appear to be the appropriate corrections. If the percentages were approximately the same the Americans might seem to have an advantage because the turnover per ton of steel was somewhat greater,[1] but against this the cost of new plant tended to be slightly greater too, more especially so after devaluation.[2] The more substantial advantage for the American industry possibly was that since the firms were large, much larger than the British, the profits would provide very large unit sums.[3] The same advantages would be enjoyed over depreciation allowances; there is, however, no indication in the statistics that the American industry gained significantly otherwise over depreciation in the years from 1947 to 1950, though from 1951, with a return to the wartime practice of accelerated depreciation for approved schemes, it was otherwise, and the United States firms had some advantage.[4] But this stage was only just starting when the Productivity Committee was writing, and the advantage was not very great. Despite their sensational diagram they did acknowledge that the American industry's profits were not by American standards

---

[1] If turnover is divided by tonnage of steel sold the average in the United States was £63 in 1951, £64 in 1952. The United Kingdom figures were £40 and £50 respectively. This does not mean, however, that these were the average prices of the steel sold, because steel firms carried on other activities which came into their turnover.

[2] As seen later however there was surprising similarity in cost of plant.

[3] The American figures quoted in the Productivity Report were for 26 firms with 92 per cent of output, the British for 26 firms with 80 per cent of output.

[4] Up to 1950 the United Kingdom firms had the benefit of initial allowances introduced in 1945. For the vagaries of United Kingdom initial and investment allowances, above, p. 155.

attractive; the steelmakers 'found difficulty in the stock market in competition with more remunerative industries', and so relied largely on ploughing back profits. During the five years 1949–53 the increase in common stock of the principal twenty-five companies was $52·9 m., by comparison with the sums reinvested ($1809 m.) a trivial sum.[1]

Table 23. *Profits as a percentage of turnover in the iron and steel industries*[a] *(all figures are a percentage of turnover)*

	Trading profit	Net trading profit	Total income	Total income less tax	Dividends interest, etc.	Balance retained
1937	11·0	9·1	11·1	9·1	5·0	4·1
1948	12·2	10·8	11·2	5·9	2·3	3·6
1949	11·6	9·5	10·2	6·6	3·8	2·8
1950 (a)	11·3	9·5	10·0	6·1	3·5	2·6
(b)	11·3	9·5	9·8	5·5	2·5	3·0
1951	13·8	11·6	12·0	6·6	3·0	3·6
1952	13·4	11·9	12·3	6·5	2·9	3·6
1953	10·4	8·5	8·9	4·9	2·7	2·2
1954	10·7	8·2	9·5	5·9	2·3	3·6
1955	11·8	9·3	10·4	6·4	2·4	4·0
1956	12·1	9·4	10·6	6·4	2·8	3·6

[a] These come from the *Annual Reports of the Commissioners of Inland Revenue*. There was a change of basis in 1951; 1950 figures revised are given in line (b). The change of basis was due to a reliance from 1951 on a mixture of income tax and profits tax statistics.

Profits as a percentage of turnover provide a basis for the useful comparison between profits in the same industry in two countries, and in addition they are a useful indication of changes in the pre- and post-war position (again with the proviso that because of the extent of vertical integration they stretch beyond steelmaking). The figures (carried as far as the published records make possible) are summarised in Table 23. These figures, which show considerable variations (those for

[1] From 1949 to 1953 invested capital rose by $2442 m. Ingot capacity rose by 18·8 m. long tons. Of the added investment $1809 m. came from surpluses, $608 m. from new funded debt. It will be noted that if the addition of capital is attributed to additional capacity this was capitalised at $130 a ton of capacity, or £47 a ton.

1953–4 possibly reflecting the decline of export premiums), suggest that trading profit, gross and net, and total income, were slightly above the 1937 level as a percentage of turnover, but only by a small amount; and because taxation was so much higher what was left after taxation was a much smaller proportion than before the war. This was the almost universal experience of British industries.[1] It has been seen earlier that the prices of new plant for steelmaking rose much more than the home price of steel; and plant in fact became inherently more costly per ton of capacity at the same time, because of its greater elaboration, partly to deal with the lower quality raw materials, partly for greater mechanisation (partly also to make more refined products; but this involves different issues). The situation was one in which the cost of capital equipment per ton of identical product at constant prices was higher in the post-war years than before the war, and to an extent greater certainly than the slight increase (in some years only) in the ratio of trading profit or total income to turnover. The return on capital employed, that is, was lower in the post-war years, capital employed being measured not by book values but by some more realistic standard.

Profits as a percentage of turnover are of little or no value for comparing the relative profitability of different industries in one country. For this purpose there were no satisfactory data. Dr Barna was to show for a later date (1955) that profits (according to a rather individual conception) in steelmaking were below the average for all manufacturing industries as a percentage of the assets employed in the industry assessed in a new way.[2] But this, though interesting, had not reached the stage where it could be confidently interpreted. What is wanted is evidence focused on the critical point, the point of new investments, and not on aggregates.

The reports of the Iron and Steel Corporation of Great Britain showed how misleading the aggregate profits could be. The reports broke up the gross trading profit for 1951 and 1952 in the way shown in Table 24. For reasons which will be

[1] Cp. *The Structure of British Industry*, a Symposium, ed. Burn, vol. II, p. 459.
[2] In *J.R. Stat. Soc.* 1957, p. 24.

observed later, although the firms within the Corporation were nationalised and the financial results of firms were set out in new ways and consolidated, with some useful additional information as a result, their development as firms was not in general disturbed, and the results for 1951–52 may be taken as not wildly different from those of earlier years in general character.

Table 24. *Sources of profits in the industry, 1951–52*[a]

	Year ended 30 Sept. 1952 (£ m.)	Period ended 30 Sept. 1951 adjusted to annual rate (£ m.)
Profits:		
On activities within the iron and steel industry, both home and export sales, export sales being valued at U.K. controlled prices	37·3	34·7
On activities outside the iron and steel industry	8·9	6·0
From overseas establishments	2·9	2·3
Export premiums, i.e. excess of export prices over U.K. controlled prices	18·9	12·5
Profits on stocks arising from increases in selling prices	6·7	8·3
	74·7	63·8
Deduct:		
Adjustments made on consolidation (principally amounts set aside for additional depreciation)	10·3	9·4
Manufacturing and trading profit as per consolidated profit and loss account	64·4	54·4

[a] *Report and Statement of Accounts of the I.S. Corp. G.B.* for year ended 30 Sept. 1952, p. 45.

Thus a surprisingly large element of the profit came from two windfalls, sources not likely to be regularly recurrent, at least on the same scale—export premiums and stock profits. Over one-fifth of the remaining profits came from activities outside the iron and steel industry or outside the country. And all these remaining profits had to be deflated to allow for adequate depreciation in keeping with the replacement cost of plant. If the deflation was spread evenly over all the sources of profit (which was not necessarily right) the result is as shown in Table 25. These profits were related to a turnover of iron and steel of £420·4 m. in 1951 and £524·1 m. in 1952.[1] The return on turnover at controlled prices was thus 6·5 per cent in 1951 and 5·6 per cent in 1952 before tax. With tax deducted in the same proportions as from the larger profits, including the windfalls and on the total turnover, this gave average net returns on turnover of below 3·6 per cent and 2·6 per cent respectively after tax. It compared with 6 per cent and 5 per cent in the same years on the total turnover of the firms from activities of all kinds.[2] Or, to return to aggregates, after providing an average of £25 m. a year in 1951–52 for depreciation of assets of all kinds, the profits of the Corporation firms arising from steelmaking at controlled prices, and after taxation but before

Table 25. *Profits at home price less adequate depreciation*

	1951 (£ m.)	1952 (£ m.)
Profit on the whole output of iron and steel valued at home prices	27·1	29·5
Profit on activities outside iron and steel	4·7	7·0
Profit from oversea establishments	1·8	2·3
Total	33·6	38·8

[1] The return on turnover from activities other than iron and steel was not notably different from that on turnover from iron and steel; it was 5·7 per cent in 1951, 7·7 per cent in 1952, if (which is doubtful) it is right to attribute additional depreciation equally to the other activities. There is, however, little logical relation between the rate of return on steel and on other products, primarily because the amount of effort and capital employed in relation to turnover is quite different—the capital being much less for engineering products, drop forgings, etc.—but also because a large part—somewhere between 20 and 40 per cent of the turnover other than iron and steel—was earned on by-products, slag, coke, gas, electricity, chemicals and fertilisers, bricks and tiles. These were to a large extent joint products and since they were not the main object of the initial investment it would not be expected that their price alone would be by design as highly remunerative as that of the main product. In the case of engineering products, constructional steelwork, bridges, drop forgings and so on, this would not apply. It is not possible from the published data to say how much of the profit not derived from iron and steel was attributed to by-products, how much to other main products.

[2] The last two figures are referred to in the note to Table 22. The turnover is for the Corporation with outside buyers.

payment of interest, averaged about £11·3 m.[1] Gross capital investment by the Corporation averaged £55 m.[2]

These figures suggest strongly that control of home prices discriminated against the firms most effectively subjected to it. The distribution of profits between firms, and between sections of the industry, is consistent with this view. Unfortunately, the allocation of different parts of profits to sources, which is invaluable for the whole industry, was not given for the separate firms within the Corporation; so that the distribution of profits between firms cannot be attributed with complete certainty to particular causes.

In Table 26 the proportion of the Corporation's profits earned by firms in various sections of the industry are shown, firms being classified according to their preponderant activity. Exports in the same section of the trade are shown in the final column as a percentage of the value of exports in all the sections; but these exports are not solely from Corporation firms, and in some sections, notably tubes and wire, a significant proportion of the export will have come from independent firms.

The distribution of profits shown in this table is in keeping with a situation in which the operation of price control gave relatively low margins in the heavy-steel products, while proportionately higher margins were earned on the more highly finished products, which were subjected to more processes and were in general less uniform in shape, size and quality. A higher profit in relation to ingot output would, however, be normal for more finished products since they were subject to more pro-

---

[1] The Corporation in its *Report* for 1952 suggested that in 1953 the situation might be less favourable than in 1951–2, that depreciation and retained profits might give only £30 m. together. This was on the assumption that export premiums were much lower, and there would be smaller stock gains. The figure is close to the one implied in the text. Interest on loans and on the Corporation stock amounted to £10·9 m. in 1951–2.

[2] *Ibid.* pp. 48–9. The rate of return on the new investment cannot be isolated. If the additional profit of 1952 (£2·4 m. gross, £1 m. after tax) is taken as the yield on net investment (£52·4 m. less depreciation £27 m., i.e. £25·4 m.), it gives a modest return of below 10 per cent gross on the new capital if sales were valued at home prices, but the sum could only be significant by accident; how much of the change in aggregate earnings was due to the new investment could only be judged from very detailed accounts.

Table 26. *Profits according to product, 1951–52*
(nationalised firms only)

	% of profits	% of ingot output	Importance of products in export (% of total value of exports)[a]
1. Integrated firms making heavy steel and light re-rolled products	31	59[b]	31
2. Pure re-rolling of light re-rolled products	7		
3. Sheet and tinplate: (a) strip mills	22	19	28
(b) old methods	3	(3)[c]	
4. Tube production (integrated)	18	8[d]	24
5. Integrated production of wire	4	2[d]	13
6. Alloy and special steel (ingot makers)	13	7	4[e]

[a] Based on values of major products exported 1949–51.

[b] It is unfortunately not possible to isolate profits in heavy steelmaking from those in light re-rolled product making, and two firms included in this group, Colvilles and United Steel, also made alloy steel in considerable tonnages. Some pure re-rolling firms rolled chiefly alloy and special steels. Hence some of the profits in line 2 were made on ingots included in line 6, and some in line 1 on ingots which ought to have been included in line 6. Hence the ratio between profits and ingot output is probably more favourable than it would be for heavy steel alone.

[c] Some of the firms used sheet bars made by firms in line 1.

[d] There was a large output of wire and tubes outside the Corporation; hence while the profit/ingot ratio is significant, neither profits as a percentage of total profits, nor ingots as a percentage of total ingots, reflect the importance of these products in the United Kingdom industry as a whole.

[e] Only alloy bar exports are given in the trade accounts separately; I have included forgings and castings in this percentage, but alloy steel will be included in exports of tubes, wire and sheet.

cesses; the question is whether the degree of difference between the ratios is more than would be accounted for by this alone. Even if this were so, as seems a reasonable conclusion, it will be noted that the firms making more finished products played a bigger role than firms making heavy steel in export trade, which would manifestly give them a larger return than the heavy-steel firms had from export premiums. The situation was far more complex still, because the firms did not fall neatly into these categories; almost every firm was in some sense a special case. Table 27 lists the main ingot-producing subsidiaries of the

Corporation in the order of importance of their aggregate profits. It excludes all the more important re-rollers.[1]

The two leading firms made highly finished products with large exports. Both will also have gained from the possession of important fairly new plants, and Stewarts and Lloyds made two-thirds of their steel at Corby. The advantage of using home

Table 27. *Profits of main ingot-producing subsidiaries of the Iron and Steel Corporation*

	Location(s)[a]	Average profits 1951–52 (£ thousands)	Approx.[b] profit per ingot ton (£)	Chief product
Stewarts and Lloyds	H IF	12,270	10·3	Tubes, cast-iron pipes
Richard Thomas and Baldwins	IF H	9,709	6·0	Tinplates, sheets
United Steel Cos.	H U C	5,503	2·6	Heavy steel light re-rolled alloy steel
Dorman Long	C	5,096	3·0	Heavy steel, constructional engineering
Colvilles	IF	4,928	2·9	Heavy steel, alloy steel
English Steel Corporation	U	3,539	6·7	Alloy steel
John Summers	IF	2,889	5·3	Sheets
Lancashire Steel	C	2,818	7·2	Wire
Steel Co. of Wales	C	2,303	2·9	Sheets
Firth Brown	U	2,140	12·4	Alloy steel
G.K.B.	C	1,908	3·1	Heavy steel
Consett	IF	1,188	2·1	Heavy steel
South Durham and Cargo Fleet	C	1,015	1·7	Heavy steel
Bairds and Scottish	IF	739	7·0	Light
Park Gate	IH	287	0·9	Heavy and light
Round Oak	U	135	0·6	Heavy and light
Skinningrove	C	117	0·5	Heavy steel
J. Lysaght (Lincs)	H	267 (loss)	−0·7	Billets

[a] Symbols: C, coastal site; H, home ore site; IF, inland site using imported ore; IH, inland site using home ore; U, steelworks without blast furnaces.

[b] Not all firms have published their output, and I have only been able to use approximate figures in some instances, but I have reason to believe the figures are correct.

[1] Among whom Whiteheads and Guest, Keen and Nettlefolds earned the largest profits.

ore was greatly lessened by levy subsidies but certainly not entirely eliminated.[1] Richard Thomas's home ore plant played a minor part in their profits. All of which shows that caution is needed in interpreting these figures. Nevertheless, the gap between the profit per ton in the three largest of the pre-dominantly heavy-steel firms and the profit per ton in the firms making more finished products is impressive, too wide, one would surmise, to explain by 'natural causes'. Each of these three heavy-steel firms could sweeten their profits from other types of work—alloy steelmaking, rolling of light products, constructional engineering. United Steel also had the only home ore plant to be compared with Corby.[2] On the showing of these figures it might be better to make heavy steel in Scotland or South Wales than in Lincolnshire. Guest Keen Baldwins had the best (profit) record for heavy steelmaking alone; they had a fairly new plant,[3] gained from the levy-subsidy arrange-ments and the subsidy on Welsh coal, and much of their output went as billets directly to the nearby associated re-rolling plant of Guest Keen and Nettlefold, thus bearing little delivery cost. The remaining heavy-steel plants earned less per ton than the big three; in some cases it may be surmised because they only made heavy steel, in others because they were small. The one which made losses was located on cheap home ore, but was small, ageing, made the least favoured product (billets) and there were plans for rebuilding it. The returns on highly finished products were invariably high; the Steel Company of Wales only appears to be an exception because the new Abbey works was just 'running in'.

These profit data refer to a period after the demise of the first Board, and should reflect the effect of any general change of

[1] Stewarts and Lloyds as owners of the Stanton Ironworks made a large output of cast-iron pipes, which no doubt contributed well to the profits. The profits of the Stavely Company (with which Stanton might be compared, though it was bigger) made a profit of over £900,000 per annum.

[2] It is open to speculation whether the gain from this was mainly lost by reason of levies, or whether it was offset by results of other plants. The Steel Peech and Tozer (Templeborough) plant was especially handicapped in 1951 by the scarcity of scrap. The firm was starting to make great improvements in its Lincolnshire plant which were not yet completed.

[3] *E.H.S.* p. 451.

direction introduced by it, though (as will be seen later) important further changes in prices had occurred. But the general pattern of the distribution of profits in the pre-nationalisation era was similar; and although the figures in each firm are a resultant of several forces whose individual strength cannot be isolated, taken with the consolidated figures published when the industry was nationalised, they do not seem entirely inconclusive. They seem to bear some imprint of price policies under which profit margins in home trading were low or high partly for no more rational reason than that some were more easily controlled than others, exports earned differentially high margins though the types of steel which were most scarce at home were least available for export, and the levelling of raw material costs of different firms lessened the advantage of firms who were best placed to get their raw materials cheaply.

What impact would such a pattern of profits have on investment? Was it irrelevant in a régime of planning?

4. CHANGING THE PLAN

(a) The Board's function

The Board's work in supervising modernisation and development, which the Minister had set out as its first task, was in a sense truncated. The Federation had drawn up a plan, which the Government had accepted in principle, and there was no question of the Board making a plan of its own.[1] It had to vet the individual proposals of the firms, accepting the general framework of the plan. The work was not a mere formality. The Federation gave an interesting glimpse of the work. 'Emphasis was laid on speed. Accordingly the schemes submitted by firms were to a large extent studied simultaneously by the Board and the Federation's Development Committee.' the latter 'asked of proposals...whether they were necessary and adequate; whether they would conduce to the maximum

---

[1] The Federation stated (*Stat. Bull.* Oct. 1949, p. 3) that the Board *did* examine the plan as a whole and came to the same conclusion as the Government: that 'in the capacity aimed at and in the distribution of that capacity it was well conceived'. But in the whole setting it was inconceivable that the Board as instructed might dismiss the Federation plan and start again.

operating efficiency; in what order of priority they should be arranged so as to avoid congestion in the plant engineering works; and what capital expenditure was entailed. Operating costs, however, were regarded in most cases as the prime responsibility of the firms making the proposals.' How it was possible to tell that propositions were adequate or necessary or justified capital expenditure in the absence of information, and judgement, on operating costs was not vouchsafed. But the Board stepped into the breach. It 'attached particular import- ance to the economic soundness of schemes, and with its accounting experts it carefully went over the estimates of economies and earning power submitted to it. In this way it furnished a check on industry.'[1]

But little is known of what in detail was done, what was turned down by the Board, or what it changed. The Federation implied that there were instances where the Board disagreed with the Development Committee; this occurred, it was explained, 'for reasons arising from its nature as an independent external authority'. According to the Federation 'a firm who felt it had received inadequate consideration in the development plan could make representations to the Board and be sure of obtaining a disinterested judgement'. 'Disinterested' implies more than it means. Whether the Board seemed disinterested to appellants—who could not fail to notice that two of its members came from firms and two from trade unions in the industry—is not known. It was sometimes observed that the Board consulted as its own technical adviser the Federation's principal technical adviser on the plan, which did not invari- ably convey the impression of a wholly independent assessment. What criteria of efficiency the Board used, how they differed from those of the Federation and the firms, and how they applied them can only be guessed.

(b) Revised version

Sweeping changes were in fact made to the plan. Their scope was indicated by the publication at the end of 1948, near the end of the Board's life, of a revised version, with new estimates

[1] *Ibid.*

of output (not this time of capacity) at the end of the plan
period, which was now put back a year till 1953–54. The new
estimates for crude steel are compared with those in the 1946
plan, and with outputs in 1948 and 1950, in Table 28. This
upward revision of the steel plan, which reflected the revised
estimate of steel requirements referred to earlier,[1] involved a
proportionately larger increase in blast-furnace capacity. The
revision was given in terms of total pig-iron output, not, as in
the 1946 plan, for basic and haematite pig iron only. In Table 29
the 1946 plan figures have been adjusted to include projected
foundry-iron capacity at that date.

Table 28. *Planned capacity and output of crude steel (m. tons)*

	1946 plan estimated capacity for 1952–3	Output 1948	Revised estimate of output in 1953–4	Output 1950
S. Wales	3·25	3·10	3·50	3·41
N.E. Coast	3·25	3·04	3·50	3·35
Scotland	2·30	2·25	2·47	2·43
Sheffield	2·10	2·05	2·13	2·22
Lincs	1·63	1·45	1·82	1·56
Northants, etc.	1·38	0·58	1·20	0·76
Lancs, etc.	1·15	1·26	1·63	1·29
Staffs, etc.	0·65	0·76	0·87	0·86
N.W. Coast	0·25	0·38	0·38	0·42
Total	15·95	14·88	17·50	16·29

This in turn required more iron ore than the 1946 plan
envisaged. Most of the additional ore was to be imported, but
some more was to come from home sources (see Table 30).
Thus the bulk of the new pig iron (i.e. the iron not planned for
in 1946) was to be based on imported ore. But it did not look
quite like that in 1948. The increase of pig-iron output since the
war so far had depended entirely on the use of more imported
ore. This had happened, it was explained, because the use of
imported ore had been so greatly curtailed during the war; it
had 'been an important factor in keeping down the consumption of coke'. But now 'an expansion of about 6 m. tons of

[1] Above, pp. 194, 198.

home ore and 4 m. tons of imported ore will be necessary'. Plans for increasing home-ore output were under way; plans for increasing imports were under discussion.[1] The argument for using home ore on grounds of economy (as will be seen below) was still resisted. But the limit imposed in 1946 by the inadequate reserves of home ore had lost its spell in 1948; it was lost in silence.

Table 29. *Planned capacity and output of pig iron*

	1946 plan estimate of capacity 1952–3	Output 1948	1948 revised estimate of output for 1953–4	Output 1950
S. Wales	1·60	1·17	1·90	1·23
N.E. Coast	2·43	2·41	3·14	2·40
Scotland	1·25	0·77	1·40	0·74
Sheffield	0·15	0·09[a]	0·14	0·11[a]
Lincs	1·42	1·25	1·73	1·24
Northants, etc.	2·55	2·02	3·12	2·21
Lancs, etc.	0·65	0·33	0·80	0·33
Staffs, etc.	0·36	0·49	0·50	0·55
N.W. Coast	0·65	0·75	0·78	0·82
Total	11·00	9·28	13·50	9·63

[a] Estimates: the figures (which are for the Park Gate works only) are included, in the Federation Statistics, with those for Lancashire. In the *Stat. Bull.* Dec. 1948, p. 3, outputs in 1946 and 1948 were given separately. Consumption of 'hot metal' for steelmaking in the Sheffield region is a guide to the output of pig iron in this region.

Table 30. *Plans for ore supplies*

	1946 plan (for 1950–5)	Consumption 1946	Consumption 1948	1948 estimate of consumption 1953–4
Imported ore	8,300	5,568	8,030	11,750
Home ore	16,400	12,119	12,160	18,000

The Federation emphasised how much of the revised plan was provided for in the original. The readjustment in the plan involves 'not a substantial increase of new building', but using

[1] *Stat. Bull.* Dec. 1948, p. 6.

6 m. tons of new steel-melting capacity to enable 4 m. tons of extra output to be secured, with 2 m. tons for replacement, whereas in 1946 6 m. tons of new capacity were to provide 2 m. tons extra output and to replace 4 m. tons of old capacity. The conclusion might be drawn that the identical 6 m. tons of new capacity could be used for these two different purposes. But this was not what was visualised, nor what happened.

Old small works which in 1946 seemed under a threat fared much better than was expected, being not only preserved when they seemed likely to disappear, but often expanded and renovated. By the end of 1952 (when the full effects of the 1948 decisions must have been felt) three small steelworks had been dismantled in South Wales;[1] in four others some or all of the furnaces had been rebuilt,[2] and the total output of the small works, which was about 1,450,000 tons in 1937 was 1,350,000 (in twelve works) in 1952. Outside South Wales only one melting plant had been closed by 1952, apart from the new wartime electric furnace plants referred to earlier.[3] On the North-east Coast the Skinningrove and South Durham (West Hartlepool) melting shops, both due for elimination in the 1946 plan,[4] were expanded; each added a new large tilting furnace. One of the two of Dorman Long's plants which were planned away, the Acklam works, also had a new furnace (the other of the two plants, Britannia, was closed in 1953). Steel output was expanded much more by the growth of output in existing

[1] Briton Ferry Steelworks, and the Landore and Bryngwyn works of R.T.B.

[2] Bynea rebuilt four furnaces from 1947 to 1952; Briton Ferry's Albion Works had all its furnaces rebuilt 1946–52; Llanelly Steel and Partridge Jones and J. Paton rebuilt several furnaces up to 1950.

[3] Above, p. 16. The exception was at the Blochairn works; its melting shop was closed in 1952, but its plate mill was improved and provided with an electric drive.

[4] Above, p. 174. The plan said Skinningrove 'fulfils an important function', but 'no permanent future can be seen for this works in the long-term plan'. *Iron and Steel Ind.* 1946, p. 18. On South Durham it was more ambiguous. The 'South Durham light plate mill, which is in the main an efficient unit, should be improved to take care of the whole district output of light plates, and some tonnage of medium plates for the limit of the useful life of the mill' (*ibid.* p. 17). But later (p. 27) the plan said: 'it is envisaged the number of plants may be reduced to five' and the South Durham was not one of the five. And indeed on p. 17 it stated that the South Durham and Cargo Fleet plants, which both 'require rebuilding', 'should be concentrated'.

melting shops than the plan suggested and much less by the building of new ones. Except for the few instances where works were closed the small as well as the large made more steel than in 1937 or 1945.[1] This happened notably in Staffordshire, one of the two districts in which steelmaking was, according to the plan, to contract. (It contracted in neither.) In most works increased output depended partly on building new furnaces or enlarging old ones,[2] though a considerable increase was also achieved by substituting oil or tar for producer gas as a fuel in open-hearth furnaces. Oil was used by 'about a quarter of the industry' by the end of 1948,[3] and increased output by more rapid melting and because it allowed more continuous working of the furnaces which did not have to be closed down every week for flue cleaning. Possibly the use of oil enabled some works to make far more than the 1946 plan considered feasible.[4]

[1] Apart from small plants already mentioned the following had increased their outputs between 1939 and 1952, several of them appreciably. Round Oak, Bilston, Patent Shaft and Axletree, Shelton, Park Gate, Clydesdale, Bairds and Scottish, Workington. The output at Barrow, which before the war was to disappear, was slightly lower in 1952 than in 1939.

[2] A very simple guide is to be found in the *Statistical Yearbooks* published by the B.I.S.F., which include tables showing the number and sizes of open-hearth furnaces at various firms. A comparison of the tables for basic furnaces at the end of 1946 and of 1951 shows that out of forty-two firms (some of course with many works, though the table gives data for subsidiaries separately), twenty-nine had increased the size of one or more furnace (sometimes *all* their furnaces); seven of these had also increased the number of furnaces, while ten had reduced the number. Two firms had built entirely new melting shops (i.e. not replacements at the same site). Of the eight who had made no change which can be traced in these tables or had reduced the number of furnaces, one at least (John Summers) was building a wholly new shop, and another (Lancashire Steel) was building a new furnace. A number of the others were primarily alloy steelmakers, hence their interest tended to be in electric or acid open-hearth furnaces. It is not possible to trace in these tables changes in equipment—ladle cranes, charging equipment, etc.— though this certainly occurred.

[3] *Stat. B.I.S.F.* Dec. 1948, p. 4. The consumption of tar, creosole pitch and fuel oil in steel-melting furnaces and of coal in gas producers (of which some may have been for re-heating furnaces) in 1949 and 1952 was (in thousand tons):

	Tar	Pitch	Oil	Coal
1949	66	119	562	3639
1952	103	158	637	3257

[4] Thus, for example, the plan put 450,000 tons as the designed level at Cardiff (though output was larger than this in 1939) and said that the capacity 'could not readily be increased'. But output was 630,000 tons by 1952. Tar was used as fuel.

While capacity at old plants was not only used more (which was in most instances a good thing) but expanded more than was first planned, the building of three of the major new melting shops contemplated in 1946 was deferred or dropped. The new works to be built on the Northamptonshire ore field to make billets, to be sponsored jointly by Stewarts and Lloyds and United Steels, was abandoned in favour of a proposal to build a large extension at Corby; the building of the new steelworks at Lackenby was not started till 1951; the project for a new plant on the Clyde was dropped, though the designers of the plan, and the Board perhaps, were possibly still insufficiently reconciled to this to admit it.

(c)   The size of works

Hence the distribution of steel production between works fell into much the same pattern as it had in the late thirties; the number of works remained high in relation to output, though the average size grew with the growth of total output. Here, in Table 31, are approximate figures. (They are for 1953; and represent capacity more fully used than in 1952.) Since several works had more than one melting shop the average size of works exceeded that of shops; separate figures are therefore given. There was more concentration of organisation, because several

Table 31.   *Size of works, 1953*[a] (*ingot outputs, thousand tons*)

	750–1000	600–749	500–599	400–499	300–399	200–299	100–199	Under 100	Total
No. of works	4	3	3	4	7	10	20	6	57
Percentage of output	21	12	10	10	14	15	16	2	
No. of melting shops	1	5	2	5	7	14	22	10	66
Percentage of output	5	19	7	13	14	20	19	1	

[a] For 1939 see p. 79. Very small highly specialised alloy and tool steelmakers are excluded, and all works making steel for castings only. A few of the plants included, however, are essentially for special steelmaking, where the criteria of size for bulk steelmaking became largely irrelevant. Five works in the penultimate column and four in the last fall into this category, and one each in the 200–300 and 300–400 columns. No comprehensive output-by-works figures are published, but the table is based in most particulars on precise data.

firms each owned more than one works.[1] This could not give to works technical economies of scale beyond their scale, but it might give better rolling programmes, and spread sales costs and overheads, and naturally it circumscribed competition.

Possibly as a consequence of the fact that less of the additional steel output came from new works than in the plan, 'pure' steelworks, having no blast furnaces and using cold pig iron, continued to provide a surprisingly large part of the whole output. The tonnage of cold iron charged fell sharply immediately after the war, but it rose steadily to 1951 when it was as high as in 1937, and it remained as high in 1953 (and indeed in 1957). The output of steel from cold-metal shops in 1953 exceeded 6 m. tons. Of this about 1 m. tons was 'special' steel.[2] Between 2 m. and 3 m. tons was made in five works each making 250,000 tons or more a year;[3] the rest was a testimony to the survival of the host of small plants.

Table 32. *Pig iron used in steelmaking*

	Hot metal		Cold iron					
		Total	N.E. Coast	Shef-field	Lancs, Flint, etc.	Staffs, etc.	Scot-land	S.W.
1937	3860	2396	312	361	268	86	664	570
1946	4046	2046	202	328	208	115	499	619
1951	5408	2386	215	394	238	115	677	619
1953	6641	2668	131	519	144	179	764	1428
1957	9179	2849	185	711	118	182	832	637

[1] The distribution of control in 1953 was roughly as follows:

Output of firms incl. subsidiaries	No. of firms	% of whole output
Over 1·75 m. tons	3 (14 works)	35
1·00–1·74 m. tons	3 (15 works)	26
0·50–0·99 m. tons	5 (10 works)	18
0·25–0·49 m. tons	4	8
Under 0·25 m. tons	13	13

[2] About 600,000 tons were made by the Sheffield special steel makers, E.S.C., Firth Brown, Hadfields, S. Fox, Brown Bayleys.

[3] I have excluded from these figures John Summers, who were in process of becoming a 'hot-metal' shop in 1953. The largest cold-metal shop was Steel, Peech and Tozers (about 800,000 tons) at Sheffield, followed by Colvilles' Dalzell works (about 450,000 tons.)

The building of new steel furnaces at Skinningrove and West Hartlepool was symptomatic of the deferment (if no more) of almost all the plans for rationalising production and ensuring the full loading of efficient plant, of which so much was made in 1946. Rails continued to be made on the North-east Coast by Skinningrove and Cargo Fleet as well as by Dorman Longs. Though the competitors were not reduced as the plan proposed, the total tonnage of rails remained far lower than the plan visualised (about 470,000 tons instead of 650,000).[1] The manufacture of heavy plate at the South Durham works continued and the mill was improved, as the firm initially planned itself in 1944–5. By 1950 this works was the 'largest producer of sheared plates on the North-east Coast', with an output of 253,000 tons.[2] On the other hand, the new four-high light-plate mill to be built on the Clyde did not materialise. (Such a mill was, however, installed by South Durham in 1956.)[3] The continuous billet mills to be put up at Cargo Fleet, Clydeside and in Northamptonsire were not built. They had disappeared in the revised programme. One was later installed (a substitute maybe for Cargo Fleet) by Consett, where steel capacity was increased beyond the size given in the plan by the use of the Bessemer (acid) process and duplexing; but this was not in the 1948 revision. The wide-flange beam mill to be installed by Dorman Longs as one of the urgent priorities of 1945–6, to fill an essential export need, was not begun by 1953. 'Site work' had begun, it was said, by 1948. The only such beams made were made by Cargo Fleet on a conventional section mill, a practice copied from Germany; it was not, however, possible to make them in this mill with a web of over 24 in.[4] The intrusion of this firm, whose trade in heavy finished products was to be rationalised away, into this new 'heavy' trade seemed a source of some irritation.

---

[1] Thus the output of heavy rails from the North-west Coast (i.e. Workington) did not exceed 129,000 tons in any year to 1952, though the quota was 190,000 tons.

[2] *The Times*, 23 Dec. 1950.   [3] *Ibid.* 8 Jan. 1957.

[4] All that was needed was specially cut rolls; but it was a difficult and hence somewhat costly section to roll. South Durham did what Appleby Frodingham apparently decided not to do as soon as Dorman Long's plans were known. It was interesting that in the United States Kaisers decided to adapt a conventional mill to roll universal beams in 1953. Dorman Long started their design work in 1948.

The revised plan for pig iron bore the same broad character as the revised plan for steel. A number of new furnaces were located at plants where steel output was originally either to be static or to cease. On the North-east Coast there were new blast furnaces at Skinningrove and the South Durham works, the works which it was assumed in 1946 would work out their useful life but not be renewed. The Skinningrove furnace was specifically mentioned in the revised plan, and it represented some of the increase in the 1948 North-east Coast 'target' for 1953–4. A new blast furnace was 'put into commission at the West Hartlepool works' in December 1950, so it too must have been in the revised plan.[1] In addition a third furnace, not in the plan, was put up at Consett (making it one of the highest capacity plants in the country), and Cargo Fleet built a new furnace.[2] Dorman Long, on the other hand, improved several existing furnaces (to great advantage) but did not start building their projected new ones in this period at all. In Staffordshire the Shelton furnaces, of which two were originally to go when the Shotton plant was built,[3] were reprieved and part was modernised;[4] at Bilston new ore-handling plant was installed[5] and a new furnace built.[6] On the other hand, the new plants in Northamptonshire and Scotland were not built.

One result of the revision of the plan of which these instances are symptomatic was almost certainly to keep down the average size of the new and rebuilt blast furnaces, sometimes because existing ancillary equipment was used, sometimes because relatively small steelworks could not use the pig iron from very large blast furnaces. This reinforced a tendency in the first version of the plan. Whereas in the United States the new furnaces of the war period and since had hearths of about 28 ft. diameter normally, the new British furnaces in the first seven years of peace (excluding 'rebuilds' which were limited in size

---

[1] *The Times*, 23 Dec. 1950.
[2] Which was not inconsistent with the first plan, but was not mentioned in it.
[3] *Iron and Steel Ind.* 1946, p. 21.
[4] This came however in the middle fifties.
[5] *Stat. Bull.* Dec. 1948, p. 9; this was completed by 1948, but no new furnace was mentioned.
[6] Possibly, however, it was not planned until after 1948.

by existing structural steelwork) had hearth diameters of from 18 to 21 ft. for the most part. Only one furnace completed by 1952 was in the largest class though a few others were being built, all at steel plants exceptionally large by British standards. The demand for pig iron slowed down the replacement of old furnaces; there were still nineteen or twenty hand-charged furnaces making pig iron for steel in 1952, and a further twenty-five making foundry iron. The average output of a British blast furnace in 1952 (105,000 tons), though much larger than in 1937, was still much less than even in Germany (130,000 tons), where little reconstruction had so far taken place, and not much above one-third of the United States average (270,000 tons).[1] The average output of blast furnaces making basic iron in the United Kingdom was above the general British average (because most of the new furnaces made basic iron); it was 114,000 tons in 1950 (compared with the estimate of 160,000 tons for 1950 given in the 1946 plan)[2] and 126,000 tons in 1952.

Such then were the main changes in the plan for investment up to the end of the first Board's activities. Much that was originally planned remained in the revised version. Nevertheless, the changes affected in a remarkable degree the elements in the plan which seemed to arise from central planning, the things which were most emphasised, for example, in the summary, the new works which were not first projected by firms, the export priorities, the plans 'to achieve the most effective degree of concentration', and to concentrate the greatest percentage expansion of steel capacity 'on Midland home ore sites'.[3]

What happened resembled the normal pattern of boom development, which made it desirable to keep all existing plant in use and tempting to expand it all. How far did central planning, in particular the Board, salvage from the process the advantages originally sought by planning? 'The big new units it is necessary to build', the Federation wrote in 1945 in the

---

[1] For some purposes, but not for all, it is necessary to make adjustments allowing for differences in the iron content in the iron ore used. The United States–United Kingdom contrasts are then less but still striking. Cp. *Report of Anglo-American Productivity Team*, in which this is discussed with some complexity, below, pp. 270 sqq.

[2] *Iron and Steel Ind.* 1946, p. 30.   [3] *Ibid.* 1946, pp. 36–7.

plan, 'involve displacing a mixed collection of plant, some of which is still moderately good. Unless this issue is faced...the reconstruction is a patchwork job and does not achieve the best long-term result. Further, while the future costs at both new and old plant will tend to change, on balance the changes are almost certain to involve a relative worsening of the position of the older plants.'[1] This reflected the discussions of the 'Under Fifties'. Was it lost sight of in the unexpectedly easy conditions of the late forties? Was it finally adjudged wrong? It has been seen that there was a strong argument in 1947–8 for making the best use of existing plants, and for deferring more radical plans. Were the changes of plan more than the reasonable outcome of an acceptance of this argument?

(d) South Wales, Northamptonshire and Clydeside

The Board's views on individual projects only became public over the siting of the cold strip mill and tinplate plant to use strip from the hot mill at Margam. They preferred Swansea to Llanelly. If costs had to be deliberately increased by the geographical separation of hot and cold rolling, as a sacrifice to the idol of Development Areas, it was sensible to do it as little as possible. The Government overruled the Board. But the Board was at one with the firms and the Federation; there was no conflict, no unwelcome initiative.

Nor do the other changes, additions or subtractions, suggest a conflict. The indefinite deferment of the new Scots and Northamptonshire plants was presumably on the initiative of the firms; the new Clyde plant had never been welcomed by Colvilles; the new plant in Northamptonshire had been wished on United Steels and Stewarts and Lloyds. The former showed no signs of regret at its demise, the latter no impatience to get on with the substitute plan for a much enlarged Corby. Their interest, as they had stated clearly in 1945, was in making tubes; billet production offered little attraction. On the other side of the medal firms such as Skinningrove, Cargo Fleet and South Durham would be glad to claim a new lease of life; and it may

---

[1] *Ibid.* p. 31.

be assumed that the delays, for example, in building the new Lackenby plant were not imposed by the Board.

The decision to forgo a new Northamptonshire plant in favour of a large expansion at Corby could be sensibly explained by the greater difficulty and cost involved in starting a new town rather than expanding an existing one. To expand Corby offered also more of the technical advantages of large-scale working, though the Federation did not claim this. The signs are that at the end of 1948 the change of plan was only expected by the Board and Federation to delay the building of the new steelworks and billet mill for a short time; site preparation was taking place for blast furnaces, Bessemer plant and billet mill, it was said, and it would all be finished shortly after the first planning period ended in 1952–3.[1] Early in 1949 Corby was designated as a new town specifically with the object of housing the workers for the new steelworks 'which was being undertaken urgently as a matter of national importance'. The Government was co-operating. Houses were already being built by the Urban District Council at a rate of 400 a year, which was to be stepped up.[2] At this stage the project appeared still to be, for the central planners, firmly in the plan.

By the end of 1950 (18 months after the Board's demise) it was more doubtful. The Federation published another of its characteristic analyses of the problems of location. East Midlands' developments were hampered, it said, by difficulties in getting skilled labour, and these were 'aggravated by the housing preference accorded to the development areas. The policy of full employment as popularly interpreted has greatly increased the "pull" of the older steelmaking areas. It has tipped the scales so markedly in favour of the development areas as to put substantial obstacles in the way of development elsewhere.'[3] No reference was made—a strange oversight—to the fact that Corby was now a 'new town'. More new houses were built in

---

[1] Stat. Bull. Dec. 1948, p. 7.

[2] First Report of Corby New Town Corporation (in the collected reports of the New Towns, 1951, p. 89). The Minister of Town and Country Planning first discussed the matter in April 1949, and provisional designation came in 27 July 1949.

[3] Stat. Bull. Nov. 1950, p. 12.

Corby (and in Scunthorpe) by the end of 1953 than in Port Talbot.[1] The new houses built in Corby in nine years from April 1945 provided accommodation for approximately 12,000 persons.[2] There was a net increase in 1950 itself of 1246.[3] A new integrated plant on the scale spoken of would probably have needed quickly from 2000 to 3000 workers.

But, the Federation went on to show, it was really immaterial whether more steel was made from home ores, on home ore sites. At greater length and even more disingenuously than in 1946 the Federation argued that the cost advantages in using home ore were very small and likely to get less over the next 20 years. They did this when imported ore reached a slightly lower price than it had at any time since the war, for what turned out to be a brief period only. Costs of home ore they argued were bound to 'rise considerably' over the next 20 years,

[1] *Housing Returns for England and Wales*, 31 Mar. 1954, Appendix B. (The figures are issued quarterly; those I used include the first quarter of 1954.) The position was as follows:

	Temporary houses	Permanent houses completed	Houses under construction
Port Talbot	115	2467	448
Scunthorpe	100	3667	492
Corby	50	2938	521

Houses in neighbouring towns and villages would also be important; only 60 per cent of Stewarts and Lloyds' 7000–8000 workers lived in Corby in 1952 (*Corby New Town: Exhibition of the Draft Master Plan*, Oct. 1952, p. 9). Kettering housed 12 per cent, the rest were in Weldon and other local villages. Many houses were built in Kettering in these years, in Kettering Borough and R.D.C., and in the Oundle and Thrapston R.D.C. and Oundle U.D.C. (130 temporary, 2416 permanent, 522 under construction). Some of this was no doubt available for Corby workers. Similarly, many houses were built at Neath, Bridgend and Aberdare which would have housed some Port Talbot workers; Port Talbot may also have gained from building at Swansea, Barry and Cardiff. It is an interesting commentary on the argument for development areas that their use saves expenditure on social capital that so much house building was needed for the strip mill.

[2] The average household numbered 3·9 (*Corby New Town*, a Report, by W. Holford and H. Myles Wright, 1952, p. 65) and approximately 3000 houses were built. The number built to the end of Mar. 1950 was 732. In the year ending Mar. 1952, 349 houses were completed; in the following year 584. If the occupation of those built by the New Town Corporation is a guide, 310 of these 584 would have been occupied by steelworkers (*2nd Ann. Rep. of Corby New Town Corp.* p. 125, and *3rd Ann. Rep.* pp. 117–18).

[3] *Ibid.* p. 38. Presumably the increase of population was greater.

'whereas the present *high prices*[1] of imported ore are more likely to fall than to rise'. Wishful thinking perhaps, but certainly a classic misjudgement. Presumably they felt the lower price marked the return of those days of normality for which they had awaited so long. The threat of Korean prices may have been foreseen but adjudged temporary. The significance of devaluation, when the effect of the lull in demand for steel early in 1950 had ceased to affect ore contracts, was still apparently not fully recognised, which is surprising, because the Federation was well staffed to be alert and sensitive in such matters.

The Federation argued that pig iron made from imported ore costing 56*s*. per ton C.I.F.[2] would only cost 5*s*. per ton more than pig iron made from home ore when the average delivered price of this was 12*s*. per ton, and the home ore pig iron would be poorer in quality. The calculation, even at these raw-material prices, threw the balance—could it have been unconsciously—in the direction of the Federation's prejudices. The total ore cost (including sinter) when foreign ore was used was put at 93*s*. This would only pay for raw ore containing 0·93 ton of iron per ton of pig iron (which was slightly less than was required, though some more iron could of course be provided in other forms, e.g. in scrap, or scale, at a cost), and at works where iron ore was delivered directly from ship to ironworks. It did not cover any sintering costs. Yet one-sixth of imported ore was now sintered.[3] This cost figure therefore applied neither to coastal works like Margam and Dorman Long, where ore preparation and sintering was becoming important, nor to inland works like Consett and Colvilles where there was a rail-transport cost. The estimated ore cost for home ore (48*s*. per ton of pig iron) manifestly included the cost of sintering; raw ore at the major home ore plants sited near the ore fields cost 8*s*. per ton or less when charged direct into the furnaces.[4]

---

[1] My italics.

[2] The average iron content of the imports was 55 per cent in 1949.

[3] The figures were published regularly by the Federation from 1948.

[4] The average of 12*s*. a ton in the Federation article probably referred not only to ore used in the east Midlands but to ore taken from the east Midlands and used, for example, on the North-east Coast and in South Wales. The figure of 8*s*. a ton was derived from one of the major firms. The E.C.E. in its report on *European Steel*

When the Federation turned to the cost of coke, current prices were accepted as though here the relation between coal prices in different areas would be stable for the next 20 years.[1] Yet it was common knowledge that Scots and South Wales coals were selling close to or below their cost, and that Yorkshire and east Midland coals were helping to pay these excess costs, and the National Coal Board had declared its intention to make prices of particular grades of coal more nearly cover their costs.[2] It was thus likely that coking-coal costs would move in favour of home ore sites, and that the less good but much cheaper to mine coking coals of the Midlands would be used in increasing proportions (as was happening in Lorraine).[3]

Trends in 1949 (p. 50) said that reliable data for the prices of home-produced ore in the United Kingdom were not available. But reliable average *values*, used in Tables 2 etc., were published by the Ministry of Fuel and (or) Power. The value which covers some costly haematite was 8s. 6d. in 1950.

[1] The Federation took the price of coke per ton as 94s. at home ore sites and 82s. at imported ore sites. This difference they attributed to transport costs. (They allowed 16 cwt. of coke for smelting imported ores costing 66s., and 20 cwt. for home ore costing 94s.).

[2] Above, p. 25, for the development during the war. The National Coal Board price policy was set out in its *Annual Report* for 1949, pp. 45–7. The average costs and average receipts in the relevant localities are shown in the following table for 1950, from the *Annual Report* for 1950. This was a year in which the margin between proceeds and costs were exceptionally favourable.

	Proceeds	Costs (before charging interest)	Margin (before charging interest) +	Margin (before charging interest) −
	s. d.	s. d.	s. d.	s. d.
E. Midlands	43 4	36 6	6 10	
Yorkshire	47 1	42 5	4 8	
S. Wales[a]	51 1	48 11	2 2	
Scotland	47 2	46 9	5	
Durham	49 3	51 6		2 3

[a] This figure is based on South Wales areas excluding Swansea (which was largely an anthracite area, with a heavy loss), and is a more reliable guide to the coking-coal position than figures for the whole South West Division, or for the whole of South Wales. Interest, at 3½ per cent, averaged roughly 1s. 4d. a ton.

[3] There were other lacunae in the Federation's analysis of costs. More limestone is normally charged with imported ore; in steelmaking from home ores a self-fluxing mixture is normally used. The careful reader of the Federation article will also find that one point is left out of the calculation which is in favour of imported ore. It is rightly said that the use of home ore involves heavier capital cost at the

The Federation arguments were the prelude to news that 'the problem of labour supply had proved so difficult that it has not been possible so far to plan for expansion at Corby beyond a steel production of 600,000 tons a year. The solution of the labour problem depends...on the provision of houses at a considerably more rapid rate.'[1] Still no mention of the 'New Town', no figures of houses built or building or required, or of the net immigration at a rate of 1200 in 1950. Blast-furnace capacity at Kettering and Wellingborough, it was pointed out, was idle for lack of men. Kettering was, it has been seen, supplying labour to Corby; the local blast furnaces were hand charged, not attractive to labour, but their difficulties were solved in 1952 by the use of Italian labour.[2] Why not earlier?[3] The problem was not as simple as the Federation made it out to be. Stewarts and Lloyds were evidently able to absorb all the additional labour coming to Corby in tubemaking and making steel for tubes, and would find it most profitable to concentrate on this. Their original programme (which did not include a large Bessemer expansion at Corby and was not restricted to Corby) took far longer than was expected—four years for the Corby open-hearth plant instead of two, for example—and since there remained an exigent demand for tubes there was no overwhelming reason why the firm should divert capital which it could use in tubemaking into making a new product (especially an unremunerative one like billets). The time had not come when in its own interest it would wish to diversify its output. It may have seemed to Stewarts and Lloyds that there was no need to be in a hurry over expanding steel output at Corby; they had bought or had leased most of the local ores; no other firm could think of starting at Corby if they themselves were

blast furnaces—they put the difference as between £18 for an output of a ton a year instead of £13, and this difference of £5 a ton/year is estimated at 14s. a year, assuming a gross profit (before depreciation) of 14 per cent. But operating costs—labour costs, repair costs, slag handling costs—are higher using home ores. It is only worth mentioning this because the article gives an air of solidity and comprehensiveness which may mislead.

[1] *Stat. Bull.* Dec. 1950, p. 7.
[2] *Ibid.* Oct. 1952, p. 5.
[3] The employment of European labour occurred frequently in British industries from 1947 onwards.

slow off the mark; and the Federation *cum* Board *cum* Ministry price and levy policies (whatever their theoretic possibilities as expounded by the Federation and set out above) had reduced the incentive to them (or to anyone else) to take advantage of the fact that steel was much cheaper in 'real' terms to produce from Corby pig iron than from any other pig iron, save possibly Lincolnshire iron. The makers were deprived of much of the cost advantage. Finally, decisions on a large steelworks expansion announced at the end of 1950 will have reflected the threat of a slump early in the year, and possibly the shadows cast both by nationalisation and Korea.

But the decisions, and motives, of 1950 fell outside the period of the first Board. Within the narrow confines of planning for Northamptonshire in 1948 the decision the Board accepted (but possibly did not instigate) to concentrate the major expansion at Corby was possibly an improvement in principle on the plan as originally presented. Whether it was a practical or still only a nominal part of the plan had to be proved. Could the same be said of the decision to drop the project for a new Clydeside plant?

When the Federation ultimately set out to explain this change (in 1952) it attributed it to coal—'the likely future development of coking coal appeared to lie on the east coast of Scotland and the markets and ore import on the west. Hence the gain to be secured from transferring a major part of production from the centre of Scotland to the Clyde coast on purely locational and raw material grounds was insufficient to compensate for the very substantial extra capital cost which would have been involved in transferring production from the Motherwell area to the Clyde estuary. Once the decision had been taken to develop further existing plant east of Glasgow the pace of development in Scotland was largely determined by the availability of coal supplies.'[1]

The Scots coal situation was set out in a *Report* of 1944. It was familiar to the Scots steelmakers at that date, because as coal-owners they contributed much of the data. It was known in the Ministry of Supply, and it ought to have been familiar to the planners of 1946. The output of the Lanarkshire mines, the

---

[1] *Stat. Bull.* Nov. 1952, p. 2.

main source of coking coal, already declining, would continue
to decline 'during the next 30 years or so'.[1] Of the reserves of
coal in Scotland which would make it possible to sustain total
output, and even raise it, while Lanarkshire declined, the seams
in the Limestone Coal Group of the north-east Stirlingshire
coalfield alone were 'of high-class coking quality'.[2] These
reserves were relatively small, but output might be increased
from 1·5 m. tons a year, the 1939 figure, to 2·5 m. tons in 1965
and 2·7 m. in 1975.[3] 'The coking coal available in other areas—
mainly in the northern and western fringes of the Central
Coalfield—forms only a comparatively small proportion of the
coal available in those areas.'[4] The Scots supply of coking coal
on the most favourable interpretation of these figures would
only be raised a little in 20 years, after several new mines had
been sunk, and the prospect was that the coal would be relatively dear. The *Plan for Coal* drawn up in 1949 repeated this
diagnosis, but added nothing essentially new.[5]

Hence the coal argument of 1952 (and perhaps 1948) should
have shaped the plan of 1945–6. The most obvious question
raised by this coal survey was whether more pig iron and steel
should be made in Scotland at all, not where precisely it should
be made. But the 1948 revised programme took the answer for
granted as the 1946 plan had done; an even higher Scots pig-
iron output was proposed in 1948. In terms of access to coking
coal the relative advantages of a Clydeside site or a site near
Motherwell—or of the new competitive site, sponsored by the
Scottish Council, a Firth of Forth site near Rosyth—had not
changed by 1948 or 1952. If anything it would appear that the
more Lanarkshire coking-coal supplies declined the less the
relative advantage of the old steelworks sites in this respect.

---

[1] *Scottish Coalfields, the Report of the Scottish Coalfields Committee*, 1944 (Cmd. 6575),
pp. 64–5.
    [2] *Ibid.* p. 74.
    [3] *Ibid.* pp. 75–6. This passage is of interest, like all the report, in showing that
the Scots mining companies were planning their sinkings for 15–20 years or more
ahead. National planning was not *longer* sighted, though it may have permitted
more co-ordination.
    [4] *Ibid.* p. 74.
    [5] *Plan for Coal*, Oct. 1950, Technical Appendix 1, pp. 47, 49, 53–58. 1·24 m. tons
of Scots coal was supplied to coke ovens in 1948 (p. 58).

Colvilles, with whom the decision ultimately rested, made no pretence that *new* considerations about coal influenced their judgement. They had, they explained in 1949,[1] examined the proposal again carefully. It had been considered 20 years earlier 'but did not get any support'.[2] The second review confirmed that 'on economic grounds the scheme could not be justified'. Any saving, they said, due to the elimination of rail carriage of iron ore would be more than offset by the cost of taking coke to a site down the Clyde. (This was presumably even more so 20 years earlier.) Conversion costs would be the same, as they would use the same plant on either site, and the move to a new site would cause a 'social upheaval of a grave and far-reaching character'. So Colvilles, who owned a lot of land adjacent to their Dalzell and Lanarkshire Steel Company works, proposed to build blast furnaces there instead of on the Clyde. They had proposed this to the Federation and Board early in 1948.[3]

It had not been approved a year later.[4] Nor is this surprising. Whether Colvilles judgement was right it is impossible to tell from published information; but their statement did less than justice to those who proposed the more radical change. To take a small point first, the riverside location in cutting the rail haulage of iron ore also eliminated a loading and unloading operation; the longer distance over which coking coal would be carried involved no extra handling. It is well known that to lengthen a rail journey does not add as large a proportion to its cost as to its length because there are no extra terminal costs. Moreover, since only 15 to 16 cwt. of coke were needed for a ton of iron (equal to less than 25 cwt. of coal), but $1\frac{1}{2}$ tons or more of iron ore, the volume of ore transport saved would somewhat

[1] *The Times*, 18 May 1949 (the Chairman's annual speech).
[2] This was a slight exaggeration according to some contemporary accounts. Mr Brassert claimed that Mr Macdiarmid (as he then was) approved of the 'Weir scheme', and Mr Macdiarmid did not demur from this in subsequent discussions. He explained to me that he thought many British steelmakers did not allow enough for the unexpected gains derived from having entirely new works. It was in the course of negotiations on the Weir scheme that Brassert was asked to draw up the report from which the Corby works resulted.
[3] This may be inferred from the Chairman's statement (*The Times*, 18 May 1948).
[4] *The Times*, 18 May 1949.

exceed the volume of additional coal transport. The advocates of the scheme had, however, claimed much more than the
saving over ore. They thought a Clydeside site would gain by
being nearer the main Scots markets for heavy steel, and nearer
the main sources of scrap (they might have argued by 1948 also
better placed for fuel oil) and that a wholly new works, which
would be replacing plants of low efficiency and poor layout,[1]
would give more economies in production than one which was
partly new and partly an adaptation, even a radical adaptation,
of existing units. It was not the case that exactly the same kind
of plant would be used, with the same conversion cost, whether
the site were Motherwell or Clydeside; at Motherwell some
parts of the plant complex would be modified old plants, as the
proposal to supply liquid pig iron from the proposed Motherwell
blast furnaces to Dalzell and Lanarkshire showed. At Clydeside
all, perforce, would have been at least wholly new in layout.[2]

During the discussion on the major scheme Colvilles had
continued their pre-war policy of piecemeal improvement to
existing plant, not on an improvising short-term basis but on
a fairly lavish scale. By 1949 it could be seen that the piecemeal
embellishments already sanctioned and carried out since the
war had virtually decided the planning issue as Colvilles
wished, though the final consent had still to be given. The
developments at Clyde Iron Works and Dalzell have been
referred to. 'Limited expenditure' (the planners' phrase in
1946)[3] on Clydebridge steelworks turned out to be a major
addition to the melting shop. 'Limited expenditure' at Lanarkshire Steel Works turned out to be completing a policy inaugurated in 1936; the old furnaces were replaced by 150-ton
furnaces, waste heat boilers installed to provide electricity, the
mills were provided with electric drives, and the works were
linked with the adjacent Dalzell works by private rail so that
the plants could be operated together. Finally, an additional

---

[1] Cp. *E.H.S.* p. 368, on Dalzell in the twenties. Though there had been changes,
in some ways new difficulties in flow appeared to have been caused by changes
before the war.
[2] On the other hand, it would have been possible to transfer existing machinery
to Clydeside when it was good enough.
[3] Above, p. 178.

pipeline was laid from the Clyde to provide adequate water for this works and for the Dalzell and Clyde Alloy works.[1] All this must have powerfully affected any new decision by the end of 1948.

Colvilles policy of building adjacent to the old sites and incorporating old plant promised to reduce capital expenditure below the level required for a new riverside plant, probably, however, without getting such low production costs as the more radical change would have given.

They appeared to have no doubts themselves where the balance of advantage lay. In addition to a real reduction of capital expenditure, their policy, by enabling much of the investment to be spread and financed over a relatively long period, reduced the capital burden of their modernisation in balance-sheet terms in a way which if not carefully observed could be misleading. 'Since its formation', as the chairman, Sir John Craig, explained in 1949, 'the company has followed the policy of expansion without increasing the subscribed capital. In 1938 we built coke ovens, blast furnaces and a new steelworks at a cost of £2·5 m. No new shares were issued.'[2] Some £5 m. had been spent on expansions since the war by the end of 1950, and again with no new shares, and no debentures or loans, and no increase of dividend since 1946. The process is simple and circumstances favoured it. No doubt interest was always taken into account in calculating the desirability of new investments, but the directors did not have to pay the interest, and it did not figure as a cost in the balance sheet. It was of course necessary that profits should be relatively good if large sums were to be reinvested. The level of demand after the war was high, plants were often operated above normal capacity, and Colvilles benefited from the Federation-Ministry price

---

[1] *The Times*, 15 May 1950. The output of the Lanarkshire Steel Company's works in 1952 was some 290,000 tons. Colvilles were also turning the Mossend works into an engineering plant: part was a constructional engineering works, part was to be a central engineering works not only for repairs but also for the manufacture of new plant for their extensions.

[2] *The Times*, 18 May 1949. Dividends (including income tax) on ordinary shares (at 13 per cent) and on cumulative preference shares took 1·7 per cent of turnover.

policy which favoured large users of scrap and imported ore.[1] However, if a balance sheet is thought of as reflecting the cost of investments, this type of self-finance provides an incomplete picture even though the cumulative series of investments is partially recorded in the book value of fixed assets.[2] Building a new works on a greenfield site involves doing much more work in a shorter time, and more new capital must be raised in shares or loans, involving a large, partly inescapable, partly implied, commitment in interest and dividends. The classic instance at this time was the Margam strip mill; in 1953, when the fixed assets of the Steel Company of Wales were valued at £79·6 m. yearly, interests on loans and debentures was over £2·25 m., although interest rates on borrowings were exceptionally low. This was apart from dividends due on £16·9 m., which so far were being paid at a very low rate, 4 per cent.[3] The possibility of obtaining capital at virtually no cost in interest may tend to tilt the scales in favour of the expansion of existing plants and near existing sites by giving an exaggerated impression of the real advantage gained thereby in lowered capital cost to offset higher material and processing costs.[4]

(e) Rising cost of new plant

By the time Colvilles presented their major programme to the Board for approval the cost of building new plants had considerably increased since 1945, and it was being suggested that

---

[1] They might reasonably argue that but for Ministry policy prices would have been higher. Nevertheless, the relative profitability of steelmaking based on scrap and imported ores compared with that of steelmaking based on home ore would have been less but for the price policies adopted.

[2] Not fully, if, for example, the value of money falls, or if depreciation is faster in the accounts than in real life—which is often the case, since plants go on in use when 'written off'.

[3] *Iron and Steel Realisation Agency: Accounts of Subsidiary Companies* (year ended 3 Oct. 1953, Acct. no. 58). There were 3 per cent first mortgage bonds (£15 m.), a loan of £28·2 m. from the Finance Corporation for industry carrying 4 per cent, and one of £23·4 m. from the Agency. This had not all carried interest yet for a year; the interest payment for the year was £2·26 m.

[4] Cp. Sir John Craig: 'Low capital cost combined with a production cost which compares favourably with (did this mean 'is a little higher than'?) 'that of a new plant offers advantages that are likely to be even more important in the future than they are today' (*The Times*, 25 May 1952).

this had lessened—the implication was permanently—the advantage of radical change. The Federation said it had now ceased to be advantageous to replace plant for heavy steel-making plates and sections, though the margin of advantage for sheets and billets remained.[1] This belief helped to provide a rationalisation of the change in the character of the plan in its revised form.

The cost of new plant had certainly risen steadily since 1945; the Federation's estimate was an average rise of 12 per cent a year. But in part this was merely a reflection of the general inflation of these years. In the course of that inflation other steelmaking costs also rose, including the elements of cost (e.g. labour) in which modernisation could bring reductions. If the costs which were to be reduced by modernisation had risen as much as the cost of new plant the advantage of radical change would have been as great in 1948 as in 1945. But it had not in fact been quite as great; the position is set out, necessarily roughly, in Table 33.

Was it possible to judge how permanent these trends were likely to prove? Why should the cost of new plants rise more than, for example, wages, or coal prices, between 1945 and 1948? In part the answer was the rise in the price of imports both of raw materials and plant. 'The terms of trade have been against the country during the post-war years', the Federation said in 1948 'and it now seems unsafe to assume a reversal of this trend.'[2] The major source, however, was the conjuncture of prolonged boomlike demand for capital goods at home and abroad with the inefficiencies of production which are

---

[1] *Stat. Bull.* Dec. 1948, p. 2. The argument was twofold: the costs of high-cost and low-cost plants had been brought closer together, by reductions in the high-cost plants, and the cost of new plant had risen. 'A change in the balance between expansion and replacement has become appropriate as the increases in the cost of new plant over the last three years has been so great.'

[2] *Ibid.* Dec. 1948, p. 2. The price indices of imports and exports in these years were (Dec. 1946 = 100):

	Imports (A)	Exports (B)	Terms of trade (A as per cent of B)
1947	111	109	102
1948	125	119	105
1949	126	124	102
1950	143	129	111
1951	190	152	125

Table 33. *Cost of labour, transport, coal and new plant*

Year	Labour[a]	Transport	(1946 = 100) Coking coal[b]	New plant for steelworks[c]	Prices of metal goods exported[d]
1937	56	80	37	56	—
1947	115	124	110	111	111
1948	121	124	119	128	121
1949	129	124	121	134	124
1950	132	144	124	138	134
1951	144	159	136	154	151
1952	160	175	152	168	168

[a] Based on Ministry of Labour figures for earnings per hour, with 2 per cent added from 1949 to allow for a week's holiday with pay, but no account otherwise of changes in fringe wage costs.

[b] Based on *average* of movements in Yorkshire and Durham. Coke prices moved up more than coking-coal prices; this possibly reflected a lesser increase in returns from by-products, which competed with alternative products. While modernisation aims at saving coke it will normally involve using more electric power. Electric power rose in price less than coal; hence this was a movement which favoured investment—power used in place of labour rose in price less than labour. To some extent, however, this was due to unsound methods of fixing prices.

[c] The Federation's index, *Stat. B.I.S.F.* Nov. 1952, p. 7 revised. This is based on steelworks contracts, but takes into account experiences in other industries. No index of this kind can be precisely accurate; in the long run I should expect figures for later years to refer to more refined plant: for example, to say that a works to make billets cost £8. 10s. a ton/year in 1933 and £23. 10s. in 1945 (as the 1946 plan said, p. 32) was not comparing like with like.

[d] Based on Board of Trade indices.

symptomatic of adjustment after war. Rates of recovery, for example, in output and in quality were not uniform for all products either in this country or overseas. Too many orders were accepted on too optimistic assumptions. Scarcities of coal, electricity, steel, zinc, timber, skilled labour, for example (not always unexpected but not subject to precise prevision), time occupied in obtaining licences to cope with the scarcities, diversions of more goods to export to cope with the worsening terms of trade, and other such things interfered with the flow of production and building. The building of new plants was not only relatively dear, it was exceptionally slow.[1] All capital

[1] It took about four years or so to build new open-hearth shops, coke ovens, blast furnaces, or rolling mills where buildings were needed; twice as long as in the United States, or before the war in the United Kingdom. When German rebuilding got under way it was much quicker than the British.

development was hampered by these things, but steelworks development perhaps a little more than the average because it had depended before the war much on imports of plant, and with dollar imports restricted and no German supplies home sources had now to be expanded.[1] These varied pressures revealed weaknesses in organisation—lack of adequate forward planning and forward ordering in big contracts, for example[2]— which were not new but newly important, and arose not only because of the post-war maladjustments but because the greater scale and complexity of new plants required more co-ordination in their erection and more mechanical aids to speed the works.[3]

One major task of planning should have been to remove the causes of the excessive cost of new works, which was clearly remediable. The one thing that was quite clear when the sources of high cost were examined was that the trend could be temporary and was reversible. Any step which would increase pig iron and steel supplies more quickly would alleviate the situation, hence the proposals in 1947–48 to concentrate for a short time on relatively minor but quickly rewarding jobs at the expense of radical change were essentially wise, and emergency measures, including special dollar imports, would have been justified for this. To continue to place orders for plants when delivery promises were not only long but not being kept was to prolong the period of excessive cost. The proper course was probably to lighten the immediate burden of demand. Some firms accepted this view. The chairman of Stewarts and Lloyds when he first referred publicly to the project of an extension at

[1] There were parallel problems, for example, in the building of some chemical and oil refinery plant. Some steelworks plant, moreover, was made for export; and some acute scarcities were not specifically of steelworks plant—but, for example, of boilers.

[2] This was not limited to steelworks; it was referrred to at some length in some of the *Anglo-American Productivity Reports*; compare also *The Fawley Story*.

[3] Thus, for example, because of the elaborate foundations and the vast extent of new steelworks, earth-moving equipment and the like, were important, though before the war they were not much used. Such equipment was brought in under Lease Lend, and there was much more after than before the war. Nevertheless, in the early post-war years it was not uncommon to see work being done by hand on big contracts, levelling surfaces, for example, which could be bulldozed. Normal before the war it had become a costly anachronism, and source of delay. But it was on the way out.

Corby to make 400,000 tons of steel a year for purposes other than tubes said that shortages 'make planning of this large scheme difficult as the delivery of some of the key items of plant are very extended'.[1] (At this stage labour and housing scarcity were not mentioned as the chief discouragements.)

Several firms were impressed by the desirability of first making the most of existing plant, notably Colvilles and South Durham-Cargo Fleet.[2] But this could be interpreted in several ways. The effect of readjusted demands was not to reduce total demand for new capital equipment for steel; the revised plan of 1948 fixed the volume of capital work to be undertaken above the 1946 plan, not merely at the end of the planning period but immediately. The assumption which was made in practice was not that radical change should be deferred till capital costs came into line, but that it should be to a large extent abandoned in favour of lesser but more numerous and scattered changes, giving less reduction in operating costs but capable of being done generally in smaller jobs requiring lesser concentrations of investment which were capable of being financed more largely out of profits (it might be called a policy of sacrificial ploughing back) and, as at Colvilles, even without new commitments.[3] How far the assumption was made deliberately as the basis of policy, how far it was a rationalisation of what happened in face of the pressure by firms to carry out the plans which they formulated in isolation under the tempting pressures of demand for steel, is not known. It may even have been thought that for steel industry to act alone in this would mean that it lost its place in the queue for some sorts of equipment with no ultimate

---

[1] *The Times*, 28 May 1948.

[2] For Colvilles see references above. For South Durham-Cargo Fleet, *The Times*, 23 Dec. 1950: 'our policy of improving the efficiency and increasing the production of works which exist today has been justified, and has avoided capital expenditure on a considerably larger scale'. A leading personality in the Federation told me early in 1948 that he found these two firms the leading exponents of the policy of dropping radical development.

[3] To take another example. Thus Mr Chetwynd-Talbot explained that modernisation was being carried out 'without charge on the capital structure' (*The Times*, 23 Dec. 1950). Within the last 3 years, he announced in 1954, £4·7 m. had been spent on capital development of which £3·7 m. had come out of profits and £1 m. had been advanced by the I.S.N.R.A. (*ibid.* 14 Jan. 1954).

gain, that one industry alone cannot cure a disorder of this kind. But the implication of the decisions of 1948 are unmistakable. The volume of capital works done in 1947 was, according to the Federation's statistics, already at the average level for the seven years provided for in the plan.[1] The level for 1948 was above it, and activity reached its peak in 1949–50. The disease of the long construction period however remained;[2] the peak did not mean a hastening of completions, though more jobs were, inevitably, being completed, but a larger amount of work in progress. The objects visualised by those who wanted 'urgent improvisation' in 1947 were not attained, because the policy, which could be presented as making use of existing plant, was of a wholly different nature. The result of more diffuse (though larger) investment was inevitably, as seen already, more diffuse production, and so smaller scale production; the number of works expected to remain for a considerable period was greater.

[1] *Stat. Bull.* Nov. 1952, p. 7, gives the following figures of the expenditure each year from 1946 in contemporary prices and in 1952 prices:

	Expenditure (£m.)	
Year	Actual	At 1952 prices
1946	5·0	9·3
1947	30·0	50·2
1948	40·2	58·5
1949	50·3	71·7
1950	56·7	76·0
1951	62·4	70·9
1952	65·0	65·0
Total	309·6	401·6

The original £168 m. was valued at £340 m. in 1952 prices. Expenditure in 1948 was just over one-sixth of this. (The £168 was to be spent in 7½ years, *Rep. B.I.S.F.* p. 36). Later discussions (below, p. 454) were to show how much figures of this kind can vary according to what is included; but the Federation presumably knew that this sort of comparison made in 1952 was valid.

[2] The Federation wrote in 1952 as though blast-furnace construction was exceptional in taking 3–4 years, and explained it by the competition of new generating stations for boilers and heavy electrical plant (*Stat. Bull.* Nov. 1952, p.6). But delays were normal for all types of plant which involved building. Colvilles, for example, brought coke ovens into operation in 1952 which were ordered 4½ years earlier. Their new Clydebridge open-hearth plant took nearly as long (*The Times*, 25 May 1952), Stewarts and Lloyds new open-hearth shops at Corby and Clydesdale, completed in 1949, took 4 years. Consett ordered new slabbing and cogging and billet mills in the early part of 1950; they were only 'nearing completion' in Feb. 1953 (*The Times*, 12 July 1950 and 17 Feb. 1953).

(f) The Report of the Productivity Committee

While the fruits of the revised plan were slowly forming a British team visited the American steel industry, it has been seen, under the auspices of the Anglo-American Council on Productivity in the early summer of 1951.[1] A year later its *Report* was published; and though it falls far outside the period of the first Board, and outside period 1, it forms an appropriate pendant to the survey of plan adjustment in the period of the Board. The recurrent dominant theme of the *Report* seemed to be how much production costs were increased by diffusion of output.

The first post-war Census of Production in America in 1947 (whose results began to appear in 1949) confirmed what had

Table 34. *Output per man-year in steelmaking*[a]

Year	U.K.	U.S.
1937	100	100
1938	86	—
1939	—	110
1947	98	135
1948	110	—

[a] The Federation index is published on the base 1938=100. This no doubt seemed appropriate as 1938 was the last full pre-war year. But plant was then lightly occupied; the efficiency of the industry when it was all-out was better shown in 1937. The Federation's index was first published in *Stat. Bull.* Aug. 1948, p. 1. This article did not give the 1937 figure, which was published in *The Times*, 16 Sept. 1948 (City Notes). By 1939 the efficiency was being raised by the completion of new works such as Ebbw Vale, Shotton, etc. The American series is based entirely on data in the *Censuses of Manufactures* for 1937, 1939 and 1947. I used two methods of comparison in computing this; one gave the result tabulated, one suggested a rise of 17 per cent only between 1939 and 1947. I had the benefit of advice on these estimates early in 1950 from Mr Maxwell Conklin, of the Bureau of Census, and Mr W. Duane Evans of the Bureau of Labour Statistics to whom I am much indebted, and from their advice I concluded that the higher figure was the more accurate. None of these figures can be precisely correct. The problem was much discussed in the United States in 1949 in connection with a wage claim in whose support the steelworkers union alleged an increase of productivity by 48 per cent since 1939; the employers put the figure at 15 per cent. These may be taken as limiting figures. (An official United States estimate was published in 1957, below, p. 524).

[1] The leader was Sir Charles Goodeve, Director of the British Iron and Steel Research Association; the team was in the United States in May and June 1951. Its report (*Productivity Team Report, Iron and Steel*) was published in June 1952.

seemed inevitable during the war, namely, that the average output per worker had increased considerably more since 1937 in the United States than in the United Kingdom. The Federation began publishing in 1948 an index of net output per worker in the British industry, and the comparative results are shown in Table 34.

Thus although the Federation was in 1948 disparaging the comparison of productivity published by Dr Rostas, in 1943, which suggested that output per man-year was 68 per cent more in the American than in the British industry,[1] it was not surprising that the Productivity Team *Report* suggested (see Table 35) an even wider gap:

Table 35. *Labour productivity, United Kingdom–United States*[a]

	Per man-year	Per man-hour
Basic pig iron	100:292	100:346
Ingot production:		
Basic cold	100:212	100:255
Basic hot	100:186	100:221
Rolling		100:150–200

[a] *Prod. Rep. Iron and Steel*, p. 14. The weighted average for all these, the *Report* suggests, would be about 100/200 (I think, but it is not made clear, per man-*year*).

These figures strikingly confirm the value of the earlier if less elaborate estimates; but as the *Report* says they were not the most useful data 'for comparisons...intended to indicate how the British position can be improved'.[2] This the team thought should be sought in other directions, and chiefly in 'plant productivity', in the larger outputs of the units used in the American

[1] Above, p. 64, and *Stat. Bull.* Aug. 1948, p. 5. The Federation article suggested that Rostas exaggerated the American advantage by neglecting the importance of the use of imported ingots and 'semis' here. I checked the estimates in 1943 at the Steel Control with this in mind, and for other similar lack of comparability, and concluded that his ratio was if anything too favourable to the United Kingdom; 100:175 was better as a comparison of output per man-year, 100:217 per man-hour.

[2] *Prod. Rep. Iron and Steel*, p. 13.

industry. The dominant theme recurred throughout the *Report*:
'British steelworks are much smaller than American and this
is the most important factor limiting increased efficiency and
productivity.'[1] The *Report* could not be criticised for neglecting
the advantages which American makers had, for reasons, such
as nature of the fuels available, not capable of reproduction in
this country. Its authors knew all these arguments. They set
down, nevertheless, minimum sizes for British conditions which
were even higher above the British average than the figures
favoured in 1944–5.[2] Blast furnaces should have a hearth
diameter of at least 25 ft.; a two-furnace plant, the minimum
desirable, would make 500,000–600,000 tons a year, requiring
a steelworks making at least 750,000 tons of ingots. Open-
hearth furnaces using hot metal should make at least (allowing
for repairs, etc.) 132,000 tons a year; there should be at least
six—so that again minimum output should be over 750,000 tons;
cold-metal furnaces, it was said, should make 88,000 tons a year
—so a works could be efficient making over 500,000 tons of
ingots; but 'there will always be a demand for small tonnages
of steels of odd compositions and sizes' which are 'best handled
by small cold-metal works, works in which the loss in efficiency
and productivity does not become serious until they get below
300,000 tons per annum'. The minimum had risen from
250,000 tons since 1945.[3] The Americans made only 9 per cent
of their open-hearth steel from cold metal, the United Kingdom
over 41 per cent.[4] A primary mill should roll at least 750,000
tons of ingots into blooms, or 1 m. into slabs, and *preferably*
1 m. tons for either purposes.[5] In all instances there were
advantages, at a diminishing rate, in steel melting in still larger

[1] *Prod. Rep. Iron and Steel*, p. 96.
[2] Above, pp. 77–8.   [3] Above, p. 77.
[4] This treatment of the cold-metal furnaces left many logical gaps. It did not
compare hot-metal and cold-metal shop costs; it did not show when Americans
used cold metal, or discuss the mill efficiencies of American cold-metal shops. By
implication a cold-metal shop of from 500,000 to 749,000 tons could not have an
efficient primary mill. The report evaded the major issue of cold-metal shop
economy by saying that no expansions of this kind of steelworks were likely to occur
in the United Kingdom (*Prod. Rep. Iron and Steel* p. 40). But some expansions were
still occurring.
[5] *Prod. Rep. Iron and Steel*, pp. 61, 88–9.

outputs (for example in steelmaking up to 1·7 m. tons of ingots). The figures quoted were minima. Lower outputs would 'prevent the development of productivity rates to modern standards'; that was, down to the lower cost end by modern standards. For some works an output of over 1 m. tons a year was 'advisable'. It was clear from the details that new American plant was above, usually much above, these minima, which were even slightly below the American averages for heavy steelmaking in 1950.[1] Between 80 and 85 per cent of American output came from works whose capacity exceeded 800,000 ingot tons a year, over 65 per cent from twenty-nine works with a capacity over 1 m. tons a year and averaging approximately 2 m. tons. There was no question therefore of the *Report* calling for a reproduction of American practice.

Size brought with it other advantages than the saving of labour, as had long been familiar; some saving of fuel and refractories,[2] for example; and the advantages of size were not confined to the furnace processes—American works gained much, for example, the *Report* said, from the scale of their general internal transport—larger capacity wagons and locomotives 'greatly reduce internal transport costs', and the heavy railway equipment used 'reduces maintenance costs and delays. ...These are important advantages.'[3] Moreover, there were cost reductions in America which did not come from size. Work was more continuous (though men worked a 40-hour week only).[4] Fewer men were needed to man plants, partly because of better handling equipment, for example, pallets and fork lift trucks,[5] and especially for maintenance and repairs; and the plant was stopped less, for shorter times, for repairs, a tribute to better design, stronger constructions, more mechanical aids for repairs and the better organisation of maintenance labour.[6]

---

[1] The *Report* (p. 86) gave the American average as 785,000 tons in 1950, the British as 325,000. The average for *all* steelworks was in the United States 665,000, in the United Kingdom 228,000. Since 1930 the American industry's total capacity rose by 37 per cent, the average capacity per works rose by 66 per cent. In the United Kingdom the total capacity rose by 20 per cent between 1938 and 1950, capacity per works by 15 per cent.

[2] *Prod. Rep. Iron and Steel*, p. 73.

[3] *Ibid.* p. 93.   [4] *Ibid.* p. 77.

[5] *Ibid.* pp. 74–5.   [6] *Ibid.* p. 92.

BEH

There was improved processing at some stages (though this was not entirely a one way affair); coke was better carbonised and better screened,[1] more ore was 'bedded' for mixing,[2] fuels of high calorific value were almost invariably used in open-hearth practice,[3] and so on. Layouts in general were much better. Restrictions to movement 'give rise to an inefficient flow of materials'; most British integrated works are restricted by main-line railways, inability to acquire adjacent land, or by slag heaps, so that 'modern development and improved technique are to be found in particular departments...there have been greater improvements in the layout of individual sections than in the relation of sections to each other...the Americans have been much more ruthless in clearing away or moving obstruc-tions'.[4] The team evidently thought (though they discussed it rather incoherently)[5] that the Americans gained by having more finishing mills integrated with the plants that made the billets, less pure rerolling. 'Consideration should be given' [a reader fresh to the subject might think this a daring novelty] 'to expanding steelworks not only horizontally... but also vertically, by carrying the steel further into the finishing processes.'[6]

The team recognised that American results required more specialisation than occurred in Britain, a smaller range of standard sizes, and 'discouragement of special sizes and qualities and of small orders'.[7] Such developments here would not, they believed, hurt customers, and they said categorically that any increase in transport delivery costs through specialisation of

[1] *Prod. Rep. Iron and Steel*, pp. 78 and 100. Though the amount of downtime due to unplanned stoppages was less in the United States than in the United Kingdom, the team was critical of the workshops used for maintenance in the United States.

[2] *Ibid.* p. 28.   [3] *Ibid.* p. 29.   [4] *Ibid.* p. 90.

[5] Possibly for reasons of tact. No pure re-roller was on the team.

[6] *Ibid.* p. 87.

[7] *Ibid.* p. 108. They referred to discouragement by larger 'extras' on specialities in America and the greater use of merchants in selling small quantities. They exaggerated the latter point as their own statistics showed (p. 110). In America over 40 per cent of steel tubes and wire and wire products were sold through ware-houses; in Britain far less of these products were sold through merchants. But British sales of other types of steel, collectively through merchants, was a larger percentage of total sales in 1950 than American sales through warehouses of the same products. It was none the less ironical to find praise of the warehouses in

works on a narrower range of products 'would usually be more than offset by the reduction in manufacturing costs'.[1] Unfortunately, when they got to this point they ceased to give measurements. On the crucial comparison between the net gain in production costs and the added cost of providing modern plant they said nothing in statistical terms. They seemed to believe that there was, or should be, a substantial net advantage in modern methods.[2] As far as the international competitive position was concerned they showed that since American earnings per hour were now almost four times as high as British (devaluation had widened the gap) labour cost in money terms was higher in the United States than in the United Kingdom. 'Current thought' (in Britain), they said, 'is heavily dominated by the difficulties of obtaining capital equipment.'[3] They suggested that the advantage of displacing existing plant might be underestimated by assessing its depreciation too low.[4] They did not point out the possibly more real danger of assessing the depreciation for a new works too high; though they did put on record that for American income-tax purposes, which were a trifle more generous than British, a steelworks plant was depreciated over 25 years.[5] The figure was well in keeping with American works experience.[6] Some parts of a plant may wear out or even become obsolete sooner, but other parts last longer, and major units may need no fundamental change for a longer period. Past experience has not justified the view that these large investments are inherently in danger of becoming rapidly obsolete, and there is no historical justification for loading them in advance estimates with heavy charges for the risk of

America's steel-selling effort coming from a team drawn from English steelworks, since the English industry had set out between the wars to discourage merchant selling and the permitted margins for stockholders were narrow.

[1] *Ibid.* p. 87.   [2] *Ibid.* p. 124.
[3] *Ibid.* p. 87.   [4] *Ibid.* pp. 123–4.   [5] *Ibid.* pp. 120–1.
[6] Thus of the rail and structural shape mills the *Report* said 'much of the American equipment is 15–25 years old, and some very much older. Such improvements as have been made are mainly operational, to give easier and faster manipulations of stock' (*ibid.* p. 57). Again: 'One or two of the very biggest works in America laid down between 40 and 60 years ago are remarkable for the conformity of their layouts with modern standards. They have been expanded and rebuilt to the extent of 40 per cent and even 80 per cent during the last 20 years....They are still very much ahead of the majority... the initial conception was very progressive.'

obsolescence. (There are, of course, instances of badly sited plants, and plants which were unskilfully run or managed, where a large investment proved for a long time unremunerative; but that was a result of initial misjudgement.)

The team's most interesting point on this topic was that a new plant cost practically as much in Great Britain as it did in the United States, despite the fact that wages were three to four times as high in the United States and 'the labour component in the cost of capital equipment constitutes the greater part of the total'. The building of a fully integrated steelworks, including a continuous strip mill, cost about $220 per ton of capacity in the United States and about £75 in the United Kingdom.[1] The inescapable conclusion was that labour productivity was much greater in the American constructional and plant-making industries. 'Raising productivity in the steel... industry is intimately bound up with that of raising productivity in British industry generally.'[2] The same moral was drawn from a study of transport costs. Charges on British railways 'are higher despite a wage-level about one-third that in America and a more favourable load factor of the permanent way. As wages represent the largest single component in railway costs (and in Great Britain are two-thirds of the total) higher costs and lower wages can only be reconciled on the assumption that the labour productivity on British railways is much lower than that in America.'[3] Improvement must come through larger wagon and train loads, better terminal facilities, more capital expenditure.

Faced with the universality of relatively 'low productivity' in the United Kingdom the team came to conclusions which were just sufficiently ambiguous to avoid being contradictory 'In Britain, for one reason or another, we have had to become masters of improvisation.' So far approval? But 'our passion for equity and compromise has led us to spread our limited national resources for re-equipment over claimants in all industries and utilities, with the result that slow progress is made by each and an immense amount of new equipment remains unproductive for a long initial period'.[4] Our passion then, if not our reasons,

---

[1] *Prod. Rep. Iron and Steel*, p. 124.   [2] *Ibid. loc. cit.*
[3] *Ibid.* pp. 94, 112–15.   [4] *Ibid.* p. 91.

had led us astray. Had it spread limited resources too 'equi-
ably' and with too much compromise among the steel firms
themselves? Here the answer seemed to be 'no'; the first
development plan had sacrificed efficiency in order to hasten
expansion, but 'an early increase in output...was of paramount
importance'[1] and 'it has not always been possible to reconcile
this with the need to attain maximum productivity'. The steel
plan was an exception, an instance of reasoned improvisation,
not impassioned equity and compromise. The team urged the
case, however, for a still higher annual rate of capital investment
in steel, so that a capacity of 20 m. tons (a new increase in the
target since 1948) could be reached in a 'reasonable time, and
in the coal, railway and construction industries whose efficiency
greatly affected the cost of making steel'.[2] Licensing arrangements for construction should be revised to allow works to be
completed faster;[3] presumably if steel and its supporting
industries were by this means to have more new works more
quickly completed the inference was that licensing authorities
should allow less to others, but this was not made explicit.[4]
Everything might come from an increase in total investment,
for which 'bold steps will be required'; but what were the steps?
Diagnosis and prescription were both incomplete in this
technicians' report.[5]

If the minimum standards, the minimum size of works, for
example, set by the Productivity Team were right the development under the first plan put new obstacles in the way of
achieving efficiency. These standards did not command universal support in the industry. In an interesting comparison
in November 1950 (before the Productivity Team went to the
United States) Sir Andrew McCance, deputy chairman of

[1] *Ibid.* p. 20.
[2] *Ibid.* p. 124.
[3] *Ibid. loc. cit.*
[4] Indeed, it might be argued that the *Report* said the reverse; it refers to the
'close interdependence of Britain's industries'. 'No one...can go very far in raising
its productivity if it must do this alone. Only by going forward together can the
desired rate of progress be achieved' (*ibid.* p. 125). But these remarks must be
related to those quoted above about equity and compromise.
[5] It is only fair to say that the visit to the United States was a short one; but the
Report was the result of much more prolonged discussion.

Colvilles argued that 'our furnaces and theirs' (the Americans) 'are adapted subconsciously to the magnitude of the industries which they serve'.[1] He also provided a forecast of steel output to 1960, 1970 and 1980 based on a mathematical formula fitted to steel output every decade from 1870 which in his view gave 'greater confidence' than 'irrational guesswork' in estimating future outputs; steel production in 1960 on this basis, 'if there is no change in present trends', was to be 17,500,000 tons.[2] This reflected a markedly different approach than that of the *Report*, and one likely to have been influential.[3]

In any event after the developments inaugurated in 1945–48 there was no prospect of a rapid approach to the standards (below American standards) which the team deemed adequate unless output rose much above the 20 m. tons which their *Report* visualised. About one-twelfth of this, it was to be expected, would be alloy and special steel.[4] It was likely that some at least of the very small works (fifteen of which made over 1·5 m. tons in 1952) would continue production. This would leave in bulk-steel manufacture some thirty-five melting shops and thirty primary mills which, having regard to the expenditures under the first plan, were likely to remain in operation for many years, making or rolling in all below 18 m. tons of ingots, an average of 550,000 tons a year, well below the minimum of 750,000 tons. Since a few shops and mills already handled more than 750,000 tons each and were likely to go on expanding, it appeared inevitable that many others would continue much below the lowest level which, according to the team, allowed reasonable efficiency by modern standards. This

---

[1] *Production in the Steel Industry: Its Growth, Distribution and Future Course*, by Sir Andrew McCance. (The Harold Wright lecture, at the Cleveland Scientific and Technical Institute, 28 Nov. 1950, p. 15.) (He was referring to open-hearth furnaces.)

[2] *Ibid.* p. 28. This figure was passed in 1953.

[3] A projection of this approach may be found in Sir John Craig's annual statement for Colvilles in 1953; a start had been made in remodelling the melting shop and modernising part of the heavy section mill at Glengarnock which, he said, 'we regard as one of the most efficient in the country for the production of heavy sections, rails and sleepers'. 'The ingot output in 1952 was about 320,000 tons. There were no blast furnaces' (*The Times*, 9 Feb. 1953).

[4] This was the proportion in 1952.

was recognised in the *Report*;[1] what it did not point out was that so many works had been partly modernised since the war that to concentrate production in a sufficiently limited number to allow the general use of large units would involve scrapping much new plant. The point was illustrated in a more limited aspect by the fact that the hearth diameter of most of the new blast furnaces built or projected since the war was less than the minimum recommended.[2] It is hard to see how the urgent need for output could have justified the sacrifice in efficiency which on the team's criteria this involved, because a smaller number of larger furnaces, taking no longer to build and requiring less building and designing effort, could give more basic iron with possibly less coke. The *Report* assumed rightly, that the difficulty of reducing the number of plants had still to be grappled with; this would happen, it was stated confidently, in the second plan. On this reckoning the first Board had salvaged little of the object of the first plan in vetting the revised plans. But this can only be a surmise in the absence of full records of what was proposed to them, what they turned down, and why; whether, for instance, they rejected the sort of criteria of efficiency advanced by the Productivity Team.[3] The team argued that the

[1] 'If all these steelworks are expanded or even retained it will not be possible to reach anything like the minimum size for efficient operation. It will be necessary for development and re-equipment to be concentrated in the works most suitably sited for expansion' (*Prod. Rep. Iron and Steel*, p. 17).

[2] The minima were 25 ft. using imported ore, 27 ft. using home ore. The following sizes are illustrative: Skinningrove (21 ft.), South Durham (20 ft.), Cargo Fleet (20 ft.), Consett (20 ft.), Lancashire Steel Corp. (22 ft.), Clyde Iron Works (20 ft.), John Lysaght's (Normanby Park) (22 ft. 6 in.), Stewarts and Lloyds', Bilston (21 ft.). Each of these cases could doubtless be presented as one in which special circumstances justified compromise; and many of the firms may have rejected the team's standards. I have excluded elaborate rebuilding in various forms, and new furnaces for foundry or haematite iron, though the former were as significant in this context in most respects as the building of new furnaces. The only new furnaces completed by 1952 which were above the minima were at the Steel Company of Wales (25 ft. 9 in.) and John Summers (27 ft.). Summers, Dorman Longs, Colvilles and the Steel Co. of Wales were building or planning to build furnaces above the minima by 1952.

[3] Formally they could not have done so, because the team came later. But as has been seen the team's standards differed little from those of 1944–45. One of the members of the team explained before leaving that no really new data were to be expected, but it was important to get more general acceptance of the need for change from a representative group including operatives.

main future difficulty in achieving the right degree of concentration 'will be the social and welfare problems which arise from the necessary re-deployment of labour'.[1] This was not in accordance with the statements made by the firms who sponsored expansion in the smaller works, who claimed they were justified on economic grounds.

The Federation had taken a midway position in 1948. Replacement of older works in heavy steelmaking was less justified than formerly. This was not quite equivalent to committing the Federation formally to the support of putting in moderately large new units, such as blast furnaces, in so many works that the prospects of radical changes as plant wore out were lessened.

The team's *Report* implied at some points that the actual investment programme going forward was in keeping with its standards to the full extent that had been possible;[2] at other points it lamented the slowness of change in Britain, the fear and inertia that stood in the way of a higher standard of output, and the obstacles imposed by development area conceptions.[3] There was, to borrow the phrase of an Indian statesman, 'a certain ambivalence in their attitude'.[4] The course of investment from 1945 to 1950 could not in fact be reconciled with the team's standards; nor did it produce results as quickly as possible. Cheaper methods of quicker expansion were suggested authoritatively in 1947; the development projects were completed very slowly, and were so badly balanced that output fell in 1951.

The question arises why should the firms not strain after the investment policy recommended by the team if it offered lower costs and therefore greater strength in international competition and, one would suppose, better profits? Why, indeed, was it thought safe to adopt a less radical policy? Why were so many firms of all sizes prepared to develop small and medium-sized plants elaborately when by doing so they risked competition

---

[1] *Prod. Rep. Iron and Steel*, p. 88.

[2] Above, p. 277.

[3] *Prod. Rep. Iron and Steel*, pp. 87 sqq.

[4] T. T. Krishmamachari's phrase characterising the Indian Government's attitude towards private industry when he was Minister of Finance.

from larger new well-sited plants built by other firms either in Britain or abroad? Could the team possibly be right if so many firms were prepared to take the risk?

(g) Inorganic planning

This is the classic, and chronic, question of the industry in a new setting. Ever since the Board of Trade Committee report in 1916 a succession of inquiries focused on foreign competition had concluded that the natural development of firms within the industry acting on their individual initiative did not lead to as rapid reduction of cost as was possible by the use of improved processes, larger scale, more specialisation, more mechanisation. The 'fittest' who survived in the competitive struggle, surprisingly numerous, relied on many forms of toughness which have been analysed at length earlier.[1] Their plants were durable; they produced normally a wide range of products, some meeting more acute competition than others; they might, among other things, be the exclusive makers of special sections; they often had some tied or half-tied markets; they often had accumulated reserves or useful financial connections, to carry them from slump to boom when prices rocketed and losses could be recouped, business increased, plants patched and expanded. What could be done quickly to increase output might be remunerated before more radical changes could be completed; when these were completed trade might again be dull.

The 'Under Fifties' were very conscious of this particular risk when they recommended the establishing of an economic efficiency committee in the Steel Federation,[2] and Mr Shone in his address to the British Association emphasised how because of the risk of trade fluctuations and the long period needed to build a new plant there was in heavy industry 'a serious danger of misinvestment, inadequate investment, or duplication and waste unless some sort of co-ordinated plan is formulated'.

The circumstances of the post-war period at most times resembled in important respects the boom stage of a trade cycle; unsatisfied demands were an encouragement to all firms not merely to persist but to expand, often as quickly as possible.

[1] Esp. *E.H.S.* ch. xi.   [2] Above, p. 62.

There was no threat of severe slump, no reason for the smaller and medium-sized firms to suppose their defences were less good than in the past if a slump were to come, and good reason to suppose that in a slump prices would not collapse.

The large firms themselves were still not in the position of competing from strength to the extent that may be superficially surmised. The building of very large plants would not occur for most of them as a natural evolution, as would happen in Germany. The large British firms, as has been seen, each made their steel in several plants, some if not all of small or medium size, often not geographically contiguous, and sometimes in different regions.[1] Where there was most contiguity (in the case of Dorman Longs) the range of products was wide and the scale of output of individual finished products was small by the team standards. The scattered plants of the large firms included several in development areas, and others isolated so that their closing would involve pockets of unemployment.[2]

Often one or more, in the extreme case most, of the plants of a large firm were rather old, and if old usually also rather small. It happened, therefore, that medium-sized firms could be producing some finished products nearly as efficiently (or better) than a large neighbouring competing firm, on as large a scale, in as large a works, with as good connexions with consumers,[3] and could visualise expansion up to the team standards as being perhaps as easy for it to accomplish as for the larger firm. The extra market had to be found, or captured, or secured by amalgamation, by both alike. Sometimes the smaller firm might fancy its own chances in a conflict,[4] and this would play

---

[1] See *E.H.S.* p. 440.

[2] See *ibid.* p. 510. Colville's plants, for example, were scattered in the same region; Stewarts and Lloyds were scattered in different regions, making the same type of product; United Steel's plants were scattered in different regions, making different products. For example, Stewarts and Lloyds had plants in South Wales and Scotland; United Steel had a plant at Workington, and the Stocksbridge plant was an isolated centre 10 miles from Sheffield.

[3] It will be recalled, for example, that South Durham claimed to be the largest makers of plates on the Tees in 1950. Above, p. 250. They had a useful outlet in their Stockton works making fabricated tubes.

[4] It was after all a medium-sized firm that first *made* wide-flanged beams—Cargo Fleet. Above, p. 250. By 1954 they had improved their practice and were exporting to America.

a part in the small firms' approach to amalgamation. The larger firm would tend to think in terms of absorption; the management of the smaller would naturally aim at survival, and the owners of the smaller might not fancy the prospective change of management. Often a major product of a large firm was produced in what may be called a handicapped plant.[1] It could happen that none of the plants making a particular product—rails were a case in point—was likely to enjoy the benefit of lowest costs available in a well-sited large modernised plant for a mixture of reasons: development area considerations, the amount of leeway to be made up, greater preoccupation with other products.[2] In this situation there was no risk of drastic competition, or of damaging cost comparisons threatening to bring down profit margins for higher cost units.

There was one conspicuous instance where a large firm, Stewarts and Lloyds, met little or no competition, because among steelmakers it had a monopoly of much of its finished product. The main competitor, Tube Investments, whose activity overlapped only in part of the range of tubes, at this time bought all its steel, and had to buy some overseas. The urge to reduce the cost of making its steel need not in this period have been overwhelming for Stewarts and Lloyds. The inducement to expand tube-making, which required consequentially more steel, was great, with the oil industry providing the chief stimulus. The *simplest* way to expand tube production was quite clearly to expand partly at some of their works which, unlike Corby, were much *below* the team's standards. It was simplest both because it avoided all the extra problems which development at Corby involved—struggling with Government over the housing problem, organising for more labour, possibly exploring for more ore, and certainly

[1] Thus, for example, the billet production of United Steels was produced in the large but unintegrated works of Steel, Peech and Tozer (above, p. 249). Relatively high costs in this plant would enable other plants whose costs also could not be very low, who, for example, like Park Gate lacked the scale of Steel, Peech and Tozer but had hot metal, to provide billets at least for their own re-rolling on a competitive basis.

[2] Of the rail mills belonging to large companies Workington was a development area; Glengarnock lay outside the main Colville group and was unintegrated; the Cleveland iron and steelworks of Dorman Longs required much modernising.

curtailing expansion in two development areas, which would evoke protests. Being simplest it called for less resources immediately, financial and personal; the second could be more conclusive than the first. Stewarts and Lloyds had no immediate reason to combine with making tubes the manufacture of other types of steel; nothing to drive them to develop Corby in order to diversify their output, which in the long run most companies have done. In view of the unsatisfactory margin on billets there was also little or nothing to attract them to do it in the programme laid down in the 1946 plan or the revision of 1948.

What was there to persuade a small firm to forgo the opportunity to expand when the going was good, let alone to give up. (Was not this ubiquitous growth the very policy of expansion for which 'everyone' was calling?) Or to persuade the few firms with large reserves of the cheapest raw material to expand their steelmaking more than their programmes for finished steel called for? Or to persuade a firm planning a large expansion to choose a site, other than one it already had, where raw materials could be most cheaply assembled, when there was no prospect that anyone making the same finished products was likely to do this? Or to persuade firms to stagger developments, so that a few could get their improvements more quickly because others deliberately delayed starting?

The formal answer, the answer which Mr Shone put forward at the British Association, was that what was needed to secure such ends in the steel industry, so far as they were desirable ends, was now provided by central planning and the right form of prices policy. Paradoxically, however, the Government and institutional policies and attitudes, as they developed and were expressed in period 1 (as the analyses earlier in the chapter show), were more likely to encourage than to discourage the investment habits of the boom stage of a trade cycle, and the strengthening and perpetuation of the existing subdivisions of production.

This was so as has been seen to a remarkable extent. There was one conspicuous possible exception: low rates of interest, most unboom-like might in principle, have given a special fillip to large-scale labour-saving expansions. This was the counter-part to central planning, which was in future to sort out the wheat from the chaff. But the most that interest rates would do was to change the timing of investment modestly (some say not at all) in heavy industry. It is unlikely that the actual rates ruling in these years would have influenced the estimates of comparative capital costs of different investments at all. On the other hand, the low rates of interest were quite likely to encourage ubiquitous investment. While interest rates were low there was less to be said for keeping reserves in securities. Creeping inflation counselled immediate investment in the business; and the tax preference on profits retained, coupled with strong pressure against increased dividends (and against bonus shares even to acknowledge the progress of inflation, let alone saving), pressed in the same direction.

The price policies had similar complex effects. Low margins of profit where prices were controlled were not calculated either to drive firms to find the *shortest* cuts to larger outputs at once, or to encourage them to major investments if they could use their resources in other associated trades, making steel in categories where prices were not controlled, for example, or fabricating steel, it may be, into bridges or other steel structures, like Dorman Longs. In steelmaking a radical investment was likely to result immediately in a larger lowering of prices than a less radical one, irrespective of market circumstances. Price controls, by making the margins on controlled products and expecially on heavy products, and most conspicuously on billets, relatively low, were indeed accentuating during the boom the normal effects of imperfect competition in a slump. But while the narrow margins should have discouraged investment there were political cross-currents. Low prices increased the exigence of demand; the desire to counteract the campaign for nationalisation, with its emphasis on restriction, put a premium on ubiquitous expansion. All firms must establish their virtue. The proportions of investible resources coming from their varied activities bore no rational relation to the worthwhileness of pro-posed developments, largely because price controls and other associated measures had made the pattern of returns irrational.

The extent to which firms made profits either on products outside price control, or within the field of control on products with low or high margins was not uniform; and some firms gained a windfall advantage in compensation for coal mines taken over by the state, which added another fortuitous circumstance. The practice of keeping home scrap prices down by price control lessened the impact of foreign competition, so long as it could be sustained as an insular monopoly, and gave British steelmaking a misleading air of efficiency. The levy-subsidy arrangements, which also as administered contributed to keeping steel prices misleadingly low, favoured users of scrap and of imported ore in ways set out at length earlier, and lessened the prospective gains of any firm who contemplated a radical change to reduce raw-material costs. Finally, the way in which development area policies were carried out had a similar effect, with its prejudice in favour of keeping alive obsolete sites.

The bias of administrative policies and attitudes was thus unmistakable, and it reinforced the old bias. How far the mere absence of the additional bias would have changed the pattern of development is not something which can be assessed with assurance. To dispense with a moderately accurate measuring rod and 'scramble' the cost picture, and to dispense with moderately rational incentives, is not an obviously sensible proceeding in an early stage of planning. More especially is this so when the plan is to be based primarily on the projects of those who may be subject to the incentives, and is to be supplemented (if need be) by a central authority who must first assess the economic prospects of the projects. The 'new bias' reflected the contemptuous neglect of the problems of a mixed economy which characterised this phase of 'planning' and invested the word with an air of ridicule.

If a bias existed what was needed to correct it was an antidote, not a reinforcement. In official doctrine the antidotes, it has been seen, were to be found in price policy and planning. Price policy did not provide it in period 1. The impression given by all the changes of the 1946 plan during period 1 was that planning as then organised could not provide it either. It is impossible to be certain. Those primarily responsible for the additions to the plan which emerged as a result of central discussion may progressively have been persuaded that these additions, a new home ore plant, a new plant on the Clyde, no more expansion in the north-west or west Midlands, the ultimate closing of Skinningrove and West Hartlepool, for example, had been wrong or untimely, and not merely impractical because firms would not adopt them. Later developments were to suggest this was not the whole story;[1] but naturally the people involved, especially in the middle of the nationalisation dispute, were unlikely to air their disagreements.

There was, indeed, something in the comment by some Labour Party critics of the Plan-cum-Board arrangements that the central body would have little effect of a positive nature; it was possible to say no effectively at the centre, it was not possible to bring about what firms did not spontaneously, or derivatively, wish. To the extent that this was so the arrangements would tend to delay, and little else. Some people in the industry thought this was what happened. But the background of the Labour criticism was the presumption that steelmakers would not want to increase output as much as it 'should be' increased because by keeping output down they would increase profits. This threw the wrong problem into relief; the real problem, as now seen, was not the smallness of total investment but its distribution. If the Productivity Team was right, zeal to increase capacity was tangibly expressed in too many places!

Nevertheless, the step from injecting something into a printed plan to getting it done was possibly regarded too lightly; the approach took too 'inorganic' a view of industrial behaviour. In the steel industry the existing firms were the organisms which could create and execute, could evolve manufacturing plans which were bound up with an understanding and assessment of specific market possibilities and a selling strategy and marketing antennae. In the past large users had often come in and set up the up-to-date plants, which had often given cost reduction a fillip (and provide an answer to those who suppose that if

[1] Below, pp. 635 sqq.

existing firms don't make a certain change it cannot be worth making). But the scope for this had narrowed as the size of steelworks with low costs had risen. How could a central planning body implant in firms projects of which the firms were not the fathers? The experience of period 1 suggested that such projects were not conceived in the right way, and so were still-born; what was conventionally conceived proved more lusty. Could the central planning body even persuade a firm that a project of its own, which it intended ultimately to carry out, but over which it delayed, was timely and urgent, as Dorman Long's much delayed plan to build a universal beam mill was said to be in 1946? The organisms, having grown in an environment and adapted themselves to it, had evolved a habit of growth, and in the process had found ways of partly adapting the environment to their habit. It was not easy to persuade them to change their habit. But this does not seem to have been widely appreciated. No doubt some on the inside of the de-tailed planning were alive to it (and may have regretted some departures from the 1946 proposals; they were often in no position to say so openly).[1] Why it was not more widely appreciated is a little hard to follow; the difficulties in over-coming structural rigidities when the scale of low-cost operations has for long grown faster than the market, and locational advantages have changed, in an industry where the forces of inertia are great, should have been becoming familiar to serious analysts.

There were many beguiling circumstances. Much, let it be repeated, was happening in the industry. At times it was right to get expansion with little new capital expenditure as fast as possible without straining after lower costs. And the competitive pressures from abroad expected in 1944–45 had not built up by 1950. What was being done was not immediately dangerous. Obviously it might be better to raise real earnings faster and nearer to the United States level by more greatly increased pro-

---

[1] It can be fairly argued that within the Federation some occupied on this work did try hard to 'find organisational concepts that will combine co-operative thinking and effort with acceptance of the fundamental competitive economic tests and traditional *laissez faire*' (quoted from an unpublished note).

ductivity in steel and other industries; but it was not obligatory, nor was it obligatory to adapt locations to use more cheap home ore and foreign ore to best advantage.[1] The connection between a failure to secure maximum cost reduction in steel and the general economic weakness of the country internationally was not conspicuous; the British steel industry itself remained internationally strong. Was the degree of cost reduction which could be enjoyed by more radical change worth the extra effort— primarily intellectual and administrative—which would be needed? The difference in United States and United Kingdom productivities, between home and imported ore costs, and between assembly costs for imported ores in different sites, were certainly significant. They were not rigorously set out; the real costs were masked; occasional estimates from the industry were *ex parte*. The inclination was to imply that time didn't matter; a second five-year plan would allow mistakes to be retrieved. This overlooked that what was being done created new 'moments of inertia', whose danger the 'Under Fifties' had stressed. The industry seemed to lack at this time personalities of the stature of Macdiarmid, Firth and Whitehead, the tiresome chaps who broke the conventional pattern in the thirties. They were too few, it has been seen, in the thirties. No doubt in the late forties the desire to maintain a united front because of the political situation would have discouraged overt disagreement but it would hardly have kept a new Macdiarmid, in the right position, down. Outside the industry clearly opinion was influenced by attitudes in the political conflict. But socialist critics were obsessed by quantity and negligent on costs. It was the Labour Government who imposed on the Steel Board and the Steel Company of Wales a location for cold rolling chosen to keep an old site alive at the sacrifice of low costs, in the most conspicuous instance in period 1 when the high-cost horse was

---

[1] Hence commentators who knew the drawbacks of the Margam site, for example, were prepared after the decision was made and the work started to speak of the project as one of Britain's great industrial achievements, suppressing all reference to site disadvantage, though this was the main British contribution. Most had not perhaps seen the United States plants. But the silence on site, as I found in correspondence (in 1947) was not an oversight; perhaps it was thought there was no use crying over spilt milk.

19   BEH

frankly backed. The Government were at least as anxious as managements to confine the development of the industry as far as possible within limits which did not involve any agonising readjustment. Central planning as it was conducted gave an illusion that rational assessment was governing what was being done to a greater extent than it was. The obstacles to more radical change in the last analysis were emotional and temperamental, not a careful judgement of gains and losses. The politicians turned aside to decide the perfect organisation for the future without facing up to the problems of the present.

Chapter VI

THE CAPTURE AND RECAPTURE OF THE CITADEL

1. IRRESISTIBLE ASSAULT

Mr Herbert Morrison said in 1946 that nationalisation of steel was 'a matter of business'. It was 'not really a party political matter' at all. The Government suffered from a split mind if not a divided heart on the wisdom of nationalising, and Mr Morrison was perhaps the least certain of its timeliness. But when the faithful had irrevocably decided and the Bill came before the House of Commons in 1948 he stated the 'business' case for it with more perceptiveness than any other speaker. Perhaps it was because he understood better the case for the alternative, the system favoured by the Opposition, which was close to the system under the first Board.

Mr Selwyn Lloyd described this as a five-tier system. 'There are the companies, and above them, acting as a trade association, is the Iron and Steel Federation; above that, until recently, has been the Steel Board; above that the Minister; and above the Minister, at least in theory, Parliament. This has worked extraordinarily well in practice as, I think, everybody in the industry admits.'[1] Mr Morrison argued on the contrary that the system 'cramps the style of management and impedes its freedom of action'.

'It is impeded in its freedom both by the Federation and by the State. We think that under that system it is more difficult to rationalise and modernise the industry, since if it is a question of expanding here or contracting there the fact of an industry being in private hands is bound to cause the maximum of difficulty. Next we think that it is difficult for the industry to achieve the necessary freedom of movement in reorganisation

---

[1] House of Commons. *Standing Committee on Iron and Steel Bill* (abbreviated as *S.C. Steel Nat.*), 16 Dec. 1948, c. 322.

and to change the physical characteristics of many of its undertakings, when there are a large number of separately owned undertakings, even if they are not a cartel. The separate bodies of shareholders are also an added difficulty. Of course there is the political difficulty in a private monopoly of expanding or contracting the industry in particular areas, and therefore it is liable to great difficulty. Moreover in the raising of capital—and the industry must raise very large sums of capital—it cannot raise capital as well as it can be raised under State guarantee, either in speed or in amount or in the rate of interest which has to be paid. Therefore we think that also is a disadvantage.'[1]

The last point was one of Mr Morrison's foibles, and its contempt for economic measurement was somehow out of character. But otherwise he was close to the important problems of the kind discussed in the preceding chapter if not to the right answers, and in its repetitive way this passage set out potential weaknesses. This achievement would, however, have been more impressive in 1946 than in 1948, for by the later date the Government should have been able to establish that there were also real weaknesses. But they could not do this effectively because they approved of the steel industry's record so wholeheartedly, saw nothing wrong with the plan, except where they wanted to give still more concessions to Development Areas, and they adopted the levy-subsidy arrangements as their own policy to keep prices low as a valuable anti-inflationary measure and to provide cheap basic materials. They could point to no matter in which the industry had failed to co-operate with them except the promotion of nationalisation. This, of course, they said betrayed the cloven hoof. So the change to nationalisation must be made now, while things were going well Mr Strauss argued, before the 'schizophrenia' of capitalist owners 'reached a harmful stage'.[2]

The weakness of this approach was hard to conceal. A very

---

[1] *Hansard*, 17 Nov. 1948, c. 489–90.

[2] *Ibid.* 15 Nov. 1948, c. 57, 75. 'If schizophrenia has not reached a harmful stage it is better and easier to cure it before it becomes chronic.' Also 'All in the industry and...Federation did magnificently during the war...and are doing exceedingly well now'. But when private individuals *own*, they own the know-how: 'They can at any moment withdraw their co-operation. It happened over the Steel Board'.

interested observer drew the right conclusion. Referring to negotiations between Sir Andrew Duncan and the Government the Public Relations Officer of the Ministry of Supply, a believer in nationalisation, said they 'made the mistake of trying to "out Duncan" Duncan, and failed.... They cannot argue with him on productivity, on labour relations within the industry.'[1] Mr Morrison should have been able to show the experience on which his type of criticism was founded; instead the criticism appeared to be merely a speculation. He tried later in the same speech to provide an apologia for this weakness: 'the technical experts were in Steel House.... One of the incidental consequences of the passing of this Bill will be that this expert technical knowledge will be at the disposal of public authorities.'[2] Steel House alternately attracted and repelled Labour Ministers. Its 'very able staff'[3] seemed almost a model central body; unfortunately, Ministers felt powerless before it. It might have been a warning, but they did not see it.[4] Would they be masters of a nationalised Corporation?

A similar powerlessness was already uncovering itself by 1948 in the relations of Ministries with the already nationalised industries. The resignations from the Coal Board, the premature introduction of the five-day week for miners, the prolonged

[1] R. Williams-Thompson, *Was I really Necessary?*, p. 45.
[2] *Hansard*, 17 Nov. 1948, c. 493.
[3] Mr Morrison in *Hansard*, *loc. cit.*
[4] Those who drafted the nationalisation Bill were indeed supposed to destroy the power of Steel House; but a little earlier the notion of nationalising the Federation, making it the agent of the Government, not of self-governing industry, while only taking powers to buy firms if they were obstructive, appeared to have strong support. There were negotiations between Mr Morrison and Sir A. Duncan whose content was not disclosed, but it was understood they were along these lines. Mr Williams-Thompson (*op. cit.* pp. 44–5) traces these negotiations to a threat by Sir Andrew that the target of 14 m. tons set in 1947 for 1948 would not be met if the Government went ahead with nationalisation. Threats of immediate disaster were constantly being expressed, as the situation demanded, on both sides (the silliest was the statement by Mr E. L. Mallalieu (*Hansard*, 15 Nov. 1948, c. 117) in the second reading debate that 'there is enough ill-will in the industry to blow the lot sky high' in the absence of nationalisation), but I believe they were not taken seriously. The reasons for the negotiations on the Government's side were that (1) those in the Government who didn't like nationalisation at once wanted an alternative, (2) the Economic Crisis of 1947 gave an admirable pretext for a new effort at compromise, (3) some Ministers had considerable admiration for Sir Andrew Duncan.

controversy about over-centralisation in the Board, underlined in different ways that Ministers or their appointees could make mistakes. The low-price policy for domestic users of electricity with which the British Electricity Authority persisted showed its determination to pursue an autonomous policy without regard to Ministerial policy.[1] There were rumours that in the experience of Treasury officials the nationalised industries were the most inflexible and secretive in regard to investment policy. Since a Minister's contact with a Board was through its chairman, his access to the experts depended entirely on the chairman's attitude. It could, as a result of the change, be more remote instead of closer; the significance of this was hardly appreciated fully however by 1948.[2]

It was against this background, success in steel by the conventional standards understood by public and politicians, a tarnished medal for recently nationalised industries, that the Steel Bill was drafted and debated. Its form reflected an understandable desire to maintain the continuity of management in the firms so that the success should not be disturbed. Every nationalisation Bill was, of course, as put across to the public, tailored to measure. The Coal Bill under which the firms were all broken up had not been a mistake, but for steel it would be a mistake to do the same, and with minor exceptions no firms would be broken up. Not at first. Control would be put in the hands of a holding company, but the basic organisms would be left intact, would retain their names, their identity, their balance sheets, their management (so long as there was an amicable acceptance of the holding company's control).[3] This

---

[1] This became progressively clearer; it was most vigorously expressed after the Ridley Committee's *Report on Co-ordination of Fuel Policy*. This recommended the Minister to appoint an independent body to advise him on tariff policies to ensure co-ordination. He did not do so, and this reflected the understood preference of the chairmen of two of the bodies concerned.

[2] There have been times when data provided to Ministers and quoted in Parliament were sufficiently incomplete to make a balanced view of what was going on extremely hard.

[3] 'The alternative would have been that before (firms) were taken over we should cut off or dislocate them...that would create the very dislocation, the very confusion and muddle which has been urged against this Bill' (Mr Morrison, *Hansard*, 17 Nov. 1948, c. 491).

decision carried with it the controversial corollary that some nationalised firms whose unity was to be maintained were largely engaged in activities other than iron- and steelmaking, and got most of their profits, for example, from constructional engineering.

While the Government presented their Bill as one likely to cause as little as possible unneeded disturbance in the industry, the Opposition naturally asked what was going wrong now which could be put right by the Bill, to which there was no answer.[1]

The Bill proposed that an Iron and Steel Corporation of Great Britain should be established to hold the securities of companies engaged extensively in iron-ore working or the production of pig iron or of ingot steel or the hot rolling of steel. The securities would be acquired from the present owners and compensation would be based where possible on Stock Exchange valuations at certain dates. The Corporation was to have power to carry on those basic activities (called Second Schedule activities in the Bill) or any other activities which the companies whose shares they held were authorised to do by their memoranda of association, but they might not increase their authorised activities without the Minister's consent. They would have the general duty of ensuring that iron and steel was available 'in such quantities, at such prices, and...of such types, qualities and sizes, as the Corporation consider best in the public interest'. The Minister could 'give the Corporation general direction in matters appearing to him to affect the public interest', and in matters of capital development, reorganisation, training education and research the Corporation was to act in accordance with programmes 'settled from time to time with the approval of the Minister'.[2]

How would the Government choose the members of the Corporation? How would these be constrained to serve the

[1] Mr Morrison could merely resort to evasion and derision—the Bill would set managements free, but to expect a Bill to work out in detail the technical future of the industry was a 'preposterous suggestion' (never of course made) which 'illustrates the lack of practical minds of Members opposite and the unreal world in which they live' (*Hansard*, 17 Nov. 1948, c. 492).

[2] This is based on the *Explanatory Memorandum* to the Bill as first presented.

national interest, how would their powers be circumscribed, how would their work be open to scrutiny, how would their monopoly powers be kept under control, how would consumers and competitors be able to protect themselves, and, since the Bill like all similar measures gave great powers to the responsible Minister, how would his powers be defined, how would his activities be subject to scrutiny and control, how would he judge the national interest?

These questions were asked with more assurance in the Steel Bill debate than earlier because of accumulating experience; though there remained a lack of incisiveness on critical points because the Opposition was itself committed to a system which involved choosing persons who would have powers to decide the national interest and would in turn be subject to Ministerial control. They were, as Mr Morrison rightly pointed out, closer to the socialist solution than they were prepared to acknowledge.[1]

Discussion of the composition of the Corporation took a fifth of the Committee proceedings on the Bill. What was achieved was hardly in proportion to the time spent, but it showed an uneasy awareness of the dangers and difficulties involved in making appointments of this kind. On the scale it was now reaching the selection of persons to carry executive office of some kind or another at a high level in business activities was virtually a new task for Ministers, though no doubt it looked less so because so many executive jobs had had to be filled by Ministers in the wholly different setting of the war. Mr Lyttleton remarked that Government patronage had reached a scale exceeding anything in the eighteenth century. He did not suggest there was a danger of corruption; nevertheless, 'political convenience' might be met 'by having some of these posts at the disposal of the Government'.[2] The risk to which he and others

---

[1] 'What they are advocating is the acceptance of the near monopoly—through the instrument of the B.I.S.F.—and (they) are prepared to superimpose on that control a further control by the politicians, which they are denouncing every day of the week outside the House.... Why does the Rt. Hon. Gentleman, the Member for the City of London (Sir Andrew Duncan), deserve to be picked out for all this meticulous control and legislation?' (*Hansard*, 17 Nov. 1948, c. 487–8).

[2] *S.C. Steel Nat.* c. 57.

were most alive was put less obliquely by a Labour member; 'elderly trade unionists who tend to bask in the miracle of their own careers', he said, were to be avoided.[1] There was an equal danger he implied of having 'tired business men who have just failed to make the grade'. This shaft was less well directed; for though the Minister might be tempted to prefer business men who supported the right party, he was certainly likely, as Mr Strauss said, to choose people, if he could get them, who had 'proved themselves outstanding men'.[2] It was going to be difficult, however, to find someone who could grow for the first time to his full stature in the job. It might indeed be difficult to make the job sufficiently attractive for bright young men even if the Minister found the way to discover them, since the appointments were only for three to five years, subject to reappointment by the Minister. There was thus a special risk, which was not compensated for at all by salary scales, since these were lower than for jobs of comparable magnitude in private enterprise.[3]

In private enterprise directors were indeed also subject to periodic reappointment, often every three years. But as several contributors to the debates pointed out this tended to be a formality, and shareholding groups (small shareholders were powerless) were only likely to exert influence if a firm ran into difficulties. Some groups, financial or industrial, might be represented on the Board of a company, but a Board could normally be regarded as a continuing body providing for its own succession. The wisdom shown in this would naturally not be uniform; Boards are not all equally first class and it is not a foolproof system, but it both provides for continuity and ensures a degree of organic unity and organic growth. It limits,

[1] Stanley Evans, famous for his dislike of feather-bedding the farmers (*S.C. Steel Nat.* c. 322–3).

[2] *Ibid.* c. 232. The Bill said the Minister should choose from 'persons who have wide experience of, and shown capacity in, the production of iron ore or iron and steel, industrial, commercial or financial matters, administration or the organisation of workers'.

[3] An amendment to limit salaries to a maximum of £5000 a year was moved in committee by Mr Ivor Thomas, but was opposed by the leaders of both the main parties on the committee. Nevertheless, it was clear the limits in earlier nationalisation measures would apply.

too, the concentration of the power of appointment into few hands which nationalisation accentuates. Ministerial appointments at the top threatened these things. Appointments would be made from outside without the intimate knowledge of personalities and of precise needs which is enjoyed inside an industry and still more inside a firm. Mr Strauss emphasised that the Corporation 'cannot be responsible for the reappointment' of its members;[1] the Minister, being responsible to Parliament for the industry, must have absolute responsibility over the appointments.[2] It was suggested that he should appoint from panels drawn up by the Steel Federation and the Confederation,[3] and possibly the consuming interests;[4] but this he rejected on the same score. He would have rejected it too on the ground that the Corporation should not be a collection of representatives (which was sound reasoning).[5] The proposition was of course misconceived; it was desirable that people should rise to eminence within the industry, but the idea that the best people would be chosen by a sort of election within the industry flew in the face of all experience. The best man will often be the 'odd man out' until he is a confirmed success. 'Everyone's out of step save our Jock' was not such a joke as Sir Andrew Duncan with his zeal for compromise supposed.[6]

Yet the proposal only formalised a procedure which to some extent would be followed in any event. Mr Strauss said he would make informal inquiries;[7] he would no doubt have been glad if the Steel Federation would have suggested someone to serve, because he was anxious to secure the industry's collaboration at a high level. Mr Jack Jones, Parliamentary Secretary to the Ministry of Supply, said there was a T.U.C. sub-com-

---

[1] S.C. Steel Nat. c. 233.

[2] Ibid. loc. cit. and c. 63.

[3] Ibid. c. 41. These were proposed, oddly, by Lord Hinchinbrooke.

[4] Ibid. c. 42, proposed by Mr Lyttleton.

[5] Mr Peake, against the stream, asked what is a non-functional full timer? How can he fill in the time? (ibid. c. 327–8).

[6] He disliked anyone in the industry expressing publicly a dissenting view.

[7] S.C. Steel Nat. c. 65: 'Any Minister appointing people to responsible posts of this sort, in which he has to get the co-operation and goodwill of all those connected with the industry, would informally consult a variety of people and maybe a variety of bodies.'

mittee who would make recommendations.[1] It was hard to avoid something of this sort, partly because some interests almost had to be satisfied, even if this fell short of representation and still more because Ministers and civil servants (who played a large part in discovering possible names) have only a narrow range of personal acquaintance. Ministers had indeed been appointed, as a Labour member put it in a charming euphemism 'who have not the background to make wise choices, at least without a great deal of advice from officials'.[2] Ministers would inevitably have a final voice in making these choices, and their traditions as well as their perceptiveness would be important.[3]

When the spotlight turned from the membership to the powers and duties of the Corporation it rested almost exclusively on the risk of monopoly exploitation. It was no doubt a natural emphasis; Parliament had just set up the Monopolies and Restrictive Practices Commission. The prospective impact on production methods and costs was hardly considered. The Corporation obviously would have enormous monopoly power and with all nationalised concerns would be immune from the attention of the new Commission's power. It might 'exploit'[4] consumers, or it might compete 'unfairly' with small steel-makers, working on licence, or with makers of the more highly finished products, steel castings or forgings or tubes for example, or in the engineering industries in which it participated; it might,

---

[1] 'The interests of the trades union element will be taken care of inside the aggregate opinion, which is a special sub-committee set up by the T.U.C.' (*ibid.* c. 45). Mr Jack Jones, a former trade union leader in the steel industry, was conspicuously an instance of a successful unionist who was not useful in office. His contributions to the debates and committee proceedings were confused. Apparently his unsuitability was recognised in the Ministry. Williams-Thompson, *op. cit.* p. 48.

[2] *S.C. Steel Nat.* c. 42. Mr Geoffrey Cooper added: 'It may be that a Minister acts too much on the advice of officials, and too little on the advice of those who, in the opinion of all concerned, are knowledgeable.'

[3] Mr Strauss, for example, showed himself admirably in the English and especially in the City tradition in discussing the possibility of having an applied scientist in the Corporation. 'Normally it is right that technicians of every sort...should be at the service of a corporation or board...but not sit in judgement on the views of experts set before them' (*S.C. Steel Nat.* c. 115). The American and German view seems to be different.

[4] I use the term which was used by the Steel Federation.

for example, in a time of scarcity give preferential supplies to its own constructional steelworks. According to the Bill it was not to give '*undue* preference' to any consumers or class of consumer in supply or price of second schedule commodities, or to 'exercise *unfair* discrimination'. But this was 'without prejudice to such variations in the terms and conditions in which products are supplied as may arise from ordinary commercial considerations or from the public interest'. This gave no protection to users of the more highly finished products (on the ground that these products met competition) nor to those who might be faced with 'unfair competition'. It would rest no doubt with the Consumers' Council to take up violations of the 'undue preference' clause—which obviously had little if any legal force— but this was depicted by the Opposition as the Minister's creation, and the Minister, it was argued, would always tend to be on the side of the Corporation, since he was responsible for it. Even one Labour member suggested that the Minister should not appoint both the Corporation and the Consumers' Council.[1]

These provisions in the Bill probably reflected both an underestimate of the monopoly risks which they involved (derived from a habitual exaggeration of the importance of ownership and of the zeal for high distributed profits, and a relative neglect of the zeal for security, status, recognition and power), and a confused belief that privileges sought by a private firm must be good for a nationalised industry. Mr Lyttleton was most likely right in saying that the powers of Corporation and Minister were left largely undefined in part at the prompting of civil servants as a means of retaining unlimited reserve powers for use in unforeseen contingencies.[2] But there was more to it than

---

[1] Mr Beswick, in the Report stage, *Hansard*, 27 April 1949, c. 262. He argued that the Bill asked too much of one man. 'When we ask him to know the personalities of all the firms and to be responsible for a big Government department and to be responsible for other big industries we seriously ought to think whether one human being is physically able to comprehend all that is going on in the field of responsibility nominally under his control.'

[2] *S.C. Steel Nat.* c. 390. 'I know what happens. Ministers start with very good intentions, but are warned by the Civil Service, perhaps by the Parliamentary draughtsmen, the solicitors of their departments and all the rest of it, that there may conceivably arise questions about the right to exercise this or that power, and this is used as an excuse for giving this overcoat power.' An argument on these

that. When Opposition members argued that it was undesirable that a state monopoly in steelmaking should also own parts of some of the steel-consuming industries, as it created a dangerous risk of discrimination, Mr Strauss replied that he 'assumed that the various integrations and amalgamations which had taken place had been undertaken in the economic interests of the industries concerned'.[1] This implied utter confusion over the significance of amalgamations in competition as means of securing markets, and a confusion of firm and industry, which made his argument irrelevant and void, nonetheless illuminating.[2] He showed no recognition of the helplessness which a small buyer or competitor would experience in face of the new colossus, persuaded of its unerring rectitude (what else had it to serve but the national interest?), backed by a department whose officials would perchance be fired with the same rigid assurance, and be faintly irritated at people who reiterated complaints which had already been dismissed by impartial authority.[3]

Mr Lyttleton contrasted this proposal unfavourably with the system which was being replaced.[4] The Steel Federation (and Mr Shone) elaborated the unfavourable contrast; probably they initiated it.[5] Mr Lyttleton was more convincing in arguing that the public interest is not something which Ministers instinctively recognise and protect (otherwise why should not Parliament confine itself to passing votes of thanks?)[6] than in establishing the virtues of supervision by an independent Board with a Minister supervising the Board. It was known that Federation policies were the result of internal compromises, and

lines was advanced to me by senior civil servants as a reason for not attempting to define principles to govern price policy which did not leave unlimited discretion to central authorities.

[1] *Ibid.* c. 1104.

[2] How far the Minister was really confused or merely following a civil servant's brief, cleverly drawn up *ad hoc* without consideration of its general significance and in the evasive technique of answering Parliamentary questions, I cannot of course say.

[3] It was still five years before 'Crichel Down'.

[4] *Hansard*, 15 Nov. 1948, c. 94–5.

[5] Cp., for example, *Iron and Steel Bill, Discussion in Committee* (B.I.S.F.), pp. 3 sqq.

[6] *Hansard*, 9 May 1949, c. 1518.

that the unsuccessful minority had on occasion been the more progressive part of the industry. It was known, too, that there was an understanding, if not an undertaking, that all member firms would speak with one voice when the Federation had adopted a policy.[1] There were signs that a Board would try to work amicably with the Federation, which was natural and in a measure desirable, but it was liable to mean that when both had agreed on a policy, judgement, or forecast, sometimes again as the result of a compromise, they would become restive under criticism. It was, indeed, likely that the two bodies in this relation would tend in the process of working together on a basis of compromise (it might be with the same technical advisers and with some common membership) to feel a sense of unity and identity on many matters against any outside criticism, which would present virtually as impenetrable a front as a Minister and a nationalised corporation.[2] A Minister, moreover, was likely to feel the same loyalty to a Board which he appointed and which he regarded as fitted to judge public interest as to a Corporation, and would depend on it for information.

A continuation of the Minister-Board-Federation structure not only endowed the Minister and Board with duties of declaring the public interest but foreshadowed that these duties would be widely exercised in fixing prices and profits and in planning raw-materials supplies, output and investment. At least it seemed so from the Federation publications.[3] Thus though Mr Shone depicted the Federation as a concern to provide

[1] This came to be regarded as the only decent thing to do. Sir Andrew expressed to me (before the Second World War) his disapproval of company chairmen who were critical of the 'industry's' policies at their annual meetings.

[2] It was instructive that I.D.A.C. and the Steel Federation presented virtually a common front before the war, and the evidence before the May Committee, of which some was known to have been very critical of the Federation or some of its members, was not published. It was a provision in the establishment of I.D.A.C. that information given to it in evidence should not only not be published but not be available to other Government departments. But that meant that the judgement of I.D.A.C. on many matters, judgements of persons, motives, probabilities, had to be taken on trust without reference to the evidence on which they relied.

[3] They were prepared even to consider the possibility of 'approximating (the Board's) peace-time powers to those enjoyed in time of war', though this was perhaps thrown in for good measure to show how far they would go to avoid nationalisation. *Stat. Bull.* Oct. 1949, p. 8.

external economies (or common services) for the industry (such as collective research, collective ore imports) and to create conditions of more perfect competition, this involved a surprisingly wide range of central decisions.[1] And again, though Mr Shone was rightly critical of the mystical fervour with which bodies like the Coal Board might explain their decisions in terms of 'national interest' instead of in terms of 'objective economic grounds',[2] it was quite evident that the Coal Board used objective grounds of some sort (indeed it usually set them out rather well), and that its use of them could be objective, whereas the combined decisions of the Federation, independent Steel Board and Minister were capable of being less reasonable even if they were set out with a show of 'objective economic grounds', and they were equally a limitation on the power of other persons to make decisions. To emphasise that a Board's decisions might be impartial or independent tended to obscure the fact that they were decisions, and were a token of centralisation (they would, indeed, result from negotiations with another central body, the Federation) and in fact also a token of delay.

The core of the existing structure as the Federation (who provided most of the briefs for the Opposition)[3] set it out, was the competition between firms. This was at least a source of administrative efficiency (efficiency, that is, in the use of existing capital resources, in keeping costs down and producing what the customer wanted) and provided some stimulus to efficient investment, though for this function central guidance was also needed. Thus, the argument ran, although there was an appeal to Board and from Board to Minister to protect aggrieved customers and the public interest, this supervisory machinery would not be called into action so often; there would be powerful checks in the system before the balancing action of the final arbiters was called for, so that their work would be

[1] *Ibid.* Aug. 1949, pp. 1–13, the paper read to the British Association.
[2] *Ibid. loc. cit.* p. 11.
[3] There was a Joint Policy Committee representing the Federation, Joint Iron Council and the National Council of Iron Ore Producers, which acted with legal advisers and Parliamentary draftsmen, and in close cordial contact with the Joint Iron and Steel Consumers' Committee set up by the Federation of British Industries, National Union of Manufacturers and Associated British Chambers of Commerce.

restricted to balancing imponderables outside the range of objective economic measures.[1] The validity of this claim, oddly enough, never seems to have been examined in the debates; nor, although the Federation stated its case in its bulletins with great ability, was the case even set out in the debates. The proposed new monopoly was shown as a danger to consumers, to competitors, and to efficiency, because the holding company structure could not preserve the reality of competition between the constituent companies. To which the Government retorted the *new* Corporation would be much smaller than the United States Steel Corporation, conveniently forgetting, or perhaps they really did not know, that the latter has been often prodded into action by smaller competitors. But the nature of the existing organisation, monopoly in the eyes of the Government, competition in the eyes of the Federation, was never probed.

Nor was there any consideration of the 'objective economic grounds' according to which, Mr Shone implied, the 'national interest, should primarily be identified. The Federation's elaborate presentation of its own contentious approach, its claim to have found the way to more perfect competition by means of externally fixed prices, which involved changing the raw-material costs of different firms according to its assessments of long-period 'marginal costs', and changing profit margins periodically for different products to direct firm's investment programmes, escaped discussion.[2] One or two voices in the debates were raised in favour of competition as the only way of establishing the national interest, deciding what was efficient and what waste, but they showed no taste for the subtleties of the problem which experience had revealed. Did they refer to the Federation's style of competition? Did they see any other

[1] The Federation, through the Joint Policy Committee, proposed amendments to the Bill which underlined this element in their theory, namely, that both the Corporation and the Minister should have the power or duty of deciding the national interest removed from them, the reason in the case of the Minister being that 'this should be a question of fact, not of opinion' (*Iron and Steel Bill: Discussion in Committee* (issued by B.I.S.F.), pp. 8–9).

[2] This approach was analysed in the previous chapter. (It has already been given in the previous note that the Federation in a proposed amendment treated the national interest as a 'question of fact'.)

way to restore the competition they wanted? They did not say.[1] The general presumption, however, of the majorities in both main parties was that the public interest could in fact emerge from *ad hoc* decisions of persons appointed by Governments,[2] and there were no suggestions that instructions should be laid down which would limit the range of their authority and determine the 'objective economic grounds' or criteria on which they would base their judgements.

In so far as the policies to be adopted when the Corporation came into power were foreshadowed either in the Bill or the debates, it seemed apparent that the new form of centralisation would, if the Government had its way, follow the same course as the old. A Conservative member declared, 'I believe there are at Steel House the brains which are in any case to run the industry';[3] and he might by judicious cullings from the Bill have proved that the brains had already been at work as it were by proxy. The Bill provided that the new Corporation should keep a central reserve of whose uses the only one specifically set out in the Explanatory Memorandum was to check 'the undue fluctuation in prices'.[4] There was no need to put this in a Bill which also said that the Corporation should pay its way 'taking one year with another',[5] and the inclusion can only be accounted for by an insuppressible attachment to the policy of stabilising prices at a relatively low level. The Bill also gave the Government power to subsidise the import of raw materials and of steel bought at high prices, the intention again being to keep

[1] Two main instances of the argument for competition were Mr Byers (*Hansard*, 2 May 1946, c. 706) and Lord Hinchinbrooke (*Hansard*, 27 Apr. 1949, c. 262 and 2 May 1949, c. 746). The second of these advocated giving special privileges to small firms to preserve competition, indeed, to force firms into competition; but he also said competition should be 'as we now know it, regulated, without going back to the old days of internecine competition... competition between individual competing utilities'.

[2] Thus when Mr Lyttleton was asked specifically 'Does Steel House always know the public interest?' he answered 'if Steel House is not acting in the public interest there is Government control of prices and a Government to which the country can appeal'. *Hansard*, 9 May 1949, c. 1518–19.

[3] Mr Hugh Fraser, *S.C. Steel Nat.* c. 467.

[4] *Explanatory Memo*, pp. iv, 17.

[5] There was an interesting discussion on the lack of definition in this phrase. *S.C. Steel Nat.* c. 1187–99.

20

prices down when imports were dear.[1] Two Conservatives
did criticise this on the ground that it might cause too great an
expansion in steelmaking,[2] an unusually circumstantial point in
these debates, but no one alluded to the equal danger of the
same diversion of resources which the Federation policy of
spreading high marginal raw-material costs entailed.[3]

When Mr Strauss was asked on what matters he was likely
to give directions to the Corporation he instanced only the
possibility of saying what the capacity of the industry ought to
be.[4] Asked in another context whether the right capacity
would 'meet the tremendous demand there is today' his lieutenant said, 'we would not expand beyond what was economically correct'; capacity, Mr Strauss agreed, would be less than
peak demand.[5] It all sounded familiar. No wonder that Lord
Layton, expressing a view which is surprising only because he
might have been thought to speak as a Liberal, said that 'if
what is needed further in the public interest is made clear
I personally do not doubt it will be carried out by the iron and
steel industry'[6] (without nationalisation). So the harmony in

[1] Mr Strauss, *S.C. Steel Nat.* c. 423.

[2] Mr Hugh Fraser (*ibid.* c. 418) and Lord Hinchinbrooke (*ibid.* c. 421). The
main Opposition criticism of the subsidy proposal was based on the argument
that Compensation Stock would give only 3 per cent interest, compared with
6 per cent paid in dividends and interest, and therefore the Corporation would
have extra resources and should not ask a subsidy of the taxpayers! (Mr Peake,
ibid. c. 413). Mr Jennings (*ibid.* c. 415) explained that while a subsidy under
nationalisation would be a 'swindle on the public' it was right under the existing
régime because the iron and steel industry was 'hedged around by all sorts of
controls'.

[3] Mr Ernest Davies stated the case for averaging all costs in a form which
deserves to be classic: 'If one has to consider whether each unit is operating profitably one is driven ultimately to take out of production the inefficient... the need of
the country today is production' (*S.C. Steel Nat.* c. 1171–2). The whole passage is
illuminating. For example, 'Only through nationalisation is one able to get away
from the bogey of finance which operates all the time as far as private enterprise
is concerned.'

[4] *Hansard*, 9 May 1949, c. 1604.

[5] Mr Clem Davies raised the point; the lieutenant was Mr Jack Jones (*Hansard*
16 Nov. 1948, c. 259). There were socialists who advocated very high capacity,
for example, Professor G. D. H. Cole (*Why Nationalise Steel?* p. 20).

[6] *Hansard* (Lords), 25 May 1949, c. 1094. Throughout the debates the Government never advanced a more circumstantial instance to rebut this point (i.e. that
the industry had done and would do what the Government wanted) than
Mr Strauss's (above, p. 292), that opposition to nationalisation was itself a refusal

outlook of Government and Federation (and therefore of the Opposition who were largely briefed by the Federation) on the proper pattern of policy to be pursued was almost complete. Though the steelmakers were criticised by a few Labour back benchers for not moving to the best locations, the Government had insisted on even greater concessions to development areas than the firms and the Federation and Board had favoured.[1] Ministers still called in aid the Jarrow story, which was now a fantasy, a symbol of capitalism defying the public interest, which in this context was to keep old sites alive.[2]

Near identity of view on the part of Steel House and Government as to what was desirable in investment and in price policy immediately did not imply, of course, that nationalisation would make no difference. It would transfer some powers to new hands, and create a stronger concentration of power. Some of the new hands might bring new projects if not new principles. The new Corporation would wish to give at least the appearance of novelty in some of its policies, and some tokens of success would be wanted by the Minister, tokens of failure by the Opposition, so that the actions of the Corporation would have a political angle at least for some years. The privilege of getting capital at gilt-edged rates would give the industry an undue

to follow the national interest. The most impassioned statement of this irrational doctrine, by Sir Stafford Cripps, provoked the most heated exchanges in the second reading debate. 'This challenge having been put forward by private interests, it is essential that democracy should assert its rights, otherwise it must acknowledge for all time that it cannot touch these citadels of power, and that it is not the electorate but the owners of industrial property who shall determine the economic policies of this country. And the ugly alternative would then be that any such change which is to occur must be brought about by other and more violent means, and it is because we are preventing that that we say Socialist democracy is the true barrier against Communism.' Prophecy in retrospect is rarely edifying, but Sir Stafford Cripps was not at his best in these realms of abstraction and forecasting (*Hansard*, 16 Nov. 1948, c. 326).

[1] Mr Lyttleton rightly pointed out how they tried to have the best of both worlds. 'To them (the Socialists) a company which moves a plant to a new location is always a juggernaut. On the other hand, if it accepts some increase in cost by remaining in the previous location...it is bowing down to vested interests' (*Hansard*, 15 Nov. 1948, c. 92).

[2] Mr Strauss referred to it in opening the second reading debate: 'new projects which could have brought greater employment...such as that at Jarrow were killed'. Not projects which would have saved labour and lowered costs! (*ibid.* c. 55).

preference in raising capital which might add to the temptation to over-expansion.[1]

But though there would be changes as a result of the Bill, and there was the element of bias through low interest rates, the Bill did not determine what sort of changes. This was a not surprising outcome in the circumstances, indeed, was almost inevitable, because owing to the near identity of outlook on immediate policy and development the only tangible object of the Bill was to transfer power,[2] on the socialist assumption that the disinterestedness of the management which would be appointed under the Bill would prove an important safeguard of public interest at some future time. But if the Bill in transferring power had the effect, as Mr Morrison claimed, of making radical change easier, it was more important than ever to have some standards whereby to tell whether the radical changes were right. The simple faith that the transfer of power was enough was now more difficult to sustain than it would have been in 1945, and the Opposition probed its weaknesses, but because of their own tradition of entrusting the determination of public interest to independent authorities like I.D.A.C. their criticism ended in anti-climax. The gap in their thinking was to be implicitly recognised (though they did not recognise it themselves) when the plan for a European Coal and Steel Community was propounded.

One exception there was to the uncertainty about the change which would follow the Bill. The present owners knew what they would be paid—namely, whenever there were stock exchange quotations of their shares, the market value of their

[1] The difference was hard to assess. Large sums had been borrowed from the Finance Corporation for Industry at low rates of interest. It was not a point which interested the Opposition in this sense; they referred to it (above, p. 306, n. 2) in connection with compensation. Some were aware that the Corporation would gain in the competitive finishing ends of its firms by having cheaper capital.

[2] This could equally well be called a *political* or an economic object. When referred to by Mr A. Bevan it had a political flavour. For example, 'Steel was power, and they had to transfer that power from the modern private barons to the public before the future could be safe. The Government was determined to pay compensation if the alternative was to be civil disorder. It was no use to carry out reforms in a revolutionary way; they had to take the tiger claw by claw' (*The Times* 3 Oct. 1949 (reporting a speech in Glasgow)). When referred to by Mr Morrison it sounded more economic (above, p. 293).

shares on certain dates. Was it a swindle as the Opposition argued? The Government did not claim that what they paid would equal the value of the assets they acquired; they said they had done very well in buying the Bank of England,[1] and by implication might do well again. They argued broadly that if some people had been willing to sell shares at the prices realised, then the great majority who were not induced to sell at that price must nevertheless accept the valuation of the minority; and they paid no heed to the fact that when majority holdings in companies were bought and sold, carrying with them control, the price was always above the Stock Exchange value. Valuations of businesses after all must be largely guess-work; the future was in the lap of the gods, or of the Governments, who might, Mr Strauss argued, cease to support the steel industry, for example, with tariffs. These contemporary arguments, passionate and sophistical,[2] illuminating as they are in the field of political ethics, have little relevance in retrospect for the development of the steel industry,[3] though they emphasised how remote the small buyer of shares was—and the speculative buyer, and most of the Stock Exchange machine too—from what was really happening in the companies whose shares were bought and sold. The terms of the ultimate purchase of the companies, and the fact of the purchase, were significant later because of their effect on the capital structure of the industry when it came again into private ownership. That, however, was for the future.

Towards the end of the debate on the third reading of the Bill, as success in the Commons was at hand, Mr Strauss was asked the future position of the Federation. 'I invited the Federation to put any point to me', he replied, but they had done nothing about it. 'I am sure the House and country would condemn any politically inspired non-co-operation.'[4] The Bill said nothing about the Federation, though Ministers had willed

---

[1] Mr Glenville Hall (Financial Secretary to the Treasury) (*S.C. Steel Nat.* c. 720 sqq.).

[2] Mr Lyttleton said of Sir Stafford Cripps' defence of the proposal that his 'training as an advocate has got a little ahead of the desire to be fair which is inherent in his character' (*S.C. Steel Nat.* c. 715).

[3] Hence I do not propose to list the arguments either in text or notes.

[4] *Hansard*, 9 May 1949, c. 1609.

its end. The silence of the Bill on this was to be explained, it was said,[1] by the fear of creating a 'hybrid Bill'. The Government need fear no delay over an ordinary public Bill; their majority was ample, and they prepared against opposition from the Lords by further curtailing their powers. Their attack on the 'citadel' of capitalism, when they could agree to make it, and how to make it, must be irresistible. But a hybrid Bill opened the door to exceptionally prolonged proceedings, because it would involve treating this Bill much as a private Bill, and interested individuals and groups could be represented by counsel who presumably could not be guillotined. A hybrid Bill was one which 'affects the interests of specific individuals or corporations as distinct from all individuals or corporations of a similar category'.[2] This was habitually interpreted with restraint and a sense of proportion; and it was 'not the practice' to treat as hybrids Bills 'dealing with matters of public policy whereby private rights over large areas or of a whole class are affected'.[3] Hence the Bill as it was drawn up escaped. And if the Bill had merged the identity of the companies to be acquired into one or more new entities presumably the main constituents of the Federation would have disappeared, as the coal owners' organisation vanished. But as it was had the Bill introduced some discriminating action against the Federation curtailing its powers or changing its constitution there would perhaps have been a danger. The Federation through its Conferences represented not only firms which were being acquired but many others too. To terminate by statute agreements between individual firms, many of whom were to remain in private ownership, *might* conceivably be deemed an interference with the rights and obligations of *some* of the individuals and corporations in a category, and not *all* of them. The doubt could be avoided by leaving the matter until the individual nationalised firms could as members of Conferences act for the Corporation, either in ending or using the Federation.

[1] Some of my informants made this much the most important factor; others said it was one of several.

[2] Even as it was the point was raised (*Hansard*, 15 Nov. 1948, c. 47–52). This quotation is in c. 47 (from Erskine May).

[3] *Ibid.* c. 51 (also from Erskine May).

Such presumably was the calculation. The Federation might collaborate. If so well and good; if not, it was merely a matter of time. But a matter of time which had a different aspect when the Bill had passed through all stages than when it started on its way. 'Is it right or wrong, if the nation believes that for economic reasons the steel industry should be nationalised that nationalisation should not take place?'[1] Sir Stafford Cripps asked in the opening debate. At the end it was clear that the nation's belief, if it had ever been more than a politician's fantasy, was waning. The Government's decision[2] to put off the 'vesting day' and the appointment of the Corporation until after a general election was time-absorbing; and the constitution of the Federation was such that when the unstable second Labour Government was formed with a small majority and divided counsels there was a good prospect of the Federation surviving untouched, autonomous and independent until another election.

2. TENUOUS OCCUPATION

The Iron and Steel Corporation of Great Britain was appointed six months after the 1950 election had given the Labour administration a precarious majority, in September 1950, and it started formally to operate in October.[3] The Minister had been faced after all with the difficulty he had decided to avoid a year earlier. The 'men best suited for this responsible task'[4] (Mr Ernest Davies had said they must be supermen) were still 'understandably...reluctant to commit themselves...and throw up their present position'.[5] Back in 1946 the Government had tried to attract Mr Ernest Lever to the job; he had become, it was said, a close friend of Mr Dalton's for his part in

---

[1] *Hansard*, 16 Nov. 1948, c. 326.
[2] This decision was imposed, as Mr Strauss stated in the House of Commons in Nov. 1949, by the impossibility of recruiting a Corporation of the right calibre on the eve of an election (*The Times*, 15 Sept. 1950).
[3] *The Times*, 15 Sept. and 3 Oct. 1950. 'Vesting day' came later, on 15 Feb. 1951 (*The Times*, 15 Feb. 1951).
[4] *S.C. Steel Nat.* c. 227.
[5] *Hansard*, 16 Nov. 1949, c. 2042–3, for the original quotation.

the South Wales strip-mill development. But he had repelled the advances.[1] In 1950 they could still get no one of outstanding importance in the steel industry, not even its trade union leaders, as members of the Corporation. As chairman they had Mr Steven Hardie, whom Mr Morrison had wooed in Scotland. One prophecy at least was thus fulfilled, that a Scotsman would again be put in control of the industry.[2] Mr Hardie, who was 65, had, it was universally conceded, a profound acquaintance with monopoly, since he was chairman of one of the most powerful monopolies (though its monopoly was on the eve of being challenged), the British Oxygen Company. The steel firms were large customers, and they had sometimes looked with envy on what seemed to them the cheap and convenient supplies of oxygen available to American steelmakers[3] (though it would no doubt have been argued that American circumstances made this easier). Mr Hardie had come into the oxygen business himself as a large consumer, for though by training an accountant his first industrial venture had been in the scrap trade, after the First World War, near Rosyth. He still retained this interest,[4] and it had led him before the war to advocate the setting up of steelworks there on the Forth, in preference to the Clyde. From the steel industry the Minister appointed two of the lesser figures in the Sheffield industry, Sir John Green as vice-chairman, Mr Garton as a part-time member.[5] There was a general;[6] a former member (not the senior member) of a city

[1] R. B. Williams-Thompson, *op. cit.* p. 39. The plan was that he should be chairman of the first Board, and later chairman of the nationalised industry. Mr Hugh Dalton spoke warmly of Sir Ernest Lever in the debate on steel in 1946.

[2] The prophecy was made by Mr Granville, in discussing the proposal that one member of the Board should represent Scotland. *S.C. Steel Nat.* c. 350.

[3] This was not a matter brought to light after Mr Hardie's appointment; it was referred to with some vigour during the visit of the United Kingdom Metallurgical Mission to America in 1943 in discussions of such things as the advance of flame cutting—much ahead of the United Kingdom—in United States.

[4] Metal Industries Limited.

[5] Neither had experience of mass-production steelmaking. Sir John Green was labour director of Firth Browns, but not a director of John Browns, the holding company; and Mr Garton was chairman of Brown Bayleys, but primarily concerned with the ball-bearing concern Hoffman's, which was a subsidiary of Brown Bayleys. Hoffman's was an instance in which part of a company acquired under the Act was by permission of the Minister 'hived off' to become a separate company, outside the nationalised industry.   [6] General Sir James Steele.

banking house who had been a success in administering Hamburg after the war;[1] a little-known senior trade unionist from the potteries,[2] a civil servant who had not quite reached the top.[3] It was perhaps not the Board which would have been appointed if it had been more certain that nationalisation had come to stay.

Nor was the Corporation able to set to work as it would have had its survival been assured. As it was the managements behaved with frigid propriety, and the Federation 'unanimously agreed that since the Act imposed certain duties on the new Corporation facilities should be provided by the industry for carrying out these duties as necessary'.[4] But it also declared it 'necessary for those in the industry not only to continue faithfully and loyally to manage their particular firms but also to preserve, as far as possible, those arrangements which had been so successful up to the present', i.e. separate managerial responsibility plus common services. Mr Hardie asked the companies to continue to co-operate with their appropriate trade associations, and proclaimed that 'any action taken should reflect the widest possible measure of agreement'. He hoped to take control of the main Federation Committees.[5] He asked for assistance in finding four steelmakers to join the Corporation; he was offered instead the co-operation on a consultative basis of the President and three leading steelmakers, who would be 'placed at the disposal of the Corporation' by the Council of the Federation. It was a group from which the master tactician excluded himself.[6] What impact could the Corporation quickly have in this situation having powers without knowledge?

The Corporation was in one respect helped by the flux of world events which made it easier to strike an attitude. For

[1] Sir Vaughan Berry.   [2] Mr W. H. Stokes.
[3] Mr A. R. McBain.
[4] This and what follows are recorded in the *B.I.S.F. Ann. Rep.* 1950, pp. 8–9.
[5] The position was described in *The Times*, 7 Feb. 1951. Mr Hardie hoped to have representatives on the Executive Committee and Council of the Federation, and (Mr Strauss stated in later debates) the Finance Committee. This was not agreed to; the Corporation did, however, have representatives on certain lesser though important committees—e.g. those concerned with planning.
[6] Sir Andrew Duncan described this with relish.

314 THE CAPTURE AND RECAPTURE OF THE CITADEL

between the election in June 1950 and vesting day, demand for steel had been revived and electrified by the Korean war. Demand for steel had flagged so far in 1949 that the volume of outstanding orders fell by one-quarter during the year; new orders, that is, were to that extent less than production, and the total order book at the end covered four months' work only.[1] The trend continued. Deliveries of steel to home consumers were less in the first half of 1950 than in the first half of 1949,[2] not through lack of steel but lack of orders, and exports were higher; that is one reason, presumably, why Continental and American exports fell off. (To increase British exports competitively was part of the Government's plan in devaluation.) Hence, as noted earlier, at the end of May, after some hesitation and just a month before the fateful challenge, the control of distribution was abandoned.[3] So little was the new turn of fortune or misfortune foreseen.

Since early in 1949 the O.E.E.C. and E.C.E. steel experts and steel committees, in large measure the same people, had, as noted earlier, been forecasting that there would be surplus steel capacity by 1953, and it seemed at hand by the beginning of 1950.[4] Too little significance was attached in the first half of 1950 to the rapid industrial recovery in America before Korea, possibly because the probability of collapse there had so firm a grip—some people seemed almost to hope for it; and by the second quarter the revival had, it could be said, only brought production back to its average level in 1948.[5] What impetus was there behind it? The Korean war unmistakably added an enormous impetus everywhere.[6] There was no rush of orders in

[1] B.I.S.F. Ann. Rev. for 1950, p. 10. Presumably about 4 m. tons of finished steel.

[2] The figures were 7·47 m. tons ingot equivalent in Jan.–June 1950, 7·25 m. tons in Jan.–June 1949.

[3] B.I.S.F. Ann. Rev. loc. cit. The Federation undertook that in certain sections of the trade which fell within its purview exports should be kept down to a reasonable level, having regard to home requirements for particular products.

[4] Above, p. 145. The E.C.E. Coal Committee expected a surplus in the second quarter (though still a deficit of coking quality coal), and an E.C.E. report on engineering industries emphasised the 'great improvement in delivery dates' which implied that new orders were less than deliveries (The Times, 6 Apr. 1950).

[5] There is a graph in The Times, 18 Sept. 1950, in an article on 'Production and Exports since Devaluation' (survey of A Year of Devaluation, p. ii).

[6] Above, p. 146.

the United Kingdom when allocations were abolished, but a sharp increase immediately after the Korean war started, and by November outstanding orders had reached 6,908,000 tons, between six and seven months' work compared with the four months at the end of 1949.

In Britain the Government defended their final determination to go ahead in the steel nationalisation 'primarily' by this international situation. Mr Morrison, who had so far avoided the vulgar errors, asserted that 'When war broke out (in 1939) capacity was much below what it ought to have been'.[1] Without some such fantasy perhaps it was harder than ever to 'recapture the generous certitudes' of the new world.[2] The danger of 1939 must never of course be faced again. Unfortunately, despite the development plan, authorised and revised, it was likely that Britain would be short of steel at the outset of the new rearmament because she would be short of raw material.[3] On this occasion there would not be steel supplies elsewhere to fill the gap, as there were in 1939. Expansion of steel output had depended much more than had been first projected on imports of German scrap. The ratio of scrap to pig iron in the charge was higher in 1950 than in 1945, or in 1937; it had risen steadily throughout the first five years of the plan, as Table 36 (which carries the figures to 1954) shows. But once German steel output grew fast and raw materials looked like being a limiting factor in Germany, the prospect of continuing supplies of German scrap in Britain on a large scale disappeared, and the blast-furnace programme was not sufficiently advanced to compensate for the disappearance. The question also arose, however, whether sufficient ore and coke had been provided to keep the blast furnaces which there were fully active.

This gave the cue to the Corporation's chairman who by his own background was already more sensitive perhaps to the raw-material situation of the industry than to other aspects. The industry, he now said, had paid too little heed to securing

---

[1] *Hansard*, 19 Sept. 1950, c. 1735, 1749. Mr Morrison knew well that output fell below capacity in the war through lack of raw materials.

[2] To avoid confusion—this quotation is *not* from Mr Morrison.

[3] Cp. *The Times*, 29 Dec. 1950.

its raw-material base. Who should say now the Corporation had nothing to do? He must set about giving steelmaking a secure base for the next fifty years.[1] Reviving demand soon involved another major decision of policy—how far should prices be raised as prices of imports shot up? Which also, though rather later, allowed the chairman to take a line in public which (more fairly) could be called a line of his own.

Table 36. *Scrap imports, weight of scrap in charge and stocks of pig iron and scrap*

Year	Total imports (thousand tons)	Imports from Germany (thousand tons)	Scrap per ton of steel (cwt.)	End of year stocks at steelworks	
				Scrap (thousand tons)	Pig iron (thousand tons)
1937	955	Nil	11·51	409	?
1945	178	23	12·18	470	1023
1946	443	270	12·05	617	856
1947	379	325	12·10	375	452
1948	858	781	12·16	504	462
1949	2097	1925	12·55	813	797
1950	1958	1805	12·59	618	760
1951	589	481	11·67	257	380
1952	734	392	11·05	422	664
1953	861	69	11·09	648	841
1954	761	174	11·10	688	802

The influence of the Corporation on the course of events was necessarily small, though its precise achievement cannot yet be unravelled.[2] There were enough 'straws in the wind' to show that it would have made considerable changes had it remained in power. These were expressed primarily as constitutional changes within the industry, and their implications for policy and development can only vaguely be surmised. The most significant step actually taken was a review of the company

[1] This was a main theme of his first public statements.
[2] I was informed, for example, that the chairman insisted that one major company should sign contracts for the building of a new blast-furnace plant, for whose rapid completion the company ultimately got great credit; but no records to establish this kind of claim will be available for many years.

Boards. The Corporation decided that it was undesirable that directors of a 'nationalised' steelworks should also be directors of large privately owned consumer firms; that directors representing the financial interests of a former group of owners should disappear; that directors should not, save for exceptional reasons, be older than the Companies Act of 1948 laid down; and that there should be a 'proper balance' between full-time and part-time directors. The chief executives of a firm should normally be on the Board, plus part-timers with special and wide experience of value to the company. The principles were sound enough; their application for a period of nine months led to the elimination of over 50 out of 450 directors, 32 at the request of the Corporation and some others as a protest against the Corporation's attitude toward their colleagues. Further changes were at hand when a Conservative Government came into power, and all the changes stopped forthwith.[1] The Corporation henceforth, until disbanded, was to have powers without influence.

The significance of these changes of Boards was unmistakable. The Corporation acknowledged a 'statutory obligation to decentralise';[2] accordingly 'administration of the business of each company has remained with the board of directors'. But an owner can appoint a Board; common ownership in the end must mean common appointment, and the virtue of having a multiple source of appointments inherent in the former structure, an important expression of 'decentralisation', had gone. Boards were acceptable when they accepted the Corporation's principles in a wholly amicable manner.[3] It was unavoidable. Critics concentrated understandably on the distinguished names of persons removed rather than on the distinction of some of the persons newly appointed.[4]

---

[1] *Iron and Steel Corporation of Great Britain; Report and Statement of Accounts for the period ended 30th of September 1951* (referred to later as *Rep. I.S. Corp.* 1951), pp. 11–12.

[2] *Ibid.* p. 2.

[3] *Ibid.* p. 12. 'In the great majority of cases the arrangements have been made with the agreement of the boards of directors in a wholly amicable manner and the Corporation's principles have been accepted.'

[4] The most conspicuous change was in the Board of Firth Browns because the chairman (Lord Aberconway) was asked to resign, and several other members of the Board resigned. They were all Board members in the former holding company,

These changes were quite evidently and quite openly a prelude to still greater changes. The Corporation 'recognised that it would be impracticable in the early months to do other than accept the general pattern of the companies as they found it'. But they visualised changes in the company structure, a 'major reorganisation' which would 'require the fullest consideration and could only be undertaken after the most careful consultation with those concerned'.[1] Some minor changes were made. The large change which the chairman at least had in mind[2] involved a consolidation of the 298 companies into seven companies (would they have been subsidiary holding companies?), one of them to be an iron-ore company which would embrace both the home and imported ore business, the remainder probably regional consolidations of existing companies.[3] This could be interpreted to mean that the advantages of large scale were infallibly to be reaped. The ore company could be thought of as a projection of the existing collective importing arrangements (which had continued since the war)[4] into the home ore field, because it was thought by some members of the Corporation and of the staff that the best use was not made of home ores owing to the particular interests of the owners or those who leased the mineral rights.[5]

John Browns. The new chairman and managing director was Dr Sykes, F.R.S., hitherto a director and in charge of research. The incident was thought to owe something to the fact that Sir John Green had been a member of Firth Brown's Board, though not of John Brown's. The *New Statesman* criticised the change of this Board as 'perhaps regrettable' (*New Statesman*, 4 Aug. 1951).

[1] *Rep. I. S. Corp.* 1951, pp. 11, 13.
[2] He referred to it in conversation.
[3] These intentions were not, as far as I know, set out in any published document. But in the debate which followed Mr Hardie's retirement Mr Duncan Sandys said that Mr Hardie had proposed in a 'few vague letters and conversations' that the Corporation should take over B.I.S.C. (Ore), without showing what gain there would be, and had proposed what he called a 'scheme of decentralisation' which was to be a grouping of companies, but no details were forthcoming (*Hansard*, 25 Feb. 1952, c. 824–7).
[4] See below, p. 325.
[5] The view was, as I gathered, that (a) some ore quarries were too small either to be efficient mining units or to *treat* the ore efficiently (which made it better for smelting). (b) Only part of the home ore used in blast furnaces was used in appropriate mixtures—as nearly uniform as possible through appropriate 'bedding', and as near self-fluxing as possible. This happened chiefly where large firms owned a number of mining leases. (c) Much ore was made available in quantities which

These were interesting propositions. When it came to detailed decisions on plans, as will be seen, there were no signs that the Corporation brought any new light, and the chairman's only known contribution was the suggestion that the new Scots works, often talked of, should be at his favourite Forth site. Nevertheless, the concept of new companies was a token of the centripetal force of national ownership. If the Corporation was to escape cramping the style of management (to recall Mr Morrison's phrase)[1] it might do so apparently by changing the management. What benefits or drawbacks this might have conferred was never shown. The steel experience had no chance of being a test of nationalisation. Its practical influences were trivial,[2] and the atmosphere preserved by uncertainty made inferences from the experience unreliable.[3]

The time for the 'fullest consideration' which regrouping of companies would need never came. While the Labour Government was in power the uneasy truce with the Federation limited the Corporation's authority. It was significant that when this Government appointed a Steel (Rearmament) Panel in March 1951 to ensure that steel was forthcoming for rearmament the Commercial Director of the Federation[4] was its chairman, while the Corporation merely had representatives on the

suited the mining companies, either because of their facilities or because as users of ore they had, after mixing what they wanted for their own use, a residue. (d) Much ore was used remote from the mines or quarries, because the mineral rights were leased by iron manufacturers who used them at their own plants, in South Wales or the North-east Coast. The resources were cheaper to use than imported ore, even at the coast, and being tied by leases or ownership to remote users they were not available for use nearer at hand. A newcomer could not readily acquire mineral rights.   [1] Above, p. 291.

[2] For example, the publicity of the Corporation made much of the fact that since some firms had cash resources and others needed cash the Corporation could use the former as the basis of cheap short-term loans for the latter.

[3] Thus one member of the Board argued to me that the Corporation's experience showed how necessary ownership was for control; but this involved two confusions. Because of the opposition to the new Corporation it enjoyed no moral authority, no authority derived from respect for status. And of course while the Corporation was so weak the question of Ministerial and Parliamentary control over the Corporation never arose, and was not seen to be a problem by members of the Corporation.

[4] Mr E. W. Senior, who had been Director for Alloy Steel in the Iron and Steel Control and later Head of the Steel Section of the Ministry of Supply Purchasing Mission in the United States.

panel. It could be argued that a high proportion of the steel for armaments was made outside the Corporation, in small alloy steel firms or in 'pure' steel foundries. The Ministry of Supply panel appeared to use the Federation machinery for coping in detail with shortages. When the Distribution Scheme was reintroduced in February 1952, and the panel disappeared, under the Conservative Government, all agreed 'the Federation should undertake general responsibility for arranging steel production and supply in accordance with Government requirements'. The Federation was, as it frankly claimed, the 'focal point for the clearance of shortages'. And it could now call the tune more generally. The Corporation, on the other hand, were fettered until they could be dispensed with. The new Minister, Mr Duncan Sandys, within three weeks of his appointment directed that they should do nothing which altered the financial structure or management of the publicly owned companies. Until the Government's plan to re-call the industry into private ownership was completed and passed through Parliament the Corporation remained formally important; but they no longer occupied the citadel.

3. THE RETURN OF SCARCITY

The steelmakers and the first Board had not, as the discussions of the first plan showed, overlooked raw-material problems, though they had not, as was plain enough by the end of 1950, provided for the demands of 1951–52. This was as clear to the steel firms as it was to Mr Hardie. The plans had aimed from the first at a big increase in pig-iron capacity, and the revision of 1948 had pushed the 'target' up again from 11 m. tons in 1952–53 to 13·5 m. tons in 1953–54. The need ultimately to have a higher ratio of pig iron to scrap and the transitory nature of the German imports had been acknowledged.[1] But performance had fallen behind plan and continued to do so. The output of pig iron in 1952–53 was 10·8 m. tons, a little less than the original unrevised figure; in 1953–54 it was 11·6 m. tons, a

---

[1] 'Substantial quantities of scrap from Germany are unlikely...for more than a few years' (The Federation, in *Stat. Bull.* Dec. 1948). The drop came in 20 months.

lot less than the revised figure. Was it deliberate, or unavoidable?

Probably there were deliberate delays; plans put back deliberately because demand for steel fell off and German scrap was, for a time, available. The public explanation of deferments was usually the uncertainty over nationalisation. But there were respectable reasons for taking the less optimistic view of demand trends which Sir Andrew McCance of Colvilles took.[1] Though there was an official unpublished estimate in Britain completed by the Government's central planning organisation at the end of 1947 which accepted a high figure of 16 m. tons home demand for the United Kingdom in the early fifties, and consumption plus new stocks came near this in 1952,[2] the much more familiar E.C.E. survey published at the end of 1949 had used the same assortment of statistical techniques to produce for the wider market its estimate which emphasised a lively risk of excess capacity by 1953.[3] This was probably prepared in closer touch with the industry than the British figure, but it was not an industry estimate. Civil servants participated,[4] and it is likely it was accepted by the British Government as something likely to be right unless deliberate action was taken to change things.[5] In the event the E.C.E. estimate of 58 m. tons as the 'practical maximum' consumption in Europe in 1953 was 10 m. tons less than the actual consumption of 1953.[6] It would be wrong to

[1] Above, p. 278.
[2] Consumption alone was approximately 15·0 m. tons in 1952 (above, p. 151).
[3] Above, p. 145. For the techniques cp. *European Steel Trends*, 1949, ch. II passim. They were the familiar methods; projection from past outputs, projections based on supposed 'normal' ratios of manufacturing output to steel consumption; estimates based on forecasts of outputs in main consuming industries; and a summation of national 'plan' figures.
[4] The chief official on the E.C.E. steel committee, M. Tony Rollman, was a member of the Luxembourg firm ARBED. His successor on the E.C.E. committee, Miss Elizabeth Ackroyd, was at this time chairman of the O.E.E.C. Steel Committee, and was an assistant secretary of the Ministry of Supply.
[5] Economists after all were discussing what America should do to prevent a growth of unemployment throughout the western world. The economists were called 'experts' (*National and International Measures for Full Employment*, United Nations, Dec. 1949). A second report by different 'experts' with different conclusions was produced some months later.
[6] *European Steel Trends*, E.C.E. Dec. 1949, p. 21, the whole of ch. II, and p. 72 (the tons are metric tons); *The European Steel Market in 1953* (E.C.E. Jan. 1954, p. 43).

assume, however, that because in fact this was too low the high British figure of 1947 was, except by coincidence, right; it may well have been too high in relation to current trends,[1] and only 'realised' because of unforeseen and highly stimulating circumstances. This could be judged best from the degree of correlation between forecasts of steel to be used in particular industries and the steel in fact used—but these forecasts were not published.[2] They were made when the railways demand was put very high, steel economies in building were not allowed for, and an extremely austere view was taken of the output of motor-cars, for home and export. The 10 per cent of consumption for defence in 1952 naturally was not forecast. War and preparations for war are likely to change trends.

If the impetus to expansion was lessened by a sense that demand for steel would be less exigent in the early fifties than the revised plan of 1948 assumed there was an understandable motive for it, though it proved a misjudgement. There was less justification for letting up on blast-furnace development in particular, however, since steelmaking, which relied so greatly on German scrap, was obviously living on the edge of a precipice. What happened exactly in this respect it is impossible to say from published records.[3] The volume of investment, it has been

---

[1] The *total* requirement was put at 19 m. tons, including 3 m. tons for exports. The crude-steel output accepted for the revised plan was 18 m. tons, allowing possibly 1 m. tons for imports.

[2] A number of forecasters (e.g. Sir Andrew McCance) implicitly do not accept this. I observe, however, that their forecasts are at least not more accurate than others. A Marxist might no doubt argue that rearmament was introduced to fill the demand gap. Such certitude was not, conspicuously, exhibited in advance; the customary argument, in terms of 'capitalism' (or 'anti-capitalism') was that depression was unavoidable unless American economic policy became less 'liberal'. It can be argued that this happened as a result of rearmament, but this was not the route which was, in current talk, or in the documents, expected. The E.C.E. view was that the actual growth of demand due to Korea induced an expansion of engineering and steel-using industrial capacity which was greater than would have occurred by 1952–53; but once it was created those who managed it went out for civil work, hence sustained the growth in steel use. This view is, I believe, largely valid.

[3] It may be impossible from the unpublished records; for as all who have assisted in taking decisions, or in *not* taking decisions, well know, the records rarely set out all the factors on which decisions rest. The operative part of the record is the decision, and instructions to action arising from it. People in action are rarely

seen, rose through 1949–50, and the peak expenditure in the seven years of the first plan came in 1950. It was above the average for the original plan, but the plan had been enlarged. Whether there was a 1948 time-table, and whether achievements looked at in what had come to be called 'global figures' were up to it, there is no published record to show. In detail, as has been seen, there were so many departures from the original proposals, so many new blast furnaces not in the original plan, and such imposing 'absentees' that it is hard to know how a balance can be struck.[1] The new furnaces projected at Corby, Appleby Frodingham, Colvilles (1948 scheme), and Dorman Long's for instance, had not been started. How far was this deliberately concerted with decisions to build elsewhere, at West Hartlepool and Skinningrove, for example?[2] Failure to achieve the projected outputs at the terminal dates might be accounted for by the long time taken in building blast furnaces; but the argument would have been more convincing if the starting dates had been less delayed, or if (it having been decided that the time was not propitious for starting all the major projects first projected at once, on the grounds that to try to do too much at once was a source of delay) the resort to measures for making the most of existing plant by small expenditures referred to above[3] had been more widespread. As it was some of these measures were resorted to under stress of the rearmament drive, a plain indication that they were not impracticable.[4]

interested in explaining or remembering why they take a certain line. This is not always recognised by those with a passion for finding a written record which will solve the mysteries of history.

[1] The facts are set out above in another context, p. 251.

[2] I have never heard of any such linking. Of Appleby Frodingham I was told in 1950 that the new ore preparation and sintering plant was intended to give the increase of pig-iron output from existing furnaces which had been projected from the new furnaces. It had been possible to get United Steel's output as planned therefore without new furnaces. The works at Templeborough, where some members of the company's staff had pressed for the building of a blast furnace, suffered however, badly when German scrap supplies were cut. Building of new blast furnaces at Appleby-Frodingham started in 1951.   [3] Above, pp. 195 sqq.

[4] Thus third stacks at two blast-furnace plants (Ebbw Vale and R. T. Scunthorpe) were provided with auxiliary equipment so that they could be used. Obviously this might have required a reallocation of resources earlier; it could not be deemed impossible. The integrated plants may have been internally balanced, and have had no direct interest in increasing their iron output.

No doubt, moreover, it seemed to Federation, Board and Government that adequate safeguards were provided, since, as Table 36 shows, stocks of pig iron and scrap were built up from 1947 to 1950. They ultimately reached (together) 1·77 m. tons at the steelworks, in August 1950, which was equal to almost a year's consumption of German scrap.[1] (Stocks of semi-finished steel were also built up to 1·19 m. tons by August 1950; they were halved by the end of 1951.) Distribution of stocks was, however, of great importance; and though no figures were available it was known that large stocks were built up for the new Margam works, which was to come into full production in 1951, and for the reconstructed Round Oak works of the Earl of Dudley. On the other hand, the stocks for Colvilles and for Steel Peech, and Tozer soon proved inadequate and several furnaces had to be shut down.[2] Whose responsibility the provision of adequate stocks at specific works would be it is hard to judge, because though the Federation did not allocate all scrap it exerted an influence by requesting the scrap trade to fulfil some specific requirements, as seen earlier, and this would have stopped stock building elsewhere. Reallocation of the stock could not, however, have substantially altered the total impact of the cut in import supplies; the vital weakness of certain locations was their reliance on imports against whose disappearance adequate preparations were not made either locally or centrally.

At the end of 1950 a stranger scarcity began to lessen output, scarcity of iron ore. Pig-iron output was increased in the last quarter of 1950, in response perhaps to the dual influence of declining scrap supplies and rising orders, but it was not maintained at the increased level in the first three quarters of 1951.[3]

[1] It was between five and six weeks' consumption of pig iron and scrap in steelmaking, but this is a less relevant figure. Furthermore, it would not be practicable to use the whole of the stock. Stocks were drawn on heavily however—400,000 tons by end of 1950, a further 750,000 tons in 1951.

[2] Below, p. 333.

[3] The weekly average outputs per quarter for these years were (thousand tons per week):

1949	4th qr.	186	1950	4th qr.	192
1950	1st qr.	186	1951	1st qr.	184
	2nd qr.	183		2nd qr.	183
	3rd qr.	179		3rd qr.	184

Either blast-furnace capacity could not be used fully or output was reduced through use of less rich materials, less scrap, less imported ore, more home ore. Both things probably happened.[1] The use of more home ore as a part of a general development policy would have contributed to low costs, but it was only a makeshift in this situation. How far did this also uncover a position in which there had been less prevision than was to be expected?

Again it was a field in which Federation (and, at a remove, Board and Government) decisions were operative; ore importing had been handled since the war as during the war by the British Iron and Steel Corporation through a specially created subsidiary which contracted for all imported ores, arranged all their shipping, and sold them at uniform prices to all firms;[2] subject to some variations according to the efficiency of ports, and with the addition of carriage from port to works. This was much against the traditional preferences of British steelmakers who had resisted suggestions of collective purchase before the war, arguing that they got the qualities they wanted for their particular practice, and often they had financial interests in particular mines. 'Most companies felt that they were able to buy better than any other',[3] and they were encouraged by the ore merchants, who suggested that collective buying would lead to collective selling. German and Polish buying, however, was already, it was argued by the advocates of joint purchase, collective, and the purchases were on favourable terms.[4] They argued, too, that the main cost of ore was in freights, and shipping would remain competitive[5] and that collective purchase allowed a better use of ships, since cargoes could be

---

[1] Total pig-iron output was slightly higher in 1951, owing to a rise at the close of the year; consumption of imported ore (excluding manganese ore) for pig iron was 7·75 m. tons compared with 8·14 m. tons in 1950. In 1950 stocks of imported iron ore were reduced by 337,000 tons to a total of 945,000 tons (*B.I.S.F. Ann. Rev.* 1950, p. 14). By the end of 1951, when ore flowed in more freely again, stocks were raised again by 175,000 tons.

[2] B.I.S.C. (Ore). There is a useful brief account in *B.I.S.F. Ann. Rep.* 1952 pp. 30–2.   [3] I am relying on an unpublished memorandum.

[4] It was not pointed out that the Germans had much better unloading facilities and for this reason could buy cheaper C.I.F.

[5] They argued too that the trade really depended on coal freights out, ore back.

diverted to ports where either there was a vacant berth or there was a local scarcity of ore. Both these were of course a reflection on the badly scattered nature of the British use of ore and the smallness and slow unloading facilities of many of the importing ports. At the end of the war the temporary need for planned imports, partly for currency reasons and the scarcity and high cost of shipping, and the desire to keep steel prices lower than imported ore prices would without subsidy or pooling allow, all weighed strongly in favour of continuing the war system.

The implied suggestion of Mr Hardie when he spoke of securing ore supplies for fifty years was that there was a lack of ore to ship to the United Kingdom. It was well known that the United States was investing heavily in Venezuela and Northern Ontario and Labrador. Before these new ore fields were producing America was importing about 3 m. tons a year from the normal United Kingdom sources. Projected new developments of these normal sources were modest in scale. There was a plan to develop a mine at Conakry in French West Africa, a deposit leased originally by an American speculator, offered (before the war) to the Germans, and then to Colvilles, who took an option. It was not a very good ore.[1] There was a plan also to develop a new Sierra Leone deposit inland from the one already exploited.[2] But these were not spectacular, nor did they progress fast. Some of the old sources—Northern Spain for example, were nearing exhaustion.[3] A case could be argued that supplies were not sufficiently assured ahead. The E.C.E. *Report* of 1949 not only argued that if all the new steel capacity planned for 1953 were used there would be 8 m. tons too much steel—it cast some doubt on whether there would be enough iron ore for all the plants. It was not certain; not enough was known.

[1] This ore was opened up by an Anglo-French Company in which B.I.S.C. (Ore) had one-third of the capital.

[2] Sierra Leone ore was mined by a British ore-importing company. The scheme may have been delayed because of doubts as to the political security of a new investment which required a costly rail development. In 1950 this project was estimated to raise the supply of ore from Sierra Leone to 4·5 m. tons a year. *B.I.S.F. Ann. Rep.* 1950, p. 15.

[3] Hence Spanish steel companies were anxious to buy up what remained; the Orconera and Alquife companies, both owned by British firms, were sold to Spanish companies in the early fifties.

But 'in 1949 supplies just cover requirements (for Europe as a whole) without leaving a sufficient margin for meeting any sudden or unforeseen eventuality'.[1] The 'tightness' of the position was probably due to the reviving German purchases.

Nevertheless, although there may have been some temporary curtailment of the British industry's ore supply by the exclusion of Newfoundland ores early in 1950 to save dollars, the source of the scarcity from the end of 1950 was lack of shipping, which in turn was due to the conjuncture of the need for ships for the Korean campaign, and the (on this occasion) shorter lived but still acute need for ships to bring coal from America.[2] England was occupied with one of her recurrent threats of coal famine.[3] Shipping stringency continued till the summer, and though 9·35 m. tons of ore were ordered for the year only 8·78 m. tons arrived.[4] The main conclusion to be drawn from this stringency was that the shipping arrangements were not adequate, and they were altered. In future B.I.S.C. (Ore) had a large number of ships on time charter, contracted to operate for it on such journeys as it chose for several months, instead of chartered for one specific voyage only. They also began to carry out a plan discussed ever since the end of the war to have a fleet of ore carriers of their own for part of the traffic.[5]

It is likely that the crisis of early 1951 did also provoke a change in ore-buying policy, encouraging the conclusion of some longer contracts, and the study of further possibilities of jointly opening up new deposits. The prospecting of a large ore body in Mauretania began in 1951.[6] But this did not support

[1] *European Steel Trends*, p. 41.
[2] *B.I.S.F. Ann. Rep.* 1950, *loc. cit.* There were some other exceptional demands on shipping; for example, in the grain trade to India in the first half of 1951.
[3] *The Times*, 12 Dec. 1950; there was a debate on fuel in the House of Commons on this date.
[4] *Stat. Bull.* Aug. 1951, p. 3.   [5] *B.I.S.F. Ann. Rep.* 1952, p. 32.
[6] *Ibid.* 1951, p. 17. It was to be a French–Canadian–British venture. The ore was in French North Africa, and exceptionally high in quality and of easy accessibility. The nearest rail connection would be through Spanish North Africa, hence negotiations with Spain were for long a time held to be vital. An estimate of probable capital expenditure needed for the venture in 1954 was £25 m. The output was to be 4 m. By 1960 the figures were £60 m. and 6 m. tons. The ore was to come out via Port Etienne. German steel firms now had a small interest, and the adventure had a World Bank loan. Ore was to become available from 1964.

the argument that policy had hitherto been negligent. Ore buying had been relatively easy (although even so F.O.B. prices never fell to the low levels used for early estimates of post-war costs and had risen from 1946); shipping had become easy, the Government would have frowned on a lot of oversea investment and B.I.S.C. (Ore) could hardly be expected to prepare for the Korean affair with more prescience than the Government.

The changed aspect of the ore trade from 1949 was reflected in a sharp, and long-lived, rise of ore prices. It began in part as a result of devaluation, though like most of the effects of devaluation its influence was delayed. Apart from Sweden the main ore-exporting countries did not devalue as much as the United Kingdom, nor did the other main buyers of imported ore.[1] Thus the terms of trade on which the United Kingdom bought ore shifted still further in favour of the suppliers. The F.O.B. prices had been rising significantly since 1946, but the movement was now accentuated. The extreme probability of this happening when Germany came back as a buyer had been rejected, it has been seen, when post-war costs were being forecast in 1944.[2] But the effect of devaluation on F.O.B. prices seemed like an act of God; ore prices were not thought of as part of the situation which imposed devaluation, and by good fortune the level of freights fell early in 1950 as the F.O.B. cost of ore rose. The impact of Korea raised both F.O.B. prices and freights precipitately and established a new level of ore prices, at first thought to be transitory, of almost 100s. a ton or more (or, say, 1s. 9d. a unit of iron, three times the guess of 1944, and about five times the average in 1937, which was itself high for the pre-war period). The yearly average C.I.F. prices from 1946 to 1954 together with indices of the movements of freights and F.O.B. prices for three specific ores are shown in Table 37.

[1] France devalued by 10 per cent, Spain nil, Brazil nil, Canada 10 per cent; Sweden, like the United Kingdom, 30½ per cent. Among ore buyers Germany by 20 per cent and the United States of course not at all. There is a table of the rates of devaluation in 'A survey of the first year of devaluation'. (*The Times*, 18 Sept. 1950, p. iv).
[2] Above, pp. 100 sqq. I am informed by Professor Austin Robinson that similar advice was rejected by Ministry officials concerned with steel prospects in 1948.

Table 37. *Imported ore prices*

Year	Average C.I.F. prices (s.)	Indices for three typical ores[a]					
		F.O.B. prices			Freights		
		A	B	C	A	B	C
1937	22·5	68	51	70	—	—	—
1946	57·2	100	100	100	100	100	100
1947	55·0	112	100	116	91	95	112
1948	56·4	131	113	132	89	94	112
1949	57·8	152	113	143	86	90	96
1950	57·8	181	133	161	77	77	80
1951	85·2	233	167	184	178	180	120
1952	117·8	379	285	314	123	122	130
1953	113·6	438	446	330	85	93	93
1954	102·6	371	373	296	77	88	90

[a] I.e. each one is an ore of one quality from one source. The greater range of the movement of freights for A and B ores reflected greater sensitiveness on the Atlantic and Mediterranean shipping routes, and in circumstances where less of the shipping was owned or controlled by one of the parties in the trade.

There was nothing the Corporation could do to alleviate the immediate scarcities, and, as shown earlier (though it was in no way cause and effect), the first year of nationalisation was a year of lowered output, the first since the war. Output fell below the hopes—it would hardly be correct to say the forecast —of the *Economic Survey* for 1951,[1] being 15·64 m. tons instead of from 16 to 16·25 m. tons. The practice of making safe forecasts of probable outputs and exceeding the forecast had for long been followed with success, and this reversal of custom seems to have occasioned irritation. Steel users, the Federation concluded, had 'made nothing like the same effort as the steelmakers themselves to throw out all possible supplies of scrap'. They had, of course, much less incentive. There was a drive and it did not fully succeed.[2] And, particularly galling, more scrap

[1] '...It would be unwise to rely on a crude steel production of more than 16 to 16·25 m. tons, and even this may prove to be an optimistic forecast.' *Econ. Survey* for 1951, p. 13.

[2] *Stat. Bull.* Dec. 1951, p. 3. The Federation recognised that the demand for ships reduced the supply of shipbreaking scrap. They argued, however, that total deliveries of steel were as great as in 1950, therefore the total supply of bought

had gone to the iron founders, whose output rose while the steel output fell. (Perhaps some of them *had* paid higher prices for scrap). It raised 'in an acute form the question whether the distribution of these raw materials which are common to both the steel and the foundry industry has been made to the best advantage'.[1] Steel consumption had been growing everywhere for so long faster than and at the expense of cast iron that the contrast in 1951 seemed almost an outrage. Yet it was hard to pin an effective charge on anyone, because the products in which more castings were used were almost exclusively impressively necessary—ingot moulds, cranes, railways, machine tools, agricultural machinery, electrical machinery, gas, oil and steam engines, and so on.[2] Domestic gas ovens, it was suggested, could be made of sheets, as an increasing number have been, but sheets were themselves usually among the scarcest steel product.

Table 38. *Home deliveries of steel (weekly averages, thousand tons)*

Quarter	1949	1950	1951	1952
1st	296	287	289	294
2nd	288	274	283	306
3rd	256	255	257	286
4th	278	280	287	314
Average for year	280	274	279	300

The Federation argued that steel supplies to home users were in fact better in 1951 than in 1950 despite the decline in ingot output, though not as good as in 1949. There was little difference in deliveries, according to the rough figures then published, which are set out in Table 38.[3] This rate of supply

scrap should have been as large, but was not; only a small part of the difference was to be explained by more use of second-hand steel.

[1] *Stat. Bull. loc. cit.*   [2] *B.I.S.F. Statistical Yearbook* for 1951, p. 69.

[3] They were based on the sum of the output of ingots, plus or minus steel used from or put into producers' stocks, plus reusable material used, plus imports, less exports, all the data except the first being converted into ingot equivalents. It is quite evident that in the short run the material included in a month is not available for use at the same time; errors must creep in owing to the conversion factors being only approximate, and it is doubtful whether the figure for second-hand material can be comprehensive. For figures from 1950 including users' and merchants' stock changes, above, p. 151.

could be severely cramping when strong expansive forces were at work, and was bound to become more cramping towards the end of the period of constriction, since any stocks consumers or merchants had would tend to be exhausted. (The *Economic Survey for 1950* forecast that 420,000 ingot tons would be drawn from stock in 1950; the Federation thought the real figure may have been higher.)[1] Moreover, the position was less satisfactory for common qualities of steel. Total 'crude steel' output was 650,000 tons less in 1951 than 1950, but the output of alloy steel and of castings *rose*, and the output of carbon steel ingots was in fact 750,000 tons lower. When crude steel output recovered again in 1952, being slightly higher than in 1950, the output of ingots was virtually identical (the increment was in the output of castings), and carbon steel ingots, though 560,000 tons more than in 1951, were nearly 300,000 tons less than in 1950. It is not surprising therefore that even if the total home deliveries of new steel did not fall there was a widespread and acute sense of scarcity by spring 1951, both because fewer firms could rely on their own stocks and because there were shorter supplies of many of the main grades and shapes.[2] Firms were being forced to change their programmes of work according to the stocks of steel they had, and to use steel, wastefully, in such sizes (often larger than necessary) as they had or could get.[3] There were delays in completing work because one type of steel was available when its complement was missing; shipbuilders, for example, fell shorter at this time of sections than of plates.

As noted earlier, a system of priorities was reintroduced in April 1951 for alloy steel.[4] By this time the defence programme was beginning to have a noticeable direct impact, though still possibly a small one. Priorities for all steel came two months later, when steel was 'the most widespread if not the most acute

[1] *Stat. Bull.* Apr. 1951, p. 3.
[2] There were smaller outputs of rails and sleepers, heavy plates, heavy angles, tee sections and girders, wire rods, ferro-concrete bars, light bars (non-alloy), strip other than for tubes, galvanised sheets, tinplates and wire. There were increases in medium plates, heavy rounds, steel colliery arches, light sections, strip for tubes, uncoated sheets (the Margam works started in 1951) and in special grade products electric sheets, cold-rolled strip, bright bars, forgings etc. The data are fuller in the *B.I.S.F. Statistical Year Book* for 1952 (Table 55) than for 1951.
[3] Cp. *The Times*, 30 Mar., 9 May, 4 June.   [4] *Ibid.* 21 Apr. 1951.

scarcity', and there were discussions about introducing the former distribution scheme again.[1] This step was not finally taken till February 1952, under the new, Conservative, Government, and after a promise had been given of 1 m. tons of steel from America.[2] It might even have seemed that the step was too late to be needed; but though there was a sound prospect of steel supplies growing, the supply immediately may have been almost at its worst, since consumers' stocks must have been largely used up, while new demands were piling up. The direct demands of defence created an additional demand of from 500,000 to 750,000 ingot tons between the beginning of 1950 and the end of 1952,[3] and the effect of the direct defence needs was multiplied both internally and (since rearmament was widespread) externally by its indirect effects. Steel supplies at this stage thus became seriously constrictive. Output of the engineering, electrical and shipbuilding industries, which remained fairly steady from January to August 1951, surged up to a new peak in the first quarter of 1952 and then fell off—the second quarter output of 1952 was 8 per cent lower than the first, and there was little recovery in the rest of the year. Vehicle output had suffered already in 1951; it was lower in the fourth than in the second quarter.[4]

---

[1] *The Times*, 4 June and 29 June 1951. Steel could be given a symbol, D.O. for defence order or P.T., i.e. preferential treatment for urgent civil work; the intention was that P.T. should not cover more than from 7–10 per cent of total deliveries. Makers undertook to put aside a proportion of their capacity for priority work. The major steel needs for defence orders—gun forgings, tank castings and the like—were subject to planning and progressing as during the war; capacity was examined, and where gaps were discovered plans for new capacity were made. There was a good deal of uncertainty about needs, however, when it came to the point of expansion plans. The priority arrangements were not mandatory.

[2] Made on the occasion of Sir W. Churchill's first visit to the United States on becoming Prime Minister again. Above, p. 150.

[3] Cp. the White Paper on Defence.

[4] The quarterly indices were (average 1950 = 100):

Volume of output of metal-using industries

	1949	1950				1951				1952			
Quarters ...	1	1	2	3	4	1	2	3	4	1	2	3	4
Engineering, ship-building and electrical goods	94	97	98	95	109	107	110	107	115	119	110	98	113
Vehicles		98	103	97	94	107	101	108	97	105	97	106	92	107

There were marked variations in the flux of steel output in different regions. Ingot output dropped most in Scotland in 1951, and hardly recovered in 1952.[1] Basic open-hearth output fell severely in and around Sheffield in 1951, but recovered most of the lost ground in 1952. Lancashire lost severely in 1951 and did not recover in 1952. The North-west Coast lost progressively. South Wales and Northamptonshire, on the other hand, both gained progressively.[2] Ingot outputs were reflected in finished steel outputs. In Scotland outputs of heavy plates and sections were both over one-tenth lower in 1951–2 than in 1950. By contrast there was a substantial increase in South Wales, not only of sheets but of plates, these probably being in general medium plates produced on the strip mill, and not suitable for ship plates.[3] All this was bound to be reflected in

---

[1] This may have been partly due to furnaces taken out of commission owing to lack of raw material having been subjected to drastic reconstruction so that they could not be reactivated quickly.

[2] The regional positions were as follows:

Percentage gains (+) or losses (−) in steel ingot output

	In 1951 over 1950	In 1952 over 1951
Northants, etc.	+6	+9
S. Wales	+2	+7
Staffs, etc	—	+6
N.E. Coast	−5	+1
Lincs	−7	+13
N.W. Coast	−7	−7
Lancs	−8	—
Sheffield[a]	−9	+7
Scotland	−14	—

[a] Basic open-hearth ingots only. To include *all* ingots for Sheffield would confuse the rise in special steel with the fall in common-grade steel.

[3] The output of plates according to districts, not divided into heavy and medium (for which regional data are not published), was as follows (thousand tons):

	1950	1951	1952
Lancs	56	44	35
Sheffield, etc.	34	43	47
Lincs	373	352	390
N.E. Coast	772	802	792
Scotland	671	604	601
Staffs, etc.	61	62	61
S. Wales	122	233	338

the distribution of steel scarcity among consumers; scarcity was inevitably acutely felt in shipbuilding for example.[1]

As a by-product of the return of scarcity, rearmament demand and rationing, the Steel Federation examined the structure and location of the market for steel. It seemed surprised at the intensity of the concentration in the Midlands; and certainly one of the most enlightening discoveries (though the point was not made) was that expansion of steel-making capacity was rather remote from the largest and growing markets. Table 39 brings together the regional distribution of consumption and steel output by districts. Demand was not homogeneous, and the balance in which different sizes and shapes of steel were used varied from region to region. That all the major producing areas made more steel than was used in local industry was not inherently surprising, but the degree to which this was so in areas where, as in Scotland and to a lesser extent South Wales, the raw-material situation had deteriorated was rather remarkable. Concentration of exporting was a slight counterbalance; here the pull of good shipping facilities was impressive—much steel was exported from London, and the chief concentration was from the Mersey. Regional deliveries of steel for particular industry groups are shown in Table 40.[2]

The comparative divorce of markets from producing areas had the obvious significance that much of the steel had to bear relatively high delivery charges to more distant markets. (In fact, because of growing regional specialisation on particular products the amount of this unavoidable transport was higher than the table shows). Less immediately obvious, the large steelmaking areas were to an increasing extent scrap-importing regions. This was so in Sheffield and Scotland, where the local markets were often spoken of in contemporary doctrine as a

[1] Some effort was made to compensate for regional variations in steel output by the distribution of imports. Even the fall of scrap imports was partly compensated for by increased pig iron at appropriate points, though most went to South Wales. Scotland imported 6600 tons of heavy plates in 1952. Regions where output fell most tended to cut their sales to customers who were not local; they avoided long transport costs. Thus it was said Scotland sent much less steel to England, which particularly hurt customers who relied on Scots supplies.

[2] There were no statistics showing the regional consumption of the separate finished steel products.

magnet for mass-production steelmaking. It was most marked in South Wales, where local use of steel was not a fifth of the local output. The price of scrap was always appreciably higher in South Wales (this was already so in the early twenties) than in most other parts of the United Kingdom.[1] The predominant

Table 39. *Distribution of markets and production*

Regions (Ministry of Labour)	Receipts of British steel[a] (4th qr. 1950)	Export[b] (quarterly average, 1950)	Crude steel outputs in finished steel equivalents (quarterly average, 1950)
London and S.E.	439	50	—
East	92	—	—
South	100	—	—
South-west	105	—	—
Midland	505	—	160
N. Midland	155⎫	—⎫	720[c]
E. and W. Ridings	237⎭	30⎭	
North-west	313	155[d]	250
North	206	105[d]	700[e]
Scotland	289	100	450
Wales	120	115	640
Northern Ireland	37	—	—
Northants, etc[f]	—	—	150

[a] *Stat. Bull.* June 1951, p. 5. This was not quite equivalent to consumption. It was described by the B.I.S.F. as regional *deliveries*, but I have called it receipts to avoid confusion, since the total despatches of steel by steelmakers are referred to in statistics as 'deliveries'. Deliveries include re-rolled imports, but consumption would include also imported finished steel.

[b] Based on annual exports according to Ports of Departure, *B.I.S.F. Statistical Year Book* for 1951. Exports were not necessarily manufactured near the port of departure.

[c] Sheffield and Scunthorpe are joined in relation to the north-Midland and East and West Riding markets.

[d] The North-west figure excludes from the exports from Mersey to Solway 25,000 tons for Workington.

[e] The outputs of the North-west Coast and North-east Coast are combined.

[f] Unlike the remainder this is a steel industry division; it is on the Ministry of Labour north-Midland division, but to relate Corby to the same consuming area as Scunthorpe is meaningless.

[1] The differential averaged almost 5*s.* per ton between 1922 and 1938; from 1945 it rose steadily from 5*s.* to 16*s.* in 1954. In 1958, as will be seen later, the margin was reduced because the demand for scrap was reduced by the closing of the small unintegrated steel-works.

Table 40. *Estimated United Kingdom regional and industrial deliveries of finished steel. Fourth quarter, 1950 (thousand tons)*

Industry group	London and S.E.	E.	S.	S.W.	Mid-land	N. Mid-land	N. E. and W. Ridings	N.W.	N.	Scot-land	Wales	N.I.	Total
Mechanical engineering	78	15½	7	11½	41	30	42	46½	16	43	5	3½	339
Motors, cycles and aircraft	55	20	25½	19½	90	20	9½	29	1½	9	7	3	289
Constructional engineering	42	6½	3	13	32	7	17	33	40	45½	12½	1	252½
Shipbuilding, repairing and marine engineering	20	5	23	15	—	2½	6	32	49	58½	6½	20	237½
Railways and rolling stock	35	3	10½	18½	20½	17½	22½	34	15	24½	7½	2	210½
Hollow-ware	27	1½	3½	1½	42	11	14½	22	8½	5	14½	1	152
Coalmining	1½	—	1	1	12	20½	26½	10½	32	17	23½	—	144½
Bolts, nuts, screws, rivets, nails, etc.	7	½	—	—	84	2½	6	6	1½	13½	2	—	124
Metal furnishing, windows, etc.	26	4	2	2	49	5	5½	12	2	6½	5	1	120
Electrical machinery and appliances	42	6½	3	2	21	4	4	21	5	3½	2½	—	114½
Drop forgings, laminated springs	4½	1	½	1	56	3½	21½	6½	3½	10½	3	½	112
Iron and steel	3	2	½	½	19	11	18	7	12½	14	16½	—	104
Building and contracting	25½	6	6	6	7	6	6½	11	6	11	4½	2½	98
Wire manufactures	4½	1½	1½	1	10	3	18	19	5½	9	2½	—	75½
Agricultural machinery (excluding tractors)	4	11	3	4	7	4	3	4½	1½	6	1	—	49
Other U.K. consumers (including small users)	64	8	10	9	14½	7	16½	19½	6½	12½	6½	3	177
Total	439	92	100	105½	505	154½	237	313½	206	289	120	37½	2599
Per cent	17	3½	4	4	19½	6	9	12	8	11	4½	1½	100

use of steel sheets was in the Midlands, the London area, and the North-west, where the chief concentrations of motor-car making, electrical engineering and manufacture of hollow-ware were found.[1] How would the new alertness to the pattern of the market affect future planning—the location of another sheet mill, for example? How much did the pattern itself reflect a price policy which had been based upon the exploitation of local monopoly for nearly half a century and had denied with increasing regularity to users of steel located near a steelworks the natural advantages of low transport costs?

The Federation's survey of markets also showed that 'there is a considerable concentration' of consumption in a 'relatively small number of large firms'. Half the steel was used by 374 firms or public organisations who took at least 4000 tons of finished steel each a year, and almost 60 per cent by 678 firms who used over 2000 tons each, and an average of almost 10,000 tons a firm.[2] This had its bearing manifestly on the scope for using high-capacity plants in British steelmaking.

The Federation hoped that its analysis of consumption would help to persuade the Government to adopt a simpler form of distribution control than the one in force in 1950, but were disappointed. The old form (the old form M) was revived.[3] With this the priorities (P.T. and D.O.) and the Steel (Rearmament) Panel disappeared, though there were a few 'super-

---

[1] Table 40 shows that 70 per cent of the motor-car and allied industry's consumption of steel was in these areas plus the south region (i.e. Oxford); 60 per cent of the holloware, and 70 per cent of the electrical engineering consumption were in the three regions.

[2] I have converted quarterly figures to annual rates which would be a trifle too high. The details of the analysis of size distribution was in figures for the 4th quarter, 1950:

	No. of users	Thousand tons used	% of total
Public organisations	7	310	11
Firms using: Over 2000 tons	179	853	31
1001–2000 tons	188	262	9
501–1000 tons	304	214	8
101–500 tons	1304	298	11
26–100 tons	1605	90	3
Under 26 tons	?	723	27

[3] On 4 Feb. 1952. Above, p. 332.

priorities'. At first scarcity remained acute—authorisations exceeded supply, and the failing of the system in its earlier post-war phase, over-authorisation by departments was seemingly repeated. By the autumn more steel was available; crude steel output, which from January to April was much lower than in the corresponding months of 1951, rose sharply to new 'record' levels from September to December, and imports rose, rather earlier, also to an exceptional rate.[1] For the year imports were 60 per cent higher than in the previous 'peak' since the war (1949), and almost three times as high as in any other year. Exports fell slightly.[2]

Some of the delayed new blast furnaces were completed; imported ore supplies were assured; efforts to get more scrap had some reward. By the end of the year scarcity was limited to a relatively narrow range of products, being most acute in heavy plates.[3] The control of distribution lingered on till May 1953, and restraints on the use of nickel and molybdenum ended

---

[1] The rate of crude-steel output was equivalent to 17 m. per ton a year in September and nearly 18 m. per ton in November; imports reached an annual rate of over 2 m. tons (in semi-finished) a year; it was about 1·6 m. per ton for the whole year.

[2] The course of imports and exports, in ingot equivalents, was (in m. tons):

	Imports	Exports	Net export
1945	0·17	0·67	0·50
1946	0·49	2·36	1·87
1947	0·48	1·77	1·29
1948	0·53	2·01	1·48
1949	1·14	2·41	1·27
1950	0·58	3·25	2·67
1951	0·56	2·67	2·11
1952	1·82	2·61	0·79
1953	1·11	2·75	1·64
1954	0·47	2·90	2·43

[3] The B.I.S.F. Ann. Rep. 1952, p. 15, listed the scarcities—apart from plates which was 'in tonnage terms the most severe' and had 'the most widespread effects', the scarcities were in forging quality billets, middle- and high-carbon billets, free cutting billets, re-rolling slabs, tube solids and heat-treated alloy bars. 'Special steps have been taken to improve the supply of many of these products but the position is not yet satisfactory.' Alloy steel had been particularly scarce—an outcome of rearmament—and had been subject to separate allocation and also other controls; some restriction of the use of particular compositions to the more 'urgent' needs.

in the autumn.[1] Throughout the period of renewed distribution control the national Corporation had, as has been seen, 'powers without influence'; the Federation, as it claimed with great assurance, was the 'focal point'.[2]

4. COSTS, PRICES, POOLS AND PROFITS
(1951–53)

The price of imported ore rose exceptionally among steelmaking costs during rearmament, but not in isolation. Imported scrap prices rose more, though the rise at its highest was less enduring. In 1952 the quantity of scrap imported only just exceeded a third of the 1949 import, but its cost was three fifths more. Table 41 gives the figures. Imports of pig iron and semi-finished and finished steel cost more too, both because they were larger and because the price rose. The larger size of imports has been noted earlier; representative price movements were as shown in Table 42.

Table 41. *Scrap imports—quantities and cost*

	Quantities (thousand tons)	Cost (£ thousand)	Price (£ per ton)
1948	858	2,788	3·2
1949	2,097	10,249	4·9
1950	1,958	14,903	7·6
1951	589	8,731	14·9
1952	734	16,507	22·5
1953	863	16,804	19·5
1954	760	10,939	14·4

Table 42. *Prices of imported pig iron and steel*

	1949	1950	1951	1952
Pig iron (thousand tons)	262	195	300	732
£ per ton	15·9	14·6	21·8	29·5
Billets and sheet bars (thousand tons)	348	184	138	435
£ per ton	25·6	21·0	33·0	45·3
Heavy plates (thousand tons)	22	35	29	72
£ per ton	32·0	30·0	44·7	61·2

[1] Restraints in the use of tungsten were lifted in 1952. Cp. *B.I.S.F. Ann. Rep.* 1952, p. 23 and 1953, p. 8.   [2] Above, p. 320.

By comparison home costs rose modestly, but they too rose. The main elements are traced in Table 43, which continues Table 33.[1] Wages rose automatically with the cost of living, but there was a special upward adjustment in 1951 whereby the cost-of-living addition was increased by $8\frac{1}{2}$ per cent,[2] and there were increments, some automatic, some negotiated, as new plant of higher capacity came into use. The application of scales fixed before the First World War to the Abbey steel plant at Margam led to remarkably high earnings; this, however, was not generally observed till later.[3] A further increase in labour costs came in mid-1952 with the introduction of a 44-hour standard week and the increase of paid holidays from 13 to 18 days a year.[4]

Table 43. *Costs of labour, transport, coal and new plant*[5] *(1946 = 100)*

Year	Labour	Transport	Coking coal	New plant for steelworks	Prices of metal goods exported
1949	129	124	121	132	124
1950	132	144	124	138	134
1951	144	159	136	154	151
1952	160	175	152	168	168
1953	168	185	163	174	160

The second of the two increases in coking-coal prices (the rise, that is, in December 1951) varied in different regions to an extent which for the first time since the war was significant. the National Coal Board had decided to begin applying its announced policy of charging more for special quality coals (therefore more for coking coal and especially more for the best

---

[1] Above, p. 266.

[2] The addition became 1·3d. per point in the index of retail prices, instead of 1·2d. *Stat. Bull.* July 1951 and 1952. The Retail Price Index rose from 113 in January 1950, and 116 in December 1950 to 130 in December 1951 and 138 in December 1952. Thus the rise in the 'percentage addition' would have been 30d. a shift on the original basis, but was 33·8d. on the new.

[3] See below, p. 665.

[4] *B.I.S.F. Ann. Rep.* 1952, p. 47.

[5] For notes, see above, p. 266. From 1952 a second addition of 2 per cent is made to take account of a second week's holiday with pay.

coking coal) and, where possible, more for coal which was dear to mine. On these two criteria coking coal was raised on an average more than other coal (it rose by 5s. 9d. per ton, against the average of 5s. per ton); and the coking-coal price rose more in South Wales and Durham than in Yorkshire, and most of all (presumably because of cost) in Scotland.[1] 'The increases were in certain cases up to 15s. per ton', according to the Federation, 'the effect of the new prices being felt especially in Scotland.'[2] The rise in Durham and South Wales just exceeded one-half the maximum; the Scots price rose on an average by about 8s. and may have been the region where coking coal was dearest.[3] Yorkshire prices now moved up less than Durham prices, and other Midland area prices moved up less still. This process of differentiation was to continue in March 1953 and May 1954; in the second Scotland again suffered most, iron-making costs being 'expected to rise by roughly 11s. a ton'.[4] This suggested a rise of about 7s. to 8s. per ton of coal, more than twice the

[1] The average costs (before charging interest let alone profit on any funds for investing in new methods) and proceeds for all classes of coal in representative divisions or areas providing some coking-coal were, according to the National Coal Board accounts for 1950:

	Costs	Proceeds
	s. d.	s. d.
Scotland: Central West	54 3	47 7
Central East	48 1	47 0
Durham (aver. all areas)	51 0	49 4
S. Wales: Rhondda	51 7	54 3
Rhymney	59 0	54 9
Monmouth	55 9	54 6
Aberdare	47 0	54 7
E. Midlands	36 6	43 4
N. Eastern (Yorkshire)	42 4	47 0
W. Midlands	42 7	46 8
N. Western	50 0	50 8

The receipts in Durham to some extent, in South Wales still more, were raised by high export prices.

[2] B.I.S.F. Ann. Rep. 1952, p. 26. The peak rise of 15s. 3d. applied to a small proportion of Scots supplies.

[3] Before the war Scots coking-coal prices were about the same as South Wales and Durham prices in 1937, but did not rise as much in 1938. They were as high again as South Wales and Durham prices in 1943.

[4] Stat. Bull. Apr. 1954, p. 6.

average for the country as a whole.[1] Durham and South Wales prices rose by about 5s. per ton, Yorkshire by 3s., other Midland prices by rather less. When these changes had occurred the pithead cost of coking coal in Yorkshire, which was used for making steel in Lincolnshire, was approximately 90s. for a ton of coke; in Durham and South Wales it was approximately 109s., in Scotland presumably quite a bit more. Hence the cost of coking coal for making Linolnshire basic pig iron was not appreciably more than the cost of coking coal for making basic pig iron from imported ore, although only 16 cwt. of coke were needed in the best practice at the coast and 20 cwt. in the best practice at Scunthorpe. This point was not reached in 1951–52,[2] but the course was set. No doubt some of the steel-makers hoped still ultimately to divert the National Coal Board from its course of relating prices to costs, as they tried in the Federation in 1951–52. They were to prove in part successful.

The movement of home scrap prices also marked a change of policy towards greater rationality, though here no rational principle was relied on to define an ultimate object. The price had been increased since 1939 only slightly except to cover additional transport costs; but late in August 1951 the maximum price was raised by the Minister of Supply by £2 per ton, an increase of nearly one-half.[3] This was obviously a late and reluctant admission that price might increase supplies. Perhaps to counter this argument the Federation argued that less scrap than normal came forward in 1951. But the examination of scrap statistics earlier showed that a 'normal' relation between the supply of steel and the supply of scrap is hard to establish. Steelworks' circulating scrap is likely to be a larger proportion of crude-steel output when output is falling and smaller when it is rising; it will be a larger part when the proportion of alloy and special steels rises, and it will be larger when the use of imported 'semis' or of 'semis' from stock rises. All the conditions favourable to an increase of circulating scrap in proportion to ingot

---

[1] I understand it was not as high as this. The average rise for the country was 3s. 10d.

[2] B.I.S.F. Ann. Rep. 1952, p. 26.

[3] Rep. I.S. Corp. 1951, p. 21.

output were present in 1951, and to a lesser extent in 1952: and the figures confirmed that it happened.[1]

It is similarly in accordance with precedent that 'home-bought scrap' should fall short in 1951 of the expectations of increase entertained when the scrap drive was opened early in

[1] The Federation and the Corporation seemed to attribute the result entirely to the scrap drive. 'Own-arisings', according to the Corporation's *Annual Report*, 'yielded (in 1951) an extra 325,000 tons from scrapping obsolete plant and buildings and the general cleaning up of works'. This seemed a statistical figure based on the assumption that 'normal' own-arisings were 26 per cent of ingot output; if so it had little justification in the published records. The extreme variations before the war are shown in Appendix I (below, p. 689). The war and post-war figures were:

Year	Crude steel output (m. tons)	Imports + net use of stock (ingot equiv. m. tons)	Circulating scrap as % of crude-steel output
1940	12·98	2·25	27·0
1941	12·31	2·26	27·0
1942	12·94	3·01	30·1
1943	13·03	2·97	30·0
1944	12·14	2·19	31·1
1945	11·82	0·69	28·9
1946	12·70	0·66	27·1
1947	12·73	0·79	27·2
1948	14·88	0·33	25·8
1949	15·55	0·91	25·6
1950	16·29	0·68	25·9
1951	15·64	1·24	28·0
1952	16·42	1·65	27·5
1953	17·61	0·80	27·0

The percentages are on a higher level than in the preceding 20 years, for which several factors may account: more special and highly finished production, for example, and probably a greater proportion of integrated re-rolling. This table does not give all the data needed for an attempted correlation. It does not show variations in alloy steel outputs, for example (the proportion was high in the war; and it rose from 5·4 to 6·9 per cent from 1950 to 1952, and fell in 1953 to 6·1), nor does it take account of changes in *finished* steel imports, which fell by approximately 360,000 (finished) tons from 1952 to 1953, while imports of 'semis' fell by 240,000 (*semi-finished*) tons only. It is likely that some extra steel was found by steel firms in their own works as a result of the 'drive', but the proposition that in three years they found 818,000 tons (see table in *B.I.S.F. Ann. Rep.* for 1953, p. 51), which otherwise would not have been used, the result of scrapping obsolete plant and 'generally cleaning up the works' (*Rep. I. S. Corp.* 1951, p. 21, and 1952, p. 19) suggests that part of the scrap recovery which would have occurred in any case was set apart under a separate name.

1951. The tonnage of carbon steel used in 1951 was probably less than in 1950,[1] and the revival of industrial prospects from mid-1950 made it desirable to retain much existing plant instead of scrapping it because the chances of replacing it were getting less while the uses for it were getting greater.[2] By the middle of 1952 more steel was available as much more finished steel was imported; hence an increase of process scrap was to be expected. By this time too the 'drive' *was* successfully tapping some exceptional sources.[3] The decision to raise the basic price of scrap was sensible, because where there was a doubt whether to 'scrap' idle plant or just leave it unused, or whether to make the effort to salvage material, the additional price incentive could be decisive. The increase, however, still left the price extremely low by comparison with the price of pig iron; the incentive to scrap was still far less than it had been before the war.

In face of all these increased costs how much must the price of steel rise? This remained a matter ultimately for Ministerial decision, but naturally the Corporation now came largely into the discussions, and the Federation remained in.[4]

The prices fixed in April 1949 after the first Steel Board's review[5] were to remain stable, it was hoped, for at least two years.[6] So, in effect, they nearly did; there were only a few

---

[1] Above, p. 331; the increase of alloy steel would mean a smaller net yield from ingots. A leading Sheffield scrap merchant confirmed from his own experience in 1951 that in this area there was less process scrap because less steel to process. But he also showed the difficulty of judging exactly, because some steelmakers gave preference in deliveries of steel to users who would return scrap. Hence the normal merchant channels were less used, and different steelmaking districts 'poached' on each other's markets (as the merchants thought).

[2] The offer of higher prices for old machinery sometimes succeeded; the same scrap merchant told me that iron founders were buying old machines at high prices and he called it a grey or black market for scrap.

[3] There was a drive among farmers, a drive for tramrails, for household scrap, etc. *B.I.S.F. Ann. Rep.* 1952, pp. 24–5.

[4] 'Having regard to the fact that both publicly owned and privately owned companies produced similar products and to the general difficulties concerning modification of price control arrangements at the time, the Minister in agreement (with) the Corporation, maintained the Price Control Orders in their existing form.' *Rep. I.S. Corp.* 1951, p. 23.

[5] Above, p. 228.

[6] *Stat. Bull.* July 1951, p. 1.

minor adjustments. But by the second half of 1950 the cost bases for these prices were being undermined and their economic justification became more than ever obscure as demand became intense; yet steel prices remained low while most other prices rose. For a time rising costs, especially of imported raw material, could be partly offset by savings of fuel and labour as some of the more up-to-date plant now being installed came into use,[1] and the ingot levy and the levy on home-produced semi-finished steel (to help meet the losses on imports of semis) had been fixed high enough to allow a surplus to accumulate in what was now publicly christened the 'Industry Fund'. (It had apparently been so named ever since the war.)[2] There may have been, as there was during the war, a disposition to play for safety; the decisions were made before the threat of plenty in 1949–50 had had its full effect in lowering, for example, prices (and quantities) of imported steel. There may have been provision in the levy for more imports of scrap and semi-products than in fact came in; the tonnage of 'semis' was at a relatively high point in the spring 1949. There was, anyway, a surplus to draw on. The precise course of events cannot be traced because the manipulations of levies and subsidies were not published.[3] Tit-bits of information were occasionally released at times of stress in negotiations to buttress one argument or undermine another.

In April 1951, when the two-years period during which prices were to remain stable ended, the ingot levy still stood at 51s.[4] It was now quite inadequate for the expenditure which it was intended to finance. It was said at the time that less than one third of the levy had been imposed to finance the excess cost of imports of raw materials—but that by this date the excess cost incurred alone required a levy of about 50s. a ton, and in the light of the quantities and prices this seems a reasonable

[1] The Federation published surveys setting out the more impressive data on these things in *Stat. Bull.* Feb. 1950 and Mar. 1951.
[2] *Rep. I. S. Corp.* 1952, pp. 22–3.
[3] It was arranged at the time of the Steel Board review that levies should be reviewed every six months. *Stat. Bull.* Mar. 1949, p. 3.
[4] I was informed that it was made up of two elements: levy for imported raw materials, 16s.; levy for general purposes, 35s.

figure.[1] The other main use of the ingot levy—to pay for the pig-iron remission—must have required nearly 40*s*. a ton. The remission was now 75*s*. a ton, to whose cost (approximately £33 m.) the 20*s*. levy contributed little. The remission and scrap levy were intended to bring the cost to the steelmakers of using pig iron and scrap close together despite the fact that scrap prices were kept low by price control and prohibition of export on the assumption that the price of scrap in free market conditions averaged 75–80 per cent of the price of pig iron. In practice the adjustments had left users of scrap with an abnormal advantage since 1945 and they still did.[2]

[1] Here is a guess as to how this might have been made up:

	m. tons	Paid from Fund per ton (£)	Total payments (£)
Iron ore	9·0	2·0	18·0
Scrap	0·55	10·0	5·5
Pig iron	0·3	10·0	3·0
Steel 'semis'	0·4	15·0	6·0
Ferro-alloys, etc.			3·0
			35·5
Margin of safety			4·5
			40·0

The total (£40 m.) would be the yield of 50*s*. on 16 m. tons of ingots. I have assumed some of the excess of cost on 'semis' was carried by the levy on 'semis', but I have no data for this; indeed, the table is highly speculative, but may indicate the sort of calculation made.

[2] The relative costs of pig iron and scrap in April 1951 are shown in the first line of the following table; the earlier figures given assume that the levies and remissions were the same at the earlier dates as in April 1951, but this was not necessarily so:

Date	Price of basic pig iron less 75*s*. remission = *P*		*P* less 20 %		*P* less 25 %		Price of scrap + 20*s*. in Glasgow, Sheffield, Lancs		S. Wales	
	s.	*d.*	*s.*	*d.*	*s.*	*d.*	*s.*	*d.*	*s.*	*d.*
Apr. 1951	144	0	115	2	108	0	103	5	117	0
Feb. 1951	144	0	115	2	108	0	99	11	112	1
1 Jan. to 21 Feb. 1951	136	6	108	9	102	4	99	11	112	1
15 May 1950	136	6	108	9	102	4	98	11	110	11
1 May 1950	130	6	104	5	97	11	98	11	110	11

The price of basic pig iron was changed frequently. The changes from 1948 were:

	£	*s.*	*d.*		£	*s.*	*d.*
23 Aug. 1948	9	10	0	27 Feb. 1952	12	10	0
1 Apr. 1949	9	17	6	13 Oct. 1952	13	19	0
1 May 1950	10	5	6	14 Mar. 1953	14	6	6
15 May 1950	10	11	6	7 Mar. 1954	14	15	6
22 Feb. 1951	10	19	0	31 May 1954	15	10	6
13 Aug. 1951	11	15	6	6 Dec. 1954	15	15	6

Scotland, Sheffield, Lancashire and the Midlands accounted for well over half the consumption of bought scrap, and for them the price of scrap was less than 75 per cent the cost of pig iron, below the lower limit of the Federation range. Lincoln-shire, the North-east Coast and Shotton were near the lower end of the range; only South Wales was at the upper end or above it. It was particularly striking that the arrangements worked to the advantage of Scotland and Sheffield.[1]

As was to be expected, the surplus in the Industry Fund fell rapidly after April. Prices of imports continued to rise almost more certainly than was foreseen, and possibly the volume of some imports was slightly higher than at first seemed likely. It was not practicable to raise the levy without a price increase; the levy was possibly embarrassingly high for a few firms already, and other costs, wages, coal, transport, were rising, so that a large increase of price was made in August 1951.

The Minister chose this occasion to eliminate the last element of state subsidy for steel, that on imports of finished steel. Mr Strauss knew that larger imports were needed, and the burden would be a heavier one in future. The Federation and Corporation both protested that it was not desirable that the price of home-produced steel—or as the Corporation empha-sised of nationalised steel—should be burdened with a levy to pay the excess cost of a lot of imported finished steel. Hitherto the Government had paid not only the import duties on imports of steel but also the excess cost of the imported steel to the other, older, Corporation, B.I.S.C., the Federation's commercial counterpart, which imported the steel at foreign prices and sold it at home prices. By what sophistry this old arrangement was justified no one concerned ever attempted to explain. Sugges-tions that users of imported steel should bear the whole cost were brushed aside as though they were impracticable or faintly improper,[2] although it would have seemed normal in the

---

[1] Because of the large scale of cold-metal working there; Steel, Peech and Tozers at Rotherham, and all Colville's cold-metal shops in Scotland.

[2] There were signs of a change from this attitude; indeed, the Federation said that the allowance in the price increase for the cost of finished steel imports was too low if the imports came in as was hoped. 'When practicable it may in some cases be neces-sary to charge the British buyer at least part of the cost.' *Stat. Bull.* July 1951, p. 2.

United States. Mr Strauss had his way, and a further 15s. 6d. subsidy per ton of ingots was imposed in order to relieve the Government of the excess cost of imported steel now that it was rising steeply, and spread the excess cost evenly (it could not be thinly) over total consumption. This formed part of the price increase, about £1 a ton of finished steel.

The whole rise for most products (of which Table 45 gives representative samples) was over £4 a ton. Of this two-fifths was expected to pay for extra costs of imported raw materials, including ore, pig iron and semi-products, one-fifth for the above-mentioned finished steel imports, and the rest for home-bought materials, wages, railway rates, road-transport rates, coal, coke and oil. A fortnight after these price increases were announced the increase in the price of scrap followed.[1] For some inscrutable reason it proved impossible to decide on the scrap-price increase before announcing the steel-price increase, and, inconceivable as it seems, the increase of steel prices on 13 August 1951 did not make an allowance for the scrap-price increase which came on 27 August 1951.

Corresponding to these price changes there were two changes in the levies. The ingot levy was raised to 90s. 6d. on 13 August, when steel prices rose, and reduced to 64s. 6d. on 27 August, when scrap prices rose. While the degree of change within two weeks was surprising the broad explanation was clear. Since prices of steel, pig iron and scrap were raised the excess of import prices over home prices was lessened and imposed a smaller burden on the Industry Fund. The part of the levy related to home costs could be reduced when home scrap prices rose, because the pig-iron remission came down as much as the price of scrap rose, i.e. by £2 per ton.[2]

---

[1] Above, p. 342.

[2] The reduction of the pig-iron remission by the same amount as scrap prices went up, with no increase in the scrap levy, and just after pig-iron prices had themselves been raised, meant again that home scrap was less than 75–80 per cent the cost of pig iron. The calculation seems to be:

Pig-iron price	235s. 6d.
Less remission	35s. 0d.
	200s. 6d.

Of which: 80 per cent 160s.; 75 per cent 150s.

Scrap price in Scotland, Sheffield and Lancs	125s. 0d.
Plus levy	20s. 0d.
	145s. 0d.

Table 44. *Costs and prices, 1948–54*

	Indices of some costs					Prices[a]											
						Billets				Plates				Sheets			
Year	Labour	Railway rates	Coking coal	Imported ore	Home scrap	£	s.	d.		£	s.	d.		£	s.	d.	
1945	100	100	100	100	100	12	10	0	100	15	8	0	100	22	15	0	100
1948	127	134	125	78	104	16	16	6	135				—	28	16	0	127
1949	135	134	127	80	104				—	20	14	6	135				—
1950	139	155	130	80	107				—				—				—
1951	151	172	143	117	142	21	11	6	175	25	6	6	164	35	15	6	157
1952	166	191	161	162	176	25	4	6	206	29	14	0	193	40	12	6	179
1953	177	202	173	152	178	25	12	6	206	29	14	0	193	41	6	0	179
1954	185	222	180	141	183	26	2	6[b]	209	31	1	6[b]	202	42	1	0[b]	185
1954 as % of 1937	314	255	460	458[c]	203				332				303				267

[a] The prices given are the increased prices after the chief change in a year. The important relevant dates are: 1949, 1 Apr.; 1951, 13 Aug.; 1952, 27 Feb.; 1954, 31 May. *Average* prices are given in the *Statistical Yearbooks of the B.I.S.F.* The products chosen are fairly representative.

[b] These figures refer to the period 31 May 1954 to 5 Dec. 1954: from 6 Dec. there were further changes, and the new prices were: billets, £25. 15s. 0d. (206); plates, no change; sheets, £40. 5s. 0d. (175).

[c] It will be noted that 1954 was a year in which imported ore prices had fallen; the prices in 1952, 1953 and the first quarter of 1955 as a percentage of 1937 were 524, 489 and 473.

Thus the net effect of this series of changes in August 1951 was a relatively modest increase of the ingot levy,[1] less in the end than the only item publicised (the 15s. 6d. for imported finished steel).

Within a few months of these steep price increases, from 20 to 30 per cent on the major products, the steelmakers were establishing on the same premises that a further sharp increase was due, which, as finally agreed by the Minister, a new Minister (Mr Duncan Sandys) since the Government had changed, and brought into force in February 1952, was from 14 to 16 per cent on the main products. According to the Minister the new increases were not quite so generous to the steelmakers as Mr Strauss's. The first bout of increases when Mr Strauss was Minister had accepted new 'standard margins' established in 1949.[2] The second bout conceded price increases estimated to give only £56 m.,[3] whereas materials costs were expected to increase by £75 m. The extra costs were set out in simple persuasive tables; three-fifths were due to still dearer imports.[4] Despite the new Minister's claim that his policy was the more astringent, Mr Strauss was unable to resist attacking him for trying to give high profits to steelmaking to help

[1] I do not know what happened to the semi-product levy.

[2] 'The Corporation have not so far sought to revalue the standard margins which have been regarded as appropriate to the various products.' Rep. I.S. Corp. 1951, p. 23.

[3] Mr Strauss's had been calculated to yield £65 m.

[4] Stat. Bull. Mar. 1952, p. 9. The Federation in effect provided a gloss on the speech in which Mr Duncan Sandys announced and defended the price increases. The estimates of increases in annual costs were:

Increases of

(i) home costs		(ii) imported materials cost	
	(£ m.)		(£ m.)
Coal, coke, fuel oil	8	Imported ore	20
Scrap (price rise, Aug. 1951)	6	Steel	16
Other materials	5	Scrap and pig iron	10
Rail transport	$4\frac{1}{2}$		
Wages	$1\frac{1}{2}$		
Other (mainly use of higher proportion of pig iron in steel)	4		

denationalisation, and Mr Hardie proved so attached to keeping steel prices low that he resigned from what must have become an extremely inhibiting job. The small change of politics has little interest in retrospect, but this incident revealed a readiness on Mr Hardie's part to accept the traditional erroneous view that increases of steel prices were a serious source of inflation, a view to which many politicians still adhered. In its way the new Government, with its emphasis on *not* covering the cost increases (although this could be a healthy reaction against cost-plus) paid tribute, more modestly, to the same doctrine. And all therefore cheerfully fell into line over the familiar 'artificial arrangements' (as the Federation had christened them) of levies, pools and cost averaging devices.

These indeed had come into their own again to an extent which seemed to make everyone forget that in 1949 their end had been foreshadowed. The 'Exchequer losses' on imported ore, scrap, pig iron and 'semis' 'taken over' by the industry in 1949 were described by the Federation, it has been seen, as 'the result of abnormal elements in the post-war supply position which, it may be hoped, will eventually disappear'.[1] Now the devices were rehabilitated. The Federation asked for an increase of 40s. per ton on the ingot levy at the end of 1951, on account of rising import costs, and the price rises of February 1952 in fact seem to have included an even larger increase in the levy, because the ingot levy rose to 112s.[2] A little later, in 1952, apparently after prolonged discussion, the industry accepted the view that higher imported ore prices had come to stay, though not at the peak, and at length Corporation and Government were persuaded. Users of imported ore were charged

---

[1] *Stat. Bull.* Mar. 1949, p. 2.

[2] The figure was given by Mr Strauss in the committee stage of the Denationalisation Bill (*Hansard*, 16 Feb. 1953, c. 1252). The scrap levy (20s.) and pig-iron remission (35s.) according to his figures had not been altered in 1952. In the debate Mr Duncan Sandys said he 'did not think there is any secret about the amount of money levied' (c. 1260), but in fact the Federation had normally been unwilling to publish it. The *Economist* commented on the scope for giving more information on this in the I.S. Corporation accounts, and Mr Strauss's general comment, that 'It is not generally recognised how important this industry fund is' (*ibid.* c. 1252), was justified. He did not bring it notably to light when he could have done so, as Minister.

more though not the whole cost. By this proceeding pig iron became dearer, and the ingot levy fell because less had to be paid out of the pool on account of imported ore. Moreover, since pig iron was dearer either the pig-iron remission had to go up or the levy on home scrap; in fact, the latter happened. The amounts were not stated.[1] What was more remarkable, however, was that both the dying Corporation and the triumphant Federation took the opportunity in their records of these events to describe the Industry Fund as a permanent feature of the industry. They emphasised, it is true, that the steel industry's policy was to 'keep the scale' of these transactions 'down to the minimum'. The minimum was what was needed:

(1) 'to ensure that the cost in excess of the home price, of pig iron, scrap and semi-finished steel imports is shared by all steel producers', the materials obtained 'being made available, as required, without discrimination as to which firms pay the considerably higher import price';

(2) to 'spread the burden of any temporary and abnormal element in the high cost of foreign ore imported by B.I.S.C. (Ore) Ltd. on behalf of the individual firms';

(3) to 'ensure that steelmakers using mainly pig iron are not at an unfair disadvantage compared with those using mainly scrap'. This was the Federation's list.[2] The Corporation set the purposes out differently;[3] they excluded semi-finished steel from the first item, left the second intact,[4] created a new third purpose

---

[1] The events were sketched, without the significant detail, both by the Federation (*B.I.S.F. Ann. Rep.* 1952, p. 41) and the Corporation (*Rep. I.S. Corp.* 1952, p. 25). The increase in pig-iron prices of £1. 9s. per ton would relieve the pool of about £15 m. a year; if, in addition, the scrap levy had been raised by, say, 30s. a ton, yielding about £7 m. a year, this would have allowed a reduction of nearly 30s. a ton in the ingot levy, ostensibly bringing it to about 80s. a ton of ingot. The net reduction in levies, however, must have been equal to the increase in pig-iron prices unless some other object had been entertained than passing on more of the higher cost of ore.

[2] *B.I.S.F. Ann. Rep.* 1952, p. 70 (published 23 Mar. 1953).

[3] *Rep. I.S. Corp.* 1952, p. 23 (published 17 June 1953).

[4] The wording of the Corporation was in some respects to be preferred; but the Federation statement, because of the durability of the body, and its part in creating the Fund, must be regarded as the classic statement. Even the intensive 'unfair' in item 3 is illuminating. The Corporation wording was (i) to enable overseas pig

—'to spread over all the steelmakers the loss on importing foreign steel and selling it to consumers at home controlled prices',[1] and added two further purposes; to provide finance for central research; and to provide assistance in abnormal high-cost transactions and production.

Though the Corporation list was more inclusive it was less descriptive and enlightening. But it was accompanied by an encomium of the system which must have made up to the Federation for much of the friction in which the Corporation had involved them. 'Although the operation of the Fund may be said to mask real costs and interfere with the operation of normal economic forces as they affect individual companies, the Corporation consider that the Fund has been of great service both to the consumer and the industry. In the period of maximum demand with high and fluctuating prices of all iron and steelmaking materials, whether produced at home or imported, the Fund has been the means of spreading the burden. It has enabled all the plants to be kept in production and at the same time relatively low selling prices have continued to be in force.' When they discussed the impact of imported ore prices on costs and prices early in March 1952 'there was common ground between the Federation and the Corporation that it was in principle desirable to reduce the levies and transfer to the direct costs of the makers and consumers as much of the charges as practicable, although it was desired to retain as far as possible the valuable stabilisation of prices. The Corporation were of opinion that owing to the economic changes taking place within the industry, the falling freight rates and the fact that the proposal would have the effect of greatly enhancing the profits of some companies and seriously reducing the profits of others, the interests of the industry as a whole would be best served by postponing action.'

Continuity was thus remarkably preserved, and the Federation formulas were endorsed by the Corporation, without, it is

iron and scrap to be bought at world prices and to spread the excess cost over all steel production, (ii) to spread over all producers abnormal or temporary increases in costs of imported ore.

[1] The Federation excluded spreading costs on imports of finished steel from the list of chief purposes: it recorded it in brackets as occurring.

true, any supporting argument; but what could more effectively show how completely persuaded they were? Why 'relatively low' prices were to be desired for a scarce commodity at a period of rising general prices was not discussed, nor why stability was an economic advantage when stretched over a long period of economic change, as from April 1949 to August 1951. Why should the gains which were not explained outweigh so completely the drawback of 'masking real costs' of particular firms? Perhaps for a nationalised industry this drawback must seem of secondary importance. But the time was, as they said, one of economic change. Among these changes was the prospect of returning the firms to private ownership. Did this make it inopportune in 1952 to make changes which would help the low-cost and hurt the high-cost firms? Or were the Corporation pursuing the old will-o'-the-wisp of normality, the time when, for instance, normal prices would be restored for imported ore, normal prices being by implication low prices, at which the levy would become unnecessary? Were the 'economic changes' they referred to visualised as a reversion to pre-Korean price levels? So far ever since the war, seven years after, the levy-subsidy arrangements, and the pig-iron remission plus scrap levy, had been calculated to the disadvantage of home ore users and to the advantage of heavy users of scrap. This was not denied. The time for the right balance was always just round the corner. The Corporation seemed neither alert to the dangers (though in a formal sense they recorded them) nor armed to avoid them. They accepted the reinforcement of the natural bias against radical change which had characterised the administration of steel prices from 1937 onwards.

With the successive price increases the Federation brought up to date its table to show that British steel still cost less to the home user than steel in the main competing countries. Representative figures derived from their tables are given in Table 45. The prices given were not the base prices, but sample prices for specific lots, identical in size and tonnage,[1] with the addition to foreign prices of 'representative transport charges' since United

[1] The descriptions were set out in detail in the tables printed by the B.I.S.F.

Kingdom prices were all 'uniform delivered'. Details of these 'representative' additions were not published. A comparison in this form, as earlier discussions have shown, is capable of being misleading;[1] at-works prices are a more illuminating and precise starting-point, and the transport-cost comparison can be handled separately. However, even on an at-works basis the excess of foreign over British home prices for the given sizes and quantities would have remained for most products considerable.

Table 45. *Home prices for steel, Britain and abroad*

	Plates				Bars[a]		Sheets			
	Aug. 51	Mar. 52	Dec 52	Dec. 53	Aug. 51	Dec. 53	Aug. 51	Mar. 52	Dec. 52	Dec 53
	£ s.	£ s.	£ s.	£ s.	£ s.	£ s.	£ s.	£ s.	£ s.	£ s.
U.K. Price	27 9	31 16	31 16	32 9	28 0	32 8	35 5	40 2	40 2	40 16
Excess over U.K. price:										
of U.S. price	8 3	3 16	5 8	8 5	9 12	6 0	5 10	14	2 10	5 0
of German	−1 8	6 6	15 17	11 9	−4 1	4 18	18	8 15	13 0	10 10
of Belgian	9 5	5 12	5 5	9 5	2 15	2 18	15 0	12 2	12 2	11 10
of French	6 9	9 12	9 12	11 3	1 11	4 5	5 6	9 8	9 8	9 19

[a] For some unexplained reason the bar prices were left out of the tables in Mar. and Dec. 1952.

[1] Among other difficulties, price schedules of different countries favour particular sizes and order weights differently. The plate prices given are for a minimum of 5 tons of plates 20 ft. × 60 in. × ¼ in. This would amount to seven or eight plates of this size, not a big lot. The price was for an *order* of 20 tons, with *5 tons* minimum in one size. It is conceivable that British prices would favour this smaller lot more than, say, American prices. To show how differently the figures can be presented I have compared the base prices for plates and for cold rolled sheets. The American price for hot rolled sheets is much lower; the British price is for uncoated sheets, and is I believe the lowest price for any sheets (except presumably for 'seconds'; but at this period of scarcity the proportion of 'seconds' which appeared on the market seemed surprisingly small):

	Plates		Sheets	
	U.S. delivered Pittsburg[a]	U.K. delivered main regions	U.S. cold rolled delivered Pittsburg	U.K. delivered main regions
	£ s. d.	£ s. d.	£ s. d.	£ s. d.
Aug. 1951	29 10 0	25 6 6	34 16 0	35 15 6
Mar. 1952	29 10 0	29 9 6	34 16 0	40 12 6
Dec. 1952	31 4 0		36 11 0	40 12 6
Dec. 1953	32 16 0		38 7 0	41 6 0

[a] Based on tables in *Iron Age*, 7 Jan. 1954, p. 411.

But the differences were not rigorously examined in the light of the different administration of price policy in the various countries. British prices, it has been seen, were based on low profits on home sales, with high profits on exports; this principle was not adopted in general elsewhere. In America prices were not controlled, although the basis on which they were quoted was changed in the light of anti-trust doctrine.[1] Above all raw-material costs were not varied to the advantage of foreign steelmakers to the extent they were in Britain. In the United States they were not managed at all. Coal prices were not kept low by cost spreading in coal industries abroad, as they were in Scotland, South Wales and Durham, and, of course, scrap prices were not kept down at all in the United States, and were not nearly as low in any Continental country as in Britain.[2] Margins which looked substantial were in large measure tokens of dual pricing, low profits on home sales, artificially low coal prices, still more artificially low scrap prices, and the practice of milking home ore-based steel production for the benefit of imported ore steel production.

Superficially, however, the argument that prices were low partly because profit margins were too low had little to commend it when gross profits of the firms rose as they did from 1950 to 1952. For the nationalised Corporation the rise was doubtless embarrassing. This may have made them anxious to show how much of their earnings came from windfalls, export premiums, stock appreciations and ancillary activities, and may have prompted them too to put aside extra depreciation to allow for the difference between historic and replacement

---

[1] See below, ch. VIII, *passim*.

[2] The average scrap price in the United States in 1951–52 was about £15. 10s. a ton. An E.C.E. comparison of domestic scrap prices in July 1952 showed the exceptional nature of the British price:

	£	s.		£	s.
U.S.	14	13	W. Germany	14	3
Belgium	16	2	Italy	23	18
France	10	0	U.K.	6	10

(*The European Steel Industry and the Wide-Strip Mills*, p. 33).

costs,[1] though they must be given credit for courage and clear-sightedness not shown in these matters by Boards of other nationalised industries.[2]

The year following the second and last full financial year of the Corporation was marked by a fall of aggregate profits of almost 9 per cent. This could be regarded as confirming the claim that the price increase did not cover all the cost increases. In the year ending in September 1952 the Industry Fund ran £9 m. into deficit; the costs of imports had to this extent not been sufficiently provided for. This deficit was rapidly dwindling when the Corporation accounts for the year were finally published,[3] so that prices in the first half of 1953 were covering some of the costs of the previous year—the stabilising process. How far the fall in aggregate profits was due to the decline of profits on stocks or of export premiums, or to lower profits from ancillary activities, or lessened profits on home sales, there is no evidence to show. The profits of the main companies are listed in Table 46. In general, the heavy steelmakers fared better in 1952–53, whereas makers of more highly finished products, tubes, sheets, light re-rolled bars and sections, and alloy and special steels, did less well. The price adjustments included noticeably favourable increases of billet and rail prices, and it is probable that all told they were designed to turn the balance a little in favour of heavy steel.[4] On the other hand, the companies whose profits fell were also among those who had large export business, which may have begun to give lower margins. For reasons which can only be surmised the fall in many steel companies' profits at this time, though it might have been a testimony of the Government's determination to prevent excess profits on defence, was not prominently discussed.

---

[1] Above, p. 236.
[2] The British Electricity Board, for example, preferred to advance specious arguments against replacement costs and kept electricity prices too low.
[3] *Rep. I.S. Corp.* 1952, p. 66.
[4] The Federation, however, was still emphasising in 1953 the claims of heavy steelmaking for higher profit margins, using the *Productivity Report* as a basis. (*Stat. Bull.* Mar. 1953, p. 1). This could still be relevant even if there had been a recent improvement in margins.

Table 46. *Profits of principal companies, 1951–53. Net profits before taxation (£ thousand)*[a]

	Year ended 27 Sept. 1952 (52 weeks)	Year ended 30 Oct. 1953 (53 weeks)
Colvilles	4,638	4,966
Consett	1,283	950
Dorman Long	5,023	5,753
English Steel Corporation	4,114	3,487
Firth Vickers	866	649
Guest, Keen and Nettlefold	1,178	1,045
Guest, Keen, Baldwin	2,081	2,877
Hadfields	665	928
J. Summers	2,728	1,196
Lancashire Steel	2,359	2,042
Lysaghts (Scunthorpe)	−740	−363
R. Thomas	10,560	6,845
Skinningrove	72	156
South Durham	1,081	1,642
Steel Company of Wales	3,969	2,082
Stewarts and Lloyds	13,395	12,870
Firth Brown	2,225	2,163
United Steel	5,959	9,111
Whitehead	1,228	805
Whitehead-Thomas	25	22
W. Beardmore	756	706
Total	63,365	59,892

[a] This table is based on the accounts published by the *Iron and Steel Holding and Realisation Agency* (*Accounts of Subsidiary Companies, Year ended 3rd October 1953*), with some additional data from reports of companies sold back to private ownership. An examination of the accounts of 32 other subsidiaries confirms the general picture given in the text and by this table; the aggregate profits of these 32 were in the year ended 23 Sept. 1952 £6,924,000, in the next 53 weeks £5,396,000.

5. BRAVE NEW PLAN

The Corporation's contribution, if they made one, to the industry's development plans cannot be isolated. In this field too continuity is the dominant characteristic. When the Corporation were appointed the Federation had already had a special committee at work on the 'second plan' for about a year.[1]

---

[1] It was an advisory Committee on Development, and appointed by the Development Committee. Cp. *B.I.S.F. Ann. Rep.* 1950, p. 22.

The Corporation had a duty to review investment plans from time to time and to 'settle a general programme of development...with the approval of the Minister'. Hence it took part in this committee, and in its second and last *Report*, published in May 1953, it surveyed the results of the review which had 'just been completed'.

It was explained, when the drafting of this second plan was to be started in 1950, that this time the work could be more scientific. The basis would again be 'detailed schemes prepared by the makers themselves'. But there would be more time to bring to bear on these schemes the results of central examination in the light of market and raw-material prospects and of a study aided by the industry's research association of the 'principles underlying modern efficient practice up to the ingot stage'. It is hard to see why the line should be drawn before rolling.

In the end central examination probably had no profound repercussions. It was claimed that the individual pattern of development by companies was fitted into the pattern of probable requirements in 1957 as it emerged from the central survey, though when this forecast was published its authority was already slightly questionable, because there were striking disparities between what was already happening and what had been forecast, and these were only partly to be explained by 'defence' orders. It was tempting to suppose that the expectations of the firms as expressed in their plans might even have influenced the forecast. The requirements for the main finished products in 1957 as set out by the Corporation in their *Report* are given in Table 47, with one column added, which compares the growths in output which had already occurred by 1953 with the growths foreshadowed in the table (published in May 1953).

The Consumers' Council set up under nationalisation doubted whether the steel industry's plans at this time catered adequately for heavy plates.[1]

Nothing was said about the way in which the estimates of requirements (which implied a crude steel capacity of 20 m. tons)[2]

---

[1] *Rep. Iron and Steel Consumers Council*, p. 3.
[2] Apart from home-produced crude steel it was visualised there would be $\frac{1}{2}$ m. tons of re-usable steel available and $\frac{1}{2}$ m. tons of imports.

Table 47. *Supplies and requirements of finished steel*[a]
(thousand tons)

	Deliveries in 1951	Estimates of requirements in 1957	1957 estimated requirements over 1951 delivery	Delivery in 1953 over delivery in 1951
			% increase of	% increase of
Heavy steel products	4,077	4,525	11	11
Light-rolled products	3,292	4,125	25	2
Sheets	1,573	2,050	30	13
Tinplates	724	1,000	38	8
Tubes	1,095	1,400	28	−1
Wire	812	1,050	29	−6
Other products	953	1,100	15	19
Total	12,526	15,250	22	7

[a] *Rep. I.S. Corp.* 1952, p. 36, plus figures in the last column based on Table 16, in *Stat. Bull.* Apr. 1954. I have included only 'hot-rolled' products in 'light-rolled' products; 'other products' includes forgings, castings, tyres, wheels and axles, and all alloy steel; 'deliveries' on the basis used in the corporation's table were not available for 1953, but the comparison given is valid.

were made, although recent experience had shown how fallible the usual methods could be. The main concern was to set out how and where the steel itself would be made. The solution was so simple, so in keeping with the traditions set in the revision of 1948, that all the difficult questions of relative costs of raw materials in different sites could be wholly dispensed with. The extra output of steel could all be obtained by adding bits to existing works, whose combined steel-furnace capacity was already almost large enough, it seemed, for the new target. The primary need was for more blast furnaces, ore preparation plants and coke ovens (which were expected collectively to cost £86 m. out of a total of £200 m. for major schemes by 1957) and more rolling mills, chiefly finishing mills, since there was an excess of primary mill over finishing mill capacity. Rolling mills would cost £62 m. New melting shops would require £19 m. only. This was a natural corollary to the changes in the plan in 1948, the decision to defer some major projects and slow down others, and to accept development at most existing sites which often included new and by modern standards rather small blast furnaces.[1] The combined effect of partial additions, a new blast furnace here, a new steel furnace or new mill there, and of the improvements often made to plant when it is overhauled,[2] is to bring about a lack of balance even in plants initially balanced. That the balancing of all existing plants is not always the best way of expanding output to reduce costs in the long run, and can inhibit the use of the most efficient scale of plant and continue unsatisfactory layouts, had quite recently been pointed out in the Productivity Team *Report*.[3] The Corporation wrote as though whenever balancing was possible it was right. 'When the process (of balancing) was completed...it will be necessary to consider afresh whether to provide increasing production of steel from new works in the traditional areas or to break entirely new ground.' But for the present 'the fundamental problems of...location...have not been raised in an acute form'.[4] They listed again all the problems—labour supply, housing, home or imported ore, sources of coke, shipping, port facilities, strategy, transport costs and markets—which were involved. 'It is essential that these problems should be given serious and continued consideration.' Action could be dispensed with till after 1957.

The Corporation gave no picture of the probable scale of output in different districts in 1957, nor any data about pig-iron output[5] or individual blast-furnace sizes and capacities. They published a list of major schemes, the plans of major firms, which gave more definition to parts of the picture. There was now no reference to any works going out of commission, but developments at very small plants were not included in the list. Out of schemes for steelworks to cost all told £201·5 m., most of which the Corporation had approved, schemes to cost £60 m.

[1] Above, pp. 251, 279.
[2] Oil firing of open-hearth furnaces, for example, increased output considerably.
[3] Above, p. 274 and *passim*.
[4] *Rep. I.S. Corp.* 1952, p. 37. 'The way in which development has been shaped for the next five years has meant that the fundamental problems of "location" have not been raised in an acute form.'
[5] The Federation had stated that the pig-iron output associated with the 20 m. crude steel output would be 15 m. tons (*Stat. Bull.* May 1952, p. 1).

were in South Wales; the North-east Coast was to spend
£52·5 m., Scotland £30 m., Lancashire and Cheshire £14 m.,
Sheffield £10·5 m. The new home ore districts, Lincolnshire and
Northamptonshire, had schemes for £20 m. and £3·5 m.
respectively. The Black Country also would spend £3·5 m.
The predominance of the old districts was overwhelming. The
primacy of Wales reflected the expansion of demand for sheet
and tinplates, and though the concept of regional monopoly for
these products, always excepting Cheshire, persisted, the
schemes covered here were designed to extract the most from
the existing mills; it was not as yet proposed to put in new hot
rolling mills.[1] The North-east Coast expenditure was to include
the major part of the Lackenby broad-flange beam plan, including new blast furnaces, which had been an urgent priority
in 1946.[2] The expenditure covered too the further development
of the Cargo Fleet and West Hartlepool plants,[3] which were
now each to have a capacity of 500,000 tons a year (well below
the standard set by the Productivity Team); and it embraced
the introduction of the duplex process at Consett to increase
steel output, which it called 'a most interesting project'. In
Scotland the main development was to be the creation of the
integrated works at Motherwell which had been decided on by
Colvilles in 1948, and made irrevocable by minor preparatory
schemes;[4] even early in 1953 the detailed scheme which had
been submitted was still 'under consideration', though certain
of approval. Richard Thomas were adding auxiliary equipment to their blast furnaces so that three stacks could be blown
at once at both Ebbw Vale and Scunthorpe, the kind of step
which had been suggested in 1947.[5] The further development

[1] Indeed, a report of the E.C.E. on wide strip mills published in Mar. 1953 said
that the Welsh continuous strip mills, which would produce 2,660,000 tons in 1956,
had a capacity, run in American fashion, for 3,450,000 tons. *The European Steel
Industry and the Wide-strip Mills*, p. 18.

[2] Above, pp. 85, 173. The Corporation said the new blast furnaces would replace
hand-charged furnaces; they also involved the dismantling of mechanically
charged furnaces, which had been inactive through lack of auxiliary services.

[3] Above, p. 174.

[4] Above, pp. 262–3.

[5] Above, p. 196. The cost at Scunthorpe in 1952–53 was put at £1·5 m. It would
have been nearer £1 m. in 1947 prices.

foreshadowed in 1948 at Stewarts and Lloyds plant at Bilston in the Black Country now became specific; there was to be a new blast furnace, with high top pressure, and it was to work on lean ores and Yorkshire coke in order to discover the best method of working on these low-grade materials! United Steels had made useful advances in studying coke production from Yorkshire coking coal and using it with Lincolnshire ores.[1] Stewarts and Lloyds had so far always mixed South Wales coking coal with Yorkshire and Nottingham coking coals at Corby; and in the early post-war years they had planned to use imported ore at Bilston. The announcement now made was an acknowledgement of the too high cost of South Wales coal and of imported ore used inland. How far the building of a rather small furnace not on the ore field was justified economically was yet to be shown. The firm was still only 'contemplating a scheme for general development at Corby';[2] which suggested that the 'site preparation' for this plant which was recorded in the revised plan of 1948[3] can only have been rudimentary, a skeleton operation.

Though relatively little increase in steelmaking was foreshadowed in the expenditure for the home ore areas, home ore consumption was expected to rise from 14 m. tons in 1951[4] to 20 m. tons in 1957, while imported ore was to rise from 9 to 16 m. tons. Home ore output had been rising sharply from 13 m. tons in 1950 to 16·2 m. tons in 1952. It did not, even under the stresses of 1951–52, reach the level of 18 m. tons visualised in the 1948 revision.[5] Of the increase (as shown earlier) some 1·35 m. tons were used remote from the orefields, half of it in South Wales. Was the increased output of home ore in the plan to be used where it was convenient, or where it

[1] Cp. paper on 'The Quality of Blast Furnace Coke', read to the Coke Oven Managers' Association, at Sheffield, 9 Jan. 1952 (reprinted in *The Gas World*).

[2] *Rep. I.S. Corp.* 1951, p. 42.

[3] Above, p. 254.

[4] *Rep. I.S. Corp.* 1952, p. 37. The figure is a little puzzling, because the weight of ore mined in 1951 was 14,776,600 tons, the weight as charged (including calcined ore at calcined weight) was 13,528,600 tons.

[5] Above, p 245.

would cheapen a dear burden, rather than where it could be converted most economically? This was a question which presumably no one 'raised in an acute form'.[1] A 'substantial contribution' towards the imported ore was expected from 'new orefields such as that being developed at Conakry', but no other example was given, presumably because no other development was going forward. Sierra Leone still looked a solid prospect, according to Mr Duncan Sandys; Mauretania was still only a possibility. Neither was mentioned by the Corporation. Yet 1957 was surprisingly near to benefit from new ore deposits for which plans of development had not been made in detail nor accepted in principle. Perhaps the reference was almost entirely to developments undertaken in Canada and Venezuela, in which the British, firms and Corporations, had no part.

When the Productivity Team's *Report* was published in May 1952 the Federation remarked how opportune was its appearance as the details of the second plan were being worked out. But it added for the wary reader a warning. The *Report* would 'be of great value in assessing the practical possibilities of development in the context of British conditions and aiming at a minimum overall cost, when all other factors, transport, fuel, raw material and capital costs—as well as labour productivity are taken into account'.[2] There seemed an implication that the team had only really taken labour productivity into account—which was an extravagant comment, though the team's economic perceptions were, as has been seen, limited—and it was no surprise that when the second plan appeared it was 'the mixture as before'. The bias of the system reinforced by post-war policies was not removed in the period of the Corporation, and did not seem to be understood by the Corporation; forces which checked rapid adjustments of the kind recommended by the team were still uppermost. Where the bias had favoured radical technical change on a sufficient scale, as it had above all in South Wales, there was an organic striving after high technical efficiency and an effort to expand within individual works on something like

[1] Above, p. 361.
[2] *Stat. Bull.* May 1952, a statement without a page number.

the American scale.[1] This happened in the making of sheets and tinplates in which the American example had been unusually noteworthy, where the machinery used was American in design and often in manufacture, and where the users of the plant were unavoidably more than usually conscious of American standards because their own work derived from America. It was of course not in the least surprising that this happened where raw-material costs were notably higher than at more favoured sites. Welsh coal was dear (though it had not so far been charged at a price fully corresponding to its cost); scrap was dear because there was no local supply; iron ore was more costly than it need be, at Port Talbot because only small ships could use the port, at Ebbw Vale because the ore had to be railed inland. All this seemed at first sight ironic; yet it was a natural outcome of a system which damped down the forces which encouraged change, eliminated most of the advantage of low raw-material costs and restored and reinforced the waning attractions of old sites and the power of the old to resist the advance of the new.

Hardly anyone bothered about the irony or the explanation. Most people found it satisfactory that there was a lot of invest-ment. 'The grass grows if you stand still.' In the last months of the Corporation's life many firms seemed exceptionally anxious to secure approval for their new plans, and the Corporation was heavily engaged in this work for companies which were still, though it was an odd relation, their subsidiaries. These perhaps wished to stake a claim in future expansion, since such a claim could have a good selling value when they were sold back, as they hoped soon to be, into private ownership. The Minister urged on the Corporation in September 1952, when the Govern-ment plan for denationalising had been published, the import-ance of 'early decisions...on the outstanding development projects required to carry the expansion of capacity for the pro-duction of pig iron and steel beyond the level to which existing developments would take us'.[2] The Corporation responded.

[1] The E.C.E. report on *The European Steel Industry and the Wide-strip Mills* said (p. 19) that 'It is only in the United Kingdom that an attempt is being made to operate the continuous strip mills at their theoretical "European" capacity', which was much below the American.

[2] *Rep. I.S. Corp.* 1952, p. 6.

6. THE CITADEL RECAPTURED

The Conservatives, victorious in October 1951, were pledged to repeal the nationalisation of steelmaking and to revive a supervisory Board for the steel industry. Mr Attlee (later Lord Attlee), convinced that Conservatives based this not on 'national needs' but on their 'ideological prejudices', was shocked that one Government should so soon undo the work of their predecessor.[1] But it made no difference. In July 1952 the Government set out its proposals in a White Paper, and the Bill was launched four months later. It arranged ingeniously that the assets of the nationalised companies should be handed, not just to a *Realisation* Agency, but to a *Holding* and Realisation Agency which would have the duty of selling them as quickly as was practicable at prices acceptable to the Treasury, but there was no time-table, no need for undue haste, and so long as the assets were unsold the Agency would behave as the shareholder. It was contemplated the sale would not be quick; but the change-over did not depend on the speed of selling.

This was logically the first step in the policy;[2] though it came second in the Bill. The next step was to create or recreate a Board, whose duty was to be 'to exercise a general supervision over the iron and steel industry, with a view to promoting the efficient, economic and adequate supply *under competitive conditions* (the italics were not in the Bill) of iron and steel products'. A number of particular subjects were to be kept under review— prices, raw material supplies and distribution, capacity, research and training, safety, health and welfare, joint consultation except on the 'terms and conditions of employment'. The sphinx-like governing phrase was 'under competitive conditions'. What did it mean?

Mr Low,[3] the Parliamentary Secretary to the Ministry of Supply, refused to define it because he thought it so plain. 'The whole Committee' (i.e. the whole House of Commons) 'must

---

[1] C. R. Attlee, *As it Happened*, pp. 214–15.

[2] The first step, that is, other than the repeal of the former Act and the consequential winding up of the Iron and Steel Corporation of Great Britain.

[3] Later Sir Toby Low.

be aware of what "competitive conditions" means, and I do not need to waste any more time on that point.' Other members of Parliament had at least recognised it was obscure—one had even discovered the writings of economists about imperfect competition in the early thirties[1]—and Mr Low went on to disprove his own thesis. 'There are degrees of competition.... The degree of competition in an industry of enormous plants such as this one may well be less than in the engineering industry or in parts of it where the plants are not so large. That does not mean that there is an absence of competitive conditions at all. For example when maximum prices are fixed there is still competition in quality, date of delivery, development, and so on. The Committee will no doubt be aware that on at least one occasion the Monopolies Commission have sanctioned in their reports a common price arrangement and found that it was not restrictive or against the public interest. I hope the Committee will not over-estimate the point that because there *is* co-ordination and co-operation in this industry and because the plants are sometimes very big there cannot be competitive conditions; or think that the Board ought not, as we think they ought,...to have regard to competitive conditions in carrying out their duty...there is room here for supervision, for keeping under review the co-ordination and the competition inside the industry. As in so many parts of our life in this country there is room for both, freedom and order....The effect of these words[2] is to make it part of the Board's duty to keep under review arrangements which might be restrictive in any way.'[3]

One thing shone clearly through this cloudy passage; that in the Government's eyes all the practices established in the steel industry under the Federation could be accommodated within their concept of 'competitive conditions'. Although they sought to 'restore competitive conditions under free enterprise'[4] there

---

[1] Mr F. Mulley, *Hansard*, 29 Jan. 1953, c. 1257. Also Mr Fienburgh who 'was sure the Minister will have heard with the same surprise as I myself the number and extent of the books written in connection with the definition of monopoly and competition in recent years' (*ibid.* c. 1258). Mr Fienburgh, it will be recalled, was the joint author of a pamphlet favouring nationalisation of steel, which came from the research organisation of the Labour Party.   [2] I.e. 'under competitive conditions'.
[3] *Hansard*, 29 Jan. 1953, c. 1269–70.   [4] Subject to supervision (*ibid.* c. 1269).

was room for order as well as freedom, for some co-ordination as well as some competition, and competition did not need to include competition in price. Indeed, the prescription to promote the 'efficient, economic and adequate supply' of steel 'under competitive conditions' did not mean anything so positive as the uninitiated might suppose; it meant that the Board had 'a duty to keep under review restrictive agreements'. The Board was not, however, to assume that such agreements were usually undesirable, or that competition as normally conceived, which includes price competition, should be regarded as the normal means of promoting efficiency, economy and adequacy of supply. There were instances where because plants had to be very large to be efficient the British market was large enough for one unit only; Mr Low reasonably said the Board would not be given the duty of creating competitors 'for the sake of competition'.[1] But this was not treated as a limiting case. Every case, the implication was, should be judged on its merits; and the Government were not, as the sphinx-like phrase suggested to the unwary, imposing a criterion on the Board; they left the Board free to decide the merits themselves.

The Minister made a great point of saying, however, that the Board could not decide the public or national interest. A Board whose members would be chosen from members of the steel-making and steel-using industries, trade unions, the worlds of industry, commerce, finance, administration and applied science, would, he argued, be 'well fitted to judge wisely what is necessary in order to fulfil its duty of promoting the efficient economic and adequate supply' of steel and its distribution 'at reasonable prices'. But it 'is not necessarily qualified to judge what is in the wider national interest in all matters.... The Government of the day and Parliament alone are competent to judge which is and which is not in the national interest.'[2] It was like an echo of Mr Aneurin Bevan, who had chided Labour members for pitting Mr Hardie's judgement against Mr Sandys'

[1] *Hansard*, 11 Feb. 1953, c. 448.
[2] Mr Duncan Sandys, *ibid.* 29 Jan. 1953, c. 1245. On the third reading Mr Sandys said it was the responsibility of the Government to decide what are the wider national interests; he left out the reference to Parliament (*ibid.* 17 Mar. 1953, c. 2196).

when the House of Commons debated on Mr Hardie's resignation early in 1952; 'it would be wrong to argue that a Minister is a less good person to judge the national interest than the Chairman of a nationalised corporation'.[1] Both had perhaps forgotten the wise *caveat* of Mr Lyttleton in 1949, that the national interest is not something which Ministers instinctively recognise and protect.[2] Mr Sandys' nominal restriction of the function of the Board showed him aware that there were objections to delegating to a small group of people the power of deciding in an important industry what was 'in the national interest'. The question arose, was the restriction more than nominal? It was all very well to say 'the Board is qualified and competent to judge what is right for the industry';[3] but since this meant something different from the collective judgement of the industry (otherwise the Board would have no function) it must reflect standards and criteria which the industry collectively would not apply, which would produce more efficiency and economy in the industry than the firms in the industry acting individually or collectively would achieve. The implication seemed that the Board could decide what was economically and technically desirable, and not monopolistic; the Government would decide when what was desirable on these grounds should *not* be done because, for instance, it would create unemployment, locally or nationally.[4] But unless some objective standards of economic efficiency were laid down to guide the Board, as Mr Shone had suggested during the nationalisation debates they should be, this arrangement did in effect delegate to the Board part of the job of deciding the national interest.

The Board's main decisions were to be, the Bill prescribed, on planning and prices. Planning came first in the Bill. It was symptomatic that it should; demand seemed to be still conceived, even under a Conservative Government, as a quantity unresponsive to price—a quantity, too, which must almost

---

[1] *Ibid.* 25 Feb. 1952, c. 818.   [2] Above, p. 301.
[3] *Hansard*, 17 Mar. 1953, c. 2196.
[4] Mr J. E. S. Simon put it succinctly: 'The only question is, who shall if necessary ensure that other considerations shall override the economic'. The Board 'are not in a position to do so. How can they judge the strategic situation?' (*Ibid.* 29 Jan. 1953, c. 1235–6).

BEH

wholly be supplied from home production, a quantity which the domestic industry had a right (as well as a duty!) to provide. The Board was periodically to review capacity, consulting such producers and trade associations as it thought appropriate —the chief one was evidently the Federation[1]—'with a view to securing the provision and use... of such additional production facilities in Great Britain as may be required for the efficient, economic and adequate supply of iron and steel'. The plans resulting from the consultation were not to be subject to Ministerial or Parliamentary approval, though the Board would publish an account of the review. If, however, consultation with the appropriate firms or associations failed, in the sense that *adequate* plans for expansion were not forthcoming, the Board might report this to the Minister who might himself, with the approval of the Treasury, provide and use the facilities (including facilities for mining and quarrying ore in the United Kingdom or even abroad) which the Board thought necessary or make arrangements for other persons to do so 'as agents for the Minister or otherwise. The Minister might also, after consulting the Board but without waiting to be prompted by the Board, take or lease or acquire, and then use, facilities which he thought should in the national interest be run but which otherwise would not be kept in use'.

In addition to the function of making a general review to establish that enough new capacity was being provided the Board was to examine all major schemes of development, and to have power to veto such as would 'seriously prejudice the efficient and economic development of production facilities'. If it chose to veto any scheme those who put the scheme forward had a right of appeal to the Minister. The appeal would be considered in private and the Minister would not give reasons for his decision.[2]

---

[1] The approach could be to individual conferences in the Federation.

[2] *Hansard*, 12 Feb. 1953, c. 688. 'The appellant or other persons in the industry might not welcome publication.' An appeal to the Minister (who could act in secret and give no explanation) 'goes sufficiently far to provide the essential safeguards of natural justice'. The Solicitor General explained that to forbid firms to do things was not litigation; there were no two equally placed contestants. The Board had to determine matters of policy (*ibid.* c. 690).

Firms who proposed to cease operating a plant were also required by a section which resulted from a Labour amendment to tell the Board sufficiently in advance for it to take any action it thought appropriate. A further amendment, similarly prompted, enjoined the Board 'without prejudice to the promotion of the efficient economic and adequate supply' of steel to have regard in consultations about development of capacity 'to any considerations relating to employment...or otherwise relating to the national interest to which the Minister may have asked them to have regard'.[1] The Minister was prepared, after all, to delegate his function to the Board.

The main criticism voiced against these proposals was that the Board lacked powers to compel. 'We want a Board which will govern in the public interest and...will command in the public interest.'[2] Mr Mitchison, explaining during the third reading 'what is the value of nationalisation', said that it was in relation to such questions as the opening and closing of works that the public interest might not be served by private enterprise. Under the new Bill 'can one say to private steelowners "You shall spend your money here"?' Can one say 'you shall not stop using that factory or that particular works'?[3] 'Coercion', Mr Low had explained earlier, 'was contrary to the spirit of the Bill.'[4] Mr Jack Jones, former Junior Minister in the Ministry of Supply, and before that a trade union leader and a steel melter (he spoke confidently for 'we technical people'), argued that the Board should be able to compel firms to amalgamate.[5] Mr Aubrey Jones, then a member of the Steel Federation's staff,[6] agreed that competition 'does not necessarily bring about amalgamation quickly enough', and that 'some pressure from outside is necessary'. But while a firm who resisted pressure to amalgamate might be wrong, the central authority which pressed amalgamation might also be wrong. 'I have known cases where the central authority has thought that a plant should close down...but the firm has not subscribed to that

[1] *Ibid.* 17 Mar. 1953, c. 2196.
[2] Mr Fienburgh, *ibid.* 29 Jan. 1953, c. 1221.
[3] *Hansard*, 17 Mar. 1953, c. 2116.
[4] *Ibid.* 11 Feb. 1953, c. 463.   [5] *Ibid.* 11 Feb. 1953, c. 453–4.
[6] He was brought into the Federation by Sir Andrew Duncan as his assistant in 1949.

view, has staged a remarkable recovery, has vindicated itself and proved the central authority to be wrong.'[1] Was he thinking of West Hartlepool and Skinningrove?[2] His argument amounted to saying that the Board would have no infallible criterion of inefficiency. Despite this he was content that it should be able to prevent a firm from *expanding*. 'If an uneconomic unit was trying to bloat itself uneconomically' that would be an 'upsetting of the economic balance of the industry'[3] which would justify vetoing its expansion. The veto would apparently be because its production was not required. The two firms just named whose plants were planned away in the first plan, but survived, had expanded; that must have contributed to their vindication. Was it really logical that a Board might be too fallible to force amalgamation but not too fallible to prevent expansion?

The answer might be that the Board was only to examine large schemes. The precise size was not set out in the Bill, but the object was clear.[4] It was, indeed, a weakness in the system of supervision, and recognised by Mr Sandys as such (as the lesser of two evils), because a large number of small additions to capacity can be cumulatively substantial. 'A number of small schemes which are individually insignificant may collectively indicate an undesirable trend.' Nevertheless, he was opposed to the Board's concerning itself with them; he did not want the Board to have the power to 'call for the submission of any scheme of development however small'. It was 'to concentrate its attention upon schemes of major importance'.[5] He thought the difficulty could be overcome by dealing with the matter at the periodic reviews of capacity, though since the Board had no powers of compulsion the force of this suggestion was not clear. Rather surprisingly he concluded: 'It is a theoretic problem rather than a real one'. The reverse had been

---

[1] *Hansard*, 11 Feb. 1953, c. 454–5.

[2] Above, pp. 246–7. If these provided the examples it will be recalled that their survival must be held to have lessened the chances of the larger scale operations recommended by the Productivity Team.

[3] *Hansard*, 11 Feb. 1953, c. 456.   [4] *Ibid.* 12 Feb. 1953, c. 682.

[5] *Ibid. loc. cit.* Again 'the Board should concern itself primarily with large expansion schemes *in the heavy end of the trade*' (*ibid.* 12 Feb. 1953, c. 693).

true so far since the war, and Mr Aubrey Jones might have argued more soundly that the dilemma set out—how the Board could be wise enough to constrain but not to eliminate firms— was theoretic, since if a firm could not be forced to close it could not be prevented from growing.

He, and the Minister, had, however, another escape from the dilemma. For the Board not only had powers, limited powers, over development, it had powers over prices. Here after all the Board could apply the acid test. The firms would not be allowed to charge what they liked for their product; the Board would fix maximum prices, prices only remunerative to efficient firms. 'Prices should be so fixed as to make it very difficult indeed for the uneconomic unit to continue in existence.'[1] The Board could not hope to make detailed investigations to find out whether firms were, or were going to be, efficient; 'but surely', said Mr Low, 'the best test is the far more simple test, the normal test of free enterprise and competition in industry'. If an industry fixed its own prices 'that test may not be satis- factory. For that reason the Board have the price determining power. They can fix maximum prices and one would suppose they would fix them on the basis of efficient production. In that case surely the best evidence of inefficiency would be whether the company, operating with those prices, made a loss or a profit. I cannot see any difficulty in accepting that argu- ment; I would go further. If the Board thought that greater efficiency might be obtained by reducing prices further they have the power to do so.'[2] Was Mr Low, as Mr Strauss sug- gested, just 'a little naïve in his conception of the industry'?[3] Mr Sandys added another facet to the picture: 'I submit the initial approach of the Board to production costs will be to look at the prices charged by the industry and to form an opinion as to whether compared with prices in other countries the industry appears to be producing efficiently. If the prices are reasonable they are a fair indication of the efficiency of the industry.'[4]

[1] Mr Aubrey Jones, *ibid.* 11 Feb. 1953, c. 455.
[2] *Hansard*, 4 Mar. 1953, c. 434.   [3] *Ibid.* c. 436.
[4] *Ibid.* 24 Feb. 1953, c. 2016. See above, pp. 226 sqq., where the limits to the value of these comparisons are discussed.

The Bill in giving powers to the Board to fix maximum prices did not say what standards it should adopt. By a strange irony, although Ministers saw in the prices so searching a test of efficiency the Bill introduced a new variant on the honoured formula; the prices fixed should not (in the Board's opinion) '*be inconsistent with* (my italics) promoting the efficient, economic and adequate supply' of steel. The Board was to consult with such producers and such associations 'as they considered appropriate'. Unless the Minister directed the Board its power to fix prices was *permissive* only (i.e. the Board might, but did not, have to fix them), and prices did not need to be fixed for all products. Indeed, it was certain that they would not be; in particular, the special products would escape. The Minister was empowered to direct the Board to fix prices or to vary its own decisions on prices, but only if he was convinced 'it is necessary in the public interest and consistent with the efficient economic and adequate supply...'.

The glosses in the debates were thus of cardinal importance, because they made it clear that the Government meant by price-fixing the policy developed before the war by the Federation and I.D.A.C. and pursued by the Ministry of Supply and Federation since the war, the policy of externally fixed prices which eliminated price competition and was held by the Federation (and presumably by the Ministry) to promote more perfect competition.[1] Thus the Board was endowed with the function of deciding profit margins for the products whose prices were controlled with the possibility of varying them to help enforce their wishes in investment decisions; and it continued the discrimination between products with fixed and products with free margins; which was likely, unless tradition was broken, to continue a bias against the production of common-grade steel.[2]

The Bill also implicitly allowed the continuation of the Industry Fund—to be administered by the Federation, with the

[1] Above, pp. 212 sqq.

[2] It may be argued that profits would always tend to be lower for common-grade steel; but that is irrelevant. The evidence is that price control kept prices lower than they would have been; the effect may have only been to increase a difference, not wholly to establish it.

Board exercising control only by its power to accept or not accept a 'levy' as a cost for price-fixing purposes. This again became clear in the debates though it was not in the Bill. Mr Strauss, it has been seen, emphasised how large and important were the operations (of which he fully approved) under the Industry Fund, and he thought they should be under the Board's direct control. Mr Sandys replied: 'we are not setting up an organisation to run the iron and steel industry.... Under the umbrella of the Board there will, quite rightly, continue to exist a number of trade associations.... The largest and most important will be the British Iron and Steel Federation.... It is not our intention that the Board should supersede trade associations or do their work. We are providing the Board with certain powers to intervene in the event of the trade associations of the industry failing to make the arrangements which the Board considers necessary and vital to the prosperity and efficiency of the industry. The notable example of this is in regard to the provision of raw materials. We maintain that the industry must continue to manage its own affairs and *so run its own industry funds*' (my italics).[1] The Board was given power, if it thought the arrangements for importing raw materials were inadequate, to repair the deficiency; oddly enough it was then only to be allowed to sell at prices lower than the cost of the imports with the Minister's consent. But the Minister unequivocally accepted the then existing operation of the Industry Fund, just as Mr Strauss did, and showed a profound belief in the desirability of solidarity in the industry.[2]

The Board's principal control over the Fund would come through its price-fixing power, Mr Sandys argued. 'In the last resort the Federation in fixing the levy are dependent on being able to reckon it as part of the cost of production' used as a

---

[1] *Hansard*, 18 Feb. 1953, c. 1262–4.
[2] In another context Mr Sandys gave a different impression of his attitude. 'Personally I am inclined to think that the Board would do well to establish fairly direct contacts with iron and steel producers themselves, and not to rely upon getting information second hand from trade associations. However, that is for the Board to decide. I do not think we ought to encourage the Board to regard trade associations, important and useful as they are, as being an absolutely vital element in the organisation upon which they rely' (*ibid.* 10 Mar. 1953, c. 1235).

basis in fixing steel prices. Was the logic complete? If the Board regarded a levy fixed by the Federation as too high, and if as a result the levy was lowered the consequence would be that the costs of firms using expensive imports would be higher, the costs of firms using cheaper home resources would be less. Though total and average costs for the same output would be the same the spread of costs between firms would be wider, and in order to induce the same output of steel, and to remunerate adequately the makers using dear imports, the prices fixed would need to be higher. Hence it would be better for the industry if the levy-subsidy arrangements should be entirely neglected in price-fixing, supposed not to exist, unless it was to be assumed that firms must produce as much as they can so long as prices are fixed which (in some way) cover average costs, irrespective of the spread of costs. Such a doctrine would have been plainly ridiculous when private enterprise was being restored. The same argument would have applied to the case of the scrap levy and pig-iron remission; given the low price of scrap the elimination of these arrangements would have widened the spread of costs and made it necessary to fix higher prices to induce the same output. The truth was that the Federation had evolved the system as a means of keeping prices down in booms, and with the Ministry had in practice used it as a means of keeping them down at all times. What was now important was not whether the Board would allow the levy as a cost, but whether the Board would accept as desirable a system which would allow it to fix lower prices, immediately, but would, unless the management of this system was revolutionised, distribute profits in a way unfavourable to investment policies which would give lowest long-run costs.

The only warning about the familiar policy during the debates came not from the Minister but from Mr Aubrey Jones. He stated that before the burden of the high prices of imported ores after Korea had been more fully (by no means entirely) placed on the users of the ores[1] the companies through the Federation had been pressing the policy on the Corporation and Minister for nine to ten months. This he instanced as a token

[1] Above, pp. 351–2.

of the dangerous delays which national control involves. 'It was clearly wrong, as a permanent measure', he said, 'that users of home ore should to a certain extent be subsidising the users of imported ore' (as had so far happened, though he did not go into this, save for a few months in 1950 ever since the war). The pressure of the companies on Corporation and Minister he attributed to their being faced with 'the prospect of an imminent independent existence, faced therefore with the necessity, very soon, of standing or falling by their own results. Accordingly, they were pushed on by the imminence of this prospect to know the full reality of their position, a reality which they would soon have to disclose to the world.' The Steel Corporation was not under such pressure, being from the nature of the case 'content with a broad average of results over the whole industry'. Political factors too, he said, entered into these decisions. He proceeded: 'the efficiency of an industry depends in the last resort on the degree of discipline and the commercial pressure to which its producing units are subject, and quite clearly that discipline and pressure is at its greatest when units have to stand or fall by their own results. That is automatic when they are independently owned—it is not so easy' (though perhaps not impossible) 'to achieve when they are under one owner.' Finally, 'in the short time during which the Act of 1949 has been in operation there has been this incipient tendency, there has been apparent a weakening of the discipline and pressure to which the individual producing unit is subject'.[1]

In the full retrospect of post-war history the obvious comment is that if the Industry Fund lifted the pressures during the lifetime of the Corporation it had done so in fact ever since the war, and the process started before the war. Firms had not, in the full sense of the word, stood or fallen by their own results. Relief from pressure was implicit in a system which always helped users of imported ores when their ores were 'abnormally' dear without reversing the process when their ores were abnormally cheap. It was implicit too in the same treatment of imported scrap. It was not theoretically implicit in the treatment of home scrap prices, as has been seen; the arrangement

[1] *Hansard*, 17 Mar. 1953, c. 2168-9.

could have been devised to maintain a ratio between scrap and pig-iron costs which would have been less favourable to the scrap users than competitive conditions; but in effect the administration of the arrangements did relieve the large scrap users of some of the commercial pressures from rivals using larger proportions of pig iron. Furthermore, the general lowering of prices resulting from low scrap prices reduced the commercial pressure from other materials.[1] Mr Aubrey Jones' statement did not pursue all these lines, but was an important step towards the recognition of what had been happening. It did not, however, it must be pointed out, reflect a departure from the *theory* of price stabilisation hitherto expounded by the Federation, in its refined form, exclusively by Mr Shone. It was no more than a reflection that the administration of the policy had, owing to the Corporation and the Minister, perhaps been less than perfect. But it contained the germ of a criticism which if pursued must modify the theory.

These were problems which the Government might have been expected to deal with; but although Mr Sandys at one stage indicated a preference for a price structure free from pools,[2] it was ultimately not clear that the impression was justified, and the right conclusion seems to be that the decision was of the kind he thought proper to leave to the Board. He said 'full employment' was one of the considerations which might lead the Government to intervene in price policy 'in the national interest'.[3] (The Opposition characteristically supposed, against all the evidence, that the prices fixed for steel were likely to be fixed too high for 'full employment'.)[4] He added: 'We do not think it a good thing to try to define all the different aspects of the national interest; we would have a new Schedule to the Bill setting out all the circumstances which might in certain

---

[1] For all this above, pp. 226 sqq.

[2] *Hansard*, 31 Oct. 1952, c. 1288–9. The practice of buying raw materials dear and selling them cheap he said 'possesses all the disadvantages of... price averaging, in that it masks real costs and interferes with the healthy operation of economic forces. But it would be impossible to end the system overnight without serious disturbances to consumers and producers'.

[3] *Ibid.* 4 Mar. 1953, c. 515.

[4] *Ibid.* 31 Oct. 1952, c. 659 (Mr Strauss), c. 647 (Mr Fienburgh).

eventualities lead the Government to intervene in the national interest'. The suggestion that if the Government had thought it a good thing they could have produced a circumstantial schedule was perhaps the very pretension that Mr Sandys was trying to avoid. Having created a system of supervision under which the primary test of efficiency was to be the ability to make profits with prices fixed externally, the Government might, however, have been expected to think it 'in the public interest' to ensure in the Bill that there could not be a manipulation of costs which by discriminating in favour of some firms and against others would make the test substantially misleading. The House of Commons was told how important the operation of the Industry Fund was. 'Some of the big producers (Mr Strauss said) contribute many millions...a year.[1]...No doubt those who contribute very large sums may sometimes think they have to contribute too much. Others who are beneficiaries may think they do not receive enough. There are a number of conflicting interests here, which are at present sorted out at Steel House.' Again: 'the incidence of the industry fund has an enormous effect on the prosperity...of individual firms'.[2] But apart from saying that the Fund should be controlled by the Board or the Minister he suggested no criteria for the use of the fund, and apart from Mr Aubrey Jones no member showed any concern over this. Thus in the end the new measure, although it set up an organisation as Mr Sandys put it 'to lead and guide' not to 'run and manage',[3] followed the same course as the Act which it repealed in that it left those who administered it to set up the standards against which they would measure the industry's efficiency, and in many vital respects to choose and

[1] A firm making 1 m. tons of ingots a year paid over £5½ m. in ingot levies in 1952. But if, for example, it used 600,000 tons of pig iron it received in remissions £2·1 m. If it bought 150,000 tons of scrap it paid a further £150,000 levy. The net payment in levy would exceed £3·5 m. If the firm used only home ore the only advantage for it was in the lower price of its small purchases of scrap; if this were put at £6 a ton the net cost of the arrangement to the firm would be £2·5 m.
[2] *Hansard*, 18 Feb. 1953, c. 1252–3.
[3] *Ibid.* 29 Jan. 1953, c. 1242. Also *ibid.* 13 Jan. 1953, c. 1213: 'I sympathise with those who are anxious to be protected against the man from Whitehall.... It is the very essence of this Bill that companies shall be free to manage their affairs with the *minimum of control necessary to safeguard the national interest*'.

modify the stimuli which were to be relied upon to promote efficiency. Mr Sandys emphasised that, from his point of view, the Bill gave limited but *defined* powers, both to the Board and the Minister;[1] but as regards the objects which executive or consultative rights or powers were intended to advance, they were described only in the loosest and vaguest terms (e.g. the promotion of efficient, economic and adequate supply), so that instead of strictly defined powers being conferred in fact the power to define was itself conferred. Mr Sandys might claim he delegated less than his predecessors, but he did not achieve this by establishing objective economic standards and a more automatic procedure or sorting out process.

This was not treated as particularly important. Possibly for immediate practical purposes it was not, because no breach with the current practice in price-fixing or investment was being called for. When the question of what could or should be done, or had been done, was referred to in the debates in a circumstantial form, the remarkable thing was again the near unanimity. The Conservative back bencher who regarded 'under competitive conditions' as about the most important words in the Bill went on to say: 'we are not doctrinaire in these matters, for if there are too many traders in the market real hardship will fall on those less able to look after themselves'.[2] In some industries, said another back-bench Conservative supporter of competition, 'the need for stability is greater than the need for all out competition'.[3] Labour back benchers, especially from South Wales, emphasised that 'the argument we have put forward consistently is that in the organisation of modern industry we cannot be confined merely to technical factors'; hence their advocacy of locations and disintegrations which admittedly raised costs.[4] But despite the effort to suggest a

[1] *Hansard*, 29 Jan. 1953, c. 1325.
[2] *Ibid.* 29 Jan. 1953, c. 1265. Mr J. E. S. Simon.
[3] *Ibid.* c. 1364. (Mr Shepherd, 'from black monopoly to free competition there is a graduation of competitive conditions which are capable of infinite variety'. The Board, he thought, should decide 'what degree of competition is necessary and healthy having regard to the needs of stability'.)
[4] Mrs Eirene White, *Hansard*, 12 Feb. 1953, c. 618. Mrs White, it is interesting to note, appeared to regard as mistakes not only the decision not to build at

difference both sides agreed on this kind of inefficiency. As the member just quoted pointed out, Mr Sandys himself approved of the Trostre decision, although he also said 'it is unsound from any point of view to keep uneconomic plant in production, even including the sociological point of view'.[1] Mr Jack Jones, advocate of compulsory amalgamation, pleaded the case for preserving iron and steelmaking at Barrow[2]—whose activities were subsequently increased—and urged that the Holding and Realisation Agency should not be allowed, if it exercised its powers to regroup some of its assets when it sold them, to make the blast furnaces of Park Gate an adjunct of the pure steel works of Steel, Peech and Tozer. Here, too, his hopes were satisfied; the result probably did not depend on his influence.[3]

The provision in the Bill for supervision of iron foundries, which provoked a flurry, provided further evidence that competition in the conventional sense was not expected or intended, since the emphasis in justifying the inclusion was that scrap was a raw material common to steel and iron castings. The allocation would need to be controlled. There had been complaints that in the scarcity of 1951–52 too much scrap went

Jarrow but the earlier decision to move from Dowlais to Cardiff (*E.H.S.* pp. 236, 451). Mr Griffiths (*Hansard*, 29 Jan. 1953, c. 1301–2) also referred to Dowlais, and Mr Mort (*ibid.* 10 Mar. 1953, c. 1183–4), in expressing the natural emotion of those disturbed by major changes, showed how hard it may be to do the right thing in cold blood without the sense of being under compulsion. 'Nothing gives me a greater heart-ache than to see the old works in which I served my apprenticeship 30 years ago now being dismantled....' He recalled the reply of a constituent to the question, What do you think of the Abbey Works (Margam)? 'If the scaffold is made of gold and studded with diamonds it is not much consolation if its object is to cut your head of.' Mr Mort made sensible suggestions that some old hand-mill works could be converted into engineering shops, less sensible ones that the old steelworks might be used to make billets, sections and bars. Mr Aubrey Jones, on the Government side, came from Dowlais, and his brother and father had been in the works.

[1] *Ibid.* 12 Feb. 1953, c. 618.
[2] *Ibid.* 29 Jan. 1953, c. 1247.
[3] *Ibid.* 18 Feb. 1953, c. 1357. The case for establishing a blast furnace at Steel, Peech and Tozer's was strong; the Park Gate works seemed likely in 1946 to disappear when its plant had worked out its useful life. Mr Jones called it a 'very fine steelworks'. Whether the linking spoken of by Mr Jack Jones was ever a probability I do not know. I would have expected the United Steel Co. to prefer to build a new blast furnace on a modern efficient scale.

to the iron foundries,[1] who paid more for some of it whether directly or by buying 'second-hand' machinery. Clearly the problem of distribution was only an acute one because of the control of the scrap price. The complement to this control, as seen earlier, was a collective control over the distribution of scrap, which Mr Robson Brown set out clearly in the debate. 'Any firm which thought it was exceptionally smart in accumulating scrap beyond the standard or level held by the rest of the industry would find that the appropriate committee is well seized of that and would regulate subsequent supplies.'[2] Individual foresight was not to be exercised in this régime! The right technique for getting more scrap to expand output (in the absence of some large change through reconstruction)[3] was no doubt to run down stocks and demand extra from the 'appropriate committee'.[4]

While the British Government, after making a bow to competition, left its nature and processes undefined and at the discretion of the Board, the six European countries who had opted for the Schuman Plan established a régime in which the forms of competition to be adopted were prescribed by treaty and competition was to be in a large market. The significance of this was only partially observed in the debates on the British Bill. The progress of the new organisation was welcomed as a step towards the 'peace and happiness of Europe',[5] and regarded with alarm as it would sharpen the edge of European competition in international trade. Competition had been growing from many quarters, it was observed. From 1949 to 1951 'France has doubled its export, Germany has trebled its export, Japan has multiplied its 1949 export five times, and Sweden has gone up something over double'.[6] Mr Robson Brown bravely advocated a revival of pre-war style international agreements (disliked, he recognised, as 'cartels'), of which he boldly claimed 'so far as the iron and steel trade was concerned not one...was open to criticism'. But because of public

---

[1] For the complaints cp. above, pp. 330, 344.
[2] *Hansard*, 4 Mar. 1953, c. 430.   [3] Above, p. 324.
[4] I was informed of this being done (1955).
[5] Mr Macmillan, in the second reading debate (*Hansard*, 27 Nov. 1952, c. 747).
[6] *Ibid.* 29 Jan. 1953, c. 1278 (Mr Snow, Labour).

suspicion these agreements should, he argued, be brought to the knowledge of the Board and subject to its approval, although 'I do not think that there is any need for the arrangements to be broadcast'.[1] But the establishment of the Community—it formally came into being while the denationalisation was in the Committee stage in the House of Commons—both accentuated the threat of European competition and made Mr Robson Brown's way of dealing with it unrealistic. A new clause introduced into the Bill registered that 'Schumania', as the irreverent called it, was no longer only a project; under the new clause the Board was to advise the Government over their relations with the new Community.[2] The discussions of the clause revealed the profound fears of some members of the power of the Community if dominated by Germany (as it would be, they argued, if Britain were wholly outside) to compete with Great Britain. Mr Boothby (now Lord Boothby) pleaded that instead of a 'flat-out-fight' it was better to co-operate in a comprehensive trading area.[3] But the more general reaction was to resist the idea of a '100 per cent entry' into the Community and a determination not to surrender national control of the coal and steel industries because of the danger to both industries. 'I am not prepared as a representative of a mining community', said Mr Blyton, a Durham miner, to hand over control of our coal industry to the nine people in 'Saarbrucken'. He suspected the High Authority of taking the first steps 'to push us out of our traditional markets' (which 'we' had never been able or prepared to satisfy since the war—but no doubt the claim in equity was perpetual). The 'shambles of the inter-war years' must not be repeated. He wanted close liaison—agreements on marketing, discriminating practices, wages, prices and capital resources—but national control of coal and steel must not be surrendered.[4] Mr Robson Brown, a steelmaker, thought Mr Blyton sought the best of two worlds, which the new Community might not concede. But he too shared the 'doubts and fears...about entering

[1] *Ibid.* 29 Jan. 1953, c. 1273.   [2] *Ibid.* 4 Mar. 1953, c. 445.
[3] *Ibid.* c. 452–3.
[4] *Ibid.* c. 458–60. Mr Blyton's reference to Saarbrucken arose from the uncertainty where the Community would choose its headquarters. A few weeks later he would have said Luxembourg.

any commitment which would give a voice to other countries in regard to the level of iron and steel production in our own country....It was a terrifying thought.'[1]

To all appearances Mr Sandys, though less vehemently, agreed. True he appeared to rule out the probability of a revival of international cartels: 'I do not see that it is likely that any direct arrangement will be made between, say, the French, or the German, or the Belgian steel industry and the steel industry of this country, except through the High Authority';[2] but that was consistent with cartel-like agreements, quotas and the like. The general terms in which he spoke of the industry in his final speech gave no suggestion that he was conceiving the British firms as part of a more than national scale industry with competition on a more than national scale providing the competitive stimulus which was supposedly so valuable on a national scale. Despite the frequent obeisance to competition there was no discussion of tariff policy in these debates. 'We want a steel industry which is efficient and flexible, whose output is sufficient to meet the needs of our metal-using industries at home and the export trade, which charges fair prices, which provides good conditions for those who work in it, and which conducts its affairs with a sense of public responsibility....Over many long years the steel industry has co-operated with successive Governments over prices, over development, and over the level of output. There is no reason to suppose that its sense of public duty and responsibility are going to desert it now.'[3]

This was hardly the aura of competition. The new Bill, which by the inexorable processes became an Act in May 1953, was to preserve the continuity which for fortuitous reasons the Act of 1949 had not broken, continuity not merely in the composition of the firms but in the I.D.A.C.-Federation policies of the thirties which had been evolved to preserve firms from competition at a time overshadowed by extreme fluctuations of demand when international competition was dominated by the practices of extreme economic nationalism and the ideal adopted

[1] *Hansard*, 4 Mar. 1953, c. 462.   [2] *Ibid.* 29 Jan. 1953, c. 1283.
[3] *Ibid.* 17 Mar. 1953, c. 2197–8.

for the British industry was undisguisedly one of near self-sufficiency. That new circumstances might need new policies, even assuming the old policies were right in their context, was not overtly referred to.

New policies were not, however, ruled out, for though the Act was heavily weighted in favour of continuity it did not prescribe policies. The Board, when appointed, might make a change.

BOOK III

*THE NEW COMMUNITY,
ANTITRUST AND THE
NEW BOARD*
1953–1959

Chapter VII

THE EUROPEAN COAL AND STEEL COMMUNITY

INTRODUCTION

The second Board, to be set up in 1953, 'might make a change'. The new High Authority, which preceded the Board by a few months, certainly would make a change. How would these régimes impinge on the development of steelmaking? How would they compare in action with each other, and with the American régime, 'antitrust', which was itself slowly changing, and which was the background of the technical advances which Europe wished to emulate and improve on? The answers lie in the future. It is still only possible to show the differences of principle which separated the systems—each system being in some aspect a recipe for competition—and to follow the earliest operations of the new systems, the ways in which the new authorities interpreted their functions and assessed and tried their powers.

This chapter accordingly traces the evolution of the European Coal and Steel Community. A brief glance at developments in the American industry follows, to be followed in turn by a survey of the first six years of the United Kingdom's Iron and Steel Board.

1. THE SCHUMAN PLAN

The hard core of the Schuman Plan was an economic prescription. The efficiency of Europe's coal and steel industries was to be increased, which would help to make Europe economically strong and independent. This was to be accomplished by creating a large 'common market', by promoting full employment, economic stability, and more competitive conditions, and by providing shock absorbers, as it were, which would make more rapid increase of efficiency acceptable by counteracting its disintegrating social repercussions. But the plan was much more than this. It was to be the first step in a gradual political transformation into the United States of Europe. It was to be a major step towards removing the deep sources of Franco-German conflict, and by transferring the coal and steel industries of France and Germany at least from the realm of national policy into the realm of 'supra-national' government it would at once give the French a sense of security which would make them more ready for the return of German economic sovereignty and the withdrawal of inter-allied control over German heavy industry. By stimulating the growth of markets in the West it would link West Germany with the West. The subtle interweaving of political and economic objects gave the plan a great emotive appeal initially. The joint pursuit of political and economic objects remained a source of strength though it could be a source of compromise which would delay or deflect the application of the economic prescription. In this respect, and only in this respect, the political undercurrents are relevant for this study.

The economic prescription of the plan was a synthesis based on a catholic selection of post-war experiences and policies. The final spur to action came, it has been seen,[1] from the threat, unfounded as it turned out, that demand for steel would not be adequate to use all the available capacity when current expansion programmes—the unco-ordinated national plans—were completed in 1953. The more immediate experience of contracting demand in most countries in 1949 gave substance to the fear that a period of serious over-capacity might be just round the corner.

2. ANTECEDENTS

(a) The Monnet Plan and French Steel Industry

It is at first sight paradoxical, though not really so, that the chief architect of the Schuman Plan had also been the architect of the principal national plan on the Continent, the 'Monnet Plan' of 1946 in France. This proposed a large expansion of French steel capacity which was coming to fruition fast in

---

[1] Above, p. 153 *passim*.

1949–50, thus contributing to the problems of over-capacity which then seemed to need solving. A brief review of its history is a necessary prelude to a study of the later plan. It has a place indeed in its own right in the economic history of steelmaking, and planning for steel in France may usefully be compared with the British planning.

The Monnet Plan was an integrated plan for all sectors of the economy, and the steel developments were only a part. It sprang from a recognition that the French economy had been retrograde in the decade before the war, and from the belief, probably well judged, that a massive concerted effort was needed to repair the positive damage, the loss of fixed assets which had occurred because replacement had hardly kept pace with wearing out, and to make up for lost time and put French industries on a competitive footing internationally. France, they said, was at the parting of the ways; there was no time to lose. The central 'Conseil du Plan' was composed of the President of the Government and almost all the Ministers, plus representatives of industries, trade unions and scientific researchers. It was a body to be reported to, hardly a body to act. The detailed proposals for different sectors of the economy and different industries were worked out by separate mixed Commissions who were set a task to solve. The tasks were set largely by the permanent staff, the Commissariat du Plan, headed by the 'Chief Commissar', M. Jean Monnet, with M. Marjolin (later to become a leading international civil servant as secretary of O.E.E.C. and later again a chief French architect of the Treaty of Rome, and later again Vice-President of the European Economic Commission and powerful representative in fact if not in theory of a French point of view thereon) as assistant chief Commissar.[1]

The Commission for iron and steel included five heads of firms, three senior Government officials from the main departments concerned (the Ministry of Economics, which was represented by a Director of Economic Programmes, and the Ministry of Industrial Production), three professional 'experts', two trade-union leaders and two representatives of the professional

[1] *Documents relatifs à la Première Session du Conseil du Plan* (16–19 Mars 1946), pp. 1 seq.

workers in the industry.[1] They were set the task, in March 1946, of planning for a steel output of 7 m. tons (metric tons) in 1947, rising to 10 m. in 1949, 12 m. tons within two years more, with 15 m. tons as the next aim; all to be accomplished with maximum saving of fuel and labour.[2]

The plans of individual firms provided a starting-point for discussions, as in Britain. But the structure showed a purposive direct and continuous participation of the state from the start, and was an integrated process, not planning within industry followed by state intervention or supervision as in Britain. The two processes in Britain could be brought closer together in fact than in theory by informal contacts, but they constituted unavoidably a two-stage system. The Commissariat had no powers to compel, though it could advise Government departments, and no doubt over allocations of scarce materials it did so with success.[3] In matters of investment by private industry firms could and did resist (or should one say abstain?). The strength and cohesion of the French system derived much from the determination of the 'Chief Commissar'. The Planning Council was Ministerial, but the Commissariat was kept outside and almost above politics. Its ability to secure agreement over plans and the voluntary collaboration of firms in their execution was helped by the immense sense of urgency about planning in France just after the war,[4] and by the funds for investment which the Council had directly or indirectly to dispense.[5] But a power to dispense funds is ineffective when people do not want to spend. There were, for example, plans for reconstructing the highly inefficient old high-grade steel-

---

[1] The list is given in *Rapport Général sur le Premier Plan de Modernisation et d'Équipment*, Nov. 1946, p. 170.

[2] *Rapport Général*, pp. 44 and 132. Also Maurice Fontaine, *L'Industrie Sidérurgique dans le Monde et son Évolution Économique depuis la Seconde Guerre Mondiale*, 1950, pp. 145–6. The intermediate target became 12·5 m. tons for 1952–3. I have been told that the Government in 1946 wanted a target of 18 m. tons, and 15 m. tons was a compromise, not a serious aim.

[3] *Rapport sur la réalisation du plan*, 1 semestre 1947, p. 197.

[4] French industrial output was still lower in 1938 than it had been in 1929. The *Rapport Général* is full of this sense of urgency; cp., for example, 'Modernisation ou Décadence', pp. 9–20.

[5] *Ibid.* p. 106. In 1949 out of 38 milliard francs spent 15·2 came from the 'Fonds de Modernisation' (*État des Opérations du Plan*, Dec. 1949, p. 78).

works of the Centre, but nothing was done before 1952; the works had a fixed quota (10 per cent) in the French market, and it is said this made it unnecessary to change.

The investment plan for French steelmaking was basically a plan for elaborate modernisation of existing plants, including a lot of regrouping and concentration of activities but few completely new installations, and none of these fully integrated in the stage visualised in the plan.[1] This general pattern reflected the fact that most of the works were based on the Lorraine ore or, in the Nord, on coking coal, and were already basically big units.[2] The problem was which should be expanded, and which should be retained; there was no call for a major change of location, though some sites were much better than others.[3] While the initial 'optimum' for a plant making ordinary steel was to be 1 m. tons (thus considerably above the British initial figure[4]) the expansion of output from 12 m. to 15 m. tons a year was by preference to be within existing works, which would 'help to resolve the problem of concentration, which is the central problem posed by steelmaking'. The principal new installations would be two continuous wide strip mills, one at Denain (linked to existing blast furnaces and steel melting), the second 'in the East'. It was not till 1947 that the precise location at Sérémanges, almost adjacent to the Hayange works of De Wendel, from which some of the pig iron for the new plant would come, was agreed upon.[5] Neither site was large enough

---

[1] *Ibid.* p. 71. [2] *E.H.S.* p. 433.

[3] Thus, for example, the sites near the south of Nancy were less well placed for ore and coal; the directors of Pompey recognised they should not try and turn the plant into a mass-production unit, and turned to special steel. In the Aciéries de Longwy group, though the Longwy works was the largest, and was modernised, the Thionville works was better placed for raw materials and markets, and it was planned to turn it ultimately into a large plant.

[4] The Commission suggested that 12 units of 1 m. tons capacity were needed, and 12 others for very special iron and steel. These 24 works could take the place of 177 establishments. Fontaine, *op. cit.* p. 147. The author remarks that 'il est reconnu a peu près universellement que la "capacité de production unitaire type" est de l'ordre de 1 million de tonnes d'acier'. He was following the *Premier Rapport de la Commission de Modernisation de la Sidérurgie*, Nov. 1946, p. 31.

[5] There was a suggestion that Hagondage should be the site. It was largely owned by Renault, which was nationalised. The choice of site therefore was a little coloured, or so it seemed, by this consideration. Thionville was also considered.

to allow the integration of the hot strip mill plant with cold reduction plant which was admittedly a drawback. In the second case, however, the two plants could be close together, and the site, with a firm rock foundation, had the great advantage of being close to some of the best and cheapest Lorraine ore, which gave it a prospect of being one of the cheapest producers in Europe.[1] The Denain-Anzin plant would also use the cheap 'minette'—usable, the French assumed, despite its high phosphorus—and the second plant at least was to depend mainly on Thomas steel, made in the improved version of the process using oxygen.[2]

Within the formula of change the projected work was formidable in scale.[3] As in most countries a considerable effort was to be directed to ore preparation.[4] Most existing blast furnaces were to be reconstructed and twenty-four new ones built, although, after allowing for the low iron content of the ore, the average capacity of most new and reconstructed furnaces (from 450 to 600 tons a day) was to be below the American size.[5] There were to be two new Thomas steelworks, which by using oxygen in the blast would produce a higher quality Thomas steel. Rationalisation of rolling mills was to be the most important reform in the plan. New central electric stations were to be built for groups of factories; ore mining to be developed and mechanised; several new coke ovens were to be built at the steelworks (where their gas was wanted); and from 5000 to 10,000 houses were to be built by firms for their workers. Although France built far fewer new houses in the early years after the war than Britain, the distribution of house building

[1] The hot mill plant included coke ovens which used a new process utilising more local coal, a new Thomas steel plant with oxygen-cum-air blast, and there was room nearby for blast furnaces, though in 1955 most of the iron came from Hayange where a new blast furnace had been built, but some also from other works, for example, Rombas. Output in mid-1955 was at a rate of about 1 m. tons a year. This was to be raised soon to 1·5 m. tons, but more pig-iron sources were needed.

[2] But not, initially at any rate, the still more improved oxygen and steam process.

[3] There is a useful summary of detailed plans, with early achievements, in *État des opérations du plan*, 1949, pp. 174–7.

[4] 18 ore preparation plants were visualised.

[5] The new furnaces were to have a hearth diameter of 22–23 ft.

was adapted to the desired industrial development, instead of being allowed to delay or distort it.[1]

The work got well under way in 1948, and from 1950 to 1952 the annual capital expenditure was somewhat above the level of expenditure in the United Kingdom, but the range of work covered was wider in important respects, and since a higher proportion of the new French plant was imported the average price level of their work may have been higher.[2] Precise comparison, that is, is impossible. The work done was in many respects impressive, though the output targets were not achieved and some of the changes had an interim air. Output in 1952 was 10·9 m. metric tons, which was only 87 per cent of the objective set for 1952–53; but it was 40 per cent higher than in 1937,[3] and there was enough capacity to reach the target. The achievement must be measured against the task; the French industry looked up to date in the early thirties after the reconstruction of the twenties, but it had lost ground badly before

---

[1] The houses I saw in 1950 both in Moselle and in the Nord (where the coal industry built), were good, a great improvement on those built in earlier periods, and often set with a successful effort to retain pleasant natural surroundings. Houses were expected to take about 6–7 per cent in value of the total investment.

[2] The French industry was smaller; hence expenditure was higher in relation to output. But their figures covered housing. More was probably spent in coke ovens, electrical generators and ore mining (which made up 15 per cent of the French total to 1952). It was estimated at the outset that one-third of the plant would be imported. Much of this was paid for in American aid; the point about imports is made here simply because if the prices were relatively high the volume of work done in the United Kingdom was comparatively greater than the values indicate. The comparative figures were:

Volume of investment expenditure in Iron and Steel Industry (£m. in 1952 prices)

	U.K.	France
1947–8	109	68
1949	72	66
1950	76	88
1951	71	79
1952	65	84

For the British figures see above, p. 269. For further discussion of their content cp. also p. 454. The French figures come from *Rapport sur la réalisation du Plan de Modernisation*, 1952, pp. 155 and 158. Cp. also p. 44.

[3] It was also 10 per cent over the peak output of 1929, after which the French industry fell back.

and during the war, and in 1950 many plants which twenty years earlier seemed shining examples still looked down at heel.

The plan marked an important advance towards closer technical collaboration at many points between groups of firms. The setting up of a central power station, which took blast-furnace gas from several plants and supplied them and their associated steelworks with power was an imposing early instance; it allowed power to be generated on a more efficient scale. Later this was followed by co-operation of the same group of factories to provide oxygen.[1] The first strip mill was built by the amalgamated firms of Denain and Anzin who formed Usinor; the second by a combine (Sollac) whose predominant partner was de Wendel, with many neighbouring firms holding smaller percentages of the ordinary shares. A large sum was supplied as a loan by the Government. French steelmakers had set up a joint research institute, IRSID, a little earlier, a parallel to B.I.S.R.A. in Great Britain. As in Britain it was financed principally by the heavy steelmakers, and it concentrated at first on some problems of basic importance for the French heavy steel industry, in particular the improvement of the Thomas process. IRSID's income was 586 m. francs in 1949, and 879 m. francs in 1951: and in addition in 1951 it was borrowing extensively. Its resources by this time much exceeded those disposed of by B.I.S.R.A.[2]

There was collaboration too in trying to lower the cost and increase the supply of coke, and to overcome the obstacles to using Lorraine coal for the steel industry. Here the steelmakers

[1] The group was composed of the Aciéries de Longwy, the Soc. des Hauts Fourneaux de Chiers, the Soc. métallurgique de Senelle Maubeuge; and the Soc. des Usines de la Providence (Rehon). The central power station and the central oxygen plant were at Herserange (cp. *Rap. sur la réalisation du Plan*, 1947, p. 145, and 1952, p. 149, and *Annual Report of Aciéries de Longwy*, 1949, p. 9). The *Rapport Général* (1946) mentioned three group power stations (p. 133).

[2] *Institut des Recherches de la Sidérurgie*. It was under the joint control of the Chambre Syndicale de la Sidérurgie Française and the French government. Founded in 1944 it began the construction of laboratories at St German in 1947, but its early investigations were carried out largely in the steel works. Of IRSID's expenditure in 1951 676 m. francs was on capital account (for laboratories, equipment, etc.), 456 m. francs (£465,000) on operating account: the second was rising sharply. British firms may have done more individual research than French.

(who were threatened with nationalisation but escaped) col-
laborated with the coal-mining industry which was nationalised.
Lorraine steelmakers had always enjoyed low ore costs but
suffered from dear coke. Local coal was not good coking coal,
and the Ruhr coal and coke which were used were burdened
with high transport costs. The position had been worsened by
the war; the output per miner fell seriously in all European
countries (most in Germany) so that coal was scarce and dear.
The plan set out to save coke by ore preparation and by blast-
furnace design. It was hoped to reduce by 13 per cent the coke
used for a ton of pig iron. The plan also set out to make more
coke at the steelworks where modern mechanical processes
required more heat and power, and it provided for a joint effort
with the coal industry to find ways of using a higher proportion
of Lorraine coal. Systematic experiments in blending, stamping
and separating[1] brought important successes by 1950. It did
not make French steelmaking independent of German coal or
coke, however, and by 1950 its practical effects, though they
could be counted on, were largely in the future. French steelmakers were still suffering heavily from the high export prices
charged for Ruhr coal, and the high railway rates on it which
were far above those for similar journeys inside Germany.

In regard to iron ore the boot was on the other foot, the
French charged much higher prices for export than at home.
Here, too, there was a large investment programme; over
80 per cent of the ore was mechanically loaded in 1953, compared with 7 per cent before the war. Output per man-shift
(underground and surface labour) rose from 5·2 tons in 1938
(4·8 in 1929) to 6·5 in 1952 and 7·0 by the summer of 1953,[2]
and there was an appreciable increase in ore output.

[1] The separation process was developed at the Thionville plant of the Aciéries
de Longwy: the principle was that coal when crushed broke into different sized
particles, the particle size of the constituents with coking quality being distinct.
This provided a basis for separation for the whole (cp. M. E. Burstlein, La
Cokéfaction des Charbons Lorraine, Chaleur et Industrie, Sept. 1950).

[2] The most useful source is J. Raty, Les Mines de fer françaises, published by la
Société des Hauts Fourneaux de Saulnes (cp. p. 44 and passim). With an average
output of 7 tons a shift labour cost was about 9s. 9d. a ton (wages being exceptionally
high; see below, p. 575), and total costs, presumably excluding capital charges,
about 14s. 6d. (Raty said labour costs were 66 per cent of total costs). The capital

The Monnet Plan visualised that part of the expanded steel output of France should contribute to an increase of exports to help the balance of trade. Until late 1948 exports were, however, kept low by the Government by small quotas, to satisfy home demand first. The quotas were raised in October 1948 to 1·3 m. tons of iron and steel for the next 12 months. But this was just as the world market ceased to expand and export sales from other countries grew. Actual exports were one-third short of the quota, and prices for exports fell disconcertingly.

Thus as the plan was at length well under way, the rate of investment high and output growing, prospects were seen more clearly to depend greatly on the policies of other neighbour countries. This interdependence was not a new discovery; the Monnet Plan had, indeed, postulated the need for overseas markets to be open to receive French exports. But it had now become of more immediate importance; the practical dangers, as was seen earlier, seemed at hand. The need to eliminate double pricing, duplicate investment, the closing of markets, discriminatingly low export prices, seemed urgent.

(b) The German industry before the Schuman Plan

All this was the reflex of the growth of output in the other neighbouring countries and especially the revival of Germany. Belgium and Luxembourg had both come nearer to their highest pre-war outputs by 1948 than France had; their outputs dropped in 1949 through lack of export orders. Both had projects of modernisation and re-equipment in their industries which, while not co-ordinated into a national plan, would add to capacity as well as raise efficiency and thus increase output when complete, and they included the building of three wide strip mills of high capacity though not fully continuous mills on the French scale. Owing to their normal high dependence on exports their expanding capacity would have to find its outlet

cost of a new mine (capacity 550,000 tons a year) was about £4 for an output of 1 ton a year; interest and allowance for depletion would thus be fairly heavy. A modern mine would have a larger output per man than the average for all; so that a total cost of below £1 a ton was reasonable, even at exceptionally high wage-rates in 1952–53. The home price in 1953 until the market became common was 856 francs a ton (17s.). The export price (20 per cent was exported) was 1325 francs (27s.).

in competition with any increase in French exports. Italy, Holland and Austria had by now also set out on building wide strip mills, and secured American aid to do so.

Germany, so far, in 1949 had neither a wide strip mill (because her pre-war one at Dinslaken was dismantled) nor, overtly, plans for such a mill.[1] But her output rose, as has been seen, from nearly 6 m. tons in 1948 to nearly 10 m. tons in 1949, and to over 13 m. tons in 1950. It was highly improbable that she would not aim at making sheets of modern quality by modern methods.

But though output was rapidly reviving no major important developments were under way in 1948–49. Existing plant was being brought into use again, and used with great skill, often with minor adaptations, to give high outputs. The war in its final stage had damaged the plant a lot, not in general irreparably but enough to call for considerable repairs to make it run.[2] Output in the early years was subject to a relatively low limit imposed by the Allies, but a still lower limit was imposed by the condition of the plant, scarcity of labour, fuel and other supplies, including water, and the shattered state of the German economy. In the early years plant was dismantled at several works. Allied policy, decided in March 1946, allowed Germany to make 5·8 m. tons of steel a year, and for this they were to be left with capacity to make 7·5 m tons. These figures were far lower than those which Britain originally proposed, and were not accepted for long; but on their basis a range of plant which could be removed for use by allied firms, or destroyed if it was military 'potential', was drawn up, and some important plant was in fact removed. The strip mill was taken from Dinslaken to Russia; the new Hermann Göring works at Salzgitter lost some of its blast-furnace plant to France, and its steelworks plant

[1] The German rolling mill makers had evidently been very active in making or preparing to make wide strip mills just before the war, for in visits to two of them, in 1949 and 1951 respectively, I was shown large castings for the housings of such mills which were being made for export in 1939. Demag made the Dinslaken mill before the war, and had engineers working with American continuous mill makers by 1950.

[2] For example, I visited the Mannesmann works at Hückingen in Oct. 1946, when only one out of five blast furnaces was in a condition to be run, and neither of the gasometers was working because they were riddled as the result of gunfire. The labour round the blast furnace was badly clad and had no protective clothing.

400 THE EUROPEAN COAL AND STEEL COMMUNITY

and rolling mills; Bochum lost some of its forging plant, including, for example, a railway tyre rolling mill which was brought to England and subsequently sold back to the original owners, and much other plant. Much of the August Thyssen plant at Hamborn was dismantled. The heavy plate mill of the Hörde works was removed. This process was still under way until October 1949, when there were still decisions to carry out, although it was losing momentum. As early as August 1947 the permitted level of steel output in West Germany was set at 10·7 m. tons, which was based on the original British proposal of 12 m. tons for the whole of Germany, East and West.[1] In the following year, in June 1948, currency reform had released German energies and demand for steel shot up. By autumn 1948 German industrialists and publicists were reckoning their immediate home demand for steel at 14 m. tons, pointing therefore both to the inadequacy of the new 1947 level and to the folly of going ahead with further dismantling while at the same time new investment in steelmaking was being financed by Marshall Aid and the world was short of steel.[2] It made an impression; the thing could not last much longer.[3]

At the same time the future shape of the firms had become sufficiently clear for long-term planning. When the steelworks were brought back into operation after the war one by one and with allied permission, new managing bodies were installed and the old companies remained owners without control. Programmes of production were under the allied control. Till 1948 there was a prospect of nationalisation, which the British Government favoured. But by 1948 it had become allied policy

[1] For the dates cp., for example, Fontaine, *op. cit.* pp. 202–4. Fontaine attributes the British wish to raise the figure to their experience of the financial burden of the occupation; no doubt this played its part, but the full background of previous proposals, which was perhaps not available to him, gives a different picture.

[2] The argument was pushed into great detail. Thus, for example, the Thyssen continuous sheet works at Hamborn was declared essential to provide electric sheets; if its production was not available the German heavy electric industry could not be sufficiently expanded and the need of more electric current could not be satisfied (cp., for example, a pamphlet issued in Oct. 1948 by the Vereinigte Stahlwerke Aktien Gesellschaft, *Zur Frage der Demontage in der Eisenindustrie*, p. 9 and passim).

[3] It was a common view among British experts in 1944 that because of psychological reactions dismantling would hardly be a practical policy a year after war ended.

to leave this issue of ownership entirely to the decisions of the German Government when it had been re-established, but to break up the giant firms in German industry, thus eliminating concentrations of political and economic power, and to eliminate certain families entirely from steelmaking, notably the Krupp family.[1] The stage through which the transformation of companies passed is irrelevant for this book, but it was time-consuming and created uncertainties. By 1949, however, the position had become sufficiently clear, and the market sufficiently encouraging, to lead some firms at any rate to start out on major investments. Their problem was to secure adequate capital, a severe and lasting difficulty which did not, however, reduce the firms to inactivity, though it may for a time have slowed down their development. Steel prices were controlled, which meant as usual that they were kept rather low, so that the proportion of the heavy cost of large-scale investments which could be financed out of profits, 'self-financed', in the manner widespread in much German industry in the period of most rapid revival, was rather small. Exceptional sources were already being tapped, though their scale at this stage was unimpressive. For example, the Dortmund Hörde works started early in 1950 to build a new heavy plate mill, to replace one which had been dismantled. They were obtaining part of the capital for their new investment work in general, not necessarily for this work in particular, from the Land Government of Rheinland Westphalia from whom they had 'Dismantling Loans', and, somewhat ironically, from Counterpart Funds.[2] The search for funds for large investment had by this time become an important motive of policy in the industry. It was

[1] The Flick interests were also to be sold, with a similar ban. Flick, indeed, sold out; and by subsequent purchases outside Germany showed that the ban only applied to steelmaking in Germany, an unexpected outcome.

[2] *Hüttenwerk Hörde Aktiengesellschaft Dortmund-Hörde: Bericht über das dritte, Geschäftsjahr vom 21. 6. 48 bis 30. 9. 49*, pp. 12–13. The contribution from 'Marshall plan-Gegenwertmittel' was 2,700,000 M. in long-term loans. The interest rate, not given, was probably low. This was specifically for the modernising of their cogging mill, which was started in the summer of 1949. In fact, this was a much less important job than the plate mill, which became one of the finest modern plate mills, including a 4-metre four-high stand for wide heavy plates, and a 3-metre four-high stand for lighter plates, rolled from products of the 4-metre mill. There was very ample space for finishing operations (cp. below, p. 457).

not yet practicable to contemplate a rate of expenditure approaching that which was occurring in Britain and France. The first Government investment plans, in April 1949, gave priority to getting more plant into use and so continuing the increase of output. But they emphasised the need to replace makeshift mending of war damage by more permanent measures and to undertake 'fundamental reconditioning and new constructions to keep pace with new techniques' (especially, it was said, in the field of fine-gauge sheets, i.e. wide-strip mills). They proposed an expenditure of about £25 m. in a year.[1]

Although the allies divided up Vereinigte Stahlwerke into eight main firms, and divided Krupps, the scale of production in many of the works had already been restored to a high level. In 1949–50 half the German ingot output was made in plants whose output exceeded 900,000 tons a year, and 75 per cent in plants making approximately 500,000 tons a year or more. A year later almost 75 per cent was made in plants whose ingot output was 600,000 tons or more, and averaged 946,000 tons.[2] With

[1] This was the figure fixed by the central co-ordinating body. The 'Functional Economic Agency for Steel' had proposed some £38 m., of which £14 m. for repair of war damage and reconstruction, £12 m. for backlog repairs, the rest for modernisation and rationalising. The plan was the nearest approach, in my knowledge, to the British Annual Economic Survey. I am not sure whether it was published, and only possess a stencilled copy.

[2] The figures for three years are as follows (thousand tons). I have included the two substantial works which fell below the outputs referred to in the text. It will be observed that the August Thyssen works and the Watenstadt-Salzgitter works were still not operating.

12 months ending	Sept. 1949	Sept. 1950	Sept. 1951
Rheinhausen	884	1,116	1,232
Ruhrort Meiderich	979	1,131	1,290
Oberhausen	884	1,029	1,206
Westfalenhütte	697	982	1,095
Hörde	793	917	975
Hückingen	509	727	902
Dortmund	494	757	865
Haspe	421	544	655
Ilsede Peine	434	507	639
Bochumer Verein	391	492	599
Total	6,486	8,252	9,458
Maxhütte	362	395	454
Georgmarienhütte	282	331	356
Total ingot output, all works	8,638	10,946	12,743

two exceptions the largest plants all made both Thomas and
open-hearth steel; they had therefore at least two melting shops,
though their blast furnaces and rolling mills respectively fed
and were fed by both shops, i.e. they could (though they might
not) enjoy to the full the advantages of large scale. And the
production of steel of the different types was in most instances
on a scale which was large in English practice.[1] Moreover, the
scale was growing rapidly; and this concentration was an
immense advantage in modernising, though many parts of the
works were old, and since dismantling presumably usually took
the better and newer plant this characteristic of the Westphalian
industry became more apparent. During the rationalising in
the twenties, what was new attracted most attention, but as
often happens in an expanding industry a surprising amount of
old plant survived.[2]

(c) Threat of over-production and criticisms of existing international institutions

The E.C.E. *Report* in 1950 which, it has been seen, suggested
to politicians and the public that there was a possibility
of over-capacity in 1953, assumed German capacity remaining within the limits set by the Allies. By the end of 1949

---

[1] In 1949–50 the division between Thomas and open-hearth steel in the major
plants was:

	Thomas	Open hearth
Rheinhausen	660	450
R. Meiderich	672	509
Oberhausen	584	446
Westfalenhütte	486	496
Hörde	442	474
Hückingen	309	413
Dortmund	463	294
Haspe	346	198
Ilsede-Peine	417	90
Bochumer Verein	—	473
Maxhütte	300	92
Georgmarienhütte	—	320

[2] I have been surprised at this in America. We were informed in 1943, for
example, that a Homestead melting shop, destined for scrapping but still in use,
was over 40 years old. In 1955 I saw a Thomas and open-hearth shop in Westphalia
(an extreme, but not an isolated case) which dated back to 1895.

this was already unrealistic. Output had been fairly close to the capacity limit (legalistically it should have fallen below it) for the second half of the year; it passed it in January–February 1950, and showed unmistakable signs of continuing to grow.

This contributed inevitably to the sense of imminent risk in 1949–50, and to dissatisfaction with the existing machinery of international control. The E.C.E. did little save collect information and present it in useful reports. The O.E.E.C. had been charged with the duty of co-ordinating investment policies in steel and other major sectors, and was conceived as a principal vehicle in what was widely spoken of by the end of 1949 as the economic integration of Europe, though what form this integration was to take was obscure. Proposals for a customs union, and for a development area policy (proposed by Dr Stikker, then Dutch Minister of Foreign Affairs) were discussed, and their difficulties were made plain; not least by the British delegates. 'Double pricing'—the practice then normal whereby exporters of scarce goods, coal and steel and iron ore, for example, charged higher prices for export than at home—was complained of, without being eliminated.

The weakness was in the constitution of O.E.E.C. Its steel committee, as the Steel Federation put it in its *Statistical Bulletin*,[1] could 'consider only propositions submitted to it by national delegations, propositions which by their nature have already achieved a measure of rigidity'. What that meant quite simply was that member nations would not accept unfavourable decisions on their own plans and in practice exercised a veto. So the O.E.E.C. 'could not get to grips with the real issue'. This was exactly what Jean Monnet was saying. He would hardly have gone all the way with the Federation in its further analysis. The Federation argued that the O.E.E.C. had 'failed to evolve a procedure whereby projects could be modified and adjusted by their study on a technical and industrial level before their submission to the Committee'. They seemed to think what was wanted was an industrialists' international association which, like the Federation but unlike the pre-war

[1] *Stat. Bull.* June 1950, p. 6.

International Cartels, would evolve common policies with regard to development, technical and market research, and raw material supplies, as well as exports, prices and production, and would be subject to international supervision also on the British model.[1] The whole should be part of a 'general attempt to lay firm foundations for healthy competitive trading'. M. Monnet would have wanted the technical discussion, but not confined to the industry level; he would have the industrial and administrative discussions combined, as in the French planning, and the political negotiating stage cut out. He wanted a central body which was not the victim of a unanimity rule, and not composed of delegates, a body having power delegated to it for a sufficiently long period to give it a corporate sense and to justify drastic change. It was a concept he derived initially from experience at first hand of the weakness of the League of Nations, when he was its first Assistant General Secretary in 1919. Monnet's judgement was that the existing top organisation was wrong in principle, and he shared the view which had become widely popular and which the American Government advocated vigorously that the pre-war international cartel, which constituted the substructure of 'industrial bodies organised by producers and lacking public supervision' to which the Federation alluded, had been objectionable because these bodies limited competition by fixing prices and sales quotas both within national industries and between them.

Between the wars international cartels had powerful political friends. The first European Steel Cartel, which was established in circumstances parallel in some respects with those in which the E.C.S.C. was born,[2] was hailed by leading politicians, Stresemann, Herriot and Loucheur, for example, as a step towards peace, a complement to Locarno, a model for the

[1] 'In the pre-war period international organisations were industrial bodies organised by producers and lacking public supervision on an international plane. In the post-war period an international supervisory mechanism has been established, but there is no underlying stratum of effective technical or industrial international collaboration' (*ibid. loc. cit.*).

[2] See *E.H.S.* pp. 424–5. Germany was about to recover tariff autonomy, and the free flow of Lorraine and Luxembourg steel into Germany was to end. The Ruhr firms who had lost their 'minette' industry were building up capacity to supply the markets they had supplied from minette-based works.

politicians themselves to follow.[1] They visualised a sort of hierarchy of such institutions bowing in world peace, and British industrialists apparently with their Government's blessing were negotiating with their German confrères on these lines not long before the Second World War broke out.[2] In retrospect it is evident that the pre-war international cartels were in their form an offshoot of economic nationalism; their members thought it axiomatic that they should retain as much of their home markets as they wished, and from this negotiating basis they agreed on export quotas and prices, and on tactics designed to help them as a group against 'outsiders'. They did nothing to open up their own large internal markets to each other to provide the stimulus of a larger free market. The common pursuit of national autarchy would no doubt have ruled this out; but the steelmakers, including the B.I.S.F., showed no zeal on its behalf. They might have argued that in the political circumstances it would have been impractical, that what they did was the most that could be done to stabilise economic and social conditions at home and assure fairly continuous employment, and that they charged moderate prices at home in relation to their costs.[3] Self-government by industry under benevolent inter-government supervision—the Federation's post-war formula—could work out differently in different political environments.

Political trends in the first years of peace, under pre-

[1] Ervin Hexner, *The International Steel Cartel*, ch. x. Published in 1943, this book is exceptionably valuable. Its author was a member of some sections of the cartel on behalf of the Czech industry, before he became a professor at the University of North Carolina. He sets out the political aspects, the approval of Governments, extremely well. The following extract from Stresemann's comment on the first E.S.C. in 1926 may be taken as typical: 'I welcome this agreement though clearly recognising the dangers...of the concentration of such great power in a few private hands. It has been the object of my life to realise in the political field what has been accomplished in economics by this pact. Groups of industries which a short time ago regarded their interests as irreconcilably opposed...met to bridge their differences and to regulate their production in conformity with their mutual requirements and with the demands of the world market.' And so on.

[2] *Ibid.* pp. x, xi. The idea of a hierarchy of cartels was, it has been seen, revived during the war by the 'Hundred Industrialists' (above, p. 59). The prime mover, I have been told, was Lord Macgowan, the chairman of I.C.I.

[3] Cp. Hexner, pp. 175 et seq.

dominantly American leadership but with socialist thinking leading to a similar attitude on this matter, were antipathetic to this form of organisation; and the Schuman Plan was based on an opposed premise, that a group of Governments should create conditions which would allow the units in the industry to reach maximum efficiency, that to the extent possible they should be impelled to efficiency by competition in the forms familiarly known as such, including price competition, and that any concerted action on price, output or investment should be wholly on governmental (or inter-governmental or supra-governmental) initiative.

3. THE TERMS OF THE TREATY

Hence in the plan it was proposed that certain economic conditions should be established and certain rules laid down (for example, as to price policy), and that a new central authority should be created. The conditions must be such as 'will in themselves assure the most rational distribution of production at the highest possible level of productivity while safeguarding the continuity of employment and avoiding the creation of fundamental and persistent disturbances in the economies of the member states'.[1] The authority must progressively establish and sustain the conditions and enforce (and abide by) the rules, but it would nevertheless have important powers of decision and action and (despite the lack of full discretion in deciding the international interest, whether, for example, minimum prices should be fixed and if so how) a high status.

By the time the first proposals had been converted into a treaty acceptable to the six countries of 'Little Europe' the authority—the 'High Authority'—had in the process of negotiation become surrounded by other political and judicial institutions which made its 'supra-national' powers more acceptable and less mysteriously menacing than they initially seemed to national governments.

[1] *Treaty establishing the European Coal and Steel Community* (English version), Art. 1, para. 2.

The High Authority was 'responsible for assuring the fulfilment' of the treaty's purposes.[1] It was to have nine members, eight to be chosen by the member Governments 'by agreement among themselves' (which implies unanimous agreement), the ninth to be chosen by the first eight. No more than two might come from one nation. They were to hold office for six years (with arrangements for partial replacement every two years), and were to 'exercise their functions in complete independence, in the general interest of the Community... they shall neither solicit nor accept instructions from any government or any organisation', and shall 'abstain from all conduct incompatible with the supranational character of their functions'.

There was, however, to be an Assembly,[2] composed of representatives of the Parliaments of all member states (or chosen by general election), to whom the High Authority would report annually, and which would meet at least once annually to discuss the report. If it passed a vote of censure on the High Authority with a two-thirds majority the High Authority must resign. There was also to be a Council of Ministers,[3] to which each member Government would send one representative, which was to harmonise the action of the High Authority and that of the national Governments responsible for the general economic policies of their countries. The Council could submit matters for consideration by the High Authority. It would meet periodically to deliberate, and the treaty enjoined that on many matters its concurrence, unanimous or by a simple or weighted majority according to the topic, was necessary. There was to be a Court which was to decide whether the High Authority (or any other Community institution) interpreted and applied the treaty properly. And there was to be a Consultative Committee[4] attached to the High Authority, to be appointed by the Council, who should choose from lists of producers, workers, consumers and dealers,[5] the lists to be drawn up by appropriate associations though the persons chosen were not to be

[1] *Treaty*, Art. 8. (For this para. cp. Art. 8–17.)
[2] *Ibid.* Art. 20–25.　　　　[3] *Ibid.* Art. 26–30.
[4] *Ibid.* Art. 31–45.　　　　[5] *Ibid.* Art. 18–19.

delegates. The High Authority was obliged to submit its general objectives and programmes to the Committee, and to consult on other matters, but was not obliged to accept their guidance.

Even the manner of appointment of members of the High Authority was a check to supra-nationalism. Since it was recurrent, and by Governments, the members would reflect the trends of national politics. This was to become clearer within a few years than it was at the outset. The treaty fell short too of what seemed the original intention, that the new community should be created for perpetuity—it was a treaty for 50 years.[1] But this had the virtue of promising a long enough life to encourage major industrial adaptations. The substance of the original proposal was, within the limits of reasonable expectation, largely retained.

The characteristics of the common market which the institutions of the Community, and especially the High Authority, were to establish and maintain were set out in the Treaty at length with what seemed precision.[2] The market must be regularly supplied, with due regard to the needs of third countries. All consumers in comparable positions must have equal access to the sources of production. Prices should be the 'lowest which are possible without requiring any corresponding rise either in the prices charged by the same enterprise in other transactions or in the price level as a whole in another period, while at the same time permitting necessary amortisation and providing normal possibilities of remuneration for capital investment'. Conditions must encourage enterprise to expand and improve facilities, and promote rational use of indigenous natural resources without inconsiderate exhaustion. They must promote improved living and working conditions, and make possible the 'equalisation of such conditions in an upward direction'. International trade must be furthered, and equitable limits set on prices charged for exports. Regular expansion and modernisation must be furthered under conditions which preclude any protection against competing industries outside the Community, 'except where justified by illegitimate actions of such industries or in their favour'.

[1] *Treaty*, Art. 97.   [2] *Ibid.* Art. 3.

The treaty proceeded to abolish and prohibit as incompatible with the common market all import and export duties or their equivalent on coal and steel within the Community, all discriminating measures among producers, buyers or consumers, especially as concern prices, delivery terms, transport rates, all measures which hampered buyers in the free choice of suppliers, all subsidies or state assistance or special charges imposed by the state, and restrictive practices tending towards the division of markets or the exploitation of consumers.[1]

Finally,[2] the positive steps to be taken were defined in broad terms. The Community should accomplish its aim 'with limited direct intervention'. It should provide information, organise consultations and define general objects. It should 'place financial means at the disposal of enterprises for their investments and participate in the expenses of readaptation'. It should 'assure the establishment, the maintenance and the observance of normal conditions of competition and take direct action with regard to production and the operation of the market only when circumstances make it absolutely necessary'. It should publish the justification of its actions and take the steps needed to ensure the observance of the rules laid down in the treaty, and it should do all these things with as little administrative machinery as possible in close co-operation with the interested parties.

Since it was not supposed that the conditions of the treaty could be realised at once, a transitional period of five years was provided, during which weak coal and steel areas were to be given special aid, and subsidies allowed. Where enterprises were forced to adapt themselves radically to the new circumstances the High Authority was directed at the request of Governments to make grants to some enterprises, to give temporary aid to workers deprived of employment, to help them move and to provide new training, and to study and finance re-employment programmes. The most far-reaching special arrangements for subsidies were made about coal. In regard to steel the High Authority was, among other things, given power to limit the increase in the flow of steel from one community country to

---

[1] *Treaty*, Art. 4.   [2] *Ibid.* Art. 5.

another, and to fix production quotas for supplies within the Community, and Italy was permitted to continue to charge duties on steel coming in from other Community countries.

The special purpose, as set out in the treaty, of establishing the lowest prices which could be maintained with slight variations for a long time and which would ensure continuous and adequate supplies, provide for adequate depreciation and normal returns on capital so that modernisation and expansion were appropriately encouraged was a purpose which those who propounded the British Iron and Steel Federation's policy might have claimed as their own. They might even have agreed in principle that consumers in comparable positions should have equal access to sources of production,[1] and would certainly have agreed that inconsiderate exhaustion of resources must be avoided.

The essence of the treaty was not, however, in the purposes which it set out (though it was enlightening and enlightened that it set them out as it did, and did not leave them as undefined and therefore as optional as they were in the British law analysed in the last chapter), but in the methods whereby they should be achieved. Indeed, the purposes, as the treaty implicitly recognised, were not fully defined without the definition of method. 'Normal possibilities of remuneration for capital invested', for example, is a phrase which begs many questions, though it avoids the characteristic 'dirigiste' concept of 'reasonable' remuneration. 'Regular expansion and modernisation' is given meaning by the qualification that protection from competition is precluded. The key to the treaty is to be found in its categorical prohibitions of discriminations, subsidies and restrictive practices, and in the phrases which enjoin the Community to rely on 'limited direct interference', to 'take direct action with respect to production and the operation of the market only when circumstances make it absolutely necessary', and to 'operate with as little administrative machinery as possible'. The emphasis was on the creation of conditions which, as M. Schuman said in the initial

[1] Though the policy of uniform delivered prices in the B.I.S.F. sense, even in zones, was hardly in keeping with this.

announcement of the plan, would induce enterprises to develop spontaneously in the right way.

Though the bias of intention was thus unmistakable, much of the body of the treaty was concerned with the circumstances in which the High Authority should not merely as it were 'keep the ring' and see that firms obeyed the rules, but should intervene with the free play of competition, which gave it almost an air of ambiguity, as though what was supposedly bringing more competition would in fact establish more *dirigisme*.

Thus if there were a shortage of orders so that the Community 'is faced with a period of manifest crisis', the High Authority should establish production quotas, and establish import restrictions in some circumstances. If, on the other hand, coal or steel were scarce, then the Council, if it was unanimous, and the High Authority if the Council were divided, should institute rationing both of coal and steel and raw materials for steel, including scrap.[1]

The chapter on prices was mainly devoted to clarifying what were regarded as discriminatory and unfair competitive practices. Purely temporary and local reductions of price, for instance, were ruled out, and unequal treatment of different buyers, especially according to nationality, in comparable circumstances. Price scales and conditions were to be published by 'enterprises' (an enterprise might be a nationalised industry or a part of one); and they must be prices for base points 'normal' for the location of the enterprise. Prices charged must not be more than those in the lists, and might only be less within a narrow and defined margin, namely, the margin resulting from the use of a base point nearer to the consumer. The High Authority would have the power to reduce this margin. Enterprises might 'align their quotations on the prices offered by enterprises outside the Community'. This came near to American 'F.O.B. Mill' delivered price theory, but, as will be seen later, was possibly somewhat remote from American practice.

But apart from these amplifications of the definition of competitive price policy, the treaty gave the High Authority powers

[1] *Treaty*, ch. IV.

to fix both maximum and minimum home prices[1]—if it deemed this necessary to achieve the sort of prices which were set out as an object of the Treaty[2]—and maximum and minimum export prices. Minimum home prices were to be fixed if a 'manifest crisis exists or is imminent'; export prices if it 'appears necessary' and can be supervised.[3] The High Authority was to take advice from the Consultative Committee and the Council before fixing prices, but much was evidently left to the High Authority's discretion. In regard to coal prices the High Authority was specifically authorised to allow 'compensation' schemes between the mines in particular mining areas, if this was the best way of avoiding prices being raised to become equal to the costs of the dearer production 'temporarily required'.[4] Presumably the compensation schemes would also be only temporarily required. By more general powers to set up or permit 'financial arrangements common to several enterprises', where such arrangements seem needed for the objects of the treaty compensation schemes could also in fact be established for steel or scrap.[5]

The High Authority was also empowered to help investments by lending or by guaranteeing loans. One object was no doubt to lower the price of loans and establish a uniform Community price. Here again there was great scope for discrimination; and since the High Authority had the right to require enterprises to submit all their plans so that co-ordinated development might be 'encouraged', this financial power might turn out to be not merely discriminatory in favour of coal and steel, which it was bound to be (if it made new capital cheaper), but a means of exerting a central influence. The High Authority also had an obligation to provide funds for, and to help make plans for, the

[1] *Treaty*, Art. 61.   [2] Above, p. 409.

[3] Export prices could be fixed (a) if the limits observed by enterprises in fixing them appeared to be inequitable and inimical to the fostering of international trade (Art. 3f): (b) when it appeared necessary to avoid dangers to enterprises within their common market (Art. 61c), i.e. when price-cutting was hurting firms financially.

[4] *Treaty*, Art. 63.

[5] Art. 53. Presumably the special provision was made for coal because it was intended to use the power at once, and it was no doubt reassuring to, say, Belgium to have it in black and white.

creation of new industrial activities when the new competition brought about by the Common Market deprived some workers of jobs. This was clearly, however, a form of intervention which was to ease the operation of competition, not to take its place.

Much of the treaty fell into this category, that is, providing safeguards for competition. The scope which should be given to trade associations and within which combines of firms should be allowed, for example, was carefully prescribed. The right to form trade associations was formally confirmed, and the treaty assumed that associations of 'enterprises' would in fact be used to obtain information and for purposes of consultation, provided that workers as well as employers participated in some way in the work. All such associations were to be obliged to give full information about their activity to the High Authority,[1] and associations tending to restrict the operation of the common market, by fixing or 'influencing' prices, controlling production, technical development or investments, or allocating markets or sources of supply, were forbidden. Agreements among 'enterprises' either to specialise in making, or to buy or sell jointly, some specified products, might be authorised, if this would substantially improve the production or marketing of the products, and was essential for this and did not confer powers of fixing prices or limiting competition. What precisely was to be permitted was a little obscure. What was ruled out seemed clear enough, and all was at the discretion of the High Authority.[2]

Mergers or other processes which would concentrate control of several enterprises in one hand would (unless on a small scale) also require the High Authority's authorisation, which was not to be given if the resulting integrations would have power to influence prices, control or restrain production or marketing, or impair competition in a substantial part of the market, or establish privileged positions of access to supplies or markets.

The treaty proscribed both discriminations in transport charges (which had particular importance in relation to traffic which crossed the frontiers within the Community) and restrictions on the movement of coal and steel workers to seek work

---

[1] *Treaty*, Art. 48.　　　　[2] *Ibid*. Art. 65.

within the Community. These were measures designed to free the market. But the High Authority was given power to intervene if wages in coal or steel in any of the six countries fell below the general wage level in the same country, or if wages were lowered to reduce costs and thus to compete through lowered wages; which was interventionist, and a restriction, not a promotion of competition, though the original suggestion of equalising wages was dropped.

Finally, the treaty dealt with the relations of the Community with the outside world. This was one of the least developed sections. The Council was given powers to fix maximum and minimum duties on coal and steel for all member countries *vis-à-vis* third countries. Export and import licensing were left within the control of each member country, but subject to supervision by the High Authority, who might also recommend retaliatory measures, including quantitative restrictions where third countries 'dumped' their steel, or indeed where imports from a third country into the Community increased sufficiently to threaten to damage Community production seriously whatever the source of its success. The arrangements for the transitional period made the purposes a little clearer. The Benelux import duties on steel were lower than those of France and Germany. For a time it might be necessary therefore to make arrangements whereby steel from third countries would not come in at Benelux rates to France and Germany,[1] until they should have 'harmonised' their duties with Benelux. In order to ease this process Benelux agreed to be prepared to raise its duties by 'two points'; but it was implied that the general aim was to harmonise duties down, not up. The six countries were at once to negotiate with third countries, particularly Britain, and the High Authority was to act for them, but no indication of the relations expected or hoped for was given.

How the Community would work, if it would work, could only become clear after several years. It was complex, there were divergent views on the emphasis to be placed on different

[1] Otherwise foreign steel might be imported into Benelux and thence into Germany or France which would lower the protection still maintained in intention by these countries.

elements, there was distrust and opposition among French, German and Belgian steelmakers, and the High Authority had to learn its job.

4. THE TRANSITIONAL PERIOD

(a) The first steps

The first step to a Common Market was the easiest. It was to remove customs or export duties on and quantitative restrictions on movements of coal, steel, iron ore and scrap within the Community. Double pricing within the Community went at the same time. This was completed, almost as quickly as the treaty prescribed, seven months after the High Authority was appointed. Duties on steel went on 1 May 1953. To mark the occasion M. Monnet, the inevitable first president of the High Authority, made what some aver to have been his first and last visit to a steelworks to start to tap a Luxembourg blast furnace and so make the first 'Europe' pig iron.

This breakdown of barriers was a dramatic symbol, though French and German duties on steel had for some time been suspended, and for the transitional period some protections would remain. There was a special régime for Belgian and Italian coal mines. Coal produced in Germany or Holland was subject to a levy for the assistance of these mines, which also had state aid, and were to be rationalised and modernised where possible or otherwise closed. This went too slowly in Belgium for the High Authority:[1] and the full integration of Belgian coal-mining in the Community was still not possible in 1957.[2] In Italy, at Sulcis, there had been more success. Various subsidies were allowed at the outset to continue on coal-mining in France, but they disappeared progressively in the transition period. Italian coke and steel retained the benefit of protective duties, at a diminishing rate, through the transitional 5 years; duties on steel dropped from a level of 15–20 per cent in May 1953 through

[1] 6ème Rap. Gén. vol. II, p. 48.
[2] The subsidising of Belgian coalmines by German and Dutch coalmines had stopped by the end of 1958; they refused to continue it. Belgian Government subsidies continued. It was hoped to rationalise sufficiently by 1962 to bring this to an end. In 1958 employment in uneconomic pits naturally rose.

five stages to nil in February 1958,[1] and within that period steelmakers in other E.C.S.C. countries might not align their price to the Italian.

(b) 'Interpenetration'

The High Authority were able nonetheless in the first two years or so to point to striking extensions of trade between the Community countries, most impressive in steel, but of some significance also in coal, coke, ore and scrap. In scrap the chief development was a considerable flow into Italy from the rest of the Community. In 1957 the trade in scrap between the E.C.S.C. countries was three times the 1952 level, and 70 per cent flowed from the northern partners into Italy. In iron ore, the internal trade of the Community rose from 9·4 m. tons in 1952 to 13·5 m. tons in 1955 and 14·3 m. tons in 1957. Over 95 per cent was French ore, and nearly 90 per cent went into Belgium. It was the familar minette trade. Germany took 379,000 tons of minette in 1952, 1,065,000 tons in 1957.[2] Changes in the movement of coal in the Community were only partly of concern for steel. The position in regard to *all* coal (whether coking or otherwise) and coke is shown in Table 48.

At first Germany and Belgium increased their exports, until 1954 and 1955 respectively. Germany exported less to France, Holland and Italy in 1955 than in 1952, after large increases; exports to France had just recovered in 1957, and were one-seventh over the 1952 figure, but there were further drops to Holland and Italy. The Belgian record was fairly similar—increased sales to everybody until 1955, more to France and less to the others. The main increases in coke sales between the Community countries (which hardly changed after 1955) were from Holland and Germany; the main recipients were France and Luxembourg.[3] This was traditional, and the increases in

---

[1] *6th Ann. Rep. Comm.* vol. II, p. 23.

[2] Germany took also about 400,000 tons of minette from Luxembourg, slightly less in 1957 than in 1952.

[3] The main flows of the trade in 1957 were (thousand tons): Germany to France, 3627; Belgium to France, 467; Germany to Luxembourg, 3086; Belgium to Luxembourg, 173; Netherlands to France, 788; Netherlands to Luxembourg, 450.

these fuel trades within the Community were small compared with the growth in steel output.

The trade in pig iron and steel (it was mostly steel) within the Community rose impressively from 1952 to 1955. Thereafter it fell back, to make further slight advances in 1957 and 1959. The figures are given in Table 49. The trade rose from 8 per cent of E.C.S.C. consumption in 1952 to 15 per cent in 1955.

Table 48. *Coal imports into E.C.S.C. countries 1952–57*
(thousand metric tons)

	From each other		From third countries	
	Coal	Coke	Total	From U.S.
1952	16,315	8,104	22,264	16,302
1953	19,916	7,075	13,823	6,689
1954	23,600	6,990	13,924	6,164
1955	23,236	8,992	23,048	15,935
1956	19,707	9,173	28,046	30,389
1957	19,822	9,338	44,007	37,872
1958	16,745	8,400	31,845	25,820

In these figures, from the *6th Gen. Rep.* 1958, vol. II, pp. 356–7, the Saar is included in France. In some other series the exports of the Saar and France to other E.C.S.C. countries are treated as separate trades; the result is to raise the aggregate trade. It does not change the trend. Cp. E.C.S.C. *Informations Statistiques*, Mai/Juin 1958, p. 69. The peak in 1954 comes out at 26,865, falling to 22,042 in 1957. No coke figures are given in this table.

'Interpenetration', to use the Community's word, not only extended rapidly to 1955, it also changed its pattern greatly from 1955 to 1957. Up to 1955 German imports from the rest rose impressively; thereafter they receded and did not touch the 1955 rate till the first half of 1959. In 1957 it was France and the Netherlands who were the growing consumers but both dropped heavily by the first half of 1959. Until 1955 German consumption of steel ran ahead of her production; in 1955 she had a net import in trade with *all* other countries of 600,000 tons.[1] French and Dutch industries expanded very markedly in 1957. The growth of trade within the Community was, as the table indicates, complex. It was not a case up to 1955 merely of Germany importing more; she exported more to other com-

---

[1] She was a net exporter in 1952–4 and in 1956–7.

Table 49. *Interchange of iron and steel by Community countries within the Common Market*[a] *(thousand tons), 1952–59*

Exporting country:	1952	1953	1954	1955	1956	1957	1958	1959 1st 6 mths.
Germany	302	497	771	832	918	1500	1279	578
Belgium and Luxembourg	1254	1241	1879	2483	2216	2209	2140	1122
France and Saar[b]	481	952	1304	1943	1608	1552	1503	1160
Italy	2	5	7	62	49	72	86	49
Holland	68	118	255	344	289	382	410	221
Total	2108	2810	4216	5664	5080	5715	5418	3130
Country of destination:								
Germany	786	998	1679	2564	1999	1874	2114	1362
Belgium and Luxembourg	212	320	313	507	530	540	424	266
France and Saar	28	110	443	782	901	1218	1283	497
Italy	323	440	505	483	424	533	566	399
Holland	759	941	1276	1330	1227	1550	1030	604

[a] *8ème Rap. Gén.*, édit provisoire. The original table gives a full subdivision of the exports of each country to each country of destination, and for all quarters of 1954. The table includes pig iron; the deliveries of pig iron in the total exports (which are taken from another statistical source) were:

1952	271,000 tons	1955	640,000 tons
1953	324,000 tons	1956	592,000 tons
1954	459,000 tons	1957	641,000 tons

[b] The trade of the Saar is not given separately.

munity countries. So with all the other members. The full explanation would need to be in terms of particular trades, the geographical advantage of individual works, the demands for particular products in relation to the facilities for providing them at the particular time. The immense growth of German motor-car output called for large imports of sheets from France in 1954–5 which would not be needed when Germany had more wide-strip mills. This was one of the possible interchanges discussed, it has been seen, in 1949–50, when it was feared that the two French wide-strip mills would find it hard to be fully occupied. To some extent therefore the large German import of 1955 was inherently unstable. Repercussions of this were plain in the attitudes of French and German steel-makers; the former were gloomily afraid that the High Authority would do too little to co-ordinate investment and avoid needless duplication of plant—the Germans were afraid there would be too much interference.

Much of this growth of trade between the Six would have occurred in any case. How much was facilitated by the new arrangements cannot possibly be stated. It cannot even be assumed that duties would have impeded all the trade had there been no treaty—the German Government, like the British, freed steel imports from duties when it seemed advantageous to do so.

In their third annual report the High Authority claimed— was it apologetically?—that the interpenetration of markets (which they illustrated by picturesque diagrams) 'has not harmed the trade with third countries'. How could they tell? It was not an unambiguous remark. Certainly the Community countries' imports of steel from third countries more than doubled between 1952 and 1957, from 452,000 to 1,077,000 tons. Like the 'interpenetrations' this reflected the expansiveness of the economies. A high proportion of the imports were of 'semis'. Would more have come from third countries if there were no Community preference? In most years the United Kingdom had little 'surplus', and United States steel was dear. Exports to third countries grew, quantitatively, much more than imports from them, from 5,955,000 tons in 1952 to 9,122,000 tons in 1957. This outdistanced exports from the United Kingdom and the United States.[1] Of course, if the Community organisation was already giving the member countries more of each others' business it must have been at the expense of third countries,[2] and might be expected to increase the Community steelmakers' export strength. It is, however, sterile to speculate further about these trade statistics. How far did the High Authority succeed in progressively making the market more common, establishing the free, fair—orderly—competition envisaged in the treaty? The following sections, which deal with

[1] A further gain came in 1959. Since the Community did not count tubes among steel products these figures do not match others which include these.

[2] This would not have been so in absolute terms if the existence of the Community appreciably increased economic activity; but I think no one would claim this for it in these years. Even so the Community steelmakers would be expected to make a *relative* gain.

this, fall into two groups. The first group, dealing with policy in transport, scrap and labour, covers what may be regarded as two complements to the removal of tariffs and quotas—namely, steps to remove national discriminations in transport charges and national barriers to the movement of labour—and the most notable instance where the Community prevented the removal of restrictions exerting its normal competitive influence. The second group covers the central problems—policy on prices, on cartels and amalgamations, and on investment. These are followed by an account of the relations between the Community and the British industry.

(c) Transport

In respect of transport the High Authority made progress faster than was expected in removing discriminations. They could point out in retrospect that what happened was no more than was prescribed in the treaty; but action depended on inter-government agreement and this was secured on some points sooner than first seemed likely. Its effect was already by 1955–56 on the grand scale with regard to rail rates, where 'direct international tariffs' were introduced for coal, coke and ore early in 1955 and for iron and steel and scrap in May 1956. As a result the specially heavy costs involved in crossing frontiers were eliminated.[1] The scope of these changes was widened in

---

[1] For the details, *3ème Rap. Gén.* vol. III, pp. 3 sqq. The reductions were achieved by dropping the fiction that a journey across a frontier was two journeys, including two sets of terminal charges and losing the advantage of falling rates per ton for long distances. There were also specific national discriminations which were removed. Examples of the changes (which at this date applied to coal, coke and ore only) showing progressive reductions at various stages were (the figures were all given in French francs):

	Original rate	Early 1955	May 1955	May 1956
Coke: Gelsenkirchen to Homécourt (whole trains of 950 tons)	2331	1992	1694	1599
Lusterade (Holl.)–Thionville (whole trains of 880 tons)	2018	1660	1488	1316
Coking coal: Alsdorf (Ruhr)–Saar (whole trains of 900 tons)	2157	1959	1688	1539
Iron ore: Sancy (Lorraine)–Ougrée (Liège) (1130 ton train daily)	850	784	674	606
Luxembourg–Duisburg	1243	1067	973	912

1957 by agreements with Switzerland and Austria.[1] The High Authority also had removed many discriminations within member countries for particular works and areas by 1957.[2] There remained striking differences in the general level of railway rates on different products in the six countries, and in their rates of 'degression'.

The High Authority hoped to 'harmonise' these; but great obstacles were met. The new British method of fixing charges on the railways which allowed unpublished contracts, and relied on competition of road, rail (and water) was unacceptable to the High Authority—it seemed anarchic. The extent of the differences which arose with unharmonised rail rates was emphasised by the Belgian steelmakers,[3] who have vigorously pushed the case for a liberal régime of competition between different forms of transport. So far the efforts to bring road and water transport into some system of harmonisation have met with great obstacles, and such agreements as there are have probably had little or no impact on charges. The impression in 1958 was that further advance on transport matters might be made mainly through the new European Economic Community.

(d) Uncommon market for scrap

If the High Authority's taste for a market economy was limited in regard to transport it was still more so in regard to scrap. In this field they were drawn at once to restrict the effect of the opening of the market in 1953. Increases in the price of scrap due to scarcity acquired an air of impropriety in an age accustomed to assessing 'right prices' in terms of 'reasonable returns' to resources employed. Scrap prices could never be properly geared to average costs of production. High prices could only increase supplies a little at best. The total supply was determined irrevocably by the amount of steel used in the

---

[1] *6th Gen. Rep. E.C.S.C.* vol. II, p. 76. [2] *Ibid.* pp. 79 sqq.

[3] Cp. *Groupement des Hauts-Fourneaux et Aciéries Belges, Rapport Annuel*, 1957, pp. 42–3. Thus for carriage of iron ore within France for 235 kilometres the rate was 61 Belgian francs, but from France to Belgium it was 84·75 francs, in the same conditions (for example, one whole train of 1320 tons, in 60 wagons, a day). The whole Belgian discussion is of extreme interest.

past. High prices for all scrap could therefore never be right, the argument ran, except for extortionate speculators.

The creators of the Common Market in coal and steel, it quickly became clear, were imbued with this attitude. They looked at the steel industry and assessed not its demand for scrap but its 'needs' or 'requirements'. It was the outlook and terminology implanted by wartime and post-war allocations, not disturbed by the Common Market idea. 'The High Authority drew up a balance-sheet showing availabilities and requirements of scrap. This revealed, for the Community as a whole, a deficit of 500,000–600,000 metric tons, which under normal conditions could be considered as a constant figure and mainly represented the requirements of Italy.' It was only a small deficit, about 6 per cent of the total of 'bought scrap' used in the Community. 'But as world prices were much higher than the average prices in the Community, and likely to remain so—because world scrap collection at present largely corresponds to the steel consumption of 15–20 years ago and is thus catching up with world steel production only after a certain delay—this marginal requirement of the Community was destined to become a disturbing feature, forcing prices upwards.' Whether steel-makers might be 'requiring' the impossible, as the terms of this race to 'catch up' implied, the High Authority did not at first pause to inquire; nor did they explain how it was that Europe's average scrap price was below the world price (or what in the circumstances a 'world price' was), although Europe had to import from the world. Indeed, it might even have been supposed there was a European price, whereas, as has been seen earlier,[1] there were different national prices, not kept as low as the British price, but not free, all reflecting local circumstances and local price controls and restrictions on export. The national industries wished to be insulated against anything which would raise their scrap price nearer to the world price. The 'danger was especially acute in view of the peculiar situation of Italy, three-quarters of whose iron and steel industry is based on scrap, which might well cause an

---

[1] Above, p. 356, n. 2. The High Authority did subsequently speak of the 'national markets' as having been 'subject to very different systems'.

excessive price increase on the common market if she tried to procure from the latter the additional tonnage she needed'.[1] Put in other words, Italy, before the Community was formed, had to import scrap and pay world prices. It would be an advantage to her to buy within the Community where prices had been kept lower as a result of price controls and bans on export. The effect of such buying would be to raise prices in other Community countries nearer to the level, for example, in the United States. 'It was necessary to avoid the violent disturbances' which Italy's deficit might cause. So the High Authority 'felt that it should encourage consumers in the Community to cover the deficit by imports at the common expense from third countries'.

A voluntary scheme[2] was introduced whereby imports of scrap into the Community were made at the common expense, the cost to be borne by steelmakers in proportion to their use of scrap.[3] It was to be a premium 'to ensure that each (steelmaker) would obtain supplies at reasonable and comparable prices, in a market where there were to be no more periodic upheavals of the proportions customary in the past'.[4] And just to make sure, a maximum price was fixed for scrap in the common market, and Governments of member countries were recommended to 'control' the export of scrap to third countries (for unless scrap exports were banned how could a maximum price, which was only useful if it was below the price outside, be imposed?).

So the common market in scrap, which opened in February 1953, was by March, as it seemed, securely stabilised. The probability that Italy would buy more scrap within the Community was borne out; she bought considerably more mainly from France and Germany, and reduced her imports from third countries.[5] This did not push prices up; the initial

[1] *2nd Gen. Rep.* vol. III, pp. 2, 20.
[2] 'The principle of this mutual insurance was accepted by almost all...on the basis of voluntary association' (E.C.S.C. *2nd Gen. Rep.* p. 101).
[3] Their use of all types of bought scrap, whether bought in the Community or bought outside. The payments covered the excess of the cost of the imports over the price of scrap in the Community countries.   [4] *Ibid. loc. cit.*
[5] Inter-community countries trade in scrap rose from 36,000 tons per month in 1952 to 60,000 tons per month in the 2nd and 3rd quarter of 1953 and 160,000 tons per month in the 4th quarter of 1954 (*2nd Ann. Rep.* vol. III, pp. 1, 15, § 46).

maximum fixed was \$36 per ton (almost £13), a relatively high figure compared with controlled prices, though low compared with the United States price at the same date.[1] It proved possible to reduce it by two stages to \$30 in January 1954, and under pressure from scrap merchants[2] it was abandoned in April 1954 when the price in general was about \$26.[3] The compensation scheme (or 'péréquation') on imports was to be sufficient control. During this fall in scrap prices the industry in Italy was particularly helped and was able to reduce its prices.

The High Authority recognised that a fall in demand for steel and a rise in world ore supplies, and not its operations alone, hastened the fall in the scrap price. 'Equilibrium had been restored...between requirements and supplies of scrap.' But they certainly attributed much to their compensation scheme, and reckoned that its cost was equal to an increase in the average scrap price for all users of less than \$2 per ton.[4]

The cost was not in practice spread over quite all users however,[5] because of the 'voluntary' principle, which the High Authority decided in 1954 to replace by compulsion against the wishes of some German and Benelux steelmakers. Compulsion was resorted to because some firms had delayed in taking 'necessary decisions'. 'The common market for scrap' then had 'the maximum freedom compatible...with the desire to keep it in that state of stability at which it has now arrived'.[6]

There was not the remotest hint that the forecasters foresaw the impending rise of demand which in the second half of 1954 rudely undermined this 'state of stability'. Within four months the standard price had risen to \$32 per ton and by January 1955 it was \$38, and some was bought, exceptionally, in France at \$44 and \$48. This was so near the 'world price' as to make all special arrangements seem of little value, particularly in France.

---

[1] The price in Holland, the lowest, was then \$22; the price in Italy \$55. The fixed price was at merchants' yards; delivery costs added about \$2 (cp. 3ème Rap. Gén. § 88).

[2] 'Among consumers there were some who supported this' (ibid. vol. III, p. 2, §81).

[3] Bulletin of the E.C.S.C. Feb. Mar. 1955, p. 6.

[4] The figure given was less than 5 per cent of the first maximum price, for example less than 5 per cent of \$36 (2nd Ann. Rep. vol. III, pp. 2, 21 (§81)).

[5] I understand that the exceptions were of minor importance.

[6] 2nd Ann. Rep. vol. III, pp. 2, 24, § 86.

Again the High Authority pondered what it should do to re-establish stability. This time it was not so easy. They prolonged the 'péréquation' arrangements for buying imports for a further three months, and there was an increase of imports, so that the High Authority argued there was no shortage of scrap, and that equilibrium was being maintained at least as late as the spring of 1955.[1] The price rise was thus treated as largely speculative.[2] It was perhaps encouraged unintentionally by the maintenance for some time of the selling price of imported scrap at $30 per ton, because buyers who could get some scrap so cheaply would then more readily buy other supplies at high prices.

The divergent interests of member countries now came into the open. The French felt that purchasers from other Community countries, especially Italy and Germany, were pushing up the price of scrap in France. The French Government therefore suggested that the situation should be declared a state of scarcity which required allocations, and they objected to a continuation of the collective purchase of imports in its existing form as it was most helpful to those making a large proportion of open-hearth steel. These enjoyed the greatest scope for using more of the scrap which was kept cheap by collective action. The scheme was thus of most value to Germans and Italians whose Governments announced in their turn that they were hardly prepared to continue the 'péréquation' system if there were allocations. The High Authority (as a result, they said, of a profound study) discovered the obvious, that if steelmakers want more raw materials to expand output, they must in the long run make more pig iron. Strangely they had to learn the hard way, despite Britain's warning experience. They decided, as the British had, to find a mechanism which would 'compensate' for the discouragement to the users of pig iron created by the 'divergence between the prices of scrap and pig iron'. The policies of keeping scrap prices down and encouraging scrap imports must be prevented from leading to an 'unconsidered' expansion in the use of scrap. Hence the High Authority must set against the financial advantage they gave to scrap users some counterbalancing advantage to users of pig iron. If the market

[1] 3ème Rap. Gén. ch. III, pp. 1, 30, § 83.   [2] Ibid. § 87.

had been left alone this would of course have been unnecessary, but they regarded this as the 'worst' course.[1] They had created for themselves the same problem as the British, and they proceeded to look for the same kind of solution.

Among the principles which guided them, as they now said, in their scrap price policy was this: 'the cost of scrap for steelmakers...should not rise above a level reasonable by comparison with that paid by steelmakers in the chief competing countries'.[2] Which countries—Britain or the United States? The Germans had complained of Britain's policy over scrap prices vigorously in 1953 as a subsidy on exports at the time when the mutual elimination of all such subsidies was being discussed;[3] it was not a policy whose immediate advantage could be enjoyed in perpetuity. Less rationally it was objected that scrap prices would naturally move more violently than in America because America supplied E.C.S.C.'s marginal scrap.

So the Community continued 'péréquation' for imported scrap ('it was the keystone of the arch'), on a compulsory, not a voluntary basis; and set out while lowering the scrap price to encourage at the same time expansion of the production of pig iron for open-hearth steelmaking by a complicated scheme whereby bonuses were paid to open-hearth steelmakers who increased the proportion of pig iron and lowered the percentage of scrap which they used for their steel. It was only because the price of scrap was kept artificially low that this was necessary. Nothing could show more forcibly how remote the Community had become from reliance on the market in handling questions of raw-material supplies.[4]

---

[1] *3ème Rap. Gén.* ch. III, pp. 2, 12.   [2] *Ibid. loc. cit.*

[3] The British official attitude, as I understood it, was that it was impossible to try and deal with all such sources of inequality—you must concentrate on removing straightforward Government interventions by way of tax policy. This looked singularly like skilful 'evasive action'.

[4] The text of the High Authority's decision on the bonus scheme in its first form was published in the *Journal Officiel*, 26 July 1955, p. 869. The restriction of the bonus on the greater use of pig iron to the open-hearth process was specifically explained as due to the need for technical advances before this greater use could be advanced in other processes. Presumably this referred to electric furnaces. The use of oxygen in the Thomas process was opening up the scope for more use of scrap in this process.

But the High Authority refused to fix a maximum price again for scrap. They appeared anxious now to maintain a competitive market internally, keeping the price stable by the volume of imports, but not keeping the price, on their estimate, low. Low prices such as there had been in Britain they thought undesirable.[1] They demonstrated their desire for competition as they announced their pig-iron bonuses by refusing permission to German steelmakers to buy their scrap through a central agency on a quota basis. The Germans were told brusquely to break it up.[2]

The High Authority hoped that their bonus would have an immediate as well as an ultimate effect, bringing into use existing unused blast-furnace capacity. But increased scrap imports were still sought. Imports rose from 500,000 tons in 1953 to 750,000 tons in 1954, and by the end of 1954 were at a rate of 2 m. tons. By mid-1955 the aim was to get 3 m. tons a year. It must come mainly from America. But here too home demand was rising exceptionally; and domestic users succeeded in impressing on their Government that scrap was a strategic material, whose export should still therefore be subject to restriction. European purchasing became thus a matter of Government negotiation. After a 'profound study' (the High Authority never act without this) of the internal needs of the United States and of other countries' demands, an agreement was reached early in 1957. By the end of the year the upper limit of purchases was lifted by the United States; the market had become weak, and within a few months this 'act of liberalisation' was extended to the end of 1958.

While the negotiations in the United States were taking place the levy policy moved a stage further. Instead of the levy being at a standard rate it was to be raised in future at a discriminatingly higher rate for any consumer who 'consumed larger tonnages of scrap, made the deficit worse, and obliged the Community to import more'.[3] Steelmakers in France, Germany, Belgium

---

[1] *6ème Rap. Gén. E.C.S.C.* vol. 1, pp. 4–9.

[2] *Journal Officiel*, 26 July 1955. The object presumably was to buy more cheaply. The collective organisation could buy outside Germany, if need be pushing up the price, while keeping it down in Germany. The French were complaining that in Germany scrap was cheaper than in France; the Germans bought more in Holland.

[3] *5th Gen. Rep.* April 1957, p. 96.

and Italy challenged the legality of this. The Belgians, believing in a market economy, were scathing critics of the High Authority, who by 'keeping the price of scrap abnormally low' provoked an increase in demand for scrap which 'bore no relation to supply'.[1] Because of their concentration on Thomas steel they naturally disapproved of anything which artificially cheapened scrap in relation to pig iron. The great gainers from the arrangements were in fact the Italians. Yet ironically it was only the Italian firm among those who protested against the new policy who won their case before the courts. The others protested on grounds of substance; the Italian firm claimed that the High Authority wrongly delegated their powers to an agency, and by its methods introduced long periods of uncertainty over costs which made proper pricing impossible. This was upheld by the Community Court, but not until July 1958. The substance of the policy, the practice of discriminations—which in effect implied that any new use of scrap must in some sense be worse than any existing use—was upheld.[2] But by this time the situation had utterly changed; raw materials were plentiful, scrap prices had fallen,[3] and there was vacant blast-furnace capacity. So the whole scrap policy was changed again. In November 1958 the High Authority proposed that the 'péréquation' arrangements over scrap should stop; but although ultimately the High Authority visualised a free market for scrap, they still wanted to manage the market for the time being to establish 'structural equilibrium'. They proposed therefore retaining powers to institute 'péréquation' machinery whenever blast-furnace capacity was occupied to the full; but for the time being they proposed to retain bonuses for increased use of pig iron. This would ensure that unused capacity 'at home' was used before scrap was imported, and would help

---

[1] *Rap. Ann. Groupement des Hauts-Fourneaux Belges*, 1957, p. 36.

[2] The successful case brought by the Italian firm Meroni is reported in the *Journal Officiel des Communautés Européennes* for 17 July 1958. Other cases were reported in *ibid.* 17 July, etc. The High Authority argued it was acting in the interest of the whole against a 'structural weakness'. Some interests must suffer; for example, the Ugine works which needed more scrap for new ferro-chrome furnaces, planned in 1955, which could not use pig iron, but only scrap.

[3] The price was $34 in Dec. 1958; it rose in 1959 to $44. *8th Gen. Rep.* Graph 2.

to absorb the mounting stocks of coal. The High Authority thus did not contemplate taking the risk of relying on the market yet. But the Council of Ministers did not unanimously agree on this programme of transition to freedom. They chose freedom at once with no future commitment. All the machinery of 'péréquation' was ended.

(e) Labour cards—and development areas

The High Authority succeeded in working out provisions according to which, in keeping with the treaty, member Governments would allow free movement over their frontiers of qualified workers in the coal and steel industries. The basic principle, incorporated in the treaty, was that such freedom should only be allowed to skilled workers; the theoretic basis of this restriction is indeed hard to find, except that without such a restriction the freedom of movement could not be limited in practice to the two industries. The approved qualified workers would have a labour card giving freedom of movement.

During the first year when the system of cards operated (September 1957 to September 1958) only 258 cards were issued, nearly one-half in Italy, and only thirty-five to workers in the steel industry. No jobs were offered in steelworks however to holders of labour cards. Indeed, only twenty-eight workers with a Community's labour card got a job through the Labour Officers set up under the scheme or directly, and none of these was in the steel industry. They were miners. The High Authority in its report explained why so little happened. In the frontier areas there were other existing arrangements whereby men on one side of the frontier got jobs on the other side; in Benelux there was already freedom of movement; skilled workers are not those most likely to be unemployed; and this year in particular was one of mounting difficulties in all the countries so that none was short of labour.

Meantime the High Authority did a lot of work establishing just how much labour cost in the different member countries— finding out how much must be added to wages on account of bonuses, social charges, paid holidays, free or cheap housing, other payments in kind, and the costs of recruitment.

The result for 1953, with approximate changes to 1958, is given in Table 50.

Table 50. *Costs of wages and associated payments in steelmaking*[a]
(*average per hour*)

Currency	Basic wages 1953	Total cost 1953	Total in dollars		
			1953	1956	1958
Luxembourg (B.f.)	32·07	47·56	0·95	1·15	1·32
Belgium (B.f.)	30·36	40·29	0·81	0·99	1·10
Saar (F.f.)	162·82	261·33	0·75	0·99	1·11[b]
Germany (M.)	2·05	3·06	0·73	0·91	1·06
France (F.f.)	134·15	255·10	0·73	0·96	0·99[b]
Italy (lire)	226·90	408·05	0·65	0·77	0·86
Holland (florins)	1·50	2·18	0·57	0·82	0·94

[a] *3ème Rap. Gén.* ch. v, pp. 16–17. The last column is based on a table in the *7ème Rap. Gén.* vol. II, p. 225.

[b] The Saar and French averages in dollars reflect the result of the devaluation of the French franc in Oct. 1957: for 1953 and 1956 the exchange rate was 350 francs = 1 dollar, for 1958 420 francs = 1 dollar.

This was not necessarily a complete basis of comparison. If gross earnings, including 'fringe' and 'social' benefits, are equal in two countries but are paid for in one country partly out of general taxation, in the other as additions to wages, the total cost to the Community must be broadly the same; what significance should be attached to differences in methods of payment? Did it warrant any 'adjustment' to make trade in the Common Market 'fair'?

This did not become a practical issue, but the view seemed to gain ground that it was of minor importance. When the cost of social services was largely covered by general taxation, as in Great Britain, a great part of it was spread in effect over all industries in proportion to their profit (one might almost say to their turnover). Hence industries with high labour cost, like coal-mining, were less burdened under such a system than where the costs were specifically related to wages and paid by employers as a proportion of their wage bills. This was therefore a situation where the tax system introduced a distortion, but it was one of several types of distortion which might, it was agreed, be to some extent mutually compensatory. The discussion then became much more sophisticated than it seemed when the idea of the Community was first broached.

Elaborate studies were also made of the comparative value of earnings of steelworkers to the recipients in different parts of the Community, as a complement to the studies of the comparative cost of labour. The High Authority found the differences in real income, in so far as any measure was possible, less they said, than they expected—less, they thought, than variations between incomes in different industries in one country. They were nonetheless wide. The general indication of their provisional results—to call it more would be inaccurate—is given in Table 51.

Table 51. *Indices of real incomes, European countries, 1953*

	A Married man without children	B Married man with two children	Real income B as % of real income A
Luxembourg	100	100	119
Belgium	85	82	116
Germany	71	66	108
Saar	71	69	114
Holland	70	67	113
Italy	59	68	115
France	66	75	133

These figures (like those in the preceding table) mark a striking change in the position of the Belgian and Luxembourg workers from their pre-war position when they were the lowest paid.[1] They also show the differentiating influence of the high rate of family allowance in France. It was of interest, as some High Authority experts pointed out, that the highest real incomes, as well as the most expensive labour, were found where the additions to basic wages were in proportion the smallest.[2]

The High Authority said the differences which these tables showed had already been lessened by increases in the lower wages by the time the analyses were published. At the end of

[1] See *E.H.S.* p. 422.   [2] See Table 50.

1958 the differences were still wide, though some of the proportions, as Table 50 showed, had changed. The Saar had caught up Belgium, France had gone ahead of Germany but had not caught up Belgium, Holland had gone ahead of Italy—and the cost of labour in Italy was proportionately more below that in Luxembourg than in 1953. The High Authority identified two trends—lower earnings in 1953 moved up towards the 'leader' (sic) of 1953—but the steelworkers in the 'leader' succeeded in doing still better for themselves.[1] This was an unduly elaborate presentation of the obvious. Whether the existence of the Community greatly affected the changes is doubtful. The elaborate comparisons may have had some effect on negotiations; but local conditions probably had more. The labour history of the 'Six' in these years, as the E.C.S.C. reports show, was extremely complex, in changes of hours and conditions of work as well as wages and state social benefits (which naturally were normally only changed for *all* industries in one country). Coal-mining wages and conditions were pushed up in several of the countries by difficulties in attracting labour, and the same affected steel a little.[2] This is perhaps why coal and steelworkers' wages moved up more in Germany than other wages; in France they moved more than the average, but in company with many other industrial jobs. So, too, in Belgium and Italy.[3] There was relatively little movement of labour between the various countries, except the traditional movement from Italy to Belgium and France.[4]

The achievements with most immediate practical results which the High Authority could point to on the 'labour front' were with 'development area' problems. These were steps which no doubt checked movement of labour. Reorganisation of the highly inefficient high-grade steelworks of the Loire, whose character is described later, made some steelworkers redundant but created alternative occupations requiring new training. This 'readaptation' was undertaken jointly by the French Government and the High Authority. Again, the High

---

[1] *Informations Statistiques*, Mai/Juin 1958, p. 146.
[2] *5th Gen. Rep. E.C.S.C.* (Apr. 1957), p. 184.
[3] *Informations Statistiques*, Nov./Dec. 1957.   [4] *Ibid.* Mai/June 1958.

Authority decided to assist the Italian Government in providing new industrial developments to absorb some of the labour
which became redundant as the Italian steelworks were
modernised. There have been one or two other instances, in
France, of help where modernisation or partial closure caused
unemployment. The Community was drawn into more far-
reaching action on these matters over coal. Its expenditures all
told on readaptation were, however, relatively small, $4·5 m.
in 1956–57 (nothing earlier); and of this $4·1 m. in Italy, the
rest in France.[1]

(f) Prices in and out of the Common Market

The provisions in the treaty about prices[2] lay at the heart of
the new system. When the frontier barriers were lifted in May
1953 the firms had to publish their price lists and abide by the
new rules. It was not wholly to their liking.

As if to underline the conflicts of opinion within the Community the French, Belgian and Luxembourg steelmakers had
signed the Convention of Brussels two months earlier whereby
they jointly fixed their export prices. They were joined by the
Germans and Dutch in September.[3] These had all decided that
after all it was possible, and legal, to revive an international
cartel in part—for export trade only, as in the pre-war model,
and outside the Community organisation. Austria in time joined
the Convention, which thus went over the Community borders.

The immediate motive came from the price fall in export
markets which began in mid-1952,[4] after the Korea stimulus
had tailed off. The new 'cartel', which as far as possible kept
out of the public eye, fixed export prices but not quotas. Indeed,
some of its members were opposed to quotas. Its headquarters
were in Brussels, and it appointed the same Swiss firm to inspect

---

[1] *E.C.S.C. Financial Report for 1957*, p. 22. This sum did not include the money
given to meet losses in the Belgian coal industry raised by levies on the coalmines
whose costs were below the average in the Community. The levies were paid by
German and Netherlands mines until the latter part of 1958. As seen above, the
Belgian Government also subsidised Belgian mines.

[2] Above, p. 412.

[3] Henri Rieben, *Des Ententes de Maîtres de Forges au Plan Schuman*, 1954,
pp. 475 sqq.   [4] Above, p. 154.

the works records, and ensure that members kept the rules, as the E.I.A. used before the war. The formation of an international export cartel was based on national associations, and the German industry set up a special Rolled-steel Export Association (Walzstahl Ausfuhrgemeinschaft—W.A.G.).[1]

Was it a challenge to the High Authority? The High Authority was inclined to think it was, and there were other disturbing manifestations both of association activity and of highly individualist activity in regard to home prices.

Firms, for example, discussed their price schedules in national trade associations before publishing them, and there was such a degree of uniformity in some of the base prices fixed for basic Bessemer steels that some international discussions must almost certainly have taken place. Though in Germany the former basing points were retained—there was in general one basing point only for each product—the number in France was increased. In Belgium and Luxembourg this could not be so, since home prices in the Belgo-Luxembourg Economic Union had been uniform to all buyers at the point of consumption (on the British model of 'uniform delivered price', but more rigidly than in the more recent British practice); they had to introduce basing points, and did not welcome it.

The maintenance of trade association price agreements could be regarded as a natural outcome of post-war official price-fixing.[2] Though formally Government price-fixing had ceased in Germany before May 1953,[3] it had been normal for the Governments to fix or influence the fixing of coal and steel prices in all member countries. The habit and machinery of price agreement had acquired an official *cachet*. Even so it was to be expected that some adaptation in national price levels would occur, that they would be assimilated into a more unified pattern, and initially this seemed to begin to happen. Would it continue, so that the common market was really unified in its price structure?

---

[1] Rieben, *op. cit.* p. 477.   [2] *Stat. Bull.* Nov. 1953, pp. 5–7.

[3] *Ibid. loc. cit.* The article refers to certain price changes after the formal removal of Government control as 'the result of Government intervention'. It was known that this pressure was continued.

The B.I.S.F. reflected the expectation that it would in an examination of the system in the autumn of 1953. The 'natural result' of the system should be 'the establishment of a number of localised spheres of influence served by individual producers, each enjoying a local monopoly, but each forced to keep his prices within bounds through fear of losing customers to a more competitive neighbour. The spheres of influence would be determined largely by production costs on the one hand and the choice of basing points on the other.' It was a curious comment in one respect, since the nature of the system in its basic form (on which the B.I.S.F. comment was passed) was calculated to limit the effect of local monopoly, not to emphasise it, whereas the British system, by averaging transport costs for a wide area, virtually gave the effect of local monopoly an official status.

At the beginning it looked as though price competition would tend to unify the market, or at least to give the market an appearance of unity in its price structure. Although it was said steel users showed every inclination to buy from their former suppliers, they pressed these to align their prices to any lower price offered from other basing points. Sellers, however, were prepared to do better than their quoted prices implied; probably all firms reduced prices below their list prices without revising their lists in the latter part of 1953, when demand was shrinking.[1] There was thus not only association price-fixing but universal price-cutting, and this price-cutting was accompanied by discrimination by individual firms between different groups of customers. This practice was advocated, as the B.I.S.F. said, by some Community firms who held that competition should be uninhibited by rules. Every sale should be considered in isolation, and producers should adjust their prices to the circumstances of individual bargains. It was the policy adopted in the Transport Act of 1953 for British Railways, but it was not

[1] The High Authority in its *2nd Gen. Rep.* sect. III, pp. 2, 16, 74 sqq., explained that most firms raised their prices at the start of the Common Market in May 1953 though business was falling off. 'Thus there arose a situation in which price schedules were maintained while the prices actually charged were considerably below the published prices, although there were admittedly great differences from one country or product to another.'

within the terms of the treaty. The High Authority found itself, however, under pressure from firms to devise some more flexible formula which, while not necessarily allowing unrestricted competition, would allow competition to have some 'bite'. The High Authority was probably looking for competition to be expressed primarily in changes in price schedules; the firms appeared more concerned over the possibility of competing in individual negotiations, and of making changes quickly in response to the market.

Early in 1954, while the markets were still weak, the High Authority decided that firms should be allowed to raise or lower their prices within limits of an average of $2\frac{1}{2}$ per cent in any consecutive period of 60 days above or below their published lists, without publishing new lists, subject to the proviso that all buyers were treated alike. Once prices were raised or lowered more than this allowed, amended price lists must be issued.[1] The High Authority also now started 'policing' the market, making spot checks of the books of firms lest the price provisions were being broken. The immediate effect of the new decisions was a reduction in the scheduled prices; most firms also immediately conceded the $2\frac{1}{2}$ per cent which they were allowed to cut off their prices before issuing further new lists.[2] But the economic situation rapidly changed in 1954, demand quickened, the prospect of excessive cuts receded and a risk of excessively high prices took its place. Some lists were raised, and firms instead of charging $2\frac{1}{2}$ per cent below their lists began to charge $2\frac{1}{2}$ per cent above.

By this time the legality of the High Authority's action in permitting firms to depart, upwards or downwards, within the average $2\frac{1}{2}$ per cent limit from their published prices lists, provided this was done without discrimination for all buyers within any period of 60 days, was challenged by the French and Italian

---

[1] The arrangement was not too easy to grasp. Apparently it was permitted to raise or lower prices by *more* than $2\frac{1}{2}$ per cent within a period of 60 days if this was not done for the whole of the 60 days. Thus if the volume of sales remained constant per day, prices might be reduced by 3 per cent for 30 days, but this had to be offset by a lessened reduction in a consecutive 30 days, when the average must not exceed 2 per cent.

[2] 2nd Gen. Rep. loc. cit.

Governments. The Community's Court, called into action for the first time, decided in favour of the Governments, and the High Authority's decree was annulled. Price-list prices must remain inviolate, subject to the provision allowing firms to 'meet' prices based on other basing points, and to meet prices of imports. And as if to underline their own intention that rules should be kept the High Authority fined two firms, one of them Belgian, for disregarding them, and warned four others.[1]

The course of *published* prices during the period in which these discussions were taking place, reduced to a uniform currency, dollars, is illustrated in Table 52, which carries the story to 1958. It is impossible to give figures showing the course of prices charged and realised at works, because though these certainly diverged from list prices no statistics of realised prices are available.

The relations of quoted prices for Thomas steel merchant bars and plates during the boom years, it will be seen, remained fairly constant, with Belgian prices rising sharply and remaining above the French and German; these rose, but much more gently and not so much—like prices whose increases are governed by cost increases—until in October 1957 the French price dropped in dollar equivalent, an outcome of devaluation. This, amounting to 20 per cent, was offset partly, but not wholly, by price increases in the domestic currency.[2] German prices for steel rose again in November 1957 by 4–5 per cent. Yet it was now into France that steel was flowing increasingly. Belgian prices in the Community reached their highest point in May 1957. They fell sharply in March 1958, by 7 per cent, so that they

---

[1] *E.C.S.C. 3ème Rap. Gén.* ch. III, pp. 2, 10, 112–13. It is not clear whether they were fined or warned for charging discriminating prices above or below their list prices. The same firms would be expected to do both; at the time of the *announcement* the likelihood would be that some prices charged were in excess of their published lists. Later proceedings against other firms are described in the *6ème Rap. Gén.* vol. II, pp. 60–1, where the general nature of the rules disregarded are given.

[2] French prices in francs for merchant bars (B.B.) were:

	francs
10 Sept. 1956	31,500
18 Apr. 1957	32,450
5 Aug. 1957	33,910
8 Nov. 1957	36,410

Table 52. Base prices of representative products in E.C.S.C. countries, 1953–59[a]
(all prices in dollars, less turnover taxes)[b]

Product	Country[c]	Basic Bessemer (Thomas)									Open-hearth (Siemens Martin)				
		May 1953	Feb. 1954	Jan. 1955	June 1955	Mar. 1956	Mar. 1957	Jan. 1958	Oct. 1958	Jan. 1959	May 1953	June 1955	Jan. 1958	Oct. 1958	Jan. 1959
Merchant bars	Germany	92·1	87·5	87·5	89·6	89·6	95·2	99·2	99·2	96·45–99·20	96·2	96·5	109·0	109·1	109·0
	Belgium	91·5	85·5	92·0	99·0	103·0	110·0	98·0	90·0–102·0[d]	90·0–102·0	106·6	116·0	132·0	100·0–117·0	100·0–117·0
	France	90·3	86·1	86·1	86·1	86·2	90·0	86·7	86·7	82·4	98·9	100·3	104·4	104·4	95·2
	Luxembourg	90·5	85·0	87·1	95·0	101·0	106·0	103·0	100·0	100·0	—	—	—	—	—
	Holland	91·7	85·9	99·6	107·3	110·8	115·5	100·0	97·5	88·4	97·5	109·0	116·0	—	112·5
	Italy	—	—	—	—	—	—	—	—	—	123·2	121·6	108·0–126·0	108·8–121·6	96·0–121·6
Heavy plates	Germany	103·5	95·8	95·8	98·1	98·1	104·0	109·1	106·5	106·5	109·3	108·8	122·8	119·8	119·75
	Belgium	104·5	98·0	104·0	110·0	115·0	128·0	130·0	100·0–122·0[d]	100·0–122·0	124·5	126·0	142·0	112·0–138·0	112·0–138·0
	France	104·6	101·4	101·4	101·4	101·4	106·3	102·4	102·4	97·25	117·7	116·0	120·9	130·9	110·2
	Luxembourg	104·0	97·0	99·4	103·5	111·0	124·0	124·0	118·0	118·0	111·2	111·3	127·5	122·5	112·5
	Holland	106·1	94·8	97·9	101·3	101·2	115·0	115·0	110·0	100·0	140·8	139·2	171·2	152·0	152·0
	Italy	—	—	—	—	—	—	—	—	—	—	—	—	—	—
Wide strip in coils (not rolled)	Germany	115·4	112·7	105·1	107·7	112·1	117·5	121·3	116·0[e]	—	121·1	118·2	—	129·0	—
	Belgium	113·0	106·0	106·0	106·0	106·0	106·0	112·0	108·0	—	126·6	117·4	—	122·0	—
	France	116·3	104·3	106·9	106·9	106·9	111·1	105·7	107·0	—	—	—	—	121·0	—
	Luxembourg	110·0	103·0	113·0	103·0	103·0	105·0	110·0	108·0	—	—	—	—	—	—
	Holland	—	—	—	—	—	—	—	—	—	125·1	129·1	—	125·0	—
	Italy	—	—	—	—	—	—	—	—	—	139·2	134·4	—	132·8	—

[a] Based on figures in *Informations Statistiques*, published by E.C.S.C., and tables in succeeding General Reports, plus circularised data for Oct. 1958.

[b] The deductions are 4 per cent from German prices, 4 per cent from Dutch prices in 1953–54, 9 per cent in 1955, 5 per cent in 1956–58.

[c] The relevant basing points except for Oct. 1958 were: Germany: Oberhausen, Essen, Oberhausen; Belgium: Seraing or Charleroi; France: Thionville, Montmedy; Luxembourg: Luxembourg; Holland: Utrecht, Velsen; Italy: Novi Ligure. In Oct. 1958 the Belgian figures appear as a range because they differed for different basing points (see text). The lowest figure was Clabecq, the highest for Cockeril-Ougree.

[d] See note c.

[e] These were November figures, published after Dutch prices had been reduced by 5 per cent.

were broadly the same as the German for merchant bars, but still significantly above for plates. In both countries prices were above French prices. In October 1958 another striking change occurred, for three Belgian works, excluding the Cockeril-Ougrée group, reduced their prices for plates, and one of them, Clabecq (with a history in price reductions), cut its price for merchant bars sharply. The total reduction during the year amounted to 20–25 per cent. These Belgian prices were now the lowest in the Community; they had dropped below the French. Cockeril-Ougrée presumably found themselves aligning their prices to those of their compatriots. It will be noticed from Table 52 there were minor adjustments in German prices between March and October 1958, whose significance is referred to later.

Two months later a further reduction in Dutch prices—there were several in 1958—brought their plate prices in line with the Belgian. The final word in 1958 rested, however, with the French; not that they reduced their prices, but devaluation again brought another sharp cut in their prices in the currencies of all other countries. These domestic prices were raised, in francs; the reduction in dollars is shown in Table 52.

The Belgian (and Luxembourg and Dutch) price movements had the characteristics of competitive market prices; they rose and fell with the state of demand. When Germans were buying more from them at a time of boom their base price rose, well above the German home price. When Germans were importing less and exporting more in the Community the Belgian home price fell, below the German level.

The unresponsiveness of prices to markets in Germany and France unmistakably pointed to 'artificial' stabilising forces. The French and German Governments, in fact, continued to exert influence in different ways, though formal Government price-fixing, whose object had been to keep prices low, ceased when the Common Market opened. But the French Government continued to peg the prices of goods made with steel, and Dr Erhard urged that low steel prices were a condition for freedom of other prices and a necessary anti-inflationary force, in the liberal economy. He could not always have his way *in toto*; and in 1957 when German prices *were* almost all raised, those of the Salzgitter works, still Government owned, were not. Since the object in France and Germany was to keep steel prices low, or at least to contain increases within narrow limits, the justification for changes was found in increased costs; hence the German and French home prices rose in recession when Belgian prices fell. At Community headquarters these Government interferences with prices were spoken of ruefully in the early years; at the end of the transitional period the High Authority in its sixth annual *Report* underlined the danger that investment for expansion might be checked and the disparities between different countries might distort the distribution of development between different sections of the industry in the Community (rightly or wrongly). Countries must needs, however, the High Authority conceded, be interested in the price of important commodities like coal and steel; the object of the treaty, they concluded, is to maintain through the Council of Ministers a harmony between policies of member states and the High Authority, so that these are mutually compatible and serve the objects of the Community.

But Government interference spelled association prices. In 1957 the clash between Watenstadt Salzgitter and the rest in Germany exemplified a lack of complete unity, though in odd circumstances. In June 1958 the other German firms announced that their differences with the state works were composed; uniform prices were announced. This the High Authority looked upon as collusion, and fired a little, possibly, by a recent examination which they had made of American anti-trust procedures they began to probe this as something beyond the pale of Community rules. Without naming the country—no doubt this was politic reticence—the seventh *Report* of the High Authority referred to the incident; an 'infraction' of the Treaty had been revealed when an important works raised its prices for certain products to the level charged by other firms, because at the same time for other products a uniform price level was restored by a different procedure. The firms whose prices had been high reduced them by half the difference, and the low-price firm (i.e. Salzgitter) raised its prices by the other half.

This could only have happened, the *Report* implied, as a result of collective agreement.

By the time this *Report* was written an immediately more disturbing question of harmony in policies of member states as this affected prices had become acute through French devaluation. French steel had become for the second time in little over a year much the cheapest, in dollar equivalent, not as a result of increased efficiency but through a currency change. Germany, with Professor Erhard in the van, protested. Competition within the Community should be based on efficiency. Yet it had been widely argued that France needed drastic financial reform, including devaluation, to restore her economic stability in the world. Nevertheless, it was proposed by the High Authority that an export tax of 4 per cent should be put on sales of French steel to other members of the Community, and only Holland in the Council of Ministers of the Six opposed this on the ground that the French financial reforms which caused the difficulty were obligatory and desirable. Would the French accept the decision of their fellow-member states? That the question could even be asked was significant. It seemed to be lost sight of when demand revived in 1959.

A competitive pattern is more easily discernible in regard to basic Bessemer merchant bars than for plates, or hot rolled coils, or for open-hearth steel. In Germany open-hearth steel was 5 per cent dearer than basic Bessemer in 1953, about 10 per cent in 1958; in Belgium the margin was steadily about 16 per cent, in France it rose from 10 to 20 per cent. At the end the French open-hearth price was very close to the German, but that had the appearance of chance rather than of competition. Prices for basic Bessemer plates were closer together in 1953–55 than in 1958; in open-hearth qualities they diverged at all dates. Prices of wide strip in coils were close together in 1953 and 1955 but not in 1958. Prices of cold rolled sheets rose relatively to other prices, a reflection presumably in part of the demand for motor-car sheets. The E.C.S.C. *Report* for 1958 set out to explain the contrast between the price pattern in the Community and in Britain and the United States in this respect. Strip mills were newer on the Continent; more sheet was still made on old mills; the new mills were not run fully because they had as yet too little steel capacity behind them, hence the steel firms spread their overheads over an output below their real capacity. Finally, it was pointed out that because the United States had so many mills of the type, this allowed more specialisation and cost reductions arising therefrom. The prices for these products in Community countries, motor-body sheets, electrolytic tin-plate, electrical sheets, fell in 1958 in reality when they did not in appearance, because foreign low quotations for import were increasingly being 'met'. This is referred to below in regard to international comparisons.

Italian prices were at most times for most products much higher than those of the others of the Six, but fell notably after spring 1957. Thus for merchant bars, made only in open-hearth steel, the price fell from \$132 to \$128 (September), \$124·10 (December) \$116·8 (February 1958), \$111·5 (May) and \$108·8 in October.[1] The fall was less for most other products, but still often substantial. Presumably with recession the effect of the final disappearance of duties was being felt, though the High Authority still did not give an unconditional *carte blanche* to all other Community steelmakers to align their prices on the Italian. When firms *did* so they were to declare their sales to the High Authority. This condition was soon dropped.[2]

In 1955 the High Authority claimed that the Community had lessened the fluctuation of prices as the Six had passed from near slump to near boom. This cannot be said to have resulted from the Authority's actions. It was true that when Governments kept prices stable in France and Germany the effect, hitherto domestic only, was shared in some degree by other member countries. The impact of national policies became wider and more irrational. That was an uncovenanted outcome of the common market, and at first was frowned upon by the High Authority because of its origin in national Governments.

[1] All prices from the *6ème Rap. Gén.* vol. II, p. 394, except the last figure—from *Bulletin Mensuel d'Information*, May–June 1958, p. 5. The reduction in May was by the chief producers only. The figure for Oct. 1958 was the lowest of a range; presumably this was nearest to the Thomas quality bar, and the higher figure of the range is now comparable with the other Continental open-hearth figures.

[2] *8ème Rap. Gén.* vol. V, p. 4. Sales at aligned prices were small: trade had improved.

Not that the Authority disapproved of stable prices; they joined with socialists, cartels and others in emphasising their importance, as a means of helping users to make forward plans on a solid basis.[1]

But for the Common Market the intra-Community transactions of 1955 might have taken place at the high export prices characteristic of boom, and imports might have been subject to import duties (though the German Government suspended import duties in 1952–53 just as the British Government did). The High Authority was inclined to claim that the new régime had damped down the fluctuations in export prices; but this was a dubious claim. The past price fluctuation which they had most in mind was possibly that of 1949–53, which they had set out in a special report on the common market at the time when duties were first removed. Export prices in France, Germany, Belgium and Luxembourg had certainly moved with some violence (Table 53).

Table 53. *Export prices for merchant bars,*[a] *1949–53*
(*$ per ton*)

July 1949	96	Jan. 1952	140
Dec. 1949	58	June 1952	110
June 1950	53	Dec. 1952	100
Dec. 1950	120	Feb. 1953	82[b]
June 1951	150	Apr. 1953	84[c]

[a] *Establishment of the Common Market (Special Report)*, May 1953, p. 7.
[b] Some contracts at 72.   [c] Agreed price.

These were prices at a period of great disturbance. First, German exporters advanced when markets as a whole were shrinking, which caused a sharp contraction of French, Belgian and Luxembourg business, and a price collapse. Then war broke out in Korea, with an immense expansion of demand, with exceptional import markets in the United States and (for special temporary reasons) in the United Kingdom too. But the price collapse of 1949–50 had made all participants long for a cartel restraint, and in 1953 that cartel restraint occurred.[2] The final

[1] *6ème Rap. Gén.* vol. I, pp. 40–1.   [2] Above, p. 434.

price in the table was an agreed export price. The Community was deciding in the summer of 1953 whether this was permissible within the treaty or not! The practice continued; and when subsequently the High Authority said that the price increase on exports to third countries between early 1953 and early 1955 had been limited to a rise from $80 to $100 per ton (it was, as the table shows, a rise from about $72 at the bottom), they were speaking of a cartel-controlled price, not a price resulting from the Community. Moreover, the rise in 1954 occurred when exports rose relatively little; in 1951 the Community countries exported almost 10 m. tons to third countries, including almost 2 m. tons to the United States. In 1954 the figure was below 7 m. tons. The lower and higher price levels in the range quoted by the High Authority were both determined by the firms in concert.

The export price continued to rise till 1957, but thereafter fell sharply, from $112 in March 1957 to $84 in March 1958 for the cheapest merchant bar steel, to take the official figure of the Brussels Conference. In January 1959 the lowest Conference figure was $80. But sellers who had been taking lower prices than the Conference fixed from mid-1957 continued to do so after the Conference reduced the formal price; so much so that according to the High Authority's annual *Report* the actual prices charged were between 85 and 90 per cent of the Convention prices, as in 1953–4.[1] Reinforcing rounds were selling for $75 F.O.B. in January 1959 just over £27 a long ton. Ship plates—open-hearth steel—sold for $100, about £36. 5s. 9d.; the British home price was £42. This was much more disturbing for British exporters than the bar price.

The High Authority regarded the disparity of price movements for Community and third-country trade as a 'special difficulty' which had its dangers. To the extent that exports fluctuated in quantity more than home trade it was, they said, inevitable; but there was a risk that firms based mainly on exports would turn to the home trade when export prices fell and cause disturbance; moreover, using industries in the Community would suffer if export prices were very low. The steel-

[1] *7ème Rap. Ann.* vol. ii, p. 71.

makers might suffer as buyers of raw materials, if they set a bad example. It was to everyone's interest therefore to keep home and export prices in line.[1] How bring this about if Community prices were determined by individual states?

The High Authority expressed its views thus in the sixth *Report* when export prices had begun to fall sharply. A year later their *Report* showed that some Community producers were giving to Community buyers deferred rebates in pig iron if they bought only in the Community, a reappearance of a familiar device of economic nationalism. So far it had not appeared, apparently, for steel.[2]

While the High Authority was thus concerned at the way in which prices oscillated more in the export trade than at home they also published tables to establish that the home prices of steel in the Community rose much less from 1953 to 1957 and 1958 than home prices in the United States and the United Kingdom. They based these necessarily on schedule prices (and these, it has been seen, present difficulties because 'extras' can be varied differently from the quoted base price) and they produced a weighted 'community' price index. The results for three products are given in Table 54. As Table 52 shows the trends in the different member countries varied widely. But the contrasts between Community and other price trends was clearly significant. How far they were related to differences in movements of material costs, how far to variations in relative efficiency, or of profit margins, was not rigorously explored in the High Authority *Reports*. Some elements in this are returned to later.[3]

Though the High Authority did not fix prices they adumbrated views in their sixth *Report* about what they should cover, partly because difficulties of re-rollers had made them alive to the risks that integrated firms could conceivably charge monopoly high prices to drive out one-stage firms. The High Authority's views, stated with great solemnity, were highly con-

[1] *6ème Rap. Gén.* vol. I, p. 43.

[2] *7ème Rap. Gén.* vol. II, pp. 54–5. It was used in coal pricing.

[3] It is *not* to be traced straightforwardly mainly to German recovery, because in fact from 1953 to Feb. 1957, i.e. *before* the franc devaluation, the rise in the French index was less than that of the German index.

ventional. Prices *must* include a good margin for new investment, because expansion would now need costly greenfield
works, and profits from existing production must contribute
some, though not all, the necessary finance. But though this
contribution must enter into the prices of semi-products, the
truth was that large integrated works with mass-production mills
could have great technical advantages; the re-roller must more
and more concern himself with small lots and special products!
'Thus a precise division of labour would be arrived at between
integrated works and rerollers.'[1]

Table 54.* *E.C.S.C., United States and United Kingdom price
indices compared (May 1953 = 100)*

	Jan. 1954	Jan. 1955	Jan. 1956	Feb. 1957
Merchant bars:				
Community	97	95	100	108
United Kingdom	100	99	107	118
United States	105	109	118	128
Plates:				
Community	98	95	102	111
United Kingdom	100	103	109	129
United States	105	108	115	124
Sheets:				
Community	98	100	104	109
United Kingdom	100	88	93	106
United States	104	107	115	124

* *5th Gen. Rep. E.C.S.C.* vol. I, p. 104. In later reports the E.C.S.C. presented
the information in a different form, but the burden of the demonstration was the
same. The following price indices, May 1953 = 100, are taken from the *7ème Rap.
Ann.* vol. II, p. 66. They show that the Community prices not only rose less but that
in the recession they fell more than the British, while the United States still rose:

	Jan. 1957	Jan. 1958	Jan. 1959
Community prices:			
Thomas steel	104	106	101
Open-hearth steel	110	111	105
United Kingdom prices	121	133	131
United States prices	127	135	140

Because Community prices were often 'aligned' on competition they fell more in
the recession than the index. The difference in this respect, however, is easily
exaggerated. For indices distinguishing movements in the separate Community
countries see below, p. 565.

[1] *6ème Rap. Gén.* vol. I, p. 39.

(g) 'Agreements and concentrations'

Though national prices for steel and cartel prices for steel exports remained, the High Authority set out resolutely to ensure that competition was not ruled out of the Common Market by cartels or trusts, as exemplified most notably in the German industry between the wars. There must be no explicit internal price or quota agreements, and no price leaders.[1] The general principles of the treaty were clear enough—no amalgamations or agreement should be allowed which gave power to fix prices or limit output; but subject to this limitation, amalgamations or agreements which added to efficiency were to be allowed; they were desirable. But how was the balance between the gains from large-scale or from technical integration on the one hand and the losses to competition on the other to be struck, especially as a series of small losses to competition might add up cumulatively? The special difficulty was recognised; technical studies show that while there is always a level of output beyond which further increases of scale will not lower costs, this level is constantly being displaced by technical progress in favour of a higher one.[2] To apply the Community principles in specific cases led to much heart searching; the approach was necessarily pragmatic; each case must be decided on its merits.

The High Authority inherited from the Allied High Commission the task of determining how much reconcentration into large vertical concerns there should be in the German steel industry, and this presented the first tricky problems it had to face over steel. Cartel issues arose much more over coal (though in 1958, as just seen, the High Authority was worrying about collusion in steel prices).[3] The new régime meant that over concentration the German industry would not be subject to discriminating rules. German firms wanted to restore their former characteristic integrations from raw-material production

---

[1] *6ème Rap. Gén.* vol. I, p. 37.   [2] *Ibid.* p. 34.

[3] The question of the steel export cartel arose; it was legal without authorisation because not restricting within the Common Market. Scrap-buying cartels were disallowed; but associations of German steel firms to subsidise imports of United States coal by means of a levy on sales of steel and equalise costs of Ruhr and United States coal were allowed. *6ème Rap. Gén.* vol. II, pp. 92–3.

to finished engineering. Backwards to coal the Community appears to have accepted readily enough at the start. (It had been resisted by the Allied High Commission.)[1] Several instances of links of steel and coal were referred to in the annual *Report* for 1954–55 as permitted. The case for technical advantage could be made with some plausibility, even perhaps some strength; though an even stronger case—for the steel firms, though not for the economy—possibly rested on the desirability of maintaining a link with one or more of the more modern mines with low costs, and of avoiding the risk of cartel prices or prices to cover costs of marginal mines.[2] That this was a real issue was proved by the discussions over central selling for Ruhr coal, and the break up of 'Georg', the central sales syndicate, by the Community; but this lies outside the scope of this study. Production costs in the Ruhr varied in the ratio of 2:1 between the poor mines and the good ones, being highest especially in the south-eastern parts of the field, near Dortmund and Essen, and lowest in the north and near the Rhine. In their sixth *Report*, after listing integrations which they had authorised, it seemed almost that the High Authority might be having second thoughts about its wisdom over the coal–steel links. These now tied up 14·5 per cent of the Community's total coal production; and since it was all German coal, and with the exception of Arbed all the concerns were German,[3] it meant that nearly one-third of German coal was 'tied'. The High Authority in 1958 was 'looking into' certain economic disadvantages which might flow from this for users who did not own mines and for coal mines which were not owned, and studying remedial measures.

How far was integration of steelworks with engineering,

[1] At first no such links were to be allowed: then firms could have mines to supply up to 75 per cent of their coal needs, but this was barred where particular families thereby had excessive power.
[2] The commercial value is a little obscure. Under the Community arrangements all buyers pay the same price. As coal sales are to be by groups of firms presumably the steelworks buying from its own coalmines will pay the group price. If there is a scarcity it cannot rely on steady supplies; all users must be treated alike. Nevertheless, to invest in a good mine will probably pay well, and possession will almost certainly give some greater regularity of supply.
[3] Mannesmann, Hoesch, Hörde, Thyssen, Gutehoffnungshütte, Klöckner, Phoenix-Rheinrohr. *6ème Rap. Gén.* vol. II, pp. 107–8.

diesel-engine making, steelworks plant manufacture, ship-building, and the like, desirable? Firms like Klöckners and Gutehoffnungshütte wanted to restore the old links, and informally it appeared to have happened in the second instance at any rate by 1953. Yet where branches of engineering were themselves concentrated in relatively few large units, such integration, which could have little technical advantage, though it might be a guarantee of steadier supplies to the engineering concerns (and so by implication meant less steady supplies for someone else) was obviously a source of imperfection in the steel market. How were the gains and losses to be measured? There seems to have been hesitation about this in the High Authority's thinking. There were no retrospective reviews. Nevertheless, a new instance of this problem was presented in 1955, when it was announced that the Hörde Verein[1] would, subject to a Bundestag decision, buy from the Government the Howald shipyard, the largest of the Hamburg yards. (The next biggest yard, Deutsche Werfte, was already closely linked with the Oberhausen steelworks and the Gutehoffnungshütte group). A member of the Hörde firm stated in 1955 as a reason for the purchase that plate prices were not remunerative. Obviously the yard would give a useful tied market for some of the output of the firm's new plate mill. By 1958 several other similar links had been authorised, one other with shipbuilding, several with other engineering—wagons, cars, machinery of various types—none apparently involving steel consumption on the same scale as in shipbuilding.[2]

Outside Germany the more usual form of concentration had been horizontal. Two Lorraine firms formed a large combine[3] mainly specialised on steel tubes; it more or less matched the two large German tubemakers.[4] Two groups of French special steelmakers amalgamated. Most impressive of all, perhaps, was the union of Cockerill's and Ougrée in Belgium in 1955. This caused some perturbation, because while it gave great scope for

---

[1] Above, pp. 400–1. It will be recalled this was largely under Dutch ownership.
[2] Listed in *6ème Rap. Gén.* vol. II, pp. 109–10.
[3] Lorraine-Escaut, which included the Aciéries de Longwy.
[4] Mannesmann and Phoenix-Rheinrohr.

specialisation within these two great plants (which were adjacent at Seraing) they were respectively controlled by the Société Générale and the Groupe de Launoit, the first and second financial groups—vast holding companies—in Belgium. These controlled other steel companies, including some outside Belgium, together with most of the industrial firms who were large users of steel in Belgium. Might it therefore be a dangerous concentration of power?[1] The claims of rationalisation were successful; in the list of concentrations the High Authority recorded that the combine made only 4 per cent of the Community's steel, and no reference to the real complication of veiled vertical links appeared.[2] Apart from these types of change a number of joint selling organisations working for groups of companies obtained the High Authority's authorisation. Of the amalgamations for which official approval was sought none appears to have been turned down by the end of the Community's sixth year, though several were still under examination.

A new phase was clearly opening on this front by the end of 1958, for German companies, whose preoccupations had been with reconstituting vertical links, were now also proposing horizontal mergers, which looked like reviving and in some ways intensifying the old pattern. The Krupp family had not yet sold the Rheinhausen steelworks; it was no doubt difficult to find a buyer, but there were no signs of selling pressure. The family now sought from the German Government the right to remain in steelmaking (which would involve agreement between the German Government and the Allies). If Krupp's obtained this they wished to restore the former breadth of their steel-making, and to this end they bought through Rheinhausen a majority holding in the Bochumer Verein. The Swedish owner willingly disposed of his majority holding. The High Authority agreed to the merger but emphasised that the obligations of the Krupp family and the responsibilities of the German and allied

---

[1] For a detailed survey of these and other Belgian groups, which present a fascinating picture, cp. *Holdings et Démocratie Economique*, published by the Fédération Générale du Travail de Belgique in 1956.

[2] *6ème Rap. Gén.* vol. II, p. 107.

Governments were unchanged. But the works were complementary, not competitive, and their capacity did not spell monopoly.[1] Because of Krupp's resources the High Authority would keep a 'special check' on the group's future capital schemes. Other unions were also proposed. Mannesmann were coming close to Hoesch; they had a joint tube works, but complete fusion was in the wind. Dortmund–Hörde were seeking the right to amalgamate with the Hüttenwerke Siegerland, an important customer for sheet bars.[2] Most striking of all perhaps the August Thyssen Hütte and Phoenix-Rheinrohr (another firm in the Thyssen family) were planning to unite.[3] These presented imposing problems in themselves. Beyond this it seemed that Dortmund Hörde, Thyssen's (A.T.H.), Phoenix-Rheinrohr, and Rheinstahl all sold much of their output through Handelsunion which was the descendant of the selling company of Vereinigte Stahlwerk. Was this the shadow of the giant returning? The High Authority seemed to be likely late in 1958 to delay its decision on the amalgamations of producers (which were all, like the Krupp plan, unions of complementary not competitive plants, creating units with eggs in many baskets and large joint resources) until the significance of these common selling arrangements was clarified. The investment controls insisted on for the Thyssen merger by the High Authority—acting by bare majority and under strong French political, not industrialist, pressure reflecting deep fears—led the firm to abandon it in May 1960. Would it make any difference?

(h) Investment in the Community

The first five years of the E.C.S.C. were years of fairly high investment, with a drop in 1954 and no significant rise until 1957. The new level was not fully sustained in 1958, nor, probably, in 1959. In Table 55 the figures for annual expenditure for each country are given, converted as usual for E.C.S.C.

---

[1] Rheinhausen and Bochum together made about 3·2 m. tons in 1957.

[2] Dortmund Hörde arranged to have slabs hot rolled by Hoesch into coils for Siegerland, avoiding building a hot strip mill with Hoesch not fully loaded.

[3] August Thyssen Hütte made 2·54 m. tons in 1957, Phoenix-Rheinrohr made 2·42 m. tons.

into dollars, and the totals have been adjusted roughly to eliminate the price changes; the method has been to use the German index of prices of investment goods, which cannot be very precise.[1] There was no uniform Community pattern; the re-equipment of the German industry gathered momentum up to 1955, hardly checked by the recession of 1953, while investment in the French and Italian industries notably fell off till 1956,

Table 55. *Capital expenditure in E.C.S.C. countries, 1952–58*[a]

	1952	1953	1954	1955	1956	1957	1958 planned
(a) In iron and steelmaking (including coke ovens, excluding iron-ore mines) (in $ m.)							
Germany	163	196	210	288	247	273	244
Saar	20	20	16	19	25	42	28
France	188	188	126	108	150	195	210
Italy	105	69	36	36	51	75	68
Belgium	29	37	33	33	45	61	71
Luxembourg	20	24	25	22	19	31	24
Holland	21	8	8	16	26	34	21
Total	545	542	453	524	572	710	666
In 1957 dollars	*567*	*569*	*487*	*544*	*589*	*710*	*656*
(b) In iron-ore mines							
Germany	6	4	7	9	9	8	10
France	19	18	18	19	29	35	31
Italy	3	5	4	3	8	3	2
Luxembourg	1	1	—	1	2	2	1
Total	29	28	29	31	48	48	43
In 1957 dollars	*30*	*29*	*31*	*33*	*49*	*48*	*43*

[a] The figures come from the *Reports on Investment* in 1957 and 1958. The figures for 1958 are planned expenditures for iron and steel making, actual for the mines. The total expenditure for iron and steel in 1958 was $629 m. Expenditure on iron and steel planned for 1959 was $585 m. (*8th Gen. Rep.*).

[1] The figures are taken from *Wirthschaft und Statistik*, which appears to have no index of prices of building and contracting (other than for structural steelwork). The index used is (1950 = 100):

1952	127	1955	124
1953	125	1956	128
1954	122	1957	132
		1958	134

No better index was available, but this leaves something to be desired.

and in Italy recovery was then only partial. In Holland, with one large plant only, investment was naturally spasmodic. In Belgium and Luxembourg it was relatively low in these years in relation to output; but it rose significantly in Belgium in 1955, a result perhaps of the Cockerill-Ougrée merger.

These figures suggest that for the E.C.S.C. as a whole from 1952–55, as for the French industry earlier, investment was at first higher in relation to output than in the United Kingdom, but not in 1956–57 and in 1958 it fell behind. It sustained or was associated with a higher rate of expansion—43 per cent from 1952 to 1957 compared with 32 per cent in the United Kingdom. This was still, for much of the time, a period of reconstruction for the German industry. The comparative figures are given in Table 56.

Table 56. *Investment in United Kingdom and E.C.S.C. steel industries (at 1957 prices)*

	Crude steel outputs		Total investments		Investment per ton of output	
	E.C.S.C.	U.K.	E.C.S.C.	U.K.	E.C.S.C.	U.K.
	(m. tons)		(£ m.)		(£ per ton)	
1952	41·1	16·4	213	60[a]	5·2	3·7
1953	40·1	17·6	214	59	5·3	3·7
1954	43·1	18·5	185	62	4·3	3·4
1955	50·7	19·8	206	68	4·0	3·4
1956	55·2	20·7	228	85	4·0	4·1
1957	58·9	21·7	268	95	4·5	4·4
1958	57·1	19·6	236	103	4·1	5·3

[a] Revised Iron and Steel Board series (*Ann. Rep.* 1957, p. 23) excluding expenditure on minor schemes, repairs and maintenance, iron foundries, and fringe industries.

How far equal expenditure gave equal results is not easy to discover; but the erection of new plant and new works in Germany at any rate was much faster than in Britain. It is convenient to defer further discussion of the comparison. The High Authority interested themselves in the balance of what was done, and in its adequacy, as they assessed it. This they did in pursuance of their duty to declare general objectives, which amounted in practice to proposing a highly general development plan. This followed familiar routines; demands were projected on a full employment assumption, the amount of steel needed at varying dates was forecast, and the plans of firms were assessed in relation to the forecast.

The balance of investments changed greatly in these years. From 1952 to 1954 54 per cent of the whole investment (excluding iron-ore mines) was in rolling mills, 30 per cent in steel melting, blast furnaces, coke ovens and ore preparation plants. In 1957 the percentages were 40 and 45 respectively; in forward plans for 1958–59 they were 31 and 52. In 1955 the High Authority thought too little was being spent on the earlier stages, and said so in a provisional inquiry into investments; they saw too little provision for more pig iron (hence the twist in its scrap policy) and pointed to a lack of balance between new rolling capacity which was designed to add 9 m. tons, over 25 per cent, to capacity, while steel melting was rising by 13 per cent only, and blast-furnace plans were to add 4·6 m. tons only. They thought it might be better to slow down building rolling mills, as these were going ahead of the market, rather than hasten the expansion of steel melting. At this time the plans visualised a steel output of 49·3 m. tons in 1957![1]

The change in proportions of investments in different stages which occurred after 1955 was thus in line with the High Authority analysis. Though in 1958 the balance was still not deemed quite right, there was still (the 1958 *Report* argued) too little home ore expansion, and on what was deemed a reasonable assumption about scrap the investment plans were estimated to promise 71·2 m. tons (metric) of steel in 1960, whereas the High Authority thought that it *ought* to be possible to supply 73·5 m. tons (having regard to possible demands). Investment was, despite this, falling off slightly. 'Experience shows', the 1958 *Report* said with solemnity, 'that a period of great economic growth is normally followed by a certain prudence in investments. The present level...does not warrant, on balance, any alarm.'

That the comments of the High Authority in 1955 foreshadowed the changes in investment pattern in 1956–58 did not

[1] Cp. *Résultats provisoires de l'enquête sur les investissements*, May 1955, passim.

mean that they were the main cause of the change. Study of
the regional details shows that in France expenditures on
rolling mills fell by nearly one-half from 1952 to 1955, and
thereafter rose; the German pattern, however, dominated the
total, with an immense growth in expenditure on mills up to
1955,[1] followed by a sharp fall. The figures appear to reflect
what may be deemed a natural pattern in German reconstruction. The units in a scheme which had to be made of full
capacity at the outset were the rolling mills, with what in
modern mechanised production is their extremely elaborate
ancillary equipment. Steelworks to provide them with ingots,
and blast furnaces to provide pig iron, did not have to be made
at the outset capable of keeping the mills going at full capacity.
It was possible to expand these parts of a plant by degrees, and
it would often be sensible, because the market for rolled products
could not always be expected at once to be capable of absorbing
the whole output of a modern mill working full out. This
situation was particularly likely when a large proportion of an
industry was being reconstructed at the same time—which had
happened in a measure in France, and was happening in much
greater measure in Germany[2].

In the early years of the Community the pattern of development in Germany differed markedly from that up to 1951,
though there was no dramatic change of direction. Nor was
the change traceable to the new supra-national régime. By
1951, as those who spoke for it made clear, the German industry,
no doubt partly because of Korea, was visualising a rapid
expansion to 19 m. tons. Within steelworks already restored to
large-scale activity radical replacement programmes went
ahead with greater intensity. By their side works which had
remained mainly inactive in 1951–52, as a result of dismantling,
especially Thyssens, Bochum and Salzgitter, were now restored
and newly equipped. Finally, at the end of 1955, a start was
made on a brand new giant steelworks at a new location, in
Bremen.

---

[1] The figure rose from $80 m. to $189 m. between 1952 and 1955; it was
$100 m. in 1957 and $70 m. (planned) in 1958. *Rapport sur l'enquête*, 1958, p. 55.
[2] In 1959 very large spending on mills was again envisaged (*8th Gen. Rep.*).

By 1955 all major German steelworks had one or more impressive new mill units (but were by no means in general wholly renovated; there were remarkable admixtures of the ancient, the middle aged and the modern). The Hörde works near Dortmund and the former Hermann Göring works at Watenstadt-Salzgitter both, for example, had four-high heavy plate mills to make heavy plates up to 4 metres wide, of high capacity.[1] Plates of the quality rolled in this kind of mill, which is more rigid and less susceptible to distortion by heat than the older two-high mills, were much demanded of United Kingdom makers, but it was not till the end of 1958 that a four-high heavy plate mill was operating in the United Kingdom. Thyssens' started up the first continuous wide-strip mill in the post-war German industry in 1955—the hot mill only. (This replaced the Dinslaken mill, now in Russia.) A cold-strip mill came later, in 1956, but other cold reduction mills had been built by 1955 elsewhere—for example, at Siegen and Oberhausen—and were fed from Thyssens'. At Oberhausen the primary mill, billet mill, and merchant bar mill, projected or started in 1953,[2] were complete by 1955. At Westfalenhütte (in the Hoesch group) there was a semi-continuous (Steckel) mill, one of the early results of reconstruction (1950–51), and a two-stage continuous billet mill (capacity 80,000 tons a month) completed in 1955. Mannesmann had a massive new electric welded tube plant; Bochumer Verein (a much dismantled works) a new billet mill for high-grade steels which was the highest capacity mill for this type of steel in Europe, and was characterised by several impressive innovations.[3] It would be easy to extend the list.

[1] Thus, for example, the Hörde mill at this date had a 4-metre universal mill (by Sack) to make thick plates, and a 3-metre stand. The shears had three rotary cutters so that plates could be cut in half when their edges were being sheared. The wide stand was being used partly as a primary mill for the narrower mill. Output was 50,000 tons a month. A primary mill of 120,000 tons a month capacity was to be built to supply both slabs and blooms, and the universal mill would then roll 65,000 tons a month.

[2] Above, p. 197.

[3] For example, it had an open-hearth steelworks under the same roof as the mill, which lessened transport and possibly heat losses; the reversing gear used for the electric drive of the primary rolling mill reversed much faster than the conventional Ilgner cycle equipment (this improvement has since been used in the United Kingdom); the movement of all steel was recorded at a central control

In several instances these plants were running well below capacity in 1955 because they were 'short of steel'. It was a common complaint. Most of the works were mixed works, with several mills to feed, and though their ingot output was often around 1·5 m. tons a year, and had been boosted in the Thomas plants by the use of oxygen,[1] it needed further supplementing, and this was already planned or being planned. Sometimes the problem of getting a satisfactory flow of products in an old site caused difficulty, and stimulated ingenuity.[2] There were already some fine new melting shops, and large new or reconstructed blast furnaces; and as seen earlier a lot of trouble was taken to make the most of the existing blast furnace capacity by charging scrap and by high top pressure, and other devices. There were also important technical advances in stages before rolling or forging—at Bochum, for example, the introduction of the process of vacuum casting for large ingots, whereby steel for very exacting uses, rotors for turbines and the like, was cast in vacuum and so largely freed from hydrogen and nitrogen, a familiar source of weakness.[3] At Oberhausen a 'rotor' (rotary) furnace was being developed for steelmaking, using oxygen, and based on Swedish experiments, which showed promise of combining high quality and cheapness.

station where the flow of material was determined. The finishing mill was three-high, as the size of order for special, largely alloy, billets was not large enough for a continuous mill.

[1] For example, Oberhausen, above, p. 197. Hörde installed a Linde oxygen plant; Hoesch used oxygen in their Thomas melting shop; Klöckner at Haspe were among the chief experimenters in using oxygen plus steam in the Thomas process.

[2] Hörde were in particular faced with this difficulty. This was the works where the Thomas process was first introduced on the Continent in 1879 (see *E.H.S.* p. 106). They had by 1955 built modern American soaking pits to feed the plate mill, carrying the ingots through an insulated passage to the mill, under a new covered-in scrap yard. Their Thomas plant dated back to 1895; there was one very old open-hearth plant, one more modern, with 80-ton furnaces built in 1923, and two 200-ton tilting furnaces built in 1937. The locating of new steel shops and flow of pig iron to it appeared still to be under discussion in the autumn of 1955.

[3] The process was announced early in 1955. The Russians developed vacuum degassing in the ladle by the end of 1955 (*Advances in Steel Technology in 1956* (E.C.E.), p. 16). If one read some United States advertisements in 1958 one might suppose the Americans were the sole inventors of pouring in vacuum; in fact, they derived it from Germany, and were the most active seekers after licences in 1955. The French were next in the queue.

Greater emphasis on iron and steel melting after 1955 was a corollary of the pattern up to that date in Germany. It was only a shift in balance; other impressive mill developments were to come, not least at the new Klöckner works at Bremen. Inquiries in the United States for mill equipment for this works were reported in technical journals in the summer of 1955,[1] and site work started in June 1955. The siting of this plant impressively confirmed the contemporary value of a deep-water site which is also near a market. It was to use primarily imported ore (its harbour would handle 25,000-tons ore ships), and was especially well located for Swedish ore; but Salzgitter ores could presumably come cheaply enough by water. Probably it was also designed primarily to use imported coal, though Ruhr coal could come by water. That the imported American coal might be the cheapest was possibly not clearly perceived in the early planning. The plan was on the American scale. First reports spoke of 2·5 m. tons ultimate capacity; but two years later this was almost doubled. Already by the end of 1957 a steel-works and the hot strip mill were working.[2] The cold mills, and a tin-plate plant, were well advanced; a four-high plate mill was to come. Though some early references to the works had arisen over the prospect of buying mills in America, only the coiler of the hot mill was American built, though all the plant incorporated American features—but it was a striking character of the German reconstruction that almost all the plant, including the mills, were built by German firms—Sack, Demag, Guteshoffnungshütte, Schloemann or Krupp—using, where appropriate, and it often was appropriate, United States patents and know-how. One of the chief executives at Bremen queried in 1957 whether this may have had a disadvantage. All German plants tended to be tailor-made and the Americans made standard mills; he thought it might bring large gains to do the same in Europe.[3] Elsewhere on the Continent mills in particular were

---

[1] *Iron Age*, 26 May 1955.

[2] The new plant at first used iron from existing blast furnaces; a little foundry iron had for long been made in the northern German ports.

[3] Thyssens conspicuously used more imported American plant than was normal. The President of United Engineering commented later that if there is a tailor made product in America it is the rolling mill.

commonly American; in part this was a reflection of aid, but not wholly so. Though the major shipyards were, as has been seen, tied to other steelworks the Bremen works would command a local market, so they hoped, by lower prices, with minimum delivery costs.

Was Bremen a comment on Ruhr sites in general? These had the disadvantage, even the best of them (probably Thyssens at Hamborn was the best) of having to bring iron ore by Rhine barge from Rotterdam or by canal from the north German ports.[1] The big German works were well served with inland ports and canals; nevertheless, the transhipment of imported ore was unavoidable. Though Ruhr coal remained good it was no longer so cheap. The Watenstadt plant claimed that in 1952 its pig iron, from Salzgitter ores, cost 20 D.M. a ton less than pig iron made in the Ruhr, though only 8 D.M. cheaper in 1953 when imported ore was cheaper.[2] At this time the Ruhr makers gave another picture, but after imported ore prices had again risen it was an accepted view that the Salzgitter based home ore works had much the lowest German costs. Would Bremen come next on the list? While Bremen was being built other plans for major new steelworks in the Community all visualised coastal sites—in France near Dunkirk, in Holland at Europort,[3] at the mouth of the Rhine, below Rotterdam, where ore was also to be stocked from 80,000-ton ore carriers. The Italian seaboard plant at Cornigliano antedated Bremen, but was much smaller. Expansion to 2 m. tons capacity started in 1960.

Investment in iron smelting and steel melting showed increasingly the results of efforts to use fuel and capital more efficiently, and to use poorer raw materials, often for higher grade products. High-grade ores were still sought and imported; more from Sweden (where the chief enterprise was nationalised) more from North Africa and Canada and South America. The leading German steel firms were progressively associated in the

[1] See E.H.S. p. 270.

[2] The works when restarted used the original blast furnaces, built in 1937–38; but none of the original steelworks and rolling mill buildings were used in the reconstruction. The mills had been taken away, the old buildings were left unused.

[3] This would make sectional material and so be a complement to Ijmuiden.

opening up of new resources with the other major interests, not only in the Community. Britain and Canada had for long been linked with the French in Mauretania, for example, and the Germans came in too. There was increasing stress on ore preparation, bedding, sintering and the like. The Krupp-Renn process was used for low-grade Salzgitter ores, at the mine and in the Ruhr; it was an alternative to the blast furnace for reducing ore (though the product might be put through the blast furnaces), and it used a cheaper grade of coal. Improved Thomas and other processes extended the scope and efficiency of converters; in this work collective research was particularly rewarding, but it appeared as though it would be less so in the work on low-shaft blast furnaces to use poorer fuels in reducing low-grade iron ore. Similar trends were found in all countries, including Russia.

As the Germans went ahead with their investment plans, with immense confidence, their neighbours changed the character of some of their plans or went ahead faster to meet the challenge. It was symptomatic that as seen above the two great Liége companies, Cockerill and Ougrée-Marihaye,[1] decided to combine in 1955, so that with a joint output of over 2 m. tons of ingots they could plan their modernisations to take fuller advantage of the economies of large scale.[2] In France, Longwy and Senelle Maubeuge, who were neighbours, joined to form the new firm of Lorraine-Escaut in 1954, with an ingot capacity of about 1·5 m. tons, one purpose being to become the largest producer of steel tubes in France and comparable with Mannesmann and Phoenix-Rheinrohr, the chief German tube firms. In the Massif Central four firms making high-grade steels near St Etienne joined forces.[3] It was an old plan, part of the original 'Monnet' plan; but there had been no compulsive force before the Schuman Plan, since under the older régime the district had been guaranteed a quota of output.[4] The rationalisation of these works was to lead to the specialisation

---

[1] Above, pp. 450–1.
[2] There had been partial modernisation at both works, but of limited scope.
[3] Above, p. 433, where the social effects are referred to.
[4] The works were understood to be singularly bad; it was, however, almost impossible to get access to them.

of each plant, which would allow an efficient scale of operation for their high-grade steelmaking. Le Creusot formed the core of another similar group. Another sign of the pressure of competition was the progressive conversion of one of the smaller Lorraine Thomas plants, the Pompey works near Nancy, from common-grade Thomas steel to high-grade electric steel. The metallurgical director came from Poldi, and the conversion was being carried out in 1955 by a singularly cosmopolitan group.[1]

It was now accepted as more compelling that for most steel production very large works and a higher degree of specialisation than had so far been achieved in France, despite the project for twelve large works only, was essential. Hence as work on the first plan was being completed an ambitious second plan was being devised. Its evolution gave an impression of a conflict of régimes which seemed inappropriate within the new Community. The steel firms put forward plans—perhaps their total should not be called *a* plan—to cost £290 m. within four years. The Commissariat au Plan deemed this excessive in its claims on French resources; it visualised more expenditure on steel-*using* industries, with the expansion of French steelmaking fitting into this, and absorbing less capital than the steelmakers wished, £225 m. instead of £290 m. But the Commissariat obviously doubted whether there would be a market for the more ambitious expansion plans.[2]

All must in any event fit into the Community system,—hence there were to be no fixed targets of output; the industry was to 'strengthen its competitive position in the common market'. Nevertheless, the tonnage to be lopped off the plans of the companies for blast-furnace steel melting and rolling capacity were set out, and it was broadly said that no new rolling mills at all should be embarked upon; and it was implied that

[1] The firm had one English director, the late Mr Gerald Steel, of the United Steel Companies. The Thomas steel plant was to be converted (when I visited it) to the L.D. process, i.e. the converters were to be top blown with oxygen; the Thomas steel was already being duplexed. The electric furnace capacity was large for France; American soaking pits had been installed and a new Swedish high-capacity bar mill was being installed to make alloy-steel bars to exceptionally fine tolerances.

[2] The Commissariat still planned for steel, and the Government influenced locations.

financial controls would bring this about.[1] The general decision, especially against more rolling mills, was in line with the E.C.S.C. judgement. Yet other countries in the Community were not following the same lines, not taking Community judgements as a basis of investment policies, nor (except perhaps in Italy where most steelworks were nationally owned) fitting steel investment into a national plan. It was not surprising that in the French steel industry there were complaints that the High Authority was doing too little in this respect. The Germans were equally adamant that the Authority was likely to do too much. The French had always half hoped that the High Authority would prevent excess capacity, which specifically meant would refuse to allow new strip mills in Germany until the French mills were fully employed. M. Ricard, leader of the French industry's syndicate in 1955, was quite frank in his dislike of a free competitive régime for this sort of thing, and he felt more hopeful over it all, though with what good reason was not entirely clear, when M. René Mayer followed M. Monnet as President.

That the existence of the Community was a stimulus which hastened some radical changes in France and Belgium is likely. Market interpenetration could not be wholly neglected.[2] How far the High Authority's conscious and deliberate activities really had a decisive shaping effect is much more doubtful. The scrap policy was intended to have it; but though the measures adopted caused immense irritation and their logical application had some ridiculous effects and some firms were certainly dissuaded from increasing open-hearth capacity, it is unlikely that firms needed much prodding to extend their iron production and secure more iron ore supplies. The High Authority could show preference for particular types of investment when it made loans, or extended its guarantee. From 1954 it raised $165·9 m., largely in the United States, and it lent exclusively to provide capital for coal-mining, coke-making, iron-ore-mining, ore preparation or iron-smelting projects, and for housing.[3] But the

[1] The position was summarised in an article in *Stat. Bull.* Aug. 1955.
[2] E.C.S.C. *Financial Report*, 1957, p. 19.
[3] *Ibid.* p. 21. Cp. also pp. 15–16.

sums it provided were a relatively small part of the total invested in the industry (less than 10 per cent), and the channelling of this proportion into the earlier stages might well be regarded as making more of other resources available for other stages. All the more was this so perhaps if, as was, strongly argued, the firms could not have raised money for themselves in America—which is not quite certain (they would no doubt have had to pay more dearly). The money was lent, as those who devised the plan had envisaged, at rates of interest[1] which were low for the time in Europe, hence on preferential terms, which may have increased the propensity to invest in this industry; but though it should have been objectionable to liberal economists in principle its effect was probably not profound.

(i) Relations with the United Kingdom

From the outset M. Monnet, and with him most ardent supporters of 'Europe', hoped that Britain would be closely and organically associated with the Community, if not a member. But when the idea was first revealed to the world in the Schuman Plan the British Government's attitude was reserved and distant. They hoped the idea, which was to advance peace by bringing Germany and France together, would succeed in its political object. They would not commit themselves in advance to accept the principle of 'pooling' (the Common Market) or of delegation of sovereignty in a limited field to a supra-national authority. They did not, as Mr Attlee made clear, claim unlimited sovereignty and were making concessions of sovereignty in the interests of common defence, and would make more. The French claimed a preliminary commitment as a prior condition of Britain's taking part in the formulation of the treaty, which was deemed excessive[2] for reasons which could be made to appear good. The claim was possibly politically unwise. It stirred the latent fear of and revulsion from federalism which

[1] E.C.S.C. *Financial Report*, 1957, p. 21.

[2] Cp. correspondence published as a White Paper (13 June 1950). It is strongly argued that the full records will show that the French did not want British participation in the negotiations, and changed their ground frequently when agreement seemed in sight. For what is public see W. Diebold, *The Schuman Plan*, pp. 48–60.

was widespread in Britain. Those who shared these feelings often persuaded themselves that federalism would fail through continental Europe's own dissensions; to support it was to chase a chimaera.

There were a few voices raised in opposition to this view, notably in the *Economist*, which at the outset (before the French terms were known) argued that Britain should take part in the scheme[1] and later traced both the Government's attitude and the French exigent demand to the Government's profound isolationism. 'It is difficult to find anyone on the Continent or in America or even in unofficial circles in this country who has not now been driven to the conclusion that the British Government's desire is to sabotage any move towards European economic unity under cover of accepting them in principle.'[2] Despite Mr Attlee's moderate and friendly words about the prospect of future collaboration, it became immediately clear— from the party's pamphlets, if proof were needed—that the Labour Government's attitude was partly doctrinal in origin. They had nationalised the coal and steel industries; this was to be the key to efficiency and full employment. If European countries did not use the key what benefit could come from association with them?[3] M. Monnet said that his scheme would accommodate nationalised and private enterprise industries; it was, as it were, above the conflict. But how could it fail to lessen purely national control of a nationalised industry? On an even narrower basis it was argued that the two British industries must have a first call on business in the local market; free access for foreigners to the British market was unthinkable after the experiences of the early thirties.[4] English Socialists no doubt felt some vindication of their opposition in the fact that the German Social Democratic Party also opposed the plan, as did the Communists, but not the Socialists, in France.

---

[1] *Econ.* 20 May 1950.
[2] *Ibid.* 10 June 1950. There are different views of what happened in all this; it is therefore relevant that the editor of the *Economist*, which is quoted extensively here, was on terms of friendship with M. Monnet.
[3] *Econ.* 17 June 1950 (*Socialism contra Mundum*).
[4] This view has been referred to already as expressed in the debates on denationalisation. Above, p. 383.

The *Economist* dismissed as ridiculous the theory that nationalisation had brought full employment—why had full employment occurred so universally in other countries? When it advocated British participation (and hence influence) in the Schuman Plan it was alive to the dangers—the political risk of creating a neutral Europe and the economic risk of creating an international cartel in sheep's clothing—but emphasised that the time was admirably suited economically for Britain to contemplate participation in the Common Market. Her lower prices made her amply competitive. There was, when the plan started, a risk of steel surplus. The *Economist* accepted the E.C.E. analysis that the sellers' market was coming to an end, so that there was a risk of cartel restriction, which the Schuman Plan, if it were properly directed, should circumvent by arrangements which would see production concentrated in the plants with lowest costs. If this happened Britain should do well. The conclusion that the British industry was in a good position to enter a Common Market in Europe, was sound enough for the time being; though the same data could lead other people to argue that there was no need to tamper with the coal and steel industries—why not leave well alone?

Once Britain refused to accept the French terms for participating in making the treaty they became onlookers only, being kept informed through an official observer from the Paris Embassy. The *Economist* maintained for some time its initial interest. It soon recognised that the plan in its economic approach, its attempt to find a way between, or better perhaps a synthesis of, *laisser-faire* competition and national planning, was 'bolder than either friends or critics had at first imagined'.[1] It recognised that the fear the plan would set up a cartel behind a façade was unjustified.[2] But by this time Korea had swept away the spectre of surplus steel and the immediate risk of a restrictive cartel. The plan was discussed more and more for its political implications; and as the end of the technical discussions on the form of treaty approached the *Economist* itself was uncertain of its political value. 'The problems of West European co-operation and military security have become too

[1] *Econ.* 8 July 1950.   [2] *Ibid.* 26 Aug. 1950.

urgent and too far-reaching to be settled by a local industrial agreement alone.'[1]

The 'local industrial agreement' now stirred little interest in Britain. It did not become a practical problem again till the Community came into existence in mid-1952, when M. Monnet at once sought some tangible form of association with Britain. The British Government expressed again their desire for the 'closest possible association' and announced the setting up of a permanent British delegation under Sir Cecil Weir to proceed to Luxembourg at once and lay the foundations for 'intimate and enduring association'.[2]

By now there was a different Government. In opposition Conservatives had seemed more ready to take some part in the Community than the Socialists. But they too, when in power, were found to have given hostages to isolationism. They had their own recipe for steel, forged in collaboration with the British steel firms. They were creating an Iron and Steel Board to be charged with the function of making the steel industry efficient by price and investment control and other loosely defined functions. Some Ministers thought British steelmakers could stand free competition with European makers, but they would not wish to impose it against the steelmakers' will. In the early days of the delegation what was done was limited to establishing contacts, observing what was happening, and discussing possible forms of joint action.[3]

The question whether Britain should join the Community was often approached by an examination of Britain's trade in steel with the Community countries. Britain's sales of steel to them were relatively small; it was thought they were likely to remain small, because the Community was a large net-exporting area. The conclusion was sometimes drawn that

---

[1] *Ibid.* 16 Dec. 1950. The conclusion was that if Germany could be convinced that its political aspirations would not be thwarted, and France that rearmed Germany will not bring war with Russia, the plan might still achieve its political object.

[2] *The Times*, 23 Aug. 1952.

[3] There was a Joint Committee which first met in Nov. 1952, and there were a few working parties of 'experts' from the Community and the United Kingdom industries.

because of this there was little or no advantage to Britain to enter the Common Market. The same argument more broadly stated was used in 1947–49 against the idea of a European Customs Union; European countries are not sufficiently complementary, but mainly competitive, making the same things; hence a customs union would be valueless. This dismissed implicitly, and seemingly without noticing it, one main argument for the large market, namely, that it derived value from the scope it gave for larger units without unavoidable monopoly, and for the replacing of less efficient by more efficient methods and locations. The emphasis on the smallness of exports to the Community was a producers' argument, and in character insular.

The users of steel might have been expected to be more concerned with the prospective influence of a Common Market on their steel supplies. There were few overt signs of any such interest among consumers however, though many often depended on imports. The imports were, of course, relatively dear.

A large majority of the leaders of the Steel Federation was seen at an early date to be opposed to Britain's entering the Common Market.[1] This attitude was an implied premise for an article on the British steel tariff in the Federation's *Statistical Bulletin*. There was understandable reluctance to give up the advantage of the low scrap price, low coal prices, and, as might happen, Imperial preferences (though France kept North Africa out of the E.C.S.C. Common Market). The majority of the firms were prepared to see import duties put on a fairly low level, but thought permanent low duties necessary as a protection against unfair competition, as well as anti-dumping duties.[2] They did not seem to take the idea seriously that the E.C.S.C. might eliminate dumping.

The issue came to life again when the British Government was asked late in 1953 to take a further step in association. They

[1] There was at least one exception; an important member of one major firm was prepared for a very large measure at any rate of free trade with European producers. There were possibly some waverers. But an appearance of unanimity was preserved.

[2] The Federation published an enlightened statement of the case for this double-barrelled defence in *Stat. Bull.* Mar. 1955.

were anxious from a political angle to make a gesture because the European Defence Community was showing signs of foundering.[1] They were unprepared to make any specific economic concessions if for no other reason than that the steel-makers themselves were nervous of association. Most members of the Government were probably unprepared for a Common market, many being protectionists by instinct though committed to freer trade. The Government were criticised for subordinating their policy to the pressure of the interested industrial groups, and for rejecting expert advice contrary to the line they adopted, but they were probably following their own preferences. To define the conditions which govern competition has indeed been usually regarded as a function for Governments; but in regard to steel, as has been seen, this Government had refused to define the conditions and had delegated the function. It was characteristic of the decisions which had so effectively for so long taken the edge off the forces most likely to provoke more radical change.

The upshot was an agreement to establish a Council of Association, which was to provide a means of 'continuous exchange of information and consultation' and 'when appropriate' of 'co-ordination of action'. The Council was to consist of not more than four representatives of each party to the agreement, the British members to include at least one Minister, and in addition a representative from the Iron and Steel Board and one from the National Coal Board. The Community had succeeded nominally in ensuring this was an association of Governments, though in substance it was on this point a compromise.[2]

A long list of topics, the obvious topics,[3] which would be the subjects of a consultation or action was included. A separate

---

[1] The Minister in charge of negotiations, Mr Duncan Sandys, had been prominent in the European movement before he became Minister, and he was personally sympathetic to effective association.

[2] The Chairman of the National Coal Board *is* an industrialist, even though a state appointee; the Chairman of the Iron and Steel Board is clearly so closely associated with the industry that he can hardly be deemed detached about it as a Minister or a Government official in theory would be.

[3] The topics included conditions of trade, supplies, raw materials, pricing, subsidies, investment, development plans, substitutes, research, health safety and welfare.

clause provided that if either party visualised any new restrictions on trade in coal or steel to meet difficulties arising from a decline of demand there should be prior consultation if possible and early consultation in any event. Another clause provided that the Council should examine from time to time existing restrictions on mutual trade in coal and steel 'with a view to making such proposals for their reduction or elimination as may be agreed for the mutual benefit of the Community and the United Kingdom'. The first such review should be in time for the Community Governments to take it into account when the Community's five-year transitional period with its temporary subsidies and protections came to an end, and the Community would among other things have to choose its own permanent tariff policy within the limits set by the treaty.[1]

The agreement was a commitment to nothing more than more discussion, but it implied an expectation of action. Moreover, it specified matters in which there must be early discussions, and some at least of those who drafted it thought this must end in some action. How discuss restrictions without doing something about them? Such seemed to be the tactic. Within the Government there was a hope that as British steelmakers saw the High Authority in action they would gain confidence in its stability, integrity and effectiveness. For the Community even a slight movement towards action was an advance for Britain. Yet it was little more at first than a change from marking slow time to marking time. The non-committal project evoked little enthusiasm in Europe, and was not ratified by all the various Governments until October 1955. The first meeting of the Council was held in Luxembourg a month later. Would the British Government and industry with their tradition of price-fixing and investment control and self-sufficiency adapt themselves to the quasi market economy of the Community?

---

[1] These were set out in the Convention containing Transitional Provisions (§ 15). Among other things it was provided that Benelux would be prepared to raise their protection by at most two points to assist the harmonisation of the tariffs of all member countries at the lowest level in any Community country, and even so the High Authority might find that some countries were justified in practising higher duties. Countries were free individually to use their steel duties as a basis for the negotiations of concessions by the G.A.T.T. procedure.

The High Authority appeared to have given up hoping for early results of practical significance.

However, the Council met within a month of notification, and set up three standing committees to deal respectively with trade relations, steel and coal questions. The first was to find a formula for tariff agreement before the end of the transitional period, but was initially more busily occupied with restrictions on exports of steel and coal imposed by the British Government because of the boom. After the first year's work it was explained in respect of coal that 'judicious recasting of the United Kingdom's programme of exports to the Community' had occurred, mainly a recasting of grades exported. Whether this meant that the exports to other countries had been *more* reduced, or merely reduced in qualities which the Community wanted, was not explained.[1] What was done in steel was not described, except in terms of satisfaction, till a year later. 'The United Kingdom authorities', it was then stated, 'indicated their readiness to examine any case of special hardship that might arise.' No market economy here![2] Through 1957 pressures of scarcity dropped. In its second year the main achievement of the trade relations committee was the almost obligatory general agreement on tariffs. There were signs at the outset that within the Iron and Steel Board the case for a 15 per cent tariff was argued more strongly than in the Federation or the Government. The utmost discretion was maintained, lest, it may be supposed, public discussion should affect the decision. Negotiations were very prolonged.[3] When the results were announced the lower tariff party had won. The British Government, now pressing its Free Trade Area project, was clearly moving in greater sympathy with European movement. In November 1957 the agreement was signed, whereby for a large range of iron and steel goods the United Kingdom maximum tariff was to be 10 per cent *ad valorem*, the

---

[1] *E.C.S.C. 5th Ann. Rep.* vol. i, p. 56.

[2] *Second Annual Report of the Council of Association between the United Kingdom Government and the High Authority of the E.C.S.C.* pp. 12, 13.

[3] A delightful phrase in *ibid.* (vol. i, p. 58) gives a clue: 'These talks, which are still in progress, have brought to light a nnmber of elements for a possible future agreement on parallel action to lower tariffs'.

Community's (which after all was practically settled by the treaty and in early discussions after its ratification) from 2 to 13 per cent according to product. 'An important step towards the objective of eliminating trade barriers between the Community and the United Kingdom'—so it was described. Earlier, when Britain's anti-dumping law was being passed, there had been an agreement that dumping questions over steel should be matters for the Council. By the time the agreement was signed the background had, as just mentioned, notably changed; the European Economic Community had been agreed upon, the free-trade area negotiations were on their tortuous frustrating course. So this trade relations committee had 'examined, on an exploratory basis, possible conditions for the inclusion of coal and steel in a free-trade area'. What did the explorers discover? This alas was not divulged.[1] The E.C.S.C. and the United Kingdom Iron and Steel Board both, it was rumoured, saw good reason why coal and steel should be treated as special cases, with a régime of their own, an oasis of special treatment designed no doubt to steady the progress of a competitive world.

Apart from matters of commercial policy the Council compared forecasts of future trends, exchanged information, set up a working party to compare prices (including extras), made some progress towards action for 'keeping down the amount of scrap consumed by the iron and steel industry', and set out to make special studies, for example, of the plate and tinplate position, to see how capacity was likely to be related in the long run to demand. Probably all this did not amount to a great deal immediately; obviously it involved considerable but vague possibilities of intervention. The United Kingdom through the

---

[1] *Ibid. loc. cit.* The British Blue Book on *Negotiations for a European Free Trade Area* (Jan. 1959) shed a little light on how ideas had moved (pp. 94–5). A working party (membership undefined), on which the High Authority was 'also represented', had unanimously recognised the impossibility of applying 'pure and simple the E.C.S.C. rules throughout the Free Trade area'. In considering what *could* be done some preferred applying as far as possible 'the general rules of the Free Trade Area, with the minimum of special rules'. Other countries wanted supplementary rules to ensure 'equal advantages for consumers and producers' by clauses to eliminate price discrimination and market fluctuation. A draft protocol with alternative texts had been prepared. Which appeared to mean that nothing had been agreed upon.

Council co-operated with the High Authority's work on medical research—such co-operation would probably have occurred in any case—and a United Kingdom representative was on the High Authority's Technical Research Committee; but again this was a new piece of machinery continuing what had been done earlier, though bringing some new funds to the work. This all had the air, perhaps inevitably, of an interim arrangement, overshadowed by uncertainties outside the control of the two industries directly involved.

(j) Before and after

By the end of 1958 the E.C.S.C. was much nearer the 'local industrial agreement' of which the *Economist* wrote in 1951 than it had been in its earlier years, if only because its model had been copied, and modified, in the European Economic Community, and there was another industrial agency, Euratom, and logical evolution pointed to the industrial communities becoming satellites of the European Economic Community. The change was symbolised by the changing calibre of the members of the Board. M. Finet, third President, was not a Monnet or a Mayer. As a 'local industrial agreement' nevertheless, the E.C.S.C. seemed as if it might be entering upon a new more incisive phase, with a closer adherence to the economic prescriptions of 1950–51. This was not just because the transitional phase was over. Partly it was because the High Authority had played itself in, and partly because some problems had become more conspicuous, some had grown, and some were better understood. The E.C.S.C. had already in its first five years changed the relative costs of making steel in different parts of the Community by its work on transport costs and in respect of double pricing of coal and ore, and by its policies on scrap, and the free access to all of the Community market was already an important factor for many works—it was not equally so for all. Belgian makers in particular felt that in times of slackening trade they had much more chance of selling in the rest of north-west Europe than they had before the Community. But the net economic effect of the new régime so far, on costs certainly, and probably on the pattern of trade and in other respects, was wide rather than deep, hardly in proportion to the immense outpouring of Community literature. In some directions, in regard to scrap notably, it was not calculated to encourage investments which yield lowest costs.

Ultimately its effect on investment should be the chief token of its economic importance. In the first six years it was hard to judge whether or how much it had influenced either pattern or quantity, or how much of its effect came through its mere existence, how much through positive actions of the High Authority. The existence of the wider market almost certainly had stimulated some greater effort in French, perhaps in Belgian, investment; it may have contributed something to the move to deep-water sites on the coast. By 1959 the further French devaluation had begun to exert market pressure on Ruhr steelworks to find ways to reduce their costs. The High Authority claimed that they induced a greater investment in the primary stages of steelmaking and by the end of 1958 they had instituted a comparison of costs in new works on the coast and inland. The presumption that the E.C.S.C. had added to the incentives to make radical changes in order to reduce costs is reasonable, though the addition, and the effect, was small. Outside the discussions and writings of the High Authority the focus of investment activity remained predominantly, even aggressively, national. Thus in France the Commissariat au Plan co-ordinated projects and on critical issues the Government made the decisions—and provided money. In Germany the firms, entering into larger mergers and making co-operative arrangements of varying types over investment research and operations, talked primarily in terms of strengthening the competitiveness of their firms as part of the industry in the Federal Republic. There were exceptions, but they were minor. It was the same in all the Community countries.

There seemed by 1958 a possibility that the competitive pressures in the E.C.S.C. might be strengthened. There were even murmurings that the scrap price (whose management had led the High Authority to its most dirigiste activities; in general it had resisted the temptation to dirigisme rather strikingly) might be permanently freed, though there was no formal indication of such sacrilege. Under pressure in discussion a historical rationalisation of the treatment of scrap was evolved: the High Authority could not take the strain of a high increase in scrap prices in its earliest years; if the E.C.S.C. had done nothing, the Americans would have embargoed scrap exports; it was necessary to discriminate in favour of Italy at the start, but though this could have distorted investment it probably did not, because, *deus ex machina*, the price of coal in Italy had become unexpectedly favourable as United States coal in Europe became cheaper than German. Italy might now be the best place in the Community to make steel from imported ores. All this suggested that the bastions of the scrap policy were being undermined (although the pig-iron bonus of 1958 was in the old, uncommon market, tradition). The pressure behind policies to stimulate further price competition between steel firms, to break down state price policies and eliminate association action, was being increased. It was virtually certain that transport discriminations would lessen, though this was likely to be more via the E.E.C. than the E.C.S.C. Contrariwise the consolidations in Germany seemed a potential limitation of competition. Increasing interest in vitalising price competition and containing amalgamations revived interest in some quarters in bringing Britain more intimately into the E.C.S.C. system— for with large units and a multiple basing point or analogous pricing system multiplicity of bases and diversity of locational interest are fundamental requirements. Britain could be the antidote to a Rhine-Ruhr-Moselle cost axis. The inspiration in all this came from the arrangements in the United States of America (was the E.C.S.C. not after all creating the United States of Europe?). They did not, like British politicians, cry for American style achievements, but seek to achieve them only by insular, un-American methods. How then (was it known?) did the American model work?

Chapter VIII

ANTITRUST AND AMERICAN STEELMAKING

1. THE F.T.C. ATTACK

The high efficiency of the American steel industry in the decade before the Second World War, which provided such a spur to changes in European steelmaking in the decade after the war, and was most notably embodied in the wide strip mills which spread through the industry with dazzling speed,[1] was achieved in the doldrums of the thirties, when the industry only once worked at more than 70 per cent of its capacity for a whole year and for six years was working at between 20 and 40 per cent of capacity.[2] However, such quick adoption of technical change was in the tradition. Hence during those years Americans were more conscious of economic ills than of achievements, and though the working of the economy in low gear was increasingly thought of as a symptom of general economic policy which restricted demand the temptation to explain it also in terms of malignant disease within the individual industries most severely hit was irresistible. The Federal agencies whose duty (and as it seemed whose pleasure) it was to enforce the antitrust laws, declared boldly that the practices of the steelmakers in regard to prices bred over-capacity, kept inefficient plants alive, made prices needlessly high, and led to

[1] Already in 1936 there were 21 built or building (Walter Tower, Secretary of the American Iron and Steel Institute in an address at California on 6 Feb. 1936, reprinted by the A.I.S.I.).

[2] The figures were:

	Per cent		Per cent
1930	67	1935	41
1931	39	1936	63
1932	18	1937	72
1933	29	1938	36
1934	32	1939	65

restriction of output for the sake of profits. The industry which Europeans came increasingly to admire for its efficiency was thus depicted as grossly and dangerously inefficient owing to monopoly distortions, which the Federal Trade Commission sought to root out. 'The industry has become addicted to monopoly as to a habit-forming drug. . . . A cure is necessary if the steel industry, together with American business in general, is to be restored to health.'[1]

Some American economists now doubted whether the former purity of the competitive market, if it had ever existed, could be revived; they debated whether in view of the economies of large scale in the heavy industries, the attraction of vertical integration with raw-material suppliers and using industries, and the consequently forbidding costs of entering the industries, the era of competitive capitalism had irrevocably ended.[2] These doubts were repugnant to the F.T.C. 'Even though a modern steel plant may be physically large it is relatively small in comparison with the total steel business of the United States. If monopoly is to be permitted in such industries the Commission can see no escape from. . . placing them under Government control', which among other things would tend toward the 'rise of an authoritative state'.[3]

In this setting the mixture of ideas and practices was compounded, out of which an eclectic selection was made, years later, to provide the price provisions of the Schuman Plan.

On the eve of the war, when the opponents of monopoly had succeeded in promoting a vast official inquiry to investigate the concentration of economic power,[4] the 'excess capacity' of the steel industry had become a godsend, the failure to eliminate

---

[1] Temporary National Economic Committee (subsequently referred to as T.N.E.C.) (cp. below, n. 4), Monograph No. 42, *The Basing-Point Problem*, p. 5.
[2] Cp., for example, Arthur Robert Burns, *The Decline of Competition*, 1936, pp. v and 522 sqq.   [3] *The Basing-Point Problem*, p. 8.
[4] This was conducted by T.N.E.C. under the chairmanship of Senator O'Mahoney of Wyoming, and including, apart from members of the Senate and the House of Representatives, representatives of the F.T.C., Department of Justice, Department of Labor, Treasury, Department of Commerce, Securities and Exchange Commissions. It had its own expert staff and issued masses of reports which were little noticed in the United Kingdom, presumably because the United Kingdom, but not the United States, was at war.

old plant as new was introduced could be recognised as fortu-
nate, if not far sighted, and the steelmakers, accused of charging
excessively during the slump, were able, as will be seen later,
to raise prices by up to 10 per cent by merely charging their list
prices instead of cutting them as they had been doing.[1] After
the war had led to further expansion, this enlarged capacity
seemed in the 'full-employment economy' more often too little
than too great, so that managements were now accused not of
keeping too much capacity alive but (as was seen in Chapter III)
of expanding too slowly. The same remedies, however, were
propounded for the post-war as for the pre-war situation, and
the F.T.C. succeeded in one of their main objects. The 'F.O.B.
Mill' system of quoting prices was substituted for the basing-
point system in July 1948. It was done voluntarily by the
industry, in anticipation of a 'cease and desist' order. Attention
was then returning increasingly, on the anti-trust front, to the
preoccupation of the early years of the century, the risks involved
in large mergers.

Part 2 of this section examines the way in which prices
were settled in the 15 years before the war, and the forms which
competition took. These are considered in relation to the F.T.C.
criticism that the system bred inefficiency. In part 3 the
obscurities which have persisted about the 'F.O.B. Mill'
system of settling prices are observed. Part 4 examines how
far the settling of prices has followed or departed from pre-war
patterns—in so far as it is possible to find evidence—and the
effect it may be thought to have had on development. Finally
in part 5 the development of policy towards mergers is traced.

2. THE BASING-POINT SYSTEM
IN OPERATION, 1926–1943

The F.T.C. attack on the basing-point system started in 1921
when there was only one basing-point, Pittsburgh, and the
system was synonymous with 'Pittsburgh Plus'. The American
steel industry, it has been seen, had been moved to avoid violent
price-cutting by the same forces as the European industries.

[1] Below, p. 487.

Price agreements and production quotas were ruled out by the Sherman Acts.[1] The creation of the extremely powerful United States Steel Corporation had been in part a response to instability, and its mere existence helped for a time to lessen instability. It became a 'price leader'. The Gary dinners[2] involved perhaps more than leadership, but there were no new formal agreements; firms adopted an 'open-price' policy (i.e. their prices were published), but departures from the 'open' price occurred. Until the early twenties the United States Steel Corporation prices which others followed were all based on Pittsburgh; users were charged as though all mills incurred rail-transport costs from Pittsburgh, even though a Chicago mill might be selling to a Chicago neighbour. As the proportionate importance of Pittsburgh declined the objections to this single basing-point grew formidable. In periods of low demand some Chicago mills used Chicago as a basing-point from 1911 onwards, though only spasmodically. It was established as one in 1917 by order of the War Industries Board, but this was rescinded under pressure from the United States Steel Corporation. Pressure from consumers in the Middle West grew irresistible; the F.T.C. was forced, unwillingly, to lodge a complaint against the United States Steel Corporation for using the system in 1921, and two years before its prolonged investigations ended in 1924 with an order that Pittsburgh plus was to be abandoned, Chicago had been made a basing-point by the United States Steel Corporation for bars and sections, though not for plates, sheets or wire. After the court's decision several other basing-points were adopted quickly, for the major products, either by the Corporation or by its smaller rivals. Thus Pittsburgh plus was succeeded by a multiple basing-point system under which base prices were published for a number of basing-points.[3] The prices at different points were not necessarily identical. The delivered price consisted of the price at the basing point (base price) plus the transport charge to the

---

[1] See *E.H.S.* pp. 346–8.   [2] *Ibid. loc. cit.* pp. 284–5.
[3] A. R. Burns, *op. cit.* pp. 305–7. New basing points included Duluth, Birmingham, Cleveland, Bethlehem, Coatesville, Sparrows Point, Lackawanna, Buffalo and Gary. (Not *all* points were used for *all* products.)

consumer from the basing-point, which was always the published rail freight regardless of the method of transport used. The convention was that all steel producers would quote a price equal to that combination of base price plus transport charge most favourable to the customer. (Standard extras and rebates for deviations from the basic sizes and different quantities ordered—'net-extras'—were also included in the final price.)

Thus all steelmakers would normally offer any individual consumer identical delivered prices. But the prices were not, as in Britain, uniform over wide zones for every customer, irrespective of delivery charges, and they were not identical 'at the mill'. Thus, to take the simple case, so long as a mill located at a basing-point was delivering to customers whom it could supply at transport costs lower than those which mills at other basing-points would incur it would obtain a 'mill net yield' (as it was called) equal to the basing-point price plus net extras. The same was true for mills at other basing-points; each had a territory within which it would obtain the full basing-point price. But directly a mill sold in the territory of a basing-point other than its own its 'mill net yield' would be less than the basing-point price on which the price was quoted. The mill then was said to be 'absorbing freight'. The position was more complex for a mill which was not located at a basing-point at all; it would be nearer some markets than any basing-point was, hence its 'mill net yield' would be greater than the basing-point price on some sales, and was likely to be less on others. Where it was more it was said to be charging 'phantom freight'.[1]

Assuming that the system worked smoothly, that prices quoted by different firms to the same customer were always identical, and that there was no price-cutting, the multiple basing-point system was one of concerted price-fixing, though the 'concert' took the form of following a leader. The F.T.C. said the system kept obsolete mills in operation, with new efficient mills working below capacity, and resulted in avoidable cross-freighting when sellers sold in each other's 'natural territories'. This discriminated against the consumers near the basing-point, who

---

[1] Firms were said to charge 'phantom freight' also when rail freight was charged from a basing point but a cheaper form of transport was used.

were therefore contributing to the higher costs of supplying more distant markets. If any seller accepted a lower 'mill net yield' in his sales to one customer than to another it was a form of discrimination. The F.T.C. thought this was not only in a straightforward sense unfair, but that it actually raised the average level of prices, and thus checked the expansion of industry in general, as well as distorting location.

The 'system' was, however, not always observed to the letter. It was a restraining influence; but firms did compete with each other by selling below the prices which the 'system' determined. How often, how much, for how many buyers, for which buyers, was not known. The Temporary National Economic Committee, however, gathered some information. For one month, for example, for February 1939, the average price cut made by the United States Steel Corporation for a number of products was published. This could not be taken as representative, and it was not an average. At the same time other data was also published by the Corporation in evidence, for the T.N.E.C. inquiry showed that the combined effect of price cuts and freight absorption varied according to the state of trade. Competition grew more intense as trade shrank, as was to be expected; and to some extent, possibly a large extent, it was price competition. The evidence for this was the fluctuating difference between 'mill net yield' and the quoted (or as the United Steel Corporation said 'reported') base prices. Three years later a wartime study published by the Bureau of Labour Statistics added a great deal more information on some points. The February 1939 figures provide the best starting-point (see Table 57). Thus the average price reductions or concessions, sales below the base price, not to be confused with formal allowances for large quantities of standard goods (these would enter into net extras), were from 2·5 to 3 per cent for the heavy products and about 6 per cent for sheets. Sheets were the product where because of the crop of new strip mills competition was most acute. Freight absorption exceeded price reductions in Pittsburgh. It was less than price reductions at Chicago. This is to be explained by the need of Pittsburgh to sell a larger surplus at a distance outside its 'natural territory'.[1] Price reductions and freight absorption at Pittsburgh[2] were greater than average extras, but this was not so at Chicago. Hence mill net yield at Pittsburg was less than the base price, by almost 2 per cent for structurals and plates, and by 9 per cent for sheets. In the Chicago example mill net yield was slightly greater than the base price.

Table 57. *Mill net yield and base price ($ per long ton), February, 1939*[a]

	Heavy structural steel		Plates, Pittsburgh	Cold rolled sheets, Gary and Irwin
	Chicago	Pittsburgh		
1. Base price	47·04	47·04	47·04	71·68
2. Extras	2·22	3·25	3·45	0·92
3. 1+2	—— 49·26	—— 50·29	—— 50·49	—— 72·60
4. Freight absorbed	0·78	2·73	2·67	3·25
5. Price reductions	1·30	1·39	1·66	4·21
6. 4+5	—— 2·08	—— 4·12	—— 4·33	—— 7·46
7. Mill net yield	47·18	46·17	46·16	65·14
8. 1−7	−0·14	0·87	0·88	6·54

[a] I have used the collection of *U.S. Steel Corporation T.N.E.C. Papers* published by the Corporation in 1940, vol. II, p. 134. In this table prices in cents per pound have been converted to dollars per long ton.

These figures do not show the distribution of concessions; price reductions were not necessarily restricted to distant sales, and the F.T.C. stated that concessions were normally made to large and powerful buyers, at the expense of small and medium buyers and the state.

It was clear from the second set of figures published that those for February 1939 were only in a limited sense representative. The second set showed the difference between base price and mill net yield for a number of products at a number of basing-points from 1926 to 1938. The comparison reveals great variations in the differences for the same product in different years and different conditions of trade. It is unlikely that average extras would fluctuate greatly from year to year as a proportion of

[1] The average freight paid and added was not given in this table. But for a selection of products and plants the freight paid averaged $5·71 a ton, the average added to the base price in calculating the delivered prices was $3·72.

[2] *United States Steel Corporation T.N.E.C. Papers*, vol. II, p. 130, for sheets at Pittsburgh and Gary.

base price,[1] and the implication is that the variations occurred in either price reduction or freight absorption, or both. The total of these appears almost always to have been greater than in February 1939; but there are no published data to show how they moved individually. Table 58 shows the position for structural shapes at Pittsburgh. Charts at the end of this volume give other comparisons, which bear the same general interpretation, though the extent of price reduction and freight absorption was always less for Chicago than for Pittsburgh, and the sheet trade was better off, not worse off, prior to 1938–39 when the collective effect of all the new plants was just becoming effective. The contrast between the trend of sheet prices

Table 58. *Extent to which mill net yield fell below reported base price 1926–38. Structural steel at Pittsburgh*[a]

	In cents/lb.	As % of base price	Ingot capacity occupied	Base price rising or falling
1926	0·13	6·7	89	R
1927	0·07	3·8	80	F
1928	0·10	5·4	85	R
1929	0·13	6·8	90	R
1930	0·07	4·1	67	F
1931	0·15	9·3	39	F
1932	0·19	12·0	18	R
1933	0·11	6·8	29	R
1934	0·09	5·1	32	R
1935	0·04	2·2	41	—
1936	0·10	5·4	63	R
1937	0·17	7·7	72	R
1938	0·08	3·7	36	F
Feb. 1939	0·04	1·8		

[a] Based on *United States Steel Corporation T.N.E.C. Papers*, vol. II, p. 78. For convenience it may be remarked that 0·10 cent per lb. = $2·24 per ton.

[1] Extras did become higher and a larger proportion of the base price during the 12 years (below, p. 489). It is unlikely, however, that the extras which ought to have been charged would change as a proportion of the base price much, and certainly not sometimes up and sometimes down from year to year. It is conceivable that big changes in the relative importance of different uses for steel could have significant effects of this kind, but is somewhat unlikely. Any concessions over extras, the charging of less than was due, must be thought of as a price reduction, though it was not always recorded as such (below, p. 485).

and prices of heavy products and bars is an indication of the profound effect of the strip mill in lowering costs.

The extent to which mill net yield fell below quoted base prices was thus never as low as in February 1939 except in 1935. This was one of the untypical years of the decade, during which the N.R.A. code[1] operated, though only till May. It operated also in part of 1933 and the whole of 1934; and while it was operating nominally and to a large extent practically there was a régime of open prices without secret price cuts. It is at first sight surprising that 1934 was not the year of minimum concessions; but this may in part at least be explained by the fact that it was a year of rising base prices; it was likely therefore that at any given month some mill net yields were based on lower base prices than those currently 'reported'.[2] It was possible in these figures to have conflicting trends. In 1935 the reported base price was the same for the whole year. When the N.I.R. act was declared unconstitutional the codes were dropped; but the larger steel firms wanted to sustain the code practices, and possibly no smaller firm was ready immediately to restore the old ones. It is impressive that the largest excess of base price over mill net yield was in 1932, when the industry reached its lowest ebb, an output equal to 18 per cent of capacity, and in the previous year, a year of shrinking output in which the effect of concessions was partly offset by sharply falling base prices. The third year of maximum excess was 1937, a year of relatively good output, when the base price rose in the first four months by 10 per cent, more than in a whole year in the rest of the period 1926–38, and the mill net yield rose in the end much more—by 20 per cent—but after a time lag.

Reductions of price and freight absorption were thus in 1926–38 almost certainly more as a rule than they were in

[1] Below, p. 502.

[2] Prices were normally quoted for a quarter, but buyers liked to secure quotations for longer periods if they could secure low prices, and presumably if they thought a rise was likely. Sometimes they were able to get prices fixed for a whole year (see evidence of Charles Hook, *T.N.E.C. Hearings*, vol. xx, p. 10813). Such long contracts were less likely in periods of falling prices. They should be regarded as analogous to concessions to some extent. In 1930 prices were falling; hence this kind of concession would not occur. It is possible that the high margin of 1928 reflected price-cutting in anticipation of the falls which occurred in 1930.

February 1939 (that is more, jointly, than 8–12 per cent for Pittsburgh: the percentage was smaller for Chicago), though possibly not so much more than this as the size of the excess in the table suggests because of the effect of changing base prices.

The wartime statistical examination of a large sample of consumers' experiences filled out this picture in important respects, though it did not provide a continuation of the series of 'mill net yields', nor any further information of freight absorption.[1] The data were collected from a sample 'representing every major steel-consuming industry in every major industrial area', but subsidiaries of steel companies and warehouses, and 'certain very large consumers in the automobile and container industry', were excluded from the inquiry.'[2]

Since large concessions were made to these large users the price data collected understated the extent to which realised prices fell below quoted prices.[3] The investigation, however, filled in some important gaps. It identified, as the earlier did not, how great were the concessions made on extras. The concessions could be 100 per cent; hot rolled sheets which were pickled and oiled were sometimes sold without the extras for these processes being charged. All such facts may not have been elicited in the inquiry, but at least it gave an indication of the widespread cutting of extras, which was greatest for cold rolled strip. In the second quarter of 1939, of the orders for this product examined 28 per cent were charged less than half the appropriate extras, and a further 15 per cent between 50 and 80 per cent. Unfortunately, the data refer to numbers of orders only, without weights. In some instances concessions were made by 'downgrading' the product sold into a category where either base prices or extras were lower. This is the kind of thing which inevitably escapes any statistical sieve.[4]

[1] *Consumers' Prices of Steel Products* prepared by W. Fazar and Fay Bean, supervised by Kenneth Hunter under the supervision of W. G. Keim (*United States Department of Labor*: Bureau of Labor Statistics), an inquiry conducted at the request of the Iron and Steel Branch of the Office of Price Administration.

[2] *Ibid.* p. 20. The omission was because the Office of Price Administration was planning to get data from another source.

[3] *Ibid. loc. cit.*

[4] It can happen under a rigid price control. In the United Kingdom the proportion of 'seconds' in sheets has been known to vary according to the state of trade.

The most useful general data provided were of two kinds. First, for eight products the orders examined were put into categories showing the price paid as a percentage of the price which according to published prices should have been paid, and the spread of price reduction (by whatever means) is indicated.

Table 59. *Variations of delivered prices as percentage of published prices, 2nd quarter, 1939*[a]

	% of number of orders for							
Delivered price:	H.R. sheets	C.R. sheets	H.R. strip	C.R. strip	Merchant bars	C.R. bars	Plates	Sections
Under 69·9%	—	—	—	3	—	—	—	—
From 70 to 79·9%	5	—	16	10	—	—	—	—
From 80 to 89·9%	33	29	22	28	4	3	9	9
From 90 to 99·9%	48	61	42	41	73	54	74	83
From 100 to 100·9%	3	7	6	—	5	26	8	6
101% and over of published prices	12	4	13	18	18	17	8	2
*97–99·9%	8	25	10	20	57	41	55	58

[a] Based on the detailed tables in the Appendices in the report, pp. 81 sqq.

* This is given separately because in a few products there was a large bunch of small concessions.

Thus most buyers obtained steel at prices below those published,[1] but in markedly different degrees, the concessions being much greater for strip and, in a lesser degree, for sheets than for the heavy products and bars. This confirms the impression given by the figures for February 1939 of the effect of the greatly enhanced competition arising from the strip mills. Added to this was the powerful influence as buyers of the manufacturers of cars and of cans, although as has been seen their purchases were largely excluded from the sample. Even in the sample, however, about 40 per cent of sheet and strip orders (in number, not weight) were sold at prices 20 per cent or more below the quoted price. These figures emphasised, as those for 'mill net yields' do also, the worthlessness of international

[1] 'Published price' meant 'The sum of the published base price at the basing-point nearest the consumer plus published extras applicable plus rail freight from the basing-point to the consumers' plant' (*Consumers' Prices of Steel Products*, p. 2).

comparisons which build up American prices from published base prices, extras and railway freights.

Similar information is given of these prices for five later quarters (not consecutive quarters) up to the second quarter of 1942. They are remarkable because of the change of pattern. With the war concessions became unnecessary, and the pattern is entirely different in the final periods. Sales at or below published prices in the second quarter of 1942 are shown in Table 60.

Table 60. *Percentages of sales at or below quoted prices, 2nd quarter,* 1942[a]

	H.R. sheets	C.R. sheets	H.R. strip	C.R. strip	Merchant bars	C.R. bars	Plates	Sections
Below quoted price	3	3	2	2	Nil	2	Nil	3
At quoted price	94	94	98	91	98	96	85	97

[a] Sales above quoted price can be calculated by differences—except that in some of the columns in the Table there is an uplift in rounding-off both items.

The American steelmakers thus were able to increase the real price for their product sharply at the beginning of the war (when costs also tended to rise) with no increase in their published basing-point prices, and this they did. They eliminated concessions on base prices and extras, enforced more rigid interpretations of extras, introduced new extras, and went further in some cases and charged freight from the mill, their own mill, not the basing-point. They adopted in fact an 'F.O.B. Mill' base price and cut out freight absorption.[1] This had always been done at times when users were ready to pay a premium for early delivery, but it became more widespread. The sample examined, as has been seen, understated the extent of the elimination of concessions by leaving out major buyers who had the largest concessions, and because no account was taken of rebates received at the end of a year and based on the year's business; but the broad picture is that prices of bars rose least, by about 2 per cent, by this means; sections by 4 per cent, plates by 6 per cent, sheet and strip by 10 per cent. The figures are given in Table 61.

[1] *Consumers' Prices of Steel Products*, p. 3.

Table 61. *Invoice prices as percentage of published prices*

	H.R. sheets	C.R. sheets	H.R. strip	C.R. strip	Merchant bars	C.F. bars	Plates	Sections
2nd qr., 1939	92 (98)	95 (102)	92 (98)	91 (102)	99	99 (101)	97	97
3rd qr., 1939	88 (95)	92	86 (95)	89 (100)	98	98	97	96
2nd qr., 1940	94 (97)	95 (98)	95 (97)	91 (98)	99	98	98	98
2nd qr., 1941	99	99	100	94	99	98	100	99
4th qr., 1941	100	99	—	97	100	99	102	100
2nd qr., 1942	101	100	100	101	101	100	103	101

In general the quoted prices—the base prices—did not vary in the period. The figures in brackets indicate where there were differences; otherwise the base price is 100 throughout.

Mill net yields may have risen more in relation to base prices than delivered prices did, because there may have been less of the 'cross-freighting' which reduced yields but did not raise delivered prices. The figures arising from the survey of 1943 were thus only analogous to the 'price reductions' of the February 1939 figures (Table 57); but they supplemented these because they identified and measured concessions on extras whereas the earlier set did not.[1] The comparison of mill net yields and base prices, illuminating as it was, suffered from the defect that it exaggerated the importance of the base price alone. The survey of 1943 showed that prices of all the strip and cold finished bars and virtually all sheets, over 70 per cent of merchant bars, 40 per cent of plates, and 34 per cent of sections included some extras, and that for many products extras were a large part of the price.[2] The range of 'extras' had

[1] The United States Steel Corporation figures for Feb. 1939 appear to be concerned only with the extras which were charged and paid, not with extras which might have been charged. Above, p. 482.

[2] The ratio of base prices, extras and freights was set out (p. 15) in the following table:

	Base price (av. of sample 1939–42)	Extras	Freight	Delivered price
H.R. sheets	74·6	19·8	5·6	100
C.R. sheets	89·6	5·8	4·6	100
H.R. strip	75·2	17·8	7·0	100
C.R. strip	60·0	35·0	5·0	100
Merchant bars	87·1	6·0	6·9	100
C.F. bars	69·8	25·3	4·9	100
Plates	86·3	3·3	10·4	100
Sections	83·8	1·5	9·7	100
Average	78·9	14·3	6·8	100

grown much since 1925, even for products like structural shapes,[1] which made them a larger element in prices, and a growing field for concessions. For most products they gave more scope for concessions than freights.[2]

'The price the consumer pays for steel', the 1943 survey concluded, 'does not depend as much upon the pricing system used as it does upon the degree of competition among the mills.' This conflicted with the F.T.C. judgement, that there was 'momentary competition from time to time' which was 'quickly cured';[3] that only 'vestigial traces' of competition remained which 'still crawl here and there under the surface';[4] that 'occasional variations from the perfect identity' (of prices) are observed, but only during 'short periods when there was a temporary flurry of price cutting';[5] that secret discounts 'may continue' to have some influence with large and influential users, but medium and small buyers (and the Government) paid the full price.[6] The emphasis and interpretation implied by the F.T.C. was evidently wrong; it is impossible to sustain the view that concessions were limited to large influential users only when they extended to 40 per cent or more of orders (i.e. orders by *number*, not by weight) and the statistics show a continuity of concessions over many years on a substantial scale, so that the implication that after a 'short flurry' of price-cutting the list prices were adhered to was misleading. The picture can easily be adjusted to become near the truth. When a 'short flurry' occurred it no doubt was at a period when one firm was making a vigorous effort to get new business, or when one buyer was exerting heavy pressure, playing one seller off against another. The initial sign of this was a substantial price reduction first by one firm, then followed inevitably by others, and accompanied by some shift of business, which was usually the

---

[1] For these, for example in 1925 there were list extras for special size, special cutting, special length, inspection, United States Navy inspection. In 1940, in addition, extras could be charged for chemical composition, milling, painting, special marking, protected shipment, surface finish, test requirements, restricted physical test, quantity, Federal specification (*Consumers' Prices of Steel Products*, p. 17).

[2] The average freight for the listed products ranged roughly from $3·5 to $5·8 per ton in 1939–42.

[3] *The Basing-Point Problem*, pp. 4–5.   [4] *Ibid. loc. cit.*
[5] *Ibid.* p. 1.   [6] *Ibid. loc. cit.*

initial object of the exercise. The 'flurry' was brought to an end in some instances—probably always, but the records are limited —by discussions and correspondence between some or all of the parties affected. The bigger firms, especially the United States Steel Corporation, could threaten retaliation. Big buyers too could threaten; if they found that one of their suppliers had given a better price to a rival they could threaten anti-trust proceedings under the Robinson Patman Act, and these things they did. Concessions thus tended to have to be spread, and this too no doubt had a restraining influence.[1] A 'flurry', a period of large-scale new concessions, would therefore be brought to an end, but the concessions remained. This process on varying scales was probably the normal means whereby firms expanded their share of the business to the extent that this was done by getting new customers. Though concessions were not cancelled when a 'flurry of competition' ended they were obviously not permanently invariable; but the records give little or nothing about the reverse process until after 1939 under the influence of war, when the list prices were declared maxima and firms nevertheless wanted to cover rising costs and no doubt to avoid the losses or improve on the low profits which depression had entailed. The fluctuating gap between mill net yields and base prices substantiate the judgement of 1943 that prices reflected the degree of competition, which was determined partly by general demand and partly by changes in supply, such as the development of the strip mill. There could be additional special factors of a different kind; it is possible that the traceable concessions on sections were particularly low because a large tonnage was used by constructional engineering subsidiaries of the major steelmakers, for example, by the American Bridge Company, part of the United States Steel

[1] An illuminating set of documents in *T.N.E.C. Hearings*, vol. xx, pp. 10,988 sqq., traces the spread of concessions on tinplates to the large tin-can makers in 1936–8. This involved concessions by one maker to one user being made the basis of wider concessions. In the process two of those concerned discussed 'control over the Metal Trades Journals in the publication of prices on tinplate and the elimination of such comments as are foreign to the subject (from our standpoint)'. Price concessions on past deliveries were assumed. There was also an interesting discussion of tube prices; here there was resistance to a concession and a threat of retaliation which seems to have worked (*T.N.E.C. Hearings*, vol. 20, pp. 10830 sqq.).

Corporation, which according to the F.T.C. had at one time at any rate advantages in cheap steel not given to competitors.[1]

What was the effect of competition in this form, on steelmaking, and on steel consumers? The F.T.C. complained that the basing-point system bolstered up old and ill-sited plant. The location pattern of the industry indeed changed slowly; but it did change. Pennsylvania gradually grew proportionately less important, and within Pennsylvania Pittsburgh lost a little in importance to Bethlehem.[2] As Pennsylvania lost ground Maryland and Delaware, New York, Alabama and, rather later, California and other western states gained. The relative importance of Ohio, Illinois and Indiana changed little. The United States Steel Corporation held that this relative stability was explained by relative raw-material costs; Pittsburgh gained so much by nearness to coal that her raw materials for pig iron cost less than at most other sites of plants using Lake ores.[3] Hence although Pittsburgh had to sell more outside her

[1] *The Basing-Point Problem*, p. 4. The inquiry of 1943 did not deal with sales of subsidiaries.

[2] The distribution of United States ingot output is indicated approximately in the following figures (percentages of total ingot output):

	1929	1932	1937	1941	1944	1953
Pennsylvania (Pittsburgh-Bethlehem)	36·2	27·7	30·9	31·1	30·6	27·7
Ohio (Cleveland, Youngstown)	21·5	28·2	21·9	20·9	20·9	19·4
Indiana (Gary)	12·5	10·7	12·1	13·0	12·6	12·4
Illinois (Chicago)	7·9	7·1	8·8	8·1	8·3	8·1
New York (Buffalo, Lackawanna)	4·6	4·2	5·7	5·4	5·2	5·3
W. Virginia (Weirton, Wheeling)	3·2	3·3	4·2	3·7	3·7	3·8
Maryland, Delaware etc. (Sparrows Point)	3·0	4·4	4·6	5·0	5·2	5·4
Alabama	2·9	3·7	3·8	4·1	4·6	4·0
California	—	—	1·2	1·1	1·7	2·6

[3] They reproduced with approval (*The Basing-Point Problem*, p. 17) figures giving the cost of ore, coal and limestone for 1 ton of pig iron in 1937 as: $6·313 at Weirton, $6·425 at Pittsburgh, $6·452 at Cleveland, $6·647 at Buffalo, $6·832 at Detroit, $7·324 at Youngstown, $7·595 at Chicago. These cannot be regarded as stable or even precise perhaps for 1937; but they are not widely different from some published since the war for 1939 referring to the material for 1 ton of finished steel. This assumes a scrap charge of about 50 per cent, which would keep most of the figures too low except in depressions. These are of interest because they cover

'natural territory' and so absorb more freight than, say, Chicago, it could afford to do so. The price figures for February 1939 quoted earlier show that there was a greater degree of freight absorption at Pittsburgh than at Chicago on sales of structural steel. The centre of gravity of the consumption of steel tended to move towards the Middle West; nevertheless, Pittsburgh remained fairly well located for much of it.[1] The freight absorption which might reasonably have provoked most consideration or concern was that involved in sales to the growing markets on the extremities—in Houston, for example, but above all in California. Basing-points were established at 'Gulf Ports' and 'Pacific Coast Ports' in 1934, although there were no plants at the first and minor ones at the second, in order to facilitate competition with imports; but even before that

a wider range of sites. They are only approximate, calculated from published prices and freight, not works costs (figures are in dollars).

Centre	Iron ore	Coal	Limestone	Total
Birmingham	0·95	1·49	0·15	2·59
Provo	2·30	2·46	0·26	5·02
Duluth	1·15	3·79	0·37	5·31
Pueblo	2·89	1·95	0·79	5·63
Pittsburgh	4·67	0·36	0·62	5·65
Bethlehem	1·17	4·18	0·51	5·86
Cleveland	2·67	2·94	0·45	6·06
Youngstown	4·19	1·94	0·34	6·47
Detroit	2·66	3·52	0·31	6·49
Buffalo	2·67	3·43	0·45	6·55
Chicago-Gary	2·66	4·32	0·37	7·35
Sparrows Point	4·63	3·98	1·05	9·66
San Bernardino	2·51	7·44	Negligible	9·95

(From Walter Isard and William M. Capron, 'The Future Locational Pattern of Iron and Steel Production in the United States', *J. of Political Econ.* vol. LVII, no. 2, Apr. 1949, p. 121.)

[1] The United States Steel Corporation put the following in order of precedence as steel-consuming centres in 1937: (1) Detroit, (2) Chicago-Gary, (3) Pittsburgh, (4) Cleveland, (5) Los Angeles, (6) Youngstown, (7) Milwaukee, (8) San Francisco, (9) Newark, (10) New York, (11) Cincinnati, (12) Houston, (13) Buffalo, (14) St Louis, (15) Toledo. The products used in different areas varied considerably. Thus 55 per cent of Michigan's consumption of steel was in sheets or strip; and this area, centre of car production, used 28 per cent of United States output of hot rolled sheets, 43 per cent of the total output of hot rolled strip, 60 per cent of cold rolled sheet, 37·4 per cent of the cold rolled strip. The Michigan demand was also highly seasonal, because it was a motor-car demand (Isard and Capron, *op. cit.* p. 130).

prices of steel sold there had been subject to large 'reductions'.[1] The Texas demand rose from oil, and delivery of pipe was possibly in the main by water, by sea, or down the Mississippi. There was no local production at all. California, where initially the large demand came from canners, and later also from oil,[2] could also be reached by water, through the Panama Canal; but only one major eastern plant (Bethlehem at Sparrows Point) could load directly on to vessels in the trade, and even then the freight could not be insignificant. There was a little production in California, based on local or imported scrap, and pig iron from Colorado, but it did not quickly expand. Was this an instance where eastern price-cutting stopped a natural development? When firms gave up making price concessions and absorbing freight in 1942–43, Far Western consumers of steel found prices rise exceptionally;[3] and subsequently steel production has become more vigorous—Kaiser went into steel among other things—but the general American pattern has only changed fairly gradually.

If distribution of production among firms, not among places, is taken as the criterion of the influence of prices, then the period 1929–39 did witness a remarkable change. It is most simply illustrated by the change in the relative importance of the main firms from 1929 to 1938, which is shown in Table 62. This shows that six out of the leading eleven steelmakers fared much better than the United States Steel Corporation in getting business in these years. They increased their turnover faster, in general much faster. They were all small, some very small, compared with the Corporation. In 1937 their collective turn-over exceeded that of the Corporation by less than 5 per cent; but in 1929 the Corporation's exceeded theirs by 40 per cent. The participation of the Corporation in the steel business only was not as large as these figures suggest; the Corporation had greater interests than the other firms outside the manufacture of steel, in the production of raw materials, in transport, and in

---

[1] *The Basing-Point Problem*, p. 43.

[2] In 1937 one-fifth of Pacific coast steel consumption was tinplate; a sixth was in tubes (Isard and Capron, *op. cit.* p. 128).

[3] *Consumers' Prices of Steel Products*, p. 19.

Table 62. *Turnover of main United States steel firms (in each column 1929 = 100)*[1]

	U.S. Steel Corp.	Bethle-hem	Republic	Jones and Laughlin	Youngs-town Sheet and Tube	National Steel	Inland	American Rolling Mill Co.	Wheeling	Otis	Pitts-burg
1930	78	76	a	72	69	75[b]	75	76	78	64	88
1931	48	55	a	44	37	73	45	57	53	42	52
1932	24	28	35	22	20	49	22	39	36	21	26
1933	35	35	51	35	31	72	38	60	53	42	21
1934	39	49	71	37	39	88	60	78	58	52	38
1935	52	57	100	50	54	120	91	109	80	69	32
1936	74	84	168	75	80	142	143	160	96	90	53
1937	93	123	185	93	89	169	162	163	108	98	88
1938	51	78	104	60	52	105	109	100	75	43	59
					Value in $m.						
1937	1396	418	250	117	144	146	111	115	90	32	35

a No figures available for 1929–31; the initial figure (for 1932) is assumed for convenience to be 3
b No figure for 1929; it is assumed that the 1930 figure was 75 per cent of 1929.

the manufacture of products from steel; it made bridges, railroad and oil-well equipment, ships, barges, cement.[2] In 1913 the Corporation had made 53 per cent of the total United States ingot output; in 1929, when turnover was much over half that of the main firms, the ingot percentage was 39; and in 1937 and 1938 it was 37 and 33. The Corporation's importance in different branches of the industry did not keep in line with the average. It retained its importance most successfully in rails and structural steel. Its position in heavy plate-making was unimpaired till 1929, but then fell away sharply. It lost ground particularly in wire rods, tubes, tinplate, sheets—in the more finished products.

The steel companies who thrived most in competing with the Corporation were thus in general making products for the growing industries, especially the motor trade, canning, oil and natural gas. Two of those whose growth was not markedly different from the Corporation's—Jones and Laughlin and the Pittsburgh Steel Co.—were Pittsburgh-centred, and the former

[1] *T.N.E.C. Hearings*, Part 31, 'Investment profits and rates of return', p. 17,766.
[2] There is a brief survey of the United States Steel Corporation in *T.N.E.C. Hearings*, part 31, pp. 17,746 sqq. It is followed by short studies of the other companies. There is greater detail later in the volume. Thus the investment in transport, mainly in seven railways, represented 14 per cent of the total investment, and gave 24 per cent of the income 1925–37.

Table 63. *United States Steel Corporation output as percentage of United States steel output*[a]

	Ingots	Rails	Heavy sections	Plates	Sheets and strip	Wire rod	Tin-plate	Tubes
1913	53·2	55·5	54·0	53·1	44·8	58·4	58·6	50·4
1920	45·8	58·1	43·9	46·4	32·9	56·0	45·1	43·4
1929	38·8	50·6	41·8	51·9	22·8	45·7	38·8	34·8
1937	36·6	52·3	44·7	39·8	24·2	36·9	32·5	31·5
1938	33·2	54·5	44·4	30·6	24·3	31·0	35·5	29·3

[a] *T.N.E.C. Hearings*, Part 31, p. 17,747.

and larger was heavily concerned in the rail and structural
trade. The thriving firms were, with few exceptions, little concerned with building or railway steel. Probably some of them
were more alive to the significance of the newer markets, and
they were often well located to supply them, whereas the United
States Steel Corporation was extremely strong in Pittsburgh.[1]
All, with two possible exceptions, were large enough to use the
characteristic American production methods.[2] Possibly they
were more technically alert. It was the American Rolling Mill
Company who first successfully developed the wide strip mill
(in 1939 their patents were licensed to thirteen other American
steel firms, including the United States Steel Corporation,
Republic, and Youngstown and to some foreign firms).[3] Weirton

[1] Thus the National Steel Co. had a plant at Detroit (Great Lakes Steel Co.);
the Otis Co. was at Cleveland and could send sheets, etc., by water to Detroit.

[2] The ingot capacity in 1937 of the firms listed was:

	m. tons	% of total		m. tons	% of total
U.S. Steel Corp.	25·8	35·3	Youngstown	3·1	4·3
Bethlehem	10·0	13·8	Inland	2·8	3·8
Republic	6·5	8·9	A.R.M. Co.	2·6	3·6
Jones and Laughlin	3·7	5·0	Wheeling	1·8	2·4
National	3·4	4·7	Otis	0·9	1·2
			Pittsburgh	0·8	1·1

[3] *T.N.E.C. Hearings*, Part 19, evidence of Charles Hook, President of Armco,
gives the story, pp. 10,689 sqq. Armco started its development in 1925; previous
experiments 15 years earlier by other firms had failed. The development cost
$7 m. The investment in mills to 1939 had been $500 m., for a capacity of 13 m.
tons, reducing the price of sheets by 40 per cent.

was a pioneer in cold reduction (1930), Crucible one of the pioneers in electrolytic tinning, though here the Corporation was among the first to develop the process on a commercial scale in 1936–37. Most of the companies were integrated, having some at least of their ore and coal; but at the consuming end their strength lay in their contact with growing demands, and possibly the cultivation of specialities for the newer industries.[1] There was possibly an element of reciprocity; users may have deliberately encouraged the smaller firms (which were still large enough to be efficient and have low costs). Probably too the antitrust legislation helped because discriminating attacks by a large firm on small ones *seriatim*—'price-raiding' the F.T.C. called it—were an offence. Finally, it is evident that the embarrassment of railways, building and shipbuilding in the thirties must have handicapped the older companies.

The price competition among American firms which the published records show in the home trade, and which had some effect, as the changing size of businesses shows, made the agreement between American steelmakers and the European Steel Cartel largely ineffective. This agreement, referred to briefly earlier,[2] was arranged conspicuously in order to avoid any impression that the Sherman Act was being contravened. Sir Andrew Duncan made a much-publicised visit; the American Attorney General was called in to meetings and to examine records of discussions. No restraint was placed on competition from European firms in the United States;[3] and competition from Europe, especially from Belgium, which had led to demands from American steelmakers for added protection and a more vigorous Anti-Dumping Act in 1936, continued

---

[1] Thus Republic concentrated on alloy steels (which the car trade took largely) and was an early maker of electric welded tubes.

[2] *E.H.S.* p. 482.

[3] One of the negotiators in the steel arrangements said later to me that I.C.I.'s great mistake in their American arrangements in the thirties was failing to establish clearly and specifically and conspicuously that no restraint was put on competition from Britain or Europe. But the long discussions of the steel agreement before the T.N.E.C. showed that many Senators did not accept the view that if an agreement of this kind were made it would have no effect on the home market. They held that an implied result of the agreement would be the reduction of European competition in the United States home market (see *T.N.E.C. Hearings*, Part 20, pp. 10,922 sqq.).

vigorously; the United States was one of the areas where the European cartel allowed prices to be cut. The agreement, covered by the Webb Pomerene Act, restrained price-cutting, and provided for quotas both between the countries, and within the United States between firms who were prepared to agree in respect of their exports. There were a number of separate arrangements for different products.[1] But whereas in Europe, and the United Kingdom, export selling was largely in the hands of central selling agencies, the American firms sold independently and there were always outsiders.[2] There was, too, immense suspicion about what the 'insiders' did. A leading British sheet firm believed that no American firm charged the full extras on exports, and having regard to internal United States practice this seems likely.[3] It was also currently believed that one at least of the bigger American firms stimulated one or two smaller firms to cut prices on exports rather than at home— they protected important individual home orders for themselves in this way. The United States Steel Corporation and Bethlehem appeared to adopt what some observers described as a browbeating attitude in trying to retain large slices of export business when nominally price competition was no longer allowed to determine it. But this only provoked opposition.[4] In many

[1] American participation in the international tube, tinplate and rail agreements was usually effective (*T.N.E.C. Hearings*, p. 10,986); the breaks in these were not due primarily to United States firms. A more general heavy product agreement first proposed in 1936 covering plates, sheets, etc., was never completely organised, though the United States Steel Corporation and Bethlehem felt under an obligation in regard to it, and liable for fines, and quotas were apparently fixed. (One British informant told me there were no quotas; but the evidence by United States participants to the T.N.E.C. was quite specific on this.)

[2] They were especially important in sheets and plates. For example *ibid.* pp. 10,948, 10,957. Outsider competition in plates came not solely from firms listed in Table 62, which were the largest, but notably from two Philadelphia firms, Central and Worth. Of the larger, Inland and Weirton were specifically spoken of as low-cost outsiders called in to the Dudley discussions as though they were price cutters (*ibid.* p. 10,967). Inland led the price-cutting in tinplate at home (*ibid.* p. 10,992). A form of central selling for export was vaguely proposed in the United States (*ibid.* p. 10,955).

[3] A British group headed by the Earl of Dudley visited America to complain of the United States failure over sheets in Feb. 1938 (*ibid.* p. 10,948).

[4] The Corporation and Bethlehem clearly thought that as they had had most of the export trade they should continue to have most of it (*T.N.E.C. Hearings*, p. 10,969).

export markets American selling, most conspicuously by some of the smaller corporations, was a seriously 'demoralising' force in 1938 despite the agreement.[1] It was notably so in Sweden, in Holland and in South America. In both these areas the European cartel agreed to price reduction by European exporters to meet the American competition.[2] At least one American firm joined the international agreements in some products but not in all, and from this favourable position used the familiar 'coupled bargain' technique. The agreement as a whole was in a precarious position on the outbreak of war.[3]

Thus the American industry was not held completely rigid by the basing-point price system as it worked (or as some might say did not work) in the thirties. Whether all the changes in location or relative importance of firms were for the best is another matter; but obviously there was an impressive technical development, with much improved 'productivity', and a high rate of capital investment, and in the newer products significant reductions of prices, and at many points in the industry relative newcomers had scope to grow. All these were features in the industry likely to benefit consumers; but could it be that discriminations involved in their attainment offset the gains?

The discriminations practised during the operation of the basing-point system were of two kinds, and their effect on consumers differed. The practice of freight absorption allowed

[1] *T.N.E.C. Hearings*, Part 20, pp. 10922 sqq.

[2] The technique was that firms wishing to reduce prices below the agreed figure consulted the management committee. The reduction was only allowed if business was thereby secured from a non-cartel country (or firm). The United States did not operate on this basis. The United States firms in the agreement appear to have encouraged European firms to 'get' business in competition with price-cutting American outsiders (*ibid.* pp. 10,956 sqq.). The Belgians were the chief price reducers. In determining agreed prices the United States makers usually asked for the highest figure, the Continent for the lowest, with the United Kingdom in between, and therefore commonly successful. The competitive price cuts in Sweden were around 17s. to 20s. a ton, when prices for bars, for example, averaged £4. 17s. 0d. a ton gold. It was said that British steelmakers were anxious to see United States competition in Sweden rather than in other north-European markets, as Sweden was a better market for the Germans than for the British.

[3] This account is based on unpublished information from participants. The best published authority on the cartel is Ervin Hexner, *op. cit.*, and the *T.N.E.C Hearings* give a lively picture.

people to get all the steel they used as though it came from the basing-point most favourably situated for them. If production were or could be sufficiently large at or near that point the price level on this base was one which in the long run they should have been able to enjoy for a long time; the price could correspond to long-term 'real costs' of supply.[1] There was nothing inherently misleading in freight absorption from this point of view, no necessary encouragement of 'uneconomic' sites; though if all steelmakers sold a large proportion of their output of identical products in each other's 'natural' markets, average transport costs would as shown earlier be needlessly increased. The extent to which this happened was not measured in the published records. An outside limit was set, for February 1939, in the figures published above. Freight absorption at Pittsburgh, for whom it was largest, averaged about $2·7 per ton for sections and plates, $3·4 for sheets.[2] In part this was offset by Pittsburgh's advantages in raw-material costs,[3] in part it represented deliveries to deficit areas whose supply would have involved more freight than from the nearest basing-point in any case.[4]

It is not worth over-refining the argument on this,[5] because the other form of discrimination, price cuts to particular customers (possibly according to a pattern), was an equally or more important factor. It was open to sellers to get business either by concessions or freight absorption, or by both combined. What effect was the effort to get business, on a big scale, likely to have on the development of consuming industries? To this there can be no determinate answer. Large users, who were most likely to get concessions, were likely to include those for

[1] It may be thought that if the full transport was always charged at any location the incentive for the growth of steelmaking at the most favoured basing-point would be greater; but the higher price might discourage the growth of the demand.

[2] Above, p. 482. For particular trades it was of course much more than the average. The figures for sheets cover Pittsburgh and Gary; Gary sent sheets to the Pacific coast by rail.

[3] Above, pp. 491–2.

[4] Thus Michigan in 1937 could supply only approximately one-third of her own steel, and none at all of some finished products. It is, of course, open to speculation whether this deficiency would have been less had expansion of capacity been differently located; but there is no ready answer without detailed study, and a growing market does not at once offer scope for large-scale units.

[5] There is a vast literature on it; and the problem is not one limited to steel.

whom the cost of steel was most important. The bias in favour
of larger users offended the F.T.C.; but if it added to the forces
which helped large-scale industry to develop it was conceivably
favourable to the rapid growth of general industrial efficiency,
unless it was on such a scale as to check seriously the growth
of relative newcomers and rising smaller firms in consuming
industries, which was so important in steel itself. But the concessions were, after all, competitive; the steel firms spread the
net of concessions wide. Although in appearance arbitrary, this
system of clandestine concessions may have been relatively
rational in operation.

The profit figures (Table 64) show the net effect of the policy

Table 64. *Profits before tax as percentage of total investment
(in main United States firms)*[a]

Company	1929	1930	1931	1932	1933	1934	1935	1936	1937	1938
U.S. Steel	12·18	6·16	0·95	*3·52*	*1·75*	*0·81*	0·63	4·56	8·64	0·22
Bethlehem	8·93	4·71	1·10	*2·03*	*0·41*	1·21	1·97	3·72	6·92	1·97
Republic	11·52	0·24	*2·21*	*3·90*	*0·53*	*0·08*	3·75	6·35	5·65	*0·95*
Jones and Laughlin	11·56	5·06	*0·84*	*3·89*	*2·24*	*1·34*	0·06	2·95	3·47	*1·79*
Youngstown	12·92	5·19	*1·22*	*4·07*	*1·93*	0·90	3·12	7·50	8·49	*1·33*
National	b	9·85	5·78	*2·83*	3·85	6·66	10·33	11·38	15·44	5·98
Inland	16·63	8·95	3·44	*1·39*	2·40	6·73	12·82	14·20	13·15	5·37
A.R.M.Co.	10·46	2·37	*0·81*	0·24	1·78	4·04	7·93	9·68	9·37	*0·60*
Wheeling	7·61	4·05	*1·61*	*2·80*	0·77	2·13	5·46	6·06	5·84	1·99
Otis	13·06	4·61	*2·44*	6·77	*2·79*	4·92	11·24	10·95	10·44	*1·60*
Pittsburgh	10·93	4·90	*2·09*	*3·86*	3·89	*1·84*	2·85	0·50	5·18	0·57
Weighted average	11·53	5·47	0·58	2·96	1·03	0·41	2·24	5·52	8·16	0·90

Italicised figures are losses.

[a] *T.N.E.C. Hearings*, Part 31, p. 17,760, where the figures are given from 1917.
In some respects net income before interest or tax as percentage of turnover is more
interesting. The following are calculated for a few of the firms:

	1929	1930	1931	1932	1933	1934	1935	1936	1937	1938
United States Steel	15·63	10·26	2·56	*18·55*	*5·99*	*2·38*	1·33	6·06	9·29	0·45
Bethlehem	17·23	12·64	3·88	*13·31*	*2·08*	4·31	6·19	8·05	10·66	4·37
National	—	15·92	11·48	9·04	8·72	12·09	14·64	14·73	17·83	11·97
Inland	21·13	15·59	10·28	*9·09*	8·32	15·45	20·54	16·98	16·42	10·69
A.R.M.Co.	11·72	3·98	*1·95*	0·79	3·66	6·33	9·53	9·47	11·65	*1·05*

[b] The National Steel Corporation was formed in 1930.

was not to keep profits at a high level; the profits of the industry, from 1929 to 1938, were poor, except for one or two of the most successful smaller firms.

What determined the lower level of prices, the extent of concessions, cannot be identified from the data. The F.T.C. complained that the Steel Corporation fixed prices on a break-even point[1] of below 40 per cent of capacity till June 1938, and even then on a break-even point of about 50 per cent.[2] The Corporation retorted that had prices been lower sales would not have increased significantly (demand being in the short run at any rate inelastic), but the firm would have had larger losses. Though there remained gaps in the argument the conclusion was probably sound. The Corporation pointed out that the 'break-even point' was not capable of being forecast exactly, since the prices of different finished products did not bear the same relation to costs, a clear indication of the competitive influence in prices. The break-even point would not be the same for different firms; for some of the newer firms whose plant was newer than much of the Corporation's[3] and whose locations were better for the rising markets, the break-even point would have been lower at any price than the Corporation's; they would in that sense have been in a better position to cut prices lower. National, Inland and Armco lost least at the depth of

---

[1] The 'break-even point' was the volume of sales as a proportion of full capacity which at the prices fixed would just avoid losses, at which all costs, variable and invariable with output, and including depreciation and interest, would be just covered, so that below this scale of output the company made a loss, above it a net profit.

[2] *The Basing-Point Problem*, p. 3. The United States Steel Corporation appeared to show in a monograph that 50–55 per cent was the break-even point for the prices realised in the latter part of 1938; read without reference to other evidence it would imply that the realised price was the price as published, but that of course was not so *T.N.E.C. U.S. Steel Corp. Papers*, vol. I, pp. 235, 278. The F.T.C. argued that because output rose in 1939 above the 1938 level after a price reduction the high elasticity of demand for steel was proved (*The Basing-Point Problem*, pp. 124–5). If it was necessary to disprove it (it was a lawyer's, not an economist's, argument) the Corporation succeeds.

[3] In 1928 the Corporation started a survey of the state of its plants and discovered a large proportion of its equipment in need of replacement. A firm of consultants was employed to reinforce the internal survey from 1935 to 1938. This work led to capital expenditure of over $300 m. from 1935 to 1938, apart from depreciation, repairs, etc (*T.N.E.C. Papers*, vol. XXXI, pp. 17,771 and 17,804).

the depression—indeed, only Inland of these three lost at all, and only in 1932—and the first two of these three made good profits in 1938 when most firms did poorly or badly. Concessions which such firms were prepared to make, which on balance did not make them unprofitable (though individual concessions may have involved losses), may in the most active sense have performed the function of 'price leadership' in the industry.[1]

The F.T.C. was inclined to treat the whole process of price-cutting as a minor affair, and in principle objectionable, and when the National Recovery Administration made a special investigation at the instance of the President in 1934 it gave qualified support to the basing-point system but on the assumption that the prices announced by firms were adhered to. During the Code period such adherence was legally binding; the investigators supported this provided that there were more basing-points and that a limit was put on the amount of freight to be absorbed; it should not, they suggested, in any circumstances exceed $5 per ton.[2] This implicitly accepted the view that satisfactory competition could not be imposed, and that within limits freight absorption was economically defensible.[3] Those who

[1] Mr Hook, of Armco, described the process as it was happening in Nov. 1939. *T.N.E.C. Hearings*, Part 20, pp. 10,813–4. The motor-car industry had been strong enough to get 'some of the units' to cut prices and 'we have all followed'. In the fourth quarter of the year some had sold at $8 under the 'announced price'. 'Somebody found out'—as happens in contact with buyers—and 'may have gone a little bit lower'. Then 'there was that seesawing back and forth until they got down to a point...so low that nobody wanted to go any further and it just stopped...'. 'Then somebody feels that the base has been established and they will announce a price probably on that base unless they feel that they can get it up and announce somewhere between the low and the announced price that was supposed to be in existence.' Mr Hook said there had been 'considerable sales below cost'. He did not like it. He would not like to be the first—but 'none of us think we are the first—and sometimes we are misled'—of course by the buyers. However, Mr Hook made it clearer than some of the other leaders that the 'posted price' was only a guarantee to a buyer that he 'won't be charged more'; but 'if he can work it (and) get lower prices' that was in the scheme of things. Firms with costly new mills will be anxious to run their mills full and will therefore try to do so by concessions. Despite Mr Hook the posted price was not an infallible guarantee always that higher prices would not be charged; there *were* premiums at times.

[2] Burns, *op. cit.* pp. 327–8.

[3] For example, Burns, *op. cit.* p. 331: 'It may be that conditions of production suggest a scale of operations in excess of that necessary to supply demand from any

advocated it may have thought some collaboration over investment planning desirable. They shared the desire to avoid destructive competition.

In retrospect the competition of the thirties is seen to have been fierce as between the larger firms but to have stopped short of being destructive. Nevertheless, the number of small works fell sharply between 1930 and 1940;[1] and although the F.T.C. might have regarded this as a result of unfair discrimination, and sometimes came close to pretending that the economies of large-scale and integration were not established,[2] this fall was a token of competitive pressure from technical advance. In addition, the United States Steel Corporation, and doubtless other of the older firms, felt themselves under pressure to make radical replacements of old plant. The Corporation made losses and did not fully cover depreciation in the years 1931–34, and in these years its new investment fell to low levels,[3] but when its profits began to recover its new investment to replace old plant was heavy. The American system allowed a degree of price flexibility during the depression which was the antithesis of the stabilisation of prices in home markets aimed at by the German cartels for example, and which the British industry was setting out to establish under the Steel Federation with the blessing of I.D.A.C. before the war and which has been followed since the war. Yet flexibility was not, as much discussion in Britain has implied it must be, demoralisation. The lowest cost firms in a market did not set out to expand their sales irrespective of production costs and irrespective of the repercussions of their price policies on those of other, often older and larger firms.

one area of concentrated demand. If full freight were charged from A to B the delivered price in B might be so high that a plant of less than the most economical size might be attracted into existence at B, although a plant of the most economical size could supply A and B. Partial freight absorption to B may prevent this outcome and also permit sales in A at a lower price than would be necessary if there were separate plants at A and B.'

[1] *The Anglo-American Productivity Report*, p. 86, shows a reduction from 163 works melting steel in 1930 to 134 in 1950. During the war the number was increased; after 1945 a few works were abandoned, but the net effect of war and post-war change was probably to add to the number of works. The fall in number was in works of below 200,000 tons capacity.

[2] Some doughty opponents of monopoly have echoed this in England.

[3] *T.N.E.C. Study*, Part 31, p. 17,798.

504 ANTITRUST AND AMERICAN STEELMAKING

They could not afford to do this. Price concessions were not initiated by firms *in extremis* on the way out, but by firms on the way in. Aggression was limited to what would give practical results, and the result sought was an increase of orders for new plants among customers whose orders were attractive and well located, secured at prices which did not by their full effect on the whole market involve losses for the low-cost firms. This would not lend itself to precise calculation; firms were in a measure playing for position, but by and large price-cutting probably stopped when the low-cost firms thought the *average* 'at works' price which they obtained (not the *lowest* price, since there was discrimination) would cover their costs, including depreciation, at a breakeven point higher than the Corporation's 50 per cent.[1] At that point a counter-attacker could avoid further retreat.

3 'F.O.B. MILL' PRICING

The war brought price control and steel allocations and the pricing system just surveyed fell into abeyance. How far was it restored after the war when price control was taken off, in 1946? Before tracing what evidence there is on this, which is much less than for the years 1926–43, it is useful to observe the discussions of the change which superficially might be thought fundamentally to alter what went on, and was presumably meant to do so by the F.T.C. It was as a result of their pressures that in 1948 the 'F.O.B. Mill' pricing system was adopted by the steelmakers. The basing-point system was formally banned by an order drawn up by one of the F.T.C. lawyers at the end of 1949.[2]

How much difference this has made is not yet clear; indeed, it is still not quite settled how much difference its sponsors, or the Government, want it to make. The F.T.C. in its T.N.E.C. documents adhered to the formula of the Pittsburgh plus judge-

---

[1] It needs hardly to be repeated that competition varied in different products— it was particularly acute in sheets in 1938—and in different localities, so that the effect on rates of profit in different products would not be uniform; for large composite firms like the United States Steel Corporation the profit range from product to product was likely to be wide.

[2] *Iron Age*, 8 Dec. 1950.

ment, though that applied to a single basing-point only. Steel-works should quote prices 'F.O.B. Works', with the transport cost clearly stated separately. But having lauded the virtues of an 'open', i.e. published, F.O.B. price the F.T.C. experts added that 'to fulfil this purpose' (of competition) there must be no obligation to maintain any announced price for any time what-soever'; and they pointed out that the Clayton Act safeguarded 'the right of a seller to discriminate in price for various reasons, among them being discrimination in good faith to meet competition'. The Robinson Patman Act of 1936 'now safeguarded the right of a seller to discriminate in price...to meet an equally low price of a competitor, but he has the burden of proof on that question.... The right of self defence against competitive price attacks is as necessary as the right of self defence against personal attack.'

At this date, however, they still regarded the attack on the basing-point system as an attack on identical delivered prices (in the sense appropriate to the basing-point system). But the doctrine of justified discrimination was full of ambiguities, and the only point which was absolutely clear was the undiluted opposition to collusion. This remained a cornerstone. But with the passage of years it proved difficult to draw the line between the discrimination justified in meeting (not under-cutting!) a competitor's price and the discrimination which results in the uniform delivered price of the basing-point system. The question was immediately asked in 1949, what was gained by the banning of the old system if wide discrimination were allowed? Would it not reproduce a multiple basing-point system with every works a basing-point? To which many people now retorted, Why not? Democrats, it seemed, were less likely than Republicans to make this retort.

But the uncertainty resided in the law, as well as in opinion, and competing amending statutes were drafted. It was mani-festly impossible therefore to forecast what effect the change to F.O.B. pricing would ultimately have. It might be virtually nil. The state of the discussion in 1955 was summarised by the *Report* of a committee appointed by the Attorney General in 1953 to survey the Antitrust Laws and by subsequent discussions in Congress antitrust committees. The majority of the Attorney General's committee leaned strongly towards delivered pricing and freight absorption, and their attitude marks a significant departure from those of the thirties.

'Delivered pricing', they argued, like 'other methods of price quotation, standing alone is wholly equivocal', that is, neither good nor bad in principle, since it might mean competitive meeting of other firms' prices, taking competition into rivals' territory, or it might mean collusion. Uniform delivered prices obviously made it easier for trade associations to operate and police price agreements. 'Collusion', however, 'can flourish under an F.O.B. mill system' as well as under a delivered price or basing-point price system; so antitrust policy 'is not advanced by the alternative of F.O.B. mill pricing'. Indeed, 'whatever else, delivered pricing encourages the interpenetration of geographic markets, thereby creating wide opportunity for that competitive price shading which keeps terms of sale flexible and responsive to market shifts'.[1] Interpenetration was impossible without freight absorption because 'informed buyers will never pay more to one seller than to his rival for identical goods'.[2] It was 'undeniable that *all* "delivered" prices might be regarded as discriminatory in a purely theoretical economic sense', the *Report* adds, 'but in the world of business such theoretical discriminations...must as a practical matter leave buyers cold'. The antitrust laws are concerned with 'injurious' handicaps on buyers; and it is the actual price paid by buyers 'which determines their competitive standing *vis-à-vis* each other' and must be the 'significant index of legality'.[3] The final conclusion was that 'antitrust policy is served when sellers are free to meet competitors in distant markets by quoting "delivered" prices to equalise the freight advantages of more favourably situated competitors', but 'delivered pricing employed to effectuate price fixing conspiracies' should be 'relentlessly pursued'.[4]

---

[1] *Report of the Attorney General's National Committee to Study the Antitrust Laws*, p. 215.

[2] *Ibid.* p. 216. This is not quite true; at times of scarcity buyers are prepared to pay premium prices, as is shown at various points in the text.

[3] *Ibid.* p. 217.   [4] *Ibid.* p. 219.

Many members of the Attorney General's committee disagreed with the majority report on these points,[1] and its finding was not regarded as final. Perhaps it was felt to be a Republican-weighted decision. When one of the Congressional committees which discussed monopoly later in the year questioned Mr Weir, President of the National Steel Corporation, he underlined the continuing uncertainty. Business men are 'confronted by the dilemma of what they can and cannot do, price-wise, in meeting competition'. He wanted it to be settled that 'simple good faith in meeting an equally low price of a competitor...is adequate', and that to this end a seller might 'lawfully absorb freight'. This was not, he was at pains to point out, reviving the 'discarded' basing-point system. A Congressman fell into the error of supposing that Mr Weir was proposing that a 'fabricator could get the same price wherever he was located', which 'would tend to get' fabricators 'to decentralise'. The American steel price structure has never worked in this way wholly to conceal differences of transport costs, and the freight absorption proposed would not have this effect; but Mr Weir did not point it out, perhaps because he liked the Congressman's feeling for relatively small firms, which was now again a major preoccupation.[2]

4. DETERMINATION OF PRICES SINCE THE WAR

The conditions which resulted in almost continuous price-cutting in the thirties were not repeated except for relatively brief periods between 1945 and 1958. There were brief recessions, it has been seen, in 1949 and 1953–54, and a deeper recession in 1957–58. A reproduction of the price policies and practices of the thirties would not therefore be looked for except spasmodically. What has to be asked is whether there was a more fundamental change of attitude than this alone would induce. Steelmakers were said to have learned from the thirties

---

[1] Cp. in particular Professor J. M. Clark, *ibid.* pp. 219–20.
[2] Cp. evidence in proceedings of the House Monopoly Subcommittee Antitrust Investigations, on 14 June 1955, reported by *Congressional Intelligence Inc.*

that price-cutting when business is bad is useless—you got no more orders. Price cuts were good when business is good. President Eisenhower was taken to task as not understanding this when he called for price cuts early in 1958 as an anti-recession move; prices now were related more and more, it was pointed out, to costs. And because of their agreements with trade unions the steel firms had really built-in inflation; the agreements had promised wage increases irrespective of other counter-balancing cost reductions.

Prices rose steeply from 1945 to 1959, but though the upward movement was checked on occasion it was not interspersed with falls. The trend is shown in Table 65.

Table 65. *Index of steel prices in the United States, 1945–59*

Jan. 1945	100	Jan. 1953	182
Jan. 1946	102	Jan. 1954	192
Jan. 1947	119	Jan. 1955	199
Jan. 1948	135	Jan. 1956	214
Jan. 1949	155	Jan. 1957	233
Jan. 1950	159	Jan. 1958	247
Jan. 1951	171	Jan. 1959	253
Jan. 1952	171	Jan. 1960	253

Based on the *Iron Age* composite prices for ten major products. Some products rose a little more, some a little less.

These indices are a reasonably good guide to the movement of published prices, though they overstate the rise in base prices of some products a little (the effect of compositeness, since prices did not all vary equally) and they take no account of 'extras'. These were altered on several occasions, the net effect being probably to make extras a larger addition to the price (following the trend remarked earlier); but since the sizes selected for the base price were drastically changed in some instances—to the advantage, for instance, of users of the widest strip—no easy averaging is possible. For the present discussion all these matters can be neglected.

The steepest rise, from 1946 to 1948, was the reflection of pent-up inflationary forces plus the post-war scarcity. The check during the recession of 1949 was sharper than in 1953–54 or 1957–58, and the average rate of increase was much less after 1951 than before it. The complete standstill in 1951 was due to price control. In 1959 the market was free.

It is abundantly clear from market reports that this picture of a markedly upward trend with occasional rests or slow-downs does not give a full account of what happened, either to the mill net yields of sellers or the prices which customers paid. In evidence to the T.N.E.C. the United States Steel Corporation emphasised that concessions to customers were often important, though trade journals could not readily discover this unless a trade 'broke right open'. One must not look in market reports for a complete and balanced picture, the sort of thing available in the official records for 1926–43. But what is clear is that when demand was high many users of steel paid more than the 'F.O.B. Mill' price immediately suggests, and in times of poor trade some, perhaps many, paid less, while at such times steelmakers were often involved in extra costs in manufacture and selling and delivery.

In times of acute shortage there were mills who regularly charged premium prices; they were spoken of as premium mills, and were usually marginal plants with high costs. In most acute shortages all mills, including the integrated plants, have been said to be charging a premium (in autumn 1950, for example). At such times all plants charged fully for transport and there was no freight absorption, so that users normally buying outside the range of the nearest mill would be liable to pay more. Moreover, at such times plants which were relatively isolated were likely to fix F.O.B. prices that were higher than those in the main centres; Great Lakes at Detroit (part of the National Steel Coy.) would do so for instance, and Granite City in Illinois, and Kaiser at Fontana. Kaiser in August 1948 raised prices by \$35 in order to cash in on a sellers' market to pay off a loan.[1] Some mills, Kaiser's among them, sold ingots or slabs or sheet bars for re-rolling not within the trade but to users who had them re-rolled or forged on commission; this was called 'conversion' business, and the price for conversion steel sometimes rose very high.

[1] *Iron Age*, 9 Apr. 1949.

These were all formal and avowed practices. In addition, defective steel and 'seconds' sold to better advantage,[1] and there were 'grey markets'—dealers who were not regular merchants had steel to sell at very high prices. Possibly some of the regular merchants, the 'warehouses' who hold stocks, may have become involved in 'grey market' operations. When there were scarcities of some products but not of others firms who made both used their power to provide the scarce article as a means of selling the less scarce on a coupled bargain basis (though an assistant to the President of Bethlehem insisted that 'Tie-in dealing played a minor part if any in Bethlehem's sales').[2]

Higher and premium prices clearly became quite extensive at the peak of a boom; for example, in October 1955 it was said 'The boom' had 'reached the point where going mill prices were becoming academic for many consumers', who turned to warehouses and brokers 'more and more', and would take better quality steel (as well as worse quality) to get supplied.[3] This is no substitute for a statistical reckoning, but it shows the practices were not negligible in scale.

From boom to recession the way pricewise was largely by a reversal of the practices just set out. Large firms anxious to get more business as local business thinned out began to 'absorb freight' again over a wider area, and if need be on a substantial scale.[4] They sought of course the cheapest freight—truck, for example, or water.[5] (Truck delivery gained rapidly in the late forties.) Freight absorption did not occur simultaneously on the same scale for all products.[6] Premium prices were

---

[1] *Iron Age*, 13 Jan. 1955.

[2] *New York Times*, 29 Apr. 1958, report on Bethlehem merger case.

[3] *Iron Age*, 27 Oct. 1955.

[4] It was said Eastern mills were absorbing $10 a ton to sell in the West in 1956–58 (*ibid.* 15 May 1958).

[5] *Ibid.* 14 July 1949. Firms were 'crashing through the Great Lakes freight barrier by truck'.

[6] Cp., for example, *ibid.* 15 Oct. 1953; an article entitled 'Map freight absorption policy' deals with the probability of a main 'battle' in the West Coast over wire products, and soon over tinplate—because canners had stocked against the threat of a strike and Kaiser was bringing in a new plant—whereas Eastern suppliers would not absorb freight on plates, wide-flanged beams, or seamless tubes, as these were still in short supply.

eliminated.[1] Warehouses cut prices, sometimes quite drastically.[2] It was liable to happen regionally, because conspicuous difficulties piled up in sensitive markets, especially in large markets distant, in varying degrees, from the cheapest production, like Detroit, Texas and California, where freight absorption could be important as a source of competition, where in two instances imports could affect prices,[3] and where one very large single consuming industry could severely rock demand. It is to be noted that some large steel firms owned large 'warehousing' concerns—Inland for instance owned Ryersons—so warehouse price cuts were not necessarily wholly outside the industry. 'Seconds' and reject steel became more difficult to sell except at favourable—that is cut—prices. Buyers reduced stocks, cancelled orders, relied on buying at exceptionally short notice, almost for immediate delivery, and shopped around to see who could supply fastest; all of which reduced customers' costs and tended to raise manufacturers'. Orders were smaller, and makers were sometimes prepared to sell in 'less than car-load lots',[4] thus competing with merchants.

In each wave of recession some firms have reduced their base prices; there were, that is to say, local changes which changed the open competitive situation. In 1949 they appear to have been particularly widespread, but they are difficult to interpret with confidence at that period because the industry was just settling down to the 'F.O.B. Mill' system. At first old basing-point prices were apparently often continued as 'F.O.B. Mill' prices and freights were not absorbed; demand was still high and competition did not *force* absorption. Thus for many consumers 'F.O.B. Mill' meant initially higher prices—it 'cost them a pile of dough'.[5] But by the spring steelmakers had to compete for orders, and this involved both adjustments of mill prices and fairly soon a return to freight absorption. Changes

---

[1] Thus Lukens, 'the last premium alloy plate mill in the East', came into line with the other mills (*ibid.* 1 May 1958).

[2] Thus warehouse prices were cut by $30 a ton at Los Angeles in Dec. 1957, and only partially restored later.

[3] Imports had serious impacts on prices in Texas and California on several occasions.

[4] *Iron Age*, 17 Apr. 1958.   [5] *Ibid.* 11 Jan. 1949.

in 'F.O.B. Mill' prices were fairly widespread but cannot be treated as representative, being partly an adjustment to the new system and only partly a 'response to changed competitive conditions'.[1]

In 1953–54 the market disturbance seems to have been lighter, though there were some conspicuous parallels in the regions where price cuts were announced; thus in November 1953 Kaiser's reduced the price of billets at Fontana and Acme Steel, Chicago, and Detroit Steel brought down the prices of cold rolled strip.[2] In 1958 stainless steel sheet prices were reduced by United States Steel and Allegheny Ludlum in February, a lead that others followed.[3] Stainless steel tube prices were cut; here the start was not by a conspicuous leader and the process of 'following' was spread over two or three months.[4] The most interesting changes came in June; a reduction by $2 per ton on sheet prices at Granite City (Illinois) in the first week, and a similar one by the Great Lakes Steel Corporation in the second week.[5] The Granite City Steel Company was a small but rapidly expanding firm. It had been conspicuous in 1948–49 for setting a high price on the introduction of 'F.O.B. Mill' which it could not maintain when freight absorption returned;[6] but it raised prices notably, by $10 per ton,[7] in October 1950 when the Korean frenzy was on. Output was 530,000 short tons in 1949, 1,152,000 in 1956; more capacity was coming into use in July 1958.[8] The reduction of price meant that Granite City became the cheapest supplier to St Louis— its delivery by truck competing with Chicago delivery by water. Chicago suppliers would need to compete by freight absorption;

---

[1] Thus Kaiser's reduced prices at the end of March; Inland, Carnegie-Illinois and National Tube had made some cuts by the end of April, Great Lakes (Detroit) early in May, Sheffield Steel (Houston) in June (*Iron Age*, 31 Mar., 21 Apr., 5 May, 23 June).

[2] *Ibid.* 19 Nov. 1953. A list of price changes initiated outside the United States Steel Corporation, most of them instances where differentials between basing-point prices were being reduced, is given in Administered Prices, *Hearings*, Part 3, p. 954. (For a fuller description see opposite, n. 2.)

[3] *Iron Age*, 13 Feb. 1958.   [4] *Ibid.* 26 June 1958.
[5] *Ibid.* 5 and 12 June 1958.   [6] *Ibid.* 4 Jan. and 10 Mar. 1949.
[7] *Ibid.* 5 Oct. 1950.

[8] *Ibid.* 26 June 1958; an addition of 120,000 tons in July 1956, and the target for end 1958 was nearly 1,600,000 tons.

the effect of the change was thus a real reduction of price for all users in the 'natural' Granite City market area, a change in their comparative costs. Granite City's net income per cent of sales had recently been well above the average for the industry.[1]

The Detroit change reflected the dip in the motor-car business, and was presumably designed to make freight absorption by the steelmakers from outside the area more costly. Detroit normally held its mill price above those in the chief producing areas. Ingot output as percentage of capacity in Detroit tended to be rather below the average for all districts, though it was not the worst sufferer. Great Lakes was part of the National Steel Company, which had seemed to exhibit some 'lethargy brought on by years of success', and its net income as percentage of sales had been below the general average (though as a percentage of the stockholders' investment it was high for the industry; but as its chairman said this could be misleading; the investment was valued very conservatively, being reduced by special allowances for depreciation not made in the accounting methods of the other companies).[2] The price cut may have reflected the revitalising influence of George Humphrey, who, on ceasing to be head of the United States Treasury, became Chairman of National Steel in succession to E. T. Weir.[3] Senator Kefauver had asked Humphrey in November 1957 at one of the recurrent Congressional inquiries into steel prices why National, the largest producer of sheet, never led a price change, but always followed United States Steel. He thought National should bring prices down because scrap was cheap—but Humphrey then firmly said 'We do not intend to go down'— and pointed to a substantial drop in profits already. He had, however, only recently taken over, and the market for steel had

[1] *Iron Age*, 2 Jan. 1958, p. 328.
[2] The profits-on-investment figures were discussed in the Sub-Committee on Antitrust and Monopoly of the Senate Committee on the Judiciary, United States Senate, Hearings on Administered Prices. Oct.–Nov. 1957 (referred to subsequently as *Administered Prices, Hearings*), cp. *Hearings* (Part 3, evidence by George Humphrey).
[3] *Business Week*, 31 May 1958, had an interesting article on Humphrey's plans, especially with regard to the development of Brazilian iron ore.

not followed the expected course between November 1957 and July 1958. This change in base price was a favourable change in comparative costs for all users in the ambit of the Great Lake works.[1]

It was in no wise contradictory that these reductions occurred when people were expecting a general increase of prices due to the 'built-in inflation' of the agreement to increase wages, which was duly implemented on 1 July though the steel firms had tried to persuade the workers to forgo their claim. The prospect of an increase of price in July led to hedge buying in June, and less buying in July. The general price increase was delayed, but not for long; it started at the end of July.[2] The lead, this time, came for many of the main products not from United States Steel, but from other companies; United States Steel was 'tired', it seemed, of the traditional criticism. In sheets the lead came, at the end of July, from Armco, Jones and Laughlin and Republic; in rails, towards the end of the series, from Bethlehem. (It had been assumed, however, that whoever 'led', the scale of change would be the one chosen by United States Steel.)[3] The rise was in general less than had been forecast, a concession to the dull though now more promising market. The relative changes at Detroit and Granite City were not of course affected; they were a change in the basic pattern.

Among the overt price changes of the first half of 1958 were three reductions of export prices by the United States Steel Corporation, designed 'to bring the prices more in line with domestic delivered prices at the seaboard'.[4] Hot rolled sheet came to 5·14 cents per lb. in February, 5·01 in May; cold rolled prices were 6·49 cents in February, 6·22 in May, all at New

---

[1] It was said at once that the McLouth Steelworks (Detroit) would follow Great Lakes, and that United States Steel Corporation and other companies would compete by further freight absorption.

[2] *Started*, because the first change was in sheets; other products came later— rails, for example, in September (*Iron Age*, 4 Sept.). To be quite precise, the *first* increases of price were by a small company, the Alan Wood Steel Co. (Pa); but in announcing price rises on 2 July they said they would remain competitive if other firms did not do likewise (*ibid.* 3 July 1958).

[3] For example, *ibid.* 2 July 1958.

[4] *Ibid.* 27 Feb. and 22 May 1958.

York or Philadelphia. The final prices seem to have allowed freight of $1·7 per ton on hot rolled sheets and $3·4 on cold rolled from the points with the lowest F.O.B. 'Mill' prices.[1] The two stages of price-cutting were possibly dictated by the price falls in oversea markets rather than by domestic conditions; but that can merely be surmised. After the price increases of July were announced United States Steel raised some of its export prices, but by slightly lower percentages than in the domestic market. Presumably *pro forma*, and to avoid the appearance of dumping, it had to be done.

Freight absorption according to the Court decision was legal so long as firms were meeting, but not undercutting, another firm's price. But how far were there further concessions? On this there is hardly any evidence; but in the nature of things it is unlikely there would be. In practice the very possibility of 'meeting' competitors' prices gives some latitude, as the reply of National Steel, for example, to questions by Senator Kefauver's sub-committee on Administered Prices shows. The company would sell to any of its customers at its F.O.B. price plus freight. But 'many customers...located closer to the mills of another producer...have been unwilling to pay the price. In meeting such a situation...if it decided to bid for the business it quotes its F.O.B. price plus full freight less a competitive allowance which is sufficient to reduce its price to what it thinks is the prevailing market price for the particular area.' This it finds out by conference with customers and from all other sources available.[2] It is not a situation in which a precise figure is always obvious; indeed, it can vary much according to the means of transport chosen, and where trucks can be used the position would be more obscure than if rail transport were universal, because rail rates are more public. Price 'meeting'

[1] The lowest F.O.B. mill prices were 4·95 cents and 6·05 cents respectively at Pittsburgh, Ashland (Ky), Weirton (W.Va), Chicago, Cleveland, Sparrows Point. Sparrows Point had no rail cost to Baltimore; its rail cost to Philadelphia was $3·9 a ton in 80-ton minimum car-load weights. Bethlehem (Pennsylvania) had the same rate to New York. The other centres had higher freights. (I have used a comprehensive survey of rail freights for steel from upwards of 50 originating points to about 100 receiving points in 1954; an extremely useful guide.) (*Iron Age*, 7 Jan. 1954.) Rates had possibly risen by 1958.

[2] *Administered Prices, Hearings*, Part 4, p. 1395.

could clearly easily become price shading, given a little customer encouragement.[1]

In proceedings to stop the proposed merger of Bethlehem with Youngstown, which are discussed later, one witness said that in the wire-rope business undercutting was drastic; a discount of 20 per cent was standard some years ago, but now a firm would give 35 per cent discount. This in the Middle West; in the Far West the bargains were better, and 'a 40 per cent mark down is standard'. Everybody was doing it. It was to be inferred that it was part of the conflict between integrated and unintegrated wire-rope makers, those who made and those who bought the wire. Wire prices rose more steeply than the average from 1954; it was said wire-rope prices rose less than the average, but without records this cannot be established. There is no reason to suppose that competition of this kind was limited to wire rope. It would be expected to vary in intensity according to the state of affairs in different branches of production. And so, indeed, it turned out; stainless steel, where price reductions occurred early in 1958 and continued after the summer price increases, recalled the position of sheets in 1938–9.

The United States Steel Corporation announced a reduction in the price of stainless plate in August 'in the light of the present market conditions'.[2] An article in *Iron Age* said that 'stainless men go underground when the subject of price is mentioned'. 'To what extent it (competition) takes the form of price-cutting can only be surmised.' This looks like the kind of situation referred to above where, as the United States Steel witness put it, the market 'broke wide open'. In this trade an immense expansion of capacity was becoming effective at a time when demand was not only slack but seemed unlikely to expand as had been forecast in 1955. Ten new mills, eight of them Sendzimir mills making wide strip, were coming into operation;[3] output was 260,000 tons a year compared with an output of 450,000 tons in 1955, a present capacity of 600,000 tons, and a 1955 projected consumption in 1960 of 800,000 tons (which was

---

[1] The earlier suggestion of Charles Hook (above, p. 502) that the customer often starts the price-cutting will be recalled.   [2] *Iron Age*, 14 Aug. 1958.

[3] The new mills reflected technical advances as well as expanding capacity.

now slated for 1965).[1] Historically ways of making concessions otherwise than by straightforward reductions of the base prices —by describing goods as less good than they are, cutting extras, and so on as well as by various forms of coupled bargain—are legion.

Writing in the early fifties a high official of United States Steel treated the *Report* of 1943, which gave particulars of the extent of price concessions of various kinds, as indicative of the competition in the industry; 'actual prices', he wrote, 'are highly competitive and frequently vary from published prices'.[2] The trade journals leave the impression that publication of full records would show that practices current in the years 1946–59 were not far removed from those of the inter-war years surveyed earlier in this chapter. Price competition was not eliminated as it had been in the United Kingdom.[3] It did not, however, degenerate into indiscriminate price-cutting; the concentrations within particular areas and in relation to particular products suggest that it was used to change the proportion of trade held by firms in specific markets and was guided by a sense of relative strengths and comparative advantages. If this was so it is superficially strange that it does not seem to have been referred to in Senator Kefauver's inquiries of 1957–58; but if these proceedings are regarded as strategic exercises in the antitrust campaign rather than a search after objective truth the omission is readily comprehended. Neither side would have stood to gain much from further publication of evidence on this sort of price competition. The F.T.C. had tended to treat it as trivial and undesirable because discriminatory.[4]

[1] *Iron Age*, 4 Sept. 1958. The change in the stainless steel position was also reflected in reductions in prices of 'clad' plates (i.e. carbon steel plates with a stainless sheet welded on); base-price reductions, some considerable, were announced by Lukens, other makers stated their prices would be competitive. (*Iron Age*, 28 Aug. 1958).

[2] *Competition in Steel*, by David F. Austin (Vice-President, Sales, United States Steel Corporation).

[3] In the United Kingdom of course competition by freight absorption could, and did, occur; some firms notoriously cultivated customers at a distance when trade was bad, and left them high and dry when trade was good.

[4] Above, p. 502. It is of interest that the staff economist who advised Kefauver also treated as of no interest instances where F.O.B. differentials were narrowed. Cp. *Administered Prices, Hearings*, Part 3, p. 956.

After the summer price increases a new warehouse price policy blossomed which for some buyers seems largely to have offset the effect of the increases. Quantity rebates and extras for orders of upwards of 5000 lb. were considerably increased; on orders below 2000 lb. they were considerably decreased. The object was presumably to capture or recapture more large orders; possibly some mills had been competing with warehouses—now increasingly called 'service centres'—but mainly presumably it was inter-warehouse competition.[1]

5. THE DILEMMA OF SIZE

For the antitrust zealots administered prices spelt the end of the competition which gave their free-enterprise economy its vitality and was one of the baneful effects of the growing dominance of too large firms. The attack on them was associated with the attack on mergers of large firms, into which the F.T.C., sensing a new wave of such mergers, began to direct greater efforts in 1954–55.[2] In 1955 proceedings were started to prevent a merger of Bethlehem Steel Corporation with Youngstown Steel and Tube Company, second and sixth in order of size among American ingot producers. They succeeded in 1958.

The judge who made the decision said that the Clayton Act bars all trusts, good or bad.[3] But the critics of the big firms could not be so detached. They set out where possible to show that, apart from the theoretic possibility or even probability that domination by larger firms might cause inefficiency, restriction of investment, or lack of enterprise in discovery and slowness in exploiting technical advance, such inefficiency could be observed and demonstrated. In the early post-war years the industry was most criticised, as has been seen, for not expanding capacity fast enough. After 1955 this was a hard

---

[1] *Iron Age*, 21 and 28 Aug. 1958. After the price increases of 1957 the warehouse prices rose more, in general, than the F.O.B. mill prices. *Iron Age*, 11 July 1957.

[2] *Report on Corporate Mergers and Acquisitions*, May 1955.

[3] *Iron Age*, 27 Nov. 1958.

case to make. The Kefauver Committee instead devoted much attention to what it deemed signs of technical inefficiency. By 1957 the wealth of new technical development in the industry throughout the world had become conspicuous enough to begin to catch the politician's eye. Much of it was taking place on the Continent. The improved converter processes, the use of oxygen in steelmaking, rotary steel furnace processes, continuous casting, teeming in vacuum, were instances. While it was not quite suggested that all such things should be discovered in the United States, lively doubts were expressed whether they were taken up vigorously enough. Were the big firms too concerned to protect their heavy commitments in conventional plant? Some American licensees of European patents and some American inventors were prepared, not surprisingly, to support such a view.[1] The record was not uniform. In some fields, continuous casting for example, there seemed to have been relatively little United States effort after an initially much-advertised start; but advances had been modest everywhere, though the Russians were talking of a big expansion in prospect. United States firms had gone quickly into vacuum teeming, were pioneers in developing large vacuum melting furnaces, and large

---

[1] The Koppers Corporation, for example, in respect of continuous casting, and Mr Sendzimir in respect of his planetary mill, whose initial history in the United Kingdom was not encouraging. The staff of the Kefauver Committee produced evidence (*Administered Prices, Steel*, Part 3, p. 827) that during the war the Office of Price Administration had figures which showed that the man-hours per ton in making certain products were higher for a group of older multi-plant firms than for a group of newer firms; viz. (in labour-hours per net ton (2000 lb.) of finished product):

	Hot rolled bars	Hot rolled sheets	Cold rolled sheets
Group I (U.S. Steel, Bethlehem, Republic, Jones and Laughlin)	15·3	12·2	15·9
Group II (Inland, National Steel, Armco, Youngstown	12·7	11·4	14·4

But this was almost to be expected and might mean no more than that the older firms had some older plant (which was almost inescapable). It did not mean that the older plant was due for immediate replacement, with prime costs above (or even approaching) total costs of new plant. Nor did it establish that the new plant of the old firms was less efficient in design or management than plant in the new firms. Figures of this kind became available to some British steelmakers during the war and appeared to be a great stimulus to planning modernisation.

electric arc furnaces for 'commercial quality' steels. The United States Steel Corporation allowed that 'some form of oxygen steelmaking will undoubtedly become an important feature of steelmaking in this country'; but the lead in introducing it had not been taken by the bigger firms.

The Kefauver Committee staff economists evolved the seductive theory that a chain of new processes, direct reduction of ore to avoid the expense of blast furnaces, oxygen steelmaking to avoid the capital outlay on large open-hearth plants, direct casting to avoid cogging, and planetary mills to eliminate continuous wide-strip mills, would allow much smaller plants than those considered customarily to be economically efficient. It was ingenious, but United States Steel seemed to show it was illusory; the circumstances for which these processes looked like being suitable were not so uniform as to suggest the processes would interlock. Direct reduction was not, or not yet, an alternative to the blast furnace where good coke was cheap;[1] the oxygen converter process made mass-production steel, continuous castings had so far succeeded most for special steels, as had the planetary mill.[2] The chief witness on the oxygen process went out of his way, moreover, to say that 'the small operation is inherently a high-cost operation'; every time his firm had expanded it had lowered its costs.[3]

His story helped those who wanted to keep the way open for small plants, however, as well as advocates of bigness, because his company, the McLouth Steel Company, had only started making steel in 1949, and pig iron in 1954. It started as a re-rolling plant making hot and cold rolled strip in 1934. It integrated backwards to reduce costs; it chose first to use large arc furnaces, but later introduced oxygen-blown converters (which needed blast-furnace hot metal, hence McLouth built blast furnaces) for greater cheapness. Some of the converter output was finished in the electric furnaces. The firm was clearly very successful; they had, they thought, on the Lakeside at Trenton in the outskirts of Detroit, a good location (where they

---

[1] Bethlehem Steel were however satisfied enough with their H-iron experimental plant in California to plan extensions by 1960 (*Iron Age*, 3 Mar. 1960).

[2] *Administered Prices, Hearings*, Part 3, pp. 1058–9.   [3] *Ibid.* Part 3, p. 792.

ANTITRUST AND AMERICAN STEELMAKING   521

still had a slightly higher base price than the price common at
the major centres after the price changes of 1958). By 1957
their ingot capacity was over 1·5 m. tons, to rise to 2·0 m. tons
in mid-1958.[1] This was good going; but it showed that a small
firm energetically run at a good site could grow, in spite of the
'oligopolists'.

In 1958 the main focus in international technical comparisons
had switched from Continental Europe to Russia, and so on to
the advantages of largeness. United States Steel asserted in
November 1957 that 'the distinguishing feature of the American
steel industry is its tremendous productiveness', which it
improved consistently (in general by constantly improving
current methods, which was the sensible starting point) and
which 'other countries have been unable to emulate so far'.[2]
After the visit to Russia this conclusion was challenged in regard
to the earlier stages, especially in regard to ironmaking. Blast
furnaces of comparable size, it was stated, produced 30–40 per
cent more in the U.S.S.R. than in the United States; a result
of using more sinter, higher pressure and blast temperature,
high top pressure, uninterrupted blowing during tapping (which
United States operators had given up), and so on. These were
differences of degree; the Russians were pushing United States
practices further than the United States operators. Individual
furnaces with a 26 ft. hearth were reported as producing
2500 tons a day, equal to over 750,000 tons a year; furnaces
with 30 ft. hearths to make 3000 tons a day were to begin
operating in 1958, furnaces to make 5000 tons a day (approaching
2 m. tons a year) in 1960. (In the United Kingdom a furnace
making 500,000 tons a year was a rarity; the average in South
Wales, where it was highest, was 235,800 tons in 1957. The
average for the United Kingdom was 145,500 tons. In the
United States the average was 280,000 tons in 1955, with almost
400,000 in states, Maryland and West Virginia for example,
where most plants were new.) In open-hearth shops in the

---

[1] *Ibid.* pp. 776 sqq., evidence of Mr Groner, attorney to the McLouth Steel Co.
This plant was the first which the Russians visited in 1958; they showed most
interest in its electric furnaces, not in its oxygen process (*Iron Age*, 23 Oct. 1958).
[2] *Administered Prices, Hearings*, Part 3, p. 1059.

U.S.S.R. the normal 'tap-to-tap' time was one-quarter less than in the United States. They had about 'twice the handling equipment of a typical United States shop'. There would be two charging machines, for example, available to feed one large (440 tons) open-hearth furnace.[1] But there were also differences of design and practice; they used deeper 'baths', and used all-basic furnaces, with suspended chrome-magnesite roofs, which lasted four times as many heats as the American.[2]

Whether Russian practice was very efficient, or merely very productive, was not established. American observers envied the Russians, what Europeans had often envied Americans, the benefit of 'long runs on common grades'. They had relatively simple programmes ordered a year ahead and only subject to slight changes quarter by quarter. The Russian operator could 'order practically anything he wants if it will increase output. He may not always get it because mill equipment deliveries are behind schedule and new plants have priority. Once the equipment is installed amortisation rates are so low they can almost be ignored.' The Americans envied the Russians' low wage costs (still low despite a recent 'new deal' for steelworks labour) and the co-operativeness of the labour. But on the economic side of the operation judgements were, and could only be, impressionistic.

It did seem probable, however, that Russian blast-furnace development would provide a stimulus, that some net economy was expected from the use of more sinter, and the other practices which were more normal or pushed further in Russia than in the United States. But it was plain that if there *were* net gains from Russian methods they came from larger scale, not smaller scale, operating; they underlined the advantage of bigness.

Here was a real dilemma. Could the growth of firms which

---

[1] The United States had *larger* open-hearth furnaces than the U.S.S.R.—there were 550 ton fixed furnaces at Great Lakes and Weirton (which the Russians visited; *Iron Age*, 23 Oct. 1958). To use two charging machines for a furnace was not unknown in the United Kingdom; it happened at the new Lackenby tilting furnaces of Dorman Longs, for example. But it was said to be easier than with fixed furnaces.

[2] Such roofs were familiar in the United Kingdom and United States, but very costly.

enabled the use of larger-scale methods be allowed to proceed undisturbed without in the end making the entry of newcomers and expansion of smaller firms increasingly difficult? Obviously it had not done so yet—the smaller firms could still get on— witness McLouth and Granite City.[1] But was there a danger point? The motor-car industry looked like a warning. They had reached a position of 'triopoly' (the almost complete hold of General Motors, Fords and Chryslers, to which the judge in the Bethlehem merger case referred under this name). Mr Weir, the creator of the National Steel Company, with superb indifference to the fact that his company was formed by an amalgamation in 1929,[2] argued a year or so before his retire-ment[3] that firms had to become bigger because demand was growing; but they should grow naturally, not by amalgama-tion.[4] But as Bethlehem deployed their case it became clear this was not conclusive.

Before turning to the arguments of the merger case it is to be noted that growth of efficiency continued in the post-war years (according to the most-quoted standards) approximately as fast as since 1929, though 1919–29 remained an outstanding decade, and the flexibility of the industry as indicated by numbers of firms and location of production was not significantly if at all less than in the thirties.

The decline of man-hours required to make a ton of steel is shown percentage-wise in Table 66. Whatever lay behind the peak figures of 1919–29 the subsequent rate of development was cumulatively impressive. From 1947 to 1955 the rate of improvement in labour productivity, percentage-wise, was similar in the United States and United Kingdom; output per worker per year—including *all* workers, and irrespective of changes in average hours worked—rose by 27 per cent between

---

[1] Cp. also Barium Steel, below, p. 532. And in 1958 the Kaiser Steel Corporation was expanding by adding an L.D. steel plant from a capacity of 800,000 tons to about 2 m. tons.

[2] *Investment, Profits and Rates of Return for Selected Industries*, T.N.E.C. Report, Part 3, p. 17756.

[3] To be succeeded by Mr Humphrey; above, p. 513.

[4] Evidence to House Monopoly Subcommittee Antitrust Investigations, 14 June 1955, reported in *Congressional Intelligence Inc.*

Table 66. *Decline in man-hours per unit of output, United States steel industry*[a] *(average annual figures)*

	Per cent
1919–29	5·9
1929–39	3·1
1939–47	2·8
1947–55	2·8

[a] *Man-hours per Unit of Output in the Basic Steel Industry*, 1939–55, p. 6 (United States Dept. of Labor (Bureau of Labor Statistics), Sept. 1956).

1948 and 1955 in the United Kingdom and 28 per cent in the United States.[1] But the United States started from a much higher figure; the average addition to output therefore was quantitatively much greater in the United States, and the figures gave no sign of the United Kingdom catching up. The Bureau of Labor Statistics (unlike the Kefauver Committee) recited at length the technical advances made and being made in the United States industry to explain the continuing fall of man-hours per unit of output; a professional, not a political, approach. Labour productivity reflects the most characteristic strength of the United States industry; but productivity improved in other respects too. Thus fuel consumed per ton of steel was 15 per cent less in 1955 than in 1947.[2] What was happening with productivity of capital is obscure. The cost of new plant was still surprisingly little more (at the current exchange rate) in the United States than in the United Kingdom and on the Continent. In 1950, as seen above, the cost per ton of annual output of a new large integrated plant making a highly finished product was about the same. In 1957 the position had changed little. The President of Bethlehem told the Kefauver Committee that a new plant would cost about $300 an ingot ton.[3] In Britain the figure was about £100, rather more than

[1] For the United States figure, *ibid*. p. 8; for the United Kingdom *Development in the Iron and Steel Industry: Special Report for 1957* (Iron and Steel Board), pp. 85–6 (referred to subsequently as *Development Report for 1957*).

[2] Based on consumption of coal, oil, purchased electricity and natural gas, and indices of output by the Bureau of Labour Statistics for labour productivity. Possibly a rash calculation.

[3] *Administered Prices, Hearings*, Part 2, p. 600.

less; so that the United States plant would be hardly more costly,[1] although United States wages were three to four times the United Kingdom level. This was in line with the general contrast of the cost of new plant in Europe and the United States,[2] and is readily comprehensible for steel plants because much of the new plant used in Europe came from the United States, and much was made in Europe to United States designs or in association with United States firms.

Table 67. *Indices of costs of new works*[a]

	Producers finished goods	Construction
1945	[b]	74
1947	100	100
1949	114	114
1950	117	123
End 1956	156	170

[a] Based on tables in *Administered Prices, Steel*, Part 4, p. 1496.
[b] Not available.

Nevertheless, in the United States the steep rise in the dollar cost of new plant since 1946 was a source of concern to the firms, and United States Steel and other firms gave illuminating data to show the trend. The most general indication of the rise of costs was given in indices of the cost of producers' finished goods and the cost of construction. They rose as shown in Table 67. On this basis the rise from 1950 (the date of the Anglo-American Productivity Team's visit) was 33 and 38 per cent respectively. The Kefauver Committee reports included many interesting details of costs of particular units of new plant in different firms at different dates, covering 30 or 40 years. The firms were particularly anxious to stress to the Kefauver Committee the impact of this on their prices, especially in view of the degree of self finance.[3]

How far the increase of costs of investment was due to inflation, how far to changes in the character of the plant which

[1] *Development Report for 1957*, p. 71.
[2] Milton Gilbert and Associates, *Comparative National Products and Price Levels*, 1957, pp. 54–6.
[3] Above, p. 234. But some were also anxious to challenge the view that all the industry's finance for expansion came from re-invested profits: statistics of capital raised in the market were given in *Administered Prices, Steel*, Part 4, p. 1510.

increased real cost per ton of output was not disclosed or analysed. Plant to use lower grade raw materials, and plant like the continuous strip mill which immensely increased the extent of mechanical handling and the size of the material handled and produced, and either in order to save materials, labour or fuel or to produce a different product, introduced new processes or new controls, were quite likely to raise the capital cost per unit of output. A great deal of typical American development for many decades has been in the second of these categories, and some recently—the use of 'taconites' for example—in the first. But as the *character* of the processes and products became more stabilised further developments—those probably now most common—especially increases in size of units and speeds of operation, might reduce capital costs per unit of output. (Thus a cold rolling mill for strip producing 7000 ft. per minute probably has lower capital cost a unit than one producing 5000 feet per minute.)[1] The balance in recent development could not be guessed. Discussions suggested growing interest in reducing capital cost per unit of output, and the prospect was that there would be more in future. It was as though the burden of capital cost was no longer accepted as immutable—labour saving might be associated with capital saving.

As to the numbers and location of firms and plants, the predominance of the few largest firms was rather less, measured in terms of ingot capacity, in 1958 than before the war. Some new and smaller firms had grown fast. Some small firms had disappeared; but where they had steel melting, and not merely re-rolling facilities, they disappeared by absorption, and it is possible that no steel melting site was abandoned as such between the outbreak of war in 1939 and 1958.[2] The geographical

---

[1] Early in 1959 the rapid introduction of the use of tonnage oxygen by way of a 'lance' through open-hearth furnace roofs was being written up. The use of basic roofs with this was normal. The changes could add 10 to 20 per cent to capacity of existing open-hearth shops (*Iron Age*, 15 Jan. 1959).

[2] This was in effect stated by the President of Bethlehem to Senator Kefauver (*Administered Prices, Hearings*, Part 2, p. 637). Whether this applied to ingot producers only, or to makers of steel castings too I do not know. In this context I have only ingot makers in mind. A few steel-melting plants were kept alive by political pressure despite unfavourable costs (see *Corporate Mergers and Acquisitions*, p. 130).

distribution of production nevertheless continued to change, if only by accretions, not deletions. The location of production responded to changes in location of markets and raw material sources.

During the war the established leaders of the industry observed that the war was strengthening smaller rivals; they thought it would make it more difficult to keep prices stable.[1] The Government sponsored some new plants—Kaisers at Fontana, the Geneva plant at Utah (later bought by United States Steel) and, on a smaller scale, the Lone Star works in Texas.[2] Some firms grew (not necessarily very large) because they made special steels, like Allegheny Ludlum. Some consumers began making steel, or made more, because they found it advantageous, when steel was scarce (or when their requirements were exacting), to supply themselves (Timken's, for example, and Babcock and Wilcox). Ingot capacity of firms was expanded at varying rates between 1938 and 1956; of the nine largest firms in 1938 five expanded less than the average, two expanded more. Most of the firms whose rate of expansion was notably above the average were relatively small in 1938, or did not exist; Colorado Steel and Iron, Detroit, Barium, Sharon, and of course Granite City and McLouth, and, finally, Kaiser's, who made a further great spurt forward in capacity in 1958. Indeed, the structure of the industry, though characterised by the largeness of the firms and plants which made most of the steel, was in no sense monolithic. There were sixteen firms with a capacity of over 1 m. long tons a year in 1956, and fifteen of them *made* over 1 m. tons. By the end of 1958 there were nineteen firms with over 1 m. tons capacity, and they had 87 per cent of total capacity. Forty-four plants each capable of making over 1 m. tons had 83 per cent of all the capacity. The position is shown approximately in Table 68.

The smaller plants were mainly makers of alloy and special steels, many using only electric furnaces, though there were a few small plants in isolated areas, whose remoteness from major steel centres made steel prices high (and might make scrap prices low). Among the small to medium-sized plants were some of

[1] This became evident in wartime discussions.   [2] *Iron Age*, 13 Aug. 1953.

those owned by consumers—Timkens (650,000 tons) for instance and Babcocks (200,000 tons). (Self-supply clearly yields economies in transport of scrap and finished product which would offset some diseconomies through smaller scale operating. It could give special quality control too)[1]. Fords, with a capacity of 1·5 m. tons in 1956, ranked among the moderately large producers.

Table 68. *Sizes of United States firms and plants (beginning of 1956 and 1959) (long tons)*

	20 m.	10 m.	8 m.	6 m.	5 m.	4 m.	3 m.	2 m.	1·5 m.	1 m.	0·75 m.	0·5 m.	0·1 m.	—
From ...	40 m.	20 m.	10 m.	8 m.	6 m.	5 m.	4 m.	3 m.	2·0 m.	1·5 m.	1 m.	0·75 m.	0·5 m.	0·1r
To ...														
1956														
No. of firms	1	1	1	—	—	5	—	1	3	4	5	3	20	31
No. of plants	—	—	—	—	1	2	3	6	6	17	10	11	30	50
(% of capacity)	—	—	—	—	6	10	11	15	11	21	8	6	9	5
1959														
No. of firms	2a	1b	—	3c	2d	—	—	3	3	5	3	7	20	40
(% of capacity)	44	9	—	15	9	—	—	5	4	5	2	3	3	1
No. of plants	—	—	—	2	2	1	6	12	9	12	7	11	28	56
(% of capacity)	—	—	—	11	9	4	15	21	12	11	5	5	6	2

Based mainly on tables in *Iron Age* and *B.I.S.F. Stat. Handbooks*. The figures are net after deduction of from 9 to 10 per cent average per year for operating time lost in rebuilding, repairing, and holiday. No pure steel foundries are included.

a United States Steel Corporation and Bethlehem Steel Corporation (with 28 and 16 per cent of capacity respectively).
b Republic Steel Corporation.
c Jones and Laughlin, National, Youngstown Sheet and Tube.
d Inland, Armco.

The F.T.C. refined the analysis of concentration by examining the position for specific finished products, and in specific areas. This showed, as was to be expected, more concentration in some products than in ingot production, and less in others, and it put in relief an interesting contrast between the British and American situations. In 1956 four or five firms in the United States (not for each finished product the same four or five firms) made all the rails, steel piling, wheels and axles and electrical sheets, 92 per cent of structural shapes, 80 per cent of the tin-plate. There was *more* concentration, therefore, in these branches than in ingot production. But in some other products the concentration was *less* than in ingot production—thus, for instance, in making hot and cold rolled sheets,[2] one of the trades in which

[1] British Timken at one time complained much of the difficulty in getting the steel they wanted. In 1958 Timkens in the United States were making some vacuum melted steel.
[2] For all figures see *Administered Prices, Steel*, Part 3, pp. 936 sqq.

new firms had found it most attractive to enter, and in making most types of tubes. In Britain sheets and tubes by contrast were the products where (because of the large size of the technical 'optimum' in relation to the market) concentration was greatest, and greater in degree than for any major product in the United States.

The geographical distribution of production continued to change, as Table 69 shows. Change was not dramatic, and it came by the choice of some new sites and the greater expansiveness of some regions, not by absolute shrinkage of any major area. Some inertia is inherent in the nature of the plant.

Table 69. *Distribution of United States crude steel*[a] *capacity, 1942–58* (percentages)

	Jan. 1942	Jan. 1949	Jan. 1954	Jan. 1958
Pennsylvania	31·7	29·5	27·4	26·3
Ohio	22·0	20·1	19·6	20·0
Indiana, Illinois	20·3	20·2	20·8	20·2
New York, New Jersey	5·3	4·9	5·3	5·4
Maryland, Delaware	5·3	5·5	5·1	6·3
Alabama, Kentucky	5·3	5·2	5·2	5·1
Michigan	3·7	4·1	5·2	5·1
West Virginia	2·5	2·5	2·2	2·4
Colorado	1·3	1·3	1·2	1·3
California	1·1	2·3	2·5	2·3
Texas	—	0·6	1·4	1·6
Utah	—	1·3	1·5	1·6
Minnesota, Missouri	1·2	1·2	1·3	1·3
Other Far West	0·2	0·3	0·3	0·4
Other South	0·2	0·2	0·3	0·4
Total (long tons)	79·0	85·8	111·0	125·6

[a] Includes a small tonnage of steel for castings; but not the steel for castings made by firms who only make castings.

The shifts were a response partly to growth of markets, especially in the Middle West, in the Far West, and in Texas; hence the expanding importance of California, Utah, Texas and Michigan in Table 69. They were also partly a response to changes in the raw-material situation, the use, for instance, of oil and natural gas, but above all greater reliance on new ore

sources, primarily from oversea, and most from Venezuela and
Canada, though some came from Africa, and the development
of further African sources was in view.[1] Greater dependence
on imported ore favoured the development of deep-water sites.
Hence the newest United States Steel plant, the Fairless Works,
was on the Delaware, a parallel to Bethlehem's Sparrows Point
plant. This shift was not isolated in Table 69; the Fairless works
was in the same state as Pittsburgh.[2] The St Lawrence Seaway
promised to give both larger markets and good access for
Canadian ores to steel plants on the Great Lakes. By early 1959
a crop of new steelworks near Chicago seemed a possibility;
demand was much more broadly based there than in Detroit,
and when the seaway was opened Chicago was expected to
become a major inland seaport.[3] Export markets would thus be
added to the home market; but by the same token imports
of steel would also have better access, even imports from
Japan.[4]

In the short run the rising or waning fortunes of different
producing areas were shown more by the variable course of
production in them than by capacity changes. In Table 70
production in the main district is shown for the years 1955–58
as a percentage of capacity and as a percentage of output in
1947–49. These figures show considerable flexibility; with output
in the Pittsburgh-Youngstown area contracting most, and

[1] *Administerd Prices—Steel.* Part 2, p. 604, where Mr Homer of Bethlehem Steel
emphasised the long time needed to bring a new source of ore into use—3 or
4 years exploration to establish it was 'a good thing to do': 2 or 3 years to work
out details, 5 years to develop the mine before it produces. 'We are now thinking
about Africa', he said.

[2] The Fairless works was to use ore from Venezuela, to be brought in very large
ships. Initially, however, the ships could not be filled because of unexpected
obstacles to deepening the Orinoco and the Delaware.

[3] *Iron Age*, 26 Feb. 1959. National had just announced their plan to build a
works between Gary and Michigan City; at first a cold rolling and tinplate plant
finishing hot rolled strip from their Great Lakes plant (Detroit). Great Lakes would
increase its steel output by using oxygen in the open-hearth plant and would install
a new 80-in. hot strip mill. The new plant would probably have steel making
facilities later. According to *Iron Age* hot and cold strip mills for Fords were
'almost certain to materialise', and Bethlehem owned land near to National's
new site and 'has openly stated it wants it'.

[4] *Iron Age*, 26 Feb. 1959, the same issue that underlined Chicago steel plant
plans wrote about the 'Surge coming in Steel Imports'.

Chicago a little (presumably because the car industry had contracted) by 1957, while in other districts output was sustained or increased. The contraction was thus highest in the region which sent most steel to other regions, for which therefore sustaining output would involve heavy freight absorption. An analysis of outputs of firms as a proportion of their capacity shows there were similar, indeed wider, fluctuations.[1]

Table 70. *District outputs as percentages of capacity and of 1947–49 output*

	% of capacity			% of 1947–49 output		
	1955	1956	1957	1955	1956	1957
East	93·9	89·6	89·0	152·3	152·4	152·5
Pittsburgh, Youngstown	92·7	89·6	78·6	123·1	122·1	111·4
Cleveland and Detroit	93·2	92·1	88·3	168·7	166·3	166·7
Chicago	94·1	91·5	85·2	143·0	139·2	136·1
South	88·0	74·4	87·7	152·2	133·7	163·0
West	92·2	93·2	91·2	146·3	148·4	157·9

The Presidents of Bethlehem and Youngstown (Mr Homer and Mr McCluskey) set out their reasons for the merger to a Senate Antitrust Committee (the 'Kilgore Committee') in 1955 (the case was set out before the Court on the same lines in 1958).[2] They argued broadly that the two firms were essentially complementary, not competitive—Bethlehem's plants and markets were in the East and West, Youngstown's in Ohio and Indiana, serving the mid-Continental market. Though Bethlehem sent some steel from Lackwanna (New York State) into parts of the mid-Continental market (mainly Detroit) it was not a strong seller there, because it had a $10 freight. It wanted to produce in the area, but could not make a wholly new plant, which would cost upwards of $250 an ingot ton, remunerative. (The figure had become a little higher, $300, in 1957.)[3] No firms,

---

[1] This is mentioned not only to complete the picture but because it is occasionally suggested that price leadership was accompanied by some implicit acceptance of stable trading quotas. Nothing in the figures supports this. Outputs of firms as percentages of capacity are given in the annual analyses published by *Iron Age* early in January every year.

[2] Reported in *New York Times*, 11 Apr.–6 May 1958.

[3] Above, p. 524.

on current profit margins, Mr Weikel, the assistant to the President of Bethlehem, said in 1957 could afford a wholly new plant on the profit margins now earned.[1] To use the existing plant of Youngstown would be remunerative, and much cheaper, only $135 an ingot ton. Mr Homer said prices were based on a capitalisation of about $100 an ingot ton, which certainly represented the average book value of the steel firms;[2] but it seems hard to credit that prices were based on book values. Another witness had stated that the Barium Steel Company was going to build a new plant on the Delaware, using the oxygen Bessemer process, of 2 m. tons capacity, but with a narrow range of finished product, mainly plates and structurals, in Bethlehem's eastern market. It would cost $177 per ingot ton.[3] Youngstown wanted to expand, and to modernise more, and to make a wider range of products, but could not find sufficient resources to do all they wanted. Bethlehem, who made most products (though not seamless tubes or electric welded tubes, which were among Youngstown's products), could provide the funds from profits. When it had done so the joint concern would be a much more effective challenge to United States Steel, it was argued, since it would be in all the major markets. However, there would be no question of monopoly; in the twenty-eight mid-Continental states the two firms after their contemplated expansion would make 12 per cent only of the consumption, and there would be several larger strong competitors apart from United States Steel. There were possibilities of rationalising too; Youngstown's Labrador ores could go to Bethlehem's eastern plants, Bethlehem's Mesabi ores to Youngstown's western plants, e.g. at Chicago.

The case for the 'B and Y' merger was inherently strong as presented; its substance could only be assessed from an intimate knowledge. But it was not a case with any appeal for lawyers and economists steeped in antitrust tradition. A few economists supported the claim that the merger would increase competi-

---

[1]   *New York Times*, 29 Apr. 1958.

[2]   The figure is given in the *Iron Age* annual financial analysis; it rose steadily from $58 a ton in 1948 to $86 in 1958.

[3]   *New York Times*, 18 and 23 Apr. 1958.

tion.[1] There were sceptics who feared that the antitrust laws were 'based on earlier concepts' and involved 'a danger of using an obsolete framework of obsolete techniques'.[2] And some who were sure 'competition must be maintained between centres of administrative control' were convinced that where technology determined that such centres must be large, and therefore few, the right results would depend on the 'mores' of those in control; they must 'integrate their operations' (such as price-fixing) 'to the prosperity of the whole economy'. The market would not be enough; a simple competitive system did not *and could not* exist.[3] But the great majority of economists was strongly against anything which threatened to establish a situation whereby another industry would be dominated by a very small number of major firms. Judge Barnes, in charge of the Antitrust Division of the Department of Justice, in his evidence to the Kilgore Committee, argued that in some industries where this state of affairs existed—he did not specify which—'competition between companies continues to protect the consumer interest'; but 'as we understand it it was this sort of trend (i.e. to domination by a few firms) that Congress condemned and desired to halt when it adopted the new Clayton Act anti-merger provisions'.[4] There was thus for him no question of trying to sort out good and bad giant firms or trusts. For some of the other witnesses there was at least a problem. One, for example,[5] thought it an advantage to have firms as large as United States Steel and General Motors. 'Though small firms effectively produce some kinds of research, certain kinds the large multi-product plant most effectively developed',[6] and these kinds were 'crucial for national survival.... To maintain our equality or superiority with Russia we need large firms to

[1] Professor Cook, from the Harvard Business School, and Professor Ben Lewis from Oberlin gave evidence to this effect (*New York Times*, 3 May 1958).
[2] Professor Buckingham, to a *Congress Subcommittee on Economic Stabilisation* (Automation and Technical Change), 14–28 Oct. 1958, p. 41.
[3] *Ibid.* pp. 622–8, Dr Edwin G. Nourse.
[4] *Kilgore Committee*, part I, p. 300.
[5] Mr Weston, associate professor of finance, University of California (*ibid.* p. 436).
[6] The United States Steel Corporation by 1958 had experimental plants to carry out development on pilot plant scale for all stages of production.

develop some of these things.' He also thought very large firms were needed to give full scope for outstanding administrators. He was naturally against breaking up United States Steel—a policy which had some supporters. Professor Griffin of Michigan, also opposed to splitting the giants, found that on the subject of bigness in business 'the American people have a certain "split-mindedness"'. A sample inquiry by his university showed three-quarters of the people believed that big business was good for the country; but many who liked the fruits hated the power it conferred. 'A very difficult indeed insoluble problem is presented.' To put a legal upper limit on the size of firms would remove the motive to improve products or lower costs to secure more customers. Even so he was prepared to disallow some mergers, whose purpose might not necessarily be to serve consumers better.[1] But which mergers should be disallowed he did not specify.

Very large firms stood to gain less progressively as they grew from the more familiar advantages of large-scale operating (excluding the advantage of bigness for research, and the commercial advantage of selling all types of product in all markets), but were in an increasingly strong position to squeeze unintegrated small ones, if need be by offsetting losses in some parts of their business with high profits in others. For the same reason mistakes in investment decisions could be masked. Judge Barnes presented the opposition to the 'B and Y' merger as protection for the eighty small firms in the industry, 'most of them not even integrated'.[2] The pressure that was eliminating these in the thirties was still strong and still at work; the F.T.C. report on mergers gave instructive examples, and treated narrowing margins between prices of semi-finished and finished steel as a discriminating effort to dislodge the unintegrated,[3] though it was possibly, as in the United Kingdom, due to a decision no longer to show them special favour.[4] The Depart-

[1] *Kilgore Committee*, pp. 389–92.
[2] *Ibid.* pp. 300–2.
[3] *Corporate Mergers and Acquisitions*, pp. 113, 133. Steel plants did not disappear when bought up, some re-rolling plants did.
[4] Threatened localities always had a political protector, again as in the United Kingdom.

ment of Justice brought in evidence of alleged discrimination against unintegrated firms in the merger suit.[1]

There was much more emotional impetus behind the antitrust attack than contrariwise, and its official advocates and administrators had increasing finances for the work. When in due course the case was decided the judgement appears to have accepted the antitrust arguments exclusively. The merger would infallibly eliminate *some* competition—because at present some buyers could buy from either of the companies, some fabricators who competed with Bethlehem bought their steel from Youngstown, who in turn at present bought from independent fabricators but would not do so if amalgamated with Bethlehem—and so on. The 'net balance' of competition was not struck or not deemed relevant. To agree with this merger because it would allow Bethlehem to compete more on the level as regards size with United States Steel would, so the judge argued, make it impossible not to agree to a crop of mergers among smaller firms to come nearer to Bethlehem's size.[2] There was a disposition to read this part of the judgement as ruling out *any* other mergers among the bigger firms in the industry;[3] but it did not necessarily involve this. The Department of Justice and F.T.C. did not take the line that all mergers were to be banned; indeed, they welcomed mergers in the motor-car industry which kept alive some competition with the 'big three'. They thought it their function to exercise discretion. Some Senators thought this left them too much control, and wanted a tighter law, more precisely defining what mergers should be banned. Manifestly a law which banned any merger which would remove some element of existing competition (even if it created or strengthened other competition) might impose a rigidity of structure in which the characteristically American methods of reducing costs would have less scope. Much of the early aggressive United States advance was based on mergers.[4] The situation would be aggravated if the market for steel expanded less fast than in the last decade, which some

---

[1] *New York Times*, 16 Apr. 1958.
[2] Argued first in the Kilgore Committee by Judge Barnes, Part 1, p. 300.
[3] *Iron Age*, 27 Nov. 1958.   [4] *E.H.S.* p. 187.

people thought likely, and if the moral of Russian practice was that labour and capital could be saved by larger unit outputs. Nine of the sixteen largest firms in the United States industry were smaller, most of them much smaller, than the six groups which were likely to make 80–90 per cent of West German steel in 1959. There was a danger of sacrificing some substance of real cost reduction for a shadow of competition; a danger of damping down the growth of the forms of competition which in this kind of industry at this stage of its development were the only ones which could be expected to be effective. Whether this would happen could not yet be forecast with assurance.

It was not an imminent risk. Critics of concentration found in the anomalous rise of published steel prices and dividends from 1955 to 1958 (while consumption fell and rising capacity was progressively less occupied) new evidence of the immediate danger of administered prices. Though realised prices rose probably less than published, steelmakers joined the critics in calling them inflationary. It was due they said to the trade unions. The critics said that in conjunction with other rigid or rising administered prices they reduced total consumption. The pattern of demand for steel suggested unforeseen secular trends not to be explained mainly by aggregate demand.[1] By 1959–60 published prices were static or slightly falling—and wages still higher.[2]

[1] The trends of output, prices, turnover, wages and related costs, material costs, depreciation, margins, ploughback, and expenditure on new fixed investment (output in m. long tons, the rest except prices in dollars per long ingot ton) from 1953 to 1958 were:

	Output	Price index	Turnover	Wages, etc.	Materials	Interest	Dividends	Depreciation	Plough back	New plant
1953	94·2	100	139	47	65	0·6	3·5	6·5	4·4	10·6
1955	98·2	110	143	48	62	0·6	4·4	7·5	6·5	7·3
1957	94·3	130	165	59	72	0·7	6·1	8·1	6·3	18·5
1958	72·5	135	171	66	72	0·9	7·4	9·3	4·3	15·6

Turnover per ton rose much less than published prices: (was it partly because many steel firms made other products?). Labour cost rose steeply and material costs little. Depreciation plus ploughback did not rise significantly after 1955 though investment rose; ploughback fell more than depreciation per ton rose in 1958. (*Aggregate* depreciation fell: the effect of fast write offs was ending.) For the beginnings of controversial examination of these data in relevant contexts cp. Charles L. Schultze, *Recent Inflation in the United States*, and Otto Eckstein and Gary Fromm, *Steel and the Postwar Inflation*, papers for the Joint Econ. Comm. of Congress, Sept. and Nov. 1959.   [2] *Iron Age*, 19 May 1960.

Chapter IX

THE BRITISH INDUSTRY SINCE DENATIONALISATION: THE RECORD, 1953–1959

1. BOARD AND AGENCY

The members of the new Iron and Steel Board were appointed at the end of May 1953, those of the Agency to dispose of the state-owned companies to private ownership a fortnight later. Sir Archibald Forbes came back to be chairman of the second Board, and Sir John Morison, a member of the firm of accountants Thompson McLintock and Co., who handled the business of several steel firms, and were accountants of the Iron and Steel Corporation of Great Britain, became chairman of the Agency. Morison was Director General (Finance and Contracts) in the Ministry of Supply during the war. Both Forbes and Morison had been close advisers of Sir Andrew Duncan on the strategy of denationalising. The Scots ascendancy in administrative bodies dealing with steel remained undisturbed. Sir Lincoln Evans was also back, as a full-time member of the Board; a hard pill for many Socialists.[1] Mr Shone was its other full-time member—a subtle translation which threw the balance between Board and Federation much in favour of the first. The steelmakers were represented on the Board by Sir Andrew McCance from Colvilles and Mr Rollason from John Summers, who was also on the Board of United Steel. Thus there was a

---

[1] It became known through an action which Sir Lincoln Evans took against an attack upon him by *Tribune* that the executive committee of the Iron, Steel and Kindred Trades Association had decided to associate with the Board a year before Sir Lincoln Evans accepted the invitation: that the committee had circulated the minute of this to all branches: that he had asked and obtained the approval of the Executive Committee before accepting the invitation, and would not have accepted otherwise—and that only 24 out of 662 branches passed resolutions deprecating his acceptance (Law report in *The Times*, 12 Oct. 1954).

member who was associated with home ore development, but
he would not see this in too great isolation. The other part-time
members of the Board included the chairman of Allied Ironfounders, three company chairmen or deputy chairmen from
consuming industries,[1] and two former trade unionists—one a
Welshman, formerly secretary of the Union of Blastfurnacemen,
Ore Miners, Coke Workers and Kindred Trades.[2] The Agency
included among its members Sir John Green, the second chairman of the defunct Iron and Steel Corporation of Great Britain.
Some continuity from Corporation to Agency was probably to
be desired.[3]

The British steel industry had now emerged from the cramping
period of raw-material scarcity. Output was rising, and the
scene seemed set again for steady but not immodest expansion.
The Corporation, it has been seen,[4] had been busily sanctioning
development plans which had been based, not quite formally,
on an output of 20 m. ingot tons in 1957, and which involved
no agonising reappraisal of locational advantages, since everything would be done by adding to and balancing existing plants.
How long would this seem enough to the firms, the Federation,
the Government, or the new Board? The Board had clearly
been chosen with great respect for continuity. But it was likely
to seek to establish a *raison d'être*. What would the members wish
to change? What would they add to the momentum, impetus,
and inertia, of the industry?

Such questions are dealt with in the next chapter. Before
turning to them it is convenient to sketch lightly the progress
of the work of the Agency, and to survey the comparative
growth in the industry of production and facilities, of markets,
exports and imports, costs and efficiencies, and scientific
development.

[1] Mr Beharrell of Dunlops, M. Charles Connell, a Glasgow shipbuilder, and
Sir Percy Lister, of R. A. Lister's.
[2] Mr J. Owen. The other trade unionist was Sir Andrew Naesmith, formerly
General Secretary of the Weavers Union.
[3] There was much continuity of staff.
[4] Above, p. 365.

2. DISPOSALS

Disposals went much better from 1953 to 1957 than at first seemed likely. This owed much to the improvement in Conservative political prospects—the steel share market fluctuated with the political outlook, and disposals went in corresponding waves. But Sir John Morison was extremely skilful in evolving schemes with market appeal. The Agency worked through a consortium of eight principal merchant bankers. The City was willing to be helpful, but not sacrificial.

Transactions fell into two groups. Some companies belonging to the Corporation were sold by private treaty, but most of the larger companies were sold by offers to the public. The sales by private treaty again fell into two groups: sales back to firms of companies they had previously owned and sales of companies to firms not previously connected with them. In the first category were the sales of English Steel Corporation back to Vickers and Cammell Lairds, of the Darlington and Simpson Rolling Mills back to Crittalls and Dorman Longs (Dormans were still nationalised when it happened) of G.K.B.'s Cardiff plant, and John Lysaghts (Scunthorpe) and Brymbo to Guest, Keen and Nettlefolds, though the first transaction was complex because originally G.K.N. were only part owners, and G.K.B. had links with the Steel Company of Wales. There were several other sales in this category, the sales, for example, of Templeborough Rolling Mills, Arthur Lee's, Birchley Rolling Mills, Lilleshall, Charles Bagnalls. The second category included some noteworthy instances. The second sale of the disposals operation was of Round Oak to Tube Investments, who later also bought Park Gate, and one or two smaller units from the Agency. Firth Browns, after being denationalised, bought Beardmores (which had been spoken of as unsaleable, but it gave Firth Browns more capacity cheaply and quickly); Darwins bought Sheffield Forge and Rolling Mills. Of these new ownerships the first was of particular interest, because it marked the entry of a new firm into steelmaking (albeit Tube Investments had had an interest in Stewarts and Lloyds in the past) and continued the tradition of large users of steel coming in to make steel. Sometimes the consumer in doing this introduced new techniques and new standards of efficient production; the developments at Corby and (less comprehensively) at Ebbw Vale in the thirties were instances. Would it happen this time? Tube Investments bought their way into steelmaking by acquiring two small, hardly well-favoured, plants. They did so perhaps primarily to ensure regular supplies and qualities. Both works had been modernised in part. Round Oak was not integrated with iron-making, and Park Gate's ironmaking was down at heels and could not within its existing scale be modernised. Together (the plants were, however, far apart) their steel output was too little to occupy a modern primary mill by the Productivity Team standards. Round Oak was bought in 1954 for £5·8 m., Park Gate in 1955 for £5·6 m., which did not look low prices in comparison with those at which other companies were sold.[1] The works soon involved more capital outlay.[2]

The major disposals operation was selling firms back as independent public companies by offer of shares to the public. It was symbolic that the first two of the major firms to be put on the market were United Steel (November 1953) and Stewarts and Lloyds (June 1954), both well based on cheap home ores.[3] John Summers and Dorman Longs followed in the autumn of 1954, Colvilles in January 1955, Consett in December 1955, South Durham a month later, and the Steel Company of Wales, completely hived off from Richard Thomas and Baldwins, in March 1957; this, indeed, a monster operation, and an impressive token of success. After this only one major steel firm remained to be sold, Richard Thomas and Baldwins; and the Agency estimated at the end of 1958 that companies representing five-sixths of its inheritance had ceased to be its subsidiaries. That did not mean that they had all been

---

[1] The ingot output of Round Oak was about 250,000 tons, of Park Gate 320,000 tons; hence the cost was about £20 per ingot ton a year. The price paid for United Steel Co. ordinary shares was £17·5 m.; prior charges held by the Agency were worth £15·3 m. Ingot output was 2·4 m. This gives an average of £13. 10s. per ingot ton.

[2] Thus at Round Oak the mills were rearranged and electric furnaces put in.

[3] Lancashire Steel was sold after United Steel and before Stewarts and Lloyds, but it was not a comparable operation in scale.

entirely sold; the large scale of the divestiture of control depended partly on the Agency retaining large holdings in many
of its former subsidiaries.

This was dicated by two considerations. To sell back the steel
firms entirely, even if there were no exceptional risk, would have
involved finding an immense sum of money, because the value
of the firms had been greatly added to, since they had been
bought up, by the continuation of investment, not to mention
the effect of inflation, and the purchasers would be faced with
large prospective calls for still more capital because of the
development programmes on which most of the firms were
engaged. But there was an acute political risk. There had been
threats by several labour politicians that compensation would
be meagre if the firms were renationalised—some threats,
indeed, that there would be no compensation at all, though
these looked hardly serious. Hate and spite were likely to colour
such an operation. These complex difficulties were met by
offering the equity of the companies on terms which made them
attractive and on a scale which the market seemed likely to
absorb. It was essentially the equity which must be sold,
because with it went control. Hence the line adopted was in
general to canalise all the funds which 'the market' would
provide into the purchase of the *equities* of firms; the Agency
remained the provider of money at fixed interest, often with a
promise of additional funds to meet the cost of committed future
capital investment as it arose. This was not the invariable
pattern, but it was the commonest. In a sense, too, the size
of the equity offered was tailored to fit the market. In the
early stages of the operation the equity was relatively small
in relation to the compensation paid for the equity on
nationalisation.

This became less so, with the exception of Whitehead's, as
later sales took place, as Table 71 shows. In the same table the
value of the Agency's holdings of debentures and preference
shares in former subsidiaries is shown at September 1958. This
was not quite the whole story; the Agency had advanced
£16·5 m. to the Steel Company of Wales out of £40 m. which
it had undertaken to advance as an unsecured loan as the

need arose. The fourth column of the table shows approximately the investment in each company per ingot ton of output at the time of resale.

Table 71. *Equity and fixed interest ratios*

	Compensation for ordinary shares	Proceeds from sales of ordinary shares on re-sale (£ m.)	Book value of securities retained by Agency (£ m.)	Investment per ingot ton on re-sale (£)
Nov. 1953 United Steels	15·46	17·50	15·27	14
Jan. 1954 Lancashire Steel	6·06	4·95[a]	Nil	21
June 1954 Stewarts and Lloyds	23·43	17·50	12·09	20
Oct. 1954 John Summers	6·25	11·03	10·74	19
Nov. 1954 Dorman Longs	7·16	16·88	10·29	13
Jan. 1955 Colvilles	7·45	13·00	9·23	12
Feb. 1955 Whiteheads	4·84	3·94	0·79	—[b]
Mar. 1955 Firth Brown's	6·06	6·88	Nil	50[c]
Dec. 1955 Consett	6·41	12·75	0·78	15
Jan. 1956 South Durham	0·81	11·00[d]	Nil	20
Mar. 1957 Steel Co. of Wales	—[e]	40·0	61·82	60[f]

[a] £4·5 m. Preference Shares were also sold at 21s. per share.

[b] Re-rollers only.

[c] Basis of calculation includes £3 m. debenture sold to the public; the figure is not broadly comparable with the others as all the output was special steel.

[d] £3 m. Debenture Stock was sold at £97.

[e] Some shares were held by other firms who were bought, hence there was no real compensation price.

[f] Takes into account £16·5 m. unsecured loan from the Agency.

The compensation in 1951, it will be recalled, was not based on a valuation of assets, but on the Stock Exchange values of those shares which had been sold in a reference period; it was low, and did not reflect relative values of assets realistically. It was the starting-point naturally in the book values on which resale was based. The contrast between the position of a firm like Colvilles and the Steel Company of Wales, whose significance has been discussed earlier,[1] was aggravated. The figures in Table 71 must only be taken as giving rough comparisons. The assets of the different firms varied greatly in scope. Dorman Long's, it has been seen, made a large part of their profit

[1] Above, pp. 262–4.

as constructional engineers; United Steel and Stewarts and Lloyds had a large home ore base, and so on. For comparison, the average investment on what appears a fairly similar basis in the major United States steel firms rose from $73 (£26) in 1950 to $86 (£31) in 1953 and $103 (£37) in 1956. In this respect the capital structure emerged in the United Kingdom relatively more favourable in comparison with the United States after renationalisation than before. Moreover, the drawback inherent in a heavy fixed-interest burden was less menacing, or looked less so, so long as inflation went on and business expanded. Inflation reduced the real burden progressively. The firms renationalised first gained from the earliness in two ways: the fixed-interest burden was assumed in an earlier stage of inflation, and also in an earlier stage of the third expansive cycle, when interest rates were lower. The arrangements made by the Agency secured or made possible for all the firms the financing of the development and expansion to which firms were committed at the time of re-sale. More than this the Agency could not do.

By the end of 1957 some firms were seeking the means to finance a further stage of investment. Colvilles and South Durham both raised capital by the issue of convertible debentures[1]—the new popular device—early in 1958. Presumably they could not sell more ordinary shares; and they complained that the political insecurity raised the cost, though by this date all new industrial capital was fairly dear. South Durham and Dorman Longs both secured undertakings from the F.C.I. to provide some resources in the future as they became necessary for the investment programmes. By the end of the year complaints of the dearness and difficulty of raising capital became more frequent. The election risk was nearer, and at the end of 1958 began to look dangerous. Stewarts and Lloyds postponed making an issue by deferring some investment because demand for tubes was growing more slowly than they had expected;[2]

[1] Colvilles raised £6 m. of 6 per cent convertible debentures, issued at £99, in Jan. 1958; South Durham raised £8 m. 6 per cent convertible second debentures, issued at £95, in Mar. 1958.
[2] Annual Report, *The Times*, 16 Jan. 1959.

and other firms may have been moved by the same sort of experience. New decisions in favour of investment on a large scale at this date, concerned with new strip mills (which are considered later) were set off with a new method of financing—direct loans from the Treasury. (The details are referred to later.) This continued the increase of fixed-interest liabilities, and for the disingenuous nationaliser it was another proof that private enterprise could not finance steel expansion!

The Federation published an analysis of the ownership of the public companies early in 1959[1] to show that the number of owners was large—in some companies over 30,000—and that most holdings were small. (The Agency at the outset of re-sale had said preference would be given to small buyers, as well as to former investors.) Less than 6 per cent of owners held more than 1000 shares, and only 0·6 per cent over 10,000. Several of the big owners were institutions—insurance companies (including the Co-operative Insurance Company with over 500,000 shares in six companies), the Church Commissioners, with over 2 m. shares, and the coal-miners pension fund with over 1 m. shares, and so on. The analysts could, had they known how to spot them, have found among the shareholders the names of good Socialists of the rank and file, who had taken a chance. Of such were the profit grabbers of political fiction. There were, too, the familiar unidentifiable bank nominees among the larger holders. The proportion of ordinary shares held by the ten largest shareholders was given for 12 companies as shown in Table 72. All this repeated the pattern already established earlier in the public companies,[2] though it was now on a larger scale (and with more insurance companies in). It need hardly be pointed out that a body of ten having even one-tenth of the voting power when most owners were small and wholly unorganised could wield significant power.

Most of the boards of the companies went straight on—into and out of nationalisation. The chief exceptions have been mentioned. Firth Brown's board changed during nationalisation; and after it Sir John Green, who had been a member of

---

[1] *Steel Review*, Jan. 1959.
[2] *E.H.S.* pp. 254 sqq.

Table 72. *Percentage of shares held by ten largest shareholders*

Company	Per cent	Company	Per cent
Steel Co. of Wales	28·0	South Durham	14·5
Lancashire Steel	24·2	Dorman Longs	11·3
John Summers	21·8	Consett	10·7
Whiteheads	20·5	United Steel	9·6
Firth Brown	15·2	Hadfields	9·5
Stewarts and Lloyds	15·2	Colvilles	9·3

the Board before nationalisation, returned as its chairman, and Dr Charles Sykes remained managing director. The Steel Company of Wales acquired a new chairman when it was separated from Richard Thomas and Baldwins—Mr Harald Peake.[1] The leadership of Richard Thomas and Baldwins changed too with the retirement of Sir Ernest Lever, who was succeeded by Mr Geoffrey Eley.[2] In both instances a Welsh company went to the City and found an English—Etonian—financier to head it. In the number of important companies in which members of the founding families played an important dominant role, before nationalisation, this continued, not because majority ownership gave them control, but because there seemed in effect implicitly to be a principle of family succession. This appeared conspicuously so in John Summers, United Steel, South Durham and Stewarts and Lloyds. Colvilles became in 1956 on the death of Sir John Craig the one company to have as its chairman a distinguished scientist and engineer, Sir Andrew McCance.[3] It was more common for a technical man to hold the second place as Dr Charles Sykes in Firth Browns, but still not very common.[4] Leading executives

[1] A vice-chairman of Lloyds Bank, and director of the National Bank of Scotland, the Bank of London and South America, etc.

[2] A director of the Bank of England, the Equity and Law Life Assurance Co., chairman of British Drug Houses, and member of the Board of several industrial companies. At one time a financial journalist.

[3] The former chairman and managing director, Sir John Craig, had worked up from office boy, and was the son of a steelworker. He became head of the firm as the three family heads died rather young. His own son is a director of the firm.

[4] Thus, for instance, the managing director of the Steel Co. of Wales, Sir Julian Pode, started as District Accountant in G.K.B. at Port Talbot, and later was secretary and assistant managing director.

provided, however, increasingly the body of the Board. In an increasing number of companies, possibly in most, it was possible for an able young man on entering to feel that all jobs were open to him for which his training and gifts fitted him, except it might be the ones which carried the last word.

The offers for sale published by the Agency all carried prominently a standard description of the Industry Fund. It came first in the particulars given in the prospectus. It was a curious description. 'The object of the Fund is to secure the availability of steel in Great Britain at the highest practicable level consistent with market requirements by spreading over the cost of steel the excess cost above home prices of imported pig iron, scrap, semi-finished and finished steel, and in addition abnormal or temporary increases in costs of imported ore: provision is also made for central research, assistance in abnormal and high cost transactions, and the maintenance of a balanced relationship between the cost of scrap and pig iron.' It was explained that the fund was fed by levies, at rates determined from time to time by the Executive Committee of the Federation, and that the levies were calculated 'to secure over a period that the fund is self balancing, and the obligations of contributors continue until all liabilities incurred...have been satisfied'. Who except someone with intimate knowledge would have supposed from this that here was an arrangement which consistently for years had transferred large sums running into millions of pounds from low-cost to high-cost producers, and weighted the scales against home ores and in favour of scrap, and that the way it was managed would influence immensely the relative values of the companies which were being sold? There was no guarantee that the policy would not change. Yet it was not thought necessary to reveal how much the fortunes of the individual companies sold had in fact been changed by these manipulations. None of the public's watchdogs worried!

When in 1958 the convertible debentures were put on the market an even stranger description of the scheme was given, one still more remote from the descriptions published by the Iron and Steel Corporation and the Federation in 1953.[1] The

[1] Above, pp. 352–3.

objects 'may be described as the provision of common services for the Iron and Steel Industry, including the importation and distribution of raw materials, ingots, semi-finished and finished iron and steel products and other operations designed to assist in ensuring that adequate supplies of iron and steel are available... at reasonable prices: these operations include provision for central research, training, assistance in abnormal and high cost transactions and the maintenance of a balanced relationship between the cost of scrap and pig iron...'.[1] There was no indication that the last two functions had involved the significantly large transactions under the Fund. Was it to be inferred that this was unlikely in future? Perhaps it was.

3. COMPARATIVE GROWTH, 1953–1958

The 'brave new plan' of 1952–53, discussed in Chapter VI, took an output of 20 m. tons in 1957 as a 'satisfactory figure on which to base programmes of raw material and plant development'.[2] This figure, as has been seen, was well passed in 1957, though the recession output of 1958 was within the limit. The contrast between expectation and performance extended to estimates of requirements of different types of steel and raw materials. It was shown earlier that even when published the guesses about demands for types of steel looked out of line with what was already happening,[3] and so it proved increasingly. The contrast between forecast and performance is shown in Table 73.

The first projection of home ore requirements for the 20 m. ingot ton output was 20 m. tons in 1957; this was revised down to 17·6 m. tons in 1958 by the beginning of 1955, when the steel output was visualised at 22 m. tons. Output in 1957 was 16·9 m. tons. The tradition of post-war plans and performances in this respect was thus maintained. Imports of ore were to be 16 m. tons according to the 1952–53 estimate, 15·7 m. tons in 1954, and the figure in 1957 was 15·96 m. tons. In the recession

---

[1] From the Colville prospectus (*The Times*, 13 Jan. 1958). (The same wording was used in the South Durham prospectus.)

[2] *Rep. I.S. Corp.* for year ended Sept. 1952, p. 35.

[3] Above, p. 360.

in 1958, however, the import of ore fell rather more proportionately than production of home ore. Though less ore was
to be available according to the 1955 than to the 1952–53
programme, there was to be no less pig iron, indeed perhaps
rather more.[1] In fact, the output of 21·7 m. ingot tons in 1957
was produced with an output of pig iron (for all purposes and
including blast-furnace ferro-alloys) of 14·28 m. tons. Between
1952 and 1957 the average home ore used in making a ton of
basic pig iron fell from 30 to 23 cwt; the average imported ore
rose from 16·4 to 19·7 cwt.[2]

The ingot output of 1957 depended much more upon scrap
than had been envisaged, presumably in 1952 and certainly
early in 1955. Instead of the pig iron/scrap ratio changing, as

Table 73. *Finished steel deliveries, 1957, forecasts and performances*

	Estimated requirements of finished steel in 1957 (published June 1953)	Deliveries of[a] finished steel 1957	Actual as % of forecast
Heavy steel products	4,525 (11)[b]	5,622	125
Light products (excl. wire rod used in U.K.)	4,125 (25)	4,245	103
Sheets	2,050 (30)	2,303	112
Tinplates, etc.	1,000 (38)	1,033	103
Tubes	1,400 (28)	1,252	89
Wire	1,050 (29)	879[c]	80
Other products	1,100 (15)	1,411	128
Total	15,250 (22)	16,745	110

[a] These are based on statistics of net deliveries to consuming industries, including deliveries of imported finished steel and exports of finished steel, and the product groups have been matched to those used in the 1953 estimates, which were accompanied by statistics of deliveries in 1951 which act as a guide.

[b] The figures in brackets are the percentages by which the forecasts were to exceed 1951 supplies. Above, p. 360.

[c] Wire rods consumed; the figure should of course be reduced by a small percentage to account for process losses.

[1] The figures are obscure. In 1952 the B.I.S.F. said the plan was for 15 m. tons of pig iron (*Stat. Bull.*); in 1955 it was for 15·15 m. tons including blast furnace ferro-alloys. The 1952–53 programme suggested 15·3 m. tons.

[2] This includes the ore which was used in sinter for basic pig iron.

was premised in February 1955, from 53:55 to 58:49,[1] it moved in 1957 only to 55:52.[2] Circulating scrap to be used in 1957 was put at 25 per cent of the ingot output—but the percentage had never been so low during the war or since; the average from 1940 to 1953 was 27·5 per cent,[3] and the percentage realised in 1957 was 27. Presumably this was a case of forecasters playing for safety. Imports of scrap also kept up much more than was visualised. An upper limit seemed to be set at 800,000 tons, partly because imports from the United States were deemed unlikely, partly because the price was high. This it indeed was, against the British fixed price; but it came in nevertheless on the 1951–53 level and a little above, though not as high as in 1949–50.

Table 74. *Imports of scrap into United Kingdom, 1952–57*

Year	Thousand tons	£ per ton	Year	Thousand tons	£ per ton
1952	728	22·5	1955	1272	17·2
1953	862	19·5	1956	982	22·5
1954	760	14·4	1957	664	24·5

Although pig-iron output rose less than was first foreshadowed there was a big rise in the proportion of pig iron charged as hot metal in steel manufacture. In 1952 6·2 m. tons were charged hot, 2·5 m. tons were charged cold. In 1956 the figures were 8·2 and 3·0 m.; in 1957 9·2 and 2·8 m. A striking change had occurred, though the use of cold metal was still very extensive.[4] In the open-hearth process 24 per cent of the pig iron was still charged cold. (It fell to 19 per cent in 1958.) The percentage was 9 in the United States in 1950.

The fallibility of many of the early figures in the second plan

---

[1] *Development of the Iron and Steel Industry, 1953–1958* (Iron and Steel Board), Feb. 1955, p. 23.

[2] Instead of 12·75 m. tons of pig iron and 10·8 m. tons of scrap, the figures in 1957 were 12·028 m. tons of pig iron and 11·46 m. tons of scrap. Stocks of scrap increased by 400,000 tons during 1957.

[3] For the details above, p. 343, n. 1.

[4] In several districts it rose in 1957, for example in Scotland, west Midlands, Sheffield. The biggest fall was on the North-east Coast; the next, South Wales.

is not unimportant because at the time they seemed tentative and in retrospect can be explained or understood. The view, in particular, on the market for finished steel seems to show either how much the prospect of an investment boom such as occurred in 1955–57, at home and abroad, was discounted, or alternatively, how much its implications for the production of heavy-steel products of all kinds and qualities—plates and sections, forgings and castings—were written down. There were, as has been seen, doubters in 1952–53[1] who thought the plans for plate production inadequate—neglecting the shipbuilders' need of very wide plates for welding, and the prospect of big demands for the oil, chemical and nuclear industries, including a big requirement of plates up to 3 in. thick, all in addition to the normal demands of constructional and general engineering. Some of those in the Steel Federation who thought the provision for plate capacity was adequate in 1952–53 were complaining later in private that much that should have been available for ships was being used for large welded tubes by South Durham, who had a reputation for, as it were, breaking the rules, and had built a new plant for the purpose of making these tubes.[2] But this was precisely the sort of thing the experts should have been looking out for. The German steel industry manifestly accepted the desirability of providing new and better quality plate supplies ahead of the British.[3] Development of heavy-section mills was also possibly delayed excessively, though this did not have so wide an impact. Indeed, in 1953 the constructional steelmakers were complaining (as they did again in 1958) that Government advice on steel economy had driven people too much to the use of ferro-concrete.[4]

When the new Iron and Steel Board made its first analysis of development plans in 1954, it could not fail to recognise that 'significant changes have taken place since 1952 both in the prospects of demand for the different steel products and (which

---

[1] Above, p. 359, and *Final Report of Iron and Steel Consumers Council*, pp. 2–3.

[2] It was an extension of the Stockton Malleable Works, once an open-hearth plant in the company. The pipe plant started operating late in 1955. Annual Report in *The Times*, 8 Jan. 1957, and Prospectus for Debentures (*The Times*, March 1958).

[3] Above, p. 457.

[4] *Final Report of Iron and Steel Consumers Council*, p. 5, and *The Times*, 24 Sept. 1958.

is more obscure) in the possibilities of supply'.[1] This analysis, as seen already, envisaged a higher crude steel output, and it also planned for more plates and acknowledged the need to have four-high mills to give plates of better quality.[2] This forecasting and planning will be considered later. While it is correct to say the figures published in 1953 were underestimates in general, and markedly so in some particulars, it is to be recalled that forecasts made later in 1953 on the Continent, by E.C.E., and by the new E.C.S.C., were also hesitant.[3] By the end of 1954 the fact of expansion in demand could not be overlooked. The question then was whether it might still be underestimated.

That the 'possibilities of supply' were larger by February 1955, as the Board put it, presumably meant that the capacities of new plant visualised by 1958 could be enlarged within the general rubric of the second plan, where increased output was to come mainly by the 'balancing of the different stages of production at the main consuming units'.[4] The rubric implied that there would be no startling change in geographical distribution of production; and so indeed, as Table 75 shows, it was. South Wales remained at the top; the loss in 1958 reflected the closing of small open-hearth plants, but a large replacement was in the plan. Scotland alone of the major old districts had slipped noticeably since 1937, but the fall in 1958 was aggravated by the special falling off in demand for Scotland's main products. The Lincolnshire and Northamptonshire home ore districts edged a little forward, but Lancashire 'etc.' much more, because of the integration of Summers' plant at Shotton and the healthy demand for its sheets. The Northwest Coast lost more relatively than the rounded percentages allow, but not much in absolute tonnage. This is not the picture of an industry responding vigorously to changed raw material or transport circumstances; for this quinquennium at least such things were written out of the programme.

So, too, were drastic changes in the number of firms and of

---

[1] I.S. Board, *Development of the Iron and Steel Industry 1953–1958* (referred to subsequently as *Development, 1953–1958*), p. 1.
[2] *Ibid.* p. 15. [3] Above, p. 153.
[4] *Rep. I.S. Corp.* for 1952, p. 36.

plants. Within the general rise of output there could be a rise of some importance for most firms and many plants, and very broadly this is what occurred.

Table 75. *Distribution of ingot output, 1937, 1953–58*

	1937		1953		1957		1958[a]	
	Thousand tons	%	Thousand tons	%	Thousand tons	%	Thousand tons	%
S. Wales and Monmouthshire	2,629	20	4,015	24	5,022	24	4,344	22
N.E. Coast	2,825	22	3,351	20	4,258	20	3,801	20
Sheffield	1,739	13	2,257	13	2,703	13	2,460	13
Scotland	1,895	15	2,220	13	2,512	12	2,075	11
Lincolnshire	1,299	10	1,853	11	2,288	11	2,210	12
Lancs., Flint, etc.	1,092	8	1,343	8	1,932	9	2,064	11
W. Midlands	702	5	874	5	1,026	5	946	5
Northants, etc.	418	3	755	4	980	5	925	5
N.W. Coast	385	3	387	2	361	2	322	2
Total	12,984		17,054		21,087		19,198	

[a] Based on 52 weeks. For statistical purposes this was a 53-week year, and output in 53 weeks was 19,570,000 tons.

The number of firms and of plants in different size groups according to output in 1957 is given in Table 76.

The number of plants had been reduced by the closing of a small number of the very small. A concerted effort had eliminated four and a half plants in 1951[1]—as referred to earlier—

Table 76. *Size distribution of firms and plants, 1957 (according to scale of ingot outputs)*

Size (thousand tons)	2500–3000	2000–2500	1500–2000	1000–1500	800–1000	600–800
Number of firms	1	3	3	1	2	1
% of output	14	30	23	6	9	3
Number of plants	—	1	Nil	3	2	5
% of output	—	10	Nil	16	9	16

	500–600	400–500	300–400	200–300	100–200	50–100
Number of firms	1	Nil	1	3	8	4
% of output	2	Nil	2	3	5	1
Number of plants	2	3	7	6	14	12
% of output	7	7	12	7	9	5

[1] The Stockton works of South Durham, the Britannia plant of Dorman Longs, the Blochairn works in the Colville group, the Bryngwyn works of R.T.B., and half the Barrow steelworks. A description of the Federation committee procedure on this is given in the *B.I.S.F. Ann. Rep.* 1951, p, 26.

and in 1957–58 a few more of these went—some of Richard Thomas and Baldwins' small steel plants in South Wales were closed because at length the market for tinplate would not sustain the old hand mills. It had done so far longer than was at first expected, but when the end came it was rather sudden. The Board's view early in 1955 was that output of sheet and tinplate from hand mills might well be as large in 1958 as it had been in 1953.[1]

The figures in Table 76 must be slightly qualified both because several of the plants had two steel-melting shops, which lessened the scope for economies of large scale, and because, contrariwise, a few of the plants which were nearly contiguous and were within one firm were in some respects worked as a unit; having, for example, a common source of coke, or molten pig iron, or gas and power, or interchanging ingots for some purposes (which gave the possibility sometimes of more technical gains from vertical integration, but also gave scope to have larger units of plant or more specialised operation of plant at some stages).[2] It was possible, for example, to have a blast-furnace plant with high-capacity units, even though a particular melting shop could absorb only part of its output; but the diseconomies of the smaller open-hearth melting shop in itself (through discontinuous loading of equipment, use of small units, or the production of steel at infrequent intervals only) were not lessened; and transport within a rather widely scattered complex of plants is not to be disregarded as invariably a negligible cost.

Table 76 must be read with two further qualifications in mind. Some of the smaller plants were making highly specialised qualities. The table neglects the large number of plants making below 50,000 tons of ingots, and so excludes many of the makers of alloy steels. But most of the bigger ones came into the table; in five of those making less than 100,000 tons,[3] seven making

---

[1] *Development of the Iron and Steel Industry, 1953–1958*, pp. 17–18.

[2] The two principal instances are the linking of some Colville units (above, pp. 259 sqq. and below, p. 644), and of Dorman Long's various plants on the North-east Coast. The third stage of the developments at South Durham visualised a close link between a new works at West Hartlepool and the existing works.

[3] Brown Bayley's two of E.S.C.'s Sheffield plants and their Openshaw plant, and Baker and Bessemer.

from 100,000 to 200,000 tons,[1] and one, Samuel Fox of Stocksbridge, in the 300,000–400,000 ton group. The last-named plant had become the largest alloy-steel plant in terms of tonnage in the country, making sections and bars and billets however, not forgings or castings, and stainless steel ingots to be rolled in Sheffield itself.[2] The alloy and special steel plants listed accounted for about 8 per cent of the ingot output. It is not to be assumed that the smallness of their scale is appropriate to the work done; indeed, the disparity between Fox's scale of production and that more normal in the United Kingdom is expressive.[3] But clearly these do not come into the class of plants to which the *Productivity Report* referred in laying down a size of 750,000 to 1 m. tons capacity as the minimum for efficient operation of an integrated plant. How far some other plants making mainly steels for a special purpose—tubes, for example—or making small lots of bars should also be set aside is more dubious; there are some borderline cases. It surely remains significant that 48 per cent (of which 8 per cent was alloy and special) of ingot output was made in plants below the Productivity Team standards, and a further 8 per cent in plants at or below the minimum of the team's range.[4]

The further qualification to bear in mind is that it was not a fixed situation; several big developments were in hand or planned. What was projected for 1962 was set out by the Iron and Steel Board in 1957.[5] The changes seemed to show that about 57 per cent of ingot output in 1962 would be made in

---

[1] Colvilles' Hallside works, Taylor Brothers, Brymbo, Beardmore, Hadfields, Firth Browns.

[2] At the Shepcote Lane works of the Firth-Vickers Steel Co., with which S. Fox (a branch of United Steel) was now associated. This is an instance of another kind of link allowing scale operation.

[3] Cp. above, p. 17, for wartime comments.

[4] It is useful to look at the figures from another angle. Following the team's basis of calculation—they gave an average of 325,000 tons per year for 40 bulk steel plants in 1950—in 1957, 36 bulk steel plants made an average of 520,000 tons, compared with a minimum desirable of 750,000 to 1 m. tons. Since the team's report the minimum for a strip mill had been put much higher. Cp. *E.C.E. Report* on the wide-strip mill, 1954, where it was emphasised that the European outputs from these mills lagged badly behind the American.

[5] *Special Report*, 1957, p. 50, gives the data concerning ingot outputs of principal firms; data on plants must be derived from multiple sources.

melting plants above or on the borders of the Productivity Team's standard, compared with 52 per cent in 1957;[1] with the same qualifications of course, and the three instances of partial integration of plants referred to above. The increase of output depended partly on three new melting shops which were additional, and not replacements nor offset by the closing of works. Concentration was not in the programme.

The Board itself made a qualitative analysis of the plant in the industry as it expected it to be in 1962. It divided plant in several sections of the industry into 'excellent, good, not so good, and poor'—in iron smelting, steel melting and three types of rolling—with the result shown in Table 77.

Table 77. *Proportion of 1962 output likely from various grades of plant (percentages)*[a]

Class of plant ...	First class modern of economic size A		Efficient though older B		Plant well below average, useful in time of high demand C		Obsolete D	
Product ...	1955	1962	1955	1962	1955	1962	1955	1962
Pig iron	24	34	54	55	18	9	4	1
Steel ingots	21	35	54	48	14	11	7	5
Billets	16	26	58	48	12	13	4	3
Plates	20	76	20	12	50	12	0	0
Other heavy steel	0	27	67	67	34	7	0	0

[a] Balancing percentages for some products refer to unclassified small plants making special quality steels.

An interesting feature of the table was that 'efficient but older' plant (not 'modern of economic size') might actually be responsible for a larger proportion of output; it was visualised that a considerably larger tonnage of both steel and pig iron would be made in this category of plant—8 m. tons of pig iron in 1962 compared with 5 m. in 1955, 13·25 m. tons of ingots in

[1] The largest changes were: Steel Co. Wales, from 2 m. to 3 m. tons; J. Summers, from 980,000 to 1,650,000 tons; Consett from 950,000 to 1,500,000 tons; South Durham, a new plant of some 800,000 tons. The new Newport plant, not listed in the *Special Report*, has been counted in.

1962 compared with 10·75 m. in 1955. This reflected in respect
of pig iron the building between 1953 and 1957 of several blast
furnaces with hearths of about 20 ft.—at Bilston, Irlam, Cargo
Fleet and West Hartlepool for example—whose relative smallness by the Productivity Team's standards was explained by
the size of the steelworks they were to feed. In steel melting
it mainly reflected the addition of new furnaces in existing
shops or enlargement of old ones, but some new open-hearth
shops were planned at below the team's standard size. These
things were consistent with the introduction of modern instru-
mentation, changes of furnace design, use of new fuels, better
charging methods, and the like, which greatly improved performance.

The conclusions to be drawn from the Board's qualitative
prognostic analysis must depend upon an assessment of what
was a practicable and desirable speed of approach to an
'economic size' of works. Obviously everything cannot be
renewed and 'best' at once. What were the cost differences
between the best in category A and the worst in category B, and
what was happening in other countries? In the two previous
chapters the extensive nature of changes on the Continent and
in the United States, and in Russia, has been shown. The cata-
logues of changes in the United Kingdom, issued frequently by
the Board and Federation, made an impressive show, but they
were not ideally designed to provide a perspective. It could be
assumed that most of the new units of plant were good of their
kind within their scale and for their specified purpose, and that
when there were compromises they were ingenious and carried
out skilfully, and would impress a layman. The answers to more
subtle questions—were the things done the right things? was
the choice of scale or of type of plant right for minimising costs?
how much was in a sense routine? how much innovation was
involved? how much technical leadership was being shown, or
being neglected? were often inevitably obscure. Some things
stood out. Though the development of the strip mills was
necessarily derivative, it was distinguished, and the Port Talbot
works in particular, while the inadequacy of its port facilities
became increasingly plain, was a notable plant. When at length

Dorman Longs in these years built the universal beam mill announced in 1945—it began to roll beams in 1958—it was a fine plant, and though it owed much necessarily to the American firm who *made* the mill itself, a great deal of the whole design (including the mill design) was made within the firm, and United States and French firms were soon in the market for the detailed design.[1] The development of ironmaking at Scunthorpe by Appleby Frodingham was outstanding, and by the use of self-fluxing sinter, and by using *only* sintered ore in the blast furnace, and finally excluding even sinter 'fines' (which were resintered), remarkable results in furnace outputs and coke consumption on low-grade ore were achieved.[2] The other Scunthorpe firms, with their main interests in South Wales, did not make similar pioneering advances. Doubts still remained over the siting of the Colville development area near the Dalzell works, at Ravenscraig, though there were no doubts about the quality of the plant itself.[3]

Among things *not* done in the period or done slowly development at Corby and the tacit dropping of the plan for a new Corby works—site preparation was announced in 1949— are of interest primarily in relation to location which is discussed later. The most conspicuous gaps in the British development (apart from the possibility of more concentration, larger units

[1] The mill was designed to be easily adapted to make ordinary girder sections if the demand for universal beams was not adequate. The primary mill was also used to feed a continuous billet mill, though how continuously it would feed this mill was not immediately clear. The output of the beam mill was put at 400,000 tons per year, but this seemed to be a conservative figure. Naturally the mill early in 1959 was still not fully run in or fully extended, and still had some 'teething troubles'.

[2] By the end of 1958 a furnace using only screened sinter was making 11,800 tons of pig iron a week at a coke consumption of 16 cwt. per ton.

[3] Technical enterprise was conspicuous in some smaller firms; the Ductile Steel Company, a re-rolling firm (which also made electric welded tubes and had a machinery-making works) to take an outstanding instance, pioneered the use of a 'Planetary' mill for hot rolling, to produce strip close to the tolerances of cold rolled strip; they also introduced a new French method of pickling strip for tube making and an almost fully 'automated' cold rolling strip mill (for strip up to 18 in. wide) a German mill with German electronic controls. The object in each of the mills was to give something, in quality, which large strip mills could not, or could not as yet, provide. For the planetary mill, an American perspective, see *Administered Prices*, vol. III, pp. 752 sqq.

and locational shifts) were the slow adoption of four-high plate mills and the slow advance of steelmaking techniques. The failure to increase and improve heavy plate production was the most glaring case of misjudgement in the first ten post-war years. None of the five firms mainly involved was quick off the mark; and Colvilles, who might be expected to lead, were with one exception the slowest off the mark. South Durham had the first new four-high mill—for medium plates, 8 ft. wide only—in operation in 1956. Appleby Frodingham had a medium and a heavy mill working by the end of 1958.[1] South Durham and Consett had four-high mills for wide heavy plate (136 and 132 in. wide respectively) on order by 1958, to be installed by 1962 or earlier. Colvilles had decided to install one at Clydebridge by 1962 and one at Dalzell later. Dorman Longs had still to decide; but their decision was complicated by the fact that they used a higher proportion of plates for constructional work than the other firms, and this particular demand was being lessened by their new beam mill, whose installation was an operation which absorbed their most creative energies.[2] It was surely significant of the slowness of the big firms that the small Midland plant of Patent Shaft and Axle Tree (controlled by the Vicker's group) was being doubled in capacity (from 130,000 to 250,000 tons) in 1958 and installing a four-high plate mill.[3] English Steel Corporation in 1956 57 converted and modernised an armour mill to make the thick plates which had seemed a Colville speciality.

The developments in steelmaking made first in various Continental countries, the Bessemer process with oxygen or oxygen-and-steam blast, the Austrian 'L.D.' process (a top-blown converter process using oxygen), the Swedish and German rotor furnaces, made headway on the Continent and in the United States faster than in the United Kingdom. Of new steel-melting capacity completed in the United States in 1958 almost one

---

[1] The medium mill was not new, but had new heat treatment facilities.

[2] They had immense leeway to make up at most parts of their extensive plants at the end of the war (cp. above, p. 86) and they got off to a slow start.

[3] The project was to produce plates mainly for Cammell Carriage and Wagon Works, about 20 miles away, whose consumption for steel railway wagons was expected to take a large part of the mill's output.

half was for a pneumatic process.[1] By this time certainly the point had registered in the United Kingdom; it was announced that several new melting shops would adopt one of the pneumatic processes,[2] and 'tonnage' oxygen generating plants were being set up, either at works (as at Corby) or independent of the works, supplying a bulk supply by pipe, which in the United Kingdom seemed to be likely to be more common. But the completion of such plants had been common much earlier on the Continent. Early in 1959 two steel plant-makers in the United Kingdom announced they could supply plant for oxygen steelmaking.[3] The use of oxygen by means of an 'oxygen lance' in the roof of an open-hearth furnace had made some headway in the United Kingdom, as it had also in the United States;[4] but though this had great advantages, it was not equivalent to having a plant designed initially for a pneumatic process, having in addition to high thermal efficiency the other familiar advantages of the Bessemer processes—frequent casts of ingots produced quickly in smaller batches from a smaller number of melting units than in the open hearth, requiring less soaking capacity to feed the mills steadily, and less heavy crane and ladle crane capacity, and less duplicated charging equipment—offered. All the capital equipment was used more continuously. There were savings in space and transport, significant savings indeed in labour, fuel and capital cost.

[1] *Iron Age*, 5 Feb. 1959. Of total new capacity of 6·2 m. tons, 2·6 m. tons was in this category. This did not include use of oxygen in open-hearth furnaces which was advancing very quickly (*ibid.* 15 Jan. 1959). In the E.C.S.C. £11 m. was spent on L-D or Rotor plants from 1956 to 1958, and production from this type of plant was 900,000 tons in 1958 (E.C.S.C., *Investment in 1958*, July 1959, p. 20). This did not of course include oxy-Thomas, which was widespread and older. As far as I know no L-D or Rotor steel plant was being built for a United Kingdom firm in 1958.

[2] Cp., for example, the *B.I.S.F. Ann. Rep.* 1956, p. 22 (Apr. 1957); of seven new steel melting plants in the *third* plan (1958–63), three—Consett, Steel Co. of Wales and R.T.B.—were to have 'steam/oxygen blown Bessemer converters'. Two were for making sheets.

[3] Head Wrightsons were associated for this work with the German firm, Pintsch-BAMAG, who had made complete plants for the oxy-Thomas, L-D, and Kaldo processes. Davy-United and the British Oxygen Company were associated with Linde.

[4] Above, pp. 517 sqq. The advance in 1958–59 seems to have been faster in the United States than in the United Kingdom.

It could be explained that developments naturally started outside the United Kingdom because on the Continent those who used the Bessemer process had an inducement to improve it to widen the range of qualities it made well. Why, however, should the deficiencies of the open-hearth process, especially its extremely low fuel efficiency and the inconvenience of the increasingly heavy tonnage taken at one cast in the most efficient practice, not have acted as a stimulus to the search for an alternative? It can be said that one of the new processes, the L.D., would not retain all its advantages when using the high phosphorus pig iron of the United Kingdom industry—it might still show some economy. The argument was not valid in regard to improved converter processes. One may wonder whether the confused costing which the fixing of a low price for scrap, and all the consequential procedures, introduced obscured the economic issues. The newer processes were basically good for converting pig iron into steel; it is probably best in a technical approach, as well as in economic and cost analysis, to treat the making of steel from scrap and from pig iron as inherently distinct, conceivably best carried on in large measure separately. The normal pre-war Continental—especially German—practice of having Bessemer and open-hearth shops associated in one works came close to this. And for their open-hearth furnace they used a special quality of pig iron.[1]

The question may of course equally be asked why the United States industry did not tackle the replacing of the open hearth; and a tentative conclusion seems that while the United States provided Europe with the main stimulus in steelworks engineering the Continent provided the main stimulus everywhere in

---

[1] How resistant the British industry seems to have been to the possible economies of the new processes shines through the first report of the Board on *Development of the Iron and Steel Industry, 1953–1958*, pp. 9–10. Thus 'The relatively high yields of the tilting process...tend to compensate for the lower fuel and capital cost of the Bessemer process...the extent to which the use of oxygen will grow will depend on whether large supplies can be obtained at sufficiently low cost...whilst it is not yet certain that large electric furnaces would be correspondingly competitive with the open hearth in this country, because of the cost of power. The industry is watching closely the progress that is being made in the United States.' Read in the context of the technical history of the industry—and the Blue Books—over many decades these phrases have a familiar tang.

the metallurgy of the steel processes. British work in making new steels—new recipes for special purposes—and in the control and detailed improvement of the chosen process, was important. Radical adventuring was rare. B.I.S.R.A., indeed, announced the development of a new method of making steel direct from ore—'cyclosteel'[1]—but this had a long way to go, and later appeared to be becoming analogous as a means of reducing ore to the sponge iron and H-iron processes referred to earlier,[2] which dispense with the blast furnace but make a raw material for steel, not steel itself. The initiative of the Continent in metallurgical processing was shown again in the Bochum development of casting in vacuum,[3] and in the start of vacuum melting, though here, as in the use of large arc furnaces the United States firms went ahead.[4] In the United States in 1958 electric furnaces provided almost 10 per cent of the steel capacity (almost 12 m. tons) of firms who made ingots,[5] and output of this type of electric furnace steel was over 7·5 m. tons in 1956, about 7·5 per cent of the crude steel output of the ingot makers. The position in Europe in 1957 is shown in Table 78. In these figures the ingot outputs are of most interest, and most comparable. The high proportion of electric steel in Italy and Sweden is obviously related to these countries' lack of cheap indigenous coal, and their access to hydro-electric power. Nevertheless, the much more rapid growth in all the Continental countries covered, and the greater importance of electric furnace ingots in their output are striking. This does not accord well with the suggestion sometimes made that British makers have been more preoccupied than others in producing high-quality steels and that this limits the scope for large-scale operations.

[1] E.C.E. Report on *Technical Advances in Steelmaking in 1956*, p. 65.

[2] Above, pp. 170, 520.

[3] Russian metallurgists developed a process of subjecting steel in the ladle to a vacuum treatment. Above, p. 458.

[4] The last of the series of E.C.E. reports on Technical Advances in Steelmaking gave the position thus: the United States had electric furnaces of 180 tons capacity, the German 130 tons, the United Kingdom 80 tons. The U.S.S.R. was relatively backward.

[5] For example, it included electric furnaces for castings only where the foundries were owned by ingot makers.

It is convenient at this point to recapitulate briefly, and at some points to expand, what has been said on the degree of concentration of production and mobility of location in different countries before tracing the changes in comparative costs and examining what relation there is between these and the changes in price relations from 1953 to 1958.

Table 78. *Output of electric furnace steel in Europe, 1957*

	Thousand long tons			Ingots as % of total ingot output	Total as % of crude steel output	Increase of total since 1953
	Ingots	Castings	Total			
Italy	2366[a]	146[a]	2512	36	37	66
Germany	1024	302	1326	4·4	5·5	138
U.K.	790	417	1207	3·7	5·6	17
France	946	151[b]	1097	7·0	8·0	63
Sweden	1074	30	1104	45	45	39
Belgium	358	46	403	6·0	6·7	69

[a] It is assumed that *all* castings given in Italian statistics were made from electric steel.
[b] Excludes castings made by firms not members of the Chambre Syndicale de la Sidérurgie Francaise.

The contrast between the size of firms and works in the United States and the United Kingdom can be seen from Tables 68 and 76, and it would be expatiating the obvious to underline it. The high degree of concentration in the German industry by 1949–51,[1] which reflected the pre-war situation, was amplified by 1957–58, and is illustrated (with some approximation) in Table 79. The twelve works in Germany, making on average 1,500,000 tons, produced three-quarters of the German output; the six British works, making on average 1,200,000 tons, made one-third of the British output. The concentration of production in *firms* was less sharply contrasted; the ten largest in Britain made 75 per cent of total output[2] in 1956; in Germany the ten largest firms made about 85 per cent in 1957.[3] But this

[1] Above, p. 402.
[2] Figures from *Development of the Iron and Steel Industry*, 1957, p. 50.
[3] The figures, drawn from annual reports, do not cover exactly the same 'years'

was changing; the consolidations planned by the end of 1958,[1] together with the immense expansion of Klöckner at Bremen, suggested that in a few years three-quarters of German ingot output would be in the hands of five firms[2] each making well over 3 m. tons, and on average about 5 m. tons. There were further vertical consolidations, too, to secure outlets, including re-rolling and analogous outlets.[3]

Table 79. *Number of works providing over 800,000 tons in 1957 in United Kingdom and West Germany*

Size groups (thousand tons)	From 1800 to 2500		From 1500 to 1800		From 1200 to 1500		From 1000 to 1200		From 800 to 1000	
	U.K.	W.G.	U.K.	W.G.	U.K.	W.G.	U.K.	W.G.	U.K.	W.G.
No. of works	1	4	Nil	3	Nil	2	2	1	3	2

Though French output had almost reached 15 m. tons, the goal of producing output in twelve works making upwards of 1 m. tons had not been reached by 1958. But the average size of plants making bulk steel was not less than in the United Kingdom, and the variation in size was less; no works made as much as the Steel Company of Wales at Margam, but where a works of 200,000–300,000 tons capacity, like Pompey, survived it depended on making alloy and special steels, and there were probably as many plants in France making over 800,000 tons a year as in the British industry with its much larger total output. Inasmuch as total output grew faster than in Britain, the average scale of plants grew faster. In Belgium and

[1] Above, pp. 451–2.
[2] A.T.H.—Rheinrohr (Thyssen); Rheinhausen—Bochum (Krupp); Mannesmann–Hoesch; Klöckner; Dortmund–Hörde. Outside these five there are several other extremely powerful firms, e.g. Gutehoffnungshütte, Watenstadt Salzgitter, Rheinstahl (this, however, strongest in engineering and shipbuilding).
[3] Dortmund–Hörde's link with Siegerland (above, p. 451) as an outlet for a hot strip mill is a clear instance: A.T.H. made several links—with tinplate making, for example, and, in association with Armco, with the French firm Chatillon-Commentry to postpone introducing finishing plant for grain-orientated electric sheets. Within the large firms there were a number of medium- and small-sized plants, usually with specialised markets and often to make high qualities; and there were a lot of small specialist firms.

Luxembourg this was true too. In these industries one firm in each held upwards of one-third of the total output—Cockerill-Ougrée, the new combine, in Belgium, Arbed as of old in Luxembourg. The adjacent works of the first made a unit of over 2 m. tons capacity. Some of the other plants were of only moderate size. In Holland most production was in one modern plant of about 1 m. tons capacity.

There were plans for a second giant in Holland near Rotterdam, at 'Europort'. This conveniently draws attention to the somewhat greater response traceable on the Continent and in the United States to changes in locational forces, the second contrast, alongside the more rapid concentration of production with resulting scope for specialisation, which is to be noted.

4. COMPARATIVE PRICES, COSTS AND MARGINS

(a) Prices

How far, if at all, do these differences of technical and structural development account for the divergent price trends from 1953 to 1958 which have been illustrated in some respects in Chapter VII? The most easily established point is that steel prices rose less in each of the six countries of E.C.S.C. than they rose in the United Kingdom and United States; the more difficult problem is to compare *absolute* prices in the different countries at the end of the five years. In regard to the first the data given earlier in other forms is conveniently summarised and supplemented by the indices adapted from the *7th Annual Report* of E.C.S.C. and shown in Table 80. Thus in all Continental countries and for both their main qualities of steel the divergence of trend from the United Kingdom/United States trend was very marked by January 1957.

For the comparison of absolute prices a useful starting-point is one published by the Iron and Steel Board for December 1957,[1] while Continental prices were still all at their peak. They include an estimated delivery cost for United States and

---

[1] *Ann. Rep.* 1957, p. 46.

Table 80. *Evolution of quoted prices for finished steel, 1953–58*

Prices for May 1953 in each country = 100:
All Continental prices on dollar basis.

	Jan. 1954	Apr. 1954	Jan. 1955	Jan. 1956	Jan. 1957	Jan. 1958	Jan. 1959
			Thomas steel				
Germany	96	96	97	99	104	109	110
Belgium	100	95	96	109	111	117	103
France	100	97	97	97	102	98	93
			'Basic steel'				
U.K.	100	100	101	107	121	133	131
U.S.	100	100	108	118	127	135	140
			Siemens Martin quality				
Germany	96	96	97	101	109	114	114
Belgium	100	92	92	106	116	116	99
France	100	98	98	106	111	105	95
Holland	100	95	101	109	118	118	110
Italy	100	98	97	101	112	108	97

(In the original table the base figures (May 1953) for the Community country prices were calculated as percentages of the E.C.S.C. weighted index. Here the figures are recalculated with the base year for each country individually = 100.)

Continental prices (the E.C.S.C. in its comparisons always makes a subtraction from United Kingdom prices to give comparisons 'at works'). In Table 81 the figures given by the Board for Luxembourg, Italy and the Netherlands, and prices for billets and boiler plates, are excluded solely for simplification.[1] These comparisons involve, it must be repeated, many hazards. The selection of particular sizes and extras, for example, may favour one country against another. This is brought out by the vagaries of the comparisons. But in their figures it appeared that for a few of the sizes and categories of steel chosen for these tables, German (or in one instance French) open-hearth steel was as cheap or cheaper than British.[2] For many

[1] The Luxembourg figures are interesting because slightly below the Belgian. The Dutch for open-hearth steel were above the United States prices. Italian prices were also above the United States prices except for re-rolled bars, and for these they were above the open-hearth prices of all E.C.S.C. makers.

[2] These prices are in italics.

Table 81. *Comparisons of home prices (December 1957)*

	U.K. open-hearth £ s. d.	U.S.A. open-hearth £ s. d.	Germany: Basic Bessemer £ s. d.	Germany: Open-hearth £ s. d.	Belgium: Basic Bessemer £ s. d.	Belgium: Open-hearth £ s. d.	France: Basic Bessemer £ s. d.	France: Open-hearth £ s. d.
Plate:								
Basis quality 6 ft. × 3 ft. × ⅜ in.	42 15 0	51 17 0	41 17 6	46 17 0	47 19 6	55 19 0	40 8 6	47 2 6
Structural 20 ft. × 5 ft. × ¼ in.	45 2 6	54 13 0	—	51 2 6	—	60 0 0	—	51 3 0
Ship P. 403 20 ft. × 6 ft. × ⅝ in.	46 15 0	49 9 0	—	55 4 6	—	65 11 6	—	57 10 0
Heavy sections:								
Angles structural 8 in. × 8 in. × ¾ in.	41 12 6	48 17 0	43 8 0	46 19 0	46 7 0	54 6 6	40 2 0	46 10 6
Angles basis quality 5 in. × 5 in. × ½ in.	40 10 0	50 9 0	39 13 6	43 4 6	42 3 6	50 3 0	35 18 6	42 7 0
Channels structural 6 in. × 3 in.	42 17 6	53 5 0	39 4 6	*42 15 6*	45 12 0	53 11 6	37 19 0	44 9 6
Joists structural 7 in. × 4 in.	41 13 6	53 13 0	38 3 0	*41 14 0*	44 11 0	52 10 6	36 19 0	43 9 6
Joists basis quality 12 in. × 6 in.	40 6 0	51 5 0	36 6 6	*39 17 6*	42 3 6	50 3 0	34 10 6	41 1 0
Re-rolled bars:								
Basis quality 1½ in. diameter	41 0 6	52 1 0	38 13 0	42 4 0	41 6 0	49 5 6	35 1 6	41 10 0
Ferro-concrete ⅝ in.	41 0 0	52 9 0	38 3 6	—	40 3 0	—	34 13 6	—
Basis quality flats 3 in. × ¾ in.	41 0 6	52 17 0	39 17 0	43 8 0	42 9 6	50 9 0	36 3 6	42 12 0
Re-rolled sections:								
Basis quality angles 2 in. × 2 in. × ¼ in.	42 18 0	54 9 0	39 3 0	*42 14 0*	41 15 6	49 15 0	35 12 0	*42 0 6*
Wire rods:								
Soft basic 5 G	42 6 0	57 3 0	38 7 0	*41 18 0*	40 0 0	45 8 6	35 19 0	*41 4 6*
Hot rolled strip:								
Basis quality 1½ in. × 16 G	49 2 6	58 1 0	46 9 0	51 6 6	44 14 0	52 13 6	42 6 6	49 3 6
Basis quality 12 in. × 10 G	45 10 0	51 5 0	44 11 0	49 9 0	43 12 6	51 12 0	41 7 6	47 4 6
Sheet:								
General purpose cold reduced strip mill 6 ft. × 3 ft. × 20 G	53 16 0	57 17 0	64 15 0		60 2 6		58 17 0	
Full finish extra deep drawing strip mill 8 ft. × 4 ft. × 20 G	53 16 0	63 17 0	81 12 0		80 6 6		74 6 0	
Tinplate (ex-works):								
Basis quality hot dipped (per box) 28 in. × 20 in. × 108 in.	3 8 0½	3 13 5¼	4 13 2¾		4 8 1¼		4 11 8¾	
Electrolytic quality 8 oz. coating 34 in. × 23 in. × 90 lb.	2 18 0	3 0 8½	4 4 11¾		4 10 8½		4 5 0	

NOTE. The foreign prices shown do not include turnover or similar taxes.

purposes basic Bessemer steel was satisfactory, even better in some respects than open hearth; wherever this was so German and French prices for steel now tended to be below British in heavy steel and light re-rolled sections and bars. The differences of price are strikingly erratic; the wide margin of advantage enjoyed according to these figures by United Kingdom buyers of ship plates is particularly surprising, since the Continent had done so much more to improve its plant. The high level of Continental sheet prices stand out in the table.

It is possible that even for December 1957 this sort of presentation exaggerated the margin when Continental prices were above British; partly because if British steel were offered the Continental maker could 'align' his price to the British, and still more because Continental makers were 'aligning their prices to one another's. This certainly became significant as prices fell and competition grew more acute through 1958.[1] Average prices fell more than quoted prices; but how much? In the quoted prices gathered by the E.C.S.C. for the beginning of 1959 the Thomas steel base prices were customarily below British prices; the open-hearth base prices approximately the same or lower in all the 'Six' except Holland for merchant bars; in all except Germany and Italy for heavy plates; and in Germany and France for girders[2]. In a number of specifications, however, extras for quality, on plates at least, still brought the Continental prices appreciably above the British, as in Table 81. There is thus no simple picture; for a range of uses Continental users outside Italy got their steel cheaper than British; for some other uses it was dearer. Since over half the steel made in the north-west Continent was basic Bessemer, and since some open-hearth steel was cheaper on the Continent than in the United Kingdom, it could be that on average steel, other than sheet, was cheaper. Continental users were relatively better off for sectional than for flat products. If the position is looked at from the point of view, not of the domestic user, but

[1] *7ème Ann. Rapp.* vol. II, p. 67.
[2] *Ibid.* These tables are unsatisfactory in one respect in that the Belgian prices given are the prices of Cockeril–Ougrée who did not quote the lowest prices.

of the maker and the relation between prices and costs then it
has to be taken into account that export prices were sharply cut
in 1957–59, and fell below British home prices even for ship plate.
It is hard to suppose that this had no repercussion in many
domestic sales, at least for indirect exports.

(b) Costs and Margins

It remains to trace (to the extent it can be done from the
outside) the trend of costs, to distinguish those within the control
of steelmakers, and to show the effects of Government or
Community policies. Because the Continental competition was
closer the trends of costs in various parts of Europe are dealt
with in most detail. Various categories of cost are looked at
seriatim, starting with raw materials.

(1) Coal.

British steelmakers had a considerable apparent advantage
at most times, in most places, after the war, because coking coal
prices were lower for them than for Continental makers, but
between 1953–58 this advantage was considerably lessened. This
is illustrated in Table 82, which shows the movements of pithead prices in some important Continental coal fields and in
four British mining areas (all converted into dollars), together
with the C.I.F. price of United States coal at Rotterdam. The
prices at which British coking coals were sold in 1958 remained
below those at which coking coals mined on the Continent were
sold, but in some districts the British was dearer than United
States coal. The striking fact was, however, that United Kingdom prices rose by nearly 60 per cent, German by 33 per cent,
French prices on this basis not at all, while prices of United
States coal fell, after a steep rise. Prices of French coal rose in
francs, but the increase (44 per cent from 1953 to 1959) was
offset by devaluation.

This was one of the categories of cost over which the steelmakers in Britain had no direct control. (They had *some* control
in Germany, through ownership; but none in France.) The
question arises whether more of the cheaper coal might have
been used. It will be considered in relation to location questions,

and in this context it is important that the relation of cost to price in Britain still varied greatly from region to region in a way which was likely to discourage the greater use of the cheaper coal and mask the relative real costs in resources in different steelmaking regions. In Scotland the mining costs (for *all* coal), before allowing for interest, exceeded the selling price by 11s. a ton in 1957, in South Wales by 2s. 7d., in Durham by 1s., while in Yorkshire the selling price exceeded the costs by 4s. 8d.

Table 82. *Prices of coking coal, 1952–58 (in dollars a ton)*

| | Ruhr | France | | U.S. Rotter-dam C.I.F.[b] | U.K. | | | |
		Nord	Lorraine		Durham	Yorks	Scotland	S.Wales
1952	13·9	18·7	100[a]	20·1	—	8·7	7·6	—	—
1953	14·6	18·8	102	20·3	14·3	9·5	8·1	—	—
1954	14·2	18·8	102	20·1	14·1	10·2	8·2	—	—
1955	14·9	18·1	97	19·6	18·9	11·2	9·1	10·8	10·4
1956	15·7	18·1	97	19·6	20·8	12·5	10·7	12·2	11·9
1957	17·7	20·2	130	20·0	17·2	13·3	11·6	13·5	12·6
1958	18·5	19·8	127	21·4	13·1	13·8	12·0	14·1	13·1
Jan. 1959	18·5	19·0	146	20·1	13·2	13·8	12·0	14·1	13·1
Jan. 1959 as % of 1952	133	102		100	92	159	158	—	—

[a] Index of prices in 'francs'.   [b] Described as slack/coking fines.

In France and Germany output per man-shift rose appreciably (by 10–15 per cent in France, and about 13 per cent in the Ruhr) from 1953–58, whereas in the United Kingdom it had become static;[1] there was, therefore, a solid foundation for some lessening of the British advantage. Wages increased in much the same proportion in Germany (38 per cent) and Britain (36 per cent), despite the disparate changes in productivity. The cost of labour a shift in the United Kingdom remained in 1958 considerably above the cost in Germany though output per man-shift was now similar.[2] The rise of earnings in French coal-

[1] The productivity figures are published by the E.C.E. in their *Quarterly Bulletin of Coal Statistics*; the British average output for all workers, after being static for five years, rose in the first quarter of 1959; whether this was a new turning point—it possibly was—remained to be seen. French and German figures were also up again in 1959 and rose faster than the British through 1959.

[2] Average output per man-shift in the first quarter of 1958 was 1·260 m. tons in the United Kingdom, 1·259 m. tons in West Germany. Average wages for German miners reached 2·95 DM. per hour in 1958 (E.C.S.C. *Bulletin Statistique*,

mines from 1953–58 (wages rose by 56 per cent by the autumn of 1958, total cost of labour a man/hour by possibly a little over 60 per cent) were higher, in national currency, than in Germany or the United Kingdom; but the international impact of this was counteracted by the two devaluations—November 1957 and December 1958. In dollars or sterling the rise in cost of labour to the autumn of 1958 over 1953 was about 30 per cent; had there been no increase of wages after the second devaluation it would have been below 5 per cent. In the autumn of 1958, before the second devaluation the cost was over one-fifth above the German, and possibly slightly below the British; the second devaluation brought it appreciably below the British and nearer the German.[1]

The fluctuations of the United States price was determined almost entirely by Atlantic freights; the F.O.B. price kept remarkably steady despite large wage increases because these were offset by increased productivity. The low cost in Europe at times when freights were low was a measure of the cost advantage which the United States steelmakers—who did not have the freight cost—had in respect of coke. Many Continental steelmakers used some American as well as indigenous coal; when American was dear this raised costs for makers whose indigenous coal was cheap, notably the Germans. There was an arrangement whereby the excess cost of United States coal

Jan. 1959, p. 64). Presuming total cost of labour, including holiday pay, bonuses, pay in kind, costs of recruitment and training, etc., was almost 150 per cent of the wage itself, as in 1956 (E.C.S.C. *Informations Statistiques*, Sept./Oct. 1957, p. 378), the cost for a $7\frac{1}{2}$ hour shift was about 58s. in 1958. In the United Kingdom the average shift wage alone was by then about 58s. 6d.; including allowances in kind it was about 62s. Holiday pay added about 5s., insurance, etc. 3s., and for the other items in the German cost and for the direct taxation which may be regarded as the cost of social services provided on the Continent by direct employers payments there are no figures. But the ascertainable margin was substantial. Why then did German coal cost more than British? Partly no doubt because there was less supporting of high cost by low cost mines, and partly because the industry made profits on a scale sufficient for dividends and some reinvestment. But this falls outside the scope of this book.

[1] The French total cost was nearly 560 francs/hour in the Autumn of 1958, for example, 71s. a shift. The net effect of the second devaluation, plus wage increases, cannot be guessed precisely; as the November 1957 precedent it might be followed by an early increase of costs by about 8 per cent which would give a shift cost of, say, 65s.

was spread evenly over all the firms. When United States coal became the cheaper the situation was reversed.

Whether the apparent advantage in coal price which the United Kingdom makers retained was a real one may be doubted. Table 82 shows that the coal costs of Continental firms came down much closer to those in the United Kingdom by 1957–58. But quoted coke prices, in Germany at any rate, were actually lower than in Britain throughout (from 1953–58), because the ratio of coke price to coal price in the Ruhr was 1·3:1, whereas in the United Kingdom the average was nearer 1·6:1;[1] thus in 1957 the average price of coke sold by the N.C.B. was 142s. 6d. at the ovens, in Germany the average was 125s.[2] Presumably in Germany the proceeds from 'by-products' were higher, and this was more likely a result of higher prices (for gas, and tar derivatives) than of a larger yield, though yields vary according to the nature of the coal.[3] If in fact the price of coke-oven gas was higher in the Ruhr this would raise the notional fuel or power cost in later stages of steelmaking in a vertically integrated works.[4] Since there is no reason to suppose that the relative selling values of by-products in the United Kingdom and Germany (or elsewhere on the Continent) changed appreciably in these years, this problem can be neglected. It does not affect this marked lessening of the advantage initially enjoyed by British firms in coal prices. For France, Belgium, Luxembourg and Italy the lessening was greater than the table shows, since they all imported some coal from Germany, and as seen above the E.C.S.C. eliminated double pricing which had favoured 'home' users, and removed transport discriminations on traffic which crossed frontiers within the Community.

The significance of differences in coal prices was reduced naturally by every fall in the quantity of coal used per ton of

[1] In Scotland, for the N.C.B., the ratio was nearly 1·7:1.
[2] German figures from *Wirthschaft und Statistik*.
[3] For earlier relative movements of coke and by-product prices, above, p. 27. There seems no reason to suppose that differences of efficiency play a part in this difference of ratio. The prices which coke ovens obtained for gas in the United Kingdom were often in long contracts at very low prices, for example, 6d. a therm, which was far delow the cost in any 'total gasification' process in use, or the price which any commercial gas-producing concern would find it necessary to charge.
[4] This would be true, too, of any tar, etc. used as a fuel.

output. In Britain and the United States, it has been seen, advances in fuel efficiency were continuous and considerable in these years. British makers reduced coke consumption in blast furnaces between 1953 and 1957 more than the Germans; but the net advantage was relatively slight because the British makers considerably increased their use of sinter per ton of pig iron in these years, whereas the Germans reduced it. The total blast furnace fuel picture was roughly as in Table 83. The average coke consumption per ton of pig iron in Belgian blast furnaces was less than in either Britain or Germany in 1957, it fell from 18·4 cwt. in 1953 to 17·6 cwt. in 1957. The Luxembourg consumption was much higher; so was the French, though not so much. It had not fallen between 1953–57,[1] and the use of sinter remained small. The investment plans for 1958–60, however, promised a great extension of sintering.

Table 83. *Coke and coke breeze consumed (cwt. per ton of pig iron)*

		U.K.	W. Germany
Coke in blast furnaces	1953	21·2	20·2
	1957	18·9	19·2
Coke breeze for sinter	1953	0·9	1·5[a]
	1957	1·2	1·1[a]
Total	1953	22·1	21·7
	1957	20·3	20·3

[a] Assuming a consumption of 2 cwt. of breeze per ton of sinter.

(2) *Iron ore.*

The distinction between steelmaking based on home ores and steelmaking based on imported ores, so important in Britain, was important in varying degrees for most Continental steel-producing countries, and increasingly so also, as has been seen, in the United States. On the Continent the German industry, like the British, derived a diminishing part of its ore supply from home sources in the period 1953–58 (in 1957 about 30 per cent of the iron content of the ores used in Germany came from home ores, compared with 40 per cent in 1953). As in Britain there

---

[1] The average was 20·58 cwt. in 1953 and 20·61 cwt. in 1958.

were some home ore based plants (Salzgitter, for instance, and Peine-Ilsede) and some home ore was railed or canalled—for example, to plants in the Ruhr based mainly on imported ore. The French industry used almost exclusively home ore, and the small import of ore became progressively less important in these five years. Belgium and Luxembourg were mainly based on home ore and imports from France; imports from oversea, mostly from Sweden, accounted for about one-quarter the iron content of ore used by them in 1957, and very slightly more in 1953. Most of the overseas ore was probably used in Belgium. The Dutch industry used overseas ore only.

Table 84. *Prices of Lorraine ore (average F.O.T. mine: in francs and sterling)*[a]

Jan. 1953 (pre-E.C.S.C.	Francs	Sterling s. d.		Francs	Sterling s. d.
Home	854	18			
Export	1325	27	July 1956	1379	28
Feb.–Dec. 1953	1290	26	Jan. 1957	1477	30
Apr. 1954	1173	24	Nov. 1957	1772	30
Apr. 1955	1163	23 6	Jan. 1958	1630	28
July 1955	1215	25	Jan. 1959	1780	25 9

[a] Prices from Feb.–Dec. 1953 to Jan. 1958 from *6th Ann. Rep.* E.C.S.C., II, p. 44; pre-common market price from *Gen. Rep. on the Activities of the Community*, Aug. 1952–Apr. 1953, ch. IV, p. 33; the price for Jan. 1959 is based on *7ème Rap. Gén.* p. 84, which states that the average rise of ore prices in Jan. 1959 was 9 per cent. It states also that the average reduction in dollar prices was 6 per cent.

In regard to *home ore* Britain had the cheapest supplies, but the margin of advantage over French, Belgian and Luxembourg steel-producers lessened between 1953–58. This was first because average output per man rose much more in the French and Luxembourg mines and quarries than in the British. But the net effect of devaluations in October 1957 and December 1958 was a contributing factor, and as with coke and coal the elimination of double pricing by the Community in 1953, and subsequent reductions of transport discriminations, also lowered the cost of French ore in Belgium and Luxembourg.

The prices of Lorraine ore since the E.C.S.C. are shown in Table 84.

Thus for French buyers the Common Market brought immediately a steep rise in nominal price, but most users owned much of their ore supply. For Belgian and Luxembourg users it brought the price at the mine down: though here, too, since most of the Belgian firms had interests in French ore mines, the gain was somewhat academic. In 1957 (when wage costs had risen by over 50 per cent)[1] while there was still a boom demand in Europe, the Lorraine ore price was 15 per cent higher than in 1953, but it was less than 8 per cent above the 1953 level in 1958, and it was back at the 1953 starting-price in January 1959, which was below the pre-Community price for Belgium and Luxembourg. These had gained in freights—a typical railway rate from Lorraine to Liége, it has been seen, had fallen from 17s. 6d. in 1953 to 12s. 6d. in 1956.[2] The cost of French ore was thus much cheaper at Belgian works in 1958–59 than in 1952–53.[3]

There are no British quoted home ore prices to put by the Lorraine figures. The British price was of course much below the French: a cost of 8s. charged into nearby furnaces, it has been seen, was given as representative in 1952.[4] The difference reflected the dominance of underground mining in Lorraine, of quarrying in the United Kingdom. The extent of mining in the United Kingdom was beginning to grow, however, especially in Lincolnshire, which would bring average costs up.[5] The only guide to comparative costs is a comparison of labour costs, which is given in Table 85, where German and Luxembourg costs are included with French and British.[6] This picks the

---

[1] *7ème Rap. Gén.* vol. VI, p. 28, and below.   [2] Above, p. 421.

[3] It is of interest, nevertheless, that the reduction in price in Jan. 1958 was said to be because of the competition of overseas ores, presumably Swedish, whose price had fallen.   [4] Above, p. 256.

[5] In general, however, Lincolnshire gained through the greater thickness of the ore bands, which were close on 20 ft. thick (or more) in N. Lincs., but around 8 ft. in Northants. Outputs per man were surprisingly high in underground mining in Lincs.; about 15 tons per man per day early in 1959 compared with 28 tons per day in neighbouring quarries. These were extremely good figures. The *average* output per wage earner for *all* iron ore *quarries* in 1957 was given in the Ministry of Fuel and Power Annual Statistics as 4,550 tons per year—say 18 tons a shift.

[6] Above, p. 431. The E.C.S.C. published figures covering all the costs, though for this table the 1958 figures are projections from 1957, with only the basic wage changes of 1958 available. For the United Kingdom an addition of 15 per cent to wages has been made—it may be slightly too little.

French ore story up from the point at which it was left in Chapter VII.[1]

How far were increases of output per man associated with increases in other cost elements, more particularly the capital costs arising out of the investments in expansion and mechanisation responsible for the more efficient use of labour? Output increased from 41 m. tons to 60 m. tons in France between 1952–58, and from 14 m. tons to 18 m. tons in Germany. The investment in French ore mines was £48 m. from 1952–57, even if all this was for the expansion and, none for greater mechanisation at existing mines or for ore treatment, the cost of capacity to produce a ton a year was below the £4 estimated by Jean Raty in 1953,[2] it was little over £2. 10s. The average was no higher per ton of new capacity, on the same lines, for investment in the Lorraine fields alone from 1955–57, though the average

Table 85. *Labour costs in ore production, 1953–58*

	Output of iron ore per man per year (O.M.Y.)		Increase in O.M.Y.	Increase in cost of labour per man/hour,	Labour cost per ton of ore (sterling equivalent)	
	1953 (tons)	1958 (tons)	1953–58 (%)	1953–58 (%)	1953 s. d.	1958 s. d.
U.K.[a]	2420	2730[b]	13[b]	34	4 6	5 2[b]
France[c]	1460	2100	44	70	10 0	9 6[d]
Luxembourg[c]	2330	2880[d]	24	25	6 6	6 6[e]
Germany	710	770	8	48	9 6	13 0

[a] *Ministry of Fuel and Power, Statistical Digest,* and *B.I.S.F. Statistics.*

[b] United Kingdom figures for 1957 only. A projection for 1958 is, O.M.Y. 2520, labour cost per ton, 5s. 9d.

[c] E.C.S.C. Statistical Bulletins, and *Information Statistique* (esp. Sept./Oct. 1957) and *Memento de Statistiques* (1957 ed.).

[d] The devaluation of Dec. 1957, by 20 per cent, was followed by wage increases, but it may be assumed that the sterling costs of labour fell to between 8s. 6d. and 9s. a ton.

[e] The Luxembourg cost was appreciably lower in 1957, when output was 7·8 m. tons, workers numbered 2400, and output per man/year was 3250 tons.

[1] Above, pp. 397–8.
[2] The figures are based on the *Reports on Investments in the Community* published annually. For Raty, cp. above, pp. 397–8.

cost estimated for future development was higher,[1] but not up to the Raty level. And while the 1958–59 estimates presumably 'benefited' from the first devaluation, the forecasts were made long before the second.

There is, therefore, no reason to suppose that the fall in labour cost in ore mining by 1958–59 in France was offset by a substantial increase in capital cost, nor indeed by increases in other costs, explosives, power, drills, steel, materials for maintenance, and the like, though there may well have been some increase here. However, the movement of labour costs was probably an index of the trend in comparative costs in Britain and France, while for Belgium and Luxembourg their relative gain as users of French ores was greater than the change of labour cost alone.

As regards *imported ores* from overseas there is a presumption that their price at the mine or their F.O.B. prices will be roughly the same for all buyers. Since the ores vary in iron content, other constituents, and reducibility, since ores from a large source are of different types, since furthermore contracts are not published and the decision to use one ore rather than another in a particular blast furnace plant is a managerial decision based on cost data which are not published, the presumption is not subject to statistical proof. The judgements of managements in this respect are sometimes questioned;[2] and no doubt there are more and less skilful managers and buyers. But it seems improbable that this was the source of any great differences.

International pooling of interests in developing new ore

---

[1] An estimated expenditure of $61·9 m. was expected to add 6·07 m. tons of capacity, i.e. a cost of $10, or £3. 11s. a ton. (But higher in sterling except for devaluation.) Obviously these figures are not as solid as those of expenditure and output.

[2] Thus it has been suggested by some Swedish experts that the Germans and Belgians gained by taking the high phosphoric ores which are most plentiful in the Kiruna ore-field, whereas the British preferred a lower phosphoric ore which was not so plentiful, which involved a less straightforward planning and for which the price was higher. The less phosphoric ore was, however, for some years preferred in Britain as being cheaper in use, and possibly the neglect of the Thomas process contributed to this. Ultimately the price difference led to a British demand for 'Kiruna D' which the Swedes could not satisfy, being fully committed by rapidly expanding Continental contracts. Though prices of low phosphoric ores rose more in the boom in Sweden they fell more in 1958–59.

resources extended in these years, and would inevitably tend towards uniform F.O.B. prices.[1] Though German firms did not purchase all their ore collectively as the British firms did through B.I.S.C. (Ore)—perhaps they would not have been allowed to under the E.C.S.C. rules—many joined forces for particular purposes[2] and several were associated, along with French firms, B.I.S.C. (Ore) and Canadian interests to push the Mauretanian scheme further in 1957–58, though they were careful to explain they were only committed to exploration.

Significant differences could arise from freights when F.O.B. prices were identical. No doubt it was presumably for this reason that C.I.F. prices of imported ores at British ports were normally higher than those at the main Continental west coast ports, for example, Rotterdam and Antwerp. This was the result of the great subdivision of the British ore trade, and the large part played in it by ports with poor navigating conditions and usually not deep enough for large ships.

The subdivision had not been eliminated by the post-war changes or made unimportant by improvements in ore handling equipment; on the contrary, the drawbacks arising from the subdivision and the character of the ports used grew more serious. When the Iron and Steel Board first listed the places where better unloading plant was installed it hardly seemed aware of this.[3] But the importance of reducing shipping costs —always much in the mind of B.I.S.C. (Ore) but relatively neglected otherwise, or so it seemed, in planning—had been so far recognised that by 1954 B.I.S.R.A. was conducting operational research on the design of optimum ships for British

---

[1] Some contracts specifically linked prices for a particular ore to those paid by other buyers of the same ore, or to those charged by sellers of other ores in other countries. Thus the F.O.B. element in the Venezuelan ore price for ore sold to the United Kingdom was fixed as the F.O.B. price of sales to the United States; in Canada some ore was bought by the United Kingdom at prices governed by the Mesabi ridge price, and some at a price based on the average paid by the United Kingdom buyer for *all* imported ore (on an iron content basis). When, as with Venezuela, a C.I.F. price as well as a F.O.B. price was fixed, a precaution against risk on a costly freight, the freight element was subject to escalation clauses based on movements in fuel prices and wages.

[2] I gathered that German firms did most of their ore purchasing in *three* groups.

[3] *Development of the Iron and Steel Industry, 1953–1958*, p. 30.

37   BEH

conditions. In a measure it took the form of fitting ships to
ports, finding the best size of small ship (9000 tons) for small
ports, and the best for medium ports (15,000–16,000 tons), with
due emphasis on the lower costs of the latter.[1] But early in 1957,
within a singularly short time of the publication of their result,
it was being said that 'a radical reappraisal of ore carrying
technique and economies may soon be necessary'.[2] By early
1956 the average sizes of ore ships used for imports to the United
States, the Continent and the United Kingdom respectively
were 21,500 tons, 14,500 tons and 10,450 tons. The 15,000-ton
ship which in the discussions of 1943–44 experienced ore
importers had looked upon as the big ship for which ore ports
should be able to cater, was now itself beginning to pass
into the medium if not the 'small' category. Yet British ore
ports, improved though they were, still had an unsatisfactory
record in 1955–56 in dealing even with 9000 ton ships. 'The
average time taken to discharge cargoes is still far too high, and
varies from one to eight days, including time waiting for a berth
varying from nil to four days.' Discharging costs for 9000-ton
ships varied from 3s. 11d. to 7s. 1d. per ton, and costs were
rather higher for larger than for smaller ships, which 'would
indicate that further developments are now overdue'.[3] There
was still a disposition to discuss the problem solely as one of
fitting ships to ports, not as one of fitting expansion of steel
output to the best ports. Yet the anomaly of the situation in
which ore was unloaded at sixteen or more ports, a dozen of
which handled over 500,000 tons of ore in 1956 and only two
above 2 m. tons, when the lowest shipping costs were to be
achieved in high powered last ships of over 20,000 tons, whose
operation became much cheaper if they were unloaded within
12 hours and so given a quick turn round, did not pass unnoticed.[4]
There were only five ore ports which could handle 20,000-ton
ships at all, only one (the Tyne) which with no further improve-

---

[1] The ultimate recommendations owed much naturally to the practical advice
given by B.I.S.C. (Ore).

[2] *The Shipping World*, 30 Jan 1957, p. 160.

[3] From the article in *The Shipping World* by Mr Peter Duff quoted above.
Discharging costs included port dues.

[4] Cp., for example, I.S.B. *Ann. Rep. for* 1956, p. 15.

ment would handle them at all times.[1] Had all the ore ports been able to do so, however, unloading equipment capable of turning round a 20,000-ton ship in 12 hours, which the shipowners wanted, would have been worked far below capacity (approximately 5 m. tons a year if *one* ship only was turned round each day—and with every further increase in ship size this capacity figure became larger). As a compromise solution, with an obvious analogy to the Rotterdam situation, the plan was evolved of developing Milford Haven as an ore port, with stocking facilities for Canadian ores which could not be shipped in the winter when the source of supply was ice-bound. Large, 80,000-ton ships could be accommodated, and the ore would be reshipped in smaller boats to all the small ports, or railed direct to works. The reshipping would cost upwards of 10s. a ton. This scheme was an indication of the growing advantage of the Continent as ship sizes increased. It was deferred, and—with grim irony—a plan to make a deep channel and berth at Port Talbot for 60,000 ton ships, to cost £15 m. at least, was next prepared. For east coast ports if reshipping was to be tried it looked more promising to try Rotterdam. Importing directly to the point of use in ships of 20,000–40,000 tons still seemed capable of being the most economic operation.

Rotterdam, Amsterdam and Antwerp could handle big ore ships easily and quickly, they could give the quick turn rounds which the shipowners liked. Hence they enjoyed much lower freights. The development of the big faster ore ships (there were some sixty ore carriers of from 16,000 to 87,000 tons deadweight, of 14–16 knots, built or building by the end of 1956, none owned in the United Kingdom) was thus likely to maintain or increase the freight differential in favour of the Continental compared with British ore ports, and it seems to have done so.

It appears traceable, for instance, in the Swedish ore trade from Narvik. From 1953–58 the rates to the United Kingdom

---

[1] The five were Glasgow, Immingham, Middlesbrough, Newport, the Tyne. Navigation conditions were less than perfect at Glasgow and Newport. Immingham could be developed fairly easily to handle 30,000-ton ships, and at greater cost to take ships up to 40,000–50,000 tons.

east coast ports were consistently higher than to Rotterdam or Antwerp, but the difference was considerably wider from 1956 to 1958 than from 1953 to 1955. Freights from Narvik to East Coast ports in the United Kingdom were from 4s. 6d. to 6s. 3d. a ton of ore higher than to Rotterdam or Antwerp from 1953 to 1955, and 7s. 9d. or 8s. 9d. higher from 1956 to 1958.[1] For West Coast ports of the United Kingdom the difference was 2s. higher—10s. a ton or more. Since the longer the journey the greater the advantage of using large ships, it may be supposed that the advantage of the Continent for *all* ore imports was still larger. Data were becoming harder to interpret because B.I.S.C. (Ore) was carrying an increasing amount of ore in its own ships or in ships on long term charter, and some Continental firms, Thyssens for example, were buying some ore ships.[2]

The extent to which ore imports at particular British ports suffered from this wide freight differential is not known, because B.I.S.C. (Ore) varied its selling prices for ore to the works, according to scales which made some allowances for the size of ship used and the rate of unloading. Some particulars of the scales are known, but not their average impact at different ports. At the most favoured ports the differential may have been halved, i.e. if the average was 10s. a ton it may have been

---

[1] The contract freights from 1950 were as follows. To get the true difference it is necessary to subtract about 2s. 3d. from the gross differences, the average cost of unloading ore in Continental ports, which was included in the freight to the United Kingdom but not to the Continent.

Year	East Coast ports s.	Rotterdam–Antwerp s. d.	Gross difference s. d.	Net difference s. d.
1950	20	12 3	7 9	5 6
1951	19	18 6	6	−1 9
1952	35	31 9	3 3	1 0
1953	25	16 6	8 6	6 3
1954	22	15 3	6 9	4 6
1955	25	16 6	8 6	6 3
1956	32	21 0	11 0	8 9
1957	36	25 0	11 0	8 9
1958	26	16 0	10 0	7 9

[2] See, for example, Thyssen's Annual Reports for 1957 and 1958. Having bought the ships they sold them to a shipping firm but held them on a 12 year time charter.

reduced to, say, 5s., but more than this seems unlikely.[1] If the average was halved at one to two ports it was considerably exceeded at the less favoured ports.

Where comparisons *can* be made between the C.I.F. prices the differences appear to exceed the freight and unloading differences set out above, but not by much, and the variation is erratic. In Table 86 the C.I.F. prices (based on trade statistics) of ores from Sweden, Venezuela, Algeria and Canada imported into Britain, Germany, Holland and Belgium are compared. The differences can hardly be attributed entirely to freight differences. Most large exporters of ore sold ores of different compositions and price, and the mixture of ores bought by different users were not uniform and might vary from year to year. Table 87 shows that Britain bought one Swedish ore whose price was far below the British average in Table 86. It seems nevertheless reasonable to regard the almost invariably higher averages for the U.K. in Table 86 as largely an indication of freight differences.

In interpreting these figures, allowance must be made for the fact that when a British works used ore at the point of import it

Table 86. *Average prices of imported ores (shillings a long ton C.I.F.)*

	Sweden				Venezuela		Algeria		Canada		
Year	U.K.	Germany	Belgium	Holland	U.K.	Germany	U.K.	Holland	U.K.	Germany	Holland
1950	51	65	53	57	—	—	61	54	65	60	—
1951	71	111	67	74	—	—	99	94	120	93	—
1952	123	113	100	107	—	—	125	116	99	86	—
1953	112	108	95	108	—	—	125	115	79	77	—
1954	105	94	81	104	—	104	105	108	77	75	—
1955	112	93	83	96	—	97	110	111	98	90	85
1956	121	102	93	108	112	111	115	116	117	92	103
1957	134	109	97	114	117	115	123	117	120	108	113
1958	128	114	91	114	113	114	115	100	102	105	86
1959[a]	114	97	83	95	116	111	104	93	99	95	67

[a] All figures are provisional, and the Continental averages are for 10 or 11 months only.

[1] Maximum reductions of price were 4s. for the use of ships of 15,000 tons, and 4s. for unloading at a rate of 5000 tons a day. There were additions to prices for very small ships and very slow unloading, but this will have affected a small tonnage only. If one assumes that the average difference of freight, etc. occurred half-way on the scale, the maximum reduction of average differential would be 2s. for the use of large ships, 2s. for the use of more efficient unloading. Port Talbot, to take one example, could have the second, but not the first.

escaped the additional cost of barge or rail transport which ore taken into Rotterdam or Antwerp incurred. Ore to Ijmuiden or Bremen (and prospectively to Dunkirk and Europort) escaped this too. For Ruhr works it amounted to about 6s. per ton.[1] A surprising number of works in the United Kingdom were of course burdened in this way too.

Table 87. *United Kingdom imported ore prices, F.O.B. and freight constituents*

	N. African						W. African						Swedish[a]					
	F.O.B.		Freight		Total		F.O.B.		Freight		Total		F.O.B.		Freight		Total	
	s.	d.	s.	d.	s.	d.	s.	d.	s.	d.	s.	d.	s.	d.	s.	d.	s.	d.
1950	38	0	25	0	63	0	22	0	31	0	53	0	36	0	20	0	56	0
1952	79	6	40	0	119	6	47	0	50	0	97	0	70	0	32	6	102	6
1953	92	0	27	6	119	6	73	6	38	0	111	6	73	6	24	6	98	0
1954	78	0	25	0	103	0	61	6	36	0	97	6	66	0	22	6	88	6
1955	73	2	35	0	108	2	55	0	43	0	98	0	65	3	26	0	91	3
1956	77	6	43	0	120	6	57	6	57	6	115	0	73	0	33	0	106	0
1957	85	0	47	0	132	0	57	6	65	0	122	0	79	9	35	3	115	0
1958	83	10	36	0	119	10	59	0	42	0	101	0	78	9	28	0	106	9
1959	70	2	33	0	103	2	49	0	47	0	96	0	70	6	25	0	95	6

It remains to compare the trends of home and imported ore prices in the United Kingdom, and on the Continent those of Lorraine and oversea ore prices. It has been seen earlier that from 1949 to 1952 the relation changed in the United Kingdom very much in favour of the use of home ore.[3] The great rise in prices of imported ores in the United Kingdom similarly changed the Continental situation in favour of users of minette. In the period for 1953–59 the relation did not revert to the 1950 position, though there were ups and downs in imported ore prices. The 1957 peak price was, however, 10s. above the 1952 peak. In 1958 the average was nearly 10s. above the 1954 recession level; however, in 1959 it was likely to get near to the 1954 figure. In Table 87 the contract prices of three typical

[1] In the spring of 1959 the rate to Duisburg from Rotterdam was DM. 3·30 per ton. Unloading from the importing ship into barges cost DM. 1.

[2] This column represents trends, but while the freight was normal for all grades of ore, the F.O.B. price which is for Grängesberg ore was much lower than other Swedish ores. This ore had a high (5 per cent) Silica content, and a relatively low Fe content—58 per cent: whereas the Kiruna ores were normally about 64 per cent Fe.

[3] Above, pp. 256, 329.

ores imported into Britain (for which indices have been given for earlier years)[1] are given to 1959.

The fluctuations of freight and F.O.B. prices did not coincide, but whereas in 1958 freight fell sharply and F.O.B. prices fell little, in 1959 the positions were reversed, the net effect in the two years was a fall of about one-fifth, back to 1954 levels except for the Swedish ore. F.O.B. prices had fallen below 1954 except in Sweden, freights had remained above. Freight levels in 1959 were not remunerative,[2] and the F.O.B. prices were recession prices.

Because the cost of producing home ore in the United Kingdom had risen between 1953 and 1959 the imported ore prices of 1959 left the home ore user with a smaller margin of price advantage in buying ore than he had had in 1954—though still a large one. On the Continent where growth of efficiency and currency changes had brought the dollar cost of French ore down, the margin between Lorraine ore prices and oversea ore prices was not much less in 1959 than in 1953.

(3) *Scrap*

The period 1953–59 ended with a remarkable change in the ratio between United Kingdom and Continental prices for home bought scrap. By 1958–59, moreover, the price of imported scrap had lost the importance it had in the boom, when as seen earlier there was almost a gentleman's agreement between the United Kingdom and the Community not to buy too competitively in the United States. The change which came over the scene is illustrated in Table 88.

The most impressive symptoms of the change in the United Kingdom was that the ban on exports of scrap which had started informally in 1937 was lifted. Scrap-merchants had large stocks of scrap, and some of the most unattractive scrap, turnings, was being dumped. The ban was only lifted temporarily. Price control was also lifted, though the merchants did not change

---

[1] Above, p. 329.

[2] Ships could be obtained for 15s. per ton per month on short-term charters for a single voyage—it was of course a marginal rate. A price of 24s.–28s. per ton was remunerative for British owners of modern ships of 10,000–15,000 tons. At the peak the marginal rates had risen to 60s., and 45s. had been common.

the home price level as a result, though they *did* change the important differential which made scrap dear in Wales. This they did, it was explained, because the small open-hearth plants were beginning to go out of use, so that scrap would not have to be drawn from so wide an area.

Table 88. *Scrap prices—international comparison*
(dollars per ton)

	June 1953	Feb. 1957	Jan. 1958	Jan. 1959
U.K.	16·8	28·0	30·8	30·8
Germany	33·3[a]	42·5	36·3	31·2
France	28	46·0	34·0	25·5
Belgium	52·0	51·4	35·3	28·0
Italy	55	51·2	38·4	33·6
Holland	28·0	48·0	35·7	31·0
U.S.	41·0	55·5	35·0	40·5

The United Kingdom price is a delivered price; the Continental are F.O.T. at a merchant's yard.

[a] Before June the German figure was much higher, approximately $45.

Until 1958 the home price of scrap had been kept down by control and the ban on exports, but it had not been kept down quite so firmly since the advent of the second Board. The price rose broadly in step with the published basic pig-iron price; both rose by about £5 a ton, and the margin between them remained about £8 a ton. On the Continent, as has been seen, prices were subject to the mixed influences of boom and Community—they rose high in the boom, and must have raised Continental steelmaking costs unfavourably compared with British. Indeed, when the péréquation is taken into account, scrap cost more to Continental than to American steelmakers. But the rebound in 1958 brought the Continental scrap price down to the British level. This was in keeping with the general type of price movement in a more or less competitive market for scrap analysed in earlier chapters. Probably the strenuous purchasing of scrap imports in the boom when their use was cheapened by subsidy made the rebound in recession a little more severe than it would have been, the residue of imports delivered on contract after the need for them had gone was possibly larger than it would otherwise have been. The French price here again was brought down additionally, in dollars, by devaluation.

Continental steelmakers were for a short time at no disadvantage compared with British in the price they paid for scrap. This was a substantial change; if scrap had cost as much in the United Kingdom as in Germany in 1957 the average cost of steel would have been nearly £2 per ton more: if it had cost as much as in Belgium or Italy nearly £3 per ton more.[1] How permanent the change would be turned largely on the future of British policy. The change in relative costs involved was not one which depended even in part on a change of productivity, as the other changes so far discussed—in coal, ore and shipping costs—did. It would be significant of course if Continental scrap costs would always come down to British in a recession, it would be still more significant if costs in all the countries moved normally together. But it was clear that British policy had not moved so far. The ban on exports was revived in 1959.

(4) Labour costs

(a) *The price of labour.* The average cost of labour per man-hour, including all the fringe costs which the E.C.S.C. brought into the picture, was highest in the Community (it has been seen) for Belgium in 1957, but not greatly less in France and Germany. The British figure, if it had been calculated, would have been in the same range, possibly on a par with, or above, the Belgian, and above the others. Holland and Italy had appreciably cheaper labour. In 1958 German average earnings rose slightly more than British, but otherwise, the United Kingdom earnings (in dollars or sterling) rose more than those

---

[1] The difference in the market price was about £5 per ton in the case of Germany, £8 in the case of Belgium and Italy. Home-bought scrap used in the United Kingdom was equal to about one-third of the output of finished steel. If the calculation were done the other way, and the reduction of cost for the Continental makers if they had enjoyed British prices were examined, then the German gain would have been less, possibly 25s., the Italian more, possibly about £5—because the Germans used less bought scrap per ton of steel than the British, while the Italians used much more. Complications arising from levies, scrap levy in the E.C.S.C., ingot levy in the United Kingdom) to pay for high cost imports are neglected. The scrap levy in E.C.S.C. may have forced down the market price of scrap.

elsewhere in the Community. French wages rose in francs sharply from 1957 to 1958, but this was partly because of the devaluation of October 1957, and the net effect of both, devaluation *and* wage changes, was a fall in the cost of French labour in sterling or dollars. For a contrast the American figures are also given in Table 89, which gathers together in the main data which have been looked at in another context earlier.

Table 89. *Changes in earnings and the cost of labour*
(Europe and United States 1953–58)

	Indices of		Average cost per hour, 1957		Average of direct wages
	Direct wages per hour as (1953=100)	Total cost per hour as (1953=100)	Direct wages	Total cost	per hour (end 1958)
			d.	*d.*	*d.*
U.K.	134·9	—	73	88[a]	76
Germany	138·8	138·2	58	86	62
Belgium	131·0	134·3	68	92	69
France	139·4	142·1	53	89	50
Italy	124·4	123·2	40	68	42
Holland	138·7	156·9	47	78	48
U.S.	127·2	131·8	234	275	260

For the Community these are published in the E.C.S.C. *Informations Statistiques* for Nov., Dec. 1958, pp. 542–3. The 1957 figures for France take no account of the devaluation of Oct. 1957, but the 1958 figure is based on an exchange rate of 1175 francs=£1. From the end of 1958 the rate was 1380 francs=£1.

[a] This is simply direct wages plus 20 per cent. Known items to add are National Insurance contributions (about 3 per cent), paid holidays (about 6–8 per cent). In addition the 'total' in the E.C.S.C. calculation included voluntary pension schemes (which were being introduced into the British industry) the annual charge arising from provision of housing at below commercial costs, provision of sports facilities, the cost of recruiting and training workpeople, including the earnings of apprentices. A full comparison should probably include part of the income and profits tax paid by firms as this was necessary to contribute to the general funds from which the cost of some social services was drawn. But even neglecting this the other items would probably amount to about 20 %.

(b) *Output per man.* The statistics suggest that in all the six countries of the E.C.S.C. output per man in the steel industry grew more from 1954–57 than in the United Kingdom, although the statistics are far from perfect; only the British industry publishes an index of productivity based on a measure of volume of output. Table 90 relies on this series for the United Kingdom, for the rest it is based on E.C.S.C. statistics of employment and output (in tons) of finished rolled products.[1] The use of these statistics should ensure uniform coverage, but the use of quantities only can be misleading. The proportion of high-value to low-value products changes. The probability is that high-value products were becoming a larger part of output in Germany and possibly in France. Tonnage of rolled products may give a misleading result if the proportion of imported semi-products used changes, but this could not seriously distort in this period.[2] The year 1954–55 was used as a starting-point, partly because the E.C.S.C. labour figures do not go back further, but also because 1953 was such a bad year for the Six that it would exaggerate the rise in their efficiency to 1957. To go back to 1952 or 1953, as a base year, would confuse the recovery from a period of under-utilisation of capacity in either the United Kingdom or the Continent with the increase of productivity in the later phase of expansion and modernisation.

Table 90. *Output per man per year in European steel industries (as a percentage of 1954)*[3]

	1957	1958
U.K.	109	99
Germany	117	115
France	128	135
Belgium–Luxembourg	111	107
Italy	152	150
Holland	117	121

The increase in output per man rose more in Germany per hour than per year because during the years 1956–58 hours of work were reduced, by successive agreements: for blast furnace

---

[1] *Bulletin Statistique*, March 1959, pp. 208–21, 235.

[2] Thus in Germany to take ingots as a basis of the calculation would change the figures in Table 90 to 115 and 114. The tonnage of 'semis' used in Germany was appreciably higher in 1957 than in 1954; the correct index figures should presumably be between those based on ingots and those based on finished steel, but nearer the latter.

[3] The numbers of workers in the E.C.S.C. countries is taken as the number at the end of the year, since this is the only figure available for 1954.

workers from 56 hours a week, first to 48,[1] then to 42,[2] for open-hearth and electric furnace and roughing mill workers from 48 to 42, and for other workers from 48 first, to 45,[3] then to 44.[4] In France too, hours of work in continuous processes were reduced from 56 to 48 hours a week from May 1958.[5] In Britain the hours worked per day were approximately the same in 1954 and 1957, but there was an additional paid week's holiday; this would raise the British figures by about 2 per cent. The average hours worked in Germany in 1957 were 46·5 (close to the United Kingdom figure), compared with 50 in 1956, and 50·7 in 1954;[6] to allow for this would bring the increase in output per man per hour to 28 per cent, and possibly more in 1958, when average hours worked was again lower.[7]

The fall of output per man in the United Kingdom in 1958 (and lesser falls in some other countries) was solely a reflection of the drop in demand; the number of shifts worked per week was reduced in many works because work was lacking, and the number of workers employed was reduced much less than output fell. In France and Holland output was higher in 1958 than 1957. France thus had the dual benefit of a fall in the price of labour (in other currencies) and a further rise in output per man in 1958.

Did output per man in any or all of the E.C.S.C. countries equal or exceed that in the United Kingdom after these relative gains? The only figures which are in any sense precisely comparable are of numbers of process workers employed in blast furnaces and steel melting furnaces. They are given in Table 91.

If 'process worker' covered broadly similar grades the German and French outputs per man per year at blast furnaces exceeded the British in 1957, but the French men worked a longer week, the German by the end of 1957 a shorter one than

---

[1] March 1956.   [2] Agreed in April 1957, in force Feb. 1958.
[3] Dec. 1956.
[4] This agreed in April 1958, came into force in Jan. 1959.
[5] Efforts to obtain reductions in other E.C.S.C. countries had smaller results—sometimes more paid holidays. Cp. the *Ann. Rep.* of E.C.S.C.
[6] *Wirthschaft u. Statistik*, May 1958, p. 302.
[7] Average not available.

the British. In steel melting it was more complex, because different processes were used. It may be said reasonably that the British and German averages were equal in 1957, though the German was higher in 1956.[1] The figures naturally reflect, among other things, the great labour economy of the Converter process. It may be concluded that the British output per man in the open-hearth process was considerably better than the German, but the Germans like the French reserved their open-hearth furnaces for quality steel, the British made ordinary quality steel in theirs.

Table 91. *Output per process worker at blast furnaces and steel furnaces in 1957 (tons per man per year)*

| | Blast furnaces | Steel melting furnaces | | | |
		Bessemer	Open-hearth	Electric	Total
U.K.	1174	—	—	—	961
Germany[a]	1450	1800	760	360	940
	(*1573*)	—	—	—	(*1000*)
France	1254	1540	615	340	1060
Belgium	920	—	—	—	970
Luxembourg	729	—	—	—	1200

[a] The figures in italics for Germany are for 1956. The fall in 1957 presumably reflects the reduction in working hours then partially in force. The German figures are calculated on the basis that the number employed through the year was the mean of the number employed at the end of the year and at the end of the previous year. There are monthly figures of total employment in the industry which justify this, sectional figures are, however, only available for the end of each year.

The absolute figures are not conclusive. The trend figures appear to be. There was a more marked trend to higher outputs per man in Germany than in Britain, and whether or not throughout the industry outputs per man hour were yet normally larger by 1958 in parallel operations, as they may already have been, the trend if it continued would soon make them so.

[1] This could be because of the reduced hours and reduction of 4-shift working in 1959. German managements said that, despite union assurances, productivity fell when the reduction in hours occurred.

Wages and salaries plus associated costs were calculated as a percentage of turnover by the Iron and Steel Board for the United Kingdom. They amounted to 20 per cent in 1954 and fell to 18 per cent in 1956 and 1957, returning to 20 per cent in 1958. German firms publish their turnover, and their wages and salaries and associated obligatory social charges and voluntary payments, so that the cost of the labour supply can be given as a percentage of turnover. For a group of five important firms the percentages from 1952–53 to 1957–58 are set out in Table 92 by the side of the Steel Board's figures. For 1956–57 and 1957–58 a percentage for a larger number of firms (responsible in 1957–58 for 63 per cent of ingot output) is given— in both, the figure is slightly below the average for five firms. The most obvious comment is that these figures are surprisingly close together. There is, however, a slight indication of a relative fall in the German compared with the British figures. During these years the average price of German steel rose less than British. Therefore, since German earnings, plus social insurance, fringe benefits and the like rose as much as or a trifle more than the British, and were roughly identical[1], an identical movement of wages and associated costs as a percentage of turnover implied a relative fall in such costs in money terms per ton of product to the advantage of German production.[2]

Table 92. *Wage and salary costs as percentage of turnover, United Kingdom and Germany*

	1952–3	1953–4	1954–5	1955–6	1956–7	1957–8
U.K.	—	20	19	18	18	20
Germany	19·8	21·0	17·5	17·9	17·1 (16·8)[a]	18·0 (17·7)[a]

[a] Figures for a larger number of companies covering (for 1957–58) over 62 per cent of ingot output. A description of the basis of the German figures is given below, p. 600.

[1] Above, p. 586.
[2] There is a complication to be noticed here. The average value of turnover divided by ingot output for the five German firms rose more than *prices* (whose increase is indicated in the tables on p. 565). But this is because the proportion of the higher priced steels in the output of this group of firms rose. To take one simple indication, the proportion of steel made by Bochumer Verein and Thyssens rose by comparison with the outputs of Dortmund Hörde, Rheinhausen and Hoesch.

To the extent that the percentages themselves diverged, and the percentage in Germany fell relatively to that in Britain, this relative fall in German labour costs will have been greater. Table 92 therefore confirms the results of the survey of relative 'productivities'. Prices in the two countries had come relatively close together by 1957–58, hence the actual average labour cost per ton of steel cannot have been very dissimilar. If the trend of the period 1952–58 continued they would of course progressively diverge.

(5) *Inland Transport costs*

Relative movements of these are obscure. The data would be extremely complex if they were published, but in fact they were either not published at all or not published in comprehensive form. An increasing amount of road transport of steel-finished products affected some rates by provoking competition in rates. This did not affect greatly the cost of raw material transport. In the E.C.S.C. countries competition of water and rail was of some importance. In the United Kingdom the average increases in railway rates can be set out, but at the end of the period the changes are difficult to assess because while increases of rates on raw materials were introduced, special terms were offered to firms who used rail transport for the distribution of a high proportion of their output. The increase in transport costs in the United Kingdom was appreciable in these years. The Continental literature refers little to general increases of rates, and the likelihood is that the increases were smaller than in the United Kingdom. The general level of Continental rates seems to have been lower at the end of the period than the British rates.[1] There were considerable changes of particular rates, fixed for particular works. Many were reviewed by the High Authority as being discriminatory. The operation of the E.C.S.C., as shown earlier, reduced some inter-community-country rail rates, hence for particular firms and regions transport costs fell.[2]

[1] This view was taken by Shone and Fisher in March 1958 (*J. R. Stat. Soc.* 1958, III, p. 293).
[2] In the following table the United Kingdom data used in the foregoing international comparisons are adapted and at some points amplified to provide a continuation of tables for the United Kingdom alone given earlier in the text

(6) *Margins*

Information about the sums allowed for depreciation and obsolescence, reinvested out of profits, absorbed in taxation and interest, or paid in dividends, or otherwise retained in the business, was not collected or assembled on a uniform basis to allow precise comparison between what happened in the United Kingdom and the E.C.S.C. countries. What is required in this context is data giving these items as percentages of turnover, but although most of this information is available for the large German firms it is not for many of the British. Nor are there

(especially ch. v, p. 266, and ch. vi, p. 340). The figures may be linked also with those in *E.H.S.* p. 477.

(1946 = 100)

Year	Labour	Trans-port	Ore		Coking coal	Scrap		Cost of steel-works plant
			Home	Im-ported		Home	Im-ported	
1953	168	185	206	203	163	177	552	174
1954	177	205	219	183	175	200	415	178
1955	193	219	219	191	192	215	484	189
1956	214	230	223	209	219	250	636	205
1957	227	253	231	221	234	290	692	220
1958	235	273	259	201	242	312	435	224
1959 (first half)	243	273	268[a]	193	242	312	—	227
1959 as per cent-age of								
1937	434	340	390	470	650[b]	352	320 (472)	405
1953	145	184	130	95	148	176	79	130[c]

[a] The home ore index is based on figures published since the war by the Ministry of Power. The series was discontinued after 1958, and the figure for 1959 is an estimate, but based on information which suggests a slightly smaller increase over 1958. There was a fall in the proportion of haematite ores and of Cleveland ores from 1946, so that the price and cost of the East Midland ores will have risen slightly faster than the index—but the average for these ores will have been below the average for *all* ores (14s. in 1958). The comparison with 1937 is based on data from the *Ann. Report of the Secretary of Mines*, but the average value in 1937 has been calculated on 1946 *quantities* of different grades of ore at 1937 prices.

[b] It is of interest that the price of coking coal had risen far more than the prices of other materials—notably much more than transport, which had risen much less than labour.

[c] Thus while the cost of new plant had risen slightly faster than the cost of labour from 1946 to 1952, cost of labour rose much faster from 1953 to 1959.

any collective statistics such as the Iron and Steel Corporation
of Great Britain published in its brief day. From such data as
are available, however, it seems most probable that the proportion of turnover absorbed in depreciation and reinvestment rose
in the United Kingdom between 1953 and 1958 and fell in
Germany. This relative change was slightly offset by a growth
in the proportion of turnover taken by income and property
taxes in the German industry which did not occur in the United
Kingdom. Dividends also rose proportionately more in Germany
than in the United Kingdom, though they were still a smaller
proportion of turnover in 1958. Interest on debentures and
long-term loans took a larger proportion of turnover in
Germany. Of these items the first was by far the most
important. In Belgium self-finance was initially in this period
more important than in Germany, but it declined sharply in
1957–58. In France a reverse trend is found, but devaluation made
this a matter of much less significance in the case of France.

The profit-and-loss accounts of ten large British steel companies are aggregated in Table 93, together with their ingot
outputs, and balance-sheet data on the value of their fixed
capital assets and net current assets. Manifestly it would be
better to have a wider coverage; but there are important firms
which are parts of wider groups (English Steel Corporation of
Vickers, Guest Keen Iron and Steel of Guest Keen Nettlefolds,
Park Gate and Round Oak of Tube Investments) for whom the
information is not published. For those firms for whom it is
published, comparability is not perfect where the structure of
companies changed when they were denationalised. In the case
of Firth Brown's, where a drastic change has taken place, the
figures have had to be left out.[1] The limits on the value of this
kind of data are familiar. The valuation of 'capital employed'
possibly understates what it sets out to give (which is basically
a written off 'cost'), though not to the extent that some figures
suggest.[2] Trading profit is separated from other sources of

[1] Firth Brown's purchased Beadmore's from the Agency.
[2] For example, the Board said, in one report, that assets whose value was
£680 m. would cost £1200 m. to replace, but the replacement would have been
with different plant. The steel firms have revalued assets, as the table shows.

BEH

income, which are divded into investment income and other exceptional items. Transfers to Asset Replacement Reserves were introduced—on the precedent presumably of the Iron and Steel Corporation of Great Britain—to bring depreciation up to the level needed to cover replacement costs. Taxation is the companies' provision for taxation on the profits recorded in the accounts, which may ultimately differ from taxes paid, and give rise to exceptional credits. Different companies draw up

Table 93. *Summary of profit-and-loss accounts of 10 firms representing about 75 per cent of total output of crude steel, 1953–8*

Year ending 30 Sept.	1953 (£m.)	1954 (£m.)	1955 (£m.)	1956 (£m.)	1957 (£m.)	1958 (£m.)
Capital employed						
Fixed assets plus Net current assets	354·1	394·5	458·1	519·8	579·6	685·0
Gross trading profits[a]	63·0	74·7	98·3	97·7	117·7	114·9
Add other income[a]						
(a) Investment	2·3	1·3	1·8	1·7	1·8	2·6
(b) Exceptional items	2·7	2·6	1·5	1·0	−0·3	5·4
Total income	67·9	78·6	101·6	100·4	119·2	123·4
Deduct						
Depreciation	14·2	15·4	17·7	19·5	23·9	26·4
Transfers to fixed asset replacement reserve	—	4·3	8·1	10·6	12·2	12·5
Debenture and loan interest (gross)	3·2	3·6	4·2	5·6	7·2	8·9
Profits before taxation	50·5	55·3	71·5	64·7	75·9	75·9
Taxation[b]	27·1	27·7	36·0	33·5	41·0	40·8
Profits after taxation	23·4	27·7	35·6	31·2	34·8	35·1
Dividends (net) Ordinary	3·8	4·5	5·7	6·3	9·3	10·0
Preference	0·3	0·6	0·9	0·9	1·1	1·1
Profits retained	19·2	22·6	29·0	24·0	24·4	23·9
Total of gross trading profit remaining in the business	33·5	42·2	54·8	54·1	60·6	62·6
Aggregate output of ingots and castings of the firms (m. tons)	12·8	13·4	14·4	15·2	16·2	15·3

[a] 'Other items' is a combination of debits and credits, mostly 'exceptional'. The principal credits are in respect of provisions for taxation which have proved to be excessive and are not required. The principal recurrent debits are payments to outside shareholder interests.

[b] Taxation in the accounts of course means estimated liability for taxation: it is a provision, and as the former note indicates this sometimes proves excessive.

accounts in different forms, and some rearrangement has been necessary to preserve uniformity.[1]

Trading profits grew faster, it may safely be said, than turnover from 1953 to 1955—how much cannot be shown. The Inland Revenue Statistics on Iron and Steel covering 2300 companies, many of them iron foundries,[2] showed trading profits rising from 10·4 per cent of turnover to 11·7 per cent in these years, for the ten steel companies the increase was probably more.[3] From 1955 to 1957 profits appeared to have risen less than turnover, but trading profit was probably a higher proportion of turnover in 1958 than in 1955 (or any other year in these six); an interesting situation since this was a year of recession, but not for all the companies. Prices were by and large held, raw materials became cheaper, enough possibly to offset the contrary effect of higher wages combined with lower outputs. It is the purpose of price stabilisation that price changes should not be drastic, and there is inevitably a risk of a lag between a fall of costs which, according to the formulae, justify a reduction (or rise) of price and the actual change of price.

It is convenient to discuss the remaining items as percentages of trading profits, with an eye on these as percentages of turnover and capital employed. These are set out in Table 94. In this table Depreciation and 'Transfers' are combined in one figure for the reason indicated above.

Depreciation, plus transfers—which did not rank for tax allowance because these were based on historic cost—thus rose fairly consistently through the period as a percentage of trading profits. The surplus retained in the businesses in addition was fairly steady at a high level as a proportion of trading profits up to 1955, and then fell. The year 1955 saw a 'peak' in the pro-

[1] This has been done with the guidance and help of accountants familiar with the data.

[2] Above, p. 232.

[3] Finished steel deliveries rose from 1953 to 1955 by about 17 per cent, prices by nearly 6 per cent. This suggests a rise of turnover by about 25 per cent. (Since steel firms make things other than steel the figure is very approximate.) Trading profits of the ten firms rose by 55 per cent, which would mean profits as a percentage of turnover rising by about 25 per cent, from, say, 10 per cent to 12·5 per cent (but this is only hypothetical).

portion of gross profits which in one way or another 'remained in the business'. If profits themselves were, say, 12 per cent instead of 10 per cent of turnover, then the profits kept in one form or another for reinvestment rose from 5·25 per cent of turnover in 1953 to 6·7 per cent in 1955. On the same hypothesis it was near 6 per cent in 1957, and 6·5 per cent in 1958.

Table 94. *Use of company income, 1953–58*[a]

	1953	1954	1955	1956	1957	1958
Depreciation plus transfers (%)	21	25	25	30	30	32
Profits and other income retained (%)	29	28	28	24	21	20
Total (%)	50	53	53	54	51	52
Shillings/ton	50s.	63s.	76s.	72s.	75s.	82s.
Provisions for taxation (%)	39	35	36	33	35	33
Shillings/ton	42s.	41s.	50s.	44s.	50s.	54s.
Debenture interest, etc. (%)	4·7	4·5	4·2	5·5	6·0	7·2
Shillings/ton	5s.	5s. 6d.	6s.	7s. 6d.	8s. 9d.	11s. 6d.
Dividends (ordinary and preference) (%)	6·1	6·4	6·5	7·1	8·7	9·1
Shillings/ton	6s.	7s. 6d.	9s.	9s. 6d.	12s.	14s. 6d.
Total all items, shillings per ingot ton	103s.	117s.	141s.	133s.	146s.	162s.

[a] For some purposes, and some items, it may be thought more useful to consider the various items as percentages of trading income, this makes only a small difference, and Table 93 provides the basis for this adjustment.

In cash terms, 'per ingot ton', it rose from about 48s. in 1955 to over 80s. in 1958. Large as the increase was, it was slightly less than the increase in capital investment in fixed assets between 1953 and 1958 in the whole steel industry according to the Board's figures. This rose by 114 per cent, from £49 m. to £105 m., whereas profits retained rose by 90 per cent. The trends of the other items stand out clearly. The fall in the proportionate importance of taxation was an outcome partly of net falls in the rates of the taxes: possibly new investment allowances brought a change too, but not initial allowances. Dividends and interest, both 'gross', rose appreciably after 1955. Dividends plus interest were 3 per cent of 'capital employed' as assessed in balance sheets in 1953, 4 per cent in 1958. The year 1953 it will be recalled was a year of low profits.[1]

In some respects it is highly misleading merely to look at the aggregates and neglect the different experiences of the individual firms. The experience of the firms was in fact surprisingly varied. It would be impracticable here to trace and discuss the changes for each from year to year, but Table 95 sets out some comparisons of the 1953 and 1958 balance sheets for the ten individual firms.

The gross trading-profit figures reflect both the varied impact of recession in 1958 and (together with the capital figures) the varied pace of expansions since 1953. Tubes and tinplate suffered worst in this year of the recession; heavy sections fared not much better, but sheets did extremely well, and South Durham, for so long 'booked' for absorption into a regional consolidation, showed its particular vitality. The net profit figures for 1952 and 1953 set out earlier,[2] show that in the recession of 1953 the heavy steel firms profits rose, whereas the sheet and tinplate firms' profits fell, as did also those of the tube and re-rolling firms. This necessarily must be taken into account in interpreting the growth of dividends. The Richard Thomas figures—*not* a result, in any sense, of national ownership—are to be explained perhaps by difficulties arising from sustaining in operation old plant in West Wales, largely for social reasons,[3] and the difficulties arising from the fact that the development of the sheet and tinplate business had been deliberately *not* balanced within Richard Thomas and Baldwins

---

[1] Above, p. 358. The Inland Revenue statistics showed trading profits as a percentage of turnover in 'Iron and Steel' from 1951 to 1955 as:

Year	Per cent		Per cent
1951	13·8	1954	10·7
1952	13·4	1955	11·8
1953	10·4	1956	12·1

The statistics are not yet available for later years.

[2] Above, *loc. cit.*

[3] The same considerations influenced United Steels at Workington, but Richard Thomas and Baldwins had a much greater problem to deal with and no plant with the advantages of Appleby Frodingham to offset it.

itself while Richard Thomas and Baldwins and Steel Co. of Wales were associated.

Though total trading profits of these ten firms fell slightly from 1957 to 1958, half the firms made higher profits. The Steel Co. of Wales, South Durham, John Summers, and Lancashire Steel all had substantial increases. Of these, two, John Summers and South Durham, raised their dividends; the other did not.[1] The more anomolous situation was found among the other firms, whose trading profit fell in 1958, in some cases

Table 95. *Balance sheet items for individual firms*

	Steel Co. of Wales	United Steel Co.	Stewarts and Lloyds	John Summers	Colvilles	Dorman Long	Richard Thomas and Baldwins	South Durham	Consett	Lancashire Steel
Capital employed										
1958 (£000,000)	161·9	98·3	89·9	54·5	60·3	77·6	58·5	34·4	26·4	22
% over 1953	80	117	68	85	153	161	54	207	40	54
£ per ingot ton/year^a	76	36	68	40	33	40	34	42	30	40
Gross trading profit										
1958 (£000)	22,025	20,010	16,815	12,349	11,126	10,072	8,031	6,697	3,723	3,874
% over 1953	187	91	17	370	98	29	6	214	63	65
% over 1957										
£ per ingot ton/year	10	7	13	9	6	5	5	8	4	7
Depreciation plus transfers										
1958 (£000)	8,608	5,479	4,454	4,216	2,500	4,249	3,997	1,650	1,750	1,100
% over 1953	158	213	139	226	185	150	174	266	65	186
Net dividends (ordinary)										
1958 (£000)	1,380	2,157	1,265	1,242	747	1,035	841	552	503	160
% over 1953	276	212	85	317	171	219	6	1,234	171	107
Surplus^b										
1958 (£000)	1,659	5,319	4,245	2,124	3,673	1,836	1,747	2,039	530	777
% over 1953	170	65	—	1,765	92	−40	−56	92	113	−6

a The drop in output in 1958 was large enough in some firms to raise this figure much above the 1957 figure, especially for Stewarts and Lloyds. The broad variations are significant. Some of the figures (for example Stewarts and Lloyds) are high because of the integration with tube-making, and the Steel Co. of Wales, partly because of the high cost of the type of plant used, including the electrolytic tinning. The Steel Co. of Wales is also high because almost the whole of the plant is fairly new. The contrasts of the Steel Co. of Wales, Richard Thomas and Baldwins and Summers' figures are of particular interest. It is to be noted that some firms do not regularly publish their ingot outputs, hence for some of them even the approximations here involve a slight hazard.

b Because this item is much influenced by the occurrence of special credits or debits, such as when an excess provision for taxation is brought into income, the contrast of one particular year with another is liable to be especially misleading for this item.

1 The Steel Co. of Wales, however, announced in advance a higher interim for 1958/9.

heavily, in others slightly. But of these, none reduced its dividend, while two, Dorman Long and United Steel, paid out more.[1] The dividends were well covered, but the motives of these increases were obscure. Dorman Long had been much criticised for low payment in 1957: the Chairman possibly took into account that the major outlay on the Universal Beam Mill was now made. The worst of the recession in the industry, however, lay ahead, and it was hardly to be supposed that slightly higher dividends were going to ease the way for raising new capital before a general election. Was it thought necessary to keep up the spirits of shareholders, or to reward their courage, or whet their appetites?

The sums absorbed in Germany in depreciation, interest dividends and taxes are shown in Table 96. (Expenditure on wages and associated items, reproduced earlier,[2] is shown again as a percentage of turnover because it is useful to be able to relate them to the figures here included for turnover and ingot output.) Depreciation is the chief, though not the exclusive, source of 'self finance' in Germany. Not much more appears in balance sheets however, certainly not enough to disturb the trends shown in Table 96. Expenditure of a capital nature, arising basically in repair and maintenance, which was treated as a current expense paid out of revenue was said by experienced observers to reach an extremely high figure, equal in amount to the depreciation, but this naturally does not enter into published accounts. Similar items occur in British practice: whether on as large a scale as in Germany is not clear.[3] It will be observed that the trend of depreciation both as a percentage of turnover and in shillings per ton was the reverse of the trend of 'profits retained' in the United Kingdom (the gross figures, that is, including depreciation, transfers and surplus). Depreciation in Germany was at its highest from 1952-3 to 1954-5, and thereafter fell to a somewhat lower level. The explanation is simple:

---

[1] Both raised the rate per cent of their final dividends.   [2] Above, p. 590.
[3] Relining of furnaces is always treated as a current revenue cost, but clearly the borderline between the rate and type of wearing out whose remedying counts as a revenue cost and that which counts as capital replacement must be arbitrary, though the *extreme* cases will be clear enough. Andrews and Brunner, *op. cit.* include some interesting data.

in the first three years there were special tax concessions, 'Investment Help', whereby exceptional depreciation was allowed, which most other industries did not enjoy,[1] and to which most other industries contributed. There is no reason to suppose that when the 'special depreciation' ceased firms made compensating contributions to investment from surpluses[2]

Table 96. *Wages, depreciation, interest, taxation and dividends as proportion of turnover in five German steel firms 1953–58*[a]

	1952-3	1953-4	1954-5	1955-6	1956-7		1957-8	
Turnover (DM. millions)	2493	2392	3238	3761	4770	*7030*	4170	*8212*
Ingot output	6011	6464	8248	9009	9657	*12212*	9171	*14228*
Wages and related costs (% of turnover)	19·8	21·0	17·5	17·9	17·1	*16·8*	18·0	*17.7*
Depreciation (% of turnover)	10·8	10·8	11·1	8·2	7·7	*6·8*	7·7	*6·6*
Depreciation (shillings per ingot ton)	78s.	67s.	72s.	57s.	57s.	*65s.*	58s.	*62s.*
Net interest (% of turnover)	1·0	1·7	1·6	1·7	1·9	*1·7*	2·4	*2·3*
Taxation (% of turnover)								
(1) Income and property	1·5	1·4	1·8	2·6	2·7	*2·4*	2·4	*2·2*
(2) Other	3·0	3·3	3·6	3·4	3·1	*3·3*	3·1	*3·2*
Dividends (% of turnover	Nil	0·5	0·8	1·3	1·4	—	1·7	—

[a] The series from 1952–3 to 1957–8 covers August Thyssen Hütte, Bochumer Verein, Dortmund Hörder, Hoesch, and Rheinhausen. The figures for Bochumer Verein and Dortmund Hörder are from the consolidated accounts, the others are not. The additional columns with figures in italics cover additional firms. Those for 1956–7 include the consolidated August Thyssen Hütte data (which adds data from the Edelstahlwerke and Niederheinische Hütte) data for Hoesch-Walzwerk (a re-rolling plant), and the consolidated accounts of Phoenix Rheinrohr. For 1957–8 figures for Klöckner are also added; those covering steel and engineering, but not coal. The additional figures suggest that the sample of five may be taken as a general guide; the higher depreciation percentage in the 'five' for 1956–7 and 1957–8 results from the high figure in August Thyssen Hütte, which has less effect in the larger sample: but the figure in shillings per ton is *not* smaller, but higher, in the larger sample. The accounting years are calendar years or years ending 1 October.

[1] 'Investment Help' was for coal, steel and power industries.

[2] Several German firms analysed, in very summary form, the financing of their fixed capital investment since currency reform or since a subsequent date when they were reconstituted. Thus Dortmund Hörder in their Report on 1957–8 state

(though some had accumulated reserves out of 'Investment Help' on which they drew later). This downward trend, which in shillings per ton was from 77s. in 1952–3 to 60s. (or 65s.) in 1957–8 may be compared with the upward movement of funds retained in the British firms from 48s. to 80s. It is not an absolutely precise comparison: something, but only a little, must be added to the German figures to cover other 'plough back', and the range of activities covered are not identical. But the broad contrast is almost certainly reliable. When the allowance of special depreciation ceased in Germany there was naturally a rise in the cost of income and property taxation— because more income was liable to tax. (Though taxation on income and property rose as a percentage of turnover in Germany, it was much smaller than in the United Kingdom. 'Other taxation' was in fact heavier: it was largely turnover tax. The two together were about the same in shillings per ton in 1958 as taxation in the United Kingdom.) The ending of special depreciation in Germany reflected the improvement in the capital market: firms were able to raise more money, mainly as long-term loans and debentures, rather less by share issues, and at fairly high rates of interest.[1] The increasing resort to loans is

that of a total investment since currency reform (1948) of DM. 673 m., D.M. 430 m. came from normal depreciation, DM. 82 m. from special depreciation, DM. 74 m. from other reserves—security for pension funds—(i.e. other internal resources) and DM. 87 m. from long-term loans. Klöckners' figures to the end of 1958 were: total expenditure on new fixed assets, including participations, and stock increases, DM. 932 m., of which DM. 409 m. from normal depreciation, DM. 176 m. from special depreciation, DM. 225 m. from loans and long-term credits, DM. 52 m. from share issues. Of their expenditure of DM. 153·4 m. in 1957–8, much on the Bremen works, depreciation provided DM. 66·5 m.; new long-term loans DM. 45·9 m.; stock reduction DM 12·1 m., DM. 27 m. was drawn from reserves, apparently accumulated out of special depreciation in the past. In Mannesmann's report for 1958, it was emphasised that all the net additions to assets were financed by sums *subscribed* (new shares, debentures or loans) apart from a 'quite insignificant amount from "resources retained"'. For Thyssens depreciation fell, owing to the exhaustion of depreciation allowances from 'Investment Help', from DM 135 m. in 1956–7 to DM. 91 m. in 1957–8. Recourse to other sources did not rise to match, because investment on fixed assets fell from DM. 177 m. in 1956–7 to DM. 133 m. in 1957–8.

[1] Typical rates were, for example, debentures for Phoenix Rheinrohr at 8 per cent in 1957, 7 per cent in 1958; long-period loans for Rheinhausen, 6½ per cent in 1956, 8 per cent in 1956, 7½ per cent in 1957; loans for Dortmund Hörder, 7 per cent 1954, 7 per cent 1958. Thyssen debenture bonds, 7 per cent in 1954, 7½ per cent in 1957.

reflected in the growing importance of interest as a cost—it was a much larger item in the German industry than in the British (being in the United Kingdom some 12s. per ingot ton, in Germany almost 20s.)

The rise in the amount of gross profits retained in the United Kingdom was a symptom of the rising rate of investment: the fall of depreciation in Germany did not on the other hand betoken a much lower rate of investment in Germany, as has been seen in chapter VII; though the figures per ingot ton given there relate to the investment in fixed assets for iron- and steel-making and iron ore mining coming within the scope of the E.C.S.C. The depreciation figures taken here from balance sheets necessarily cover a different and wider range of activities,[1] so that there is no possibility of comparing the two to say what proportion of total investment in iron and steel was 'self financed'. For individual firms it varied greatly in particular years according to the intensity or otherwise of their investment. For Dortmund Hörde in 1957–8 depreciation appears to have exceeded the gross value of new fixed investment: for Klöckners'[2] it was only 44 per cent of new investment, but a further 18 per cent seems to have been drawn from reserves. In this context it is not necessary to establish the average; figures of 45 per cent and 60 per cent have been given.[3] Information was given every year to the E.C.S.C. on this, but not published by the High Authority, and not published for Germany, though the Belgian firms through their 'Groupement' published it in Belgium, and it appeared for France in the reports of the Commissariat au Plan and in statistics published by the Commission des Investissements and its successor.

[1] They cover, for example, some engineering, some coal-mining and some shipping: tube-making was outside the range of the E.C.S.C.

[2] See p. 600–1, note 1.

[3] They were given to the author, both by responsible sources. They might refer to different ranges of investment (the larger percentage referring to fixed investment only and excluding circulating capital) and were not necessarily contradictory (though to isolate investment financing for fixed capital alone is liable to mislead.) The second figure seems more in accordance with the company reports which have been examined. To establish a figure from the examination of balance sheets, however, is somewhat forbidding, and in the absence of experience and familiarity with intricacies of German company law would appear dangerous.

A move away from self finance and towards a greater dependence on the capital market as a source of funds for new investment was indeed favoured by the Erhard 'school' in Germany: what was happening, partly because prices and margins were being lowered by competition, although largely as a result of the ending of favourable tax provisions, was widely welcomed. Had it gone far enough? It was a corollary that dividend payments should rise—as a source of investible funds and an inducement to investors. This was happening, though the proportion of turnover paid as dividends (the figures in the table are gross) remained in 1958 relatively low.

To sum up then, the comparison of these British and German figures seems to show that the sums absorbed for investment (gross), taxation, interest and dividends, rose appreciably for the British industry from 1953–8 as a cost per ton. They rose considerably more in the British than in the German industry. This was mainly because the sums used for investment in fixed capital rose per ton of product steeply in the United Kingdom, and fell slightly in Germany. Changes of the other items were less material. Initially the United Kingdom investment from own resources was much below the German: by 1958 it appeared to be higher. This was partly a result of a much increased rate of investment in the United Kingdom industry, partly a reflection of difficulties of raising money externally in the United Kingdom market, where the position got worse as the election of 1959 approached, whereas in Germany the market was becoming more favourable for the industry.

In the Belgian industry, figures published show that 'self finance' was the main source of capital expenditure up to 1956, but thereafter fell in importance. In 1955 and 1956 depreciation, reserves, and 'provisions', supplied 82 per cent and 83 per cent of the total: share issues provided four-fifths of the remainder. in 1957 internal resources provided 67 per cent, share issues 25 per cent, and bonds and loans, though still small, rose a little in importance. In 1958 long-term loans provided about 36 per cent.[1] In France self finance was never as high a proportion

---

[1] *Groupement des Hauts-Fourneaux et Aciéries Belges: Rapport Annuel* 1958, p. 68. The data for 1958 are incomplete, and the contribution of share issues was not included.

as in Belgium in 1955–6: but it grew in importance in 1956–7. The figures from 1953–8 were as shown in Table 97.

The trends are clear—fall in supplies from public funds and bank credits, more from the money market but more still from firms own resources, which in 1957 provided 60 per cent of the total. In francs per ingot ton the investment by firms thus rose from 3850 francs in 1953 (but only 2600 in 1954, and less in 1955) to 5000 francs in 1957 and 4460 francs in 1958. This amounted to approximately 80s. a ton in 1953, and over £5 a ton in 1957 until the devaluation of October when it became approximately 85s. a ton. After the final devaluation the the figure for 1958, if it were sustained in 1959, would have been 65s. a ton. The pattern of financing in France differed widely from both the German and the British: but the effect in terms of expenditure of firms' own resources in investment was closer to the British than to the German. The cutting edge of French prices in 1957–9 came of course from the successive devaluations, which influenced German prices and presumably German margins.

Table 97. *The financing of investments in French steelmaking, including iron ore mines (000,000,000 francs)*

Source of finance	1953	1954	1955	1956	1957	1958
1. Firms own resources	37·7	26·1	26·4	54·5	70·5	64·2
2. Money market	14·6	23·9	35·6	25·6	35·5	37·0
Shares	(3)	(1)	(8·6)	(3·4)	(15.5)	(4·0)
Bonds	(11·6)	(22·9)	(27)	(22·2)	(20)	(33·0)
3. Public funds	36·4	25·1	16·8	16·1	3·5	11·0
4. Bank credits and loans by special institutions	11·8	−11·5	−3·8	−9·2	5·5	13·0
	100·5	63·6	75	87	115	125·2

European costs were below American: paradoxically this was due wholly to the high level of United States labour costs, despite the much greater output per man in the United States. Productivity was not sufficiently higher to offset the high level of earnings—three times or more the European levels.[1] As a

---

[1] Above, p. 586.

result labour cost (including fringe benefits, etc.) was from 32 to 36 per cent of turnover in each year from 1951 to 1958 compared with 17–20 per cent average in the United Kingdom and Germany.[1] The main material costs were lower in the United States than in Europe; fuel costs always, and ore costs except possibly in comparison with European firms who were using local ores. Capital costs it may be inferred were broadly the same. Coal was much cheaper in the United States: the margin by which it was cheaper became larger from 1953 to 1958. Lake ores delivered at the lower lake ports, were considerably cheaper than Swedish or other oversea ores used in the United Kingdom or by the 'Six': though the margin became smaller between 1953 and 1958.[2] The Venezuelan and Canadian ore prices were governed by Lake ore prices: and freights on these to the United States were naturally lower than to Europe. The price of scrap was a market price: it was normally above the British price when this was kept extremely low by price control, but was normally below the Continental prices in a boom, which was natural while Europe imported from the United States. Similarity of capital cost may be inferred from the fact that new plant cost approximately the same in the United States and Europe. The United States gained by being pioneers in steel-works engineering; their large home market and considerable export business—much to Europe—gave scope for repetitive work in plant-making; the use of high-capacity units brought down investment per ton of output, and they used capacity more intensively than most European makers. Interest rates were also generally lower.

United States steelmaking, though technically stimulating, was not commercially disturbing. There was, however, a lively prospect that the relative cost position *vis-à-vis* the British of

---

[1] Cp. *Annual Statistics* of the A.I.S.I.

[2] Mesabi ore (51·5 Fe) delivered to lower lake ports rose from $9.70 a long ton in 1953 to $11.45 in 1957. For Pittsburgh there was an additional rail cost of about $3 a ton, but Pittsburgh had very cheap coal. English plants located on home ore, and Continental plants using minette, had cheaper ore than most United States plants, but dearer coal. The net difference was probably small: it is possible that Appleby Frodingham had a net advantage in burden cost over most United States plants. (Mesabi ore remained at $11.45 (82s.) in Mar. 1960.)

several groups of Continental steelmakers would continue to improve. It was based in different areas on different sources: rising efficiency in ore mining and preparation in France, good access to United States coal and cheaper labour in Italy, greater concentration and so specialisation of finishing in Germany, improvements of cheaper steel processing in all of them, and so on. If demand for steel kept up, the impact of this change on the United Kingdom might not be very conspicuous, though it could still be quite profound. How were the policies of the Iron and Steel Board stimulating British steelmakers to respond to this situation? In the next section the Board's activities are examined with this question in view, first in regard to prices, then in regard to development, raw materials supply, self sufficiency, and the like.

Chapter X

THE BRITISH INDUSTRY SINCE DENATIONALISATION: THE BOARD IN ACTION

1. PRICE POLICY

Political critics of steel prices at the time when the Iron and Steel Corporation of Great Britain was about to be dismantled said the prices were too high: and they continued to say it afterwards. In the light of their probable effects on demand, investment decisions, the balance of trade and commercial relations and if the object was to simulate the effects of (or secure the results that might be expected from) 'competitive conditions' they were, it has been seen, too low. The twin pursuit of stable prices and low prices, as the analyses in chapters v and vi has shown, had led to the evolution and perpetuation of price control practices which kept profit margins on products subject to price control (especially heavy steel and above all billets) relatively small, and reduced the advantages which firms would have obtained 'in competitive conditions' from using home ores, or from being especially well located to use imported ores, or from operating on a large scale giving advantages to specialisation, or from having first-rate facilities for making cheap hot metal at times of brisk demand for steel. The system gave no price advantage to a user of steel who was located where steel could be made most cheaply; and it was implicit in the arrangements that while prices were kept down when demand was brisk, no firm would reduce its prices out of step in a recession. How much the distortion of incentives from the competitive pattern influenced decisions on production or investment was open to question. Some of the distortions which occurred arose from the way in which the system was worked. The interest of the decisions by the second Board on steel price policy lay in their handling of these controversial matters: margins, 'special arrangements', 'uniform delivered' prices, and the like.

The Board decided at the outset that the best way for them to carry out their function of supervising prices was to fix them—'at least for the present'. Against the background of the debates of 1953, and the past history of the members, it could not have been otherwise. After six years there were still no signs that the Board saw the position differently. But in exercising their wide discretion they responded to some of the earlier criticisms, especially those of the way the system was administered. They made no dramatic changes. What did the cumulative effect of their decisions amount to? Several changes were made every year, some general, some relating to few products only. Most followed precedents. Every year, however, some precedents were broken.

A general price review in 1954 made the first breaches.[1] The main change was an increase in margins. The methods of assessing production costs, of spreading marginal costs and keeping scrap cheap, were unchanged. But depreciation and obsolescence were newly estimated and were based on replacement cost. An increased importance appeared to be given to the risk of obsolescence.[2] (The 'historic cost' of assets was, however, still treated as the appropriate basis for calculating 'reasonable profit'.) 'Having arrived at what they considered to be the allowance' (for depreciation and obsolescence) 'necessary to sustain a healthy industry the Board made it clear to representative organisations of producers that they would expect that the amounts set aside.... for these purposes would not be less than the allowances made in prices.' There was to be no nonsense about a free capital market. Perhaps this found its explanation partly in the political setting of the industry.

The review of 1954 also led to a revision of 'extras', which had remained in a few instances unchanged since before the war, and in some products had been outdated also by changes

---

[1] *Ann. Rep.* 31 Dec. 1954, pp. 16–22.

[2] This had already been accepted in the accounts of the Iron and Steel Corporation of Great Britain, above, p. 236.

of technique, particularly in sheets. The changes whose details were worked out by the trade associations for the Board[1] were expected to add £5 m. to the cost of 'extras', and made it possible to limit the average increase of base prices to 3 per cent instead of 4 per cent.[2]

In 1955, the Board announced that if some consumers wished to have fixed price contracts to cover some orders the Board would be prepared to agree (subject to being satisfied on the details), even though the price might be above the current maximum.[3] Apart from this the Board in its report emphasised how much the Industry Fund was now stabilising prices—a surplus of £15 m. built up in 1953–54 had been dissipated. Although users of imported ore had been subject to two increases, high prices of imported ore, scrap, pig iron and semi-products were all being spread over the whole industry in the traditional way through the device of an ingot levy. The Board had expressed their approval of all this in 1954, and gave no indication of the large sums transferred in the exercise. They showed a more critical approach in 1954 to the scrap arrangements which 'had certain inherent objections, notably the introduction of some artificiality into the aggregate cost of iron and steelmaking, and the possible inequity to steel-consuming industries which throw up more scrap than others'.[4] They knew it allowed British prices to be lower than if scrap moved freely in world trade: indeed they published estimates of the difference. But 'they were advised' the system was well established, made for stability in steel prices, did not check supplies of scrap, and was not complained of by customers. So 'for the time being'

---

[1] The Board (like Sir Robert Shone, in *J. Ind. Economics*, Nov. 1952, p. 45) treated the correct determination of 'extras' as a responsibility for the makers, though the Board checked the results. When firms criticised extras Shone said broadly that it was their fault if the extras were open to criticism.

[2] *Ann. Rev.* December 1954, p. 22. An important change in zone extras occurred in Dec. 1953, though how far due to the Board is not clear. Till then many shipyards (e.g. at Birkenhead) outside the zones free from delivery extras nevertheless were counted as 'in' such a zone (above, p. 230). Belfast shipyards had a reduced extra—8s. 6d. instead of the standard, viz. 22s. 6d. in 1948, which rose to 25s. in 1949, and 30s. in 1953. From Dec. 1953 no shipyard received such special privileges.

[3] *Ann. Rep.* 1955, p. 21.   [4] *Ibid.* December 1954, p. 18.

it would stay.[1] In 1955, however, they concluded after an examination that the arrangements were in fact giving a significant advantage to scrap users, as a few critics had for long declared. The value of scrap in relation to the price of basic pig iron was being taken at 77 per cent: now it was decided it should be 85 per cent,[2] and the levy on scrap and remission on pig iron, described earlier,[3] were adjusted to have this effect. This did not, of course, meet the fundamental criticisms of the scheme. It was most interesting as a belated recognition that the system had for all this time since the war been loaded in an avoidable way in favour of scrap users. The acknowledgement of the deeper issues which the first report showed was not recalled in the second. From year to year the price of scrap was raised, but though by 1958–59 when world prices slumped it was for a short time close to the world price the increases were matched by increases in pig iron prices, so that the margin between these was not lessened. As a proportion it fell.

The next year, 1956, brought a second comprehensive price review. On this occasion a radical change was made in estimating all costs. 'The Board made a detailed examination of the capital and production costs which might be expected to be incurred at a new integrated plant incorporating the most modern techniques favourably situated for raw materials and markets and efficiently operated.' The Board attached the term 'technical costs' to the results of this inquiry. Prices based on such an estimate would by implication include, not only depreciation and obsolescence, but also profit margins based on replacement costs. In a sense the issue would not now arise. The Board did not use the new basis exclusively: they used both the new and the old, the old one (the one used continuously from 1937 and during and since the war) taking as its basis the average production costs of all save a small band of high cost producers, to which the Board added a margin. In 1956 the amalgam of the old and new bases did not please all the firms,

---

[1] *Ann. Rep. loc. cit.* The price of good quality scrap was raised by £1 a ton to encourage good sorting and preparation.

[2] Or 92½ per cent of the transfer price of molten pig-iron.

[3] Above, pp. 207 sqq., 222 sqq.

and some—Lancashire Steel Corporation for instance—were highly critical in public,[1] but by 1957 difficulties had apparently been smoothed over.

The logic of this approach to price fixing, though not self evident, was not explained.[2] If new plants had lowest costs, what was a fair profit margin for them—and should no one be allowed to charge more whatever the state of demand? It was not explained how far the costs estimated for the new plant visualised greater specialisation which would increase the economy of using very costly plant. The key to the practicability of the new approach was easy to understand where the results of the two methods were much the same, which happened, the Board said, over a wide range of products. Substantial savings from the use of new plant were broadly offset in this range by 'the cost of remunerating the much greater investment required for new plant than the investment in existing plant of comparable capacity'. Just where this close correspondence was found was not made crystal clear. The exceptions were surprisingly important. It was not found for heavy plates, sections and joists, where savings in operating costs did not offset the greater cost of remunerating capital: or in the lighter sections of the industry where continuous rolling contributed major savings in operating costs which did outweigh the added capital cost.

One obvious comment was that though the 'technical costs' were 'based largely on the known or forecast costs of recent or current development projects' there was singularly little experience in Britain of new plant in heavy plate and section rolling. The performance and capacity in use of new plant usually much exceeded its designed or announced capacity so that theoretical capital costs would tend to be too high. Risks of obsolescence were possibly being over-insured. A second obvious comment was that in the heavy steel section much new capacity was wanted to make products not obtainable from the old plant—wider plates, and better plates with more uniform

---

[1] Cp. report of Annual Meeting (*The Times*, 12 Feb. 1958).
[2] It differed from the proposal of a wartime working party on post-war prospects that minimum prices should be based on the costs of the most efficient firm.

thickness and better surface, or thin plates subjected to heat treatment, and large universal beams. Thus the contrast between costs in new and old plant for heavy steel even if valid was of limited application: but it gained in interest from the perennial complaint that margins in heavy steel were insufficient. Presumably it led to higher margins for these products. Certainly the increases in prices in December 1956 were much larger for plates and heavy sections than for other products.[1] Was it altogether a coincidence, moreover, that as the policy of increasing 'extras' so that these corresponded more adequately with the cost of providing special sizes, qualities or quantities was pushed further, a particular feature of it in 1956 was that extras for heavy plates and sections were raised?

In 1956 the Board shed some light for the first time on the size of the Industry Fund operations. In Table 98 the main information published for 1956–58 is shown, together with estimates of the levies and remissions per ton, which are given in brackets. Thus the operations were on a smaller scale proportionately in the 1955–57 boom than in 1951–53, when the ingot levy reached over 80s. a ton. They were still important: and the operations

Table 98. *The Industry Fund, 1956–58*

	1956 (12 months to 31 Mar. 1957) (£ m.)	1957 (9 months to 31 Dec. 1957) (£ m.)	1958 (12 months to 31 Dec. 1958) (£ m.)
Cost of centrally purchased goods[a]	146	126	97
Excess cost spread	35	22	9
Research, finance administration	2	1	1
Ingot levy	36 (35s.)	31 (40s.)	18 (19s.)
Scrap levy	20 (70s.)	17 (80s.)	17 (80s.)
Pig iron remission	20 (42s.)	18 (42s.)	22 (42s.)
Deficiency (−) or surplus (+) in the year	−1	+7	+4

[a] This includes for 1956 and 1957 £3 m. and for 1958 £1 m. for 'payments in connection with the movement or production of materials within the United Kingdom'.

[1] For sheets the line taken was to have two prices—one for products made in old plant, one for products made on new plant. In Europe, as has been seen, the higher costs of the old plant determined the price of the product—this was the competitive solution.

over scrap were as important in 1956–57 as they ever had been. The Board had said in 1956 and 1957 that 'the intention is that users should bear the full cost of ore imported on their joint behalf but that temporary abnormalities in cost may be taken up by way of the Industry Fund'.[1] This was self contradictory if any abnormality taken up by the Fund was financed by the whole industry, partly therefore by the home ore users. But 'temporary abnormalities of cost' could 'be taken up' by the Industry Fund by reserves collected only from users of imported ore, at times when ore was cheap. From 1958 users of imported ore paid the full cost or more—the price charged them by B.I.S.C. (Ore) being by 1960 above the cost. This was indeed important.

By 1958 the high costs which were customarily spread had disappeared; even in 1957 the ingot levy had yielded a surplus, which it continued to do in 1958 until the ingot levy was reduced. Imported ores were relatively cheap; by 1959 they were as cheap as they were ever likely to be. There was no need to import scrap or pig iron or semis, and imported scrap prices were hardly above home scrap prices. These, it has been seen, were freed from control, and export of scrap was, for a limited period, permitted by the Board of Trade. The ingot levy was 'reduced to small proportions' by the end of 1958.[2] The shrinkage of Industry Fund operations in these circumstances was no indication that the levy would not be up again soon. The scrap levy-remission arrangements remained; Government price-fixing in scrap was replaced by industry price-fixing (with suppliers and consumers agreeing). The surplus earned in 1957 and early 1958 in the Industry Fund (partly used perhaps to offset the deficit of 1956) was a symbol of changes in costs which together with rising efficiency due to new plant led to the slight reductions in prices in 1958, 1959 and 1960.[3]

[1] This quotation is from *Ann. Rep.* 1957, p. 26. The same point was made in *Ann. Rep.* 1956, p. 23. In the *Ann. Rep.* 1958 (p. 28) the reference to temporary abnormalities was excluded. But the intention to use the Industry Fund for stabilising steelmaking costs, and running into surplus and deficits for this purpose was stated clearly enough (p. 31).

[2] *Ann. Rep.* 1958, p. 31. The 'average' of 19*s*. a ton for the year possibly included a few months at the much higher figure for 1957.

[3] Efficiency measured by the index of labour employed divided by the index of output fell in 1958, but the price-fixing always assumed a normal rate of output.

In 1957 a further large increase was made in margins for depreciation and obsolescence because 'technical changes which have occurred or are in prospect' had reduced the 'probable effective life of a plant'. Perhaps it was the prospect that new steel processes might be used that was most disturbing. There were no further changes of principle, no general review. More increases of 'extras' occurred—this time larger extras for smaller quantities were singled out for notice, especially for plates. The principle of charging extra for products sold at a distance from main producing areas was extended a little—to basic pig iron and in a strange way to sheets.[1] In 1959 the extras for small quantities were in effect raised again, but by a different method. Base prices were now reduced for orders of 10 tons and more of one size and kind. This was all in the direction followed in the United States as a means of attracting for mills larger unit orders, giving an advantage to large users, and encouraging stockholding, whether by users or merchants.

The home market prices fixed by the Board, like those fixed by the Government earlier, were maximum prices. In many parts of the industry there were agreements or arrangements that they were to be regarded also as a minima. Whether this was proper after the new Restrictive Practices Court had been established in 1956 was highly doubtful, and the Board appeared to decide in this sense (though it disclaimed in its 1958 report any function to examine practices in relation to the Act of 1956). After discussion with the Federation a new formula was arrived at. Understandings or agreements were to be replaced by recommendations 'giving guidance by the associations to their members on prices but without imposing any obligation'... individual producers 'are expressly free to exercise their own judgement'. The guidance was to be in the form that the association 'having regard to the need to maintain a healthy

---

[1] Until 1957 the price of sheets was the same delivered anywhere in England and Wales. In July 1957 an allowance of £1 per ton was introduced in Monmouth and Glamorgan and within 25 miles of Shotton. It was withdrawn from the Shotton area in March 1958. While this might encourage use of sheet in S. Wales it did not relate prices to delivery cost in England and Wales, and as strip mill plans showed it was not part of a policy which would induce minimum costs of supply. It created a new anomaly.

and expanding industry recommends that the maximum prices determined by the Iron and Steel Board should in general be regarded as appropriate selling prices'. The Board undertook to satisfy themselves that maximum prices fixed by associations themselves for such products as forgings and castings (where the Board had no automatic right to fix prices) were reasonable, so that the same formula might be used by the associations. The Board (whose chairman as a leading member of the milling industry had been associated with price recommendation schemes dating back a long time, of which the Restrictive Practices Court were to disapprove) thought the arrangements, which deprecated price competition without ruling it out entirely, were 'acceptable, and...compatible with the Iron and Steel Act 1953'.[1] Would the Restrictive Practices Court regard them as compatible with the Act which gave it jurisdiction?

The Board's attitude on this was a logical outcome of the doctrine that prices were fixed by it to provide competition, to be a substitute for price competition which because of the nature of the industry, the high cost and durability of its plant, its susceptibility to boom and slump, and other factors, did not satisfactorily eliminate inefficient firms, but often impoverished efficient ones.[2] The Board was constantly assessing and distributing the incentives needed for higher efficiency. Knowing what was happening through the whole industry it could judge right prices better than any firm. The idea of price competition (other than competition in absorbing freight) possibly seemed an intrusion, a relapse to an old system which had not worked. In the light of the doctrine on which steel pricing had been based for over a decade the Restrictive Practices Act of 1951 was no doubt an anomaly.

In retrospect it could be seen that most of the Board's price policy had been foreshadowed by Sir Robert Shone in the early fifties—writing for example in the *Journal of Industrial Economics* in 1952. He argued for higher margins, and for basing depreciation and obsolescence (and interest and taxation too) on replacement costs and by implication for higher margins on heavy steel. He had suggested that the costs in new plants were

---

[1] *Ann. Rep.* 1957, pp. 35–6.   [2] Cp. above, chapter v, section 3(*d*).

an appropriate basis for price-fixing during expansion (it would raise prices for some products, while it lowered others, he wrote), and had argued broadly that

it must be a very questionable policy to keep steel prices down below the world level, particularly in an industry...where heavy sums are inevitably needed for maintenance and expansion....It is even doubtful whether it is really in the interests of the steel-using industries to receive supplies at well below the world level. Sooner or later costs and prices in the various countries will move closer together and it cannot be expected that there will be a substantial permanent advantage in steel prices in favour of users in this country. Now would seem to be the time to be putting aside the substantial amount needed for the maintenance of the industry's output and making sizeable contribution towards the funds needed for faster expansion.[1]

By the time the Board began making changes of the type Shone adumbrated the comparison of British costs with Continental had become as has been seen less favourable than in 1951–52. In 1959 the most individual characteristics of the British price system all remained. Prices were still fixed by an outside body applying their own criteria. Stabilising devices—ingot levy, scrap levy, pig-iron remission, scrap price fixed low, scrap exports banned—were still in force, still maintaining therefore the 'artificial benefit of the low price of scrap' and ruling out the impact of short-term variations in its value, but not now discriminating against users of home ore, and discriminating much less than formerly in favour of steelmakers using a high proportion of scrap.[2] Prices were still 'uniform delivered' in the sense of being absolutely the same, including transport costs, for users in a remarkably large area (made up of several

---

[1] *J. Indust. Econ.* November 1952, pp. 53–4.

[2] Cold metal steelplants would still seem to gain if high costs of imports were spread by an ingot levy. From 1955 to 1959 the average scrap/pig iron cost ratio was at least as high in Britain as in the E.C.S.C., and much higher in 1958–59. The E.C.S.C. ratio was affected by *péréquation* and export prohibitions, and after 1957 scrap was cheap through recession, large eve of recession imports, and low activity in the United States. The *average* ratio in Europe had little obvious significance (cp. pp. 223 sqq) because relative price *movements* were a factor in short-term decision making. Continental export prohibition was suggested as a reason why Britain should not free her scrap price and exports: the argument is dubious in logic, and was not the determining one.

'zones') irrespective of their nearness to a works within the area or the different production costs of works in different sites. Coal prices were still low in relation to costs in divisions where costs were high and vice versa. Though the effect of some of these things was less conspicuous in 1958–59 than formerly this was partly an effect of recession: the presumption was that the spreading of some high import costs would revive when raw material imports became dearer (those who did not use these imports were possibly already contributing to a reserve for this in 1958) and that the discrepancy between the United Kingdom and 'world' scrap prices would be revived. Only radical changes which could not be taken for granted could avoid this.

Thus it could not be said after the first six years of the Board's activity that the distorting effects of the steel price system were now all avoided. There had been big advances to greater rationality and there might be more, but there was still a long way to go. Did it matter? What difference would it have made for instance if British prices had been arrived at by the methods and as a result of the conditions (described earlier) which operated in the United States or those in the E.C.S.C. countries? Did the British arrangements prevent investment and development conforming to the standards of competitive conditions? Or were they consistent with if not conducive of such conformity, and was everything put right by the planning activities of the Board?

Before turning to the Board's planning, which is the subject of the next section, it is appropriate to remark that the arrangements and customs about prices in the United States and E.C.S.C. did not prove destructive to the steelmakers or steelmaking, and had so far proved at least consistent with, possibly a source of, rather more radical adaptation to changing economic and technical situations than happened in the United Kingdom. That might be because adaptation was easier: but at least it makes one major premise in the theory of British central control doubtful—that if there were price competition it would weaken the industry instead of promoting investment appropriate to 'competitive conditions'. This view possibly gave exaggerated significance to a transitional stage on the way to oligopoly, which in Britain was made additionally difficult by foreign dumping facilitated by the existence of tariffs in the dumping countries and free trade in the United Kingdom.

Some apologists of the British system were inclined to accept this view implicitly—and that the disturbing transition was over: and they argued, seductively, that the oligopolistic situation as it had emerged in the United States and on the Continent led to a situation where price behaviour was much the same as under price fixing in Britain. But the record in the United States and the E.C.S.C. countries as traced earlier shows that there was a greater degree of flexibility in their pricing—in the United States always, in the E.C.S.C. area because different national groups behaved in different ways—as well as (and perhaps a reflection of) an absence of the subsidising and levelling practices which deliberately eliminated effects of marginal prime cost movements and prevented prices exerting any influence on the behaviour of consumers in the short run.[1] United States and E.C.S.C. prices also of course gave an interest to consumers to be near a steel producer. There can be little doubt that in the absence of the arrangements peculiar to Britain prices in Britain would have been slightly more flexible and somewhat higher in general, and the profits earned, if in total higher at certain periods, would have been very differently distributed between the firms and more favourably for those whose costs were inherently lower. Of course if it had been true that the systems in other countries produced similar price patterns to the British, then the desirability of maintaining a special organisation to bring about in Britain what happened in any event elsewhere without such an organisation might seem doubtful; though if it were thought that the main object of the Board was political, to give people an assurance that their interests were being taken care of, it was better that the activities of the organisation should be superfluous than that they should be harmful.

[1] Though export prices were not fixed in 1959 inflexibility of British prices appeared in 1959 to extend to heavy steel exports sold centrally through B.I.S.C. It was said that to cut prices would hurt home users. British merchants in order to fulfil export orders sold large tonnages of Continental steel. One or two smaller British steelmakers seemed likely to withdraw from the collective arrangements.

2. THE BOARD'S PLANNING

The Board's approach to their responsibility for planning and development showed no unconventional freshness. They did not for instance propose leaving the British industry open to free international competition, or treating Europe as one common market (as a means of ensuring efficient economic adequate supplies 'under competitive conditions'), although they discussed estimates of demand with the E.C.S.C. and E.C.E., and exchanged information on investment plans and recognised that progressive removals of duties in Europe might increase trade in steel both inwards and outwards. The Board specifically thought that lower import duties on steel would have little effect on direct trade in steel—and felt they could not judge how a Free Trade Area would increase indirect exports of steel to Europe.[1] As has been seen, however, the tariff agreement which emerged out of the deliberations of the Council of Association was surprisingly protective for a Government presenting itself as more free trade minded than the French, and there is no reason to suppose that the Chairman of the Board, or the Board as a whole, disapproved of what was done. Nowhere in the Board's reports was it suggested that because large-scale operating had so much economy to offer in steelmaking the scale of the British market might be disadvantageously small. Perhaps they thought their terms of appointment ruled out such ideas. They took the view that British costs and prices would be 'competitive' for export trade: and therefore may have felt that it was irrelevant whether international competition on even terms in the home market really occurred. For whatever reason, their planning was, like the Socialists' and the Federation's, 'Little England' planning. Britain would use x tons of steel; she might export y tons; she would, however, also import a little steel, without however 'undue reliance'. The quantity imported could be curtailed if demand as a whole contracted, exports when demand was exigent: and this would not necessarily be left to natural market forces. Import duties, relatively low now but not insignificant, could be suspended when imports were

[1] *Special Rep.* 1957, p. 27.

'needed', and restored, as happened for most products, but not for sheets in 1958–59, when imports were not 'needed'. Exports would if need be be subject to licensing restrictions. (There were, for example, export quotas for sheets, raised in 1957, lowered in 1958 as motor-car output rose.)[1] Such autarchic devices and approaches were taken for granted. Perhaps it was implicit in the functions of a national supervisory authority that they should be. Perhaps it was regarded as a transitory state. It was never criticised by the Socialists in opposition. All took the principles for granted; they only criticised the execution. Did the Board, and the British firms, put the probable British requirements of steel high enough, and were the Board or the British firms doing or proposing the right things, and enough of them to provide for the probable requirements? The questions acquired an air of inevitability and rightness. The Board's views and actions are set out and analysed in this section *seriatim* in regard to requirements, capacity, home ore, strip mills, and technical advances.

(i) *Changing views of demand.* The Board published two estimates of demand in their first six years, and at the end were engaged on a third. The first two it has been seen reflected the rising *tempo* of industrial activity, especially of investment, in the middle fifties: the third would obviously have to take into account the setbacks of 1958. The Board's first reaction was to think the recession should be disregarded and not influence investment, while they were peering further ahead to the needs of 1970.[2]

The second development report contained the Board's main published work in this field up to summer 1959. They described it as the result of 'a complete review of the probable level of demand in 1962'. This was made in 1955–56 and was published with small adjustments at midsummer 1957.[3] The 'intellectual

---

[1] I.S.B. *Ann. Rep.* 1958, p. 8: 'In 1957 there had been a temporary increase in the quota to offset a temporary recession in home demand.' In 1954–55 the Board had reviewed the desirability of continuing exports of sheet and tinplate because there was a shortage (and sheets and tinplate were being imported): they decided exports must continue to keep goodwill and advised that licences be granted at 'about the present level' (I.S.B. *Dev. Report* 1953–58, p. 18).

[2] *Ann. Rep.* for 1957, p. 19; *Ann. Rep.* for 1958, p. 18.

[3] The *Special Report* of 1957 was published on 24 July 1957.

processes and economic considerations' on which it was based were set out by Sir Robert Shone and Mr H. R. Fisher in the important paper to the Royal Statistical Society referred to earlier.[1] The work was done by the Board in collaboration with Government departments and the Federation, and was an ambitious statistical exercise. Its central assumption was that industrial production would rise between 1954 and 1962 at a rate of $3\frac{3}{4}$ per cent (compound) per year. This would combine the virtues of giving full employment, growth, and solvency for Britain in international interchanges. But it was not just *any* industrial growth that would fill the bill. There were compatibilities to be satisfied. The rise of $3\frac{3}{4}$ per cent depended upon a growth in the working labour force of from $\frac{1}{2}$ to 1 per cent, and a rise in productivity by 3 per cent per year. This would require using a higher proportion of national income for industrial investment than in 1954, and the expansion would require more raw material imports, hence more exports (an increase of 6 per cent a year). These emphases helped to design the pattern of industrial development which was necessary if the central assumption was to be realised. Capital goods industries must expand for home needs, and metal and metal-using industries would have to provide most of the extra exports. The prospective increase in industrial output was examined sector by sector. This brought out still further how much expansion would be concentrated, as they thought and hoped, in sectors where much steel was used: not only in the capital goods industries, but also in certain industries supplying final consumers, the making for example of motor-cars and domestic electric equipment. The results were interpreted in terms of steel requirements which are set out as in Table 99. The figures as first set out appeared in a table boldly entitled 'Use of Finished Steel in 1962'. They were revised in the Royal Statistical Society paper and carried the less flamboyant title used here.

Industry would thus become more 'steel-intensive', and demand for steel would grow faster (4·15 per cent a year), on the assumptions of this estimate, than industrial output in general

[1] *J.R. Stat. Soc.* Part III, 1958, pp. 10 sqq.

(3·75 per cent).[1] The 'elasticity of steel consumption to industrial production', as Shone and Fisher described it (to the discomfort of Sir Charles Goodeve who had the physicist's old-fashioned idea of elasticity) was to be 1·11. This was a notable departure from the basis of the Board's previous estimate, when the so-called elasticity was taken as 0·9. (In the United States the signs were, Shone and Fisher agreed, that there this

Table 99. *Projection of steel consumption*

	1954 estimated consumption (thousand tons)	1962 projected consumption (thousand tons)	Net rate of increase (%)
1. Merchant shipbuilding, ship repair and marine engineering	960	1,105	15·1
2. Coal-mining	638	848	32·9
3. Home railway track and rolling stock	870	790	9·2
4. Fixed investment in dwellings	154	132	−14·1
5. Fixed investment in other new buildings and works	1,300	1,976	52·0
6. Building repair and maintenance	70	90	28·6
7. Other metal-using industries' output:			
(a) Defence	580	563	−2·9
(b), (c) Fixed investment in plant and machinery, road goods vehicles and public road passenger vehicles	1,975	2,926	48·2
(d) Passenger cars for the home market	430	812	88·8
(e) Exports of engineering products	2,450	3,951	61·3
(f) Intermediate supplies and additions to work in progress and stocks of finished goods	1,970	2,491	26·4
(g) Consumer goods for the home market	465	757	62·8
8. Other steel users	580	789	36·0
Total	12,442	17,230	38·5

[1] The 4·15 is the annual rate which compounded makes 38·5. I have again used the revised figures of March 1958. The original figure for the annual rate of increase in home demand for steel was 4·24 per cent.

'elasticity' was appreciably lower—below unity: the pattern of
United States recovery after the recession was to suggest that
it was continuing to drop.)[1] The analysis by sector provided a
basis for projections of the future home demand for the individual finished products.[2]

As to exports, the Board thought world markets would continue to grow significantly, more than the E.C.S.C. thought,
and that since 80 per cent of exports throughout the world still
came from the United Kingdom, United States and the
E.C.S.C., and British costs would remain competitive, a larger
trade could be obtained profitably, provided there was no
dumping. It was 'possible that other naturally cheaper producers would take a larger share' of the market, but 'in the
remote future'. They fancied immediately the prospects of
exports for oil pipe line and for tinplate. They reckoned on a
growth of exports (in ingot equivalent) from 2·9 m. tons in
1954, and 3·3 in 1956, to 5 m. tons in 1962. They illustrated
their insular preoccupation very frankly by stating that 'To a
limited extent the United Kingdom's share in export markets
can be varied without prejudice to the long term maintenance
of exports. To prepare to meet a high export demand is therefore equivalent to introducing some flexibility into the ability
to meet fluctuations in home demand.'[3] Such a policy might
not endear a supplier to his oversea customers. Might not the
Belgians, French and Germans, if not the Americans, do just
the same? For how long did the Board count on relative scarcity
of steel persisting in export markets?

A home consumption of 17·23 m. tons finished (equal on the
Board's conversion factor to 23·48 m. ingot tons) plus 5 m. tons
for export gave a total of 28·48 m. tons—to which 0·33 was

---

[1] An alternative forecast which the same authors set out at some length, using
the familar device of evolving an equation from the historic growth of steel
consumption gave a lower elasticity (unity) and a lower probable consumption.
On this occasion only the years of peak output and high employment were taken
in establishing the trend, which is not an entirely persuasive procedure. It is
surprising what a range of forecasts has been possible using this technique; but
since the authors in this instance by-passed the result it is pointless to examine the
basis of the equation. A comparative study of these trend equations would make
an entertaining exercise.

[2] Below, p. 630.   [3] *Special Rep.* 1957, p. 26.

added for normal annual additions to stocks: the whole, rounded upwards, giving 29 m. tons as the estimated demand for 1962. To this the Board thought a further 1 m. tons should be added for contingencies. 'Unexpected increases in demand have materialised in the past, and some insurance is desirable against scarcities such as those which have hampered manufacturers in the post-war years....' So 'a margin of 3 per cent additional demand' was taken into account on top of an estimate of demand assuming full employment. Quite a good safety margin.[1]

The Board recognised that there was 'much uncertainty' about prospects in particular sectors, but 'in total' they argued 'the uncertainty' of steel demand arises chiefly from that affect-ing the course of the national economy as a whole'. It was as though the whole was not made up of the parts; yet their own argument was that the nature of the parts would determine the 'steel intensiveness' of demand: and manifestly it would affect the general balance and pattern of all industrial activity. It would affect profoundly the demand for particular types of steel. Through 1957–59 prospects in several sectors began to be assessed very differently than in 1955–56. Shipbuilding prospects worsened (how could there be a revival in world demand, it was being asked in 1959, without international restraints in shipping to remove 'surplus' capacity?) Moreover shipbuilding efficiency rose faster outside the United Kingdom. Railway programmes were varied —wagon building, for example, was seriously cut, some main-line electrification delayed. The prospects of expansion in nuclear engineering became clouded. Changed defence programmes and other uncertainties cast a shadow over aircraft manufacture. Coal surpluses changed coal investment plans—notably stopping open-cast mining completely. Oil supplies had grown so fast, and tanker capacity so much exceeded needs, that the markets for tankers and for oil-country exports, which appeared so bright to the Board in 1956, contracted sharply. Would it make any difference to steel requirements in 1962? The buoyant demand for motor-cars, which went ahead of the Board's expectations, could be used to bolster the 'swings and round-

[1] There were unavowed margins in rounding off figures too.

abouts' approach (if one demand disappoints another compensates). The advance in demand for tinplate was less in proportion to the growing use of containers than had been expected—as Shone and Fisher remarked in 1958. The export experience of 1958–59 also seemed to veer away from, and to raise doubts about, the forecast of 1957. Was the Japanese export rising faster than the Board expected? Would the French and Belgian challenge and to a less extent the German, always succeed when markets were not large enough to absorb all that the major steel exporting countries would like to export?

When Sir Robert Shone discussed the Board's forecast (or should it be judgement)[1] early in 1958, with recession pronounced, he stressed the *general* factors that might determine whether demand reached the Board's figures. He was convinced that to make all factors compatible the Government must depress consumption to encourage exports and investment and higher productivity—a traditional British planners' approach.[2] He did not discuss at all whether the collection of investment errors, incompatibilities of another order, which had a profoundly damping effect in 1957–59, could be avoided. Clearly if they could be avoided a given rise in productivity could be obtained in less time with less investment and less interruption of growth. By 1958, moreover, steel industry experience was showing forcibly, what might be supposed to be elementary, that quality as well as quantity of investment counted, and that it varied. Thus the oxygen steel processes saved capital as well as labour and fuel. The leadership of other countries in developing new methods in steel might be a warning—was there sufficient 'intellectual element' not only in steel but in British industrial expansion in general? The withdrawn economist may avoid this issue by saying it is not within his competence to judge or influence: the forecaster (or maker of judgements) cannot choose this escape. The steel industry illustrated early in 1959 another variable in the

[1] As Mr Christopher Saunders insisted it should (*J.R. Stat. Soc.* 1958, Part III, p. 303).

[2] The formula is: if you want *A* you can *only* have it at the expense of *B* and therefore you must reduce or prohibit *B*. The German approach was—you must see you get *A* and let *B* look after itself.

investment situation though Sir Robert Shone would not be expected to foresee this instance a year earlier. A decision was made
to sanction not one but two new strip mills and is examined in
section IV when there was only a demand in prospect at the
time they would both be completed and for some time after
for less than the full capacity of one. This meant that two
costly plants would be provided to work for some years much
below capacity, instead of one a less amount below capacity.
How much capital waste of this kind did the steel requirement
estimate of 1957 envisage?

When the economist statisticians discussed this estimate in
1958 much admiration was expressed for the exercise but
characteristically divergent views on its value and status. For
Dr Barna (who had recently surveyed the extent of German
investment and the growing surplus capacity in British industry)
'although all forecasts are subject to errors the way the reasoning underlying the estimates is set out should help the steel
industry to reach better decisions on its investment policy'. He
would, however, have liked to have had the effects on steel
demand of various economic 'models', based on different
assumptions,[1] and he would have liked more comparison with
Germany and the United States. Mr Schumacher, economist
of the N.C.B., on the contrary, asked 'is it worth while going
to all these lengths of estimating...if I have all these figures
they give me the idea that I know the future'. All concerned
with coal knew by 1958 the vanity of economists' forecasts. He
asked 'what difference does it really make whether we use the
factor 0·8 or 1·0 as the relationship between industrial output
and steel consumption if we really do not know whether
industrial output is going to rise by 3 per cent, 4 per cent, 5 per
cent, or 2 per cent?' In fact of course the choice of the factor

---

[1] Dr Barna among others raised the question whether it would make a difference to the steel intensiveness of industry if increased industrial production
occurred more for the consumption industries and less in capital investment, quoting
United States experience that in the United States it did not. Shone and Fisher
thought that it would matter for the United Kingdom, though possibly not now in
the United States. This problem was discussed with some elaboration in a study of
Long Term Trends and Problems of the European Steel Industry published by the E.C.E.
in 1960.

1·1 instead of 0·9 (the 1954 factor) raised the estimate of requirements in 1962 by about 850,000 ingot tons: but Mr Schumacher's simplified approach would have given a figure only 430,000 tons below the Board's figure—which was not a significant difference and became less so when the Board added a 1 m. ton margin for safety.[1] It was certainly not ridiculous to suppose that some of the changes in particular sectors discernible in 1958 might prove to be more than 'temporary aberrations' from the Board's projection.

Indeed though Dr Barna thought the explanation of the method of the forecast would help the steel industry it is arguable that it was primarily to the Government that Shone and Fisher addressed their message. How far, they were asked, was their emphasis on the steel intensive economy 'a "best guess" of what will in fact happen, how far... a desirable—or perhaps they would say necessary—objective of policy?'[2] To which they replied 'It is certainly more than a guess about the future.... The projection does involve taking a view about what is necessary for an expanding and dynamic British economy.' 'Steel must be provided to support as high a rate of increase in national output and income as seems reasonably likely to be *possible*'[3] (not probable). Prophecy was mixed with preferences.

The steelmakers were naturally more concerned with simple prophecy—the best guess.[4] They thought the Board's figure

[1] Shone and Fisher's reply to Schumacher's criticism (*ibid.* p. 310) appears to miss its point. They show that if they assumed a growth of 3 per cent a year in industrial output and a factor of 0·8 steel consumption would have risen by 2 m. tons by 1962, whereas if they took 5 per cent and a factor of 1·2 it would rise by 8 m. tons. Schumacher obviously was thinking of the difference between 3·75 per cent and a factor 1·0 and 3·75 per cent and a factor 1·1.

[2] The questions were asked by Mr C. T. Saunders, who at the time when the inquiry had been started by Board, Federation and Government was deputy head of the Central Statistical Office, and so associated with the early stages of the work. (*Ibid.* p. 304).   [3] *Ibid.* p. 309.

[4] The only contributor to the discussion who came from the steel industry, Mr E. T. Sara, economist and head of market research of United Steels, said boldly that the right criterion for a steel firm in deciding to put in new plant was its profitability (*ibid.* p. 307). It sounded almost profane in a discussion where the quality of investment was not mentioned. He was rebutting Dr Barna's implication that if anything the Board's figures were too low (cp. below, p. 629).

for 1962 was 1 m. tons too high. The area of difference when
the estimates were being made was in fact narrow. It was
concerned exclusively with the questions—how large would
demand for motor-cars, domestic electric equipment, tin cans
at home and tinplate abroad, be in 1962? By whatever mixture
of chance and good guiding, the one sector of home demand
which in 1957–59 did better than was expected was the one
whose prospects the Board had rated higher than most of the
steelmakers.

(ii) *The missing million.* 'Some forward view has to be taken',
Shone and Fisher argued 'in planning for new plate mills, sheet
mills, blast furnaces, and it seems well to set out these views as
explicitly as possible though events may show they have to be
revised again and again.' The practical object of the Board's
forecast was to see how far capacity projected by the firms was
likely to be sufficient, and the sum had to be done for each
particular finished product, not just for ingots, though lack of
ingots could limit the output of finishing plants, and in general
aggregate finished steel capacity would normally exceed ingot
capacity, though in some plants this might not be so.

Before looking at details it is to be remarked that the Board
aimed at seeing firms committed early in 1957 to a capacity of
29 m. tons, that is capable of supplying the total probable
demand as they saw it in full employment in 1962, but excluding
the million tons for insurance. A million tons would come from
recovered material, imports, and the normal ability of plants to
make more than their recorded capacities. These were normal
sources[1] (or normal potential sources). Rather surprisingly the
Board envisaged imports at a much lower level than had been
usual at times of high demand. Imports had exceeded 1·75 m.
tons in 1952, 1955 and 1956.[2] The figures give the impression of

[1] Thus re-usable material was put formally in the statistics at over 300,000 tons
every year—sometimes much more.

[2] Dr Barna made the surprising statement in the Royal Statistical Society
meeting that 'experience has shown that at the time of a domestic shortage imports
may also be difficult to obtain'. Britain had been able to increase her imports very
satisfactorily in booms since 1950–51. One difficulty had been that users were
unwilling to start buying abroad because prices were higher. Shone and Fisher
pointed out that 'frequently peaks do not occur throughout the world at the same
time'.

people playing very hard for safety. It was no doubt comforting —to go back to the Royal Statistical Society meeting—to hear Sir Charles Goodeve and Dr Barna say how much better it was to have too much than too little capacity, but Shone and Fisher showed they had reservations on this. (Apart from their cautionary remarks the subject was discussed loosely and lightly —not, indeed, even defined.)[1]

That the Board wanted by the beginning of 1957 to see firms committed to plans which would supply 29 m. tons in 1962 arose partly from the fact that it still took an astonishing long time to build new plant in Britain, and for a large new works the Board accepted five years as a minimum period.[2] The Board recognised that the building of plant took longer in the United Kingdom than before the war. They did not point out that it took longer than in other countries. They were solely concerned that plans should take account of the long period of construction. In their reports at any rate they did not suggest that the long period might be reduced.[3]

It is nonetheless interesting that despite the immense divergence between plans and performance in the years from 1946–51, which has been set out above[4] (and although the Board made warning noises about uncertainties) the summation

[1] Dr Barna merely discussed a scarcity of steel which *reduced* industrial output: which may have been the situation in the period 1946–49, and 1951–52. How much scarcity of one product reduces output is always impossible to judge, because the operation of one limit obscures the nearness of the next. The situation which Shone and Fisher referred to, which was more apposite in the later period (however undesirable the amplitude of fluctuations it betokened), was one in which steel might be scarce at the height of a boom. In this situation in which by definition there is no possibility that the highest level of activity will be maintained, it is likely that scarcity of steel will not reduce total output in the long run appreciably, and not where it will have a cumulative effect, but will merely delay a little output. A strong case could clearly be made against providing capacity merely to avoid this.

[2] *Special Rep.* 1957, p. 7.

[3] The long period of construction was a weakness which affected most British major construction projects—coal-mining, for example, and oil refineries, wind tunnels for aircraft testing. By 1957–58 the N.C.B., after insisting for years that the long period was inevitable, was successfully reducing the period to a remarkable extent—by employing first German and later South African mining experts to sink shafts.

[4] Above, pp. 242 sqq.

of plans for 1962 was generally taken so seriously—as though the pattern would be adhered to, and as if there was little scope for variation upward: and this despite the potential impact of oxygen in increasing capacity of existing open-hearth plants (as the use of oil had done notably after 1946), and of more sintering and high top pressure adding to blast furnace outputs, to mention just one or two possible sources.

Table 100. *Finished steel; summary of production and demand (thousand tons)*

Product	Production 1956[a]	Estimated demand 1962[a]	Estimated production 1962[a, b]	1962 Surplus (+) deficit (−)
Plate	2659	3800	4200	+400
Heavy rails, fishplates, soleplates and sleepers	614	730	700	− 30
Heavy rolled products	2621	3295	3175	−120
Wire rods and bars in coil	1218	1685	1555	−130
Hot rolled strip	1284	1860	1850	− 10
Light sections and bars	2983	3215	3380	+165
Cold rolled strip	412	600	645	+ 45
Bright bars	485	585	640	+ 55
Sheet	2216	3345	3065[c]	−280
Tinplate, terneplate and black-plate	918	1535	1400[d]	−135
Tubes, pipes and fittings	1439	2140	2000	−140
Heavy forgings, tyres, wheels and axles	522	470	610	+140
Steel castings	331	350	330	− 20
High-speed tool and magnet steel	54	55	55	Nil

[a] Gross figures, i.e. including the material required for further conversion into other products shown in this table.
[b] Production estimates for products derived wholly or partly from billets assume that the billet deficit is somehow made good.
[c] Including production from hand and mechanised mills.
[d] Including production from hand mills.

The Board's summary of the balance of supply and demand for steel in 1962, assuming both their estimate of demand and the completion of all the expansion schemes which they had sanctioned, is set out in Table 100.

The most striking figures in the table were the projected

excess capacity for plates and the deficiency of capacity for sheets and tinplate. The Board remarked that the surpluses and deficits in their table 'will partly cancel out', because most steelworks 'have a surplus of finishing equipment' which gave flexibility.[1] The excess of plates was still, in mid-1957, envisaged as remote: 'it is likely plates will be scarce until the new mills[2] come into production.' This showed no inkling that there might be idle shifts for plate mills in 1958–59. Only the prospective deficit in sheets and tinplate worried the Board. It did so because the supply as projected for 1962, inadequate as it was, included 300,000 tons of tinplate from obsolete mills, mostly hand mills which should already have been out of use. Hence there was not only a prospective deficit, as they saw it, of over 400,000 tons to provide for—there was obsolete capacity to replace, and hence room for at least 900,000 tons of new capacity, which 'would be fully adequate as the initial load' of another strip mill (whose full capacity would necessarily be much higher). This, however, no firm according to the Board, wished to provide by 1962. And this meant that the proposals of the firms so far *approved* by the Board would provide capacity not for 29 m. tons of ingots but only for 28 m. tons. (One wonders by what processes of rounding and persuasion the total of 28 m. tons was reached). However the Board was holding in suspense judgement on a proposal by Richard Thomas to put up a new integrated plant to make semi-products at Newport. It was understood these would include semis for Whitehead's, and possibly slabs for Ebbw Vale. This plant might be enlarged to include a strip mill later. But the proposal under discussion 'might be accompanied by the closing of obsolete capacity elsewhere'—which meant no doubt some of the old Welsh open-hearth plants. The Board wanted a commitment on a strip mill at Newport—but not on a billet mill, which was reserved for home ore. Yet it cannot be assumed, as the sequel showed, that a proposal for a strip mill would have been immediately approved. There were other small expansion schemes in the offing and if the Board had said 'yes' to Newport the firms' proposals would have come close to 29 m. tons, but not in the

[1] *Special Rep.* 1957, p. 7. [2] Above, p. 558.

pattern of finished steel output the Board favoured. The missing million was really just the missing strip mill.

The discussion over Newport showed that the Board were not perfunctory over firms' proposals. It showed too that their examining procedure might be a source of delay. But there is no guide to the normal procedure. Did the Board try to concentrate production in fewer and larger plants? How far this concentration did not *happen* and was *not* envisaged has been seen already.[1] Did they try to discourage expansion at high cost sites—except where obsolescence put plants beyond saving (as with hand tinplate mills)? Between 1955 and 1957 they approved developments likely to result in higher output in a great number of the small scattered firms.[2] They made no suggestion that this was a policy of transition. 'The present proportions of really unsatisfactory plant are not high', they wrote, though 'the absolute as opposed to the relative amount of poor capacity is not negligible....' Of the few works receiving 'various forms of indirect subsidy' they said 'ultimately such works must be sufficiently improved to be self supporting, or they must be closed. Some are so badly located that they would not be worth improving.'[3] This is not language to suggest that radical changes in the number or siting of plants were needed. It is not on record that any development in an old site was discouraged to leave room for development where ore was most cheaply imported or where coal was cheap or on home ore sites (though it was recognised that old sites might be obsolete and more home ore production was desirable, and a new works on home ore *might* partly replace some existing ones). It is hard to avoid the impression that the elaboration of the projection of demand was not reflected in an equal degree of sophistication in the planning of what was to be done. The emphasis on sheets and tinplate, moreover, might reasonably have emerged without the elaborate exercise in projecting demand, because it

[1] Above pp. 552 sqq.
[2] For example, to take small and not medium plants, Park Gate, Round Oak, Briton Ferry, Patent Shaft, Bynea Steel, Shelton, Barrow, Millom, Neath Steel, Brymbo.
[3] *Special Rep.* 1957, p. 67.

rested primarily on a judgement or guess about the probable output of motor-cars and domestic electric appliances. A trend towards a greater use of flat products had appeared to be firmly established since the war; scarcity had led to substantial imports of sheets (and even tinplate) and of hot rolled coils for several years—just as it had of plates. The areas in regard to which doubts whether enough was being done were reasonable, were not obscure and could be identified without profound observation.

How far pressure by the Board had led plate-makers to decide on the programme which has been sketched earlier is not evident; but by the time the *Special Report* was issued the Board's criteria were more than satisfied. The spotlight fell thus on sheets: and what happened over the strip mill is the most illuminating passage in the subsequent history of the Board. As a prelude to discussing it it is convenient to sketch the Board's attitude on home ore.

(iii) *The Board and home ore.* The Board, in their first Development Report, 'regarded the development of home ore as one of the crucial matters in the future' of the British industry. They saw the light, it seemed, almost at once. The cost figures as even Federation documents had shown were indeed overwhelming. But they had not led the Federation overtly to the conclusion apprehended quickly by the Board, and the Federation case which seemed to disparage the idea of using more home ore and to make it appear immaterial whether or when it happened proved surprisingly seductive. The Board did not discuss reasons, and in their brief treatment of the subject in this first report the resistances with which they were confronted, and which may have accounted for the Federation's attitude, stood starkly out. The ore producers said expansion might mean more underground mining, higher costs, labour difficulties and, the classic objection, more new houses.

The Board, therefore, called in as consultants a geologist and a mining engineer. Their reports were most encouraging. The great extent of reserves, over which doubts had been skilfully cast, was again established. Over 2000 m. tons 'proved' and 'probable', nearly 1000 m. tons 'possible'. Increased supplies could be obtained, the consultants said, above the $17\frac{1}{2}$ m. tons planned (but not obtained) for 1958 'without excessive cost'.[1] The distribution of the reserves is given in Table 101. The Board found themselves justified therefore in pressing for expansion. No plant, they said, needed an ore reserve giving it more than a 60–70-year life. On this basis if all of 3000 m. tons of ore could be worked an annual output of 40 m. tons would allow this criterion to be satisfied, even if all sites good

Table 101. *Iron ore reserves in the United Kingdom*

| | | Principal orefields | | | | | | |
| | | Northamptonshire Sands | | Oxford-shire and S.W. North-ampton-shire | Leicester-shire and S. Lin-coln Marl- | | | |
	Froding-ham	N. of river Welland	S. of river Welland	Marlstone	stone	Minor orefields	Totals	Units
'Proved and 'Prob-able' reserves in 1954 as reported to I.S. Board	860	490	370	270	36	Uncer-tain	—	Millio tons
1956 extraction	4·49	2·82	4·88	1·93	0·95	1·18	16·25	Millio tons
Expected extraction rate 1962	6·4	4·3	6·3	2·5	1·4	1·1	22·0	Millio tons
Approx. expectation of life after 1962 at 1962 rate of extrac-tion (years)	130	110	50	100	20	—	—	Years
Possible 'reserves as reported to I.S. Board' (not taken into account in above calculations)	530	150	150	110	30	—	—	Millio tons

[1] It is interesting to compare this with the fears expressed by an Oxford economist about the time when the Board made the sensible decision to find out. Mr G. R. Denton, in a contribution to *Oxford Economic Papers* (vol. VII, no. 3, Oct. 1955), p. 280, on 'Investment and Location in the Steel Industry; Corby', wrote 'the estimates—such as they are [this was *before* the figures given in Table 101 were available]—of the extent of the Northamptonshire ores...do not suggest that the long term advantages may be such as to warrant the more ambitious schemes for expansion sometimes proposed' (the only one specifically proposed had been for one more works)...'the ores cautiously described as "possibly workable" far outweighed the "known workable ore"' (for the reason that borings had not been taken: but Mr Denton seems to imply the hopes were obviously likely to be mis-placed)...'The Lincolnshire field, developed sooner...is expected to be exhausted earlier.' Despite his disparaging tone Mr Denton seemed prepared to visualise a use of a further 8·6 m. tons of *Northamptonshire* ore a year—which would provide the basis for a supply of between 2 and 3 m. tons of finished steel a year. The present writer had never met anyone whose ambitions, on current knowledge, for Northamptonshire alone exceeded this.

for the use of home ore were deemed quite unsuitable for using
imported ore—which was not so. There was always a possibility
that at the end of seventy years lower grade ores than were
deemed commercially usable in 1957 would have become usable,
but this did not need to be brought into the discussion, though
the alert minded participants were alive to it. The Board did
not state a case for a 40 m. ton annual output, but they pressed
the companies to plan an output of 22 m. tons for 1962 (the
companies would have preferred 20 m. tons) and they said a
'substantially higher figure' should be aimed at. Expansion
should occur in Oxfordshire, the Northamptonshire Sands, and
the Frodingham field. They had persuaded Stewarts and
Lloyds and United Steels, the two largest companies, to
collaborate in surveying the ore field north of the river Welland
'which has not yet been test bored'. They hoped these companies would exploit this field as soon as possible after 1962—
to provide ore for new steel capacity of their own use or for some
other steelmaker.

Early in 1959 Mr A. G. Stewart, chairman of Stewarts and
Lloyds, stated that his firm were negotiating with forty-four
landowners to bore over an area of 24,000 acres: they had
already sunk 100 bore-holes. It would be 'some time before it
is possible to arrive at any conclusions'.[1] They were planning also
to expand the output of the Oxfordshire Ironstone Company
near Banbury—on which the new steel works projected in 1946
was to have been sited—because a 'substantial increase in the
demand in this field' was indicated in a few years' time. It was,
so one gathered, to be taken to Newport. In general his company
were 'still planning to increase our ironstone capacity within
the next few years', but some of it 'may not be required quite
so quickly as was previously anticipated'. Demand for foundry
iron had fallen even more than for basic iron for steel. Because
of difficult conditions the pace of development of their underground mining in Rutland 'was relatively slow'. Possibly this
was not embarrassing because their investment plans as a whole
had been based on an 'expectation of a more rapid expansion
than has taken place or seems likely in the immediate future'—

---

[1] Annual Report, in *The Times*, 16 Jan. 1959.

and the firm had 'rephased the rate at which some schemes are progressing', to an extent which would reduce investment by £6 m. in the then current financial year (1958–59).[1]

The dynamics of the development of ore mining showed clearly through this. The company expanded its ore mining in response mainly to its own needs, the needs of its steel tube production and its foundry iron production, though also for other specific needs—such as the expanding use visualised at Newport by Richard Thomas and Baldwins. The company's total investment programme was large, and the money was not easily got (partly at least because of the nationalisation threat). To invest knowingly some time ahead of need was deprecated. Quicker expansion of ore mining was difficult because of legal and institutional problems, and in the case of underground mining because of lack of experience. Obviously it would have been easier to move faster if a start had been made earlier—with exploration, and with deep mining (if such was to be needed). But the company's own interests did not require this, and it had not got a lot of unemployed capital resources. Its business was making tubes, not mining ore.

The same was the situation of the United Steel Companies. They had developed underground mining impressively, with what seemed attractively low costs[2]—it was a relatively new technique in the United Kingdom (though normal in Lorraine) for which new machines and plant was developed by the company.[3] But the mining was subsidiary to the steelmaking, and the company 'with its foot in many products and many regions' had many outlets for investment which did not call for home ore at all, or for which it was of small importance. The Appleby Frodingham steelworks had grown much (and its technical

---

[1] Capital expenditure had been £16 m. in 1957–58: it expected to be the same in 1958–59. The replanning kept it, that is, at the level of the previous year.

[2] But they were cautious—the next mine might have higher costs, they said.

[3] The techniques visualised leaving a considerable amount of ore behind in pillars and to provide a roof: this added to the advantage of open-cast working. Modern drag-lines make open-cast working to much greater depths possible and economic. (The most impressive depths are in coal working. Coal, however, though in thinner seams than the East Midland ore, is more valuable.) The development of economic underground mining methods which leave less ore behind was clearly desirable.

development as seen earlier was distinguished) but the prospects for its outputs of heavy plates and sections, and of pig iron for Steel Peach and Tozer, did not appear to call for a high rate of expansion of ore mining.

It was probably the same with the other mining companies—most of them also owned by users,[1] though not on a scale comparable with the holdings of Stewarts and Lloyds and United Steel. None of the users had an obviously overwhelming reason within their own tradition for radical expansion of their mining. The foundry iron producers had falling demands or aging plants or both.[2] The steel firms had their steelmaking either entirely remote from the orefield, which reduced, often very greatly, the advantage of using the ore, or they had scattered interests, with their main focus of interest in those of their works which were not on the ore: as Richard Thomas and Baldwins and Guest, Keen Nettlefolds in South Wales. It had been seen that the financial attraction of using these ores had been lessened consistently by the pricing arrangements.

The problem facing the Board, therefore, in urging the use of more ore, on the orefield, was the one which had dogged the earlier projects. Who would take the initiative? Where was the organism, to revert to an earlier phrase, in which the germ of rapid growth would be nurtured? Would the firms whose raw material costs were necessarily highest be interested, as the Steel Company of Scotland was in the early days of Appleby?[3] What product or products would be made if a new plant, or a major expansion, occurred in or near the orefields? In the past the only positive proposal, made in the first plan and repeated later, had been that a new plant should make soft billets to sell to re-rollers, a product for which no one was likely to want to build a new plant because the margins were always unattractive, partly because of the bias of price control, but also because it gives little scope for the specialisations which give better

[1] Staveley, Sheepbridge, Dorman Long, South Durham, R.T.B., G.K.N. (including Lysaghts)
[2] The I.S. Board assumed there would be a contraction of this business—the old foundry iron furnaces would not all be replaced as such. Some had made basic pig iron for the Welsh open-hearth plants which were obsolete.
[3] *E.H.S.* pp. 275, 338.

margins. It was plain that in general re-rolling and billet-making were better integrated. The proposal savoured of the proposals made by the Federation about the projected steel-works for Jarrow in 1936–37: it might make those products which had the least attractive prices. The new Board was not specific, but in the 1955 report in discussing new billet mills the Board did remark that the location of such a mill 'may be influenced by the outcome of the review of home ore development'. Historically the route would have been for one or more re-rollers to form a large enough group to build the billet mill (the last major instance of this happening was Corby), but the scale of the operation, and possibly also the price policy, ruled this out. Product-wise the obvious opening was for a home ore works to make wide strip. A new strip mill was needed—at once or within a few years. There was no production of sheets by new methods in the East Midlands or on the East Coast at all. No one now pretended that the home ores were unsuitable for sheet, though some occasionally still said they were more easily used for other products. There was even one firm, Richard Thomas and Baldwins, with two feet in the home ore fields[1] who made sheets and wanted to make more. But they were strongly drawn to South Wales[2] (where, indeed, perhaps under pressure from the Board, they would use some home ore).

The Board by implication suggested that any major new use of home ore should be somewhere on one of the orefields, but the question was not discussed. Manifestly when very cheap ore was taken to the coast it might still be cheaper to use than imported ore, and it could be particularly advantageous for the firm concerned when used to make a self fluxing burden for a blast furnace. For a planning body which was considering the best way in which the ore might be used this was not necessarily conclusive. Was it a good thing to take cheap Midlands ore an expensive rail journey to be smelted with relatively

---

[1] A steelworks and ore mines at Scunthorpe, ore mines at Irthlingborough.

[2] The possibilities of their Scunthorpe plant for an oxygen Bessemer plant and a strip mill were examined, but the site was not suitable. Other sites were, however, available.

dear coal, so that it might be made into sheet which would be transported back to be used in the Midlands? Near the orefield fuel was cheaper—or could be.[1] If there had been a free market in ore and no subsidies in coal prices the relative costs would have been more obvious. The price mechanism would have given a guide, if it did nothing else. As it was this did not happen. However the Board implicitly assumed local use of ore was cheapest: and it also seemed to imply that a new works on a new location was desirable. This remained, however, in dispute, though there was little or no open discussion. One of the Federation's most respected technical advisers was saying early in 1959 that there should be *no* new sites at all—existing works should be expanded, as the Germans were doing, up to a minimum of 3 m. tons capacity. (And the next strip mill, he added, should be at Scunthorpe.) The Board's analyses made no concessions to such ambitions. They were, after all, waiting for more information: and it was hard for them to put the case for 3 m. ton plants when they were assessing so many lesser units as in the top class.

(iv) *The Government, the Board and the strip mills.* In their first Development Report the Board said that 'it is reasonable to conclude that additional strip mill capacity will be required in the near future'[2]—because of growing demand (especially for motor cars and containers) and the obsolescence of the hand mills, which still supplied over 700,000 tons a year. The problem was not one, they said, which could be resolved quickly, because the width of the new mill, its location and capacity had all to be carefully considered. From early in 1955 the case for the new strip mill, and the claims of rival sites, were increasingly discussed in public, and examined—with greater caution—in the industry.

Richard Thomas and Baldwins—now virtually Richard Thomas again—naturally had a particular interest in this after

[1] The coal was much cheaper; but methods of using some of the cheaper coal to make metallurgical coke had still to be developed. There was no doubt that this could be done. There were supplies of good (not the best) coking coal in North Staffordshire which will be mined efficiently and more cheaply than in South Wales.

[2] I.S.B. *Dev. I.S. Ind.* 1953–58 (Feb. 1955), p. 18.

the termination of the joint administration of Richard Thomas Baldwins and the Steel Co. of Wales in 1955, and the sale of the Steel Co. of Wales by the agency as a wholly separate company. This in a sense undid for Richard Thomas the benefits they were to derive from the amalgamation with Baldwins in 1944; and it left them owners of much of the obsolete capacity without sufficient counterbalance. They had the possibility of developing their Scunthorpe plant, using oxygen blown converters, looked at: but the site was not adequate. By the end of 1956 they had laid their plans and submitted them to the Board.[1] As the Board reported them in 1957[2] they included a new integrated works at Newport which would make semi-products. 'In certain circumstances this might be accompanied by the closing of obsolete capacity elsewhere.' While it might be that the new works would at some stage be enlarged to include a continuous hot strip mill and the complementary finishing equipment, 'it has not been decided when or where this development should take place'. It would be hard to improve on this for ambiguity.

Elsewhere in the report the Board stated (as seen earlier) that they thought plans for a new strip mill should be in the current development programme, whereas the industry thought the mill would be wanted rather later. Were they now saying that Richard Thomas and Baldwins wanted to build a strip mill at Newport, or that Richard Thomas and Baldwins were uncertain *if* they would build a strip mill there, or certain that they would but not *when*: or were they saying that Richard Thomas and Baldwins wanted to build a strip mill at Newport but the Board were not yet convinced it was the best site? When the Board said the *industry* thought the Board exaggerated the demand for sheets and tinplate in 1962, did the industry include Richard Thomas and Baldwins?

Possibly the answer is 'no'—there were from time to time signs that the firm's view and the Federation's view diverged, indications too that the Agency, whose approval would be

---

[1] Sir Ernest Lever referred to this in his annual statement at the Annual General Meeting reported in *The Times*, 22 Jan. 1957.
[2] Above, p. 631.

needed by the firm since it remained nationalised, needed some persuading in the early days.[1] To make semi-products was certainly never the sole object of the Newport project: though Whiteheads' obviously provided a big local outlet for billets, and Richard Thomas and Baldwins were already supplying billets from some of their obsolete West Wales works. They submitted a scheme for an integrated works at Newport with a continuous strip mill but no billet mill to the Board in the spring of 1958, thus committing themselves fully to what they had always intended to do. Despite all the urgent pressures exerted by the Board in spring 1957 the scheme now submitted was not immediately approved by the Board. Newport was well placed for sending ingots (or slabs, if there were the right primary mill) to Ebbw Vale where there was not enough room for iron and steelmaking on a scale adequate to load the continuous strip mill fully. The unsuitability of the Ebbw Vale site, whose choice had solved political difficulties in 1935, grew progressively public. Newport was a better site clearly for a strip mill than the existing Welsh strip mill sites. Iron ore would come in much larger ships than to Port Talbot—in ships of up to 30,000 tons—and it would not have the uphill train journey to Ebbw Vale, though it would be used 4 miles inland. It was nearer than Port Talbot to home ore, if any of this was to be used. It was nearer than Port Talbot to the home market, and should prove better for export since there was a general export business from Newport, which the local authority was working hard to build up, though most ships which picked up at Newport also called elsewhere—often at Liverpool. If more Midland exports did in the end go out through Welsh ports however, Newport was the best of the Welsh ports for them.[2]

That the Board should hesitate before the Newport scheme is not surprising, for Newport did not have to be a remarkable site to be better than Port Talbot or Ebbw Vale. Were there still greater advantages elsewhere? Three sites had the strong

[1] These were personal impressions. To commit Richard Thomas and Baldwins to financing an integrated strip mill may have seemed to make resale to private owners more difficult.

[2] Since Ebbw Vale would export via Newport, a works at Newport clearly had the advantage over Ebbw Vale as well as over Port Talbot in this.

support of pressure groups ouside the industry[1]—Kidwelly in
West Wales, Swansea, and Grangemouth in Scotland. Kidwelly
and Swansea were clearly less well placed than Newport for ore
markets and probably coal: their sole claim was nearness to
obsolete steel plants of the Llanelly area. Grangemouth was
Steven Hardie's favourite site in the days of the nationalised
corporation,[2] and it had the support of the Scottish Council.
To make sheets in Scotland it was said would provide the basis
on which sheet-using industries would grow. There were, however, three formidable drawbacks. A works on this site might
import Swedish ores relatively cheaply, but had no access to
any cheap home ore. Coking coal reserves were small in
Scotland, and Scots coal was dearer than in any other major
division. There was little local demand, and the site was remote
from all the major markets, and not well placed for exports.
The zealots were not daunted. If there were too little coal why
not bring some in from South Wales? But only political forces
could keep this project alive. There was a fourth proposition,
the one Sir William Firth once had in mind, to build a strip
mill at Immingham. This was, economically, the serious alternative to Newport among schemes proposed and examined.
There were three good possible sites. This project was supported
by no pressure group (though there were local interests who
hoped it would succeed). It was not sponsored by a firm. And
as a politician involved prominently in the struggle remarked,
'There is no Minister for England'. Immingham was not a
centre of unemployment, nor was it near one. The proposal to
build there was sometimes treated as though it was a plan to
use home ore, and contrasted with Newport as an imported ore
project, but this was wrong.

The prolonged discussions, or wrangles, over these alternative
sites were private: much necessarily remains unknown or
uncertain and what is more important is undocumented.
When a year had passed after the appearance of the Develop-

---

[1] 'The question...had excited considerable public attention, and representations were made to the Government and to the Board by a number of Members of
Parliament, local Authorities, and other public bodies in favour of siting the capacity
in various parts of the country (I.S.B. *Ann. Rep.* 1958, p. 20).

[2] Above, p. 312.

ment Report the Board in their annual report for 1957 reaffirmed their faith in the necessity to build a strip mill—but it could not now be 'constructed and in operation until a year or two' after 1962. The magnitude of such capacity raised 'questions with which the Government are particularly concerned in relation to its location and the social questions arising therefrom, its impact on the general policy for capital investment, and the possibility of special arrangement for financing its construction[1]? More forcefully the Board in its annual report for 1958 said that they had informed the Government that 'in the prevailing circumstances' (presumably the threat of nationalisation) the Government would have to assist in financing the project.[2] The way in which the Government interpreted its function in regard to industrial changes for greater efficiency which might cause local pockets of unemployment—it was inclined to stop such changes —plus this financial problem took the final decision outside the Board's hands. It became well known that the strip mill site was a 'cabinet' issue with certain Ministers strongly representing their departmental 'local' interests.

In the sorting out of the projects listed above the Board came down in favour of Newport. 'It was a near thing' between Newport and Immingham, according to one participant. An expert adviser, exaggerating, said the deciding factor was the cost of getting water at Immingham. Other comments by participants, which were contradictory but not the less vigorously expressed for that reason, were that whenever the case seemed to move in favour of Immingham new figures appeared to correct the swing—and that there never was any doubt that Newport had the advantage. There were indeed civil servants who spoke as though they were dealing with facts, not guesses.

The Scots would not accept defeat—even though Colvilles new chairman, Sir Andrew McCance, who succeeded John Craig at the end of 1956, publicly indicated his opposition to the plan for a new integrated plant and continuous strip mill at

---

[1] *Ann. Rep.* 1957, p. 21. This report was dated 27 June 1958. The report having set out the Government's interest said nothing about the Newport proposal though it had entered a new phase.

[2] *Ann. Rep.* 1958, p. 20.

Grangemouth and quoted the N.C.B. as saying that as it was Scotland would be 100,000 tons short of its needs of coking coal for blast furnaces by 1960.[1] The decision in favour of Newport against Immingham, with Grangemouth not in the running, did not sway the Government. And at some stage in the prolonged interchanges, to the outside world it seemed a late stage, a new project was put forward. And it was Colvilles who enabled the Scots, their pressure groups and their Minister, to make a new bid, and enabled the Government triumphantly to find a way of half satisfying both the Celtic clamours. To a diligent reader of company meetings the proposal was not entirely unheralded. In February 1957 Sir Andrew McCance's annual statement as Chairman[2] remarked that Smith and McLeans, Colvilles sheet department, had had a satisfactory year—'the demand for sheets and light plates has continued good, and the steadiness of employment is helped by the fact that these works produce sizes and qualities not readily procurable—if procurable at all—anywhere else'. But clearly all was not well. About this time Dorman Longs decided to close their sheet works (the Bowesfield works). At Colvilles 'the board recognises the changes which have taken place in the modern methods of steel sheet production'—who could fail to by 1957?—and were 'giving their serious attention to the methods suitable for the type and qualities of product for which this company has established its reputation'. What they proposed in summer or autumn 1958 (or as the Prime Minister put it 'what the board of Colvilles has agreed in principle to undertake'—which suggested some outside prompting) was that a semi-continuous strip mill making at first about 500,000 million tons should be built as part of the complex centred on the new Ravenscraig plant and using slabs from the new slabbing mill to be built there. Far from being peculiarly adapted to sheets of kinds hardly procurable elsewhere what was proposed was a modern style mill not of the largest capacity but of the type used all over the world in places where large markets could not be hoped for, to make sheets of the normal type and quality.

[1] *Glasgow Herald*, 23 July 1957.
[2] *The Times*, 8 Feb. 1958.

Sir Andrew McCance with his plan was *deus ex machina*. On 18 November 1958 Mr Macmillan broke to the House of Commons the dramatic news that there would be not one strip mill only but two, one in Wales—at Newport—one in Scotland, linked to Ravenscraig (which had been built it has been seen to sustain the old sites of Dalzell and Lanarkshire Steel, a step whose economic justification remained highly uncertain).[1] The Government would provide finance for both to the extent that firms could not provide it from their own resources. 'From my point of view, 'Mr Macmillan said,[2] 'the chief problem which had to be discussed was location rather than the size of plant'— as though the two questions could be discussed in isolation. Had the Board persuaded themselves that this was so or were they persuaded? 'The decision of the Iron and Steel Board... was that it would be a good plan to have these two installations both capable of considerable expansion': Mr Macmillan put the responsibility on the Board. 'That has made it possible to make a solution which while no doubt not acceptable to everybody seems a fair and reasonable solution of a rather difficult locational problem.' When one Scots member averred that 'the Board put its advice in the form of having a single integrated unit' the Prime Minister did not demur, he said: 'Had the technical arguments proved insuperable and it was absolutely necessary to have one giant plant I honestly don't think that would have proved to the benefit of Scotland.' 'This is a matter of judgement, perhaps a little like that of King Solomon.' No member saw fit to recall that Solomon acted with a full understanding that if his judgement were carried out it would kill the child.

Who could say now that the Government or steelmakers were not expansionist? There was, certainly, indignation in Scotland among the zealots that, out of this judgement of Solomon, they would get rather less than half the baby.[3] But they objected to

---

[1] I found English steelmakers whose opinion I sought thought a Clyde site would have been better, and the siting of the new ore dock was described by one as 'a disaster—but much was paid for by the Harbour authorities, not by Colvilles'.

[2] *Hansard*, 18 Nov. 1958, c. 1015–20.

[3] Mr Macmillan in his replies in Parliament said however that many Scots members and others who came to see him on the matter agreed that what Scotland was getting was much better than if the whole was in Wales.

this solely on Scottish grounds. Nor did the Labour opposition see anything to object to in what was to be done. Mr Gaitskell welcomed the decision and tried to raise other issues. In a pamphlet, *Steel and the Nation*, written two months later after they had had time to think—people said the author was Professor Marquand—they remarked that 'the necessary additional capacity is to be built in Monmouthshire and Scotland'. No comment was made on the substance of the decision—it was *necessary*: the only trouble was it was so late: 'can anyone now believe it' (i.e. the capacity) will be producing in 1962?'[1]

Nor did the Board when they presented their account of the events—in the *Annual Report* for 1958[2]—betray any sense of inadequacy in the decision. People had suggested that the Government had by-passed the Board and made their decision without consulting the Board. This was clearly untrue. But the Board's version of what happened suggested that the initiative remained in their hand to an extent that was hard to reconcile with other if less documented evidence. This report is indeed a classic in the art of official history. Referring to their examination of schemes they remarked that neither Grangemouth, Immingham or Swansea 'appeared to have the same net advantage on all counts as Newport or Ravenscraig'. Did these two have the same 'net advantages on all counts'? 'The Board's examination of the proposals of Richard Thomas and Baldwins Ltd and Colvilles Ltd was sufficiently advanced to enable the Board during the course of the year' (what a splendid sense of leisurely but ordered progress!) 'to consult with the Government about those aspects which concerned the Government and so to reach the conclusion that the proposals could be accepted in principle subject to consideration of detailed particulars when these were submitted to the Board.' One might suppose the Board's views on both the schemes had had an equal time to mature. Details of the Newport proposals, much the more complex, presumably a revision of those submitted a year earlier, were presented at the beginning of 1959 and received the Board's consent: Colvilles (little wonder) were

---

[1] *Steel and the Nation*, p. 13. [2] Pp. 20 sqq.

not presented till April 1959: 'the *essential parts*...have received (June 1959) the Board's consent'.

As a prelude to this account the Board set out the results of their latest survey of the market for sheets, tinplates, and light plates. 'The conclusion reached was that by *1965* there was likely to be a need for at least three quarters of a million tons of additional capacity, and the Minister of Power was informed accordingly.'[1] This was a far cry from the judgement of 1957, when the new capacity for sheets and tinplate required in *1962* was to be 915,000 tons. 'A continuous hot strip mill,' the Board then said, 'is so large a unit of plant that it could not be operated at a low rate of output. It is difficult to say what the lowest economic rate would be, but there is no doubt that 900,000 tons a year (of finished product) would be fully adequate as an initial load. The output would be expected to rise to two millions or more in the course of some years, the ultimate output depending on the size of mill adopted.'[2]

How was it in 1958 that with a smaller increase of demand foreseen, more remote in time, two mills would be able to operate at an economic rate? The secret—so the report and Mr Macmillan implied—lay in the use of semi-continuous mills. 'Experience overseas with this type of mill, as well as technical opinion in this country shows that it is better adapted and more economical than a continuous mill for rolling outputs up to at least two million ingot tons a year, and that it can be laid out in such a manner as to enable it if necessary to be converted later at a reasonable cost to a fully continuous unit capable of a much larger tonnage.'[3] Experience abroad on the Continent had shown too—but this was not mentioned—how important it was if costs were to be low to load even semi-continuous mills fully—even in 1953 the minimum capacity of such a mill run on American lines for relatively narrow sheet (44 in.) was given by the E.C.E. as 900,000 tons.[4] By 1959 speeds of working were greater, and the Board's own statement implied that the

---

[1] *Ann. Rep.* 1958, p. 19. [2] *Spec. Rep.* 1957, p. 59.
[3] *Ann. Rep.* 1958, p. 20.
[4] E.C.E. Report on *The European Steel Industry and the Wide Strip Mill* (Geneva, 1953), pp. 18–20, and chapter IV.

output of a *wide* semi-continuous mill—making, say, strip 80–90 in. wide—would be two million tons a year. Of the two mills Colvilles was at first to make about 500,000 tons a year with an ultimate capacity of at least 1 m. tons in sheets and light plate: Richard Thomas and Baldwins plant was to make 500,000 tons of sheets and tinplate (Macmillan) or (according to the Board) 'to enable the Company to produce at least an additional 600,000 tons of strip mill products' as well as slabs for Ebbw Vale. (The billet plan was now not mentioned.) These *could* with an effort be reconciled with the 1965 additional requirement 750,000 tons:[1] half of Colvilles' output would be in light plate, and would replace light plate which formerly would have been made in other existing or planned plant[2] and Richard Thomas and Baldwins could run a little below what the firm was 'enabled' to do. But at the best the implication was that Colvilles *mill* (in its fourth year of working)[3] would run at half capacity and Richard Thomas and Baldwins (in its third)[4] no better and probably much worse. Certainly each would be less well loaded than if there *were* one only. The Board denied this—apart from the light plate made at Colvilles they said the strip mill there 'will be used for the manufacture of sheet to the extent of the market demand', and so 'does not have any significant effect on the initial scale of development at Newport'. But this could only be true, even on the published data, if the steel capacity provided was wholly inadequate for the mills.[5] It was impossible to find in any of the forecasts of demand (though these might all prove wrong) justification for the view that expansion was likely to keep one new strip mill fully employed and another partially employed by 1965.

The Scottish mill was intended to attract to Scotland, as all concerned said, industries using steel sheets and strip. No one could argue, therefore, that it would not slow down the

[1] Above, p. 647.   [2] I.S.B. *Ann. Rep.* 1958, p. 21.
[3] It was to 'start operating in 1962'.
[4] It was to work partially in 1963.
[5] The new mills might be more heavily occupied than the Board's figures allowed at the expense of the other strip mills, but this is not relevant in this 'planning' context. They might be more fully employed because demand grew more.

expansion of the market for Newport—whatever its effect on the *initial* load. The Board of Trade would have a new argument in persuading firms who wished to expand who used steel sheet—motor-car makers, and makers of domestic electric equipment, possibly—to make their extensions in Scotland. A new round of expansion in such industries was expected in 1960–61. There was no reason to suppose that expansion of industries of this kind in the United Kingdom could be greater because some strip was made in Scotland: indeed since it would raise costs and prices all round the reverse was more possible.

A year later the market was viewed more favourably. Colvilles and Richard Thomas and Baldwins both expected higher initial outputs. For Colvilles sheets were seen as a welcome diversification when shipbuilding fell off. By autumn 1959 Richard Thomas and Baldwins were planning to make the Newport plant ultimately a 6-m. ton plant, and obtained approval for a *continuous* hot strip mill—whose capacity would be over 4 m. tons of sheet a year. The Steel Company of Wales, opposed in the past to plans for new strip mills which it thought premature, now sought permission itself to build a hot strip mill, but the Board demurred. The threat to prolong the under employment of the now larger Newport mill caused irritation—but it was arranged that the Steel Company of Wales should make more slabs which (for five years) would be re-rolled in the Newport hot mill and finished in the Steel Company of Wales' own plants—rather like the Hoesch-Hörde arrangement.

The decision after all to install a fully continuous hot mill at Newport, the first, frustrated, intention, was instructive. According to United Engineering, the largest makers, a semi-continuous mill was *not* the most economic for outputs much over 1 m. tons a year, and it would be costly to convert it to full continuity later. A semi-continuous strip mill had a reversing instead of a continuous roughing mill; the foundations and layout, reversing electric motor, manipulators and controls for this could not be 'adapted'.[1] A reversing roughing mill was

---

[1] The semi-continuous hot mill would cost approximately £13 m. say, for say, a top capacity of 1·5 m. tons: the fully continuous £24 m. for 4·5 m. tons. Klöckners planned to use their reversing roughing mill, resited, as a plate mill.

necessarily slower than a continuous one and fed the continuous finishing stands of the hot mill less fully: hence capital and labour and power costs were all higher per ton—the former much higher—given the same intensity of operation. The fully continuous mill would make better quality sheet because roll design and composition could be adapted to the successive stages in roughing. The Newport mill, with much larger 'backing rolls' than existing mills, was to set new standards of accuracy for British practice.

There was yet another cost consideration. No doubt a semi-continuous mill being slightly simpler to adjust to changes of gauge (because only the finishing train has to be set) and a slightly less costly asset to keep idle, was better adapted to frequent changes in the size of sheet made: so that against higher costs in actual operating it would offer lower costs when changing product. But frequent changes were still sufficiently costly—in idle time—to make it desirable to avoid them: and it was clear that it was easier to bulk orders as the volume of orders being dealt with at one plant, and by one firm, was increased. Richard Thomas and Baldwins would be able to get larger runs at Newport the more fully the capacity there was used—and because they could plan the distribution of orders between the Newport and Ebbw Vale mills they could introduce a higher degree of specialisation in each plant.[1] The division of the work between two mills was thus likely to raise operating costs and reduce the scope for reducing costs and raising quality by large runs. For the sheet *used* in Scotland there would be an offset to these additional costs through savings on delivery costs. But this is only true of such consumption as would be in Scotland in any event, not when the new mill provided the magnet to consuming industries.

It is hard then to find support for the view that dividing the

[1] It was to be assumed that since Ebbw Vale was a relatively narrow mill (54 in.) the new mill would be wider. It was later announced as a 68 in. mill. While Britain was introducing more needless subdivision of production the E.C.S.C. was explaining why European sheet prices were so much higher than Britain's or still more America's; they emphasised the importance of large orders, adaptation of *demand*, specialisation of mills in the United States on particular ranges of size, etc. (above, p. 442). Among other things of course large orders and specialisation improve quality.

Durham or South Wales coking coal were often mixed with Yorkshire to make blast furnace coke.[1]

Against Immingham it was argued that the cost of getting labour (an ultimate labour force of 7000 was envisaged) and the cost of getting water would both be higher. The first traditional anti-home-ore-argument implied that a net addition to house-building costs[2] must be involved. In fact nothing was necessarily involved except a particular locating of part of the house-building (and community building) which was going to occur in any case. The fact that water would be more costly at Immingham was perhaps more substantial, but it was to be measured in pence, not shillings, a ton of steel.

It could not be supposed to offset the advantages of the strategic site and cheaper coal and slightly cheaper ore burden, still less to have outweighed the advantages of Immingham had the project there been based almost exclusively on the use of home ore. Whether Immingham would have been the ideal site for the use of home ore would in turn have been open to argument. Why not near the Northamptonshire or Oxfordshire ores, which would also be nearer some of the major markets— as was proposed in 1935, and almost started by steel interests in association with motor-car interests?[3] In 1956 this was some-times said by one of the key personalities to be ruled out on the grounds that a new site must be capable of expanding to 3 m. tons capacity: which could not happen with a new inland Midlands' site which should be limited to 1 m. tons. This approach is now open to three obvious comments. The ore reserves as now known are much less restrictive (and many have been, as it were, released from providing foundry iron). If it were desired to expand at all sites to 3 m. tons or more—why not put in the strip mill at one of the existing sites? And if a strip mill could not be contemplated for less than an ultimate 3 m. tons capacity in 1956 at a site where steel was cheap to make, why was it sound

---

[1] There was no clear reason for supposing that costs of getting coal would move in favour of South Wales. Yorkshire conditions are good: labour relations were poor, hence in Yorkshire as in South Wales costs could be reduced by better labour relations. The conditions appear to be less faulted and more favourable to mechanisation.   [2] And associated costs—roads, sewers, etc.

[3] A company was registered to do this.

at Motherwell a few years later, for no more than 1 m. tons? Semi-continuous mills were not a recent innovation in 1958.

The cost advantage for firms using home ore, assuming it was not whittled away by the levy system, had manifestly increased greatly, as was shown earlier, after the Federation calculation of 1950, when imported ores averaged 56s. a ton. At that time the favourable margin was put at 5s. a ton by the Federation, but many items were left out of account which made it, at its smallest, higher. From 1950 the margin rapidly widened as the price of imported ore more than doubled, and was to remain more than double till the beginning of 1959 when the effect of the recession and of the surplus of shipping had its major, but necessarily transitory, effect. Though bigger ships and better unloading facilities were making the position a little more favourable for the use of imported ore, and gradually the cost of home ore would rise, the margin in favour of using home ore would remain wide for a long time, and the cost advantage in making pig iron from it be measured in '£'s' a ton of pig iron rather than in shillings. Precise calculations are extremely difficult. Technical advance was reducing processing costs for the use of both kinds of ore, if anything probably to the advantage of home ore, and the pneumatic steel processes made it less and less possible to claim that home ore pig iron was more costly to convert into good steel.[1] The reasons for putting the strip mill on a home ore site were thus exceptionally strong.

[1] I made a calculation for 1955 based on the Federation 1950 figures—above, p. 256—(giving costs of ore and coke for 1 ton of pig iron) at 1955 prices of ore and coal, with no adjustments for (1) sintering of imported ore (sintering cost of home ore was included in the calculation), (2) the movement of coal prices in favour of home ore sites, (3) the need for flux in the imported ore burden, (4) the greater volume of gas and power available as a by-product when using home ore. Neglect of these threw the calculations much in favour of imported ore. The figures, published in *The Structure of British Industry*, vol. 1, p. 274, were:

	Imported ore site	Home ore site
	(s.)	(s.)
Ore	186	64
Coke (16 cwt.)	88	(20 cwt.) 118
Total	274	182

As an offset against the wide margin in the cost of materials charged into the blast furnace the manufacture of pig iron from home ore required more blast furnace

The difficulties for the Board in regard to the strip mill were formidable. No large primarily home-ore firm showed any readiness to go in for a wide strip mill—the desire of major firms in the United States and in Germany to be associated with wide strip production was not shared in Britain (where firms seemed to recognise 'rights' to particular types of product). Possibly the Board's investigations into home ore had not matured when the investigations into the strip mill site became fairly set. And if the problem was approached from the point of view of concentrating there were conflicting considerations. If ore importing is to be concentrated, is it not better to add more to Newport (where you would import for two strip mills)? If *more* home ore were used at Immingham than in the project described earlier would it not mean a rather small scale ore import operation? If it were desired to concentrate more steelmaking in very large works and load primary mills fully, might not the addition at Ravenscraig be right?

The decision to have two mills, neither on a home ore site, was ostensibly the Government's. It was frankly political—

capacity per ton of iron—the capital outlay involved being from £5 to £7 more in *1950* practice: I put the annual cost at 15s. to 20s. a ton. The calculation probably put too low a price on coke, more especially for imported ore sites: the average price *at the N.C.B. coke ovens* in South Wales was 135s. a ton in 1955, compared with 108s. in 1950 and 105s. in 1949. N.C.B. coke in *Scotland* was priced at 145s. in 1955. In Yorkshire the price (of *all* N.C.B. coke—not all for blast furnaces) rose from 101s. (1949) to 103s. in 1950 and 104s. in 1955. But the 1950 hypotheses need revising. Now that more ores are sintered coke consumption in best practice would be 12 cwt. for imported ore, 15 cwt. for home ore (assuming *all* the ore is in each case sintered). The capital costs in the blast furnace would be reduced by one quarter (the outputs being increased in inverse proportion to the reduction in coke consumption): but the cost of providing sinter plant would partly offset this, the cost being approximately £2 for capacity to make 1 ton of sinter per year. Home ore used by plants near the mine probably cost about 15s. a ton at the plant by 1958: a little cost more, and some was taken a longish transport to provide a self-fluxing burden. Average costs of below 20s. a ton at the furnace were likely to be achieved for some time. Average costs, not marginal, were appropriate, because the use of some less accessible ore is partly to keep the averages down for many years: much more cheaply mined ore was still available. Sintering costs might be expected to bring the cost of the ore burden up to 120s. a ton. If imported ore prices (55 per cent Fe) were to be 110s. a ton—rather low as a long-term possibility—the ore burden cost after sintering would be, say, 210s. It is unreasonable to assume coke at the same price for both: but taking the South Wales (N.C.B.) price of 1958, namely 165s., and low coke usage the coke plus sinter cost using home ore would be approximately 240s., using imported ore 300s.

when they were chided on this in the Press one minister closely concerned affected surprise—what else, he asked, could a Government decision be than political? They would bring about a development which economic considerations alone would not bring about. The greatest economic advantage would be sacrificed deliberately in the interests of immediate social comfort and convenience. What was done could be fitted in to a kind of industrial strategy—and the Government were soon trying to persuade motor-car makers to go to Scotland to create a market for steel sheets. This approach was conspicuously different from that of the E.C.S.C., whose starting-point it will be recalled was that ultimate cost reduction should not be sacrificed, and the action of the Community should be designed to help the transition towards a distribution of industry which would be consistent with this. The British Government's policy would have the effect of lessening the increase of productivity, the E.C.S.C. was designed to 'maximise' it.

Mr Macmillan implied that the Board had said the sacrifices involved in his decision were not serious. The part they played is obscure. Perhaps because no firm proposed to put a strip mill on a home ore site, the Board, with the time factor in mind, wrote off a home ore site from the start, though a works at Immingham obviously could have become more predominantly home ore based as the advantages became more specific. The Board's position to discourage the Scots scheme, had they wished to do so, would have been stronger if Scots coal prices had more nearly matched the costs of production, and steel prices been basing-point prices reflecting local costs.

In retrospect it might be expected that the Board would have tried to correct the bias created by the rigidities in the industry, and the social pressures in favour of the *status quo*, the inhibiting influence of the difficulties of raising money due to political threats, and the oddities of the price system which the Board only partially controlled (it could not fix coal prices)—and still more partially removed. In these terms theirs could conceivably have been a useful function; and the emphasis to be expected would have been towards more concentration of production—naturally where raw material costs for supplying a given market would be most favourable—and more development on home ore (not with the object of making *all* steel but only *more* steel from home ore). It could be said no doubt that to make strip at Ravenscraig was concentration, but not where liquid steel was cheap to make. It could be said that Newport meant concentrating the import of ore for two works at one port—and certainly this was a point in favour. The strategic case for Immingham as an importing centre was that progressively the cheaper coal would make this a good area for using imported as well as home ore: one at least of the Scunthorpe firms was planning in 1958 to base a large development partly on imported ore, so here too the prospect was that the port would be used for more than one works. How far all this figured in the Board's considerations, or what they said to the Government, was not known: nor whether the Government neglected their strategic approach, if they presented one.

The Board only complained, in a sense, against the industry: and the basis of their complaint as regards the strip mill—not as regards home ore—seemed to become shaky when Richard Thomas began making their Newport plant, for late in 1959 they stated that they expected to have the plant operating in part by late 1961. They were planning, so it seemed, to emulate the achievement at Bremen.[1]

(v) *Gains and losses.* Before the General Election of October 1959 renationalisation of steel might have been just round the corner. After the election it was practically certain it would not come in the next five years, and seemed probable that it would not come at all. The Board and the Federation—and the firms— would go on. Would the system work differently with the threat of impermanence greatly reduced? Would there be any stocktaking, any suggestions for change?

Changes were likely to occur almost imperceptibly as firms

---

[1] The Board had said in June 1958 (*Ann. Rep.* 1957, p. 20) 'it would hardly be possible to have extensive new capacity constructed and in operation until a year or two after 1962. Klöckners began thinking of a new plant in 1952, and decided on the Bremen site in January 1954. This seems parallel to R.T.B.'s decision late in 1956 to build at Newport. The time between this decision and site work was 18 months for Klöckners, nearly 3 years for R.T.B. R.T.B. hoped to match Klöckners pace over the next stage (above, p. 459).

felt their financial independence grow. Whether there was anything in the nationalisers' taunt that private enterprise could
not finance steel expansion on the 'right' scale—whatever that
was: perhaps what the Board thought desirable—would now be
more evident. Stewarts and Lloyds within ten days of the
election announced an issue of ordinary shares. Steel shares
were at once popular (with stockbrokers recommending most
those companies whose earnings were most likely to expand
with little more capital expenditure). The Agency, it was
assumed, would soon sell Richard Thomas and Baldwins and
the remaining firms it still held back into private ownership;
how soon the prior charges held by the Agency would be disposed of, and whether Colvilles would now require less Government money, was not conspicuously discussed until the
Government decided to change the status of the Colville loan.[1]

In the changed circumstances less was likely to be done by
firms merely for appearances—because it was desirable to build
up the status of a supervisory body whose activities were a token
that there were no extortionate profits or restrictive practices.
This motive was likely to be most compelling when such a body
appeared to be inescapable as the lesser of two evils. After the
creation of the Board the influence of the Federation waned.
Many of the leading personalities in the firms meant it to be so:
the spotlight must be on the Board. But there were contributory
factors. Had Sir Andrew been independent chairman he would
not have been so self-effacing as his successor in the late fifties;
and the loss of Robert Shone to the Board in 1953 and Aubrey
Jones to the Government two years later were serious and were
not made good—it would have been difficult in the circumstances to do it at the same level. As a trade association the
Federation remained strong and efficient: its staff more or less
constant, about 300. After the election in 1959 it was felt that
recruitment at the top would become easier again. The Board
had grown quickly from the start into a substantial organisation.

---

[1] This involved a Bill, and debates. Some Tories now showed dislike of Government aid to high cost production. Lord Mills said he 'persuaded' Colvilles to
'their great act of faith'; the Minister of Power said Colvilles agreed so long as
financial assistance was available to make it 'an economic proposition' (*Hansard*,
Lords, 4 Apr. 1960, c. 660; H. of C. 28 Mar. 1960, c. 1026).

By the end of 1954 its staff was half as big again as the staff of the Iron and Steel Corporation of Great Britain had been[1] (so those who wanted renationalisation could say how well bureaucracy had been avoided in 1950–51) and it continued to grow though more slowly, being 116 at the end of 1958.[2] Would leading chairmen wish to redress the balance of power in favour of the Federation? (Would the constitutional views propounded, for instance, by Sir Allan Macdiarmid[3] come back into favour?)

Desire to change the balance might not be one-sided. The Board would feel increasingly irked if the firms became less receptive to their views and wishes, which had already been resisted, the Board felt, over home ore and strip mills. There was, moreover, a change of personalities which might prove significant. Sir Archibald Forbes expressed his wish at the end of 1957 to be relieved of his position as Chairman of the Board. He waited over a year, at the Minister's request, to complete 'certain matters of Board business'.[4] This also gave time for the choice of his successor, Sir Cyril Musgrave, whose appointment was announced in December 1958.[5] The first chairman, a prominent city industrialist, at one time President of the Federation of British Industries, was in a position to exert influence on other industrialists as one of them, on an 'old boy' basis. (One gained, in contrast, an impression of strong individualism in relations with Ministers.) The new chairman, who was Permanent Secretary of the Ministry of Supply, though having a long record of working with the aircraft industry, would not enjoy the same advantage of being an insider. As a distinguished civil servant he might be more conscious of the constitutional position—it might seem weakness—of the Board.

---

[1] The Corporation staff at Sept. 1951 was 61, but the organisation never got under way. The Board had 93 at the end of 1954 (Iron and Steel Corporation of Great Britain, *Rep. to Sept. 1951*, p. 4, Iron and Steel Board, *Rep. to Dec. 1954*, p. 1).

[2] Cost analyses, price-fixing, forcasting demand, international comparison of costs and prices, and assessing development projects and supply and international trade prospects, made heavy calls on accountants and statisticians. The Board also had technical officers. Its senior technical officer, for example, visited oxygen steel plants on the Continent in 1957 (*Ann. Rep. 1957*, p. 34).

[3] Above, pp. 67 sqq.

[4] Probably the strip mill affair was the main one.

[5] He took up his new duties on 1 March 1959.

Not that the weakness most often alleged, the lack of power to enjoin firms to carry out development projects of the Board's choosing, seemed likely to become conspicuous in the near future. The supply prospect for steel now seemed, apart from the probable side effects of the United States strike of 1959, more assured than demand. The most flourishing large demand for steel, for motor-cars, was the one for which the Government had now ostensibly overprovided though there might be interim scarcities.[1] Other industries, where the steel component was notably large, it has been seen, were flagging: and some thriving industries were conspicuously saving steel.[2] It was hard to see, for example at the end of 1959, what could make a home ore based steelworks an urgent need—even to make more billets.

If, however, stock had been taken of the situation, what was the state of the account? How was the system of 1953 working out? In what ways, in what degree was the evolution of the industry being changed by the existence of the Board? Were the Board growing more effective? Were they hampered by lack of powers? Was the division of function between them and the Government satisfactorily drawn?

The Board had made the price arrangements more consistent with the 'efficient economic and adequate supply' of steel. They claimed by 1956 already to have influenced the direction and increased the extent and rate of development.[3] They had been associated with the belated extension and modernisation of heavy plate production. They had declared themselves in favour of more home-ore based steel production. They had

[1] This seemed a particularly likely risk in 1960 because of the repercussions of the strike in the United States steel industry. There was much capacity in the United States to all appearances surplus to annual consumption at a high rate of industrial production. But stocks had been run down during the strike. When it was suspended under the Taft-Hartley Act consumers would certainly try and rebuild stocks, which would create an exceptional demand in the home industry and for imports. If the strike was not renewed the exceptional demand was likely to continue for a time. Hence the United Kingdom sheet users would find it difficult to buy imports either from the United States or Continental makers to allow them quickly to increase output of, for example, motor-cars. Against a strike in the United States the British steelmakers could not possibly prepare.

[2] Electrical generation, for instance, where much larger units were cutting the consumption of steel in relation to generating capacity.

[3] *Spec. Rep.* 1957, p. 2.

seen the strong case for hurrying up the building of a fourth wide-strip mill. They had, after a slow start, acknowledged, albeit grudgingly, some of the technical advances made abroad which were to be adopted in Britain—though they did so without committing themselves to any overt criticism of British research and development, either its quantity or its organisation. Their survey of demand to 1962 was hailed by the professionals. Their view that the steel firms were not doing enough to meet it was hailed by those who thought the firms in general and the Federation in particular were bound to be restrictionist, and by many others who thought it good to have some surplus capacity in hand. Of the Board's reports in 1956 and 1957 two economists not so committed to judgements on these specific issues remarked that if future reports 'continue to be as informative... it will be much easier for the public to understand the problems facing the industry and the policies adopted to deal with them'.[1]

The account set out on these lines could make a brave showing for the Board. But to take the last point first: it was surprising how much that was relevant to the understanding of the industry was left out of their reports. There was nothing for instance on the contrasts of costs of manufacturing in different regions, using different processes, operating on different scales, using home or imported ores, importing in different ports, using cheap or dear, subsidised or unsubsidised, coal—and nothing on the contrasts between cost trends in Britain and the Continent. (They said what was true, that it was difficult to make *absolute* comparisons of costs in Britain and on the Continent at one time, but trends were not so obscure.) There was nothing in their reports to suggest that the Productivity Team had said baldly in 1952 that if all existing steelworks 'are expanded or even retained it will not be possible to reach anything like the minimum size for efficient operation'.[2] Under the development plans up to 1962 (for an output much larger than was envisaged in 1952), the average capacity of plants making steel of mass production types and qualities would be much below the

---

[1] R. H. Edwards and H. Townsend, *Business Enterprise*, p. 464.
[2] Above, p. 279.

minimum set by the Team,[1] which further technical changes had made in turn too low. The question how far insular planning was appropriate for steelmaking was not asked: there was no examination of the advantages which might accrue from participation in a large common market, from the more stimulating competition it would provide, the greater scope for large-scale units and specialisation, and the greater smoothness with which major new units could be accommodated.[2] The possibility that new plants might be built faster, which would have expelled the fear expressed in 1957 of unavoidable scarcity of steel in 1962, was not given a critical examination in the reports. The full extent to which the British industry was depending on foreign technical innovation and foreign designs of plant was not shown; the organisation of research in Britain was at first specifically blessed[3] and never referred to critically.

So the reports confined the public's understanding of the steel industry's problems, and of policies adopted for dealing with them, within highly conventional limits. This did not mean that the Board themselves worked within those limits. Probably they did not pick up the unsatisfactory position over research and development at first: the full-time members of the Board were experienced in the industry, but their intimate connexions within it were not with the works and the processes. But they advised the Government on relations with European coal and steel industries and were on working parties dealing with it. They would doubtless have attributed their silence on this to these involvements which, however, need hardly have prevented their expressing their preference in general terms, albeit they could not have been expected to do so with academic detachment.[4]

---

[1] Above, p. 272.

[2] Since a given rate of increase of demand will more quickly provide an adequate load for one major new unit in a large market than in a smaller one.

[3] In the Board's first references to research it expressed itself completely satisfied (*Rep.* Dec. 1954, p. 27).

[4] As seen earlier the impression was that the Board collectively favoured caution in removing tariffs, and were not in favour of the more liberal terms among those considered for a Council of Association with the E.C.S.C. But Sir Robert Shone was one of the few people who supported, as an economic advantage, the heavy incidence of social service charges on employers which was characteristic of France and Germany (above, p. 430). His argument was that by raising total labour cost

They had obviously probed the possibility that expansion schemes could be completed faster, but they assumed the negative conclusion, and they did not refer to the international contrast.[1] They were certainly not unaware of the Productivity Team's views on scale, because they referred to the details. Indeed they referred to the extent to which many new blast furnaces fell below the Team's minima because of the limits to their size imposed by the size of the existing works into which they had been fitted.[2]

There remained several questions to which no answer can be given from the Board's reports. Did the Board think the gains to be derived from larger scale manufacturing operations at or above the Team's minima, concentration of ore importing in large ships at a few ports, the use of more home ore at home ore sites, the greater use of the cheaper coking coals, and the strategic siting (as defined above in connexion with the strip mill) of new mills, were large enough, either singly or in practical combinations (and combined with pneumatic steel-making) to make their realisation in any sense urgent? Did they think that the unfavourable movement of costs in British steel-making compared with Continental steelmaking were related to the slowness and compromise in Britain in adopting the radical means of reducing costs? If so did they nevertheless believe that it did not matter if time were lost? Did it seem to them not to matter if development schemes which reduced costs less than was possible by more drastic changes stood in the way of further cost reduction by establishing new sources of inertia?

There was, it has been seen, some room for different assessments of the cost advantages to be had by the different types of

to the employer it encouraged labour-saving investment. I doubt if attitudes on investment were greatly influenced relatively by this: as shown earlier, the cost of labour was not markedly different in the United Kingdom, Germany and France (above, p. 586). But the argument showed a readiness to contemplate 'harmonisation' of social charges (*J.R. Stat. Soc.* Part 3, 1958, p. 292).

[1] This topic was discussed in the *Special Report* for 1957, ch. 13, and various delaying factors—the bottleneck over large steel castings, whose manufacture was a conspicuous weakness in Britain, with much scrap and poor quality, was particularly singled out. But ways of overcoming the difficulty were not discussed: it was, as it were, taken for granted.

[2] *Spec. Rep.* 1957, p. 78.

change, in different combinations;[1] though the indications were
that what was offered by concentration, specialisation, new
process and (for some output) new location was increasing. The
Board may have felt that its problem was to check the momentum in the existing system (whereby in conditions half analogous
to permanent boom all the organisms were straining to grow)
only after the different type of growth favoured by the Productivity Team was assured and would give an equal rate of
expansion as well as better 'quality' development. They may
have repeated the adage often repeated in the first five years of
post-war growth—the best must not be the enemy of the good.
When the Board took office the Steel Corporation of Great
Britain (with some pressure from the Minister of Supply) had
given its consent to many schemes which ensured further expansion at a large proportion of existing sites without regard to the
Team's standards. The upsurge of demand from 1953 to 1955
may have made the Board hesitate to impose any check on
proposed expansions, and, so long as there were no alternative
plans, from the existing organisms or any other source, they
might have been right. Moreover, in the debates on the 1953
Bill parliamentary opinion on both sides of the House had been
very solicitous for areas threatened with unemployment if plants
were shut down: the implication seemed that if the Board could
stretch a point it should do so, though Mr Duncan Sandys
specifically said he thought social reasons should not override
economic.[2]

Of the full-time members of the Board one was Scots, one
Welsh, and they may have felt strongly for this reason the case
for stretching a point. And the tradition of trade union policy[3]
may have played its part, not only through Sir Lincoln Evans
and Mr Owen, former Secretary of the Blast Furnace Workers'
Union, who was a part-time member of the Board, but indirectly because consideration for this may have seemed likely
to contribute to the strike-free labour relations of the industry,

[1] Above, p. 633 sqq. and *passim*.   [2] Above, p. 381.
[3] Shown clearly over Ebbw Vale: it was recognised that Lincolnshire offered
lower costs, and 'as a matter of sound economic development was clearly the place
to put the (strip) mill', but the unions reacted very vigorously against it (Pugh,
Men of Steel, pp. 511–12).

and the absence of any noticeably widespread enthusiasm for nationalisation among steelworkers.[1]

There was, however, an overriding reason which made it unnecessary and perhaps impolitic for the Board to expound the reasons for their actions or inactions on these things, and in particular their assessment of the increases in cost involved in the Government's strip mill decision, namely that by the legislation which created the Board, on these things they were to leave the Government to determine the 'national interest'—to decide when some economic advantage should be sacrificed. The Board's duty was to present the economic facts to the Minister, but it was not obligatory for them to reproduce them for the public.

Whether it was obligatory for them to trim their price policy so that plants whose costs were higher than they would have been at a site chosen solely for economic reasons was not overtly discussed. If the Board applied rigorously the criterion in price-fixing that prices should be based on the costs of the most efficient works,[2] the result could hardly satisfy a new works which was deliberately below the standard of maximum efficiency.[3]

---

[1] Redundancy could obviously have been a source of difficulty. Otherwise the conditions in the industry were favourable for labour relations. They had a sliding scale based on the cost of living. Labour costs were a moderate part of total costs and became a smaller part in higher-capacity plants, which naturally made it easier to grant increases, holidays with pay, pensions, and the like; increasing size of units of plant allowed the wages of the highest paid workers to rise often to extremely high levels without being a disturbing cost. The difference between first-hand earnings and those lower down the scale remained wide. Whether what happened was always well judged, or a path of least resistance, was sometimes questioned— even by Union leaders—and it became more open to question as the costs of operation became more subject to scientific controls and the direction of managers with advanced technical training. A change in the structure seemed beginning in 1959. In the fifties trouble arose primarily with maintenance workers who were in the engineering and other unions, where there was not the same scope for some extremely high earnings, and among coke-oven workers who did not experience increases like those in the iron and steel works. A full discussion of this subject would be a digression here, and must needs be on a basis of inter-industry comparison.

[2] Above, pp. 610 sqq.

[3] It will be observed that this difficulty will not necessarily arise if the new works, though located where its costs were higher than they would have been at another site, were lower than those at other works making the same product. The Board could regard the new plant as the most efficient existing plant: it could neglect the fact that still lower costs had been a practical possibility.

And clearly if it was necessary to make concessions in price-fixing on this score (as presumably it was—for it would be ridiculous to say that private enterprise development in a high cost site was desirable unless it was also allowed to be remunerative) could this fail to have important consequences in the international relations of the industry? Was it compatible with free trade with the E.C.S.C., and the adoption of E.C.S.C. price arrangements? These arrangements would have ruled out subsidies on high cost coal, low stabilised home-scrap prices, and presumably all the Industry Fund operations which helped high cost makers. It was hardly surprising to find that in 1958 British steelmakers were interested in the possibilities of 'special arrangements for the regulation of the iron and steel and coal industries' within a European Free Trade Area if one were formed, in preference to entering the E.C.S.C. which was 'governed by rules generally stricter than those envisaged for the wider Common Market'.[1]

The cost data set out in earlier sections suggested that leaving out of account the additional capital cost involved in building two mills instead of one the strip mill decision would result in costs being between 5 and 10 per cent higher than they would have been where production costs would have been lowest.[2] This was not a published or official forecast, and in some quarters,

[1] I.S.B. *Ann. Rep.* 1958, p. 35. I understood that most steel firms would have preferred to be outside the E.C.S.C. and be in a European Free Trade Area as an ordinary industry but with special arrangements. Whether this was a formal Federation view was not clear: still less whether it was the Board's view. But it may have been. The impression was gaining ground at the end of 1959 that within the E.E.C. the E.C.S.C.'s form might be changed, and it might become an Energy Authority, leaving steel outside as an ordinary industry—but all this was vague.

[2] Above, pp. 639 sqq. Newport costs would exceed a home ore site cost: Scots costs must be above Newport. But Newport costs would for some years be higher because of the Scots operation. If there was to be a Scots operation it would have been better, obviously, combined with a home ore project. The percentage figures in the text refer to the added cost due to differences in coal cost (unsubsidised) ore costs, distribution costs, and costs of working at different scales of output. Capital expenditure was necessarily larger under the plan to have two works (though there are complications in the sum, arising, for example, from water supply problems and housing). Early capital outlay at Newport would be £120 m., at Colvilles £50 m. In the long run replacement costs would presumably be similar at all sites—but the continuous capital expenditure on maintaining and expanding would be to keep relatively high cost operations in being under the decision taken.

but not in all, it provoked violent dissent.[1] The full benefit from
the lowest cost production, it may be added, would only have
been secured if price policies had been adopted which would
have attracted users of sheet and tinplate to the low cost area:
which was the reverse of the policy which the Board of Trade
appeared to wish to follow at the end of 1959, to encourage
users to settle where it would cost most to make steel sheet.

And indeed this determination to collect using industries
round the Scots strip mill underlined that the strip mill decision
was not an isolated idiosyncratic act but a symbol of Government planning at the end of the fifties. It was not, as so much
that happened in steel development was, merely a yielding to
the forces of momentum—or inertia: though it may have appeared to give the seal of Government approval to decisions
which were the outcome of these forces. And it would have
analogous effects in reducing the extent to which costs were
brought down. It implied a judgement that this did not matter.
What the Government did could be presented as damping down
cost reduction, but not to the point where in their view the
general increase of productivity in industry as a whole was
unsatisfactory. As a compensation there was less social dislocation. The lessening was often indiscriminately assumed to be all
manifest gain—which raises esoteric problems irrelevant to this
book. How far could the damping down of cost reduction be
carried without causing difficulties in international trade?
Comparisons with past rates of growth could mislead because
the pace of industrial change in the world had become much
faster: the relevant comparison was with the world outside.
Productivity (a measure with many faults)[2] had notoriously
risen less in British industry from 1953 to 1958 than in the
industries of leading industrial countries on the Continent, and
not more percentagewise than in United States industries,

[1] *Ex parte* dissents will probably recur: and this is a matter where the full records,
showing all the hypotheses (implicit or explicit, recognised or overlooked) on raw
material costing (including coal), subsidies, Industry Fund, the basis of price-
fixing, the forcible distribution of consuming markets, adopted by the various
participants in the forecasting, will be of immense interest. But this kind of record
will not be available in full for a very long time.

[2] Cp. *The Structure of British Industry*, vol. II, pp. 421 sqq.

which meant much less in absolute terms.[1] This would be the expected outcome of a situation in which forces leading to cost reduction were damped down more in Britain than elsewhere. It was widely felt to be unsatisfactory, and a source of insecurity because Britain's economic position in the world was clearly going to be exposed to growing strains.

Britain was, with the exception of Belgium, the most dependent of the major industrial countries on imports of raw material and food. She was exposing herself to more competition from other manufacturing countries by her trade policies. Her industries were likely to face a growth in the competitive strength in common export markets outside Europe of the countries in the E.C.S.C. because of the Common Market—if the 'Six' and the 'Seven' did not come together. They would experience sharper internal competition if the two groups did come together, although they would also enjoy the outlet and stimulus of the larger market. Several Continental countries were beginning to benefit, and were likely to benefit progressively, from indigenous or North African natural gas and oil (whose exploitation might make Britain's oil trade less expansive and remunerative and the oil trade as a whole less rewarding for Britain in trade outlets). Commonwealth countries were already buying more imports from industrial countries other than Britain—they liked to choose from a wider range of goods, and to buy more cheaply if it was possible, and it was natural when they exported raw materials or food products more widely that they should buy imports more widely. (When Australia, for example, sold more wool to Japan she bought more goods from Japan.) Imperial Preference was a diminishing asset. Difficulties from the competition of exports of State industries (from Russia and the satellites) and from low wage countries (India, Hong Kong, Japan, China) was becoming greater: faster industrialisation throughout the world, made easier as industrial countries vied to provide capital goods, increased the need for British industries to replace old exports by new.

[1] Productivities in manufactures in 1958 and 1959 as a percentage of 1953 were: United Kingdom, 112, 118; United States, 111, 119; France, 146, 153; Germany, 121, 128; Italy, 138, 153; Netherlands, 119, 129.

These risks and uncertainties were certainly familiar to the Government. That they decided to lessen cost reduction, quite deliberately,[1] reflected a judgement that local unemployment was something circumstantial for which something dramatic must be done. The motives in this were no doubt mixed, part political, part compassionate. The effects of policies lessening the extent and rate of cost reduction would be diffuse and not capable of isolation, not precisely traceable to their political source. Looking back the Government might argue that, although steel expansion since the war had not followed the lines laid down in the first plan of 1946, and small works had been preserved, and almost all had expanded, and home ore development had been narrowly confined, the results could not be regarded as disastrous. Expansion may have been too slow, some new techniques had been neglected too long, some customers felt there was too little interest in their special needs, but there had been no widespread complaints of high prices, and the gradual disappearance of the British price advantage, the rise of British costs in steelmaking *vis-à-vis* the E.C.S.C. countries, was not familiar. If, therefore, by the planning canons of 1946—and the Productivity Team principles of 1952 —what had been done by the makers fell apparently short of the ideal, did not experience show that the economy was strong enough to tolerate it? Steel, after all, was an industry where Britain's natural advantages over most Continental makers were considerable so that some part of them could safely be sacrificed. To do this might lessen the rise in 'aggregate' industrial productivity, and so be a contribution to the forces which were resulting in productivity rising less—percentagewise or absolutely—in Britain than in the E.C.S.C. countries and in the United States.[2] But was this unfavourable comparison,

---

[1] Cp. *Hansard*, 9 Nov. 1959 c. 34 (Mr Maudling).

[2] I say *might* lessen the rise of productivity, because though the choice of a relatively high-cost location would certainly keep efficiency lower than it would otherwise have been, it might not keep productivity lower. For instance, if it meant using more imported ore instead of more home ore, there might be a *rise* in productivity (more than offset, however, by high import costs). Moreover distribution transport costs might be larger because of the choice of location: but the productivity in the transport might be high. All this arises from the misleading characteristics of the criterion.

it might be asked, being taken too seriously? Reassuring arguments could be found. When the Continental figures first began going ahead it was partly because Continental countries, especially Germany, were later than Britain in post-war reconstruction. From 1951 to 1955 the proportion of Britain's gross national product used for industrial investment was much below the proportion so used on the Continent and in the United States. When, however, from 1956 to 1958 this proportion rose sharply in Britain anti-inflationary policies were keeping industrial output down more in the United Kingdom than on the Continent, so that productivity in these years did not fully reflect the increase in industrial efficiency in Britain. There would be a sharp jump once the anti-inflationary brakes were taken off—and this duly began to happen in 1959. What was needed above all was that consumption should be kept in bounds. Who could tell how the comparisons with the Continent would finally turn out? Nothing had happened in steelmaking as it had in regard to fuel and power, road and rail, and aircraft production, to bring the quality of the decisions over investment into question through harsh commercial difficulties. The Government could still without running immediate risks act in regard to steel in the old tradition as though 'problems of industrial dynamics could and should be left largely to look after themselves', the politician's concern being to divert the dynamic forces in order to reduce social dislocation.[1]

In this context indeed the reverse view was seldom put that Britain should make the most of *any* natural advantages she retained because in many respects her relative position was becoming less favourable, that consequently the Government should use their influence to lessen the obstacles to maximum cost reduction, instead of reinforcing them. In the circumstances it was not surprising that (as suggested earlier) nobody appeared to examine to what extent reduction of efficiency and competitive strength enforced by Government intervention would entail protection or subsidy and make it less easy to take part in a large free trade area. To form such an area was another avowed part of Government policy: but the parts sometimes

[1] Cp. *E.H.S.* (1937–39), ch. XII *passim*, and esp. p. 324.

seemed to outsiders to be fashioned *ad hoc*, without much fuss about mutual consistency.

The Act of 1953, as was shown in chapter VI, carefully preserved for the Government the power to intervene in the way and for the purpose they did, and the Government had carefully excluded from their Act any principles in regard to price-fixing which would inconveniently have ruled out subsidy or otherwise fettered them in supporting relatively high cost enterprise. How far this was prescience, how far merely due to the protective instincts of Ministers and of senior civil servants, who are constitutionally anxious not to find their hands tied awkwardly in unforeseen circumstances by unwary commitments, is not known. The Government did not of course feel themselves bound by Mr Duncan Sandys' view in the debate that economic criteria should not be disregarded for social reasons. The Board had not been designed so that they could insulate the Government from the industry or the industry from the Government. A change in the Government's attitude was a pre-requisite therefore of any major change in the development trends in the industry: though this might itself have its origin in pressures on the Government from the Board or Federation or from individual firms or from consumers.

Suppose the Government had thought that their most useful function was to ease the way to or to encourage more radical changes in the steel industry, more concentration, more shifts of location, more technical innovation, would changes in the central organisation and arrangements have been useful or even necessary?

The problem they would then have faced was not the simple one of expanding capacity faster which obsessed most of the critics. In the absence of major strikes there was considerable surplus capacity in Europe and America collectively when the sixties opened. What was of most real importance to consumers was not to get more steel at any cost, but more steel at low cost. The problem, to set it out again, was twofold, first to hasten and extend the participation of British steelmaking in the cost saving methods (which saved not only labour, which the productivity figures showed, but fuel and perhaps most notably capital, though this had not caught the public or the political eye),[1] which had been pioneered mainly elsewhere: and second, to associate with this an adaptation in geographical distribution of production appropriate to current market and raw material and shipping circumstances, which could give many parts of the British industry useful comparative advantages, and might provide a rational economic justification for expansion which was often less rationally justified by estimates of insular demand.

Not that such estimates were undesirable: in some form they were indispensable when large expansion plans were made.[2] They could possibly have contributed more in Britain to producing the effect of 'competitive conditions' had they been less coloured by hopes, and been presented, in a less autarchic guise, as guesses of part of a larger market. There was perhaps scope for a still deeper statistical background[3] and certainly scope for more market research,[4] more intimate contact with technological trends in using industries. The ideal was to have a continuous, objective, operation. Whether it was likely to be most objective under Government auspices, as part of a machine for (among other things) coercing steel firms to expand, was a matter for conjecture.

Government actions to ease or encourage more radical change could fall into two categories. They could have been directed against practices and arrangements which discouraged,

[1] It will be recalled that apart from savings due to the intensive use of large ships, high-capacity unloading, and large furnaces, there were important net capital savings per unit of output from sintering, pneumatic steelmaking and continuous casting, and from the full utilisation of high-capacity rolling mills—by having adequate steel supplies, adequate heating, handling and cooling equipment, and by standardising and specialising to reduce roll changing and to secure uniform quality.

[2] In the United States long-term projections were published from time to time, with detailed analyses of ore requirements from different sources of supply. The forecasts were made by private enterprise. Cp. one dated Sept. 1955 issued by *Skillings Mining Review* (September 1955). The ore analysis by a consultant was based on a forecast of ingot output up to 1985 made by U.S. Steel Corporation in 1954.

[3] Input–output studies of the type made under Professor Richard Stone might have helped if they were pushed further and brought up to date: they would presumably have made the full impact of changes in demand for different types of consumer goods clearer, for example.

[4] One had an impression that market research was not always as strong in the firms themselves as it might have been. Business, perhaps, had come too easily.

frustrated or diverted enterprise and initiative, or made the *status quo* too easily rewarding: or they might have tried to compensate for (as they might have judged it) lack of initiative. How much could be done within the first category? The most obvious things to do were to change the price arrangements and by appropriate international agreements remove the remaining protection of the home market. Price arrangements analogous to the United States or E.C.S.C. model, with no Government or Board price-fixing, no Industry Fund operations to affect costs or to stabilise prices, no subsidies on coal, no ban on the export of scrap,[1] no industry agreement on scrap prices, and no association recommendation of maximum or minimum prices, but certain legal requirements (for example, prices to be published F.O.T. works—or F.O.T. basing point providing there were basing points at all major centres—but with powers to 'align') would have been an important contribution. It would have been unwelcome at the outset to many consumers, as well as to most producers. The Board might be called on like the High Authority to see that the rules were followed (though they would have no power to act on coal prices), but the anomaly whereby the same body both fixed prices and decided whether the investments of firms were 'sound' would end. Closer association in the E.C.S.C., with no tariff barrier (protection against dumping was already in force) would have given such a change in price arrangements much greater impact than if it were on an insular base only—for reasons indicated earlier. The opportunity for this had been missed twice[2]: in what form it would recur, if at all, was, in 1959, problematical.

But it could not be assumed that opening the ways for sharper competition would be enough in all circumstances to compel a vigorous reaction and force firms to break the convention or change their attitudes and the pattern or speed or technological characteristics which they had chosen for their growth. It was not certain that it would either drive some firms to contract as

---

[1] Neither of the two 'models' escaped this ban.

[2] When the Community was formed and when the Council of Association was formed: on this second occasion it is likely that an agreement on a 'free trade area' basis could have been made, but that Ministers turned it down. It probably did not have the undivided support of the Board, and certainly not that of the Federation.

steelmakers and look for new openings—it might be in the field of special steel products, for their works, or allow others, and stimulate them, to grow faster, concentrate production more or start making more products at low cost sites, try to take more business from rivals either at home or on the Continent. Nor was it likely that the way for a new entrant would be made easier. The organisms in the industry, that is, might remain for some time singularly unaffected. They were all after all expansionist in their fashion, usually in the simplest ways, but with exigent demand this had been all that was needed at least in the short run and it counted conventionally for virtue. In the absence of a severe world recession Continental exporters were likely to find the British home market less attractive than the overseas markets.

The immunity to competition which firms and groups of firms derived in varying degrees from the costliness and durability of the plant, the cost of transporting steel, their close contacts with local markets, development of profitable specialities, close links with consumers, including often complete integration in respect of part of their output, contacts through interlocking directorates with other steel companies and with banks and insurance companies, not to mention the strength some companies had through ownership of rights to work cheap home ore deposits, had if anything been increased.[1] Moreover all the major firms still had plants of varying degrees of efficiency, and none had an undivided interest in seeing the most efficient production rise at the expense of the less efficient. Firms with a foot in different regions—it applied to all the firms with home ore based plants—did not, it was plain to see, feel impelled or compelled to concentrate development where costs were or could be least. There was still no firm which would automatically devote all its resources single-mindedly to the further exploitation of home ore.[2] On the contrary there was probably no firm which would not

[1] For example, the cost for a new entrant was much greater, much of the plant was fairly new and fairly good.

[2] The announcement in December 1959 that United Steels would replace the cold metal open-hearth shop at Steel Peech and Tozers with a big electric furnace shop was symptomatic. It was to be the biggest electric furnace shop in the world. The choice of electric arc furnaces was clearly made in order to overcome the drawback of making open-hearth steel in large quantities in a cold metal shop.

have thought it almost socially reprehensible to do so. Could the spell be broken, as in the past, by a newcomer—a user of steel with an exclusive interest in having more cheap steel, someone unencumbered by slum steel property? A firm or group in the motor-car industry was the most likely source of such a venture. One car firm had indeed taken the initial steps to form a strip mill company in 1935. In the late fifties motor-car makers were often critical of steelmakers, complaining of scarcity and bothered at the high price of imports. But no car maker showed any signs of trying to make cheaper sheets. Prices, by international standards, had been low. But suppose one had wanted to—would it have been possible to get access to home ores on the favourable terms enjoyed by two or three of the firms who were well entrenched in the ore fields? It was highly doubtful. The same was true for anyone who might wish to come in—so that the only way in was probably by forming a joint company with one of the firms who owned extensive mineral rights, which would probably have been expensive and would certainly have left the last word with an existing firm. Two soundings in 1958–59 from the United States showed that new interests might be prepared to come in—but they were not specifically directed towards the use of home ores.[1]

Presumably little or no pig iron would in future be used: the economy would depend therefore on the price of scrap. Sheffield was already a scrap-importing area. United Steels now proposed to bring the scrap from their Scunthorpe works to Templeborough: had they not had this works they would presumably have used the scrap at Scunthorpe and avoided the transport. Without a large expansion at Scunthorpe bought scrap would still be needed at Templeborough. On the Continent large electric furnaces were being used increasingly at plants with pneumatic steel plants to utilise scrap. The project would cost £10 m. Had the firm wanted to build a strip mill in Lincolnshire, which naturally they considered from time to time, the cost might have been ten times this.

[1] First a United States group made soundings about securing a large interest in a steel company which happened to own a home ore mine, but not a works on the home ore. Later, in the autumn of 1959, one of the ten largest United States companies (whose identity was not revealed) made inquiries through a firm of consultants to see whether they could find a British steel company in which they could make an investment (and in which they would like to invest) on a scale which would ensure representation on the Board. Since the firm's identity was not revealed it was not certain what it had to offer and what it hoped to gain. It may have been concerned in the United States both with the high labour cost, which would make export trade increasingly difficult, and with the restraint on amalgamation in the United States (which might check its rate of growth).

In so far as the Act of 1953 supplied a possible complement to the forces of competition, which at the best must be muted, it lay in the powers of the Board to recommend the Government to start up a new State-owned steel plant or sponsor a new privately owned company. This the Board could do (it will be recalled) if they thought the existing firms were not planning to expand sufficiently, and failed to persuade the firms to plan to expand more. The whole arrangement was defined in terms which implied it was only concerned with quantity, and it was discussed mainly in these terms.

The most common criticism was that the Board's power to recommend would never be used: and no doubt it was put in the Act as a last resort, whose mere existence would add to the Board's power of persuasion. It was suggested before the election in 1959 that the Government should keep some publicly owned companies in being—not selling Richard Thomas and Baldwins, for instance—so that these could be called on to undertake the jobs which the Board might recommend. Otherwise 'the Minister would have to recruit the technical and managerial staff from the public sector'.[1] When any new works had to be staffed the problem of drawing some staff from existing companies was faced, and staff moved in fact from one company to another. Consultants, suppliers of plant and merchants could help in their different ways. The idea that an existing State-owned company would always be the right body, would have that is the necessary experience and judgement and freshness for new ideas in any field in the steel industry, was strange—but not in a world in which the quantity of indigenous steel production was everything, and quality of investment was neglected. The most interesting prospect conjured up however by the provisions of the 1953 Act was that the Board and Government might help a newcomer who wanted to get into the industry (and could possibly provide part of the market for a new works), or might stimulate a newcomer who had not thought of it perhaps because it had not seemed practical. The Government's powers in this respect covered the provision of facilities for providing more home ore (though precisely what

[1] *The Spectator*, 'Special Inquiry into the Steel Industry', 13 March 1959.

this would mean is not clear). Assistance to a newcomer would create a new organism of a type which had been familiar in the industry's past, and it would avoid the difficulties of associating State-owned and privately-owned firms in competition with each other. These difficulties tended to be glossed over—'the Board should be charged with the responsibility of ensuring that there is fair competition between the public and the private sectors of the industry', it was once blandly stated,[1] as though the principles on which this should be done were straightforward. This was far from being so: the conditions on which capital could be obtained in a State-owned company for instance, were bound to be different from those open to private enterprise, and if as might happen the State-owned company fared badly because its plant was partly idle this would not be embarrassing financially to the State as it might be to the privately-owned plants, who might be suffering at the same time through the provision of excess capacity. How, moreover, could the Board be treated as impartial arbiters on the fairness of competition when the new State competitor would be created as a result of their advice? These were no doubt trivial irrelevances to those for whom surplus steel capacity in Britain was a sheet anchor of economic well being, without which the steel industry could not 'fulfil its special role in the national economy'.[2]

The discussion of the Board's powers in the late fifties started —perhaps inevitably—from the assumption that the Board's decisions would be in some sense right. But although there was good reason to suppose that the imperfections of competition would inhibit some developments which would occur in more 'competitive conditions' this did not make it easy to identify quickly what those developments would have been. The danger implicit in a system which depended on the correctives of a Board was that it would always be catching up, doing things rather late. When the members of the Board made up their minds they had to follow a course of persuasion: if they met resistance they would usually have to persuade the Government —whether they thought more should be done, or if they wanted

[1] *Ibid. loc. cit.*   [2] *Ibid. loc. cit.*

to prevent what was proposed by a firm. These are not procedures which promise quick reactions to changing circumstances. The Board could obviously react quickly or slowly
according to the qualities of the members: being a rather large
body as constituted, its members drawn from different back-
grounds and with divergent interests, the probability was that
collective reactions would be slow and savour of compromise.
Hence perhaps the complaint sometimes heard in the industry
that the Board was just another source of delay, or another piece
of bureaucracy. The Board could escape being bureaucratic,
but it could not escape the unavoidable bureaucracy of the
Ministry.[1] Here they were liable to be dealing at different times
with different senior civil servants who when they took over
were usually new to the economic problems involved as well
as unavoidably to the technical ones. It was an unpromising
situation. The members of the Board were likely to be much
more alert to the technical position in the industry than the civil
servants, but were not likely collectively to back new developments vigorously before these were well supported by some
accepted British technical authorities. The situation in which
their greatest usefulness might in theory have been looked for
was precisely the one that existed: namely where the geographical distribution and the subdivision of the industry,
reflecting conditions which had changed, seriously hampered
cost reduction. The facts were familiar: the cheapness of home
ore, the advantages of large ships and intensive unloading of
imported ore, the shift in relative costs of coal, the advantages
in the processes which were being used of very large scale units.
It was not a situation in which daring technical judgements
were needed. It was one which needed decisive action, and
where the entrenched forces which were so feared when total
capacity was under discussion appear to have had, even among
other things by their very expansiveness, their more fateful,
subtle, little recognised effects. Here the case for central
planning intervention, perhaps only to help a once-for-all
adjustment, was clearly strong. The Board's contribution to

[1] First, Ministry of Supply, then Board of Trade, then Ministry of Fuel and
Power, then Ministry of Power.

such was, however, ineffective up to the end of 1959. Their history bore out only too well the fears that this type of organisation would be associated with an industry 'catching up'. The plate mill story is an interesting, but not conclusive example because the Board came in at a late stage. The firms' reaction to the demand was extremely late; the Board may have hastened it a little, but they were not able to keep it within reasonable bounds.[1] The gradual increase of interest in pneumatic steel-making recorded in the Board's reports grew step by step as the activity of the big firms in the same matter.[2] The Board's one conspicuous contribution to the major adjustment was their pressure to have more investigation and ultimately much more use of home ore: but despite the long background to this[3] the Board had made little headway by the end of 1959, and new forces of delay had been built up. There were no overt signs that the Board made any other effort to promote the major adjustment, but the Government were clearly not favourable to it, and there are no signs that the Government departments concerned thought it significant. Had the Board wished to assist the kind of reorganisation into fewer bigger units with more specialisation favoured by some of the 'Under Fifties' in 1944–46 the Act of 1953 hardly provided adequate power. There were no powers to reduce output at any plants: the Board might refuse to sanction expansion schemes, and presumably might refuse to sanction modernisation schemes at ill-favoured plants —but its approval was only to be withheld if a scheme *seriously* prejudiced the 'economic, efficient' supply of steel. And the aggrieved party might appeal to the Minister. This only under-

[1] Once the spate of new plate mills began the extent was possibly excessive: efforts to stop one scheme in the interests of concentration of steelmaking at good sites failed. Whether the Board collectively took any action on this I do not know.
[2] As late as May 1959 the President of the Iron and Steel Institute said (at the Institute's annual dinner): 'To blow or not to blow, that is the question'. Still a question!
[3] I find it of interest that the tonnage of ore reserves as set out in 1957 by the Board were almost exactly the same as estimates given to me when the preparation of this book was in its early stages in 1950 by the Director of the Geological Survey with permission to use them (with acknowledgements to the Director). A serious appreciation of the value of using the deposits more at any time after the war would have led to a confirmation of the size of the reserves and to their detailed exploration— so that exploitation could have started earlier.

lines the fact that the Act did not envisage the Board performing the one function which it may have been most useful to have performed in simulating the effects of 'competitive conditions'.

The Board was not given functions analogous to those given to the High Authority of the E.C.S.C.[1] to help to solve unemployment problems which market or technical developments in the steel industry[2] which it advocated might involve. The High Authority might be asked by interested Governments to explore employment opportunities outside coal and steel—in all other industries—and might help finance development in them if they were 'economically sound', as well as providing financial aid to workers for retraining, rehousing and the like. It has not in fact been heavily engaged in such work. The Board's functions did not extend into this field. There is no sign that they tried to encourage adaptation in the older areas whose advantages had lessened and where contraction of mass production steelmaking would be looked for 'in competitive conditions'. They might, for instance, have encouraged more extensive development of continuous casting, or vacuum melting, or the Sendzimir hot mill for strip; all of which might have been very appropriately developed, for example, in Scotland, but there is no sign that they did so. The Board did not appear to have formal *powers* to act on these lines, to recommend such developments not merely in general, which they could have done, but as alternatives in high cost sites. Whether this was why they did not do so, or whether in fact they were slow to see the scope for these developments is a matter for surmise. A few adaptations of this type *did* occur[3]—but not on a scale sufficient to make a significant contribution to the progress of concentration and specialisation at good sites.

It was tempting to suppose that nationalisation would have been a better medium for a radical adjustment to concentrate

[1] Above, p. 410 and E.C.S.C. *Treaty*, Art. 46, 56.
[2] For the E.C.S.C. coal and steel.
[3] For example, at the Brymbo steelworks, where hot metal from the blast furnace was treated in a pre-refining furnace with oxygen and fluidised lime injection prior to being charged into arc furnaces, to make alloy and special steels of relatively simple character and requiring no elaborate and varied heat treatments. This was described at length in the American *Iron Age*, 21 Jan. 1960.

production in fewer more specialised plants located to give lowest costs. But to do so was to be caught in what may be called the national interest fallacy which had dogged the discussion of nationalisation (and of other means of controlling industries too); to concentrate on constitutions and powers and to neglect purpose and motivation. A nationalised industry which was organised as a unit, even if only by a holding company, but still as a unit for investment planning, would plainly have greater powers of resistance to external pressures and be less subject to the force of oversea competition even if there were a European or Atlantic Community free market. Moreover, nationalisation would rule out the influx of a new company into the industry from outside, from a large consuming group, for instance, or from the industry in another country—the United States, for example—and so reduce the possibility of bringing new dynamic forces into the industry, which could have made it more prominent in technical initiative. It would rule out the possibility that one forceful competitive firm in the industry by its own independent decision alone might set a new standard by rigorous concentration on development of product and process, cost reduction and expansion. Choice of top management, and of price and investment policy must almost certainly have become centralised—which conceivably may have its most cramping effect in early stages before traditional procedures have evolved, and while there is a mixed economy. And there was no reason to suppose that the controlling forces in a nationalised industry would at once decide in favour of a kind of radical policy which would cause friction and provoke violent local and trade union opposition, would need Government co-operation, and would probably meet with Government opposition; which for a nationalised industry, as for the Steel Board, would be equivalent to a veto. The controllers would quite probably take an autarchic view, and aim at making their industry as large as possible with a monopoly of the home market and without reference to the possibility of importing, or allowing imports freely, if at all, for cheapness or special quality. They might from past associations with the industry have prejudices in favour of high cost sites—as the Chairman of the Iron and

Steel Corporation of Great Britain had in favour of a Grange-mouth site.[1] The Corporation, like the Labour Government, used with approval the devices of the Industry Fund which helped high cost at the expense of low cost production. The Labour Government set the pace in encouraging expansion of steelmaking in old established areas, and showed no practical interest in expanding on the home ore fields: when in opposition they approved of Mr Macmillan's decision on the strip mills. To suppose that those running a nationalised industry, including the responsible minister, must needs automatically serve the 'national interest' was merely a form of mumbo-jumbo. To suppose that nationalisation would infallibly have led more rapidly if at all to a use of resources less distorted (and so made more costly) by monopoly and quasi-monopoly influences was wrong.[2]

By the end of 1959 these were hypothetical issues which had lost practical importance. The more pertinent question was—would the Steel Board be an effective instrument for assisting the once-for-all radical adjustment spoken of earlier if the Government favoured a policy of more rigorous cost reduction in industry, if only because of the risks in international trade of not doing so? Obviously there was no plain answer to this. But industries where large firms dominate had proved since the war to be surprisingly chameleonic. If the Government had changed their policy the policies of some firms would almost certainly have followed suit. Some of the critics of conservatism, stabilisation and caution within the industry would have come out into the open. By implication the change of Government attitude would have brought their development area policy closer to the ideal (if not conspicuously the practice) of the E.C.S.C., so that firms would not have felt under an obligation

[1] Above, p. 312.

[2] Obviously other considerations would weigh with people in deciding whether nationalisation was desirable or not. To avoid misunderstanding I may say that I am not concerned here to set out and deal with issues which are not specific to the steel situation, for example, the part played by shareholders, the justification of dividends, nor to refer to all the problems which arose in the earlier discussions of nationalisation; discrimination in cost of capital, dangers of discrimination arising from the parts of nationalised firms in finishing industries, the dangers of complications in export trade, etc.

to keep existing ill-favoured plants active, still less to build new ones, since constructive measures would be taken to make this unnecessary. The Board's advice would presumably have been taken more readily by the Government if economic considerations (in the sense used in the debates of 1952–53)[1] were to be the overriding ones. In those circumstances the critical question would probably have been not whether the Board had enough powers but what was the quality, incisiveness and speed of its decisions. They were likely to be more independent than a committee from the Federation, where some firms felt, rightly or wrongly, they were unpopular members of the club. The members of the Board might have had such faith in their price policy in its more recent form, with its cost-equalising devices no longer looking like a one-way pendulum, as to rely on this alone to induce 'good' investments only (though they had not taken this line so far). If what was at issue was not merely how the existing organisation would work, but whether another would formally at any rate seem preferable it might well have been argued that a Government-appointed body to advise on investment in one industry alone is not satisfactory: that something like the Industrial Commission suggested discreetly in 1944 to deal with a range of industries,[2] or something analogous to the French Commissariat au Plan, would have been more appropriate. But the Government had not changed their policy by the first half of 1960—and these deep organisational issues were not stirred.

For the long run the most determining changes must be within the firms—changes of mood, associated with, and derived from, changes in the temperament and the dominant abilities of the leaders. While the Board might help in promoting concentration and more economic siting and more use of home ore, the weakness on the technical front was likely to be more intractable. No doubt pressure to have more pilot plant operations would help. One managing director of a leading firm stigmatised as the worst effect of the threat of nationalisation a slow turnover in management. It has been seen that the positions of greatest seniority in many firms still went commonly

[1] Above, pp. 369 sqq.　　　　[2] Above, p. 111.

to persons 'in the family' or to persons influential in the City. Would the balance change? There were signs that it might— that some people would come to the top who had made their way solely on their own merits and achievements including technical achievements in the industry. The British position nevertheless had to be looked at in historic perspective. The plain truth is that the relative lack of contribution to technical advance was not a new thing. The basic inventions which Britain contributed to steelmaking came from outside the iron and steel industry: already in the eighteen-sixties innovations came fast from the Continent and America and resistances to change, often based on scientific arguments and cost assessments which proved wrong, were legion. The great inquests of the nineteen-fifties, in which the participants set out Britain's lack of scientists in industry, and explained authoritatively what was lacking and what should be done, were following in a tradition over a century old, though they did it with a sense of freshness and novelty which was beguiling. Deep-seated characteristics are not easy to influence—especially by superficial remedies. The sixties opened in British steelmaking with a spate of technical changes. Some general economic factors, as well as technical pressures, favoured this: the cost of labour had risen for several years much faster than the cost of new plant, and invention (mainly foreign) had greatly lowered the capital investment required for a ton of steel. New processes developed elsewhere were now being adopted. This could give to the unwary an illusion of indigenous technical innovation which could be misleading and foster complacency. Whether any profound change was occurring—in steelmaking in particular, or in British industry more generally—only time would show.

Appendix

SCRAP PRICES AND VALUES

This appendix sets out first some data on the ratio between pig iron and scrap prices since 1909 in relatively free market conditions, then examines the statistics on supply of various types of scrap in the United Kingdom, and finally sets out what seem the likely relations of price, supply and demand at various stages of a trade cycle in competitive conditions.

The price movements themselves are not familiar. A German study of the relations between pig iron and scrap prices in five years before the First World War[1] showed that scrap prices were on an average more than 80 per cent of the pig iron prices in each country —that is, above the upper limit of the Federation's range—and showed marked variations, though the lower figure was only in one instance below the Federation's minimum.

The relations of these figures to changes of steel output is uneven.

Table 102. *Scrap prices as percentages of pig-iron prices, 1909–13*

Year	U.K.[a]	U.S.[b]	Germany[c]
1909	101	99	93
1910	86	88	98
1911	88	82	95
1912	75	84	85
1913	72	77	79
Average	84	86	90

[a] Based on hamatite pig-iron prices, North-east Coast, and heavy melting scrap prices in the same region. The ratio would be higher if basic iron prices were used.

[b] Pittsburg prices of heavy scrap and Bessemer iron.

[c] Prices of heavy scrap delivered at Rhineland West works; price of stahleisen (which was much above the price of Thomas iron). For some years the price was F.O.T. Siegen; but clearly this price would be based on production which would be more costly than Ruhr production.

[1] Dr Buchmann, Prof. Mathesius, Dr Petersen and Dr Reichert: *Zur Frage der Schrottpreise*, and *Zur Frage der internationalen Eisenpreisvergleich* (two studies for the *Ausschuss zur Untersuchung der Erzeugungs und Absatzbedingungen der deutscher Wirthschaft*, Berlin, 1927).

The initially high figures may be taken to reflect the rising output: the maintenance of the German figure until 1912 (inclusive) can be said to reflect the continuing rise, but the fall in 1913 has then to be explained. The United States figures show a more rational correlation, the United Kingdom figures rather less.

The same study covered three inter-war years, 1924–26; but this was not only a short period but abnormal, and the comparisons were for technical reasons imperfect.[1]

Table 103. *Ingot output (m. tons)*

Year	U.K.	U.S.	Germany	Year	U.K.	U.S.	Germany
1908	5·3	14·0	10·6	1911	6·5	23·7	14·1
1909	5·9	24·0	11·3	1912	6·8	31·3	15·3
1910	6·4	26·1	12·9	1913	7·7	31·3	17·3

Table 104 compares the scrap/pig-iron ratio between the wars in the United States and the United Kingdom; for much of this period the German figures, either because of the dislocation in the early years and the price-fixing in the final years, are of no significance for this purpose.

These series show similar trends in the United States and the United Kingdom for most of the time (though not in 1937–39), and a remarkable difference between the first and second decades. The overall average in each country was 80, which at first sight is fairly in accord with the Federation's ratio, though on the high side. The average was notably brought down by the depression of the thirties. In years of good demand for steel the ratio was usually considerably higher, and if an average had been taken for the period 1909–13 and 1919–30 (seventeen years which included the shattering slump of 1920–21) it would have been 83 for the United Kingdom, for the United States over 86. It was not until the latter part of the thirties, and then only in the United Kingdom, that in years of heavy and

[1] The averages were: United Kingdom 79, United States 80, Germany 64. But it was now certainly not right to take hamatite iron as the basis for a North-east Coast comparison; it depressed the British percentage without justification, as basic steel was now the standard. Similarly, Bessemer pig iron was no longer a reasonable basis for the United States. In Germany it was complex; Siegerland stahleisen was a costly high-quality pig iron, but the Germans did not use the open-hearth as their standard process for ordinary steel. The international comparison must take into account the different balance of processes employed. In France, predominantly a 'Thomas' steel producer, scrap prices often tended to run very low, because the process could use only a little scrap.

rising demand, 1936–37, the ratios were only 81 and 73. By this time price control in Britain was more effective in keeping up the price of pig iron, while by 1937 the price of scrap was being artificially depressed, exports being in effect prohibited by 1937.[1] Steel prices were also, but to a less extent, kept down. The British figures were thus no longer relevant. No year in the thirties saw a revival of demand for steel in the United States to match that of the previous decade; the percentages in 1936–37 (83, 82) did not coincide with the same pressure of demand for steel as there was in 1924–29.[2]

Table 104. *Scrap prices as percentages of pig-iron prices, 1919–39*

Year	U.S.[a]	U.K.[b]	Year	U.S.	U.K.
1919	—	87	1930	84	81
1920	—	100	1931	70	70
1921	63	43	1932	67	65
1922	73	65	1933	73	72
1923	79	83	1934	70	84
1924	91	90	1935	70	78
1925	95	87	1936	83	81
1926	92	74	1937	82	73
1927	88	86	1938	65	62
1928	94	97	1939	81	—
1929	99	107			

[a] Mahoning and Shenango Valley prices for basic pig iron, which are in line with Pittsburgh prices when these are available. Pittsburgh prices for scrap.

[b] North-east Coast basic pig iron when available; otherwise ascertained prices for Cleveland III (which are normally the higher). Glasgow area scrap prices, which were normally in line with North-east Coast prices, and in general lower than scrap prices in other major producing areas, especially lower than South Wales.

Since the war only American figures have any bearing on this problem; the percentage from 1945 to 1951 inclusive averaged 83, the range being from 105 (1947) to 64 (1949). Thus from before the First World War, in relatively free (though never wholly free) market conditions, the price of scrap has fluctuated between less than 50 per cent of the price of basic pig iron to over 100 per cent.

This acute fluctuation is not inherently surprising because the major part of the supply of scrap arises in the operations in making steel and subsequently machining, forming and fabricating it. This

[1] See *E.H.S.* p. 474.
[2] United States steel ingot output averaged 81 per cent of capacity from 1925 to 1929, and was never quite as low as 74; it averaged 59 per cent from 1935 to 1939, and never quite reached 73 (it was 72·5 in 1937).

part of the supply is likely at any time to be roughly in proportion to the rate of output and the use of steel a little earlier; if, therefore, output consumption and orders are falling process scrap—the term is used to include all scrap produced in the manufacture of steel and the use of steel—should be able to provide a larger proportion of the raw material for steel made than if they are rising. The same may be true of the scrap which arises from the 'scrapping' of old plant, machinery, building, ships—'capital scrap'; though the influences here are more complex and obscure.[1] Unfortunately, there are no statistics on scrap supply in the free market, so that speculations about how supplies ought to have behaved cannot be checked. There are statistics of how much scrap, of all kinds, steelmakers used in the United Kingdom, and this is subdivided into the amounts of the scrap they used which came from their own works (which fluctuate widely as a proportion of ingot output in an inexplicable manner) and the amounts they used which came from scrap which they had bought. But there is no information on the stocks of either category held by steelmakers until the end of 1937, and none on stocks held by scrap merchants before or even during the war. The only information on the supply of scrap is contained in the Census of Production for 1935, which gives for some industries their sales of scrap iron and steel in 1934 and 1935. Important scrap-producing industries are omitted, some of the figures are in values only, different categories of scrap are lumped together; and, of course, as is the way with all Census figures, these data do not refer to precise years, the figures for different firms relating to their financial years, so that the assembling of the figures to give a total for 1934 or 1935, even if all industries were properly covered, is quite unjustified and not to be correlated with data specifically for a calendar year.[2] On capital

---

[1] It is dubious how far it is worth pushing an analysis in the absence of data. Obviously when business is booming the inclination to scrap existing plants is lessened; new machinery is likely to be used to expand output, and 'scrapped' machinery more likely to find a second-hand use as machinery. On the other hand, a boom is associated with the replacement of an old by a new industry. In a time of slump there will be a disposition to put off repairs and even a maintenance. No doubt the end of a boom often corresponds with the completion of a bout of new plant building, and this leaves redundant plant; but redundant plant is not immediately broken up. Even machinery sold as scrap may be used again, either in whole or part. It is therefore idle to try and base a general conclusion on a few simple points.

[2] Sir Robert Shone built up on these Census figures a series of figures intended to give the tonnage of 'bought' process scrap, i.e. process scrap other than is produced by firms who have steel furnaces, from 1921–46 (*J.R. Stat. Soc.* 1947, p. 293).

scrap there are no data at all. The consumption figures are consistent with the thesis that more scrap will be available as a proportion of ingot output when this is falling than when it is rising; but more elaborate conclusions the data do not provide.

This in itself, however, would explain the general pattern of scrap-price movements. An upper limit must be set at any time by the price of steel. When demand for steel is falling, and output contracting, the scrap available will only be absorbed if some steelmakers can be persuaded to use a higher proportion of scrap to pig iron. Steelmakers using their own hot metal will have proportionately

Using *consumption* figures to show total *supply* from year to year he estimated the output of capital scrap by subtracting from this total the *consumption* of 'circulating' scrap plus this calculated figure for 'process scrap'. I do not think this procedure can give valid results or indicate the magnitudes involved. The *Census of Production* includes no figures for shipbuilding or for motor-cars, and its figures for mechanical and electrical engineering were in value only. Over one-third of the total was accounted for by the sales of the steel melting and rolling industry itself, presumably mainly by the pure re-rolling mills; the value per ton of the scrap sold by this industry was greater than the value per ton of the scrap bought, which shows that its character was not the same. It would include alloy steel scrap and scrap used as new material (for example, plate cuttings used for spades). If scrap were sold there would normally be merchants' charges as well as transport, and often some costs of preparation. Thus it is clearly impossible to step surely from value to tonnage in any of these figures. My view is that Shone attributes too high an average value to the scrap sold by the mechanical and electrical engineering industries in 1934–35, and so gets too low a tonnage. One other element in the basis of the calculation presents difficulty, namely, the great fluctuation in the percentage of 'circulating scrap', from over 26 per cent in 1927 and 24 per cent in 1929 to below 21 per cent in 1932 and then up again to 24–26 per cent in 1937–39. Shone's estimate of 'process scrap' varies closely in accordance with the crude estimates of steel consumption, but the *total* process scrap thus estimated (including circulating scrap) does *not* vary in proportion to output and consumption. With such unexplained anomalies and no stock figures a calculation based on differences is far too hazardous. The known data are as follows:

Year	Liquid steel made (m. tons)	Scrap used for steel Circulating (m. tons)	Bought (m. tons)	Imports of steel 'semis' (m. tons)	Home consumption of steel (m. tons)	Pig iron used per ingot ton (cwt.)	As % of liquid steel output Circulating scrap used	Bought scrap used	All scrap used
1927	9·1	2·4	2·5	1·4	9·5	10·4	26·8	27·1	53·9
1928	8·5	2·0	2·7	1·4	7·4	10·2	24·0	31·4	55·4
1929	9·6	2·4	2·6	1·3	8·3	10·6	24·6	28·1	52·7
1930	7·3	2·0	2·1	1·4	7·2	10·0	26·7	28·9	55·6
1931	5·2	1·2	1·9	1·4	6·1	9·1	22·7	37·5	60·2
1932	5·3	1·1	2·3	0·9	5·1	8·4	21·1	42·7	63·8
1933	7·0	1·5	3·1	0·4	6·1	8·5	20·3	40·3	60·6
1934	8·9	2·0	3·4	0·6	8·1	9·0	22·4	38·7	61·1
1935	9·9	2·3	3·6	0·5	8·6	9·3	22·8	36·5	59·3
1936	11·8	2·7	4·2	0·7	10·8	9·4	22·9	35·8	58·7
1937	13·0	3·1	4·4	0·8	11·6	9·6	23·7	33·8	57·5
1938	10·4	2·7	3·5	0·5	9·2	9·3	25·6	33·4	59·0
1939	13·2	3·6	3·8	—	12·8	—	27·0	29·0	66·0

BEH

more of their own 'circulating scrap' to absorb; and in Great Britain (but not in America) the more likely users, initially at any rate, to *buy* more scrap would be those using cold pig iron. For them it would be cheaper to substitute scrap whenever its price was somewhat lower than the price of basic pig iron delivered in their works (less the cost of any added deoxidising material required when using pig iron instead of scrap). But though cheaper it might not be cheap enough, for the competition they face is with steel made from hot metal. To produce steel ingots as cheaply in a cold-metal shop as in a works based on hot metal it would be necessary for scrap to cost less than the hot metal in the integrated works.[1] If the integrated works lowered its prices below total costs in order to secure orders the scrap price might theoretically be forced below the prime cost of hot metal.[2] Theoretically the market price of pig iron might also be determined by its marginal prime cost, which would always be appreciably higher than that of hot metal because of the additional casting costs, and costs of handling, transporting and selling. In fact the price of pig iron has rarely been completely 'free' since 1920; and the fact that scrap prices have fallen in a slump to as little as 50 per cent of the pig-iron price may reflect this. But the scrap seller, with the commodity in inelastic supply, would be the weaker seller—until the price was low enough to make holding of stocks seem not merely inevitable (as it probably would be in a measure) but preferable.

When demand for steel expanded, the scrap seller's position would become a strong one. Expansion of steel output could initially be based on stocks of pig iron and scrap, but ultimately must be based on exceptional sources of scrap (e.g. exceptional imports) and on a greater output of pig iron. The second is in the long run the only permanent basis of growth. The value of both pig iron and scrap will be raised. Even with no increase of steel prices the lowered overheads of larger scale working would have this effect. Pig iron

[1] Because the average cost of the raw materials charged—cold pig iron (which is dearer than hot metal) and scrap—must be below the hot-metal cost in order to compensate for the additional fuel cost in melting and the longer time, therefore higher capital and labour costs, of the cold-metal process. To offset these disadvantages some cold-metal shops will be nearer markets.

[2] It will be noticed that in a country where cold-metal shops are rarer than in the United Kingdom, for example, the United States, the same conclusion is valid If more scrap is to be used it must be used primarily as a substitute for hot metal However, the situation would not be quite simple; for in any integrated works the demand for steel might fall so far that it might force the closing of one or more blast furnaces, and in this situation a larger part of raw material needs might be most conveniently provided from scrap.

more costly to make (due to the use of less efficient less well-placed furnaces, or dearer ore or coke) will be used. Cold-metal steelworks will find it hard to sustain their normal proportion of scrap (since apart from new sources or stocks scrap will be relatively scarce); to expand output they must use more pig iron, but it will be cheaper to use scrap so long as its price is only a little below that of pig iron when delivered to them. Hot-metal shops might find it attractive to increase their output beyond the limits set by their blast furnaces and should find it profitable to pay more than the cost of hot metal. In boom conditions there was no reason to expect a close functional relation between steel prices and pig-iron costs, and it was the former which set the upper limit to scrap prices. It was natural enough that the striving after limited supplies of scrap ultimately pushed the scrap price, even from normal sources, above that of pig iron.

The economic significance of the widely fluctuating price of scrap, sometimes below the prime cost of hot metal, sometimes above the market price of pig iron at users' works and unrelated to this price functionally, can thus readily be seen in relation to the different stages of a trade cycle. The low price in a slump would discourage supply (having little effect on the supply of process scrap but some important effects on the supply of capital scrap), and would tend to encourage those steelmakers who were most efficient in making steel from pig iron in the open-hearth process,[1] those with the most efficient blast furnaces, using hot metal in the steelworks, and with cheap ore and coke and good sites. In a boom these could, if they had spare steelmaking capacity (which is likely since open-hearth furnaces are often rebuilt and their capacity increased), ideally afford to pay more for scrap than other works making analogous finished products.

---

[1] In cost analysis it is necessary for clarity on these issues to distinguish the manufacture of steel from scrap and the manufacture from pig iron. The cost of converting scrap probably does not vary significantly whether hot metal or cold pig iron is used. It can be converted without either. But since it is not merely a melting operation but a refining one (the analysis of different bits of scrap varies, and much is dirty and adulterated, and some has alloy inclusions) and also because the open-hearth furnace as a melting furnace is oxidising, carbon additions (for example, coke) and lime are needed, and generally it is most practical to add the carbon in pig iron. When *this* is done, and the use of pig iron and scrap is combined, then the *overall* cheapness must soon be thought of in terms of economy in converting pig iron. Here there is a great advantage in charging hot metal, a great reduction in the heat needed (cp. G. A. V. Russell, *Proc. Cleveland Inst. Engineers*, 1941–2, p. 80). In a small works the amount of iron used may be too small to use the output of a blast furnace; but this is itself a factor in deciding whether the scale of operations is itself too small.

The rapid extension in the use of oxygen in steelmaking was likely to change the relative values of hot metal and scrap, reducing that of scrap, because it was (or appeared to be) changing the relative costs of converting hot metal and scrap into steel. The increased use of electric furnaces for melting scrap was one evidence of this. While this introduced new specific factors into the determination of scrap values, and was likely to stimulate new practices in preparing scrap (which were now talked of in America) the general nature of the forces operating and determining scrap values was unaffected.

INDEX

Abbey Works, 241, 340, 381; *see also* Port Talbot, Margam

Aberconway, Lord, 317

Aberdare, 255

Aciéries de Longwy, 393, 396, 397, 450

Acklam Works (Dorman Long), 174, 246

Ackroyd, Elizabeth, 321

Acme Steel Co., 512

Acts of Parliament, *see* Legislation

Administered Prices, Hearings before the Subcommittee on Antitrust and Monopoly of the Committee on the Judiciary, United States Senate: Part 2, 524, 526; Part 3, 512, 513, 519, 520, 528; Part 4, 515

Advances in Steel Technology (E.C.E.), 170, 458

Africa, North, 101–4, 149, 327, 460, 468, 530, 581, 668; West, 101, 326, 530, 652; South, 149, 629: Iron and Steel Corporation of S. Africa, 191; *see also* Conakry, Mauretania, Sierra Leone

Alabama, 491

Alan Wood Steel Co., 514

All-basic open-hearth furnaces, 522

Allegheny Ludlum Steel Corp., 512, 527

Allied High Commission (Germany), 448, 449

Allied Ironfounders Ltd, 538

Allocations, *see* Rationing

Alloy and Special Steels, 7, 10, 14–17, 31, 33, 49–50, 218, 239–40, 248–9, 331, 333, 338, 344, 457–8, 462, 496, 516, 519–20, 542, 553–4, 561–2, 563, 630

Alquife Ore Co., 326

Alsop, R., 5

Amalgamation, *see* Integration

American Aid in Europe, 134, 137, 139, 144–5, 400–1

American Bridge Co., 490

American Rolling Mill Co. (ARMCO), 495, 501, 514, 563

Amsterdam, 579

Anderson, Alexander, M.P., 190

Andrews, P. W. S. and Brunner, Eliz., *Capital Development in Steel*, 87, 177, 599

Anglo-American Council of Productivity, *see* Productivity Team Report

Annual Report of the Secretary of Mines, 21, 592

Antitrust

division of the Department of Justice, 533, 535

investigation by House Monopoly Subcommittee, 507, 523

Laws, 506

Antwerp, 577, 579, 580, 582

Anzin, 396

Appleby-Frodingham Works (United Steel Companies), 14, 48, 87, 189, 250, 323, 557, 558, 597, 636–7

Arbed (Aciéries Réunies de Burbach-Eich-Dudelange), 321, 449, 564

Argentina, 8, 166

Armco Steel Corp., 495, 501, 514, 563; link with A.T.H., 563

Arthur Lee and Co., 539

Ashland Works (Armco), 515

Asiatic Petroleum Co. (Shell), 55

Asset Replacement Reserves, 594

Associated British Chambers of Commerce, 303

Attlee, Mr C. R. (Lord Attlee), 366, 464, 465

Attorney General's National Committee to Study the Antitrust Laws, Report of, 506

Auditor General, The, on steel prices, 26, 28, 35, 42, 44, 46

August Thyssen Hütte (A.T.H.), 400, 402, 449, 452, 456–60, 563, 580, 590, 600–1; link with Armco, and Chatillon Commentary, 563

Austin, David F., *Competition in Steel*, 517

Australia, 148, 166, 211, 668

46

Mitchison, G. R., M.P., 117, 371

Monmouthshire, 82, 614, 646

Monnet, Jean, 138, 153, 391, 404–5, 416, 463–5, 467

Monnet Plan, The, *see* Planning development

Monopolies and Restrictive Practices Commission, 299, 367

Morison, Sir John, 537, 539

Morrison, Rt. Hon. Herbert, M.P. (Lord Morrison of Lambeth), 116, 124, 188, 291–6, 308–9, 312, 315, 319; *Prospects and Policies*, 125

Mort, D. L., M.P., 381

Mossend Works (Colvilles), 16, 189, 263

Motherwell, 190, 259, 260, 262, 362, 654

Motor vehicles

fluctuations, in output, 157–8; in exports, 167; car makers' criticism of steel industry, 65; special price concessions proposed for car industry, 72; conceded, 229–30

registrations of motor cars, 158

restrictions removed, 155

steel consumption for (1953–59), 160

Mulberry Harbours, 11

Musgrave, Sir Cyril, 659

Naesmith, Sir Andrew, 538

Nancy, 393, 462

Narvik, 579, 580

National and International Measures for Unemployment, U.N. Report 1949, 134, 321

National Coal Board (N.C.B.): and coke supplies for steel industry, 197–8; liaison committee on, 198; slow in developing new coke ovens, 198; coal price policy, 257, 340–2; coke prices, 571, 655; structural problems of, as background for steel nationalisation debates, 293–4; criticised for 'mystical fervour' of its reports, 303; represented on Council of Association, 469; reduces time in developing new mines, 629

National Council of Iron Ore Producers, 303

National Expenditure, 14th Report from the Select Committee on, Session 1942–3, 5, 31, 33, 35, 36, 41, 44, 51

National Industrial Recovery Act, 484

National Policy for Industry, A, 60, 66

National Recovery Administration, 484, 502

National Steel Corp., 500, 501, 507, 509, 513, 515, 523

National Tube Co., 512

National Union of Manufacturers, 303

Nationalisation

the evolution of the case for, 113 sqq.; the armaments argument, 113–14; depression, 114–15; danger of producers' monopoly and capitalist restriction, 118–20; three constitutions before 1939, 115–17, 121–4; intellectuals versus trade unionists, 124; opposition to putting in Labour programme, 124; divisions continue, 143; and cause delays, 188; B.I.S.F. opposition, 172

the passing of the Act, 293–311; Herbert Morrison states the case for, 291–3, 295; negotiations with Sir A. Duncan, 293; influence of earlier nationalisations, 294–5; Iron and Steel Corp. to be holding company, 295 sqq.; problems of appointment, 297–9; not designed for specific policies, 305–7; no standards of efficiency, 308; preferentially cheap capital, 307–8; terms of purchase, 308–9; B.I.S.F. not touched, 309–11; vesting day delayed, 311; Corporation appointed, 311–13

an obstacle to Schuman Plan, 465; most company boards unaffected by, 544; no guarantee of better use of resources, 680–2. (For the industry while nationalised, and the ending of nationalisation, cf. Iron and Steel Corporation of Great Britain; Denationalisation)

Neath, 121, 255, 632

Netherlands

Dutch coke to Thionville, 421; scrap prices, 425, 584; wages, earnings and real income, 431–3; cost of labour, 585–6; labour productivity, 587–8

exports and imports within E.C.S.C., 417–20; joins export convention,